MAGILL'S
SURVEY
OF
CINEMA

MAGILL'S SURVEY OF CINEMA

English Language Films

SECOND SERIES
VOLUME 4
LUS-PUR

Edited by

FRANK N. MAGILL

Associate Editors

STEPHEN L. HANSON

PATRICIA KING HANSON

SALEM PRESS
Englewood Cliffs, N.J.

Library of Congress Catalog Card Number: 81-84330

Complete Set: ISBN 0-89356-230-0
Volume 4:   ISBN-0-89356-234-3

PRINTED IN THE UNITED STATES OF AMERICA

LIST OF TITLES IN VOLUME FOUR

LUST FOR LIFE

Released: 1956
Production: John Houseman for Metro-Goldwyn-Mayer
Direction: Vincente Minnelli
Screenplay: Norman Corwin; based on the novel of the same name by Irving Stone
Cinematography: Freddie A. Young, Russell Harlan, and Joseph Ruttenberg
Editing: Adrienne Fazan
Art direction: Hans Peters, Preston Ames, and Cedric Gibbons
Running time: 122 minutes

Principal characters:
Vincent Van Gogh	Kirk Douglas
Paul Gauguin	Anthony Quinn (AA)
Theo Van Gogh	James Donald
Christine	Pamela Brown
Anton Mauve	Noel Purcell
Theodorus Van Gogh	Henry Daniell
Cousin Kay	Jeanette Sterke
Doctor Peyron	Lionel Jeffries
Doctor Gachet	Everett Sloane
Anna Cornelia Van Gogh	Madge Kennedy

A biographical film about a famous person poses difficult problems to a filmmaker, for the public has numerous beliefs about the celebrity which are sacred, and the filmmaker may choose either to reinforce these commonly held ideas or to reinterpret them. *Lust for Life* reinforces many of the elements of artist Vincent Van Gogh's life that became well known through the best-selling novel of the same title by Irving Stone, but it also uses a narration of Van Gogh's own letters to his brother Theo to enlarge the scope of events and to make the film almost autobiographical.

Van Gogh (Kirk Douglas) first begins to draw while living as a missionary amongst miners of the Borinage in Belgium, but his church and his brother Theo (James Donald) insist that he leave that debilitating life because he is destructively overzealous as an evangelist. He returns to his family home in an agricultural village to regain his strength. In letters to Theo, Van Gogh explains that he has begun to draw the peasants about him and feels that they represent the goodness of hard labor and the simple life. He is encouraged by his work and hopes that he has finally found his avocation, which is, he believes, his need to communicate truth through visual means.

The ability to communicate verbally continues to elude him, however; he cannot refrain from quarreling with his father (Henry Daniell), a conservative clergyman, and his recently widowed Cousin Kay (Jeanette Sterke) is horrified when Vincent proposes marriage to her. Van Gogh is too sensual and too elemental to avoid conflict with her middle-class standards of love, and he is accused by her of "whimpering" because he cannot stand "a little disappointment in love." Van Gogh, however, proves he is a man of dangerously intense emotions and that his anguish is real when he holds his hand over an open flame until Kay's father must force him away. Leaving home, Van Gogh moves to The Hague where he hopes that his cousin Anton Mauve (Noel Purcell), a well-respected painter, will be able to teach him more about art. Van Gogh falls in love and moves in with a laundress, Christine (Pamela Brown), but he faces rejection again because his obstreperous ambition alienates both Christine and his cousin. Only Theo continues to support him and his work.

These scenes rely too much upon a simplistic yet common understanding of psychology which maintains that art is created only out of frustration. The film establishes that Van Gogh's inability to communicate with other people verbally kept him from leading a happy, normal life and that it was this frustration that made him an artist. Many experts believe, however, that Van Gogh was an undiagnosed epileptic whose fits of irrationality were doomed to increase in violence as he grew older and the condition went untreated, and that this physiological problem would have existed regardless of his personal happiness or unhappiness. The film discounts the fact that Van Gogh was self-educated in art and yet developed a remarkable genius in not more than ten years. His self-discipline must have been as enormous as his artistic zeal to enable him to complete approximately sixteen hundred canvases in this short period of time.

The film, however, does indicate that it was his fear of losing control and not being able to continue working that led Van Gogh to commit suicide. As the film progresses, he asks to be committed to an asylum and meekly submits to its regimen of complete rest. He has become terrified of his emotional instability and writes to Theo that he is afraid that someday he will not even have the ability to do away with himself. When he is finally allowed to paint again he writes, "I work in haste from day to day as a miner does who knows he's facing disaster." The climactic scene of Van Gogh shooting himself is filmed with intense restraint as the artist struggles to remain in control of his muscles in order to handle the pistol. The suicide is not an impulsive act.

Many people believed Douglas' performance to be remarkable primarily because of his physical resemblance to Van Gogh, but the characterization goes beyond excellent makeup and costuming. His performance is effective because it is deeply emotional and sensitive. Despite the many memorable scenes of dialogue, probably one of the best scenes Douglas plays is the one in which the only words are Theo's narration on the sound track. The camera films a long shot of Doctor Peyron (Lionel Jeffries) escorting Van Gogh to his room at the St. Remy asylum. They begin their walk on a sunlit gravel path but immediately step within the shade of a tall tree and must walk the perimeters of a small, three-tiered garden in order to reach the interior of the hospital. It is as if Van Gogh is stepping out of the warmth of the sunlight which was so important to his work and entering the deep, cold, and confining maze of his mind. His physical presence seems to shrink with every step. Inside the hospital, the artist and the doctor walk with their backs to the camera down a long corridor of closed doors. There is a piercing wail as they pass by one door. The doctor continues walking unaffected by the scream, but Van Gogh pauses with a slight tremor of terror before continuing on with his head bowed in resignation.

Motion pictures are technically well suited to explore the life of an artist, for as a visual medium, the film can use its many elements to correlate, exemplify, and illustrate the painter's life and emotional state. The sets, cinematography, and musical score of *Lust for Life* are designed to do more than merely re-create the environments in which Van Gogh lived. The periods of artistic study which influenced Van Gogh's painting are reflected in the set decor, cinematic compositions, and musical themes. Rembrandt and Millet influenced his drawings during his time of evangelism at the Borinage; hence the cinematography uses those masters' styles of composition and lighting to film blue-black hills of coal, the shining darkness of the mining shaft, the suffering miners at work, and the earthy hues of Van Gogh's own village hovel. When Van Gogh returns home, he has a picnic with Cousin Kay, and its background set is a pastoral painting reminiscent of the murky greens and lush foliage painted by seventeenth century Dutch landscape artists. It is known that Van Gogh became interested in Delacroix and Rubens while studying at The Hague, and here again the film's lighting and color scheme echo the influence of those painters. The Parisian sequences are brilliant with cinematic equivalents to the work of the Impressionists. There is bright translucent color and movement in the scenes to illustrate the active modernity which the Impressionists gave to Van Gogh and to the world of art.

The film translates more of the elements of Van Gogh's own style to cinematic equivalents as the painter moves to the south of France and produces the canvases for which he is best known. This achievement is more subtle than the instantaneously recognizable re-creations of "Van Gogh's Bedroom" and "The Night Cafe," among others. The film animates Van Gogh's stylistic elements of clashing colors, concentric circles of light, undulating waves of foliage, and blustery winds to intensify the film's emotional pitch prior to Van Gogh's self-mutilation.

The film's use of various visual styles are intended to carry the action and are different from the sequences which directly re-create Van Gogh's own compositions. The famous "Potato Eaters," "Fishing Boats on the Beach at Saintes-Maries," "The Drawbridge," and "The Orchard," among many others, are brought to life in the film with imagination and meticulous care. They are also important thematically as transitions between events in Van Gogh's personal life and do not directly influence the film's plot development.

Lust for Life was critically acclaimed in the United States at the time of its release. Douglas won the Best Actor Award from the New York Film Critics Circle, but lost the Oscar to Yul Brynner (who won for *The King and I*). Anthony Quinn, in a small but outstanding role as Paul Gauguin, won an Oscar, his second, for the film.

Contrary to the favorable reaction of American critics, the foreign press criticized the film for its obvious Americanism and Hollywood banality in failing to understand both the artistic process and European sensibilities. The Americanism of the film, however, may be its most original contribution to the actual reinterpretation of Van Gogh and his paintings, for it ignores the distinct European influences of a rigid social structure and time-honored traditions. *Lust for Life* minimizes the centuries of social history which are the natural foundations of Van Gogh's art and presents him as an individual struggling to realize his personal vision independent of society. The film treats Vincent Van Gogh as if he were an "American," someone with idealized "manifest destiny" and undiminishing vistas of personal achievement.

Elizabeth Ward

THE LUSTY MEN

Released: 1952
Production: Jerry Wald for RKO/Radio
Direction: Nicholas Ray
Screenplay: David Dortort and Horace McCoy; based on a story suggested by Claude Stanush
Cinematography: Lee Garmes
Editing: Ralph Dawson
Art direction: Albert D'Agostino and Alfred Herman
Sound: Phil Brigandi and Clem Portman
Music: Roy Webb
Running time: 113 minutes

Principal characters:
Louise Merritt	Susan Hayward
Jeff McCloud	Robert Mitchum
Wes Merritt	Arthur Kennedy
Booker Davis	Arthur Hunnicutt
Al Dawson	Frank Faylen
Buster Burgess	Walter Coy
Rusty	Carol Nugent
Rosemary Maddox	Maria Hart
Grace Burgess	Lorna Thayer
Jeremiah	Burt Mustin
Ginny Logan	Karen King
Red Logan	Jimmy Dodd
Babs	Eleanor Todd

The opening sequences of *The Lusty Men* deserves to be recalled in detail. The credits are shown over a number of views of a rodeo parade, which provide brief glimpses of cowboys, cowgirls, horses, trick riders, clowns, and even Indians in full tribal dress—an innocent charade of facets of the West—accompanied not by the film's musical score but by actual source music of the rodeo. Following this, the rodeo itself is presented as in a documentary, with the announcer introducing the events and contestants. Jeff McCloud (Robert Mitchum) is one of the bronc riders. With no dialogue exchanges providing exposition relating to his character, he prepares to compete, rides the bronc, and is thrown and hurt. A subsequent shot finds him limping across the arena after the rodeo is over. Alone and in pain, he traverses the empty arena in twilight as the wind blows the litter of a long day across the ground. The shot of this walk is beautifully lit in delicate gradations of black and white and composed with architectural grace. Carrying his saddle, Jeff follows a diagonal line from left to right, the camera tracking with him but continuing to hold him at a distance as he moves from background to foreground, and the half-light catching just enough of his face to stir in us a subtle sympathy. Music is totally absent during the shot. The main theme of the score, a gentle and wistful motif evoking the melancholy of a vanished West, does not appear until Jeff has disembarked from a bus and started to approach the home he left years before.

Crawling under the house to reclaim the few possessions he had left behind, he is interrupted by Jeremiah (Burt Mustin), the old man who now lives there. Until this point, the film has shown an aesthetic kinship to silent films, with sound being used not to tell the story but to provide a complementary background to the visual description of Jeff's solitude and the gaiety of the rodeo. Reflective and unhurried, the film has conveyed both mood and meaning before its principal characters begin to enact a story. When Wes Merritt (Arthur Kennedy) and his wife Louise (Susan Hayward) arrive at the house a few minutes later, the elements of a triangle become evident, and melodrama begins to mingle harmoniously with the realistic depiction of the modern West already established.

We learn that Wes and Louise are trying to save enough money from his wages as a ranch hand to buy the property and that Jeff, a rodeo star, has fallen on hard times and has sustained too many injuries to continue competing. Wes befriends Jeff and gets him a job at the ranch, much to Louise's displeasure. Her concern turns out to be justified, as Wes has already decided to try his skill at the rodeos and wants Jeff to teach him the tricks of the trade. Wes learns quickly and comes away from his first rodeo a winner. He and Jeff agree to split his winnings on the circuit, and a reluctant Louise goes with them as they leave the ranch and begin to travel from rodeo to rodeo.

On the rodeo circuit, a number of interesting secondary characters are introduced and developed. Al Dawson (Frank Faylen), a supplier of stock for the rodeos, is engaged to trick rider Rosemary Maddox (Maria Hart), one of Jeff's old flames. Buster Burgess (Walter Coy) has been gored by a Brahma bull and is drinking heavily in an attempt to escape his fear. His wife Grace (Lorna Thayer) stands by him until he is killed by another bull. Booker Davis (Arthur Hunnicutt), an old rodeo great now reduced to telling tall tales and cracking jokes about the endless punishment taken by his leg, travels with a young girl named Rusty (Carol Nugent). Red Logan (Jimmy Dodd) and his wife Ginny (Karen King) are also veterans of rodeo life.

Wes quickly becomes a spectacular competitor and begins winning a great deal of money. He promises Louise it is for the ranch they want to buy, but soon he is intoxicated by the glamour and excitement of being a rodeo star. Louise makes the best of it, while Jeff, loving her in silence, waits for a break in the marriage. Although Wes is inconsiderate and selfish toward Louise, she persists in her dream of a home of her own until he reveals that he is more interested in staying with the rodeo. After disrupting a party and roughing up a rodeo groupie named Babs (Eleanor Todd) who has designs on Wes, she finally decides to leave him, and Jeff reveals his feelings about her. She is emotionally responsive, but she refuses to return his love, declaring that his wandering and irresponsible life has made him a cripple.

The climax occurs the next day after a drunken Wes has accused Jeff of taking advantage of their arrangement to live off him because he can no longer make it on his own. Hurt by both Louise and Wes, Jeff enters four events, even though he is not in shape to compete. He manages to perform like a champion in the first few events, arousing Wes's renewed admiration. As Jeff prepares for the bronc-riding event, Wes appears beneath the chute and wishes him luck. The two men smile at each other in silent affirmation of their ambivalent friendship. Jeff gives the bronc an exceptionally good ride, but after the time limit is up, he is unable to jump off properly. He falls, his foot caught in the stirrup, and is dragged along the ground. Taken to a bed in a nearby room, he realizes that his rib is sticking through his lung. Bending over him with tears in her eyes, Louise speaks to him lovingly, as he rolls toward her and holds her for a moment, his face buried in her breast. After Jeff's death, Wes, who is sobered by the incident, makes up his mind to leave the rodeo, and he and Louise are reconciled. Followed by Booker and Rusty, who have volunteered to work with the couple on the ranch, they depart beneath an exit sign as the rodeo continues.

Although Jeff's unexpected death is deeply poignant, the ending cannot be accurately described as sad; nor does the return of Wes and Louise to their earlier dream make it a happy resolution. Significantly, a piece of rodeo life goes with them in the form of Booker and Rusty. The alternative life styles of wandering and being settled in a home of one's own both are respected and honored by the film, and there is a wonderfully achieved balance of sympathy between the three leading characters. Louise is very tough-minded and often unfair in her aggressive determination to keep her marriage within the limits of her own steady insistence on settling down, but she is eloquent in describing what the idea of a home means to her. She also remains loyal to Wes in spite of the provocations of his own callous treatment of her and Jeff's warm and appealing attentions. Her feelings toward both men are never simplified; the movie implies that she loves both of them and is coping admirably with a difficult situation. Wes reveals considerable weakness of character in the course of the story, but the energy and willfulness with which he pursues his goals is initially well-motivated, and there is an excitement in the lure of rodeo life which makes his actions understandable. As he is also driven by admiration of Jeff, his obsessiveness is never completely unappealing. Jeff himself is neither the sadly incomplete man who arouses Louise's ambivalent solicitude nor the romantic figure who is the object of Wes's hero-worship. An essentially simple man, seemingly in control of his life but unable to reconcile his deeper desires with his uncomplicated self-image, he is alienated not only from a settled world but also from the rodeo world. He is unable to relate more than casually to anyone, and the tenderness he feels for Louise comes too late to give him purpose and direction.

Other characters correspond without undue deliberateness to Louise, Wes, and Jeff while remaining highly individualized. Grace, widowed by the rodeo world, portends Louise's own possible fate. Her husband Buster, easily undone by liquor and insecurity, mirrors Wes's own incipient weaknesses. The colorful and entertaining Booker is also unambiguously pathetic, reduced as he is to depending on old friendships and memories of former glory to sustain him. Clearly, this is the direction in which Jeff's life is heading and from which he is spared by death. All of the characters blend in convincingly with the realistic atmosphere in which the rodeo action occurs, testifying to a superb ensemble of actors and actresses.

The leading roles are astutely cast and played to perfection, with Kennedy's intensity contrasting effectively to Mitchum's more relaxed style, and Hayward revealing a softness and feminine charm beneath her character's tough façade. The women in the film are given as much attention as the men, and the performances of such unknown actresses as Hart and Thayer are worthy of attention for the contributions they make to the film's detailed and complex texture. If the male in each of us can respond to the wanderlust embodied in different ways by vulnerable men like Jeff, Wes, and Booker, the female in each of us can respond to the longing for stability expressed in the characters of such strong women as Louise, Rosemary, and Grace.

Even allowing for the customary freedom with which director Nicholas Ray executed material that engaged him, the screenplay of *The Lusty Men* represents an outstanding piece of writing. Undoubtedly, this is largely attributable to the presence as coscenarist of Horace McCoy, author of the celebrated Depression novel, *They Shoot Horses, Don't They?* Although the dialogue sounds natural enough, it is largely composed of a number of almost lyrical phrases which tend to recur in variations. The phrase "broken-down bronc rider" is echoed in Jeff's rueful "broken bottles, broken dreams, broken everything." When Jeff suggests to Booker that Wes will buy the ranch, the other responds, "The only thing he'll ever buy is a fancy car, a case of bourbon and a pair of low-cut town shoes." Tired of splitting his winnings with Jeff, Wes refers to the other as "dragging your foot in my stirrup." The most beautiful line, delivered by Mitchum early in the film and repeated by him as Jeff dies, is "There never was a horse that couldn't be rode; there never was a cowboy that couldn't be throwed." Enriched by the altered context when it reappears, this oblique admission of emotional vulnerability—it is Jeff's relationships with Louise and Wes which have "thrown" him—is especially touching for being rendered as homespun cowboy poetry. Essentially prosaic, and true to the rodeo milieu, the dialogue is so persistently suggestive and evocative that it instills the characters with poetic souls.

Ray's direction of the film shines with sensitivity and care. The architectural principles of his compositions lend considerable visual tension to scenes involving the three principals but never seem studied. In one early scene, after Jeff has had dinner with Wes and Louise, Louise is doing the dishes while the two men talk. Ray places the three characters in a diagonal, with Louise in left foreground, Wes in right background and Jeff in the middle, a visual prefiguration of the romantic triangle not yet touched upon in the script. Later, as Wes collects his winnings, Louise watches him as Jeff watches her—the central focus of each character's desires and the implied conflicts of those desires subtly defined in a single moment. Close-ups and camera movement are unobtrusive, lending dramatic expressiveness to key moments. The sudden pan from Louise to Jeff when he asks her if she could become interested in another man is the only instance in the film of that particular style of shot. An exchange of large close-ups between Jeff and Wes is saved for their final encounter, with Wes viewed from a slightly high angle and Jeff from a slightly low angle. Surprisingly, Jeff looks more boyish and vulnerable, an impression made especially poignant by camera angles having the initial purpose of telling us that Wes still looks up to Jeff.

Ray makes the film both a documentary on a particular world and an affecting human drama. This approach is manifested in his simultaneous embrace of the naturalistic and the artificial. The alternating of source music and Roy Webb's score on the soundtrack is an obvious example. Certain visual aspects of the film are even more fascinating. Actual rodeos were filmed, but according to cinematographer Lee Garmes, it was necessary to film these sequences at night and light them as if they were occurring during daylight. In addition, staged scenes and actual ones had to be seamlessly woven into a single structure. That this was achieved testifies to the expertise of Garmes, editor Ralph Dawson, sound engineers Phil Brigandi and Clem Portman, and art directors Albert D'Agostino and Alfred Herman. The art directors also provided Ray with a beautiful sound-stage exterior for the trailer camp. Rather than attempting to conceal its artifice, Ray permits the set's loveliness to provide romantic counterpoint to the rugged realism of the rodeo sequences.

The kinetic energy which Ray reserves for especially intense moments in his films is another significant element of his style. Jeff's fatal mishap, for example, is rendered with such immediacy that it provokes an almost physical response. Ray also displays a facet of his work often remarked upon, the appreciation of an emotional difference between day and night. All of the rodeos in the first half of the film take place during the day, and their culmination is reached in an exhilarating montage. Following this, as personal conflicts begin to surface, a lengthy series of nighttime sequences begins during a night rodeo. A return to daylight is reserved for the climactic sequence. This is arguably the crucial reason why a feeling of serenity overrides the wave of sadness which so startlingly and forcefully accompanies Jeff's death.

To say that *The Lusty Men* is the best rodeo film ever made does it little justice. Although it treats a modern subject, it evokes the vanished spirit of the West with a more touching fervor than most actual Westerns. Extending the finest tradition of classical American cinema—exemplified by certain films of John Ford, Howard Hawks, and Raoul Walsh—it is no less emotionally reminiscent of some of the music of Aaron Copland and of folk ballads such as "Someday Soon." It strikes to the heart of the American character, exploring contradictory impulses with grace and lucidity. Only a rare maturity of vision could appreciate so profoundly both the need to wander and the need to settle down.

Blake Lucas

MCCABE AND MRS. MILLER

Released: 1971
Production: David Foster and Mitchell Brower for Warner Bros.
Direction: Robert Altman
Screenplay: Robert Altman and Brian McKay
Cinematography: Vilmos Zsigmond
Editing: Louis Lombardo
Music: Leonard Cohen
Running time: 120 minutes

Principal characters:
John McCabe	Warren Beatty
Constance Miller	Julie Christie
Sheehan	René Auberjonois
Elliot	Corey Fischer
Bart Coyle	Bert Remsen
Mrs. Coyle	Shelley Duvall
Cowboy	Keith Carradine
Lawyer	William Devane

The richly atmospheric and photographically lush *McCabe and Mrs. Miller* is one of Robert Altman's best films. It works simultaneously on a number of different levels. It is a parable of industrialization, a love story, an exploration of the Western genre in film, and finally, a kind of existential drama about the struggle for survival through isolation, set against the background of Leonard Cohen's haunting songs. It is a film that shifts tone with amazing adroitness, sometimes edging into the farcical but retreating just far enough to keep the audience focused on the characterizations. Altman's strength as a director lies in his sense of time and place, and nowhere is this strength more evident than in this period piece set in 1902 which charts the development of the shanty mining town of Presbyterian Church. Few films have portrayed the physical environment, the weather, and the land, with such visual respect as this one, filmed on location in Canada. It is almost as if the town has been hewn from the wind and snow.

Warren Beatty plays John McCabe, a small-time gambler. As the film opens we watch his horse stumble through the snow toward town. McCabe is, as related in the Leonard Cohen song, a dealer "who wants to trade the game he knows for shelter," but his reputation as a gunfighter precedes him in Presbyterian Church. At this point, *McCabe and Mrs. Miller* starts to take liberties with the audience's conceptions of Western film tradition. Instead of the cool, tough hero, hardened by killing and moral reckonings, Beatty's McCabe conveys a sweetness and naïveté. He enters some poker games and wins enough money to invest in three prostitutes. He sets up a makeshift bordello in three tents on the outskirts of the mining encampment, while he builds a permanent saloon and whorehouse. He seems unable to function effectively, however, as one of the young women attacks her first customer.

McCabe soon meets Mrs. Constance Miller (Julie Christie), an English prostitute who proposes that they go in business together. She offers to manage the finances and keep the women sanitary and their customers entertained, and finally to make the bordello into a fine institution with beautiful furniture and fancy women from Seattle. Mrs. Miller is efficient and professional, and soon the brothel is the focus of the town's leisure activities. The two entrepreneurs make money hand over fist from the prostitutes and a bathhouse that customers are required to use before they can partake of the women's services.

Word of the success of the brothel begins to spread, and soon two representatives of a big mining company come to town, anxious to purchase McCabe's and Mrs. Miller's business. McCabe, cocky and puffed up with his own importance, misunderstands, thinking that the mining company is not tendering an offer to be accepted or rejected but that the company, by virtue of its money and power, intends to acquire the business whether McCabe cooperates or not. McCabe negotiates, bluffs, and generally plays the game of a good gambler, without realizing that he is out of his league. The mining company representatives quickly tire of negotiating with the self-aggrandized McCabe and leave town. Too late, McCabe realizes his error and tries to find them and capitulate, but they have disappeared.

He seeks a lawyer. In a scene that demonstrates the screenplay's blending of farce and pathos, the lawyer promises to use him as an example or test case, portraying McCabe as a small businessman in a struggle against domination by big capital. The mining company, however, has other plans and hires three professional thugs to murder him. Although McCabe has by now fallen in love with Mrs. Miller, she has only responded to him within the context of her profession; an exchange of money has always preceded their lovemaking. When his naïveté proves potentially fatal, however, she begins to betray her real feelings for him. Still, it is not enough emotion to break through the loneliness essential to the character development in this comic but bleak film.

When the killers come for McCabe, he leaves Mrs. Miller's bed to face them, but the confrontation runs counter to our expectations of the classic Western shoot-out. Although McCabe is described throughout the film as having a reputation as a gunfighter, he seems immediately overpowered by the detachment and cool brutality of the assassins. The duel takes place in the snowbound town as McCabe seems to battle his impenetrable isolation as well as his killers. He is shot and dies alone in the snow as the film cuts back and forth from his freezing body to Mrs. Miller as she lies in her bed smoking opium.

The story of McCabe's rise from gambler to small entrepreneur, only to be forcibly taken over by big business, is viewed by some critics as a capsule version of American economic history. *McCabe and Mrs. Miller* is a film whose meaning rises from the compilation of the richness of its images. Clearly, one of the film's central concerns is the Hollywood Western. *McCabe and Mrs. Miller* depicts its characters with a realism absent from the classic Western. The men are seen in their daily lives, with their daily functions and even their mumblings. A case in point is the small concern of the bartender in one scene regarding how he looks without a beard. This is the kind of incident that one would find unimaginable if it occurred in the heightened metaphorical language of the classic Western.

The women, too, refuse to conform to the classic Western film images of saloon girls or whores, instead conveying a self-consciousness and everyday quality uncharacteristic of Hollywood. Shelley Duvall, later to become one of Altman's "repertory" players, is seen here as the mail-order bride Mrs. Coyle. When Bart Coyle (Bert Remsen) dies, Mrs. Miller takes Mrs. Coyle in as a prostitute, telling her that in marriage her sexual duties just pay for her bed and board but in the brothel, "you get extra for yourself." Mrs. Miller is seen to be both capable and in possession of much business savvy—more than McCabe. Her sexuality is her job, a fact about which she is unashamed. She is far from the fallen woman of the classic Hollywood cinema. Thus Altman has made a Western about Westerns. It is not a satire, but in its very realism, it presents some perspectives on the traditional Hollywood approach to the Western genre.

Even though the characters of McCabe and Mrs. Miller fail to really draw upon the chemistry of Julie Christie and Warren Beatty, the two actors do manage to create an energy between them that seems to tether one to the other. Reflecting on *McCabe and Mrs. Miller* in the light of later Beatty productions such as *Shampoo* (1975) and *Heaven Can Wait* (1978), it is difficult not to invest the characters with the powerful sexuality of the stars' later teamings. It simply does not exist here in that sense, however, since glamorous sexuality would destroy the realism.

The characters are created with precision. Beatty's mumblings are well placed, not accidental. The important dialogue comes through with clarity. Altman creates a collage of this clarity and mumbling, and although it has annoyed critics of the film, it works as a sort of aural pointer, emphasizing certain moments and blending others into atmosphere. Altman carried this type of mumbling to an extreme in his recent film *Popeye* (1980). McCabe seems highly articulate in comparison. Julie Christie won an Academy Award nomination for her portrayal of Mrs. Miller, which combines briskness with a muted tenderness and self-assurance with an opiated languor. Minor characters, as in Altman's later work, reveal his expertise and emphasis on the art of casting. Keith Carradine, perfectly cast as an amiable cowboy who is brutally shot by McCabe's killers, is a case in point. Shelley Duvall is also quite strong, as is William Devane as a tragically funny overblown populist lawyer.

Cinematographer Vilmos Zsigmond creates the low-key colors of snowy and wet landscapes and gaslit interiors that are particularly effective in McCabe's death scene. Admirers of the film find its editing and its storytelling economical and efficient in building the subtle drama most clearly symbolized by the last shots of McCabe's dead body being covered by snow. Other critics find this very subtlety to be the film's weakness. Rather than feeling the dramatic impulse to be muted or suppressed, they simply find it nonexistent. This film meets with fervent admiration or impenetrable disinterest, as do many of Altman's later films. Clearly, *McCabe and Mrs. Miller* is a milestone in the development of a style some find boringly diffuse and many others find totally captivating.

Rebecca A. Bailin

THE MACOMBER AFFAIR

Released: 1947
Production: Benedict Bogeaus and Casey Robinson for United Artists
Direction: Zoltan Korda
Screenplay: Casey Robinson; based on Seymour Bennett and Frank Arnold's
   adaptation of the short story "The Short Happy Life of Francis Macomber"
   by Ernest Hemingway
Cinematography: Karl Struss
Editing: George Feld and John W. Wheeler
Running time: 89 minutes

> *Principal characters:*
> Robert Wilson .... Gregory Peck
> Margaret Macomber ....Joan Bennett
> Francis Macomber .... Robert Preston

Ernest Hemingway's fiction would seem to lend itself to a natural transition to the screen. His action-filled dramas and his sparse and succinct dialogue would appear to be perfectly suited for adaptation to the motion picture medium. Successful translations of Hemingway's works on film, however, have been few and far between.

Hemingway wrote about a man's world but a world in which women still played a very important part. While he preferred a relationship in which the male was dominant, he did not degrade women or regard them as inferior. In fact his heroes sought out those women who were independently individual. His ideal woman was Catherine Barkley, the nurse in *A Farewell to Arms* (1929), and while she may have subordinated her personal desires to the wishes of her man, she was a courageous realist. His fiction did, however, include many emasculating women, women which critic Edmund Wilson described as "American bitches of the most soul-destroying sort." This is precisely the kind of woman Margaret Macomber is in his short story "The Short Happy Life of Francis Macomber," which was made into a motion picture in 1947 as *The Macomber Affair*.

One of the recurrent themes which preoccupied Hemingway's writings was what Stendhal and others had observed before him to be the ageless war between the sexes. Stendhal observed that when men lose courage and self-confidence, women take over. To Hemingway this reversal of roles constituted a breakdown in the personal moral code to which he aspired, a moral code in which physical virtues and courage were tantamount to salvation of the soul. He believed man's most noble effort to be his battle with nature and with the universe; the goal was not the winning, but the battle itself. A fight well fought and perseverance was the name of the game. "Courage is grace under pressure" was Hemingway's description of this code of ethics, and he never captured it any better than in "The Short Happy Life of Francis Macomber," his truculent study of the war between the sexes.

Hemingway incorporated these themes in his writings over and over in his sparse, laconic, direct style, underplaying emotion and emphasizing courage and virility. He wrote sparsely, telling his reader no more than he deemed necessary, which inspired one critic to state that there was more to Hemingway's "white spaces" than to his printed words. It is often these "white spaces" which prove elusive to filmmakers, with the result that the fifteen films which have been based upon Hemingway's writings are of widely divergent quality.

A Farewell to Arms, filmed in 1932 and in 1957, and *For Whom the Bell Tolls* (1943) are the most popular screen adaptations of Hemingway's writings, but by far the best is *The Macomber Affair*, because it says in cinematic terms what Hemingway said with the written word. The chief reason it did so was the script by Casey Robinson, who had an uncanny ability to capture for the screen the essence of Hemingway. He also wrote the screenplays for two other Hemingway-based films, each of which was praised for coming close to the true Hemingway. Those films are the all but forgotten *Under My Skin* (1950), which is based on Hemingway's short story "My Old Man" and which starred John Garfield (a good choice for a Hemingway hero), and the wonderfully cast *The Snows of Kilimanjaro* (1952), also based on a Hemingway short story and starring Gregory Peck, Susan Hayward, and Ava Gardner.

While Robinson tried to remain true to Hemingway in each of these three screen adaptations, none of them ever pleased Hemingway himself because each was in some way changed by the addition of romantic "mush" by studio brass. *The Macomber Affair* nevertheless remains the best screen version of a Hemingway work, first because of Robinson's script and second (very important for all screen versions of Hemingway) because of the cast. Gregory Peck, Joan Bennett, and Robert Preston are perfectly cast in *The Macomber Affair*.

Francis (Robert Preston) and Margaret Macomber (Joan Bennett) are an ill-matched couple whose marriage is disintegrating. Francis is a rich, piteously unmanly blowhard who lacks courage and sportsmanship. Margaret is a childless, selfish, and treacherous woman who is beginning to lose the bloom of youth. He regards her as a tramp but has stayed married to her because of her beauty; she thinks of him as a heel and has remained married to him because of his millions. They are members of the international social set, which Hemingway despised, and in a last-ditch effort to save their crumbling marriage, they embark upon a safari in British East Africa. The idea of the hunt means nothing to either of them; a safari is merely one more aspect of the snob appeal of their social set. Screenwriter Robinson and director Zoltan Korda establish this fact early in the film as we see the Macombers purchase the best available supplies as well as the most expensive wardrobe for their journey and hire native gun bearers, porters, trucks, and—most important of all—the best guide money can buy, namely Englishman Robert Wilson (Gregory Peck). Wilson is the epitome of Hemingway's ideal of what the hunter should be: a man who is not only an expert marksman and hunter but also a man who has a sense of honor toward his quarry.

Korda had directed two earlier films with African backgrounds—*The Four Feathers* (1939) and *Sahara* (1943)—and he adeptly maintains throughout this film the primitive geographical locations of the hunt, while Robinson's script ably equates the motivation and psychology of the three characters in their primitive emotional displays to these African surroundings. As Hemingway intended, this equation results in an excruciating dissection of the relationship of the unhappily married Macombers to their guide and the relation of all three to "grace under pressure."

From the outset Margaret reveals herself as a deceitful bitch with a corrosive concern for herself as she openly humiliates her husband in front of Wilson. Macomber immediately senses his wife's interest in the virile guide. They argue; she admonishes and they temporarily put aside their differences in the anticipation of the excitement of the hunt. On their first night out Macomber cannot sleep because the roar of the lion in the night terrifies him, and the next morning when they track the lion down, Macomber's self-doubt overcomes him, he visibly trembles and is only able to wound the animal in the hunt. Wilson insists that they must seek out the lion and kill him. Macomber reluctantly agrees, but when they come upon the wounded beast and it charges them, Macomber panics and turns and runs, leaving Wilson to finish the job.

Witnessing this shameful behavior, Margaret blatantly kisses the courageous Wilson and that evening cuckolds her husband with him. She flaunts her infidelity, and when Macomber whines that she thinks he will stand for anything, she replies, "I *know* you will."

The next lap of the hunt takes them out after three buffalo. The party shoots all three and believes them to be dead when one of the natives discovers the third is only wounded. Wilson and Macomber go into the bush after the animal, and this time Macomber, steadfast and manly, shows no fear. Margaret responds to his newfound courage with resentment and hatred. She is no longer in control. As the buffalo charges Macomber, he fires and fells the animal, but only seconds later another shot is heard, and Macomber falls dead as a bullet from his wife's gun goes through the back of his head.

Up to this point *The Macomber Affair* follows Hemingway's story, but Hollywood's code of morality was different from that of Hemingway, and the implication that Margaret shot her husband deliberately could not pass the censors. Therefore, we next see a hysterical Margaret fall into Wilson's arms crying that she did not mean to shoot her husband, and, as further demanded by the censors, Margaret appears before the local Nairobi police captain. In the police station she breaks down and confesses her true feeling for her husband: "I wanted my husband dead. I hated him. Maybe I killed him. I don't know."

The film ends with Margaret being flown off to appear before a court of justice while Wilson remains in Nairobi. The ending implies they will end up together but also hints that the seed of distrust in Wilson's mind about her innocence or guilt will probably prevent any long-term happiness for them. This ending invalidates Hemingway's story, but as most critics of the day commented, if the viewer can ignore those last few minutes of the film, this is by far the best screen adaptation of a Hemingway work. Robinson's script is properly sparse and Hemingway-esque, and Korda's direction is stylish and vivid. All three actors excel in bringing life to Hemingway's characters, and Bennett is particularly amazing to watch. Arguably one of the all-time best descriptions of a performance by an actress was given by Bosley Crowther in *The New York Times* review of the film: "Joan Bennett is completely hydrochloric as the peevish, deceitful dame."

Ronald Bowers

THE MAGIC BOX

Released: 1951
Production: Ronald Neame for Festival Films
Direction: John Boulting
Screenplay: Eric Ambler; based on the biography *Friese-Greene: Close-Up of an Inventor* by Ray Allister
Cinematography: Jack Cardiff
Editing: Richard Best
Music: William Alwyn
Running time: 118 minutes

Principal characters:

William Friese-Greene	Robert Donat
Edith Friese-Greene	Margaret Johnston
Helene Friese-Greene	Maria Schell
Lord Beaverbrook	Robert Beatty
Graham Friese-Greene	J. Charlesworth
Maurice Friese-Greene	John H. Davis
Reporter	Michael Denison
Mrs. Claire	Joyce Grenfell
Kenneth Friese-Greene	James Kenney
Orchestra Conductor	Miles Malleson
Cousin Alfred	Bernard Miles
Policeman	Laurence Olivier
Mr. Lege	Michael Redgrave
Arthur Collings	Eric Portman
Bank Manager	Emlyn Williams

The Magic Box was produced as the British film industry's contribution to that country's tribute to its past and present, the 1951 Festival of Britain, which took place on the South Bank of London's River Thames, where today stand such memorials to the arts in England as the Royal Festival Hall, the National Theatre, and the National Film Theatre. The film cost an estimated two hundred thousand pounds to produce, of which one hundred thousand pounds was provided by the government-controlled National Film Finance Corporation.

Britain intended *The Magic Box* as a monumental tribute to its film industry, and used some of the country's leading film people, such as director John Boulting, producer Ronald Neame, and cinematographer Jack Cardiff, behind the camera, as well as seventy British stars and supporting players, most of them in cameo roles, in front of the lens. The result is a film which, while not completely a monumental bore, has little to recommend it as either art or entertainment. It is well made, but no amount of expert craftsmanship can hide the basic dullness, or lack of credibility, of its story.

The problem is that *The Magic Box* is based on the life of British film pioneer William Friese-Greene and attempts to promote him as the inventor of the cinema. It was a nice claim for Britain to make during its Festival, but one that could not stand up against the more worthy assertions for such an honor long since put forward by the Lumière Brothers in France and Thomas Edison and his colleagues in the United States. Indeed, even before the film was completed, a heated argument had broken out in the pages of *The New York Times* and *Motion Picture Herald* between supporters of the film in England and the noted American film historian Terry Ramsaye (author of *A Million and One Nights*), with the latter calling the film "a perversion of history," "romantic fabrication," and "socialistic government propaganda and part of a scheme to nationalize the British film industry."

Unfortunately, the controversy was livelier and more entertaining than the film itself. *The Magic Box* opens in 1921 with William Friese-Greene (Robert Donat) leaving his home to attend a meeting of members of the British film community. In a flashback, Friese-Greene's second wife, Edith (Margaret Johnston), tells of the later period in her husband's life when the inventor was experimenting with color film, experimenting which drove him deeper and deeper into debt and obscurity. His wife leaves him, and his three sons enlist in World War I rather than be a financial burden to their already overburdened father. In the second half of the film, again told in flashback, Friese-Greene himself reminisces about his early days as a young society photographer (much as the father of the film's producer, Ronald Neame, had been), a lucrative career which he throws aside to pursue his dream, the invention of a camera to photograph moving pictures. His first wife, Helene (Maria Schell), a delicate woman, is driven to her death by the financial hardships and exhaustion which Friese-Greene's experiments create.

The climax of *The Magic Box* has William Friese-Greene succeeding in his dream and showing his first successful moving picture film, scenes in Hyde Park, to an audience of one, a bewildered London policeman, bitingly portrayed by Laurence Olivier. Upon witnessing this monumental event, Olivier comments drily, "You must be a very happy man, Mr. Friese-Greene." Frustration soon sets in as Friese-Greene sees not himself but Thomas Edison receiving credit for the invention of the motion picture. At the 1921 meeting of film industry executives, Friese-Greene makes an impassioned plea for the British film industry and for unity in its ranks. Those present are unaware of the identity of the speaker, who collapses and dies immediately after his moving address. In Friese-Greene's pockets is found nothing but one shilling and tenpence, the cost of a ticket to the cinema.

As William Friese-Greene, Donat bears a marked resemblance to his earlier characterization of Mr. Chips in 1939's *Goodbye, Mr. Chips*, for which he won an Oscar. He is the type of man who is marked as a failure in Donat's playing, just as Mr. Chips—at least on the surface—was a failure. Aside from

Donat and Olivier, none of the other players particularly stand out, although Schell and Johnston are adequate as the inventor's two wives. Among the major British stars wasted in *The Magic Box* are Joyce Grenfell, Michael Redgrave, Emlyn Williams, Glynis Johns, Margaret Rutherford, Sybil Thorndike, Peter Ustinov, and Googie Withers, not to mention former American silent star Bessie Love.

The British press was frankly disappointed with the film, and *The New Statesman* (September 22, 1951) summed up the general feeling when it commented, "We haven't been so much bored as, gently, let down. But the disappointment rankles." American critical response was polite. *Time* (October 6, 1952) called *The Magic Box* "a cinebiography that is more of a blurred long shot than a clear close-up." *Newsweek* (October 27, 1952) found the film "colorful and touching." Despite its star names, *The Magic Box* could only find an American release through the art film distribution company of Mayer-Kingsley.

Today, *The Magic Box* is forgotten. It is seldom seen in either Britain or America, while Miss Ray Allister's biography on which it was based is almost impossible to locate in any library. Even information on Friese-Greene himself is scant: most film books and general encyclopedias give him only a passing reference, or nothing at all. He did die in the manner seen in the film, but that aside, much of the material in the biography is speculative. Today his work is generally regarded as paralleling some of the Lumières' and Edison's work, but his invention was too complicated and impractical to be considered the first successful motion picture camera. The film was a good idea—as *Variety* (September 26, 1951) called it, "a picture of great sincerity and integrity"—that simply did not work. Like the Festival of Britian, it belongs, vaguely remembered, in Britain's past.

Anthony Slide

MAGNIFICENT OBSESSION

Released: 1935
Production: John M. Stahl for Universal
Direction: John M. Stahl
Screenplay: George O'Neil, Sarah Y. Mason, and Victor Heerman; based on the novel of the same name by Lloyd C. Douglas
Cinematography: John J. Mescall
Editing: Milton Church
Running time: 110 minutes

Principal characters:
Helen Hudson	Irene Dunne
Bobby Merrick	Robert Taylor
Tommy Masterson	Charles Butterworth
Joyce Hudson	Betty Furness
Nancy Ashford	Sara Haden
Randolph	Ralph Morgan

The Lloyd C. Douglas novel *Magnificent Obsession* was on the fiction best-seller lists for several years during the days of the Great Depression. It did not come to the screen until the last few days of 1935 because it had been regarded as a well-needed fictional sermon, a treatise on righteousness and the true rewards of brotherly love. Yet there was a definite audience for the cinema version when it was presented to the public, as was proved by its initial holiday engagement at the Radio City Music Hall. It was a good tear-jerker, sensitively presented and tenderly acted by a first-rate cast.

Box-office receipts and book sales have shown that in times of stress, book and cinema audiences have been drawn to any theme that is basically spiritual. Although the country was out of the worst part of the Depression which might have destroyed it had Franklin D. Roosevelt not become the type of presidential leader that he was, it was crippled anew by a recession during the 1935-1936 period, and again people were seeking spiritual salvation, so they were ready for the message contained in the Douglas novel.

In the very first reel of *Magnificent Obsession*, its heroine, Helen Hudson (Irene Dunne), is faced with a perplexing moral dilemma. Her husband, the eminent surgeon and metaphysician, Dr. Hudson, dies of a heart attack. He might have been saved, but the only pulmotor resuscitator equipment in the area is in use on the other side of the lake near which they live, pumping water from the lungs of Bobby Merrick (Robert Taylor), a worthless millionaire playboy who had smashed his expensive speedboat during a drunken spree and was nearly drowned when he was thrown into the lake. Helen is bitter that circumstances have allowed her husband to die while the life of a wastrel youth has been saved. She grows even more morose when, as a widow, she learns for the first time of the many philanthropic deeds and acts of truly Christian charity which her late husband, all unknown to her, had wrought in his life.

Consequently, she is justifiably furious when she encounters Bobby Merrick and sees for herself that he is continuing his wanton life while her husband's unnecessary death has been indirectly caused by this thoughtless, unfeeling young man. Bobby, unaware of her identity or emotions, makes a pass at her, while she burns with angry resentment. She is in the car he is driving and is so upset that she opens the door when the car is temporarily halted, and thoughtlessly steps out in front of an oncoming automobile, causing her to be critically injured. When she is brought to an emergency ward, it is discovered that while most of her injuries will mend, her eyesight is hopelessly gone.

Bobby Merrick is so jolted into an awareness of what he has twice done to the Hudson family that he vows to God that he will reform his ways and return to the medical studies he had abandoned in order to live the life of a wastrel. He himself pays for all the medical aid Helen receives, although she is unaware of it, and he does everything to bring top specialists into the case. He has had her sent to Paris for the attention of the outstanding eye surgeons of the day, and while they are waiting to see what progress surgery has done in her behalf, he takes her through Paris, describing the beauty of the city. She has gone through so much, and, having heard his voice only a few times before her accident, she does not recognize vocally who he is. It is on the top of Montmartre near the Sacre Coeur Cathedral that one of the tenderest and most moving sequences develops, when he describes what he is seeing, and she is able to envision the Paris he sees with his eyes.

Six years pass, and Merrick has become not only one of the leading eye specialists of his time, but has won the Nobel Prize, a small miracle in itself. In a Virginia retreat, he himself again operates with his newfound skill on Helen's eyes, and this time the surgery is successful, and she is able to see. She is stunned when she sees for herself that her salvation lies in the very hands of the man who had been responsible for the loss of her sight, as well as the death of her husband. Merrick is totally changed because he has taken on the philosophy of Dr. Hudson and now lives a life of brotherly love.

The last reel of this film is doubly moving for what it does not say. It could have been mawkish, and at times the situation borders perilously close to the absurd because of the happenstance of so many plot twists; coincidence abounds at every turn. Romance, however, motivates every sequence involving Merrick and Helen; she has become the only woman he loves, and with her sight restored, she sees him for what he has become, the one man who has truly followed in heart and deed in the image of her dedicated husband.

Restraint is the keynote of the entire 110 minutes of screen narrative. The three screenplay writers have understated the dialogue, and director John M.

Stahl has handled the dramatic situations with a kind of humility unusual in a director who had gained a reputation for being so volatile on occasion. Although the basic plot outline may seem corny, on the screen it is entirely believable. This is probably due to the skill of the actors. Irene Dunne had already shown in *Cimarron* (1931), in *Back Street* (1932), and in *The Age of Innocence* (1934) how delicately she could handle a scene that combined romance with pathos, and this time her skill is both adroit and free from every taint of melodrama. She had come to *Magnificent Obsession* fresh from the melodies and bittersweetness of her role as Stephanie in the Astaire-Rogers musical, *Roberta* (1935), and her interpretation of the hazards of Helen Hudson was a skillful utilization of the thought inherent behind her lyrics in the main song from that musical film, "Smoke Gets in Your Eyes."

It was Dunne who suggested to director Stahl that he would do well to consider Robert Taylor for the role of Bobby Merrick. Taylor had been put under contract by M-G-M, who promptly lent him to Fox for a Will Rogers film, *Handy Andy* (1934), whereafter his only roles had been of no consequence at his home studio, where he was regarded as remarkably photogenic and of some potential talent. After his success in *Magnificent Obsession*, M-G-M took a new look at Taylor, and before the next year was over he was playing Armand to Greta Garbo's exquisite Marguerite Gauthier in *Camille* (1936). Taylor became one of the most important fixtures at M-G-M, lasting there under contract for twenty-five years; but the first real step to the stardom he attained he took when he went on loan-out to Universal for the male lead in *Magnificent Obsession*.

The roles of Bobby Merrick and Helen Hudson continued to be harbingers of good luck when Universal remade the film in 1954 with Jane Wyman and Rock Hudson. Wyman had already won an Academy Award with *Johnny Belinda* (1948), so her ability as the blind but sensitive heroine of Douglas Sirk's *Magnificent Obsession* did not have to be proved; but Rock Hudson's career took a turn for the better when he played Merrick, for he then got better roles at his home studio, Universal, that helped him bring a becoming dramatic authority to his subsequent part in George Stevens' *Giant* (1956), a role that brought him a nomination by the Motion Picture Academy as Best Actor. Contrived as the situation is in *Magnificent Obsession*, it is presented throughout with a becoming restraint, and the audiences for both versions were willing to accept the thoughtful humility of both presentations.

DeWitt Bodeen

MAGNIFICENT OBSESSION

Released: 1954
Production: Ross Hunter for Universal-International
Direction: Douglas Sirk
Screenplay: Robert Blees; based on the novel of the same name by Lloyd C.
   Douglas and Wells Root's adaptation of a screen story by Sarah Mason and
   Victor Heerman
Cinematography: Russell Metty
Editing: Milton Carruth
Running time: 107 minutes

Principal characters:
Helen Phillips	Jane Wyman
Bob Merrick	Rock Hudson
Joyce Phillips	Barbara Rush
Nancy Ashford	Agnes Moorehead
Randolph	Otto Kruger

Magnificent Obsession was the third of ten films Douglas Sirk directed and Ross Hunter produced for Universal-International from 1952 to 1959. Six of these—*All I Desire* (1953), *Magnificent Obsession* (1954), *All That Heaven Allows* (1955), *There's Always Tomorrow* (1956), *Interlude* (1958), and *Imitation of Life* (1959)—are melodramas, and were among the most economically successful of this genre made in the 1950's. Although the "woman's picture" remains an underrated and misunderstood genre, Sirk's critical reputation has grown enormously since his own time, and his work is now the subject of at least two books— Jon Halliday's *Sirk on Sirk* (1972) and *Douglas Sirk* (1972), edited by Laura Mulvey and Jon Halliday—countless film magazine articles, and even university courses. Sirk is admired for his brilliant visual style, his ability to make radical statements about the condition of life depicted in melodrama (oppressive bourgeois values and narrow roles for woman), and his remarkable talent for taking unpromising material and transforming it into brilliant cinema.

Never was this last talent more sorely tested than in *Magnificent Obsession*. None of the major critical works on Sirk deal with this film, except to attest to its difficulty. Halliday calls it "an appalling weepie," Robert E. Smith (in his excellent notes on the film for the University of Connecticut Film Society's film series "Douglas Sirk: The Complete American Period," 1974) says, "At first glance this story would seem to be hopeless." Sirk himself says "My immediate reaction to *Magnificent Obsession* was bewilderment and discouragement. . . . This is a damned crazy story if there ever was one." He continues, "It's a combination of kitsch, and craziness, and trashiness."

Magnificent Obsesson was an extremely popular film, however, made from an "inspirational best seller" of the same title written by Lloyd C. Douglas in 1929. It was first produced by Universal in 1935, directed by John Stahl and starring Irene Dunne and Robert Taylor. These circumstances are remarkably like those of *Imitation of Life*, another Hunter-Sirk remake of a 1934 Stahl film. In 1954, *Magnificent Obsession* was a "big picture" for Universal; Jane Wyman was one of their biggest stars, and the production was lavishly mounted compared to many of Sirk's other melodramas. Audiences and critics agreed, and *Magnificent Obsession* received rave reviews, many even citing it as a superlative remake.

The plot of *Magnificent Obsession* contains many of the most difficult elements of melodrama: absurd coincidences, unbelievable tragedy and suffering, and ponderous, manipulated fate. Because of his recklessness, Robert Merrick (Rock Hudson), a rich playboy, has a boating accident and requires the use of a resuscitator kept by Dr. Phillips for his own uncertain health. Phillips (who is never seen in the film) has an attack and dies while Merrick is being saved. Phillips, a much-loved doctor, leaves a young widow, Helen (Jane Wyman), whose blindness Merrick unintentionally causes when she is hit by a car trying to avoid listening to his insistent but thoughtless apologies. He then falls in love with the blind Helen, and they become friends while he conceals his identity from her. Upon his urging, Helen's friend and companion Nancy Ashford (Agnes Moorehead) and stepdaughter Joyce (Barbara Rush) convince her to go to Europe for special treatment of her blindness. While in Europe, Helen is visited by Merrick, who finally confesses to her that the man she has come to know as "Robbie" is actually Bob Merrick. Helen forgives him and is in love with him, but because she does not want her incurable blindness to be a hindrance to his new career as a surgeon, she and Nancy disappear. At the end of the film, after several years of separation, Helen and Merrick are reunited after he saves her life and restores her sight in a delicate brain operation.

There is another thread which is woven throughout the story, but one which Sirk wisely downplayed when transferring the original novel to the screen. Dr. Phillips was an extremely powerful, kind man who helped many people, Helen learns after his death, and his "magnificent obsession" is passed on to young Merrick, first reforming him, then taking him back into medicine, where he becomes a brilliant surgeon, a man not unlike Phillips himself. Sirk weaves the miraculous and redemptive qualities of the book into the love story with dark foregrounds, occasional inspirational light, and a feeling of awe and mystery. His characters blunder about, never really guided by anything except good intentions and an absurdly mechanical fate. He infuses the awful coincidences, tragedies, and inevitable transcendent ending with a dark pessimism, managing (as he does in his best films) to turn the themes of the novel on their head with such subtlety that even admirers of the author, Douglas, loved the film. It is inconceivable, however, that they could have left the film without having been affected—even if unconsciously—by the extreme differences of the film's attitude toward the "magnificent obsession."

In the novel, this "obsession," a strangely 1970's kind of secular religion, is the heart of the book. Based on a page in the Bible (never identified) but vehemently dissociated from the church, it is a system used by Dr. Phillips and passed on in his journal, via his friend Randolph (Otto Kruger), to Merrick. Amazingly, yet entirely consistent with a Protestant ethic which bases salvation on a system of exchanges and justifies material wealth as a sign of divine approval, this system is a formula for power and success. Phillips' "teacher" calls it, "a secret formula for power," "the rule for getting whatever you want, and doing whatever you wish to do, and being whatever you would like to be." "I now have everything I want and can do anything I wish . . . and so can you! So can anybody!" writes Phillips of his teacher's lesson. When he finds the page in the Bible, he exalts, "There it was—in black and white— the exact process for achieving power to do, be and have whatever you want." It is a system of good works in which the good you do in secret gives you power—a perfect exchange system to fit (and justify) a capitalist economy. Phillips—"a materialist and a very cold blooded one at that"—uses science to explain that when your personality is hooked up to the "Main Personality" any man can essentially be Jesus—only a rich, successful Jesus. "If that's religion, I'm religious," Merrick says, "But I'd rather think of it as science."

This appalling system certainly performs the usual ideological role of melo-drama—it justifies the status quo. Sirk's film introduces an element of dark-ness and uncertainty into the neat mathematics of the novel, producing a fascinating tension between fate and coincidence. Unfortunately, the material is so murky that the film is less accessible than most of Sirk's pictures. One of the major changes made in the film which shows Sirk's creation of a foreboding tension is the role of blindness. In the novel, Helen is only briefly blind, while in the film she develops a deep friendship—possibly love—with Merrick as a result of her prolonged blindness. Sirk's characters are always metaphorically blind; Helen Phillips is the only literally blind character in Sirk's works, and her fumblings and vulnerability provide insights into other symbolic forms of blindness. Her helplessness is more complete, but not unlike that of other characters who take uncertain steps with no guide to lead them. They are driven and buffeted by forces they do not understand (material success which promises happiness but cannot deliver, love without foundation, and self-doubts that are untrue), victims (and it is here that Sirk, a Marxist, makes his radical statements) of a system which cannot fulfill its promises to them. Many of his main characters are unhappy women whose idea of hap-piness is marriage and children as in *There's Always Tomorrow* and *All I Desire*, yet we see the illusory nature of their dreams. No Sirk character really knows himself or herself, and Sirk is careful to show that this is a result of the false values and goals of bourgeois culture, not of personal failure.

Magnificent Obsession is the least accessible of Sirk's 1950's melodramas. It rewards the effort required to appreciate it, especially within the context of Sirk's entire body of work. Sirk himself likens its appeal for him to that of Greek tragedy.

Janey Place

MAJOR BARBARA

Released: 1941
Production: Gabriel Pascal; released by United Artists
Direction: Gabriel Pascal
Assistant direction: Harold French and David Lean
Screenplay: Anatole de Grunwald and George Bernard Shaw; based on the
  play of the same name by George Bernard Shaw
Cinematography: Ronald Neame
Editing: Charles Frend
Running time: 121 minutes

Principal characters:
Barbara Undershaft .... Wendy Hiller
Adolphus Cusins .... Rex Harrison
Andrew Undershaft .... Robert Morley
Bill Walker .... Robert Newton
Jenny Hill .... Deborah Kerr
Policeman .... Stanley Holloway
Lady Britomart .... Marie Lohr
Sarah .... Penelope Dudley Ward
Stephen .... Walter Hudd
Charles Lomas .... David Tree

By the time cinema had become an important form of entertainment and long before it was ever called an art form, George Bernard Shaw was a well-established, successful playwright. His critical reputation, financial security, and dislike of the mistreatment of literary works by motion picture companies enabled him to wait for a satisfactory agreement before he would allow his plays to be filmed. Because his works depended greatly upon their dialogue, he wisely did not allow silent film treatments of them. When sound films were developed, however, he began to consider the many requests of filmmakers who wished to put his prestigious and popular plays on the screen. After a long series of negotiations and two unsatisfactory films, Shaw finally found a producer whom he could trust to film his plays faithfully. The man was Gabriel Pascal, a Hungarian *émigré* whose main qualification was that he convinced Shaw that he venerated Shaw's works and would not desecrate them as Hollywood producers would. Shaw's faith was rewarded when Pascal produced a film of *Pygmalion* (1938) that satisfied the author; so Shaw and Pascal decided to film *Major Barbara* next.

As he had done for *Pygmalion*, Shaw wrote a screenplay for *Major Barbara* that embodied several changes from the text of the play. These changes, however, did not alter the structure or themes of the original. In general, Shaw added transitions and dramatized certain events that were merely described in the play. He also wrote a few new scenes, excised several portions of the play, and continued to rewrite the script and give his consent to excisions from it during the filming. In addition, three chief factors caused changes to be made that were not desired or approved by Shaw: restrictions of time and budget, decisions made by Pascal (although he usually followed Shaw's wishes), and censorship. The film of *Major Barbara* that emerged from this process, then, is generally, but not exactly, the film that Shaw wanted to have made from his play.

Like most of Shaw's works, *Major Barbara* is a play of ideas. Each of its three main characters pursues and preaches a different ideal. Adolphus Cusins (Rex Harrison), a professor of Greek, is an intellectual; Barbara Undershaft (Wendy Hiller), a major in the Salvation Army, is religious; and her father, Andrew Undershaft (Robert Morley), a munitions manufacturer, is a capitalist. To a certain extent the film (much more than the play) divides itself into two sections. The first part centers on Barbara, both her work and her romance with Cusins. In the second part, the emphasis shifts to the combination of intellectual, moral, and enlightened capitalistic ideas for the betterment of mankind.

The film opens with Cusins on a street corner delivering a lecture on the ancient Greeks as part of a workers' education project. His audience is small and pays little attention to him. Once the sound of a Salvation Army band is heard, he loses all his audience except for a policeman (Stanley Holloway) on duty. Accepting defeat, Cusins ends his lecture, and—guided by the policeman—he goes to see the Salvation Army meeting because of his intellectual interest in religious experiences. At the meeting Major Barbara is speaking to a large and engrossed crowd. We first hear her voice, then see her from the back, and finally we see her face. Barbara's intensity and sincerity immediately captivate Cusins, and he volunteers for a private prayer session just to meet her. As soon as he is alone with her, he admits that he is not interested in her religion and declares his love for her.

Barbara soon accepts Cusins and brings him into her world. We learn that she is the daughter of a wealthy munitions maker, Andrew Undershaft, although she has not seen him for many years. He lives apart from the family, which consists of his aristocratic and domineering wife, Lady Britomart (Marie Lohr), his daughter Sarah (Penelope Dudley Ward), his son Stephen (Walter Hudd), and Barbara herself. Also usually present in the house is Charles Lomas (David Tree), a rather foolish young man who is Sarah's suitor. Cusins soon becomes part of the family group as well as a member of the Salvation Army band, playing the bass drum.

At the Salvation Army shelter we see that most of the souls who have been saved are merely poor people willing to claim salvation for free food from the Army. They are not, however, happy about either poverty or their acceptance of charity. Then Bill Walker (Robert Newton) comes to the shelter. He is a tough bully who comes to punish his girl friend, who left him when she was converted. He physically and verbally abuses nearly everyone at the shelter, including delivering a particularly wicked blow to the face of Jenny Hill (Deborah Kerr, in her screen debut). Barbara then comes out and finds what he has done; she talks to him and within a few minutes has him feeling guilty and wanting to make amends.

During this time Andrew Undershaft has returned to visit his family. After he meets Cusins, he, Cusins, and Barbara have many discussions about money and religion and what they can do for individuals and for the common people as a whole. Undershaft then takes his family and Cusins to see his factory and the splendid housing and recreational facilities he has built for his workers. In addition, Undershaft also gives a large donation to the Salvation Army. When Barbara sees that the Army can be so easily bought with money tainted by being earned from the manufacture of destruction, she resigns from the organization. Finally, Undershaft convinces Cusins and Barbara that financial well-being is the first step to the social and spiritual improvement of the common people. Undershaft disinherits his own son and adopts Cusins so that he will take over the running of the factory.

The filming and editing of *Major Barbara* was handicapped by three main factors: wartime filming conditions, censorship, and the distributors' desire for a short film. Since the film was shot in England during the last half of 1940, Nazi bombing was a constant threat; often shooting was interrupted by air raids, and more than one location was reduced to rubble before the company was through using it. In addition, film distributors were accustomed to films that were about ninety minutes long and could not accept the two-hour-and-seventeen minute version that Pascal prepared. Until 1977 Pascal's full version was never shown. Instead audiences saw various versions, with sixteen to forty-two minutes excised. Most of these cuts came from the second part and reduced the development of Shaw's ideas. In addition, some minor cuts and changes were required by censors, particularly American ones.

For *Pygmalion* Pascal had been only the producer and Anthony Asquith had directed. For *Major Barbara* Pascal was both producer and director. He hired Harold French and David Lean as assistant directors, however, and they did much of the directing, although Pascal always retained overall control. *Major Barbara* overcomes most of the difficulties of its production. Hiller and Harrison give strong performances, but more notable, partly because they have more showy parts, are Morley and Newton. The film earned a few rave notices from the critics, most notably from Bosley Crowther in *The New York Times*, but its overall reception from both critics and audiences was only moderately successful.

Marilynn Wilson

MAJOR DUNDEE

Released: 1965
Production: Jerry Bresler for Jerry Bresler Productions; released by Columbia
Direction: Sam Peckinpah
Screenplay: Harry Julian Fink, Oscar Saul, and Sam Peckinpah; based on an
 original story of the same name by Harry Julian Fink
Cinematography: Sam Leavitt
Editing: William A. Lyon, Don Starling, and Howard Kunin
Running time: 120 minutes

Principal characters:
Major Amos Charles Dundee .... Charlton Heston
Captain Benjamin Tyreen .... Richard Harris
Lieutenant Graham .... Jim Hutton
Samuel T. Potts .... James Coburn
Sergeant Gomez .... Mario Adorf
Widow .... Senta Berger

Major Dundee is a film of two wars. One of them is pictured in the film. The other war, the war between director and producer, occurred during the film's production. As it stands, *Major Dundee* is approximately one hour shorter than filmmaker Sam Peckinpah had originally intended it to be. Although the film's principal star, Charlton Heston, returned his entire two-hundred-thousand-dollar salary to the producer as an act of good faith to ensure that the remaining scenes would be shot and director Peckinpah would have full control over the final cut of the film, the producer took the money but turned the film over to the editors. The producer won the offscreen war, and Peckinpah lost control of his film, but in the process, what might have been a great Western epic was turned into a severely truncated remnant of a very individualistic director's vision of the West.

In spite of its butchered form, however, *Major Dundee* remains an interesting film and an important work in Peckinpah's career. It cannot be called a great film, however; many of the scenes that were meant to establish the motivation of the main characters are now missing. The heart of the psychological concerns, which were so important in fleshing out Peckinpah's themes, have vanished forever on the cutting-room floor. What remains does, however, still show glimpses of the creative control of director/screenwriter Peckinpah, but the film has an overall incoherence and lack of continuity that obscures its meaning.

As with most of his films, Peckinpah's *Major Dundee* is concerned with a world in which violence is the rule rather than the exception. The film is set in the turbulent era of the final years of the Civil War. The opening scene was originally planned as twenty graphic minutes showing the Halloween night massacre of the B Troop of Fort Brenlin, New Mexico, and a local ranching family, the Rostes. With this scene in place, the structure of *Major Dundee* would bear a great resemblance to that of Peckinpah's later masterpiece, *The Wild Bunch* (1969), which is framed by two long and bloody battles, the first occurring during a bank holdup and the second involving the outlaws and Mexican federales. These two scenes, like the battle scenes in *Major Dundee*, reflect Peckinpah's preoccupation with violence as both a thing of appeal and repulsion. The famous choreographed scenes of violence in *The Wild Bunch* are also revealed to have their technical forerunner in the battle scenes of the earlier film, which communicate the agonies, but also the perverse excitement and fascination of warfare.

The present version of *Major Dundee* shows only the very final moments of the Rostes Ranch massacre, but this raid provides the obvious impetus for the action of the film. Major Amos Charles Dundee (Charlton Heston), commander of Fort Brenlin's prison camp for Confederates, leads a motley band of Union reprobates, black prison guards, Confederate prisoners of war, and civilian horse thieves and murderers across the Mexican border in an attempt to rescue the Rostes' three boys from their Indian captors. Ironically, this obsessive pursuit is revealed to be motivated less by the apparent need to save the boys than by the Major's own overriding need to escape his role as warden of a prison camp. The boys adapt well to their new lives as Apaches, but the Major cannot adjust to a role forced on him as punishment for his own disregard for authority at Gettysburg.

Dundee's initial image is one of an authoritative, competent officer whose main interest is in rescuing the boys, but as the film progresses, he is seen as an inflexible, guilt-ridden man whose ramrod manner barely conceals a troubled, insecure soldier whose concept of self is assured only when he is embroiled in war. Heston offers a well-controlled performance as Dundee, and even though the dialogue is sometimes inadequate in expressing character, director Peckinpah successfully uses Heston, and the other main actors, to create each character as a viable physical presence in a large-scale film that could easily have swallowed up lesser characterizations.

Dundee is given a personal and military rival in the dashing figure of Confederate Captain Benjamin Tyreen (Richard Harris). Tyreen's roles in life have been many—Irish potato farmer, court-martialed Union officer, and captured Confederate, but unlike Dundee, Tyreen's identity appears securely rooted beneath his assumption of a flamboyant, posturing appearance. Tyreen has an eloquence and personal flair which Dundee lacks, but more importantly, he possesses an understanding of himself and an intuitive knowledge of his fellows that make him a much more effective leader of men than his former friend, Major Amos Charles Dundee.

Although the other key roles of Sergeant Gomez (Mario Adorf), Samuel T. Potts (James Coburn), and Lieutenant Graham (Jim Hutton) have suffered because of the massive editing, they are still important, as is Tyreen, in pointing out the deficiencies in Major Dundee's character. Samuel T. Potts, a scout, is especially critical in his function as Dundee's friend. Potts is a wry observer of Dundee's failings, and his own levelheaded, self-effacing professionalism contrasts sharply with Dundee's chaotic leadership.

As the film details the commmand's raid into Mexico, the duality of Peckinpah's vision is apparent in his embrace of a romantic view of that country while creating a generally realistic portrait of war. The poor Mexican village that welcomes the American soldiers as liberators becomes a haven full of simple, generous people, including Peckinpah's usual selection of generous women, among them Senta Berger as the widow of the town's doctor. The command's leave-taking from the village is clearly a model for the startlingly similar scene in *The Wild Bunch*. In contrast to this romanticism, Peckinpah treats the violence in *Major Dundee* in a realistic manner that emphasizes the bloody action and aftermath of conflict: men writhing in pain from festering wounds, rows of leaking canvas bags containing the multilated bodies of the first battle's casualties, and Dundee's strained shoveling of dirt into a huge mass grave.

The Rostes boys are ultimately rescued and the Apaches are destroyed, but Dundee's command is decimated and the Major seems to have acquired little self-knowledge as a result of the costly foray. Our expectations of what a cavalry film should be have been satisfied in terms of "action," but Peckinpah turns the mythic expectations upside down. The glorious defenders of the frontier have been transformed into desperate, generally selfish men who, unlike the soldiers in John Ford's cavalry films, are not bound together in a homogeneous, lasting community. Only the figure of Captain Tyreen carries on the expected romantic tradition of the heroic cavalier. Tyreen dies in the final battle against the Emperor Maximilian's forces, but his single-handed charge against the enemy is an idealistic gesture that enables the twelve survivors to escape across the river into Texas. Tyreen may damn Major Dundee and the Major's flag, but Tyreen carries that flag into as glorious a death as is possible in the world of Peckinpah.

Major Dundee attempts a great deal, and in some measure succeeds, in spite of its mutilated form. Within its epic proportions lurk some of the techniques and creative impulses that later achieve full fruition in Peckinpah's indisputable masterpiece, *The Wild Bunch*.

Gay Studlar

THE MAN FROM MUSIC MOUNTAIN

Released: 1938
Production: Charles E. Ford for Republic
Direction: Joseph Kane
Screenplay: Betty Burbridge and Luci Ward; based on an original story by
  Bernard McConville
Cinematography: Jack Marta
Editing: Lester Orlebeck
Running time: 58 minutes

> *Principal characters:*
> Gene Autry .... Himself
> Frog Milhouse .... Smiley Burnette
> Helen .... Carol Hughes

Mention the term "Western" to cinema buffs and they will likely conjure up images of cowboys and Indians, of John Wayne and Randolph Scott, the films of John Ford and Howard Hawks, or perhaps one of the legendary Western heroes such as Wyatt Earp, Billy the Kid, Buffalo Bill, or General Custer, all staples of the classic Western film. There was, however, for a period from the mid-1930's to the mid-1950's, another breed of film Western that rivaled and often exceeded the more conventional films in the genre in terms of general (if not critical) popularity. In the heyday of the "B"-movie Western, the Singing Cowboy rode the range across a fantasy West that blended nineteenth century cattle drives with twentieth century jeeps and airplanes, all laced with a generous dose of country music.

There were a number of practitioners of this now arcane art—Tex Ritter, Jimmy Wakely, Rex Allen, and Roy Rogers, to name a few—but the first and most consistent of these musical cowpokes was Gene Autry. Autry appeared in ninety-one films between 1934 and 1968; his best work was done for Republic (1935-1947) and Columbia (1947-1953).

Among his many contributions to the genre, Autry was the author of the Cowboy Commandments, which set forth the credo of the Singing Cowboy. These heroes of the Saturday matinee were admonished to be truthful; to be gentle with children, animals, and oldsters; to be tolerant; to be patriotic; to be respectful to women, to their parents, and to the law of the land; to work hard; and to help those in distress. They were forbidden to smoke or drink; to go back on their word; and to take unfair advantage—even of a bad guy. In short, the ideal singing cowboy embodied the traditional American virtues. Norman Rockwell could not have stated it better.

Autry films featured a number of conventions that, while deviating from the norm of the traditional Western, eventually became commonplace in the musical Western genre. First of all, Autry invariably played himself; there were no name changes for his protagonists from film to film, which made it that much easier for his audience to identify consistently with Gene. In addition, Autry always dressed to the hilt in outfits that no real cowhand would be caught dead wearing. Although there was quite a bit of gunplay during the last reel, there was relatively little actual killing in Autry's films. Of course, there was also Autry's penchant for bursting into song at the drop of a ten gallon hat. Most of the songs (which featured complete orchestral and choral backgrounds, no matter how far from such amenities Gene might have been at the time) were eminently forgettable—for example, "Defective Detective from Brooklyn" in *Public Cowboy Number 1* (1937) and "That's How Donkeys Were Born" from *Gold Mine in the Sky* (1938)—but many were quite deservedly popular. "Be Honest with Me" from *Ridin' On a Rainbow* was nominated for an Academy Award in 1941.

There was a general, benevolent air of unreality in most Autry films. Indeed, his most important innovation may have been the blending of elements of traditional Westerns into contemporary settings. In this never-never land, Autry and his friends rode horses (Gene's horse was named Champion), packed six-shooters, and shot it out with the bad guys à la Tombstone, Arizona, in the 1880's. His films were set, however, in the American West of the 1930's and 1940's. Electricity, automobiles, and contemporary events such as the opening of the Boulder Dam in *The Man from Music Mountain* all coexisted peacefully with characters acting out the simple morality plays set half a century earlier.

These anachronistic plots probably accounted for the opinion, prevalent among foreigners and some Easterners, that there were still raging gunbattles between posses and rustlers on the streets of contemporary Western towns. That same fantasy also undoubtedly accounted for the films' tremendous popularity with children—it was possible to believe that such marvelous adventures were still available, and in one's own country. There was no need to travel backward or forward in time, or to Africa or the Orient, to find adventure. If parents never got around to going to Texas or Arizona on their summer vacation, well, there was still the Autry movie on Saturday afternoons.

The Man from Music Mountain is one of the best of the early Autry films. Gene had learned at least the rudiments of acting by this time (film studios, forced in their search for Singing Cowboys to choose between actors who could not sing and singers who could not act, usually opted for the latter), and Republic and its chief director, Joseph Kane, had the Autry formula down pat.

The film opens with shots of a newspaper headlining the opening of Boulder Dam on the Arizona-Nevada border. This sets the film chronologically as well as geographically—Boulder Dam was opened in 1936—and gives a fair hint of the plot. The twentieth century West lives or dies with water, a theme echoed as recently as Roman Polanski's *Chinatown* in 1974. Autry's version of the old story is much simpler, of course. Here the bad guys (land developers from Phoenix) conspire to sell lots in a ghost town on the false promise that water from the new dam will quickly turn it into a bustling metropolis.

The stage thus set, it is time for Gene and his compadres to make their appearance. They ride into view singing the title song, in which Gene describes himself as "a carefree buckaroo." They are riding their ponies home from a successful cattle drive, and they cannot help but notice the flocks of people in buses and old jalopies heading towards the ghost town of Gold River. One person in particular catches his eye—Helen (Carol Hughes), an aspiring beautician. Gene takes an immediate interest in her and resolves to help the townspeople get even with the swindlers.

To accomplish all of this, he enlists the aid of his sidekick. Most Singing Cowboys had sidekicks—loyal but often stupid second bananas who provided the films with a bit of comic relief. Often these sidekicks moved from star to star, depending upon which studio had whom under contract at the time. Gabby Hayes, for example, rode with Hopalong Cassidy until Republic persuaded him to hitch his wagon to Roy Rogers' star in 1939. Autry's first, and most memorable, sidekick was Smiley Burnette (who also later showed up in a number of Roy Rogers films). Burnette played a fat, rumpled man named Frog Milhouse; the character was known as Frog because he occasionally talked and sang in a croak.

Gene and Frog prepare an elaborate ruse that involves salting a played-out mine with gold nuggets, thus convincing the swindlers from the big city to buy back the land from the people they duped in order to reacquire mineral rights to the gold. The stratagem does not go exactly according to plan, but, many songs and a few bullets later, all ends well. Rumors of the gold strike cause state authorities to divert water and electricity to Gold River after all, and an explosion in the supposedly abandoned mine (the result of a shootout between Gene and the bad guys) reveals a new vein of gold. The residents of Gold River thus have their water and a mine as well. Gene is vindicated, and virtue is triumphant.

Kane, director of *The Man from Music Mountain*, was one of the "kings of the B's," a veteran of scores of Singing Cowboy sagas cranked out for Republic. Oddly enough, one of his later films was also called *The Man From Music Mountain*. Made for Republic in 1943, it starred Autry's chief "rival," Roy Rogers, who rose to prominence during Autry's two prolonged absences from the screen. The first of these occurred in 1938, when Autry went on strike for more money; the second was in 1943 to 1945, when he was serving in the Army Air Force during World War II. Despite the identical titles, however, the plots of the two films had nothing in common.

Autry combined his skills as an entertainer with a sharp business instinct. In 1947, he formed Gene Autry Productions and switched his allegiance to

Columbia, where he made dozens of films as well as several best-selling records, the most popular of which was "Rudolph the Red-Nosed Reindeer." In 1950, he moved into television, filming eighty-five half-hour episodes of the *Gene Autry Show*, featuring Pat Buttram as his sidekick and comic relief, and also featuring his horse Champion prominently. The television show featured what has become Autry's theme song (and the title of his autobiography), "I'm Back in the Saddle Again." Despite this already hectic schedule, he still found time to make twenty-four Singing Cowboy films (most of which were directed by George Archainbaud) for Columbia. He retired as a professional entertainer in the mid-1950's to devote himself to business pursuits which have turned him into a multimillionaire whose interests include television stations and ownership of a major league baseball team.

The Singing Cowboy, and indeed, the "B"-movie Western, largely vanished from the screen in the 1950's, although the audience for them did not. Television became the new home of such cowboys as Autry, Rogers, and their nonsinging colleagues such as Hopalong Cassidy ruled the airwaves in that medium's infancy, only to be replaced by more adult fare such as *Gunsmoke*, *Wagon Train*, and *Bonanza* by the end of the decade. Today, these films are largely curiosities—pleasant enough, but interesting primarily as an example of popular culture in a bygone era.

Robert Mitchell

THE MAN IN GREY

Released: 1943
Production: Edward Black for Gainsborough-Universal
Direction: Leslie Arliss
Screenplay: Margaret Kennedy and Leslie Arliss; based on the novel of the
same name by Lady Eleanor Smith
Cinematography: Arthur Crabtree
Editing: R. E. Dearing
Running time: 116 minutes

Principal characters:
Hester Shaw	Margaret Lockwood
Clarissa Richmond	Phyllis Calvert
Marquis of Rohan	James Mason
Rokeby	Stewart Granger
Toby	Harry Scott, Jr.
Gipsy	Beatrice Valery

The British film *The Man in Grey* is an overbearingly romantic melodrama
set in the Regency period of nineteenth century England. The film marked
the directorial debut of Leslie Arliss, who went on to make six feature-length
motion pictures between 1946 and 1954. Although generally panned by critics
in America as it had been in England, the film fared well at the matinee box
office. Heroine Margaret Lockwood was already gaining popularity in the
United States thanks to *The Lady Vanishes* (1938) and *Night Train to Munich*
(1940) and *The Man in Grey* also presented to the American public actress
Phyllis Calvert and British melodrama star James Mason, and marked the
film debut of Stewart Granger.

More interesting, however, than the snail-paced story, and certainly more
valuable in terms of cinema history, is the pomp and regality of the authen-
tically designed sets and costumes. Prior to the Victorian period, various
romantic forms were culminating in England, and this Gainsborough production pays deliberate attention to the structural and ornamental elements
of the Regency style: the integration of decorative architecture inspired by
organic modes in Greek and Roman antiquity, elaborate interiors, flat surfaces, and the general taste for French-styled furniture. Mason's clothes typify
the dress of a Regency dandy: long waistcoat, tight breeches or trousers, and
neck cloth. Lockwood and Calvert are seen in an array of period dresses,
tight-waisted with expanded skirts. The jewelry is simple, and they wear
ribbons or ornamented hats. Among the many sights in this period piece are
Vauxhall Gardens and Bath.

The screenplay, adapted by Doreen Montgomery, is based on a novel by
Lady Eleanor Smith. The film begins in the present (1943) at an auction of

the Rohan estate in Grosvenor Square. A chance encounter between descendants of unlucky lovers fades into a sequential history of their ancestors. The bulk of the plot concerns a tragic love story, together with a lengthy and cumbersome background. Clarissa Richmond (Phyllis Calvert) and Hester Shaw (Margaret Lockwood) are pupils at a snobbish finishing school. The former exudes purity while Hester, an incoming student, is at once distrustful, even spiteful. Clarissa's ample friendliness draws the dark-haired newcomer to her side. Nevertheless, Hester remains solitary in the way calculating schemers often do, and she suddenly leaves the school to elope with a navy man.

Clarissa's classical beauty and innocence do not protect her from the real world of chance after she graduates. As a convenience for the Marquis of Rohan (James Mason), it is arranged for Clarissa to be his wife. The Marquis, although well-bred and powerful, is a male version of Hester: dark and selfish. Not even a loveless marriage to a cad, however, can dim Clarissa's glow. When she learns that Hester is performing at a nearby theater, she is quickly off to applaud her friend's talent. She finds Hester dispossessed and without a husband, and the audience finds her to be as crafty as ever. Clarissa also recognizes one of the actors, for, in an earlier scene, he had mysteriously forced Clarissa's carriageman to give him a ride to a destination of close proximity to the theater. This bold, impetuous character, Rokeby (Stewart Granger), is infatuated with the blonde Clarissa. Ironically, she preserves her romantic contact by inviting Hester to share her home and her fate.

When the film finally gets around to the only dramatic tension in the plot, the audience is all too aware of the ensuing outcome. Hester becomes the Marquis' mistress and helps Clarissa and Rokeby's affair. Hester almost secures the Marquis for herself when Rokeby and Clarissa plan to run off together, but she makes the mistake of telling the Marquis, who uncharacteristically objects to this intrusion into his marriage and therefore his position at Court. The doomed Clarissa returns, becomes ill, and is left to die by an insanely jealous Hester. The Marquis, who has become increasingly evil, beats Hester to death with a cane when Clarissa's servant Toby (Harry Scott, Jr.) tells him what Hester has done.

Arliss' directorial debut lacks technical leadership. The film is neither innovative nor inspired, and the presentation is relatively artless and riddled with clichés. The viewer is presented with the ever-popular blonde innocent, dark-haired villains, and gleaming lover that had become the convention of earlier decades. The production is enhanced, of course, by the period sets and by the notable portrayals of Clarissa and Hester. Both Calvert's and Lockwood's performances turn tremendously romantic characters into believable personalities. Neither Mason nor Granger display the superior talent of their later years, probably because these are less than challenging roles. The film crawls through the Kennedy and Arliss screenplay without authority. The tragic lovers' lengthy history may have had its place in Lady Smith's novel, but it is too long for the screen. Certainly, the source is far below the great novels of other English women, such as Jane Austen or the Brontë sisters. Four years before *The Man in Grey* was released, the superior American production of Emily Brontë's *Wuthering Heights* (1939) was released, and it is a testament to the cinematic potential offered by a sound, poignant story.

The critical viewer cannot dismiss the fact that director Arliss and producer Edward Black were content to rely upon strong sets, adequate dramatics, and a weak script in the filming of *The Man in Grey*. The lack of story or directing merits mattered little to the moviegoing public, however, and the film was a hit in both Britain and the United States. The Gothic romance has proven lucrative on film many times before and since *The Man in Grey*. The matinee audience has ample material in this film to compensate for its lack of excellence: attractive stars, beautiful properties, and a tragic love affair.

Ralph Angel

THE MAN IN THE IRON MASK

Released: 1939
Production: Edward Small; released by United Artists
Direction: James Whale
Screenplay: George Bruce; based on the novel of the same name by Alexandre Dumas, *père*
Cinematography: Robert Planck
Editing: Grant Whytock
Running time: 110 minutes

Principal characters:

Louis XIV/Philippe	Louis Hayward
Maria Theresa	Joan Bennett
D'Artagnan	Warren William
Fouquet	Joseph Schildkraut
Porthos	Alan Hale
Athos	Bert Roach
Aramis	Miles Mander
Colbert	Walter Kingsford
Mlle. de la Vallière	Marian Martin
Spanish Ambassador	Montague Love
Queen Anne	Doris Kenyon
Louis XIII	Albert Dekker
Commandant of the Bastille	William Royle
François	Fred Cavens

During the 1930's and 1940's, when the studio system was at its strongest, there was not much room for the independent producer. The most successful independent was David O. Selznick, but another who had considerable success was Edward Small. Although he later turned to other types of films, Small became established with well-made productions of costume adventure classics, many of them derived from Alexandre Dumas, *père*. In 1934, he had an outstanding hit with *The Count of Monte Cristo*, and he followed it over the next seven years with *The Last of the Mohicans* (1936), *The Man in the Iron Mask* (1939), *The Son of Monte Cristo* (1940), and *The Corsican Brothers* (1941).

The Man in the Iron Mask is one of Dumas' most durable tales. Originally, the final volume in the four-volume novel *The Vicomte de Bragelonne* (1848-1850, itself following *Twenty Years After* as the third and final sequel to *The Three Musketeers*), it has taken on an independent life of its own. The novel is based on a very old legend that tells of a mysterious prisoner whom Louis XIV kept imprisoned in the Bastille with his face always covered. Apparently the mask was velvet, but legend turned it into the far more terrifying iron mask. Dumas then fashioned a fiction that immortalized the legend, according to which the prisoner was none other than the Sun King's identical twin brother. This story provides a natural *tour de force* for motion pictures—a virtuoso dual role for the lead, royal intrigue, the terror of the Bastille's dungeons and of the sinister iron mask, swashbuckling adventure, and costume romance. It also benefits from numerous filmed versions of *The Three Musketeers*.

Douglas Fairbanks, Sr. first filmed *The Three Musketeers* in 1921. It was an immense hit that confirmed the switch he had made from contemporary comedy to historical swashbucklers the year before with *The Mark of Zorro*. In 1929, he filmed the sequel as *The Iron Mask*, directed by Allan Dwan. It was the last of Fairbanks' successful swashbucklers, for he was becoming too old to perform plausibly as the athletic romantic lead. In *The Iron Mask*, however, he plays not the dual role of Louis XIV and his brother but rather the aging D'Artagnan; despite the title, the story of the Man in the Iron Mask has a secondary place in the film. It was Fairbanks' last silent film and his last major hit.

During the 1930's, two remakes of *The Three Musketeers* were filmed, neither very successfully, but the great popularity of Small's *The Count of Monte Cristo* showed that there was an audience avid for more Dumas, and the immense success of *The Prisoner of Zenda* (1937) with Ronald Colman in the dual roles of the king of Ruritania and his impersonator may also have suggested another swashbuckler with a dual role. In fact, a considerable number of swashbucklers have the lead playing dual roles of a sort. *The Prisoner of Zenda*, *The Man in the Iron Mask*, and *The Corsican Brothers* have literal dual roles—identical twins or identical look-alikes. In addition, however, numerous swashbucklers have the hero perform in dual impersonations: in *The Scarlet Pimpernel* (1934), *The Mark of Zorro*, and *The Son of Monte Cristo*, he pretends to be an effeminate fop, while he is in reality a dashing freedom fighter; in *Scaramouche* (1952), the hero doubles as an idealistic young lawyer and a comic actor; in the silent version of *The Sea Hawk* (1924), he doubles as an Elizabethan nobleman and a Barbary corsair; in *If I Were King* (1938), Colman is at first an unkempt vagabond and then a debonaire nobleman, while in *Kismet* (1944), Colman is a ragged beggar by day, an elegant man on the town by night, and further pretends to be a visiting monarch. Most of these stories had several film incarnations.

The best motion picture of *The Man in the Iron Mask* is the 1939 Small production. It was directed by James Whale, best-known for his horror classics—*Frankenstein* (1931), *The Bride of Frankenstein* (1935), *The Invisible Man* (1933), and *The Old Dark House* (1932)—and his version is by far the most macabre, almost a horror film itself in the sequences involving the iron mask and the Bastille. Cast as Louis XIV and his twin brother Philippe was Louis Hayward in his first major starring role(s). Hayward had come from England to Hollywood in 1935, on the same ship with Errol Flynn, but he did not work his way up to stardom until 1939. He had a notable supporting role, however, as the dashing cavalier who fathers Anthony Adverse in the 1936 film of that title and then is killed in a rapier duel by the cuckolded husband.

The screenplay for *The Man in the Iron Mask* by George Bruce takes considerable liberties with the novel and even more so with history. In it, Queen Anne of Austria (Doris Kenyon) gives birth to a son, the crown prince; a few minutes later, she gives birth to a second son who is his identical twin. Fearing a conflict for supremacy, even civil war, between his sons when they should come of age, Louis XIII (Albert Dekker) arranges for his loyal friend D'Artagnan (Warren William) to take the second prince away with him and bring him up as his own son in rural retirement. Only one person discovers this plot, the wily counselor Fouquet (Joseph Schildkraut), but he bides his time until the information may become useful.

A generation passes by and the first prince is now King Louis XIV, a decadent and foppish tyrant. The second son, Philippe, has grown up in Gascony with D'Artagnan and the three musketeers, Athos (Bert Roach), Porthos (Alan Hale), and Aramis (Miles Mander), who have reared him to be a dashing swordsman. During their exile, France has degenerated deep into the tyranny that will eventually lead to the Revolution. When the King's tax agents come to collect a particularly confiscatory tax, the musketeers claim that Louis XIII personally made them exempt. The royal troops reject this claim and try to arrest the musketeers and Philippe, who nearly fight off an entire regiment but are finally captured and taken as prisoners to Paris. There, Louis XIV notices Philippe's striking resemblance to himself, noting that if the latter shaved off his moustache and put on a wig, he could pass as the King's double. Fouquet suggests that this would be a useful device; the populace is enraged against Louis' tyranny, and there are plots afoot to assassinate him. Fouquet advises the King to let Philippe impersonate him and receive the assassin's dagger instead. Philippe agrees to do so if D'Artagnan and the musketeers are set free. On Philippe's first venture impersonating the monarch, a murderous mob attacks him on his way to church. They are expecting the cowardly Louis and are amazed when Philippe leaps out of the coach, sword in hand, and outfights the pack of them. Instead of having them seized for punishment, however, he promises redress of their wrongs. The would-be assassins end up cheering the King.

A similar confusion occurs with the Spanish princess Maria Theresa (Joan Bennett), who has come for an arranged marriage with Louis. The King treats her with arrogant disdain; he prefers the company of his mistress Louis de la Vallière (Marian Martin) and flaunts his infidelity. When Maria Theresa encounters Philippe, however, he acts like a gallant gentleman. Louis later becomes so obnoxious that she attempts to flee to Spain, whereupon Philippe is sent to bring her back. They fall in love, and eventually she learns that he is not the loathsome King but his twin brother. By then, Louis has come to consider Philippe a threat; his double has become too popular and crosses him too often. Indeed, his economic minister Colbert (Walter Kingsford) has been urging the sort of reforms that Philippe has advocated. Colbert's plan to have Philippe replace Louis fails, and Fouquet, eager to have his rival Colbert defeated, now reveals to Louis that Philippe is his twin brother. Louis then orders Philippe imprisoned for life in the Bastille with his face forever concealed by an iron mask. This mask, completely covering the entire head, is locked in place and is never to be removed. The mask in the Whale version is by far the most visually sinister; in the other film versions, it is simply a loose-fitting helmet with eye and mouth holes, but Whale's is molded to the face and features so that the prisoner within it both resembles a monster and is the victim of a monstrous torture, for as his beard grows, it will slowly suffocate him to death.

There is accordingly an urgent need to rescue him before it is too late. Learning with terror of Philippe's fate, Maria Theresa seeks the help of D'Artagnan and the musketeers. She manages to steal the key to the mask from Louis when he is in a drunken stupor after an orgy with Vallière, and Colbert provides the musketeers with a pass to the dungeons. After they remove Philippe, D'Artagnan takes him by a secret passageway to the King's chamber, removes the mask, and puts it on the still senseless King Louis and takes him back to the dungeon in Philippe's place.

Philippe then resumes his impersonation of the king and proceeds with plans to marry Maria Theresa. Waking up in the Bastille behind the mask, Louis is terrified, but he keeps his wits and scrawls a note on a pewter plate, which he tosses out a window. It contains instructions for the finder to take it to Fouquet. Receiving it, Fouquet loses no time. He interrupts the wedding and denounces Philippe as an impostor; when Vallière protests and tries to stop him, he shoots her and flees. He has meanwhile removed Louis from the Bastille, and he now joins him as he races in a carriage toward Fontaine-bleau to reclaim the throne. Philippe and the musketeers intercept them, and in a running fight, D'Artagnan and all three musketeers are killed. Louis' coach, however, falls off the road into a lake, and the evil king, still wearing the iron mask, is drowned. Fouquet too is killed, and Philippe, now unopposed, returns to marry Maria Theresa and rule as Louis XIV.

As history, this is patently absurd. Louis XIV was not killed and impersonated by his nobler brother but ruled France until 1715; the Sun King's extravagance and disastrous wars helped lead France to the Revolution of 1789, an event that a more noble Philippe might have prevented had he indeed been king. Fouquet and Colbert *were* rivals, and Fouquet *was* removed from office and arrested for mishandling funds, but it was Louis who deposed him. Vallière was not the voluptuous wench of the film; Martin plays her absurdly as a Mae West-type vamp, but the real Vallière was a shy, sensitive woman with a lame leg; instead of being shot, she eventually became a nun. Neither does the film have much resemblance to the novel, in which Aramis, who has become the Grand Master of the Jesuits, discovers Philippe's identity and arranges the substitution, but the plot fails, D'Artagnan arrests Philippe, and the prince is returned to prison for life.

The film was nevertheless very popular. Hayward was particularly effective, especially as the decadent, foppish, and sinister king. He and Bennett played so well together that the next year Small teamed them again in another swashbuckler, *The Son of Monte Cristo*, in which Hayward pretended to be an effeminate fop while he was really the best swordsman in France, working undercover as The Torch, a masked Zorro type, to overthrow an evil tyrant (George Sanders). Hayward went on to star in a number of swashbucklers, but the scripts and productions declined in quality. Eventually, he ended up playing D'Artagnan in a second-rate production called *The Lady in the Iron Mask* (1952), in which he rescues a princess imprisoned behind an iron mask by her evil twin and a wicked duke.

The Man in the Iron Mask was remade for television in the late 1970's, with Richard Chamberlain as Louis and Philippe, Louis Jourdan as D'Artagnan, and Ralph Richardson as Colbert. Although that film also ends with Philippe becoming king, it is considerably closer to the novel. At the same time, another movie version, at first called *Behind the Iron Mask*, was filmed, but because of the popularity of the television version, it was not released until 1979, under the title *The Fifth Musketeer* (to capitalize on the popularity of Richard Lester's *The Three Musketeers*, 1973, and *The Four Musketeers*, 1974). Filmed on location in Europe, it was an opulent production with good performances by Cornel Wilde as D'Artagnan and Rex Harrison as Colbert. As the lead, Beau Bridges was effective as the foppish king but not very believable as the dashing Philippe. The film had a brief run and quickly disappeared. The television version has excellent performances and a literate script but has less atmospheric horror and derring-do than Whale's, which for all its historic inaccuracies remains the most memorable film of that durable classic, *The Man in the Iron Mask*.

Robert E. Morsberger

MAN OF A THOUSAND FACES

Released: 1957
Production: Robert Arthur for Universal
Direction: Joseph Pevney
Screenplay: R. Wright Campbell, Ivan Goff, and Ben Roberts; based on a story by Ralph Wheelwright
Cinematography: Russell Metty
Editing: Ted Kent
Running time: 122 minutes

Principal characters:
Lon Chaney .... James Cagney
Cleva Creighton Chaney .... Dorothy Malone
Hazel Bennet .... Jane Greer
Gert, a movie extra .... Marjorie Rambeau
Clarence Logan .... Jim Backus
Irving Thalberg .... Robert Evans
Mrs. Chaney .... Celia Lovsky
Creighton Chaney (Lon, Jr.) .... Roger Smith

To many film fans, Lon Chaney was the greatest character actor who ever lived. From 1913 to 1923 he made a series of melodramas, mostly at Universal, in which he played a character, most often sympathetic, who was plain, even ugly, and usually cursed with a deformity or a crippled body. Irving Thalberg, production executive at Universal for Carl Laemmle, moved to the new Metro-Goldwyn-Mayer studios in 1924 and persuaded Chaney to come over to M-G-M also, where he would personally supervise the star's career. Chaney made the move and filmed seventeen silent features and one talking film before his death in 1930. He was known by the catch-phrase "Man of a Thousand Faces" because he was a master of makeup and character costuming.

The story of Chaney's life had all the elements for a good cinematic study, and over the years possible scripts and treatments were discussed but were always eventually abandoned because nobody could think of an actor who might be able to play Lon Chaney. Robert Arthur, producer at Universal during the 1950's, came up with the idea of using James Cagney in the role. The idea seemed better the more it was talked about, and when it was learned that Cagney was definitely interested in the project, Arthur got a good workable screenplay written with Joseph Pevney to direct and assembled a first-rate cast headed by Cagney to enact the Chaney story.

The life of Lon Chaney was more than a tearjerker or soap opera. He had been born in Colorado Springs of deaf and dumb parents, and it was young Lon, one of four normal children born to the pair, who became closest to his mother and father. He learned to converse with them by sign language. He was only nine years old when his mother became bedridden, and the first three years of her invalidism, when he tended her every day, marked the time when he became a master of pantomime. After his classes at school, he would come home and pantomime for her everything he had seen and done during the day; it was the one bright time of her lonely, bedridden days.

The screen story starts briefly with Chaney's boyhood in Colorado Springs, and then shows him, stagestruck, as a traveling actor and song-and-dance vaudevillian. He travels all over the West, especially in San Francisco and California, with the Columbia Musical Comedy Repertory Company. In Oklahoma he meets and falls in love with a singer he has hired for the show, Cleva Creighton (Dorothy Malone). Cleva is a real singer, whereas Lon has always claimed that he cannot sing a note and only fakes a song. Cleva marries Lon and bears him a son named Creighton.

In San Francisco, Cleva, who is beautiful as well as talented and very gregarious besides, comes into her own, while her husband is little more than a supporting actor, a drudge, and stagehand. She has aspirations for a career and does not intend to remain on the vaudeville circuit with a child to rear and a husband who is always busy in the theater backstage. She leaves him, and he determines to wipe even the memory of her from his life.

Cleva is not very successful and begins to drink, and it is not long before she returns to Lon, now rising as a comic performer, but he will have nothing to do with her. In a pitiful effort to gain sympathy and attention, she drinks a strong poison on stage in front of the performing Chaney, and although she lives, her throat is hopelessly scarred, and it is obvious that she will never again be able to sing or even talk properly. Chaney takes his son and goes to Los Angeles; he resists every effort Cleva makes to see him and even signs papers committing her while he divorces her and then marries Hazel Bennet ("Hastings," in real life, played by Jane Greer), who has had an unhappy first marriage of her own. She becomes a real wife to him and mother to his son.

In Southern California, Chaney finds that he can get better work and more pay in the movies at Universal, starting first as an extra and then getting proper supporting roles that become leads. A young executive, Irving Thalberg (Robert Evans), is much attracted to him as a serious actor, helps him get lead roles at Universal such as *The Hunchback of Notre Dame*, and then, when he moves to M-G-M to become production manager for Louis B. Mayer, entices Chaney to come over with him. There has been a very effective sequence already when Chaney goes over to Paramount from Universal to play a phony cripple in George Loane Tucker's production of *The Miracle Man*. Now, at M-G-M, Thalberg sees to it that Chaney becomes top actor on the lot. Hazel stays with him faithfully, and he finally manages to be rid of Cleva.

At this juncture the talking film comes in, and Chaney decides that his debut film in that medium will be a remake of one of his favorite silent roles, *The Unholy Three*. He is suffering from cancer of the throat, but does not know how serious his ailment is. Ironically, for an actor just starting his career in talking pictures, he loses the power of speech and becomes as mute as his parents had been. He dies, leaving proof in the completed film that he could have gone on to an even greater fame. His son, Lon Chaney, Jr. (Creighton originally) went on to be a well-known character actor himself but never attained the status which his father had.

James Cagney, who is a very versatile performer, gives a superlative performance as Chaney, and both women in his life, as played by Dorothy Malone and Jane Greer, are wonderfully effective. Again ironically, however, when Academy Award time came around, the picture received only one nomination—for Best Story and Screenplay written directly for the screen. The story was presented much as it really happened in real life, but the abilities of the actors and director were what made the film distinctive, as well as the beautifully delineated silent studio atmosphere, but they were not honored. The public, however, liked the picture, and it made money.

The 1950's represented an era when the biographical story enjoyed a definite vogue. At Universal both *The Glenn Miller Story* (1954) and *The Benny Goodman Story* (1955) had been well-received, and Universal now definitely had another hit in this backstage and behind-the-camera production of the Lon Chaney story, *Man of a Thousand Faces*.

DeWitt Bodeen

MAN OF ARAN

Released: 1934
Production: Michael Balcon for A. Gaumint-British
Direction: Robert J. Flaherty
Screenplay: Robert J. Flaherty
Cinematography: Robert J. Flaherty, Francis Flaherty, and John Goldman
Editing: John Goldman
Music: John Greenwood
Running time: 77 minutes

> *Principal characters:*
> Man .... Colman King
> Wife .... Maggie Dirrane
> Son .... Michael Dillane

Robert Flaherty, one of the most creative contributors to the art of film-making, reached what many critics believe was the high point of his career with *Man of Aran*. Like all of his films, especially *Nanook of the North* (1922) and *Moana* (1926), *Man of Aran* bears the unmistakable mark of his vision and philosophy.

The story of *Man of Aran* is austere, perhaps, but its beauty lies precisely in its simplicity. Flaherty uses the story's simplicity to focus on the subject which interested him most: man versus nature, pitched in a relentless battle for survival. In this film, Flaherty records and celebrates this struggle on the barren, isolated, windswept island of Aran, which is situated just off the coast of Ireland. For Flaherty, the activities of a fisherman (Colman King), his wife, (Margie Dirrane), and their son (Michael Dillane), are dignified daily illustrations of man's struggle against the impersonal, crushing natural forces of the island. An indefatigable wind blows coldly upon the island, making growth possible for only the smallest plants, and even those growing only in tiny sheltered rock crevices. The paucity of flora indicates the nearly impossible task of raising crops. The nameless wife and son drag seaweed and grass from the shore to the rugged cliffs in order to nourish the scarce soil with some life-encouraging fertilizers.

Heroic attempts to coax substance from the soil are paralleled by the fishing activities of the husband. This man of Aran daily launches his rugged dory into the violent surf in search of a few fish, which are scarce in this cold and forbidding sea. While at sea, Flaherty's tireless mariner is unceasingly assaulted by the surging wind and water. With whatever meager catch he has, he must renew his struggle against the pounding surf going back to shore, because to be on the sea in the dark is to risk almost certain death.

The saga of this fisherman's passage through the surf becomes the dynamic, dramatic element in the film. A safe return is always in question, and the anguish of the wife and son as they watch from a nearby cliff underscores the life-and-death nature of the husband's attempts to land his boat. Their expressions of joyful relief when he succeeds bear further witness to the awful consequences of failure. Nature has been stemmed once again, but tomorrow the contest begins anew, for victory over nature is transitory and must be retested on a daily basis. *Man of Aran* celebrates this daily cyclical struggle which elevates an ordinary man to the status of a hero. It is the unending, predictable daily struggle which renews the most elemental characteristic of man: his extraordinary ability to overcome the impersonality of the natural world.

Man of Aran, like most of Flaherty's films, was filmed entirely without a script and allegedly without preconceived notions; and it contains no dialogue. The story is told entirely on a visual basis, augmented only by the music of John Greenwood. Flaherty always believed that a story must come from the environment, and that the function of the filmmaker is to record without intrusion the natural conditions observed. Flaherty's cinematic philosophy was, and still remains, a significant contribution to documentary and semi-documentary films. His fascination with nature has been termed romantic naturalism (or at least naturalism), and it was in sharp contrast with the then-prevailing style of making films in studios with highly structured scripts. By comparison, Flaherty's films were recorded on the spot and then only after long observation. Flaherty spent two years observing, shooting, and editing what was to be the final version of *Man of Aran*. In the early 1930's, when filmmakers of all nations were entranced with the possibilities of sound, Flaherty's style stands singularly apart from the rest because of his unique reliance on visual perceptions.

Also distinct is the social philosophy inherent in *Man of Aran* and many of his films. By focusing on nature and man's relationship to it, Flaherty applauded an age-old battle. In theme, the film reflects an attitude which premodern or ancient man might quickly have recognized. What the filmmaker ignored, however, were the unmistakable social problems of the modern world. It is on this point that Flaherty's films have been criticized. The primary concerns of the 1930's were not the struggles of isolated islanders or Eskimos; the key issues of the day involved the consequences of the Depression, human suffering, widespread poverty, health problems, and housing. Critics felt that illustrations of modern man's struggle for survival should have been the subject of Flaherty's quasidocumentaries, not primal man's fight against the elements of nature. Some critics also felt that the same kind of visually exciting conditions existed in the slums and factories of large cities, making those sites ideally suited to a filmmaker of Flaherty's talents. Each viewer must decide for himself whether a filmmaker's most important function is aesthetic or social, and whether there is substance to such philosophical criticisms of Flaherty's works.

While some may question the importance of Flaherty's fascination with natural, timeless heroes and of his essentially preservationist attitude toward his subjects, none takes exception to the pure, hard beauty of his creations. Flaherty's films should not be missed by serious film students, and *Man of Aran* is possibly his best work. While *Nanook of the North* is more widely known, the physical deterioration of the film stock has made it available in its entirety only recently through the work of dedicated film preservationists. While *Man of Aran* has no dialogue, it cannot be termed a *silent* film in the same sense as *Nanook of the North* because of the scoring and natural background sounds. It is for this reason, perhaps, that some scholars feel that *Man of Aran* is the better film.

John G. Tomlinson, Jr.

THE MAN WHO KNEW TOO MUCH

Released: 1956
Production: Alfred Hitchcock for Paramount
Direction: Alfred Hitchcock
Screenplay: John Michael Hayes and Angus MacPhail; based on a story of the same name by Charles Bennett and D. B. Wyndham-Lewis
Cinematography: Robert Burks
Editing: George Tomasini
Music: Bernard Herrmann
Song: Ray Evans and Jay Livingston, "Whatever Will Be, Will Be" (AA)
Running time: 119 minutes

Principal characters:
Dr. Ben McKenna .... James Stewart
Jo McKenna .... Doris Day
Louis Bernard .... Daniel Gelin
Mrs. Drayton .... Brenda De Banzie
Mr. Drayton .... Bernard Miles
Hank McKenna .... Christopher Olsen
The assassin .... Reggie Nalder

While the films of Alfred Hitchcock abound in familiar trademarks such as blonde heroines, obsessive mothers, and a biting wit, they are also marked by a recurring theme: that of the innocent, ordinary person caught up in dangerous events which he or she cannot control. A common subtheme involves characters who wish for excitement to invade their otherwise mundane lives. "This family's gone to pieces. . . . Nothing ever happens. We're in a rut," laments actress Teresa Wright, as the small-town girl of Hitchcock's 1943 film, *Shadow of a Doubt*. Tippi Hedren's worldly rich girl of *The Birds* (1963) is also bored. In fact, her fateful journey to Bodega Bay, site of the fearsome bird attack, is undertaken because she has nothing else to do.

The characters of *The Man Who Knew Too Much* are tied into a similar humdrum existence. "We saw the same scenery last summer, driving to Las Vegas," sighs Jo McKenna (Doris Day), during a Moroccan vacation. When her husband Ben (James Stewart) recounts past travels, he evokes the resignation of a spectator, rather than participant, when he states, "We looked in on Lisbon and Rome." In keeping with the Hitchcock tradition, the McKennas will ultimately face excitement and terror, however, when they become pawns of an assassination plot.

Based on a story by Charles Bennett and D. B. Wyndham-Lewis, *The Man Who Knew Too Much* is a diverting and heavily symbolic film which has the distinction of being the only project Hitchcock chose to make twice. The first version was made in Britain in 1934, and offered Peter Lorre as the chief villain, with Leslie Banks and Edna Best as the tourists. Although the earlier version is revered among Hitchcock devotees, the 1956 production is more technically sophisticated in its production values, including the use of VistaVision and Technicolor (the 1934 film was made in black and white). The 1956 film (which is forty-five minutes longer than the original) also contains excellent performances and a spellbinding twelve-minute scene involving an assassination attempt which required 124 shots and utilizes no dialogue. Hitchcock called this sequence an attempt at "pure cinema," and in discussing both versions of *The Man Who Knew Too Much*, he noted, "Let's say that the first version was the work of a talented amateur and the second was made by a professional."

Actually, the story line is similar in both versions, although there have been logistical changes: the first film opens on the ski slopes of Switzerland, while the remake begins in Marrakesh. As the 1956 film opens, credits roll over scenes showing an orchestra in performance. As the musical selection comes to an end, a musician holds up cymbals, at which point the audience reads, "A single crash of Cymbals and how it rocked the lives of an American family." (This is also a change from the original, which concerned a well-to-do British couple and their daughter.) The next shot introduces the viewer to that family—with the camera lingering on young Hank McKenna (Christopher Olsen), who is seated between his parents, Ben and Jo McKenna. The initial focus on the boy is appropriate, for he will become the link to the assassination mystery.

It is also the boy who brings attention to his parents, singling them out for the events that will follow. Traveling by bus across French Morocco following McKenna's attendance at a Paris medical conference, Ben and Jo appear to be jaded tourists on an uneventful trip. Then a series of small, seemingly innocuous interruptions inevitably change their course. The first occurs when the bus inadvertently swerves, sending Hank, who is walking in the aisle, grabbing for an Arab woman's veil. A commotion breaks out, since he has tampered with an important native custom. It remains for a handsome Frenchman named Louis Bernard (Daniel Gelin), who speaks the language, to intercede on Hank's behalf, thus quelling the excitement. "There are moments in life when we all need a little help," he tells the McKennas. They are unaware that Bernard will eventually require their assistance.

Through conversation with Bernard, aboard the bus and at a hotel in Marrakesh, the McKennas reveal their backgrounds. They are from Indianapolis, where Ben is a doctor at Good Samaritan Hospital. Jo is a retired singer who had been a star in Europe as well as America, but who gave up her career because her husband did not want to live in New York. Although Bernard's curiosity is flattering to Jo, her suspicions are also stirred. At one point she tells her husband, "He knows everything there is to know about you, Ben." This line implies that it is Bernard who is "the man who knows too much," but a shift of distinction will soon follow, and Ben himself will unwittingly become that person.

The dangerous inheritance transpires in broad daylight, in the crowded Marrakesh marketplace, when the McKennas see a man being stabbed. Rushing toward the man, who is attired in Arab robes, Ben is startled when facial makeup from the man's darkened face rubs off on his hands. The victim is Bernard, who, before dying, whispers a cryptic message about an assassination plot to a stunned Ben. Like other once-bored Hitchcock characters whose lives are suddenly changed, Ben will later lament, "Why should he pick me to tell?"

Following the murder, Ben reports to police headquarters, but before revealing Bernard's message, he receives a telephone call warning him that his son has been kidnaped. If Ben reveals what he has learned, Hank will be harmed. Later in the story, when the McKennas try to tell authorities about the plot, their story defies belief.

Ben is now the man who knows too much, but ironically, he does not know enough, because Bernard's message was incomplete. Thus, in order to avert the assassination and save Hank, the McKennas must play detective. One of their fragmented clues is the name "Ambrose Chapel." Once in London, where Bernard's message takes the McKennas, they will assume that Ambrose Chapel is a person. It is one of many red herrings within the plot (typical of Hitchcock's films), and Jo will eventually surmise "It's not a person, it's a place." Prior to their investigation through the streets of London, Ben and Jo are paid a surprise visit (another interruption) by old friends who are also staying in London. The friends have dropped by for cocktails. Unable to explain their tangled predicament, Ben and Jo invite the friends to wait for them in their hotel suite while they tend to errands.

Once they decipher the Ambrose Chapel clue, they are ultimately led to the famed Albert Hall, where the assassination of the Prime Minister of an unnamed country is supposed to take place. During the twelve-minute sequence of "pure cinema," the viewer will witness a carefully calculated collision of images. The effect is heightened by the dramatic orchestration being performed (Hitchcock film composer Bernard Herrmann is seen at the podium, conducting the London Philharmonic in an orchestration of Arthur Benjamin's "Storm Cloud Cantata"), as the camera rhythmically surveys its subjects—Ben, Jo, the conductor and musicians, the hired assassin, and the unaware target. The fatal shot is to occur at the clash of the cymbals, and when Ben is unable to get to the assassin in time, it remains for Jo to issue a warning message. She does so by letting out a scream—just seconds before the cymbals are to clash. The disturbance upsets the planned assassination's timing when it causes the Prime Minister to shift in his seat, thus saving his life.

From Albert Hall, Ben and Jo go to the Minister's embassy, where they have learned that Hank is being held. Once again, it is Jo who sends a warning. She does so when she is requested to perform for the clustered dignitaries. Jo's fame as a singer is a subplot of the film which often causes complications in the McKennas' search for Hank, as well as affording an opportunity for singing-star Day to perform. In the 1934 version of the film the wife was not a famous person. Accompanying herself on the piano, Jo sings "Que Serà, Serà" so loudly that her audience is taken by surprise. For Jo, however, the song is a message, for it is a favorite bedtime song for mother and son. Upstairs in a locked room, the boy hears the song and whistles back. The McKennas are then able to retrieve him, following a shooting incident involving one of the kidnapers. The boy had been kidnaped by the Draytons, played by Brenda de Banzie and Bernard Miles, a presumably innocuous couple that the McKennas met in Marrakesh. As the reunited family descends down the embassy stairs, Jo sings "We'll Love Again."

The film's final moments, which are quite funny, seem out of step with the sinister elements that have taken place, but they are in keeping with Hitchcock's humor. With Hank in tow, Ben and Jo return to their hotel suite, where their friends (who had dozed off) are waiting. To explain their prolonged absence, Ben simply says, "Sorry we were gone so long. We had to go over and pick up Hank."

Although *The Man Who Knew Too Much* was hugely successful at the box office, critical reception was less positive. Many critics felt the film did not improve on the 1934 version, and Day's performance was not generally well liked. In retrospect, however, the film is considered to be one of Hitchcock's greatest efforts, far surpassing the original in terms of production values. The performances by both Stewart and Day are quite natural and enjoyable. With the exception of the film's song "Whatever Will Be, Will Be" ("Que Serà, Serà"), which won an Academy Award, the film was completely overlooked at Oscar time. That song, incidentally, has since come to be popularly associated with Doris Day; she sang it again in *Please Don't Eat the Daisies* (1960) and *The Glass Bottom Boat* (1966).

Pat H. Broeske

THE MANCHURIAN CANDIDATE

Released: 1962
Production: George Axelrod and John Frankenheimer for United Artists
Direction: John Frankenheimer
Screenplay: George Axelrod; based on the novel of the same name by Richard Condon
Cinematography: Lionel Lindon
Editing: Ferris Webster
Running time: 126 minutes

Principal characters:
Bennett Marco	Frank Sinatra
Raymond Shaw	Laurence Harvey
Rosie	Janet Leigh
Mrs. Shaw	Angela Lansbury
Chunjin	Henry Silva
Senator John Iselin	James Gregory
Jocie Jordon	Leslie Parrish
Senator Thomas Jordon	John McGiver
Yen Lo	Khigh Dhiegh
Psychiatrist	Joe Adams
Holborn Gaines	Lloyd Corrigan

John Frankenheimer's film based on Richard Condon's novel *The Manchurian Candidate* was a gamble in 1962. Senator Joseph McCarthy was gone, but something of the hysteria that was his legacy remained alive in America. John Kennedy had sent the Green Berets into Vietnam as technical advisers, and it was the time of the Bay of Pigs and the Cuban missile crisis. The project with which Frankenheimer and screenwriter George Axelrod were engaged was a satirical film about McCarthyism contained within the framework of a cartoon strip plot, to which was added the more paranoid elements of *film noir*. Had Frank Sinatra not expressed great interest in doing the film, it is highly doubtful that it would have been made. Although limited in budget to a thirty-nine day shooting schedule, director Frankenheimer, screenwriter Axelrod, and Sinatra (displaying a willingness to cooperate on a project which clearly challenged him as an actor) made a film which has earned itself a place in film history.

In the film's prologue, an American infantry platoon in Korea is ambushed and captured. The unconscious men are flown by helicopter into Manchuria. A few years later, all of the men except one supposedly killed by North Korean guards are repatriated. One of them, Sergeant Raymond Shaw (Laurence Harvey), has been awarded the Congressional Medal of Honor for a heroic action corroborated by his men, the only witnesses.

In reality, Raymond, Major Bennett Marco (Frank Sinatra), and the rest have been expertly brainwashed by the Communists. Raymond has been transformed into a walking time bomb who can be sent into a hypnotic trance by the sight of the Queen of Diamonds card. Once he has seen the card, he will kill whomever his American contact suggests without any feelings of guilt or remorse because he has no memory of the deed once it has been carried out. His American contact reaches him by phoning and making the suggestion that he pass the time by playing solitaire. The first call is made and Raymond turns up the Queen of Diamonds. His victim is the liberal publisher Holborn Gaines (Lloyd Corrigan) who has given him a job. Raymond carries out his mission—a triumph of the sinister ingenuity of his captors. He is now ready for more important targets.

Marco and Corporal Melvin (James Edwards), another member of the platoon, are both plagued by recurring nightmares in which Raymond murders a young private. Marco, driven to the point of nervous collapse, meets with Shaw and learns of Corporal Melvin's similar nightmares. He suspects, and is finally able to convince Army Intelligence, that Raymond has been programmed to carry out assassinations when a certain "key" in his mind is turned. Marco is put in charge of an intelligence unit and attempts to discover the key and then deprogram Raymond. Before they have accomplished anything, however, Raymond receives another phone call. His target this time is Senator Thomas Jordon (John McGiver). Raymond obeys the command, and also kills his own wife Jocie (Leslie Parrish), who is the Senator's daughter.

Working against an unknown deadline, Marco, through the aid of a psychiatrist (Joe Adams), is able to discover Raymond's "key." He confronts Raymond with what he has learned and tells him that he need no longer obey the Red Queen. Before either Marco or the audience are convinced that the deprogramming has been successful, however, Raymond manages to escape surveillance and make his way to Madison Square Garden where, at a National convention, a presidential candidate is about to make his acceptance speech. Marco and his men rush to the Garden, certain that this must be the mission for which Raymond was originally trained.

What Marco does not know is that Raymond's American contact is his own monstrous, power-hungry mother (Angela Lansbury). Not only did she order her son to kill her political enemy Senator Jordon, and, inadvertently, his own wife, but she has also instructed Raymond to assassinate the candidate at a particularly compelling moment in his speech. She has stage-managed the event to put her malleable McCarthyesque husband, Senator Iselin (James Gregory), in the White House. Their oppressive influence on Raymond has been shown via flashbacks and domestic squabbling throughout the film.

A desperate search of the Garden takes place as the convention grinds on, moving closer to the candidate's acceptance speech. Raymond makes his way to a small room near the highest level of the Garden. He appears to the audience as he has appeared before every previous murder, a lethal sleep-walker. As the unwitting candidate grows nearer to uttering the phrase which is Raymond's cue to fire, the audience is, with Raymond and Marco, caught up in the nightmare, unable to do anything but watch it unfold.

Noticing a tiny light in the top balcony of the Garden, Marco sprints up flight after flight of stairs. Raymond, from his vantage point, prepares to fire at the candidate, wavers, and then moves his gunsight away from the candidate and obliterates not only Senator Iselin, but his mother as well. Marco bursts into the room, but before he can be reached Raymond turns the gun on himself, smiles, and commits suicide. Raymond, with the Congressional Medal around his neck, has finally become a true hero.

The Manchurian Candidate was generally well received because of its fast pace, reminiscent of 1940's films such as *The Big Sleep* (1946). Sinatra's per-formance, particularly in the early part of the film in which he brilliantly portrays a man near the emotional breaking point, is unquestionably one of his best. Harvey is also quite convincing as Raymond, an essentially unlikable individual who finally captures the audience's pity. Unfortunately, Harvey had appeared in so many inferior films that some critics snidely suggested that a brainwashed zombie was all he could play. Janet Leigh does the best she can with the ill-defined role of a girl who meets, befriends, and falls in love with Marco. Their initial meeting on a train is a quirky, highly effective variation on the trite "boy meets girl" theme in which Leigh is the aggressive party and Sinatra, passive and self-absorbed, only half listens to what she is saying. In the chaotic context of the film the scene plays extremely well. Top acting honors went to Lansbury, who had played a somewhat less grotesque mother for Frankenheimer in *All Fall Down* (1962).

The brainwashing sequence was filmed three different times to correspond with the viewpoints of the "Garden Club ladies" (the procedure employed by the Communists involves the men imagining a tedious lecture on horti-culture), the Russian officers, and the nightmare of Corporal Melvin. The men slump in their chairs while the lecture drones on. Yet the tedium is interrrupted by the presence of the puppetmaster Yen Lo (Khigh Diegh), who orders Raymond to commit his first murder. Raymond follows his sug-gestion, much as a schoolboy might obey a teacher, blasting his former com-rade, the youngest and most innocent member of the group, out of his chair with a 45-calibre automatic. Sinatra and the others look on, registering no emotion. The tactic of keeping the audience in the dark as to whether Ray-mond's mind has been "cleared" generates almost unbearable suspense and makes for a climax worthy of Alfred Hitchcock. Marco frantically races to the top balcony of the Garden during the playing of the Star Spangled Banner; the Garden audience, oblivious to danger, is on its feet singing; and Marco and Raymond engage in a deadly struggle.

Ultimately, *The Manchurian Candidate* is an audacious mixture of suspense, action, and satire which, under Frankenheimer's direction, never falters for a moment. The surrealistic quality inherent in the brainwashing scenes is combined with anti-McCarthy satire. In one scene, for example, Iselin decides to charge that there are fifty-seven Communists in the State Department because he notices the number on a catsup bottle. The epilogue, in which a troubled Marco reads from a list of Congressional Medal of Honor winners, his emotion complemented by a thunderstorm outside, provides an unsettling conclusion to a film which presents the viewer with a world filled with fear, treachery, and death.

Michael Shepler

MANHATTAN MELODRAMA

Released: 1934
Production: David O. Selznick for Metro-Goldwyn-Mayer
Direction: W. S. Van Dyke
Screenplay: Oliver H. P. Garrett and Joseph L. Mankiewicz; based on an
original story by Arthur Caesar (AA)
Cinematography: James Wong Howe
Editing: Ben Lewis
Running time: 93 minutes

Principal characters:
Blackie Gallagher .... Clark Gable
Jim Wade .... William Powell
Eleanor .... Myrna Loy
Joe Patrick .... Leo Carrillo
Blackie (at age 12) .... Mickey Rooney
Snow .... Thomas Jackson

Top showmanship was revealed by M-G-M in presenting *Manhattan Melodrama*, a fast-moving modern drama that takes place almost entirely on Manhattan's East Side. It tells the story of three kids from the sidewalks of New York, three boys who grow up together when their parents are drowned in a holiday river boat accident. As they mature, their lives follow three divergent roads, yet their destinies are intertwined as they follow their individual fates. Blackie Gallagher (Clark Gable) is a rebellious roustabout with the unpolished airs of a tough gent. He becomes the owner and manager of a gambling house that has a reputation as shady as his own. Jim Wade (William Powell) is like a brother to him, but Wade is studious, becomes an outstanding attorney, and rises to become governor of the state of New York. The third boy, Joe Patrick (Leo Carrillo), devotes his life to public service and enters the priesthood.

Blackie is known as a ruthless underworld leader who has a way with women. He is drawn to a girl named Eleanor (Myrna Loy), and he sets her up in style as his mistress. Blackie's gangsterish ways alienate him from Eleanor, however, and when Blackie informs her that he has just won a yacht, she comments sarcastically, "Some day you're going to win somebody's mother." Eleanor is drawn to Jim Wade, who, like her, has class, but the affable Blackie does not object, because he considers his friend Jim a far better man than he, a man who is thoroughly honest and incorruptible.

Blackie is involved in a number of gangland killings, and it is at this point that Eleanor deserts him for Jim Wade, whom she marries. Blackie kills a gambler who has welched on his debts, but he cannot be indicted by Assistant

District Attorney Jim Wade because of lack of evidence; Wade nevertheless warns him of the dangerous path he is on. When Jim is elected District Attorney, he fires a jealous assistant named Snow (Thomas Jackson), who sets out to ruin him. Eleanor is aware of the assistant's schemes, and, desperate, asks Blackie to help Jim. Blackie seeks out the offender; the two get into a serious quarrel, and Blackie shoots and kills the man. This time he is caught and imprisoned. Wade's hands are tied; he is powerless to help Blackie and has to work, instead, to convict his friend.

Jim wins his party's nomination and is elected to governorship of the state. He refuses to stay Blackie's execution until Eleanor confesses that it was to insure Wade's own future that Blackie committed murder. Wade rushes to the prison to commute Blackie's sentence, but Blackie refuses to let him corrupt his principles. Blackie, accompanied by Father Joe, goes to his doom without bitterness. Jim resigns as governor, but leaves office with an admiring Eleanor.

Manhattan Melodrama was popular with both the critics and the public, and an Oscar for Best Original Story was awarded to Arthur Caesar. It also became known for a more sinister reason, for it proved the end for escaped gangster John Dillinger, who came out of hiding to attend a matinee of *Manhattan Melodrama*, in the company of the "Lady in Red," and as he left the movie house, he was shot down by the FBI.

Producer David O. Selznick had always believed in Powell as an actor, and he brought him over to M-G-M, where the role of Jim Wade was his first assignment. Powell's career had brought him stardom some years before at Paramount, and he was then enticed over to Warner Bros., who at first did well by him, especially in costarring him with Kay Francis in *Jewel Robbery* and *One Way Passage* (both in 1932). His subsequent career there was on the downgrade, and Warners could not afford to keep and groom him. With one film Selznick changed his future at M-G-M, where he not only jumped ahead into a place of box-office importance, but was also teamed for the first time in *Manhattan Melodrama* with Loy. They went on together for all the *Thin Man* features, a group of romantic comedies, and were paired again when he played the title role in M-G-M's biggest musical, *The Great Ziegfeld* (1936), and she played Ziegfeld's second wife, Billie Burke.

Powell and Loy were such a winning couple that they charmed the audience away from Gable, who was stuck in another tough guy role. The part of Blackie was sympathetic in spite of its violence, but it did not have the appeal of a later role that came to him in 1936, when he played another gangster called Blackie in *San Francisco*. As a running mate, Gable clicked more certainly with Spencer Tracy, with whom he costarred in a number of big M-G-M successes. Gable never again played with Powell, but he was often teamed with Loy. It was as if the characters played by Gable did not move in the same circles with those played by Powell, for only once, in this exemplary melodrama, did their paths cross; yet the paths of Gable and Loy crossed in at least six other M-G-M features.

Selznick was always very proud of *Manhattan Melodrama*. It was a class film, certainly one of his best and most popular when he was an M-G-M producer. It caught the spirit of contrasting lives in a great, ever-changing American metropolis, and it was always believable.

DeWitt Bodeen

MARAT/SADE
(THE PERSECUTION AND ASSASSINATION OF JEAN-PAUL MARAT AS PERFORMED BY THE INMATES OF THE ASYLUM OF CHARENTON UNDER THE DIRECTION OF THE MARQUIS DE SADE)

Released: 1967
Production: Michael Birkett for United Artists
Direction: Peter Brook
Screenplay: Adrian Mitchell; based on the play of the same name by Peter Weiss
Cinematography: David Watkin
Editing: Tom Priestley
Running time: 115 minutes

Principal characters:
Marquis de Sade .... Patrick Magee
Jean-Paul Marat .... Ian Richardson
Charlotte Corday .... Glenda Jackson
Marat's mistress .... Susan Williamson
Monsieur Duperé ....John Steiner

On July 13, 1808, nineteen years after the close of the French Revolution, the Marquis de Sade (Patrick Magee) is presenting a play of his own writing and direction at an asylum for the insane at Charenton, just outside Paris. The eccentric nobleman is himself a patient there, incarcerated for his ill-received views on sexuality. As is the fashion, Parisian aristocrats attend the performance, one of many such plays enacted as a means of therapy for the inmates.

Tonight's play deals with the latter days of the Reign of Terror during which the demogogue, Jean-Paul Marat (Ian Richardson), issued edicts from the bath to which he was confined for relief of a skin disease. Performing the drama are more than thirty patients of varied afflictions. They are led by a nun attendant onto the set, a semicircular, white-tiled room used as a steam bathhouse at the center of which are several sunken cells covered over with wooden slats. The splendidly arrayed spectators are safely seated up on the opposite side of a large black metal grill which separates the "stage" from the audience.

The play is introduced by the Marquis as a "series of conversations concerning life and death" and as a means to cast "some light on our eternal doubts." Its chief aim is "to take to bits/Great Propositions and their opposites." Such is an example of the rhymed couplets into which the dialogue is formed. A quartet of gaudily made-up clowns form the mocking, Jacobin chorus which also sings in this rhyme. They introduce the play and later reappear at various times to comment upon the action, to advance it, or to stop it.

The action itself concerns the murder of Marat by the zealot, Charlotte Corday. Glenda Jackson is the narcoleptic young woman who plays Corday. She recites her lines sleepily, once she is awakened and prompted by the nurse nun. Her director, de Sade, has allowed her three opportunities to call upon Marat in order to stab him in his bath. Despite much digression, in which Marat and the Marquis debate their opposing social and political views, the tale returns to the soporific Charlotte and her knife. In addition to the chorus' "musical interludes" and the disputes, the play is further interrupted by overwrought patients who must be subdued by strong-armed attendants, and by the angry *Monsieur le directeur* of the hospital who repeatedly questions the Marquis on the therapeutic value of his play or upon the propriety of raising this or that politically volatile issue. Numbering himself as one of the patricians of the audience, the fawning dandy wishes that the production of his charges offend no one among the rich and powerful spectators present tonight, and he cautions the Marquis to that effect after several outrageous or irreverent deliveries.

Such interventions are a welcome reprieve from the hysterical carryings-on of the madmen, who at one point must be shut away in the subterranean cells in order to be brought under control. The quiet of the intellectual sparring between Marat and de Sade is a much-needed respite which adds thought and depth to the film. This play-within-a-play in which actors portray mental patients who portray historical figures is actually a series of scenes of mounting intensity which climax in an unintended outburst from the lunatics, the chorus, or *le directeur*. The ideas expressed in dialogue and in behavior invite comparison to parallel circumstances occurring during the Revolution itself and in the modern day. Most clearly suggested is the asylum as a microcosm of revolutionary France. Without these challenges to interpretation, these hints at deeper meaning, interest in the film would indeed be difficult to sustain. Although no message is intended, many provocative ideas are posed or implied.

The inmates are soon to absorb the logic of the arguments between Marat and de Sade. They come to identify with the characters they play. At the final stabbing of Jean-Paul Marat, the uproar and tumult which ensues is greatly relished by the Marquis de Sade, who has for this long hour been propounding his theories of existential self-indulgence and gratification in opposition to his adversary's belief in the advancement of the socialist state through collective improvement. The patients turn violently upon the guests, the guards, and *le directeur*, breaking down the barrier which separates them and overwhelming both spectator and camera. The Marquis is glimpsed triumphantly laughing at the havoc he has fomented. The play, and the film, ends in this frightening turbulence.

The Royal Shakespearean Theatre Company, which performed the Peter Weiss play in Britain and in New York and won the New York Drama Critics and Tony Awards, brought excellence to the film version. Requiring little rehearsal to reenact the stage play for the motion picture camera, the company kept production costs under $500,000, aided by the brief, eighteen-day shooting schedule and the small sums needed for the single set and for the ragtag costumes of most players. Only two cameras were used, one the versatile and highly selective hand-held camera which roamed crazily amid the action as if held by a patient himself, with its focus alternately blurring and sharpening images unpredictably. Because of this imaginative camerawork, the film transcends the stage play, directing and concentrating the viewer's attention at important points and thereby avoiding the fixed viewpoint inherent in watching a play. The use of intensified sound together with faded or brilliantly lighted color adds dimension and variation to the potentially boring single set of the film.

At twenty-seven, Jackson's early screen appearance heralded a promising film career. In this role, however, she remains simply an actress playing a squinty-eyed, yawning young woman of an unbalanced mental state. Perhaps it is Jackson's upper-class British accent, her refined and clipped diction, which undermine her credibility as a dozing lunatic. Richardson plays a splendid Marat. His role permits him no movement about the stage because of the confines of his bath, but he counters this dramatic limitation by the power of his rational, quietly sane character which is in high contrast to the flailing, empty-eyed crazies limping about around him.

Marat/Sade is not a pleasant film to view. The sight of soiled and miserable humanity not in control of itself is both pitiable and revolting. The bizarre and grotesque chorus in their lurid paint and wigs is no less offensive. Aesthetics aside, the contrast of the wretched inmates with gorgeous Parisian gentility is as repugnant as the victimization of the patients by one of their own, the Marquis. Despite high audience attrition, the film did well because of its preselling by the successful play and its low budget. Its success, both financially and as an art movie, is due to the masterful direction of veteran Peter Brook, who broke free of the confines of the theater to create a supremely moving, infuriating, and engrossing screen experience.

Nancy S. Kinney

MARGIE

Released: 1946
Production: Walter Morosco for Twentieth Century-Fox
Direction: Henry King
Screenplay: F. Hugh Herbert; based on short stories by Ruth McKenney and Richard Bransten
Cinematography: Charles G. Clarke
Editing: Barbara McLean
Art direction: James Basevi and J. Russell Spencer
Costume design: Kay Nelson
Sound: Eugene Grossman and Roger Heman
Music: Alfred Newman
Technicolor consultants: Natalie Kalmus and Leonard Doss
Running time: 94 minutes

Principal characters:
Margie	Jeanne Crain
Professor Fontayne	Glenn Langan
Miss Palmer	Lynn Bari
Roy Hornsdale	Alan Young
Marybelle	Barbara Lawrence
Johnny	Conrad Janis
Grandma McSweeney	Esther Dale
Mr. McDuff	Hobart Cavanaugh
Joyce (Margie's daughter)	Ann Todd

Margie is the story of a girl passing through adolescence in the 1920's in a small town. The subject is essentially a very common one, and in this instance, it is not even embellished with a great deal of dramatic incident. Suggested by stories of Ruth McKenney, the author of *My Sister Eileen*, the events portrayed are to some extent a whimsical reminiscence of her personal experiences. Darryl F. Zanuck, the head of Twentieth Century-Fox, suspected that the material was too lightweight for a feature film. Nevertheless, he asked his favorite director at the studio, Henry King, to take a look at the screenplay and offer his opinion. To Zanuck's surprise, King—at that point in his career the director of such major Fox efforts as *The Song of Bernadette* (1943) and *Wilson* (1944)—not only saw a movie in the screenplay but also offered to direct it himself.

King saw *Margie* as a potentially entertaining and humorous film, but he also recognized that it could possess considerable emotional force. Specifically, he was responding to the heroine's uncertain relationship with her father, which is resolved during the climax. It is precisely this sort of insight on which the American cinema has thrived, and *Margie* is one of the most appealing examples of the transformation of an apparently modest project into a special artistic experience. Although it is not a commonly known or often-shown film, its distinction rests on two equally exceptional accomplishments. One is its strikingly individualized use of Technicolor, which has in recent years provoked the intense admiration of every audience fortunate enough to see an original print. The other is the level of profundity unexpectedly attained in the characterization of the heroine and the rendering of her experiences.

Margie McDuff (Jeanne Crain) is an only child whose mother is deceased and whose father (Hobart Cavanaugh), a respectable undertaker, elects to live apart from her, uneasy over the responsibility of rearing a girl and convinced that Margie's grandmother (Esther Dale) is a suitable substitute for a parent. Although she is pretty and intelligent, Margie is more introverted than most of her friends, and as a result, she leads a somewhat lonely life, pursued by only one boy, the rather uncharismatic Roy Hornsdale (Alan Young). Longing not to be different from her peers, she agonizes over the social poise of her friend Marybelle (Barbara Lawrence), who is going steady with Johnny (Conrad Janis), the most popular boy in school. She also has a crush on the new French teacher, Professor Fontayne (Glenn Langan), who, it appears, is romancing another teacher, Miss Palmer (Lynn Bari). Margie is a skilled debater, whose impassioned plea to "take the marines out of Nicaragua" makes an unexpected impression on her father. Unfortunately, however, her verbal command tends to desert her in social situations. She is easily embarrassed and given to stuttering when tense. Additionally, her 1920's-style bloomers have an amusing tendency to disengage themselves from her body and become exposed to public view. Her greatest trauma, however, is reserved for the prom. Wrongly believing that Professor Fontayne is taking her after Roy has caught a cold, she makes a fool of herself, and, having bragged to Marybelle, she sulks in solitude as though she will die of shame. Her grandmother assures her, however, that she will have a date. The date turns out to be her father, and she is so moved by this that she discovers in herself a new composure and becomes the hit of the party until the bloomers fatefully slip once more.

If this outline of the story makes Margie seem a somewhat more compelling character than might be expected, it is because the film is so replete with detail and mood which deepen her. Additionally, mention should be made of a prologue and epilogue which inform the substance of the main story. The film opens about sixteen years later, with the adult Margie going through her attic and discovering her adolescent possessions, arousing the curiosity of her daughter (Ann Todd). The main story is related in flashback, and when that has concluded, the daughter asks Margie who took her home from the dance. It turns out to have been the ever-gallant Professor Fontayne, now her husband, who arrives with news that Margie's father has been appointed ambassador to Nicaragua. The anguish of adolescence is therefore placed in a certain perspective, but the final effect is not what one would expect. The reason for this becomes clear on repeated viewings, when the long introductory sequence of Margie and her daughter is watched with a knowledge of the flashback. The younger Margie is very intense and emotional, investing each moment with the conviction that happiness or tragedy might suddenly overwhelm her. The mature Margie is like a different person. She speaks quietly, does not stutter at all, and moves with composure; this is not a woman who would lose her bloomers even if she still wore them. She is a completely relaxed and confidant woman, but the energy of the adolescent Margie has disappeared.

The process of growing up ends naturally in a greater assurance and equanimity. Validating this process is the *apparent* intention of the film, as is true of similar films. The fully created character, however, does lead to a certain amount of ambiguity. Far from being a typical girl of her time, Margie comes across as an extraordinary person whose sensitivity and intelligence almost overwhelm her in situations which would not have the same effect on a more ordinary girl. Her loneliness and estrangement from her father and the daring of her love for a teacher set her apart from the conventional teenage heroine because she experiences these aspects of her existence with such soulful fervor. Her rather reserved father is probably the source of her insecurities and melancholy. When he shows her he loves her, the emotional reconciliation has the effect of bringing out her poise and permitting her to relate to men with greater assurance. Margie gains something by being healed of the youthful wound prompted by her father's earlier rejection. She grows up, marries, and has a daughter of her own. If, however, in retrospect, something is gained, something is also unmistakably lost. At the end of the film, one can feel almost as if one has seen a tragedy. Margie has lived the deepest feelings of her life twenty years before, and they have been taken from her by the consequence of going on to live a stable and ordinary life.

The remarkable performance of Crain has a great deal to do with this effect. Under King's direction, she projects the differences between the older Margie and the younger Margie with surprising skill. The moment the flashback ends and the film returns to the present, we miss the animation, spirit, and vulnerability of the young Margie which have been conveyed so expressively by Crain. The three prolonged sequences of Margie alone in her room are the most memorable in the film, and King's slow and deliberate style and Charles Clarke's daring lighting demand a vibrant presence which Crain has not otherwise had the opportunity to reveal in films. These sequences contain a visual progression that is central to the film. In the first, Margie is studying, but she is distracted by the sound of music to which Marybelle and Johnny dance on the porch of a neighboring house. Getting ready for bed afterward, Margie provides her own music, singing to herself and moving with an unconscious seductiveness in the subdued light. The second sequence in the room finds the lights even lower, with Margie moving in and out of shadows. In the final sequence, in which Margie is suffering her apparent disgrace over the prom incident, there is almost no light in the room at all. Margie cries, retreats to the middle of the room, and sits, head bowed, in complete silhouette.

That long moment is the culmination of a gravitation to shadows, silhouettes, and other strikingly somber effects throughout the film. This visual approach to Technicolor in the 1940's is so bold that it can only be described as experimental. The general attitude to color at the time was to emphasize its difference from black and white, the prevailing mode of cinematography for most films. Color was used mostly for adventure films, costume pictures, and, particularly, musicals. *Margie*, although not a musical, does have songs and dances and is mostly set in period, so one can understand why the studio decided it should be shot in color. The rainbow effect expected in a film of this type, however, is avoided. While the color is not truly naturalistic in the sense that it usually is in a contemporary film, its expressive richness is subtly employed. Bright colors are used selectively, so that, for example, when Margie wears a green dress, the vividness of the green contrasts to subdued backgrounds. King's penchant for shooting exteriors on location led him to a small town in the Northwest, and as the flashback takes place in winter, the snow and ice on the streets and the bare trees have a realistic effect, creating a more dramatic atmosphere than the decorative prettiness of Technicolor permitted in less imaginative hands than those of Clarke and King.

Color in *Margie* accentuates every emotion and visual mood desired by the director and cinematographer, and is quietly dazzling in certain sequences in which the lighting is matched by the vitality of a moving camera. One such instance is the opening of the flashback, introduced by a record of Rudy Vallee singing "My Time Is Your Time," to which Margie and her daughter are listening. As the flashback begins, the camera tracks through a crowd at the high school, moving briskly in their winter costumes beneath a clear sky, as Marybelle's voice, singing the same song, overlaps and then replaces Vallee's. The shot finally ends as the camera swiftly moves to Marybelle, singing to the boys. Beautiful in every respect, this shot not only displays an imaginative use of image and sound, but also poignantly links the introspective adolescent Margie (as yet unseen) to the extroverted Marybelle through the lyrics of the well-chosen song. Another sequence that is even more technically impressive occurs at an ice-skating rink. The camera moves continuously throughout the sequence, following the skaters, a prodigious feat of lighting and camera operation in view of the difficulties of shooting such a sequence in color in this period of cinema history. The white-blue of the ice and the distinct colors of the skaters' costumes are always perfectly in focus and differentiated, and this visually complex and captivating sequence never seems remotely labored.

Margie ranks with *Leave Her to Heaven* (1945, photographed by Leon Shamroy and directed by John Stahl) and *Black Narcissus* (1947, photographed by Jack Cardiff and directed by Michael Powell) as one of the most beautiful and unusual Technicolor films of the 1940's. The two films evoked for comparison are not named at random; both won Academy Awards for color cinematography. *Margie*, completely overlooked in a year which saw only two nominations in the category, is in some ways the most imaginative achievement of the three, as its subject lacks the melodrama which served as inspiration for the daring color approaches of the other two films.

The use of color and the emotional density of *Margie* are, of course, intimately related. King has missed none of the humor and charm of the script's situations, and it is possible to remain aware that the work is superficially a slender and light nostalgia piece. In the hands of the Fox directors customarily responsible for the studio's musicals and Crain vehicles of the 1940's, it would have been a very conventional film. The mark of a great director, however, is to see something more in apparently frivolous entertainments than meets the eye. Just as Vincente Minnelli made of the similarly nostalgic *Meet Me in St. Louis* (1944) a moving portrait of idealized experience as perceived subjectively by the family on which that film centers, so King uses *Margie* to crystallize the nature of emotional intensity as it is experienced in solitude and to trace the overtaking of troubled but vibrant youth by disenchanted adulthood.

Blake Lucas

THE MARK

Released: 1961
Production: Raymond Stross for Continental Distributing; released by Twentieth Century-Fox
Direction: Guy Green
Screenplay: Sidney Buchman and Stanley Mann; based on the novel of the same name by Charles Israel
Cinematography: Dudley Lovell
Editing: Bernard Gribble
Running time: 127 minutes

Principal characters:
Jim Fuller	Stuart Whitman
Ruth Leighton	Maria Schell
Doctor Edmund McNally	Rod Steiger
Clive	Donald Wolfit
Janie	Amanda Black

The Mark is a serious-minded British production that approaches its subject—a topic once considered taboo—with intelligence and concern. *The Mark* is about a sex offender, specifically, a child molester. The story is told from the viewpoint of the psychiatrist, Dr. McNally (Rod Steiger), who is treating Jim Fuller (Stuart Whitman), who, on parole from prison, undergoes therapy. Through the sessions the film audience is a party to Fuller's improved mental health and gains insight into the problems of the emotionally distraught man. The most famous film about crimes against children, Fritz Lang's 1931 melodramatic *M* (the story of a child-murderer), concentrated on action, upon the crime itself, and upon the criminal's attempt to elude authorities. In contrast, *The Mark* is a calm, near-textbook study dominated by dialogue and a strong character portrait. Its makers have attempted to dig deep within their subject in order to paint a comprehensive picture of one man's dilemma.

The story opens with Fuller's release from prison following a three-year term. We do not initially know the nature of his offense, but the prison psychiatrist maintains that he is ready to return to society. Fuller is handsome, brooding, and serious. The story takes place in the British Midlands, where Fuller, a Canadian, takes a job as an accountant with a man named Clive (Donald Wolfit) who professes to be interested in social welfare. Fuller is exceedingly conscientious about his work, as well as uneasy around some of his coworkers. Through sessions with the psychiatrist, we learn about his background through flashbacks. He had a dominating mother and a weak father which caused Fuller, the youngest in a family of five sisters, to grow up fearing women. It is Fuller's inability to deal with women that makes him shy away from Ruth Leighton (Maria Schell), a coworker at Clive's office who knows nothing of his past, except that he is good-looking, intelligent, and unattached. It is a minor victory for her when she gets him to accept a dinner invitation to her home, considering that, by this time, we have learned Fuller's secret. His fear of women as well as his early fumblings with sex have been revealed, as well as his crime.

At this point *The Mark* becomes somewhat compromising. As Fuller's story unfolds, it is revealed that while he intended to rape a ten-year-old girl, the act was never consummated. Through the tangled shreds of his past we see that, in his fear of relationships with women, he turned to a child. After taking the child to an isolated area where she begins to cry, Fuller is repulsed by his intentions, however; he stares at the weeping child, turns to run, and vomits. When brought to trial he declares his guilt, viewing prison as necessary in order to curb his dark fears. Because Fuller did not actually carry out the rape although he did want to, he may emerge as a more sympathetic character than if he had raped the child. Nevertheless, he will carry the stigma of the crime, even though he did not commit it. This is "the mark' of the title.

Secure in prison, Fuller is tense on the outside, wondering what will happen if the old desires should overcome him. His psychiatrist is insistent. "Everybody has these impulses, but healthy people learn to live with them and control them. I think you're healthy." Is he, however, "cured?" The first real test takes place when he goes to have dinner with Ruth and meets her ten-year-old daughter, Janie (Amanda Black). Uneasy and engulfed with guilt, Fuller keeps his distance from the child, and, as time passes, he is relieved to discover that his feelings toward the child are fatherly. His manhood is also reinforced during a weekend holiday with Ruth, when he is successful in making love to her.

Fuller's relationship with Ruth and Janie progresses to the point that some of his guilt begins to erode. His past comes into full view, however, through the efforts of a scandal-seeking newspaperman. Aware of Fuller's crime, he photographs Fuller and Janie on an outing at a carnival. When the pictures and headlines scream out Fuller's past, those who have been kind to him suddenly turn away. His employer Clive explains, awkwardly, that he no longer has work for him. His landlady now refuses to rent to him, and Ruth, angered at the secrets kept from her and concerned for Janie, also turns away. Although Dr. McNally wants Fuller to stand his ground, Fuller cannot. In shame, he retreats to another city, where he will attempt to start once more.

His life there is one of solitude until Ruth finds him. Dr. McNally has talked with her and she knows that Fuller did not actually rape the child, although she is still worried about the effects of the scandal on Janie. In love with Fuller, however, she wants to give their relationship another try. As the film closes, the two are aware that life together will have its difficulties because the stigma of "the mark" may once again resurface.

Whitman, who has been relegated to mostly "B"-action pictures throughout his lengthy career, was nominated for an Oscar for his sensitive performance as Fuller; he lost to Maximilian Schell for his work in the socially stirring *Judgment at Nuremberg*. Whitman's performance, however, garnered critical raves, and the role will probably remain the best of his career.

Steiger, an actor of many dialects, including that of the Southern sheriff of *In the Heat of the Night* (1967) and those connected with his disguises in *No Way to Treat a Lady* (1968), is engagingly perceptive as Dr. McNally, a quick-tempered Irishman, messy, and a bit wild-eyed, but a passionate, caring man. Steiger gives the role a feeling of warmth and concern that is a departure from the image of the standard film psychiatrist (glasses, heavy European accent, stern-faced). Schell is also effective as Ruth, the woman whose faith in the man she loves falters only once.

Guy Green, the Oscar-winning cinematographer of David Lean's *Great Expectations* (1947), directed *The Mark*, and although Green went on to direct some glossy Hollywood efforts including *Diamond Head* (1962) and *Once Is Not Enough* (1975), his most perceptive works are intimate studies of people in conflict with their environment and, in a sense, their heredity. *A Patch of Blue* (1965) tells the story of a blind white girl who falls in love with a black man. In *Light in the Piazza* (1962) Olivia de Havilland succeeds in marrying off her retarded daughter; and Hayley Mills embarks on womanhood in *A Matter of Innocence* (1968). *The Mark* is delivered with calm objectivity. As a character study it does tend to be one-dimensional because it allows for only a narrow view of Fuller. We see his past, and his present torment, but we know nothing of his everyday likes, dislikes, or dreams.

When it was first released, *The Mark* was branded a controversial film. Yet in 1961, the year of the film's release, a handful of other films also probed subjects once considered taboo for the screen, such as *The Children's Hour*, which hinted at a lesbian relationship between the characters played by Audrey Hepburn and Shirley MacLaine. An even more bold film, *Victim*, starring Dirk Bogarde as a lawyer trying to break up a blackmailing ring, openly discussed homosexuality, even in the married character played by Bogarde.

Although it has been twenty years since *The Mark* and fifty since *M*, no other film to date has presented a character study of a child molester. Many films have had child molestation or rape as a topic but never have any other films delved into the character of the offender.

Pat H. Broeske

MARKED WOMAN

Released: 1937
Production: Hal B. Wallis for Warner Bros.
Direction: Lloyd Bacon
Screenplay: Robert Rossen and Abem Finkel
Cinematography: George Barnes
Editing: Jack Killifer
Running time: 96 minutes

Principal characters:
Mary Dwight (Strauber)	Bette Davis
David Graham	Humphrey Bogart
Betty Strauber	Jane Bryan
Johnny Vanning	Edward Cianelli
Emmy Lou Egan	Isabel Jewell
Estelle Porter	Mayo Methot
Gabby Marvin	Lola Lane
John Truble	Arthur Aylesworth

During the halcyon years of Hollywood in the 1930's and 1940's, most of the major studios had their specialities; M-G-M made the best musicals, Universal made the best horror films, and so forth. There has never been any disagreement among film scholars that Warner Bros. made the best gangster films—and there was a good reason for this. Warners, more than any other studio in the 1930's, looked to the front pages of the newspapers for story material. Depression audiences were not eager to be reminded of their plight, yet Warners managed to do it successfully on a fairly regular basis. The films might not have done very well at the box office but many of them, such as *Heroes for Sale* (1932) and *Wild Boys of the Road* (1933), have been acknowledged as classics and are fairly accurate as documents of the times. When it came to gangsters, Warners adopted a "no holds barred" policy. Although racketeers were the lead characters in films such as *Little Caesar* (1930) and *The Public Enemy* (1931), they invariably died or were imprisoned for life. In films such as *G-Men* (1935), the crooks were given no mercy, and lawmen wielded tommyguns with great aplomb, much to the apparent satisfaction of moviegoers.

Marked Woman, in keeping with the Warner Bros. policy of raiding the newspapers for story lines, deals with the "clip joint" and the unfortunates who worked there, the dance-hall hostesses who were forced to aid their racketeer bosses in robbing their patrons. The clip joint was primarily a big-city institution, and as such was prime material for the Warners scenarists. Ordinarily, at another studio, material such as this would have fallen to the makers of "B" pictures, who might use the situation as an excuse to showcase the studio's latest new leading man, make him a two-fisted cop or federal agent, and turn him loose to spend six reels shooting up assorted heavies without much rhyme or reason. At Warners, however, the clip joint got "A" treatment, with a good cast, solid scripts, and workmanlike (if uninspired) direction.

Gangster Johnny Vanning (Edward Cianelli) takes over a two-bit night club called the Club Intime and remodels it, making it the Club Intimate, a fancy clip joint. The hostesses who have been kept on the payroll are given instructions to take their patrons for a ride, have them spend lots of money, and steer them to the gambling tables. Mary Dwight (Bette Davis) does not like her new job, and makes it known to Vanning, who admires her spirit. Later, in the apartment that Mary shares with some other hostesses, she announces that she will beat the racket. Estelle Porter (Mayo Methot), an aging member of the group who is afraid of being overshadowed by the younger girls, promises Mary a life of misery but can offer no real means of escape.

One night, Mary feels sorry for one of the suckers, a young man from out of town who has paid off his gambling losses with a bad check. Knowing that Vanning will kill the young man if he finds him, Mary loans him enough money to get out of town. Touched by her generosity, the man writes Mary's name and address down and promises to return her money as soon as he gets home.

The next day brings a surprise visit from Betty Strauber (Jane Bryan), who is Mary's sister. Betty, a college girl on vacation, is unaware of Mary's occupation and believes that the girls all work in a dress shop. Her illusions are badly shaken when a policeman arrives looking for Mary. The man she had helped the night before was found dead, with Mary's name and address on his body. Mary refuses to talk, as do the other girls, and the entire group—including Betty—is taken to police headquarters. Assistant District Attorney David Graham (Humphrey Bogart) has been trying to get the goods on Johnny Vanning for some time, and he is convinced that the gangster was responsible for this latest killing. He holds the girls in jail as material witnesses, hoping that they will testify against Vanning. Mary, as Graham's chief witness, proves uncooperative—especially after she is visited in jail by one of Vanning's shyster lawyers (Raymond Hattan) who threatens her if she talks.

In court, however, Mary *does* take the stand and identifies two of Vanning's henchmen (Alan Davis and Allen Matthews). Vanning's lawyer, hoping to make her testimony useless by exposing her as a cheap dance-hall hostess, tears her to pieces on the stand, painting her as a cheap little guttersnipe. He then produces an unsophisticated sheriff named John Truble (Arthur Aylesworth) from a rural town who claims to have locked the henchmen in jail for drunk driving on the night of the murder. Graham's case is thrown out of court, and he makes a point of telling Mary what he thinks of her for helping Vanning.

Back at the girls' apartment, Betty tells Mary that she could never go back to school, since she had been arrested and dragged into court. While Mary, heartbroken, goes off to work at the Club, Emmy Lou (Isabel Jewell), one of Mary's roommates, convinces Betty to come with her to a swank party, which turns out to be in Johnny Vanning's penthouse. Betty, trying to avoid being manhandled by a drunk, puts up a fuss and Vanning intervenes. He slaps her in the face, whereupon she is thrown backward, falls down a flight of stairs and is killed. The horrified Emmy Lou is instructed to go into hiding and keep quiet.

Mary, arriving home and finding Betty gone, becomes worried and attempts to enlist Graham's aid, who informs her that Betty's body has just been found in the river. Emmy Lou is established as the girl who brought Betty to Vanning's party, and Mary promises to find her and expose Vanning. The gangster learns of this and sends men over to beat Mary brutally while the other girls watch. Hearing that Mary has been hospitalized as a result of the beating, Emmy Lou decides to visit her. At the hospital, she tearfully confesses to being the one who brought Betty to the party and promises, as do the other girls, to testify against Vanning. Graham therefore has no trouble obtaining a conviction with the girls' testimony. His victory in court makes him a hero, and he tries to convince Mary to stay, but she remains loyal to her friends, and the girls walk away together into the night.

Marked Woman is a startlingly frank depiction of racketeering in the big city. In true Warners fashion, the plight of the hostesses is not glamorized; in fact, little is left to the imagination when, for example, Mary is beaten by Vanning's henchmen. Betty's sudden death is also shocking since she has been portrayed as a lovely girl so full of life that her removal from the story is almost beyond belief. At the end of the picture, instead of remaining with David Graham, Mary chooses to stay with her friends, now jobless and walking the streets. The final shot, in which the five girls walk side-by-side down the street disappearing into the fog, is one of the most memorable endings to this type of picture.

Director Lloyd Bacon, never considered a very stylish director, handles his story and players with equal dexterity, giving the audience a full measure of time to experience each event. His sturdy direction gives us cause for thought, and he neatly handles a dynamic scene in which Bogart, ostensibly speaking to the jury, delivers an impassioned antiracketeer speech to the audience.

Typical of similar material in other hands, Columbia's *Paid To Dance* (1937) has a story line which echoes *Marked Woman*, but reduces the action to standard heroics from undercover G-man Don Terry, and is, in the main, notable only for the appearance of Rita Hayworth as one of the girls.

Ed Hulse

THE MARRYING KIND

Released: 1952
Production: Bert Granet for Columbia
Direction: George Cukor
Screenplay: Ruth Gordon and Garson Kanin
Cinematography: Joseph Walker
Editing: Charles Nelson
Running time: 93 minutes

Principal characters:
Florence Keefer	Judy Holliday
Chet Keefer	Aldo Ray
Judge Carroll	Madge Kennedy
Joan Shipley	Sheila Bond
Howard Shipley	John Alexander
Emily Bundy	Peggy Cass
Pat Bundy	Mickey Shaughnessy
Ellen	Susan Hallaran
Joey (age 4)	Barry Curtis
Joey (age 6)	Christopher Olsen

Set in the New York City Court of Domestic Relations, the funny and poignant *The Marrying Kind* is a series of flashbacks that visually show what divorce-seekers Florence and Chet Keefer (Judy Holliday and Aldo Ray) verbally tell the sympathetic judge (Madge Kennedy). Needless to say, the two married characters each present their own individual sides of the story. Recalling the time that the two met, Chet describes it as "Just a pick-up." "It so happens I remember it different," Florence interjects. In this round-about way, we learn of the events in the characters' lives from the time they first meet in Central Park and the ensuing fights over the wedding, apartment, relatives, jobs, and children, to the time the Keefers decide to separate seven years later.

We learn of the couple's thwarted ambitions. Chet invents ball-bearing roller skates in a moment of vision important to his philosophy of life, only to see someone else put a similar product on the market. Florence enters a radio contest only to lose it with a wrong answer. We also learn of the couple's jealousies. Chet is suspicious because Florence's former boss makes her a beneficiary, and Florence becomes upset because, at a party, Chet flirts with a bosomy female guest. In one charming scene during a strife-ridden breakfast, the Keefers' little girl, Ellen (Susan Hallaran), makes them all sing her kindergarten song. With glum faces, Florence and Chet begin, "Good morning to you, good morning to you, we're all in our places, with bright shining faces, oh this is the way to start a new day." In a later, unexpectedly chilling scene, we learn of the Keefer family's heartbreaking tragedy. On a Memorial Day picnic with their little children Joey (Christopher Olsen) and Ellen, the small boy goes off to swim with his friends. While Florence sings "Down Among the Sheltering Palms" gleefully, suddenly, in an electrifying moment, we learn that he has drowned. One of the unique aspects of *The Marrying Kind* is that in the midst of all the happiness comes such overwhelming despair, which is, of course, what often happens in real life.

As Florence Keefer, the wonderful Holliday is magnificently funny and profoundly moving. Following on the heels of her Academy Award-winning role of Billie Dawn in *Born Yesterday* (1950), Holliday once again plays the dumb blond that became her trademark and film *persona*. As in her roles as the pea-brained, pistol-packing housewife in *Adam's Rib* (1949), or the dizzy doxy in *Born Yesterday*, Holliday here plays an endearing wise fool.

Like Holliday's other characters, Florence Keefer speaks with the same Brooklyn accent and diction and manifests the same lunatic thinking. For example, Florence considers making living room curtains out of comic books stuck on unbleached muslin with borders of scotch tape. She also contemplates the possibilities of mint-flavored postage stamps, and as Florence seriously tells one of her relatives, she sets aside one half hour a day just to think. Florence is also deeply affecting, however, particularly when she describes the scene of her son's death, and when she later tells the judge, "I always thought the one thing I would never be anymore when I ever got married was lonesome. But the funny thing—you can be it even in the same bedroom if he seems to be thinking about different things except you."

In his first screen role, Ray is believable as the civil servant/post-office worker who suffers from nightmares caused by the pressures of work and his often nagging wife. We see his comic-frightening dream inventing the roller skates in a near-surrealistic sequence. Like Florence, Chet also ponders, meditating on such topics as why dogs do not have to brush their teeth. Playing the role of the very average and ordinary middle-class couple, Holliday and Ray are most hilarious when they do average and ordinary things. They gargle, spit, brush, pluck, and rinse. As Florence grimaces and squeals to Chet, "First you brush your teeth and then you drink beer? Ooooo!" The reality of the situation is all too familiar to the audience.

As the Keefers tell their story to the judge, they become somewhat purged of their sorrows, and they soon come to realize that their life together is worth saving. As Chet tells Florence, "I like to make a promise everything's goin' to be different, I mean, but how *can* I promise that? But I tell you what I *can* do. I can tell you I would certainly try." Pausing a moment, Florence softly responds, "If we could only remember not to blame each other for things going the wrong way . . . I would try, too, Chet. With the bottom of my heart." The film then ends as the Keefers give their salvageable marriage another go.

The Marrying Kind was written by Ruth Gordon and her husband/writing partner, Garson Kanin, who also wrote two previous Holliday hits, *Adam's Rib* and *Born Yesterday*, both of which were also directed by George Cukor. The successful collaboration of the four went on the next year to create *It Should Happen to You*. While the last two films were not as successful as the first two, they remain literate, entertaining, and excellent showcases for the talents of Holliday. She was a fine comedienne who was equally successful on stage and screen and could create great affection for her characters. After a few successful films in the 1950's, Holliday returned to the stage and appeared in only one film in the 1960's, *Bells Are Ringing* (1960), re-creating her Broadway success as the lovable answering-service operator. Holliday died five years later at the age of forty-three, the victim of cancer.

Leslie Taubman

MARY OF SCOTLAND

Released: 1936
Production: Pandro S. Berman for RKO/Radio
Direction: John Ford
Screenplay: Dudley Nichols; based on the play of the same name by Maxwell Anderson
Cinematography: Joseph H. August
Editing: Jane Loring
Art direction: Van Nest Polglase and Carroll Clarke
Interior decoration: Darrell Silvera
Costume design: Walter Plunkett
Music: Max Steiner
Running time: 123 minutes

Principal characters:
Mary Stuart	Katharine Hepburn
Earl of Bothwell	Fredric March
Queen Elizabeth	Florence Eldridge
Darnley	Douglas Walton
David Rizzio	John Carradine
James Stuart Moray	Ian Keith

In the masculine canon of John Ford's works, two films stand out as notable exceptions to the rule, *Mary of Scotland* and *Seven Women* (1965). Whereas women usually function in supporting roles, in these two films they are at the center of the dramatic conflict. There are more than a few similarities between the two films, down to the final self-sacrifice of the heroine, but it is their differences which are most striking, both stylistically and thematically. There is a world of difference between the conscious artistry and optimistic tone of the former and the latter's seeming artlessness and pessimism. Just as *Mary of Scotland* resembles *The Informer* (1935) with its oppressive studio-bound expressionism, *Seven Women* can be viewed as a disguised Western, falling in line with the director's late development from *Two Rode Together* (1961) on. With Ford's growing maturity, a greater ambiguity entered into his work as his films grew more reflective and intuitive.

Ford's own attitude toward Catholicism, and religion in general, was apparently ambiguous, and from the evidence of his films it would be foolish to draw any sweeping generalizations. Yet in three particular films, *The Informer*, *Mary of Scotland*, and *The Fugitive* (1947), Ford comes closest to articulating his religious beliefs. Interestingly, these films are his most expressionistic in style, making dramatic use of light and shadow. They also make great use of symbolism. Of course, nearly all of Ford's films make use of these devices, but the difference lies in the degree and the concreteness of the metaphors in these openly religious films.

The central conflict of this film is between Mary (Katharine Hepburn), the Catholic queen of Scotland, and her Protestant adversary, Elizabeth (Florence Eldridge). Even in the original play Mary is idealized, but in Dudley Nichols' script and Ford's handling she becomes almost Christ-like. Thus, within her is an even deeper conflict between her own ideals and those temptations which would deter her from her goals. Mary is given the choice of fulfilling her destiny, which means death, or escaping with her lover Bothwell (Fredric March). Inevitably she chooses death in the knowledge that her son will eventually rule. At the scaffold she achieves her apotheosis as Ford's camera tilts up from her face to the sky above. It is a victory in defeat which can be found in many of Ford's films.

The difference between the two queens is established through several different levels. Both are quite determined in their aims, although Elizabeth's pragmatic realism is a foil to Mary's dogmatic idealism. Most clearly, their opposing situations are mirrored through their environments. Elizabeth's court is orderly, while Mary's is a vision of chaos achieved through a combination of low-key lighting, oppressive decor, and disruptive activity. Dogs run about freely amidst the human din and confusion. Mary's entrance into the film by sea, amidst a dense fog, sharply outlines the uncertainty of her position.

Although the film does contain historical distortions, the plot is generally faithful to the events from Mary's arrival in Scotland to her eventual execution. Having lived most of her life in France, she is virtually an outsider. Immediately she comes into conflict with her half-brother Moray (Ian Keith) and his party. Her own Catholic beliefs are also at odds with those of a number of her countrymen, who are represented by the reformer John Knox. In order to strengthen her power, she agrees to marry the effete Darnley (Douglas Walton). She also finds an ally, as well as lover, in Bothwell. Gradually her position becomes more precarious as first her friend Rizzio (John Carradine) and later Darnley are murdered. Finally Bothwell is imprisoned and later dies, and Mary is left alone to face her fate.

Ford and his cameraman, Joseph H. August, achieve some chilling effects in the film's more violent moments. Rizzio, running from room to room, is dogged by sharply etched shadows. At bay, he covers himself with a sheet so as not to see his attackers. Darnley's death is no less effective with its *film noir*-like lighting. Symbolically, Bothwell dies during a windstorm, half-crazed.

Both on the stylistic and dramatic level the film achieves its high point during Mary's trial. Unable to face her judges at eye-level as they are placed in imposing seats above her, the inferiority of her position is obvious. Ford emphasizes the disparity in the setting through a judicious use of camera angles, subjectively from Mary's point of view and objectively from above.

Demanding to see Elizabeth at her trial, she is told by the judges that the English queen is present symbolically through her orb and sceptre. Invited by the judges to sit down, she flatly states that she will stand "symbolically." Only when she hears of Bothwell's death does she temporarily break down.

As successful as certain scenes are, and they certainly stand up as well as much of Ford's other work from the period, overall the film does not fully succeed. A good deal of the fault can be found in the material with its lack of historical balance, but Ford and Nichols deserve some of the blame in their unquestioning acceptance of it. On the technical side the film is on much firmer ground. Ford himself expressed admiration for the cinematography of August, and they worked together on several occasions. August specialized in low-key lighting effects even in his work for other directors, although with Ford his effects seem more relevant than merely beautiful. The art direction also plays a key role in conveying meaning to the film. Walter Plunkett's costumes are both historically accurate and dramatically apt. Bothwell's easy carelessness, Darnley's effeminacy, and Mary Stuart's seriousness are all mirrored by their apparel.

The part of Mary Stuart seems almost tailor-made for Katharine Hepburn. Shrewd, intelligent, and often proud, she can also be warmly vulnerable. Eldridge, who was married to March in real life, is no less good as the imperious Elizabeth, becoming almost sympathetic in her self-willed isolation. These two women surely dominate the film, their strength working as a foil to the weaknesses of the male antagonists.

Flawed though the work is, it would seem a major work in the *ouevre* of a less talented director than Ford. Lacking the deeper resonance of the later *Seven Women*, its failure is largely relative to Ford's more substantial films. Few of Ford's films are devoid of interest, and *Mary of Scotland* has more than most.

Mike Vanderlan

MARY POPPINS

Released: 1964
Production: Walt Disney and Bill Walsh for Walt Disney Productions
Direction: Robert Stevenson
Screenplay: Bill Walsh and Don DaGradi; based on the Mary Poppins books
by Pamela L. Travers
Cinematography: Edward Colman
Editing: Cotton Warburton (AA)
Animation direction: Hamilton S. Luske
Special effects: Peter Ellenshaw (AA)
Music: Richard M. Sherman and Robert B. Sherman (AA)
Song: Richard M. Sherman and Robert B. Sherman, "Chim Chim Cher-ee"
(AA)
Running time: 140 minutes

> *Principal characters:*
> Mary Poppins .... Julie Andrews (AA)
> Bert/Mr. Dawes, Sr. .... Dick Van Dyke
> Mr. Banks ....David Tomlinson
> Mrs. Banks .... Glynis Johns
> Uncle Albert ....Ed Wynn
> Jane Banks .... Karen Dotrice
> Michael Banks .... Matthew Garber

"Practically perfect people never permit sentiment to muddle their feelings"
is a statement that does not seem like typical Walt Disney movie dialogue.
Sentiment, in the form of cuddly animal stories, animated or live, fairy-tale
characters, or clean-cut young people having good, old-fashioned fun, was
firmly identified with the Disney Studio product by the time of *Mary Poppins*,
but no Disney film before or since has equaled the popularity and worldwide
box-office success of that film.

On closer look, some of the apparent anomalies of *Mary Poppins* can be
fitted within the Disney tradition. Mary Poppins is a prim, starched English
nanny who is never ruffled and is always, or almost always, tidy. She fits
neatly within a strong Disney tradition of cleanliness on film. Often in the
animated features, woodsy creatures tidy up, or characters get a bath. In
Fantasia (1940), Mickey Mouse has a famous encounter with brooms and
buckets as a Sorcerer's Apprentice. Mary Poppins' problem is to tidy up the
Banks household.

The Banks family lives in London during the Edwardian era. Prior to Mary
Poppins' arrival, the family is in a mess psychologically as well as physically,
and so in trouble. The children, Jane (Karen Dotrice) and Michael (Matthew
Garber), are missing, their nanny has quit, and the cook and maid are fighting.
Mrs. Banks (Glynis Johns) is oblivious to all these problems. She sings "Sister

Suffragette" to demonstrate that she has been out crusading while her own house falls to pieces. George Banks (David Tomlinson), following the pattern of a great many American film husbands, is oblivious to the problems in his home. His song, "The Life I Lead," evokes a well-ordered existence impossible to locate in reality.

Only the arrival of his children in the tow of a friendly constable alerts Mr. Banks to a problem in his home. It is time to hire a new nanny. His children try to give him a list of nanny requirements by singing "Perfect Nanny," but their father, still not communicating with them, tears up the list. Then the Mary Poppins "magic" begins to take effect after her initial appearance. Mary (Julie Andrews) represents the children's best wishes and, by extension, happiness for their family. She has a mysterious control of the London air. The children's torn list rises up the chimney and into the night sky. The next morning, the personification of Mary Poppins appears out of that sky, holding a proper umbrella which keeps her aloft. With the help of her winds, she also sees to it that all the other nanny applicants are blown off the block.

Mary Poppins gets the job, slides up the bannister to the nursery, and immediately tidies it up. Fixing messy situations is a problem of getting the medicine down with a "Spoonful of Sugar," she explains in song to the children. The lyrics indicate Poppins' mixture of fun with more serious instruction. She is an ideal combination of opposites. Not only does she represent comfortable and predictable discipline and "good upbringing"; she is also the source of fantastic adventures.

She takes the children to meet Bert (Dick Van Dyke), a street entertainer, and then transports the group into one of Bert's sidewalk chalk drawings. In a mixed live action/animated sequence, the foursome has a series of winsome adventures. After they are served tea by dancing penguin waiters, they hop on a carousel whose horses come to life and take them on a fox hunt, followed by a race which Mary Poppins wins. The word for all this excitement, she teaches Jane and Michael, is "Supercalifragilisticexpialidocious," launching into one of the film's most popular songs. The next day sees another tea party, conducted on the ceiling. Mary has taken the children to see Uncle Albert (Ed Wynn), who floats to the ceiling whenever he laughs. She and the children follow suit.

Now the movie takes on Mr. Banks's education in earnest. Mary Poppins must bring him around to see the proper priorities of life, which should be realized in his home. She suggests that he take the children on an adventure—to the bank where he works. She then tells the children that on the way to the bank, they may see an old woman who, she sings, "Feeds the Birds." The next day, Jane and Michael, with their father, do see her, and Michael tries to give her the change in his pocket to buy crumbs for the birds. His father is outraged, and once at the bank, he has the board of directors give Michael a lecture on investment. When the greedy chairman snatches

Michael's pittance, Michael grabs it back, and both children create a small riot in the bank by running away. Lost, they meet up with Bert. "Who's after you?" Bert asks. "Father is," they chorus. Bert tries to help them to understand their father by singing "Chim Chim Cher-ee," and brings them home.

Once home, the scatterbrained Mrs. Banks persuades Bert to clean the living-room chimney. While testing the chimney's draw, Michael and Jane are drawn up the chimney. Mary Poppins arrives home, and with her magic power over the air, she sends herself and Bert up the chimney, after the children. The ensuing dance with chimneysweeps over the rooftops of London, singing "Step in Time," is one of the special effects highlights of the movie.

Totally blackened with soot, the group slides back down the Banks's chimney and dances through the house. Mr. Banks's arrival home brings the celebration to a halt. Mary Poppins takes the children upstairs, unruffled as usual, as Bert tries to explain what George Banks has overlooked in life by singing "A Man Has Dreams."

Mr. Banks soon reaches a turning point after these events. He loses his job for causing a ruckus at the stuffy bank, but he realizes that he is happier away from the place, and he dances out of the bank. When he comes home, Mary Poppins is packing to leave. Mr. and Mrs. Banks take the children kite flying. Again, something is "in the air": at the park, everyone is kite-flying. Mr. Banks is rehired and given a promotion by a kite-flying chairman of the board, Mr. Dawes, Sr. (Dick Van Dyke). Mary Poppins sails off into the skies over London, unseen by a happy Banks family below.

Despite her ability to spirit children away or slide up the bannister, Mary Poppins in no way promotes a topsy-turvy world. On the contrary, she is a bulwark of reassuring conformity to conventional behavior. The most fantastic, logic-defying adventures in flying or racing are always preceded by the polite behavior of a very British tea. Mary Poppins is a paragon of "reverse psychology." If she wants to put the children to bed, she sings them a lullaby asking them to "Stay Awake." Every childhood wish to break the rules—to stay awake, or run away, or fly—is safely expressed through Mary Poppins' no-nonsense belief in good manners. The logic of cleanliness is carried throughout the movie. When Mary and the children become sooty and messy, we know matters have reached a head: a resolution is close at hand. Mary Poppins gives Jane and Michael a reassuring avenue to a fantasy life which does not endanger the security of their family, but instead restores it. If, to paraphrase Poppins, "sentiment will not muddle our feelings," neither will fantasy invade a well-ordered reality.

The Sherman Brothers' Academy Award-winning score for *Mary Poppins* was the most popular film score that the brothers have produced to date. Disney Studios went outside their own house stock company to cast the movie. It was a first film for Andrews, who was an enormous success in the role, which won her an Oscar for Best Actress of the year. Dick Van Dyke is also well cast as the genial and limber Bert, and as the extremely elder Mr. Dawes, chairman at the bank, as well. British character actors David Tomlinson and Glynis Johns are also well suited to their roles.

Peter Ellenshaw's special visual effects are one of the great delights of the film, especially the combination of animated figures with real actors and the blending of the actors into otherwise totally animated scenes. The sequences involving dancing on rooftops and ceilings, sliding up bannisters, and other gravity-defying exploits are magnificent.

The enormous popularity of this film has continued for more than fifteen years with frequent re-releases of the film bringing many new fans to the character of Mary Poppins each time it plays. For star Andrews it launched her career in films. As a wry note at the Oscar ceremony, Andrews personally thanked Jack Warner, head of Warner Bros., for not allowing her to re-create her stage role of Eliza Doolittle in the film version of *My Fair Lady* that same year. Warner's feeling that Andrews was an unknown and could not carry the film enabled her to be free to film *Mary Poppins*, and thus win her award. Audrey Hepburn, who got the *My Fair Lady* part, had to have her voice dubbed for the role by behind-the-scenes singer Marni Nixon and received lukewarm reviews and much ill-placed Hollywood animosity. Andrews, on the other hand, went on to become a star and to play in another popular Broadway musical, *The Sound of Music*, the next year. Perhaps unfortunately, the success which Andrews gained from *Mary Poppins* and *The Sound of Music* made her "typed" in the minds of many of her fans, and her career was never quite able to attain the same success in later films which diverged from her "sugar-coated" image here.

Leslie Donaldson

MEAN STREETS

Released: 1973
Production: Jonathan T. Taplin for Warner Bros.
Direction: Martin Scorsese
Screenplay: Martin Scorsese and Mardik Martin
Cinematography: Kent L. Wakeford
Editing: Sidney Levin
Running time: 110 minutes

> *Principal characters:*
> Johnny Boy .... Robert De Niro
> Charlie .... Harvey Keitel
> Tony .... David Proval
> Teresa .... Amy Robinson
> Michael .... Richard Romanus
> Giovanni .... Cesare Danova
> Mario .... Victor Argo
> Joey .... George Memmoli

Mean Streets launched a number of young artists into careers as first-class filmmakers. It was produced by twenty-six-year-old Jonathan T. Taplin, who had formerly been involved in the rock-and-roll music business, and directed by thirty-year-old Martin Scorsese. After a brief tenure as a film editor for *Woodstock* (1970), and after directing *Who's Knocking at My Door?* (1970) and *Boxcar Bertha* (1972), two unsuccessful films, Scorsese had a triumphant critical success with his third film, *Mean Streets*.

A semiautobiographical film, *Mean Streets* epitomizes all that is meant by the term "personal cinema." It is Scorsese's memoir of his boyhood as an Italian-American growing up on the "mean streets" of New York's Little Italy. Using this as a background, Scorsese creates a powerful film which is startlingly and brutally realistic. *Mean Streets* was filmed entirely on location in New York City, and is set during the frenetic days of the popular street festival of San Gennaro. The rather intense drama concerns four second-generation Italian-American youths who have become corrupted and toughened while trying to survive in a violent street-corner society inhabited by petty criminals, racketeers, and dope pushers.

In the bleak, stifling environment of the Italian ghetto, the explosiveness of gang animosities and small-time Mafia operations are dissected as they relate to the main characters. The young men who inhabit the streets of Little Italy are desperate, bored, and paranoid. Caught between his strong brand of Italian Catholicism and loyalty to his Mafioso uncle Giovanni (Cesare Danova) is Charlie (Harvey Keitel). Charlie, who seems to represent Scorsese as a young man, is too gentle and too good to be a successful gangster, and his conflict between the Church and the Mafia places him in an impossible situation from which there does not seem to be an escape.

Charlie wants to run a restaurant which is currently owned by a man who is badly in debt to Giovanni. At the same time he must please his uncle, however, he also wants to maintain a relationship to his girl friend Teresa (Amy Robinson). This is difficult to do because Teresa is an epileptic and therefore considered by Giovanni to be somehow bad; so Charlie has the pressure of keeping his relationship with Teresa a secret while he tries to remain loyal to his uncle.

Other pressure is brought on Charlie by his relationship to Johnny Boy (Robert De Niro), Teresa's wild and simple-minded brother. Johnny Boy is the antithesis of Charlie, for while Charlie tries to balance everything to stay out of trouble, Johnny Boy seems to invite it. Almost psychotic, Johnny Boy's violence erupts in ridiculous incidents of smashing mailboxes, indulging in rooftop shootings, and running up huge gambling debts which he cannot pay. When Michael (Richard Romanus), an ambitious hoodlum and loan shark, threatens Johnny Boy, demanding that he pay back the money he owes plus incredibly high interest, running away seems to be the only way out.

Charlie, who is fanatically devoted to Johnny Boy, decides to help him escape by borrowing a car and taking him and Teresa out of Little Italy. They get away as far as the Brooklyn Bridge, but there another car drives up next to them carrying Michael and another man (Martin Scorsese), who has been seen briefly at odd points during the film. They shoot repeatedly into the car, wounding Johnny Boy several times in the head and causing Charlie to crash the car into a fire hydrant. Teresa almost goes through the windshield, and when the car stops, Johnny Boy gets out of the car and reels around in a very slow, very bloody death scene. At the end of the film Charlie and Teresa, both very bloody, are taken away to the hospital, but presumably they will live.

The film is violent, but it is also an intimate drama. There are many scenes using the natural, low-level lighting which is characteristic of the bars and poolhalls where the film was shot. The realism of the scenes shot with a hand-held camera seems to bring the story into the same perspective as the characterizations, for as Vincent Canby said in his review of the film for *The New York Times*, "It [the film] never looks over their [the characters'] shoulders or takes a position above their heads in order to impose a self-conscious relevance on them." Most of the story is made up of unimportant incidents and takes place in the everyday places which would be inhabited by characters such as Charlie and Johnny Boy. The characterizations are also given in a matter-of-fact, gradual unfolding. Only De Niro seems to thrive on a flamboyant performance, but then Johnny Boy is a more flamboyant personality. As his life is the most irrational and violent of all of the characters, so is his death. Charlie, however, is more even, and therefore has more hope for a future at the end of the film.

Scorsese's career has skyrocketed since the premiere of *Mean Streets* at the 1973 New York Film Festival. He has had many successes, including several featuring Keitel and/or De Niro. His most recent film, *Raging Bull* (1980), maintains the same kind of violence-oriented characters that have populated most of his other films, including *Taxi Driver* (1976). One of his few films to prove unsuccessful was *New York, New York* (1977), which was an attempt at a lavish big-budget musical. That film starred De Niro and Liza Minnelli, and although neither a critical nor financial success, it is still a very good film and one which displays many elements of circumstance and characterizations which are evident in Scorsese's other films.

De Niro, who won an Oscar as Best Supporting Actor in *The Godfather, Part II*, in an understated role, and an Oscar for Best Actor in *Raging Bull* for a very emotional role, seems to epitomize the type of character whom Scorsese wants to analyze. His violent interior, which often erupts with disastrous results, reflects the violence which Scorsese sees as a major part of American society.

Leslie Taubman

MEDIUM COOL

Released: 1969
Production: Tully Friedman and Haskell Wexler for H & J Pictures/Paramount
Direction: Haskell Wexler
Screenplay: Haskell Wexler
Cinematography: Haskell Wexler
Editing: Verna Fields
Running time: 110 minutes

Principal characters:
John Cassellis	Robert Forster
Eileen	Verna Bloom
Gus	Peter Bonerz
Ruth	Marianna Hill
Harold	Harold Blankenship

In case the credits do not make it clear, *Medium Cool* is very much Haskell Wexler's film; he does almost everything except appear in it. It is an angry film with a great deal to say and the very definite intention of standing up and being counted. It is also a love story, an extended reflection on the ethics of television newsfilm, and a piece of American social history. The film not only records an event which was as important a part of American history in the 1960's as Watergate was of the 1970's—the riots at the Democratic National Convention in Chicago in August, 1968—but it also, by the mere fact of its tone, its message, and indeed, its very existence, became a part of that history. In no other year in American history could a film such as *Medium Cool* have been made.

Wexler made it with $800,000 of his own money, with a deal to sell it to Paramount on completion for $600,000, and a fifty-fifty cut of the profits (which he freely admitted that, given the accounting methods of the major film companies, he was never likely to see). Wexler had been a highly successful cinematographer with credits that include *The Thomas Crown Affair* (1968), *In the Heat of the Night* (1967), and *Who's Afraid of Virginia Woolf?* (1966), for which he received an Oscar. If he really wanted to make a low-budget "youth movie" in Chicago, then the studio reasoned he should be able to do so. The result was obviously not quite what Paramount had anticipated, and they released it without much enthusiasm at the end of August, 1969, a whole year after the Chicago riot and eight months after the film had been completed. The film received strong reviews; Joseph Morgenstern in *Newsweek*, for example, called it "intensely American in its images and its ambition," an exciting piece of work that demanded to be seen "by anyone who cares about the development of modern movies." Hollis Alpert in *Saturday Review* declared that "*Medium Cool* is not only more than ordinarily thoughtful, it is one of the most visually exciting films ever made." It got an "X" rating, however, because of a nude bedroom scene and never really made it into the mass market. The film's release also marked the beginning of a protracted split between Haskell and commercial cinema. He spent the next three or four years working on a number of radical projects—an interview with Salvador Allende; Jane Fonda and Tom Hayden's Vietnam film *Introduction to the Enemy*; and a documentary entitled *Brazil: A Report on Torture*. Haskell Wexler, in other words, became a radical filmmaker, a role which he had already to some extent occupied in his pre-Hollywood days, but not one to which many Oscar-winning cinematographers have devoted themselves.

Medium Cool was shot and recorded entirely on location. Wexler, his cast, and his crew set off for Chicago about six weeks before the Democratic Convention was due to start. It was not very difficult to anticipate the riots, claimed Wexler: "Anybody could have seen what would happen." His working method was to launch his actors into a scene or a situation and leave them to sort out the details. The scene in which the semi-improvised working method justifies itself most clearly is when the central character, John Cassellis (Robert Forster), goes into a room in the black ghetto and is confronted by a group of militants. The scene was shot with the minimum of preparation, with Forster placed in a position almost identical to that of the character he was playing—a white filmmaker in a room full of hostile black militants. The result is as honest a politicial confrontation as has yet been captured by a commercial American film.

Medium Cool operates on three levels which are, it suggests, totally inter-related: the personal, the professional, and the political. The central character, John Cassellis, is a news cameraman working for a Chicago television station. In his personal life he becomes involved with the problems of a poor white family in the Appalachian ghetto; in his professional life he becomes increasingly politically involved with the militant black movement and, because of the assassination of Robert Kennedy and the funeral of Martin Luther King, Jr., with national politics. All these elements come together when his girl friend's son, Harold (Harold Blankenship), gets lost in the middle of the Convention riots.

The film has a thematic rather than a linear narrative structure; it follows John through a series of experiences which are broadly "politicizing." *Medium Cool* begins with John and his soundman, Gus (Peter Bonerz), coming across an automobile wreck in which a girl lies groaning in the wreckage. They leap from their camera truck, film her, record her, and then, as an afterthought, call an ambulance. At a party, Gus defines his job as being that of a typewriter rather than a typist: "The typewriter doesn't really care what's being typed on it." It is on the personal and ethical implications of this question that the film initially focuses. The title, too, is centered on this notion, adapting and questioning Marshall McLuhan's fashionable definition of television as a "cool medium" because it supplies all the information one needs; there is no call to think about what is being conveyed—one merely receives it (or, in the case of John and Gus, records it).

Another incident opens up the question in a less theoretical way for John. Coming across a story about a black taxi driver who finds ten thousand dollars in his cab and turns it in to the police, he decides to follow it up with a filmed interview. He discovers that the police, far from being grateful for this act of citizenship, are immediately suspicious, questioning the cab driver for hours on end until the man finally exclaims in exasperation (although not really surprise): "Well, actually, it was only $1,000: I added another nine of my own to make up the ten." Only to a white reporter does the fact of police harassment of blacks come as any surprise. Refused permission by the television station to follow up the report in the black section of Chicago, he does so anyway, and finds the militants completely distrustful of him. To them he is merely after a story. John is fired by the station for using film without their permission, although the footage he has shot is turned over to the FBI for "routine investigation"—a procedure which he discovers to be common practice. (Ironically, some of the twenty hours of riot footage Wexler shot for *Medium Cool* was subpoenaed by the Justice Department and used in the Chicago Conspiracy Trial.)

Gradually, the theme of *Medium Cool* spreads from simply that of the responsibility of the cameraman for the material he shoots and the uses to which it is put, to the responsibility of the individual in modern American society; the film is not merely about the media. The issues still affect John only on a general level, however; and what brings it all together is his meeting with a war widow from West Virginia and her young son, Harold. The scenes with the widow, Eileen (Verna Bloom), and especially with Harold, a serious-looking, foul-mouthed kid particularly interested in the sexual habits of pigeons, rescue the film from complete abstraction, but they add only marginally to the theme. This theme comes to a head with the Convention riots. Inside the International Amphitheatre, the Democratic delegates are singing "Happy Days Are Here Again"; outside, America is in a state of confrontation, across a no-man's-land of generation gaps, tear gas, and baton charges.

Medium Cool ends on a note of surreal horror. Driving away from Grant Park, John and Eileen hear their deaths reported on the car radio; seconds later, the car goes out of control and smashes into a tree, killing her instantly and fatally wounding him; another car passes and a child leans out of the back window to take a photograph.

Medium Cool is a film whose power cannot be denied. Instead of the ragbag of images it could so easily have been, it presents a brave, complex, and desperately honest picture of a society in turmoil which almost succeeds in finding what Wexler set out to achieve—a "wedding between features and *cinéma vérité*." Wexler takes a risk in using the images of the Chicago riot in a way not wholly different from the way John Cassellis' television station would have used them—as images of truth, emotion, and reality, when in fact the truth, emotion, and reality come not from the images, but from the watcher's engagement with them. It is a risk, however, of which he is aware. "I as a filmmaker am guilty of the same insensitivity," he declared, "but I know that I'm guilty and am throwing the challenge back." It is a challenge the cinema avoided in 1968 and is still avoiding today.

Nick Roddick

THE MEMBER OF THE WEDDING

Released: 1952
Production: Stanley Kramer for Columbia
Direction: Fred Zinnemann
Screenplay: Edna Anhalt and Edward Anhalt; based on the novel and play of the same name by Carson McCullers
Cinematography: Hal Mohr
Editing: William A. Lyon
Production design: Rudolph Sternad
Music: Alex North
Running time: 88 minutes

Principal characters:
Frankie Addams	Julie Harris
Bernice Sadie Brown	Ethel Waters
John Henry	Brandon De Wilde
Mr. Addams	William Hansen
Honey Camden Brown	James Edwards

The Member of the Wedding was brought to the screen after considerable success as both a novel and a play. Carson McCullers adapted her 1946 novel into play form, and, produced on Broadway, it won the New York Drama Critics Circle Award in 1950. Edna and Edward Anhalt wrote the screenplay, changing little of McCullers' powerful and poignant dialogue; however, it is not merely a filmed play, since under Fred Zinnemann's inspired direction, the story is interpreted in a moving, cinematic manner.

As the film opens, the camera and music hauntingly meander through a small Georgia town, setting the tone. The camera settles on the Addams' kitchen, where most of the story is told. Here the main characters are introduced: Frankie Addams (Julie Harris), an awkward, motherless twelve-year-old girl; Bernice Brown (Ethel Waters), the Addams' earthy middle-aged black maid; and John Henry (Brandon De Wilde), Frankie's precocious young cousin. The story belongs primarily to Frankie and Bernice, but John Henry is important as the catalyst of the action both in terms of conversation and plot development. He also provides a source of comic relief.

Frankie is acutely aware that she is alone in the world. She desperately wants to belong somewhere. She is no longer a child like John Henry, but neither is she an adult. The neighborhood girls have denied her membership in their club, so she does not even fit in with her peers. Her brother, she reasons, is part of the army, and Bernice has her church, but Frankie is struggling to find a place for herself. Bernice is a kind, sympathetic woman who also feels alone in the world. She very much loved her husband Ludie, and it is apparent that part of her died along with him. Although he died twelve years earlier and she has remarried several times, his memory still affects her daily life. Yet she is a strong, resilient woman with an easygoing, common-sense approach to life, coupled with a warm sense of humor. Frankie articulates her thoughts to Bernice and John Henry. John Henry earnestly offers advice, although Frankie assures him that he cannot possibly understand her situation. Bernice listens empathetically, identifying with Frankie's pain. She offers Frankie advice and criticism and also shares personal experiences with Frankie and John Henry to illustrate various points, as well as for her own relief.

When Frankie's brother Jarvis (Arthur Franz) returns home to be married, Frankie is ecstatic. Although Jarvis and his fiancée Janice (Nancy Gates) are a very ordinary couple, Frankie deifies their relationship. She is impressed by the fact that they are a "we," and that they belong to each other. She, consequently, becomes completely involved in romantic fantasies about the couple. She desires to change her name to F. Jasmine so that she will share the letters "J" and "A" common to their names. She has decided to become part of the "we" because this is finally an opportunity to belong somewhere. Unknown to Janice and Jarvis, Frankie will be a member of the wedding. Bernice, however, realizes that Frankie is setting herself up for a lot of pain and disappointment and so chides her about the foolishness of falling in love with a wedding. Her warnings go unacknowledged, however, as Frankie continues to act upon her fantasies. In one of the few scenes to take place outside of the kitchen, Frankie bicycles to town, where she tells her father (William Hansen) and everyone she meets of her plans. Mr. Addams is a busy man, insensitive to his daughter's needs, and quickly dismisses her gibberish, sending her off to buy a dress for the wedding. She returns home with a gaudy satin bargain basement dress, and both Bernice and John Henry tease her for the inappropriate purchase.

At the wedding, the camera clearly tells the audience that the event belongs to Frankie. She is wearing a childish organdy dress which is as unsuitable as the satin one. Much of the scene cuts between the bridal couple and extreme close-ups of Frankie. Other shots reveal Janice and Jarvis in the foreground and Frankie looming physically, as well as figuratively, in the background. As the vows are exchanged, Frankie grabs her suitcase from the back of the room and dashes out into the newlyweds' car. After being pulled from the car by her father, Frankie is left lying by the roadside as the couple drives off. She is retrieved by an unidentified arm, most probably that of Bernice. It is obvious that Frankie has been shattered.

Frankie immediately acts upon her pain and leaves home. Simultaneously, Honey (James Edwards), Bernice's stepbrother, is also fleeing, running from the police. Frankie has always admired Honey and identified with him. This is partly due to his skillful trumpet playing, but largely on account of his mobility, which Frankie interprets as freedom. In fact, Honey is very talented, but rather aimless. He continually walks away from responsibilities and troubles. His freedom is only an illusion; he is just as trapped as Frankie. His character is also used symbolically to illustrate the oppression of blacks in the small Southern town. Running through town, Frankie is clearly frightened. The streets are seedy and threatening. Frankie seeks refuge in a bar, only to be accosted by a drunken soldier. He, too, feels lonely and isolated. Terrified, Frankie returns to the security of her home. There she learns that John Henry is very sick. The transition from Frankie's return home to the film's final scene is poetic. The camera moves in for a close-up of John Henry's bedroom window. The boy is obviously lying ill inside the room, and when his light goes out, it is apparent that he has died.

The next image is of the same window, but now it is daylight, and there is a nicely dressed young woman in the foreground who turns to reveal herself as Frankie. Some months have passed, and she has changed; she no longer looks pained and awkward, her hair has grown, and her clothing is finally appropriate. Many other changes have taken place. Honey has been apprehended and is serving a ten-year prison sentence. Bernice still mourns John Henry, but Frankie, on the other hand, feels him fading from her mind. Her life is filled with growth and activity, and she has friends among her peers. She and her father are moving into a house with her aunt, so they will no longer be needing Bernice's services. Although Frankie professes that she will miss Bernice, the woman realizes that she, too, will fade from Frankie's mind. As Frankie walks out the door, the film ends with a close-up of Bernice, softly humming. She is once again alone and will endure another loss.

Throughout the film, the cinematography and production design combine to express themes of isolation and entrapment. Bernice, Frankie, and John Henry are largely confined to the kitchen, creating a claustrophobic atmosphere. The close-up is used extensively to isolate and examine individual characters, particularly Frankie. The angle of vision is most often narrow and limited, further illustrating the characters' confinement. Spatial relationships are metaphorically used to reveal individuals' inner thoughts and emotions. The low-key black-and-white cinematography is well suited to the mood of the film. Alex North's music, especially the moving trumpet pieces, also adds to the textural quality of the work.

The performances are superb. Julie Harris, Ethel Waters, Brandon De Wilde, and some of the minor characters re-created their Broadway roles. It is difficult to believe that Julie Harris was twenty-five years old when she so convincingly portrayed the adolescent Frankie. Her rather plain features and very thin body add a physical dimension to the role on which she admirably capitalizes. She received an Academy Award nomination for her outstanding performance, losing the Best Actress award that year to Shirley Booth for her role in *Come Back, Little Sheba*. Ethel Waters' black servant may be a stereotype, but Waters has created a very genuine, three-dimensional woman in Bernice. De Wilde also presents a remarkably sensitive and well-shaded characterization as the young cousin, possibly his best performance.

The film did not enjoy the popular success attained by both the book and the play. Compared with most Hollywood productions, it was considered by many to be too arty. Despite its limited appeal, however, it is recognized as a significant work. It is a complex film that is at once entertaining, insightful, and moving. The film was made during one of director Zinnemann's most productive periods. The year before he had directed the enormously successful *High Noon*, and in the same year as *The Member of the Wedding*, he won an Oscar for his direction of the even more successful *From Here to Eternity*.

Debra Bergman

THE MEN

Released: 1950
Production: Stanley Kramer for United Artists
Direction: Fred Zinnemann
Screenplay: Carl Foreman
Cinematography: Robert de Grasse
Editing: Harry Gerstad
Running time: 86 minutes

Principal characters:
Ken	Marlon Brando
Ellen	Teresa Wright
Dr. Brock	Everett Sloane
Norm	Jack Webb
Leo	Richard Erdman

An interesting reversal took place in American filmmaking between World War II and the war in Vietnam. During the years of American involvement in the European and Pacific theaters of World War II, the American film industry rallied to the cause. Wartime exploits were lionized, homefront morale was bolstered, and the necessity of making the world once again safe for democracy was validated in hundreds of dramatic, musical, and comedy films. Thirty years later, American involvement in Vietnam was barely acknowledged on the screen. The aftermath of Vietnam, however, continues to be dealt with extensively in major features which cost almost as much as did the whole incursion into Vietnam. *Coming Home* (1978), *Who'll Stop the Rain* (1978), *The Deer Hunter* (1978), and *Apocalypse Now* (1979) span the entire political spectrum but all are rooted in, if not total nihilism, at least extreme cynicism, whether liberal or conservative in origin.

The problems which faced mainstream post-World War II filmmakers were different. In the early days of the Cold War, which would escalate rapidly into the Korean Conflict, antiwar sentiment could not be expressed with equanimity. Yet several films attempted to deal with the problems engendered by human involvement in an essentially inhumane and socially disorienting activity. The best-known of these films is William Wyler's *The Best Years of Our Lives* (1946), which deals with alienation, economic insecurity, and physical handicaps in true Hollywood fashion. Overtly, there is a great deal of sentiment, a few uncomfortable moments, and a happy resolution for all concerned. Underlying the plot, however, is a pervasive feeling of unease. Among other films of this period which dealt questioningly, at least in terms of plot, with the war were *Bright Victory* (1951), *Till the End of Time* (1946), and *Pride of the Marines* (1945). The least compromising of these films is *The Men*, which was a forerunner of *Coming Home*. In many ways it was more daring, coming as it did after a war during which, in its early days, the government censors prohibited any photographs of dead, wounded, or maimed soldiers to be dispensed in the States. Such photographs were considered dangerous for morale.

The Men concerns Ken (Marlon Brando), a young lieutenant who is shot in the spine by a sniper during the final days of World War II. Returning to a Veterans' Hospital, in the United States, he is bitter and suicidal, rejecting Ellen (Teresa Wright), the woman he was to have married. She persists in trying to reach him, as does the physician who is the director of the hospital. Gradually, he begins to adjust and to engage in the struggle for mental and physical rehabilitation. After the death of a friend in the hospital and another man's failed romance, Ken agrees to marry Ellen. On their wedding night, however, neither can deal with the tension and the strain of expectations. They quarrel and he returns to the hospital, having lost the ground he had gained. He gets into altercations because of his drinking and finally is expelled from the hospital by his peers. Afraid of further contact with the outside world, Ken urges the director of the hospital Dr. Brock (Everett Sloane) to overrule the Board's decision and permit him to remain in the hospital. Through the doctor's counseling and Ellen's renewed efforts, however, he is persuaded to leave the hospital with his wife. Their future together is left open-ended and hopeful, but uncertain.

The Men is usually referred to as a Stanley Kramer film. It was, in fact, directed by Fred Zinnemann, but was the product of Kramer's independent production company. During the late 1940's and early 1950's, Kramer was distinguishing himself as the producer of low-budget, socially conscious box-office hits. *The Men* was the third in a chain, preceded by *Champion* (1949), which starred Kirk Douglas, and *Home of the Brave* (1949), which dealt with racial prejudice in the military. Kramer was something of an anomaly: a creative producer of low-budget films with high production values. His method of operation was based on intense preproduction preparation. *The Men* was thoroughly researched for months at the VA Hospitals, in interviews with the paraplegics themselves, and with those who worked with them. The entire film was storyboarded by the production designer, with every frame being diagramed beforehand to determine sets, placement of actors, lights, and camera angles. The actors rehearsed for weeks before the cameras ever began to roll. Marlon Brando, in fact, lived at the VA Hospital as a paraplegic for a month in preparation for the role, which was his long-awaited and much heralded film debut, after establishing a name for himself on Broadway. He was only twenty-five at the time.

Kramer's allies in this production of *The Men* were Fred Zinnemann and Carl Foreman. Zinnemann had earlier directed *The Search* (1948) with Montgomery Clift, a film shot in Europe about the plight of postwar orphans, and Foreman had written *Champion* and *Home of the Brave*. The film was truly a collaborative effort under the guidance of Kramer.

The Men was mainly filmed at a Veterans Hospital for paraplegics in a suburb of Los Angeles. Forty-five of the patients were cast as extras, and, in minor roles, a doctor, nurses, and a physical therapist enacted their real-life roles in the film. The fusion of art and life is effective, mainly because the script and the actors strove for a realistic quality. The script had an ear for the patients' own brand of sardonic humor about themselves and military conventions, and the camera had an eye for exposing the daily life of the hospital. There is a striking montage of Brando and the other men engaging in the agonizing physical struggle of therapy to build and train their bodies to function at their highest level of capacity.

Upon its release, the film was universally acclaimed and honored by critics, the public and, especially, veterans' groups. The critics' response to Brando's performance is interesting and often amusing since they did not know quite what to make of his acting style. Brando gives a highly internalized performance. He was a student of Method acting, and had just come from Broadway, where he overwhelmed audiences with his performance in *A Streetcar Named Desire* (a role he would perform on film in 1951). While some reviewers marveled at the emotional range he conveyed with his eyes, face, and entire body, others were not quite ready for the advent of the "angry young man" on film.

The Men remains a powerful film, in spite of (or perhaps because of) the fact that it worked within existing filmic conventions and restrictions. The loss of biological function (especially sexual) is discussed only obliquely, but concern and fears are communicated nonverbally without equivocation.

Connie McFeeley

THE MERRY WIDOW

Released: 1934
Production: Metro-Goldwyn-Mayer
Direction: Ernst Lubitsch
Screenplay: Ernest Vajda and Samson Raphaelson; based on the operetta of
the same name with book and lyrics by Victor Leon and Leo Stein
Cinematography: Ernest Haller
Editing: Thomas Pratt
Musical adaptation: Herbert Stothart, with additional music and lyrics by
Lorenz Hart, Richard Rogers, and Gus Kahn; based on the music by Franz
Lehar
Running time: 99 minutes

Principal characters:
Captain Danilo	Maurice Chevalier
Sonia/Fifi	Jeanette MacDonald
Ambassador	Edward Everett Horton
The Queen	Una Merkel
The King	George Barbier
Marcelle	Minna Gombell
Lulu	Ruth Channing
Orderly	Sterling Holloway
Valet	Donald Meek
Zizipoff	Herman Bing

As far as operettas, which are hardly the most popular of film sources, are
concerned, Franz Lehar's *The Merry Widow* has had the most consistent
appeal to American filmmakers. It was filmed in 1925, although it had already
been filmed at least once previously—as a starring vehicle for Mae Murray
by Erich von Stroheim, who, in typical fashion, completely disregarded the
original story. In 1952, Lana Turner and Fernando Lamas starred in a lush
Technicolor version directed by Curtis Bernhardt, and in 1934, Ernst Lubitsch
directed what is, without question, the definitive film version of the operetta.

The 1934 production of *The Merry Widow* brought back together, for the
last time, three superior talents of the cinema. It starred Maurice Chevalier
and Jeanette MacDonald, who had worked together frequently at Paramount.
The Merry Widow was MacDonald's second M-G-M film, and the actress still
displayed the youthful charm and easy manner she had brought to the screen
at Paramount; she was still unattached on screen to Nelson Eddy, who, a year
later, would be teamed with her in a seemingly endless series of dull, weighty
musicals. Lubitsch's directorial success with MacDonald is evidenced by their
three previous films together, *The Love Parade* (1929), *Monte Carlo* (1930),
and *One Hour with You* (1932).

Lehar's score remains virtually intact, but is enhanced by new lyrics from

Lorenz Hart and Gus Kahn, two giants of the American musical theater, who bring a slightly salty flavor to the already saucy score. When Prince Danilo goes to Maxim's, the lyrics of the song tell us "That's where a man can/see ladies dance the can can" and "Each kiss is on the wine list/and mine is quite a fine list." Above all, Lubitsch's film is a fond tribute to a ruritania, destroyed by World War I, where champagne flows freely and where Kings can order their subjects to make love to save a Kingdom; or where, as the ambassador informs Danilo, it is one's diplomatic duty to fall in love with the wealthy widow, anxiously enquiring, "Have you ever had diplomatic relations with a woman?"

The Merry Widow opens in the ruritanian kingdom of Marshovia, where the King (George Barbier repeating a role he perfected in Lubitsch's *The Smiling Lieutenant* in 1931) is practically a joke, thanks in no small measure to the extramarital activities of his wife (Una Merkel). She insists on the king telling her when he will return to the palace from his cabinet meetings in order that she may plan her affairs accordingly. Fifty-two percent of Marshovia, meaning fifty-two percent of everything, even the cows, belongs to a wealthy widow (Jeanette MacDonald), and the King is determined that her money shall not be removed from his domain. In his Queen's boudoir, he discovers the answer to his problems, Prince Danilo (Maurice Chevalier at his most beguiling, full of swaggering sensuality), and orders him to follow the widow to Paris, make love to her, and bring her back to Marshovia.

Unbeknown to them both, Danilo and the widow have already met. He had heard her singing the lilting lyrics of "Villa," dressed in black and wearing a black veil, on the balcony of her mansion. Their encounter had persuaded the widow to discard her weeds and embark on a new life in Paris; "there's a limit to every widow," she announces. In one of those wonderful uses to which black-and-white cinematography can be put, Lubitsch has everything in the widow's home in black until her change in mood, at which point, clothes, shoes, and even a lap dog become white.

In Paris, the natural location for romantic encounters, Danilo is to take his orders from the Marshovian ambassador (Edward Everett Horton, as perfect as always in a flustered, nerve-wracked role), but first, Danilo tells the ambassador he plans to spend the evening at Maxim's. Tonight, Chevalier comments, with a sigh that has untold hidden meanings, belongs to the ladies of Maxim's. The widow, incognito, has also gone to Maxim's, where she, using the name of Fifi, is mistaken for one of the ladies of the establishment. In a sparkling repartee, a verbal battle of wits ripe with sensuality, MacDonald asks Chevalier if he is a banker, sighing "I'm just in the mood for a banker." "The Merry Widow Waltz" brings the two together, but eventually MacDonald grows angry with Chevalier's arrogance and leaves his private room, to be replaced by a group of Maxim's more regular girls, whom MacDonald describes as "all your todays, and not a tomorrow amongst them." With the

departure of Fifi, Danilo finds solace in champagne and presumably—
although the strict Hays code of morality could not allow this to be too
apparent—Maxim's girls. Much credit must go to the director and the scriptwriters for managing to evoke so much sexuality in a film from this period
when the Production Code was so very much in evidence.

While the ambassador tries to sober up Danilo in time for the embassy ball,
frantic telegrams arrive from the Marshovian King, which the ambassador
and his secretary, Zizipoff, played by Herman Bing in his own inimitable
style, hilariously try to decode. At the ball, Danilo and the widow meet again
and discover their true identities. The angry widow tells Danilo that Fifi has
committed suicide—"she jumped into a cold bath"—while Danilo accuses
her of being "just a rich woman looking for a thrill," and claims he fell in
love with her strictly for her money and out of "cold-blooded patriotism."

Then, however, the magical strains of "The Merry Widow Waltz" begin to
take hold of the couple. First they dance alone, and then the ballroom and
the mirrored hallways are filled with hundreds of Albertina Rasch dancers
in a scene of overflowing black-and-white beauty. The mirrors make the
hundreds of dancers seem as thousands. The music swells to a crescendo, and
the magic of the waltz transcends even the film itself. The cynicism of many
of the earlier scenes is forgotten in the romantic lyricism of the waltz.

Waltzes do not last forever, unfortunately, and the widow rejects Danilo,
who returns to Marshovia to be tried as a traitor. At his trial the widow
appears to testify on his behalf, that Danilo did indeed try to win her affections. Later she visits Danilo in his cell, a cell sprayed with perfume and
furnished with champagne. As the couple talk, a gypsy orchestra strikes up
the refrain of "The Merry Widow Waltz," and the magic of the music takes
hold again. Before it can lose its grip on the couple, a priest puts his head
through the peep hole in the door, and, almost angrily, the couple exchange
marriage vows. The widow begins, "Any man who can dance through life
with hundreds of women," only to have Danilo interrupt, "And is willing to
walk through life with one should be married."

The Merry Widow was not a great popular success at the time of its original
release, although the critics found much in it to like. Today, however, it stands
high in praise as a film which skillfully combines art and entertainment, which
dazzles the ears and the eyes, lifts the heart, and manages to be a work of
art without ever appearing to be a work of art.

Anthony Slide

MICKEY ONE

Released: 1965
Production: Arthur Penn for Columbia
Direction: Arthur Penn
Screenplay: Alan M. Surgal
Cinematography: Ghislain Cloquet
Editing: Aram Avakian
Running time: 93 minutes

Principal characters:
Mickey One	Warren Beatty
Jenny	Alexandra Stewart
Castle	Hurd Hatfield
Ruby Lopp	Franchot Tone
Berson	Teddy Hart
Artist	Kamatari Fujiwara

In 1967, Arthur Penn directed Warren Beatty in *Bonnie and Clyde*, a controversial film which brought both men international acclaim. *Bonnie and Clyde* depicts the real-life exploits of the Depression-era bankrobbers Bonnie Parker and Clyde Barrow, in contemporary, 1960's terms, with a beautifully detailed re-creation of milieu combined with the fusion of nostalgic, poetic, and psychological elements. Technically, *Bonnie and Clyde* is expert, and the film is trend-setting in its powerfully realistic presentation of violence. Three years earlier, however, both director and star collaborated on *Mickey One*, a superficially allegorical attempt at a character study. *Mickey One* fails as effective, compelling cinema, but it is ambitious and does have a finely realized visual flow. The filming of *Mickey One*, in which Penn was in complete control as producer and director, was a trial-and-error project for him. The film portends the stunning triumph of *Bonnie and Clyde*.

In *Mickey One*, Beatty stars as a small-time nightclub comedian in Detroit who has an overabundance of gambling debts. Convinced that the underworld has marked him for death, he flees to Chicago. He destroys all evidence of his identity and, with a fake social security card inscribed to Miklos Wunejeva (hence, the simplified "Mickey One"), obtains a job hauling garbage for a restaurant. He soon decides that he wants to return to nightclub performing and, hopefully, gain fortune and fame. He soon is booked by a befuddled agent named Berson (Teddy Hart) into the exclusive Club Xanadu, which is owned by slick club operator Ed Castle (Hurd Hatfield).

Mickey wants to work, but is unsure of Castle's connections and is afraid that gangsters will find him if he continues his career. He auditions for a man who is supposed to be connected with other nightclubs, but who he thinks may be his executioner. In a chilling sequence, the most effective in the film, he performs on a dimly lit stage for this mysterious person. He pauses in panic, then rambles on with some pointedly unfunny jokes. He is greeted by a profound silence. He is sweaty and panicky, and he cuts the act short out of paranoia.

Mickey tries to contact mobsters who are participating in a crap game, is manhandled by a vicious nightclub doorman, and ultimately decides to keep his commitment at the Club Xanadu. He also has a relationship with Jenny (Alexandra Stewart), a sad young woman who moves into his dreary apartment when his landlord tries to evict him. He keeps discouraging her, yet she still falls in love with him.

The hero of *Mickey One* exists in a depressing, drab world, with his original identity unknown. The gangsters who are allegedly seeking to harm him are also unknown. He is like the protagonist of Albert Camus' *The Stranger* as he helplessly, pathetically seeks information about those who are supposedly his tormentors. Presumably, when he chooses to work at the Club Xanadu at the film's finale, he is choosing to accept his position in an uncertain world. The character does not evoke any compassion in the viewer, despite his desperation, because he is a moody creature, more repulsive than ingratiating. His mind is totally enveloped in himself and his anxieties and neuroses. The antihero who became so popular in films beginning in the late 1950's may be coarse and insolent to some, but he must be at least somewhat likable in order to gain the favor of the audience. Mickey One, however, is an outright bore. His liaison with Jenny also seems superfluous. Her character has potential, but not enough information is offered as to who she is for her role to develop into an attractive personality in the story.

While outwardly Mickey has a definite personality, it is unclear what is actually in his mind; it is unclear whether he is trying to escape from gangsters who are interested in murdering him, or is really trying to escape from himself. Penn and screenwriter Alan M. Surgal have not etched a character who is totally rounded out and developed; Mickey is as baffling to the audience as to himself. The film may have been more effective if Beatty's acting had been as polished as in some of his later works. Instead, he offers a formless, bland performance.

The supporting work by Stewart and cinema veterans Hart and Hatfield, is fine, however, and Franchot Tone is also a plus as Mickey's gruff employer at the film's outset. Thirty years before, Tone had starred in and been nominated for an Oscar in *Mutiny on the Bounty* (1935) with Clark Gable and Charles Laughton. His career never attained the heights of his costars, but he was a talented actor who brightened many films, including *Mickey One*, in which he has only a few brief scenes. This was one of his last films before his death in 1968.

Mickey One is also superficially surreal. One evening, Mickey and Jenny see a Fellini-esque artist (Kamatari Fujiwara) unveil his kinetic sculpture. In a nicely staged "happening" by the artist Jean Tinguely, the piece suddenly explodes, jerks in every direction, and burns out. In another sequence, Mickey visits an automobile junkyard where he watches cars crushed, pounded, and pressed into blocks of steel. A character driving a horse-drawn junk wagon appears at various points and beckons Mickey to join him. All are supposed to be mirrors of Mickey's confusion and agony as he tries to float above water in what is to him an unfriendly, uncertain sea. The effect, however, is not as sophisticated as one might think. All of these things tend to overwhelm the film, which would have been aided instead by more character development and depth.

Ultimately, the camera is the true star of *Mickey One*, as the film's visual rhythm makes up for any lack of substance in the story. Imaginative use is made of location filming in Chicago, and Penn succeeds in sustaining a stylized, controlled mood as he details the grimy ambience of two-bit nightclubs and strip joints, cluttered junkyards, and slum neighborhood flophouses. Ghislain Cloquet's cinematography, with its harsh, dramatic lighting, graphically captures Mickey's outward world. The inward world, unfortunately, is too ambiguous, and the film's attempt to comment on survival in an uncertain, often hostile and violent world is not entirely successful. It also fails in its attempt to explore the fine line between what is actual and what is in the mind, but *Mickey One* is an offbeat, original work and a well-intentioned experiment in a cinematic character study.

Mickey One was highly praised when released. Penn's previous film had been *The Miracle Worker* (1962), in which Anne Bancroft and Patty Duke gained Oscars for their respective performances as Annie Sullivan and Helen Keller. When *Mickey One* was shown at the Venice and New York Film Festivals, its critical reception was mostly negative, and the film was unsuccessful at the box office. Beatty, who during this period also appeared in Robert Rossen's serious but unsuccessful *Lilith* (1964) and two disappointing escapist films, *Promise Her Anything* (1966) and *Kaleidoscope* (1966), was floundering as a screen star. *Bonnie and Clyde*, of course, irrevocably altered his career as well as Penn's. *Mickey One* is a direct link to the creation of one of the most influential and financially successful films of the 1960's, and a turning point in the careers of two important filmmakers.

Rob Edelman

MIDNIGHT

Released: 1939
Production: Arthur Hornblow, Jr., for Paramount
Direction: Mitchell Leisen
Screenplay: Charles Brackett and Billy Wilder; based on a story by Edwin Justus Mayer and Franz Schulz
Cinematography: Charles Lang
Editing: Doane Harrison
Running time: 92 minutes

Principal characters:
Eve Peabody	Claudette Colbert
Tibor Czerny	Don Ameche
Georges Flammarion	John Barrymore
Helene Flammarion	Mary Astor
Jacques Picoin	Francis Lederer
Judge	Monty Woolley

Midnight was first released in 1939, a great year for the American film, and the last before the oncoming war was to be reflected in filmmaking. It is a beautifully assembled comedy reflecting a high sophistication, as stylishly dressed people are moved like pawns in a game of blithe romance. It is set in Paris and its environs at a time when Paris was gay-hearted, before such terms as "occupation," "starvation," and "prisoner of war" were applicable. Many who saw the film took it for granted that Ernst Lubitsch must have been its director, for it fairly glittered with the diamondlike brilliance of a *Trouble in Paradise* (1932). It was directed by Mitchell Leisen, however, who in his lifetime never got the homage he merited. It was his best film, a light-hearted screwball comedy with dialogue that sparkles and characters who know how to dance across the surface of emotion. *Midnight* is above all just plain fun, a comedy in praise of practically nothing except sheer escapism. It is a fashionable variation of the Cinderella theme, with no message to ponder, just an evening of complete and satisfying film fare.

Eve Peabody (Claudette Colbert), a showgirl with a gold-digging penchant, has gone to the Riviera hoping to make a rich marriage. She comes close, but instead, she is paid off, and dares to risk her newly acquired winnings on the spin of a roulette wheel. She loses every cent and must board a train returning to Paris, wearing a smart gold *lamé* gown, since she had been forced to leave the rest of her luggage behind in a pawn shop so that she could buy her train ticket. It is drizzling when she arrives in Paris, where she meets Tibor Czerny (Don Ameche), a cabdriver who is fascinated with her and is willing to give her some help, at least a gambler's chance. She ditches him, however, when she sees a well-dressed crowd going into a musicale. She uses her pawn ticket, which is the same size as the invitation cards, and so enters with those attending the *soirée*. In a side-room, apart from the conventional, dreary musicale, she finds a bridge game in progress and meets Georges Flammarion (John Barrymore), his beautiful wife Helene (Mary Astor), and her lover, Jacques Picoin (Francis Lederer). Eve loses outrageously at cards, but Flammarion is on to her and not the least bit blind to her physical charms. He pays her losses and hires her to make a play for Jacques, thus enticing him away from the lovely Helene.

This is the beginning of a comedy of masquerade and mistaken identity, with the scene soon shifting to a fashionable hotel where Flammarion has provided Eve with a stylish wardrobe, a suite befitting a countess, and an invitation to join him for a weekend at his country estate. There the comedy of intrigue is intensified as Jacques is beguiled by Eve, who flirts with him openly much to the displeasure of Helene and the delight of Flammarion. Tibor Czerny discovers the whereabouts of Eve through his fellow taxi drivers, however, and soon arrives at the villa posing as Eve's husband, a Hungarian count. The mixup is further intensified, with only Flammarion knowing all of the make-believe. There are diverting sequences in which Flammarion makes a phony long-distance phone call to the Czernys, pretending to be their nonexistent four-year-old daughter, left behind in Budapest and pleading now with her parents to come home. As enacted by Barrymore, the imitation of a four-year-old on the telephone makes for a highly diverting farce. Flammarion's wife, humiliated by her lover's interest in another woman, goes back to her husband in a fit of pique.

Eve recklessly promises to marry Jacques, but before she can do that she must first get a "divorce" from Tibor, to whom she is not even married. Tibor thinks that he can help her secure the divorce, thus making her happy, by pretending to be afflicted by the insanity of which she has accused him. He gives a wonderful imitation of a lunatic, impressing the judge (Monty Woolley), an old friend who has been called in to help solve the problem. The judge remembers the existence of an old French law under which a mad man or woman cannot be divorced. He is very pleased with himself, thinking he has solved everything. Eve tells Jacques that she does not really love him, and he accepts the "blow" philosophically. Outside the house, Eve meets Tibor. Impulsively he asks her for the last time to marry him, and this time she does not refuse. The judge, coming out at this moment, sees them embracing, and asks, "Where are you two going now?" "To get married!" is their happy answer. They climb into Tibor's taxi, and the judge looks after them, feeling certain that it is not only the husband who is crazy.

Midnight skates around and through risqué situations, chancing the double entendre and rising lightly to every climax like a well-prepared meringue covering a rich dessert. It is, in its perfection, a prelude to *Hold Back the Dawn* (1941) and *To Each His Own* (1946), two subsequent features which

Leisen directed with great finesse. They had heart and often drama which was drenched in tears, however, while *Midnight* is completely carefree, filled with intrigue and laughter—a weekend's madcap adventure that ends with the lovers reunited. Leisen had demonstrated his skill for directing fun-loving glimpses of high life in *Easy Living* (1937) and *Hands Across the Table* (1935). It was not until *Midnight*, however, that he revealed how deftly he could treat the entire comedy scene, beginning with an intriguing introduction, rising to new inventive complications, and finally resolving everything with as light a touch as he had begun it.

Midnight was so successful a venture in 1939 that Leisen, who was himself fond of the film, took on the assignment of remaking it only six years later in 1945, when it became the plot for *Masquerade in Mexico*. Even in that comparatively short time, however, audiences had changed. A world war had been fought. People were tired, and, although victorious, American audiences could not treat life with the flamboyant indifference they had felt in 1939. Just as in the theater, where drawing-room comedies ceased to be the vogue because drawing-rooms ceased to exist, so *Masquerade in Mexico* failed because its characters did not have the chic of those who had masqueraded in the prewar world. Nor were Dorothy Lamour and Patric Knowles able to convey the easy skill of accomplished comedians as did Colbert and Barrymore. *Masquerade in Mexico* played out its bookings quickly and is forgotten; but *Midnight* goes on, a leading attraction of all comedy, Paramount, Colbert, or Barrymore retrospectives.

Interestingly, Leisen had received his original training as an architect. He worked in interior design, and his first film credits came as a costume designer for Cecil B. De Mille and Douglas Fairbanks. He was soon promoted to assistant director, and in 1933 Paramount gave him his first chance at full directorship. Everything he subsequently did displayed his great tastes. He had an eye for the beautiful, and his skill as a director increased with every production, reaching a brilliance in *Midnight* that made him the envy of his American and European peers. He always appreciated the advantage of good writing and top cinematography, realizing that they made his own work as director much easier. In *Midnight* he had a screenplay written by one of the finest team of screenwriters in the business—Charles Brackett and Billy Wilder, who had based their work on a story by Edwin Justus Mayer and Franz Schulz. The cinematography by Charles Lang, was outstanding. These were all worldly men who were masters of their individual crafts. Leisen had become one of the best in his field, and he attracted other top talent.

Midnight is a perfect vehicle for Colbert. She makes Eve Peabody a real person whose vices attract audience sympathy. She is a charming little gold-digger out to get all she can, but she is also good-natured and sentimental, a natural target for the arrow of love when it is shot her way. Born a French-woman, Colbert knew exactly how to play a showgirl on the loose in France.

Leisen dared to do a bit of off-casting for the Hungarian driving a taxi in Paris when he chose Ameche for the part. Ameche had made a name for himself at Twentieth Century-Fox in such big action-filled specials as *In Old Chicago* (1938) and *Alexander's Ragtime Band* (1938). Leisen borrowed him from Fox, for whom Ameche, that same year, did *The Story of Alexander Graham Bell* (1939), a completely different kind of story. Leisen must have known how Ameche hungered to play a character in a comedy of warmth and intimacy, for Ameche displays a raffish charm and easy professionalism that he never got a chance to show elsewhere.

Barrymore's forte was always comedy. He could, of course, play the costumed rogue to perfection, but from his first appearance in silents he was the master of high comedy and farce, and he has one of his last good comic roles in *Midnight*. Astor, a onetime close friend of Barrymore and also twice his leading lady on the silent screen, rarely got a chance in talking films as a comedienne, but *Midnight* gave her an opportunity to cavort in high style, always feminine and seductively groomed.

There are no disappointments in this film. Every scene is touched with a kind of knowledgeable understanding of the ways of ladies and gentlemen in polite society—ladies who can be cattish and gentlemen with the morals of mutts, but well-mannered and always fashionably dressed.

DeWitt Bodeen

MIDNIGHT EXPRESS

Released: 1978
Production: Alan Marshall and David Puttnam for Casablanca Filmworks; released by Columbia
Direction: Alan Parker
Screenplay: Oliver Stone (AA); based on the book of the same name by Billy Hayes and William Hoffer
Cinematography: Michael Seresin
Editing: Gerry Hambling
Music: Giorgio Moroder (AA)
Running time: 123 minutes

Principal characters:
Billy Hayes	Brad Davis
Susan	Irene Miracle
Jimmy Booth	Randy Quaid
Max	John Hurt
Erich	Norbert Weisser
Tex	Bo Hopkins
Mr. Hayes	Mike Kellin
Rifki	Paolo Bonacelli

Midnight Express gives credence to the persuasive power of filmmaking. It is based on the actual story of American student Billy Hayes who, in 1970, had hashish in his possession while attempting to board a plane at the Istanbul Airport. Based on a book coauthored by Hayes and William Hoffer, *Midnight Express* details the student's arrest, imprisonment, and ultimate escape. *Midnight Express* offers a stern lesson against disregard for another country's laws, but it is a manipulative film, painting a one-sided story—Hayes's version—from beginning to end. The film is also riveting and powerful, a modern horror story about the nightmare of an ordeal in a foreign prison.

Director Alan Parker heightens the drama with an especially clever, calculated use of sound. Giorgio Moroder's disco-flavored score, which received an Oscar, is frenetic and pulsating. Background sounds are brought up close, heartbeats are amplified, and the sounds of running water and dripping faucets are exaggerated. The film has a particularly strong beginning. After a quick look at the foreign locale, there is a cut to Hayes (Brad Davis), who is using adhesive tape (the audience hears each crisp, crackly sound as it is unrolled and cut) to secure foil-wrapped packets of hashish to his body. From there the action moves to the airport, where Hayes comes down with a bad case of nerves. He ducks into a bathroom, where he douses his sweating face with water and takes a series of sharp, quick breaths. After readjusting his sunglasses, he makes his way toward the inspection area. An amplified heartbeat details his fear and invites the audience's sympathy.

After making it through the inspection, Hayes boards the shuttle to the plane. His girl friend, Susan (Irene Miracle), is reading through an English-language newspaper, and upset over an item detailing the recent death of singer Janis Joplin. Hayes has a flip response. "You never take anything seriously, do you?" she reprimands. Neither of them takes note of the paper's headlines detailing a recent rash of terrorist hijackings. Once at the boarding area, however, Hayes is aware of the increased security. Susan boards the plane on her own, while Hayes tries to evade another inspection (physical searches are being conducted), but he is unsuccessful. In a dramatic sequence which takes place alongside the plane under the nighttime sky he is arrested. The tension is broken when the armed officers, on the lookout for terrorists, discover that they have found a drug offender.

Hayes is searched, stripped, and questioned. An ambiguous character named Tex (Bo Hopkins) meets with Hayes. When Hayes asks, "Are you with the consulate?" Tex answers, "Something like that." Tex has implied that Hayes's cooperation will lead to a lighter sentence, so Hayes leads the officers to a café alongside Istanbul's crowded streets where he purchased the hashish. There, he attempts to escape. Again he is unsuccessful, and imprisonment follows.

At this point in the film a narrative technique comes into frequent use, as Hayes, in letters to family and friends, recounts his arrest, prison life, and Turkish customs. He spends his first prison night in a cold cell, and is punished by having his feet beaten when he takes a blanket, the first in a series of atrocities which he will endure or witness.

In prison he becomes friends with Max (John Hurt), Erich (Norbert Weisser), and Jimmy Booth (Randy Quaid). Booth, a fellow American who was imprisoned for stealing candlesticks from a mosque, is obsessed with the idea of taking the "midnight express"—prison jargon for "escape." Erich, a Swede, is completing his term. Englishman Max, who has become a drug addict, has long since given up any hope of leaving prison. He has long, greasy hair and unkept fingernails, and one of the lenses in his glasses is broken.

Encouraged by visits from his father (Mike Kellin), an American consulate representative, and a defense lawyer, Hayes is initially determined to await his trial and serve the impending sentence. When the sentence comes, he is told he got off lucky, with a four-year, two-month term. The prosecutor wanted a sentence for smuggling rather than possession, a charge which, Hayes learns, could result in life imprisonment. Waiting out his sentence, Hayes tells Susan, in a letter, "you can drift in here and never know you're gone. . . ." He tells her of Turkish traditions and horrors, which he witnesses daily. Homosexual crimes and knifings are common; children are tortured; peacocks, not dogs, patrol the prison grounds (peacocks are noisier than dogs and they cannot get rabies).

Although his lawyer is supposed to be working for an appeal, Hayes, with the passage of time, becomes cynical about the prospect. When his sentence has dwindled to only fifty-three remaining days and he receives a summons, he euphorically believes he is being granted an early release. Instead, he discovers, he is to be made an example. A new court has been scheduled, and he will now face a smuggling charge. Speaking out at his trial, Hayes says "I think I've paid for my error." In an emotional tirade, he says, "For a nation of pigs, it sure is funny you don't eat them." He adds, "Jesus Christ forgave the bastards. But I can't." He receives a new sentence of no less than thirty years, and when Hayes returns to prison, he knows he must escape.

With Jimmy Booth and Max, he finds a way into a tunnel system running beneath the prison (connecting with sewers and, they believe, a system of catacombs weaving under the city). Their dramatic attempt has a depressing climax, however, when they discover the tunnel dead ends. They must return to their cells. Later, one of the Turkish prisoners, a man named Rifki (Paolo Bonacelli), one of the story's many Turkish heavies who capitalizes on his imprisonment, discovers the tunnel entrance. He tells the prison officials, and Jimmy Booth is taken away for punishment. Hayes now wants, more than anything, to hurt Rifki, so he steals his money. Infuriated by the theft, Rifki suspects Max and reports him to the guards, saying that he has been dealing in hashish. A terrified Max is led away, and Hayes, no longer able to contain himself, breaks into uncontrolled violence. It subsides only after he attacks Rifki and, in a slow-motion shot, chews off Rifki's tongue.

In the next sequence, titles tell us that seven months have passed; Hayes, following the outburst, is in Section Thirteen, for the criminally insane. Once inside the new (unseen at this point) section, the cameras follow an erratic chase involving Max, who is finally shackled by guards. Then the camera moves in for a closeup of Hayes. For the first time, he is glassy-eyed and oblivious to the horrors about him. The scenes here seem a bizarre combination of Federico Fellini and Dante's *Inferno*.

Hayes does not return to life until he is visited by Susan. She sees him in a small booth where the two are separated by a plate of glass. At his urging, she unties her blouse, and as he looks at her breasts, he masturbates. Susan, horrified at what has happened to Hayes, presents him with a special family photo album with pictures of "Mr. Lincoln" and "Mr. Jackson." "Don't you count on anyone but yourself," she insists. The back panel of the album contains the "pictures"—money for escape. After buying his way out of Section Thirteen and planting a kiss on Max's forehead, promising to return for him, Hayes is taken to quarters upstairs for a meeting with a prison official. The official comes toward him with apparent sexual interest, and Hayes fights back, pushing the man against a wall, where he is impaled on a hook and dies instantly. Although Hayes holds the officer's gun, and wants to send bullets into the dead body, he cannot pull the trigger.

Escape in the officer's uniform follows. Although the disguise permits Hayes through the prison's gates and onto the street, he has a momentary scare when a prison truck approaches him. When it is obvious that Hayes is not recognized, he runs and jumps, with a freeze frame capturing his last movement. Closing credits report Hayes's return to the United States, and still photographs show us his teary homecoming. Finally, a closing scene bears words proclaiming that *Midnight Express* has played a part in effecting changes in prisoner treatment, a statement which serves to underline the film's already sanctimonious tone. While the film is an intriguing character study, as a social document it leans toward the heavy-handed; thus it has garnered criticism and created controversy. It was alleged that the filmmakers enhanced the film's violence as compared to events detailed in the book. At the same time, a homosexual encounter between Hayes and Erich, described in the book, was left out of the film. Not surprisingly, the film also drew fire from the Turkish government.

While *Midnight Express* will never bolster tourism in Turkey, it is a chilling if one-sided look at one man's hellish five years in a foreign prison. Director Parker (whose only previous film was the all-child-cast musical *Bugsy Malone* in 1976) has a special flair for creating atmosphere and evoking a striking sense of contemporary terror. As Hayes, Davis makes an auspicious feature film debut, and British actor Hurt, best known for his brilliant portrayal of Quentin Crisp in the British television movie, *The Naked Civil Servant*, is a constant scene-stealer as Max.

Midnight Express, a Columbia release, is one of the first films to come from Casablanca Record & FilmWorks, the company noted for its musical performers such as Cher, Donna Summer, and KISS.

Pat H. Broeske

MIDNIGHT LACE

Released: 1960
Production: Ross Hunter and Martin Melcher for Universal
Direction: David Miller
Screenplay: Ivan Goff and Ben Roberts; based on the play *Matilda Shouted Fire* by Janet Green
Cinematography: Russell Metty
Editing: Russell F. Schoengarth and Leon Barsha
Costume design: Irene
Running time: 108 minutes

> *Principal characters:*
> Kit Preston .... Doris Day
> Anthony Preston .... Rex Harrison
> Brian Younger .... John Gavin
> Aunt Bea .... Myrna Loy
> Malcolm .... Roddy McDowall
> Charles Manning .... Herbert Marshall
> Peggy Thompson .... Natasha Parry
> Inspector Byrnes .... John Williams
> Ash .... Anthony Dawson

Doris Day appeared on the October 10, 1960, cover of *Life* magazine, illustrating the fact that she was in a "new type of role" in the Ross Hunter-Martin Melcher suspense-drama *Midnight Lace*, directed by David Miller. Day was the perpetual screen virgin and epitomized womanhood of the 1950's and 1960's, chasing the man until he catches her and, of course, marries her. Her screen *persona*—pretty, virtuous, amusing, childlike, naïve, spirited, and spunky but willing to melt into the back seat when Prince Charming comes along—reflected the role of the American woman in postwar society. Her wholesomeness and vitality radiated from every freckle. Her homespun, apple-pie, perky tomboy image was the antithesis of the blond-bombshell stereotype which Marilyn Monroe and Jayne Mansfield represented at about the same time.

Hunter, who also produced *Imitation of Life* (1959), *Pillow Talk* (1957), *Portrait in Black* (1960), and *Airport* (1969), is an advocate of screen glamour, and his films have always offered excellent eye appeal. An exquisitely gowned Day wears fashions designed by Irene for *Midnight Lace*. The costumes received the only Academy Award nomination for the film, which *Newsweek* proclaimed a "third-degree time-killer." The opposite view was taken by some other critics, however, who felt that Miller was "challenging Hitchcock" with this film. Miller had done another film in a similar vein with Joan Crawford fleeing from imaginary pursuers in *Sudden Fear* (1952).

Although *Time* referred to Day's performance as that of a ". . . silly, spoiled, hysterical, middle-aged Lolita," many felt that she gave an excellent performance and painted a convincing portrait of a woman almost driven to insanity. Often referred to as her "first dramatic performance," *Midnight Lace* was in reality the third of her suspense-drama roles (although her first non-singing one)—the first two being *The Man Who Knew Too Much* (1956) and *Julie* (1956)—and one of several dramas. She never did as well at the box office in this type of role as in her sophisticated sex comedies such as *Please Don't Eat the Daisies* (1959) and *Pillow Talk*, the latter for which she received her only nomination as Best Actress. This was despite the fact that Day was the top box-office star of 1960 and the top female star of the 1960's, appearing on seven of the annual top-ten polls, in four of which she was number one.

Midnight Lace, which is in the same vein as *Gaslight* (1943) and *Diabolique* (1955), does suggest a Hitchcockian influence, although the plot is a bit too contrived to be credible. Deliberately, and a bit too obviously, the audience is continuously misled by various suspects, in the manner of Agatha Christie novels, without the wit and justification needed to sustain the conventions of this type of story. The film is entertaining and easy to look at, however, despite its flaws. Day, vascillating between wrinkle-nosed charm and wide-eyed terror and hysteria, manages to give a highly competent performance. The vulnerability, emotional commitment, and trusting nature she projects lend credibility to her character, resulting in a believable interpretation which manages to detract from the inherent flaws in the script. She plays the part of Kit Preston, a lonely young American heiress who has been married only three months to Anthony Preston (Rex Harrison), the Chairman of the Board of a company dealing in the promotion of mining shares.

The film opens in a London fog with Big Ben striking five o'clock. While walking home through the mist from the American Embassy, Kit is taunted by a voice that says he is going to kill her. Arriving home, Kit is calmed by her husband, who teases her, saying "What's up Kitten? Swallow too much fog?," and tells her that it was probably just a practical joker. The next day when Kit goes to her husband's office to join him for a lunch date which he has to break, she is almost killed by a steel girder as she passes the building site near her apartment. She is saved by Brian Younger (John Gavin), the building contractor. Kit enters her apartment and sees her housekeeper giving her ne'er-do-well son, Malcolm (Roddy McDowall), most of her wages. It is the unscrupulous Malcolm whom Kit will later suspect of making the threats on her life. Kit gives her housekeeper money to buy a coat, and after the housekeeper leaves, Kit receives a phone call. The voice on the other end of the line tells her in the same eerie style as before, "I'm going to kill you before the month is out." She is terrified when Peggy Thompson (Natasha Parry), her sophisticated neighbor, an attractive woman in her early thirties, enters her apartment. Peggy, whose husband is away, calls Tony and tells him to come home.

Inspector Byrnes (John Williams), a Scotland Yard official, questions Kit and her husband Tony. "We'll forgive you if you blush Mrs. Preston," says the inspector, as Kit listens to recorded voices of "crank phone chaps." The inspector discreetly suggests to Tony that Kit might be making up the story as other neglected wives have been known to do, but Tony protests and the inspector promises complete cooperation.

The next day, Kit's spirits rise when her Aunt Bea (Myrna Loy), a zestful, loquacious woman in her mid-fifties, arrives for a visit. That night while Kit and Tony dress to go out for dinner with Aunt Bea and Charles Manning (Herbert Marshall), the treasurer of Tony's company and an old flame of Aunt Bea, Kit gets another phone call. She calls to Tony, but before he can get to the other receiver, she slams the phone down (the threats, one gathers, are intermingled with sexual innuendos). Tony reprimands her and Aunt Bea wonders whether Kit might be imagining things as she had when she was a neglected wealthy child.

The following day when Kit is alone in the automatic elevator, it gets stuck between floors in a suspenseful sequence in which she is once again rescued by Brian, who removes the escape hatch and drops in. They go for a drink at a nearby pub to calm her nerves. A supressed emotion continues between these two throughout the film.

Later, while Kit and Tony are attending a ballet, Tony is called to his office by an attendant. He arrives at his office to find that one of his associates has discovered that someone has "dipped their hand into the till" to the tune of one million pounds. At the ballet, Malcolm appears and puts the touch on Kit for money for his "sick mother," but Kit refuses. Malcolm becomes angry and threatens her just as Tony returns and overhears the conversation. Tony tells him to leave and to stay away from their apartment.

The next morning while Kit is waiting for her aunt to return from the beauty parlor, she gets another threatening phone call, and the voice tells her that he knows she is alone. She tries to run from the apartment, but as she opens the door, she sees a stranger, a man named Ash (Anthony Dawson), standing there. His unnaturally rigid features on a face once handsome—possibly as a result of plastic surgery restoration—shock Kit, and she retreats into the living room with Ash following. She runs out onto the terrace and sees Brian on the adjoining structure and calls to him for help, but when he arrives, the stranger has disappeared. Inspector Byrnes is called to the apartment, but he appears somewhat skeptical about Kit's account of the incident.

After the inspector leaves, Tony tells Kit that he is going to take her to Venice to give her a rest and get her away from the whole mess. Kit is delighted and goes the next day to shop for clothes. Unable to get a taxi in the rain, she decides to take a bus. As the bus approaches the stop, Kit (who later insists she was pushed) falls into the path of the bus, and it barely misses her. As a crowd gathers, Peggy pushes her way through the crowd and says she saw the entire incident as she was coming from a shopping spree.

After they arrive home, Kit persuades Peggy to tell Tony that Kit had received another phone call while Peggy was there as a witness. Peggy reluctantly agrees when she sees how important it is to Kit that Tony believe her. When they relate the story to Tony, however, he accuses them both of lying, since "the phone has been out of order all day." As Kit cries, the phone rings once again; it is the operator saying the phone is now clear. Kit is close to hysteria when Aunt Bea arrives, and when the phone rings, Kit begs her to answer. The man's voice says, "What time shall I ring you today, Mrs. Newton? You haven't called me." The others look pitifully at Kit when Aunt Bea relates the message.

A neurologist then examines Kit and suggests the possibility of "dissociation of personality" and advises that she see a psychiatrist. The night before they are to leave for Venice, Kit receives another call. This time, however, Tony is there and listens on the extension. Although terrified, Kit is relieved to know that Tony realizes that she has been telling the truth. Tony calls Inspector Byrnes and then tells Kit that the inspector wants Tony to leave, drive around the corner and come back, in order to trap the culprit, who had indicated that this was the night he would kill Kit. Kit begs Tony not to go, but he convinces her and leaves.

Tony arrives back at the apartment and tells Kit to answer the phone. The voice tells her that he saw her husband leave; then Tony goes toward the terrace telling her to put out the light. She hears the voice in the room and runs to the terrace but Tony is not there. She hears the voice saying "I'm here to keep our appointment," and stares into the apartment as a figure appears in the moonlight. It is Tony holding a pocket tape recorder. He has a look on his face that Kit has not seen before. "Oh Tony—it's you," she says. "Recordings for all occasions," Tony answers, and the voice from the recorder says, "We all meet death somewhere along the way." Then Tony says, "We have an appointment. I'm going to kill you." Kit does not comprehend at first, then she slowly begins to back away. Tony tells her that he is going to tip her by her "pretty little heels" and send her head first over the terrace. When Kit tearfully begs why, Tony tells her, "for your vulgar American money"—to make up for the deficit his coworker had discovered.

A figure then is seen running along the catwalk from the building site to Kit's terrace: it is Brian. He and Tony pummel each other into the living room. Tony pretends he was trying to save Kit from jumping off the terrace, and then smashes Brian with an ash tray. As Tony is about to kill him with a poker, a shot comes, felling Tony. Peggy and Ash stand in the door of the hall. Peggy runs to Tony and cradles his head, saying, "Tony darling—it's me, Peggy." Ash then discloses, "That's right, Mrs. Preston. Your husband and my wife [Peggy] . . . two of a kind."

As Brian and Kit walk across the street to Grosvenor Square where her nightmare began, Brian tells her that sometimes, in his business, he comes across a building that looks fine outside but is rotten inside and that it has to be torn down and a new one built in its place, "one that will last." Kit tells Brian that it takes time to tear something down, and Brian closes with, "Everything takes time—everything worth doing."

The performances of the costars—Harrison smooth and British, Loy flamboyant and warm, Marshall world-weary but charming, and Gavin handsome if slightly neurotic—all contribute to the success of this titillating chiller.

Tanita C. Kelly

A MIDSUMMER NIGHT'S DREAM

Released: 1935
Production: Warner Bros.
Direction: Max Reinhardt and William Dieterle
Screenplay: Charles Kenyon and Mary McCall; based on the play of the same
name by William Shakespeare
Cinematography: Hal Mohr (AA)
Editing: Ralph Dawson (AA)
Music: Felix Mendelssohn, arranged by Erich Wolfgang Korngold
Choreography: Bronislawa Nijinska
Running time: 132 minutes

Principal characters:
Bottom	James Cagney
Flute	Joe E. Brown
Snout	Hugh Herbert
Oberon	Victor Jory
Hermia	Olivia de Havilland
Demetrius	Ross Alexander
Hippolyta	Verree Teasdale
Lysander	Dick Powell
Helena	Jean Muir
Theseus	Ian Hunter
Titania	Anita Louise
Puck	Mickey Rooney

Max Reinhardt's reputation for spectacular stage productions began in pre-World War I Germany. One of his most famous presentations was a version of William Shakespeare's *A Midsummer Night's Dream* in which lighting and dance emphasized the fantasy elements of the play. In 1934 he staged this work at the Hollywood Bowl. One result was a contract with Warner Bros. to produce the drama for the screen. Reinhardt saw this as an opportunity to send the message of *A Midsummer Night's Dream* all over the world in a production more impressive than had ever been possible on stage. This message, as he saw it, was that fantasy can always provide us a refuge from "stark reality." Hired to assist Reinhardt in the direction of this huge project, which was to be his only film, was William Dieterle. Dieterle had admired Reinhardt ever since he had acted in some of the producer's German plays. Dieterle had already directed several films for Warner Bros. (although his big successes—biographical films on Louis Pasteur, Émile Zola, and Paul Ehrlich—were yet to come) and was to handle the technicalities of filming while Reinhardt concentrated on the dialogue and actors.

The plot of the play is a complex one, full of incident, but even though Shakespeare's text was cut back by more than half, Reinhardt was able to keep the complications of the story clear to the audience. *A Midsummer Night's Dream* is constructed around the wedding festivities of Theseus, Duke of Athens (Ian Hunter), and Hippolyta, queen of the Amazons (Verree Teasdale). Interwoven are the tribulations of four young lovers and the escapades and intervention of Oberon (Victor Jory) and Titania (Anita Louise), the king and queen of the fairies, and Oberon's fairy page, Puck (Mickey Rooney). In rustic and comic contrast to the fairies are the tradesmen, who rehearse and perform a play for the wedding celebration.

At the beginning, both young men, Lysander (Dick Powell) and Demetrius (Ross Alexander), love Hermia (Olivia de Havilland), but the fairies use a potion to change the affections of both to Helena (Jean Muir), who loves Demetrius. Later the fairies again intervene to change Lysander's affections back to Hermia so that there are two happy couples who receive permission to marry on the day of the Duke's wedding to Hippolyta. The tradesmen perform their ludicrous drama at the wedding celebration, and the film ends with Puck speaking the epilogue from the Duke's bedroom door.

Two other elements besides the plot were essential to Reinhardt in his attempt to convey the atmosphere of the play: music and dance. For the music he had Erich Wolfgang Korngold, with whom he had worked in Germany, fashion a complete score from the music of Felix Mendelssohn, the nineteenth century composer who had written music for *A Midsummer Night's Dream*. Korngold spent more than six months adapting and rearranging the music of Mendelssohn (including some not originally written for Shakespeare's play) for Reinhardt's conception of *A Midsummer Night's Dream* as a film.

Notably effective is the choreographic spectacle which frequently highlights the film. We first see the dancing fairies in an evocative scene which is introduced by shots of such animals as an owl and deer, and then we see a misty woodland in which the mist becomes a ballet of white, wraithlike figures. The choreography for these scenes was done by Bronislawa Nijinska (sister of eminent *danseur* Waslaw Nijinsky) and Nini Theilade, who plays the principal fairy. These dances are an enchanting counterpoint to the dialogue scenes and reinforce the mixing of reality and fantasy in the film.

To try to insure the artistic and commercial success of the film, Warner Bros. used a great many well-known stars, such as Olivia de Havilland, Dick Powell, James Cagney, Hugh Herbert, Joe E. Brown, and Mickey Rooney. It was such a diverse group that smooth, integrated ensemble playing was not possible, but because of the diversity of moods in the play and Reinhardt's emphasis on fantasy and spectacle, almost all of the individual performances fit well into the film as a whole. To this day, however, critics argue about which actors and actresses succeeded and which failed. Rooney's performance is the most controversial; it is regarded by some as a remarkable acting feat and by others as tiresome. Since Rooney was not yet fifteen (although he had already appeared in many shorts and nearly two dozen features), some of the responsibility for his rather manic interpretation of the role should go to the director. Herbert, Brown, and Cagney are effective in their respective roles as Snout, Flute, and Bottom, three of the amateur dramatists.

All in all, Reinhardt and his associates did well the tricky job of putting Shakespeare on the screen. Because Shakespeare wrote for a different medium and in a style which emphasizes what is said more than what is seen, it is necessary that his plays be adapted rather than simply recorded by the filmmaker, but it is also necessary that the essence of the dramas, the qualities which make them masterpieces, be preserved. Reinhardt, one could say, practiced for his filming of *A Midsummer Night's Dream* by first producing it on stage for decades. Then, at Warner Bros., he was fortunate to receive the assistance of cinematic artists and technicians. Foremost among these are William Dieterle, who codirected, Hal Mohr, who won an Academy Award for the cinematography, and Ralph Dawson, whose editing also received an Academy Award. Reinhardt's accomplishment was truly, as critic John Russell Taylor has stated, that he "translated Shakespeare instead of merely recording him."

Judith A. Williams

MINISTRY OF FEAR

Released: 1944
Production: Seton I. Miller for Paramount
Direction: Fritz Lang
Screenplay: Seton I. Miller; based on the novel of the same name by Graham Greene
Cinematography: Henry Sharp
Editing: Archie Marshak
Running time: 84 minutes

Principal characters:
Stephen Neale	Ray Milland
Carla Hilfe	Marjorie Reynolds
Willi Hilfe	Carl Esmond
Costa/Travers	Dan Duryea
Mrs. Bellane	Hillary Brooke
Inspector Prentice	Percy Waram
Mr. Rennit	Erskine Sanford
Mr. Newland	Thomas Louden
Dr. Forrester	Alan Napier

Fritz Lang arrived in Hollywood shortly after fleeing Nazi Germany, and by the time of America's entry into World War II, he had embarked upon a series of films designed to outline the dangers of Fascism, unveil its insidious and evil mentality, and awaken Americans to Nazi menace and methods. The first of these was *Man Hunt* (1941), followed by *Hangmen also Die* (1943), *Ministry of Fear* (1944), and *Cloak and Dagger* (1946).

Ministry of Fear is a film for which Lang apparently had little feeling; but, as Lotte H. Eisner relates in her book *Fritz Lang*, the director was greatly taken by Graham Greene's original novel and eagerly accepted Paramount's offer to direct the screen version. Lang's subsequent lack of interest in the film stemmed from his disagreements on matters of casting (he had suggested Tonio Stelwart for the role of Willi Hilfe) and from his inability to make changes in the script because of contractual obligations. Despite these initial reservations, however, Lang still managed in *Ministry of Fear* to create a uniquely Langian world of mystery and menace. The film, like many of Lang's best works, is a thriller, a direct link to the postwar *film noir* tradition, on a par with other classics such as *Double Indemnity* (1944) and *The Big Sleep* (1946). Many of the concerns with which Lang continually dealt are present in *Ministry of Fear*: a preoccupation with the insulted and the injured, a recognition of the ambiguity of guilt, a constant subversion of expectations, and an ultimate redemption and redefinition of identity, all placed within the framework of a powerful political statement.

The film opens with the image of a wall clock whose ticking is the only sound as the seconds crawl by. The camera pulls back to reveal a young man seated tensely in the twilight, his sight focused on the clock. We learn that his name is Stephen Neale (Ray Milland), and as he is led outside to a heavily barred gate, he is told to stay away from the police and try to lead a quiet life. As Neale voices his assurances, every indication thus far has led us to believe that he is being released from prison. As he steps out of the gate and walks away, however, we read the words, "Lembridge Asylum" on the stone wall; Lang has, in his usual fashion, set us up to expect a set of circumstances which he immediately undercuts. Neale, we later learn, had been sentenced to two years in a mental institution for the accidental death of his wife.

As Neale reenters the outside world, everything is seen to be foreboding and uncertain. The night is dark; shadows abound, and Neale walks with an understandable uneasiness. He purchases a train ticket to London and, while waiting, decides to visit a charity bazaar being held at the local fair grounds. The event is a fund-raiser sponsored by a group known as the "Mothers of Free Nations," a collection of harmless looking middle-aged women who take an immediate liking to the young man.

After visiting a fortune-teller who directs him to a booth at which a prize cake is to be given to the one who guesses its correct weight (she had also told him the right answer for reasons Neale cannot fathom), Neale wins the cake and prepares to leave the fair. As he exits, a well-dressed young man rushes to the booth and declares the cake to be his. Both he and the ladies then try to persuade Neale to give up his prize, but he refuses, and leaves. On the train, he shares his compartment with a blind man who turns out to be sighted after all, and who steals Neale's cake when the train stops because of an air raid. Neale pursues him until a bomb explosion blows the man to pieces, leaving no trace of him or of the cake.

In London, Neale visits the office of the Mothers of Free Nations, but all seems to be normal there. He relates his odd tale to a pair of young Austrian refugees who help run the organization: Willi Hilfe (Carl Esmond) and his beautiful sister, Carla (Marjorie Reynolds). Willi accompanies Neale to the home of Mrs. Bellane, the fortune-teller at the fair, in an effort to get some sort of explanation for the strange events of the previous night. When they arrive at her home, however, she turns out to be a different woman, very elegant and beautiful and very sinister.

The two men become involved in a seance, elaborately orchestrated and superbly lit to highlight its mystical nature. Among the participants is a man introduced as "Mr. Costa" (Dan Duryea) whom Neale recognizes as the well-dressed man at the fair. As the seance progresses, Neale becomes increasingly agitated. A spirit voice seems to be that of his dead wife. He jumps away from the circle and a shot rings out. The lights come on and Costa lies on the ground, seemingly shot dead.

Willi helps Neale escape (for he seems to be the only logical suspect). On the run, Neale meets with Carla, and as they spend the night together in a subway station waiting out an air raid, they begin to fall in love. The next morning, Carla takes Neale to a hiding place in a musty, out-of-the-way bookshop. That night the bookshop proprietor, an elderly German whom Carla trusts implicitly, asks the two to deliver a suitcase filled with books to a Mr. Travers, emphasizing that the suitcase should be returned. Arriving at Travers' flat, Neale and Carla find it deserted. Mystified, Neale opens the suitcase and just manages to dive to safety as the bomb inside it explodes.

He awakens in a hospital bed guarded by a Scotland Yard inspector, who accuses Neale of killing a detective Neale had hired the previous day. Neale again relates his strange tale and is naturally met with disbelief until the site of the "blind man's" death is searched. A fragment of the cake is found and inside is a small reel of microfilm containing England's defense plans. Neale's suspicions are now confirmed. He is not imagining things; he has become involved in a Nazi spy ring composed of some of England's most respected citizens. Now, however, he has Scotland Yard on his side and can act more positively. The elusive Travers is discovered to be Mr. Costa, still very much alive and the owner of a respectable tailor shop. Neale learns that another reel of microfilm is hidden in a suit just delivered to a customer. That customer turns out to be Willi Hilfe, who, as Carla reveals that she herself has just learned, is a member of the Nazi gang and plans to escape after shooting both her and Neale.

A fight ensues between Willi and Neale, Willi knocks Neale down, snatches his suit, and runs out the door; but Carla has recovered Willi's revolver and shoots her brother as he dashes out. Willi's accomplices arrive, and it looks as though Neale and Carla are doomed, but the police rescue them just in time. The epilogue shows Neale and Carla on their honeymoon, driving by the sea, the brilliant sunshine dispelling the darkness and mystery of the previous nights. When Carla mentions that there was no cake at their wedding, Neale quakes at the very thought. "Cake? No! No cake," he announces firmly as they drive happily into the future. The plot description outlined above does not do justice to the intricate story line of *Ministry of Fear*. In fact, one of the many virtues of this film is the incredible amount of information and plot development that is presented in a mere eighty-four minutes.

As stated above, *Ministry of Fear* is a direct antecedent of the *film noir* style which emerged full-blown after the war. The lighting strategy employed here, with its dominant tone of darkness broken only by hot spots and shafts of bright light, is characteristically Langian and Germanic and is firmly within the *film noir* tradition. Another basic *film noir* element, and one that Lang was to employ throughout his lengthy career, is the notion of an innocent man becoming drawn into an evil situation which he is unable to control.

Although *Ministry of Fear* is a fully realized Langian film, it is interesting to note its similarities with the works of another master of suspense, director Alfred Hitchcock. Indeed, of all of Lang's many films, *Ministry of Fear* is the one most closely related to Hitchcock's unique style. Like Hitchcock, Lang includes many comic touches in *Ministry of Fear*, humorous moments which break the tension at precisely the proper moment. Another common Hitchcockian device used here is that of ambiguity of character: that is, people possess both good and evil traits. Thus we naturally sympathize with Neale, but we must remember that he was also responsible for his wife's death. Conversely, we cannot help being attracted to the apparent kindness and vitality of Willi Hilfe, and when he is revealed as the villain, our surprise is very great indeed. Another Hitchcockian device, and one that he constantly employed, is that of (as Hitchcock called it) the "McGuffin." The McGuffin was merely the catalyst that set the action in motion; it was of no intrinsic value to the story. Here, the microfilm is the McGuffin. It makes no difference plotwise whether the film contains photos of invasion plans, secret weapons, or defense strategies. All that matters is that the characters believe it to be important, and thus it spurs them to action.

Ministry of Fear is by no means Lang's best work. Much of it seems hastily conceived, and the plot, while intricate and involving, is not unusual. It is an essential film for students of Lang's canon, however, because in it are contained all of the thematic and stylistic elements with which the great director was concerned from the beginning of his career to the very end. *Ministry of Fear* is in every sense a mainline Lang film. Its evenly paced action, its careful development and logic, its skillful blend of fantasy and documentary realism, and its ability to handle myriad intricacies, all mark it as the work of one of the greatest of all *film auteurs*.

Daniel Einstein

MINNIE AND MOSKOWITZ

Released: 1971
Production: Al Ruban for Universal
Direction: John Cassavetes
Screenplay: John Cassavetes
Cinematography: Arthur J. Ornitz
Editing: Frederic Knudtson
Running time: 114 minutes

> *Principal characters:*
> Minnie Moore .... Gena Rowlands
> Seymour Moskowitz .... Seymour Cassel
> Husband .... John Cassavetes
> Zelmo Swift .... Val Avery
> Sheba Moskowitz .... Katherine Cassavetes
> Georgia Moore .... Lady Rowlands
> Morgan Morgan .... Timothy Carey

Minnie and Moskowitz is John Cassavetes' craziest and most charming film, and also his greatest playful parody. It is a zany screwball comedy that unites the grand old Hollywood conventions about the war between the sexes with the contemporary craziness of singles bars, pickups, blind dates, and one-night stands. Cassavetes' wife, Gena Rowlands, plays Minnie Moore, a vulnerable, sensitive, WASPish museum curator reluctantly romanced by Seymour Moskowitz (Seymour Cassel, in real life, one of Cassavetes' best friends and earliest backers), a loud, brash, Jewish, long-haired, and huge mustachioed car parker, with inevitably nutty consequences for all concerned. It is Cassavetes' most playfully exuberant film and at the same time one of the most delicate, touching, and comic explorations of the differences between the sexes and of the give and take of falling in love since the screwball comedies of Howard Hawks.

In many ways, *Minnie and Moskowitz* is Cassavetes' study of how directors such as Hawks and performers such as Humphrey Bogart and Lauren Bacall (both of whom are mentioned in the film) have created our language of love and courtship, even as it is an analysis of all of the ways that life is different from the movies. It is precisely through so successfully anatomizing and parodying the old Hollywood forms of love that Cassavetes earns the authority to assert the possibility of an alternative to Bogart and Bacall in his film. Only by so meticulously dissecting, mocking, and discarding one sort of false glamour can he clear a cinematic space for the very different glamour of this delicate, unstable, breakable pairing of Seymour and Minnie.

Cassavetes' criticism of the Hollywood film goes beyond a rejection of the coolness and composure of its stars. While Hawks and Michael Curtiz, whose

Casablanca (1942) is alluded to twice, spirited their romancing lovers off to exotic nightclub sets or strange, romantic, exciting locations, Cassavetes' romance blooms in parking lots, neon-lighted take-out joints, and in the front seat of Seymour's pickup truck cruising up and down Hollywood Boulevard at night. It is significant that the music Seymour and Minnie dance to in their occasional lyrical interludes comes neither from piano players named Sam (from Casablanca) nor the musicians of the Warner Bros. Orchestra, but over the static and hiss of the radio in Seymour's truck—interrupted by reports of news and the weather.

Perhaps the most shocking and profound change that Cassavetes works upon on the standard studio formula romance (and the thing that makes *Minnie and Moskowitz* such an unsettling experience for audiences prepared only for laughter and lightness) is that the destruction, violence, and cruelty associated with the outside world (generally the world of men without women) are no longer confined there as they are in other films. Love and sex are no longer privileged encounters, protected forms of relationship, sanctuaries that exempt the loving couple from the messes of the world. There is no escape into the bedroom of the imagination in Cassavetes' film; sexual relations become part and parcel of the stupidity, insanity, and violence of the rest of the world. Cassavetes himself appears as an actor in a cameo performance to beat up Minnie brutally in a lover's quarrel early in the film. Only a few minutes later Val Avery as Zelmo Swift turns in a *tour de force* performance in one of the most stunningly cruel (and yet by turns comic) scenes ever filmed, badgering, hectoring, and shaming Minnie on a luncheon date. Sexual relations for Cassavetes are less an escape from the violence and insensitivity of the world than a sort of ultimate refinement of them into techniques of personal torture. Cassavetes' men (with the exception of Seymour) are as much emotional hustlers, manipulators, and con men in their sexual affairs as they are in their social, financial, or business affairs.

All of this is by way of arguing for the unprecedented greatness of *Minnie and Moskowitz*. It is one of the most tough-minded, unsentimental comedies ever made. Cassavetes shows an almost Shakespearean daring in his desire to include even acts of cruelty and violence that resist his own comic intentions and his film's romantic rubric. There is an openness to personal sadnesses, failures of communication, and social insensitivities so great here that at every moment they actually threaten to destroy the film, to tear its comic premise to pieces. It is that recognition on Cassavetes' part that perhaps causes the film to go soft in its last half hour. Cassavetes is finally unable to see his characters through to the end of their disturbing cinematic predicament without destroying his own film, and he chooses to save appearances.

By the third instance of sexual violence in the film (when a male friend of Minnie beats up Seymour in trying to protect her) the comic placement of Minnie and Seymour in a larger society becomes impossible. For the rest of the film Cassavetes only goes through the motions of tying up all the loose ends in the plot and providing the kind of conventionally happy ending that the entire film has been arguing against up to that point. In the final half hour Seymour proposes to Minnie and is accepted, they each phone their mothers to announce their plans, meet with both mothers-in-law in a hilarious meal in the first real restaurant of the film, and are married in a quickie Hollywood marriage chapel service. These are beyond doubt the most outrageous and comical scenes Cassavetes has ever written, and usually the ones audiences go away remembering most vividly and hilariously. Their unremitting comedy is just their limitation, however; they are so funny because they make us forget all the social, personal, and emotional problems that led up to them. As poet Robert Frost said "the best way out is always through," Cassavetes has had to stoop to a comic trick, an aesthetic sleight of hand, to get himself out of this one. This final half hour is Cassavetes' least expected course of action, a series of subtle and systematic exclusions all the more insidious because of the comic amnesia Cassavetes is brilliantly able to induce.

At the meeting with both mothers-in-law at the restaurant, Mama Moskowitz (Katherine Cassavetes) asks how Seymour intends to support himself and his bride. Seymour gives a ridiculously amusing answer about going to work for a bigger parking lot, but Cassavetes depends on our laughing and not taking the question any more seriously than Seymour does. When the final minute of the film (immediately after the marriage ceremony) suddenly jumps a few years ahead to show Seymour and Minnie surrounded by children (their own, presumably) at a birthday party in a lusciously green yard, Cassavetes depends on our not asking where the grass found room to grow in this world of asphalt and formica, wondering if the kids have to cross Hollywood and Vine to get to school, or where Seymour's truck is parked. We have been transported to happily-ever-after filmdom, and these questions do not apply. After ninety minutes of the toughest-minded, most bracing, most exhilaratingly comic exploration of the battlefields of sexual warfare ever filmed, perhaps it is unfair to complain when in the final thirty minutes Cassavetes declares a hilarious cease-fire. A filmmaker of lesser genius would never have gotten there at all, before retreating back to clarity and lightness.

Raymond Carney

MIRACLE ON 34TH STREET

Released: 1947
Production: William Perlberg for Twentieth Century-Fox
Direction: George Seaton
Screenplay: George Seaton (AA); based on an original story by Valentine Davies (AA)
Cinematography: Charles G. Clarke and Lloyd Ahern
Editing: Robert Simpson
Running time: 94 minutes

Principal characters:
Doris Walker .... Maureen O'Hara
Fred Gailey .... John Payne
Kris Kringle .... Edmund Gwenn (AA)
Judge Henry X. Harper .... Gene Lockhart
Susan Walker .... Natalie Wood
Mr. Sawyer .... Porter Hall
Charles Halloran .... William Frawley
Alfred .... Alvin Greenman
Thomas Mara .... Jerome Cowan
Thomas Mara, Jr. .... Robert Hyatt

Miracle on 34th Street is a modest comedy-fantasy with ageless appeal that has become a classic holiday staple; it is as much a part of the holiday season as Christmas trees, packages, and parades. Like the *New York Sun*'s famed reply to young Virginia O'Hanlon's earnest letter, *Miracle on 34th Street* stands as further affirmation that there is a Santa, along with a need for good will and year-round kindness. Each holiday season this film is shown on television, although when first released, *Miracle on 34th Street* was shown with complete disregard for the calendar, having its debut during the summer of 1947.

The film opens at the annual Macy's Thanksgiving holiday parade, which makes its way up New York's Fifth Avenue. Doris Walker (Maureen O'Hara), the store's advertising executive, is infuriated to find that its Santa, who is set for the parade finale, has become intoxicated. Among those to witness the unfortunate incident is an elderly gentleman with a beard named Kris (Edmund Gwenn). He kindly offers to act as a replacement for the tipsy Santa, and Doris is happy to make the authorization. (In actuality, Gwenn did play Santa in the Macy's parade.)

Doris' young daughter Susan (Natalie Wood) is watching the festivities from up above, looking out of an apartment window with friendly neighbor Fred Gailey. Gailey (John Payne), an attorney, is fanciful, displaying an almost childlike fascination with the parade. Susan, on the other hand, is old beyond her years. Her mother, who is divorced, has reared her progressively. Gailey is saddened that Susan has not been encouraged to believe in childhood dreams (since her mother "hired" Santa, Susan knows he is not real), but he is also hopeful that, through Susan, he can get close to her attractive mother. His efforts with Susan pay off when Doris arrives home from the parade, and Susan (with some prompting from Gailey) asks if their new neighbor can stay for the holiday meal.

Kris, who was a smashing success as Santa in the parade, shows up at Macy's the next day and is offered the job of the store Santa. He is a success with the children, but their parents have some worries. What should they do, they ask, when the youngsters request gift items that they cannot locate? Kris's answer is a simple referral of the parents to other stores. When word of this reaches Macy's management, there is a brief furor, and Doris is instructed to fire the new Santa. When customers begin applauding what they perceive as a holiday goodwill gesture, however, the management has a quick change of heart. Kris is reinstated, and is even photographed alongside executives from both Macy's and Gimbel's (who shake hands for the benefit of the cameras).

Kris's reign as Santa is being maligned, however, by Mr. Sawyer (Porter Hall), Macy's employee psychiatrist, who is a quack. Sawyer is upset with the fact that Kris claims his real name is Kris Kringle. He apparently thinks he really is Santa Claus. On his employment form, for example, Kris lists Donner, Blitzen, and so forth as his "next of kin." Sawyer has confided to a concerned Doris that Kris is probably insane, and he administers a series of tests to Kris. Kris patiently endures them—revealing that he has taken the same tests in the past, with considerable success.

While Sawyer questions Kris's sanity, Susan mulls over the possibility that Kris might really be Santa. She is impressed with his beard—it is real, not a fake one attached by a string over the ears as most store Santas' are, and, more importantly, Susan witnessed a mystifying incident. A shy little girl, who stood in line to see Santa, could not speak English, so, Kris fluently spoke with her in Dutch, her native tongue. The child was so grateful that she nearly burst into tears, and Susan cannot help but be puzzled by it all.

When Kris begins rooming with Gailey (so Doris can help keep an eye on the strange old man), Susan and Kris embark on a delightful exchange. She teaches Kris to chew bubble gum, and he teaches her about the marvels of the imagination; specifically, he shows her how to behave like a monkey.

The question of Kris's sanity erupts when Sawyer, who has continued scheming, reprimands Alfred (Alvin Greenman), a young store employee who annually performs as Santa Claus, for having "fixations." In anger, Kris bops Sawyer on the head, using his ever-present cane. That is the sign Sawyer was waiting for, and he quickly has Kris committed to Bellevue. Lawyer Gailey jumps to Kris's defense. When the question of Kris's mental health is put before a New York superior court judge, Gailey claims he will prove that Kris is, in fact, Santa Claus.

The newspapers gobble up the story and the presiding judge (Gene Lockhart) gets some stern words from his political aide, Charles Halloran (William Frawley). He warns that this case involves more than one man's sanity, since it will, in effect, determine the possible existence of Santa Claus. Halloran insists that the judge will be in trouble if he does not rule that there is a Santa. When the case gets under way, Thomas Mara (Jerome Cowan), conducting the state's case, relies on testimony from Sawyer to prove Kris's insanity. Gailey does some showstopping by calling to the stand Mara's own young son (Robert Hyatt). Asked whether he believes in Santa, the child nods solemnly, pointing to Kris sitting in the courtroom. When Gailey asks the boy why he believes that there is a Santa, the child reveals it is because his dad told him so. The courtroom bursts into laughter, and prosecutor Mara slumps down into his seat.

Although Gailey has employed some clever tactics, he cannot prove conclusively that Kris is the one and only Santa. Finally, Gailey's worries and the judge's political dilemma are put to rest, because the "dead letter" section of the post office has sent all the holiday mail, addressed to "Santa," to Kris, at the court. From behind a gigantic stack of letters (postal employees are carrying in additional sacks of mail), the judge shrewdly sides with the government. If it finds Kris to be Santa, "well, so be it." The decision is handed down on Christmas Eve, so Kris does not have time to celebrate the victory. He has got work to do.

Gailey and Doris have fallen in love throughout the course of the trial. Doris has also softened in her attitudes toward Kris. Susan loves him, and would like to believe he really is Santa. If he is Santa, she reasons, he will be able to give her the special present that she has asked for. On Christmas morning, however, when she rummages under the tree, Susan does not find what she is looking for. Later when Gailey, Doris, and Susan drive home from a Christmas party, taking a route that Kris has suggested, Susan cries out, and Gailey stops the car. Then Susan bolts up the path to a picturesque house—the exact dream house that she has asked Kris for. The house is for sale and resting in a corner of one of the empty rooms is a familiar cane. Susan is now a firm believer in Santa Claus, and Gailey concedes that his defense was not as brilliant as he thought it was.

One of the most popular films of 1947, *Miracle on 34th Street* competed for Best Picture Academy Award (losing to *Gentleman's Agreement*). It took awards for original story and screenplay, however, and British actor Gwenn walked away with a Best Supporting Actor Award for his portrayal of Kris. Capable, unassuming performances by Payne and O'Hara allow a polished screenplay to shine, and a young Wood is engaging as Susan. For the producing-directing team of William Perlberg and George Seaton (who were together for more than twenty-five years), *Miracle on 34th Street* ranks as one of their most successful ventures. The two also created such films as *The Song of Bernadette* (1943), *The Country Girl* (1954), and *36 Hours* (1964).

Pat H. Broeske

THE MIRACLE WORKER

Released: 1962
Production: Fred Coe for United Artists
Direction: Arthur Penn
Screenplay: William Gibson; based on his play of the same name and *The Story of My Life* by Helen Keller
Cinematography: Ernest Caparros
Editing: Aram Avakian
Running time: 107 minutes

Principal characters:
Annie Sullivan .... Anne Bancroft (AA)
Helen Keller .... Patty Duke (AA)
Captain Keller .... Victor Jory
Kate Keller .... Inga Swenson
James Keller .... Andrew Prine
Aunt Ev .... Kathleen Comegys

The Miracle Worker was a milestone in the careers of its stars, Anne Bancroft and Patty Duke. After a lackluster decade as a Hollywood starlet appearing in such artistic failures as *Treasure of the Golden Condor* (1953), *New York Confidential* (1955), *The Last Frontier* (1955), and *Gorilla at Large* (1954), Bancroft established herself as an actress of unrelenting power and skill. The acclaim that she received enabled her to win starring roles in such films as *The Slender Thread* (1965), *The Graduate* (1967), and *The Turning Point* (1978). Likewise *The Miracle Worker* was a major step forward for Duke. Only fifteen when the film was released, her success brought her her own situation comedy series on television and starring roles in both theatrical and made-for-television movies.

The Miracle Worker is a dramatization of how Helen Keller (Patty Duke), the renowned writer and lecturer who was blind and deaf from infancy, gained the capacity for understanding through the dedicated effort of her teacher, Annie Sullivan (Anne Bancroft). The project has an interesting history. In 1953, William Gibson read *The Story of My Life*, the autobiography of Helen Keller, and he was so moved by her life and accomplishments that he wrote a ballet with vocal accompaniment based on the material. The piece was not produced, but Arthur Penn proposed that he develop it further as a television play. In February, 1957, Penn directed this version for *Playhouse 90*, with Teresa Wright as Annie, Patty McCormack as Helen, Burl Ives as Helen's father, Katherine Bard as her mother, and John Barrymore, Jr., as her brother James. After further revision, it opened on Broadway in October, 1959, with Bancroft and Duke, Torin Thatcher and Patricia Neal as Helen's parents, and James Condon as her brother. For the film, Victor Jory, Inga Swenson, and

Andrew Prine replaced, respectively, Thatcher, Neal, and Condon. Kathleen Comegys appeared in the play and the film as Helen's Aunt Ev. Producer Fred Coe and director Penn were also involved in both play and film.

The year is 1887, and seven-year-old Helen Keller is unable to function under the influence of her domineering father (Victor Jory) and overindulgent mother (Inga Swenson). Annie Sullivan, herself almost blind, is hired to care for the child. Annie has been toughened by a youth spent in institutions, as well as by the death of her crippled brother. She is allowed to spend two weeks alone with her charge in a small garden house owned by the Kellers, yet Helen resists all efforts to teach her how to care for herself. Annie is determined to break Helen's will. When Helen screams and scratches at her teacher, Annie screams and scratches right back. During the two weeks, Annie is able to teach Helen how to eat with a fork, to get dressed, and even to comprehend the alphabet by touch. When Helen returns to the Keller household, however, she tries to revert to her former self. She spills a water pitcher at the dining room table, and Annie pulls her outside to a pump in front of the house so that she may refill it. As the water splashes over Helen's hand, she abruptly realizes that the liquid on her fingers is not an abstract feeling, but is W-A-T-E-R. Helen has learned that the letters Annie has been banging into her head form words, which are the names of objects. She spells out W-A-T-E-R on Annie's hand. Emotionally aroused, she runs about and spells out the names of everything she can touch—pump, tree, porch, bell, and finally, mother.

Both roles are emotionally exhausting, and Bancroft and Duke are up to them: *The Miracle Worker* is, ultimately, a *tour de force* for both. Bancroft's Annie Sullivan is a survivor, a woman determined to succeed at her task despite the tantrums of her charge. The actress triumphantly conveys a will that will not give in to Helen's obstinacy. As she sniffs at Bancroft's hand like a hungry animal, ravages the Keller family's dinner table like a maniac, and mimics her confusion out of desperation, Duke masterfully conveys the terror of a sightless, soundless world. Duke had previously appeared in child roles in such films as *The Goddess* (1958) and *Happy Anniversary* (1959), but her biggest success prior to *The Miracle Worker* was her stage performance as Helen. Bancroft had rightfully been so disgusted with her career during the 1950's that she abandoned Hollywood for the stage, and this film was her triumphant return to the cinema. Critics were justifiably unanimous in their praise for both actresses, and each was awarded an Oscar—Bancroft for Best Actress and Duke for Best Supporting Actress.

The film in its entirety, however, pales in comparison to the star performances. A major flaw is Gibson's depiction of Helen's parents, who are both maddeningly shallow. Her father, portrayed with a dearth of subtlety by Jory, is no more than a one-dimensional tyrant; her mother, limply acted by Swenson, is helplessly and superficially overprotective. Penn's direction, however, although somewhat showy, ultimately heightens the power of Bancroft's and Duke's performances. The director shoots the confrontation sequences in subjective, extreme close-up. Food, dishes, and water are splattered about, and at one point, Annie and Helen even fight on the floor. These encounters often seem to jump right off the screen and into the viewer's lap. On stage, Annie's memories of her brother's death were represented by offstage voices; in the film, out-of-focus images are superimposed over Bancroft's face. This visualization of a script which is essentially an expanded stage play assists in involving the audience in the dramatics.

Penn's film career has been an enigma. Before breaking into the cinema, he directed plays for television and on Broadway. His earliest works, notably *The Left-Handed Gun* (1958), an allegory about the myth of Billy the Kid, and *Mickey One* (1965), the study of a confused nightclub comedian, were interesting, but failures at the time. Although his direction of *The Miracle Worker* is intelligent and skillful, the film is dominated by the performances of its stars. *The Chase* (1966), the underrated tale of an escaped convict at the mercy of a violent, corrupt community, is not really his film, as he allegedly did not have final say over the production. Five years after *The Miracle Worker*, he reached his zenith with the innovative classic *Bonnie and Clyde* (1967), a poetic recounting of the careers of the notorious Depression-era bankrobbers. Diverting follow-ups were *Alice's Restaurant* (1969), an expansion of Arlo Guthrie's ballad of life on a hippie commune in the Berkshires, and *Little Big Man* (1970), an epic saga of the American West which studies the extinction of the American Indian. Penn was then inactive for a half a decade, and his latest films have been rather pedestrian: *Night Moves* (1975), and average detective yarn with Gene Hackman, and *The Missouri Breaks* (1976), a jumbled Western featuring hired gunman Marlon Brando (sporting an outlandish Irish brogue) and Jack Nicholson.

The Miracle Worker was not a financial success, despite its critical acclaim. It took in a disappointing two million dollars at the box office, perhaps because of its subject matter. *Variety* ranked it a dismal forty-third for its year in earnings, but the film remains an important credit in the progression of the careers of its director and stars.

Ronald Bowers

MR. AND MRS. SMITH

Released: 1941
Production: Harry E. Edington for RKO/Radio
Direction: Alfred Hitchcock
Screenplay: Norman Krasna
Cinematography: Harry Stradling
Editing: William Hamilton
Running time: 95 minutes

Principal characters:

Ann Krausheimer Smith	Carole Lombard
David Smith	Robert Montgomery
Jeff Custer	Gene Raymond
Mr. Custer	Philip Merivale
Mrs. Custer	Lucile Watson
Chuck Benson	Jack Carson

Alfred Hitchcock reportedly described *Mr. and Mrs. Smith* as his worst film, in an interview with French writer-director François Truffaut. Although many of his ardent admirers undoubtedly agree, the RKO/Radio comedy is not only extremely funny in spots but it also lends considerable insight into a number of images and techniques that would reappear with greater significance in the director's later films.

According to Truffaut, the film was done as a friendly gesture to Carole Lombard. "At the time," said Hitchcock, "she was married to Clark Gable and she asked whether I'd do a picture with her." In a weak moment, the director accepted, even though he admittedly "didn't understand the type of people who were portrayed in the film"; yet the "Master of Suspense" tackled the problem very seriously. He in fact had two reference points, his films *Champagne* (1928) and *Rich and Strange* (1931), that he kept in mind during the filming. His guiding impulse was to ignore the usual technique of the genre, a technique based upon simplicity and speed. The result was that, ultimately, only the acting style of the stars Lombard and Robert Montgomery would remain faithful to the tradition. Both had portrayed the story of *Mr. and Mrs. Smith* many times in other films and were experienced, deft hands at comedy. Thus, Hitchcock felt that he could legitimately focus all of his attention on the direction of the film which he wanted to construct in a manner that would be truly characteristic of his personal style.

Although this, Hitchcock's third American film, was a typical Hollywood production and did not share the success of *Rebecca* (1939) or *Foreign Correspondent* (1940), it at least stood up to some outstanding examples of its genre as reflected in the drawing-room comedies of George Cukor, Howard Hawks, and Ernst Lubitsch. It compensated for some structural weaknesses in several moments of hilarious comedy, poignant human touches, and extremely good acting. No matter how much audiences might prefer the Hitchcock of the horror, violence, and subtle restraint reflected in *The Lady Vanishes* (1938) or *The 39 Steps* (1935), they cannot help appreciating the techniques reflected in *Mr. and Mrs. Smith*'s funny scenes in the night club and in the Lake Placid Ski Lodge.

Hitchcock was for the first and only time working within the tradition of the drawing-room comedy that had been established by Noel Coward's *Private Lives* (1931) and was fully realized in Hawks's *Bringing Up Baby* (1938). Yet the originality of Hitchcock's approach becomes evident in the very first scene of *Mr. and Mrs. Smith*. A slow, panoramic dolly shot reveals a bedroom in a highly chaotic state with clothes and various other objects piled on the floor and tossed over furniture. The camera pauses for a moment before the bed. Slowly, the top of a woman's head emerges. The camera moves forward, capturing first an eye and then the face of Ann Smith (Carole Lombard). This slow, meandering shot constitutes a significant departure from the reigning laws of American comedy; it actually expresses a kind of anxiety and could easily be used to begin a suspense film such as *Suspicion* (1941). The remainder of the film adheres to the same principle.

Hollywood comedy normally achieves its expected results from the maintenance of an objective viewpoint. The audience is expected to be witness to a somewhat clinical report on madness. Yet in *Mr. and Mrs. Smith*, the spectators become accomplices of the characters through the assumption of a subjective camera. Our shifting identification with each character possibly stymies some of the merriment, yet we do laugh when the viewpoint shifts from one subjectivity to another, as long as we shift with it. The full effect of the gag, however, is lost upon those members of the audience who do not change viewpoints with the camera and instead continue to identify with the person at whose expense the joke is being carried out.

To make this nontraditional comedy work, Hitchcock needed actors whose glibness and spontaneity would allow them to roll with the punches and keep the action moving. Lombard, for example, plays the role of Ann Smith as if she has not a brain in her head, which was exactly what the director demanded. Montgomery, her counterpoint as David Smith, the confused husband, also lives up to Hitchcock's expectations with a performance that places him well within the mold of the director's ideal leading men such as Cary Grant or Jimmy Stewart, who are able to combine comedy with a certain mysteriousness of demeanor.

Mr. and Mrs. Smith does contain some traditional aspects of comedy such as Gene Raymond's performance as Jeff Custer, the perfect gentleman who gets drunk in a stuffed-shirt sort of way, and the scene in which Chuck Benson (Jack Carson) doles out advice in a turkish bath. These ploys, however, typical of Hollywood comedies, lack the originality and creativity evidenced in the scenes in which Hitchcock works, as he did in *Rich and Strange*, against a serious situation. When Ann and David try to recapture the magic of their first dates by returning to Mama Lucy's, their old haunt, the new owner watches them hostilely while they eat their favorite dish. The meal, although funny, is a failure; it culminates when David thinks that he has been poisoned and screams for a stomach pump. Thus, the disintegration of their marriage begins in both a humorous and yet a poignant manner.

In addition to a number of other eccentricities, the Smiths maintain a set of rules akin to the Marquis of Queensbury boxing regulations for solving their marital crises. The chief one is an agreement that requires the combatants, following a quarrel, to remain in their bedroom until the instigator has apoligized and been forgiven. Sometimes these bedroom escapades have lasted for as long as eight days. Although David Smith is an up-and-coming young lawyer, he never seems to make it to the office very often between fighting and making up.

After a particularly bitter fight, an embarrassed little man, Mr. Deever (Charles Halton), arrives from the town in which they thought they were married and explains that they are not married at all because of a legal technicality. To tease his wife, David delays asking her to remarry him until she reaches the point at which she becomes thoroughly fed up, tosses him out, and refuses to marry him at all. She subsequently takes up with David's partner in the law practice, Jeff Custer, a stuffy, gentle Southern aristocrat. To make her jealous, David, who has been living at his club, double dates with a vulgar clubmate, Chuck Benson, and two boisterous floozies.

Immediately after they sit down, David spies his wife and her boyfriend. Embarrassed to be seen in such low-class company, he notices a young and beautiful socialite sitting at an adjoining table and pretends to be talking to her to convey the impression that she is with him. With some glee, he realizes that his wife, sitting across the room, is becoming upset. Suddenly, however, the woman's husband comes back to the table and threatens David, after which he takes his wife away. Realizing now that Ann will know who he is actually with, David decides that he must leave as soon as possible, so he attempts to give himself a reason to leave—a nosebleed. In perhaps the single most hilarious scene in any Hitchcock film, David attempts to punch himself discreetly in the nose. Try as he might, and despite increasing pain, he cannot do it with his fist alone, so he resorts to putting a heavy salt shaker in his hand, thus adding considerable power to his bare fist. The result is a terrible nosebleed which, instead of giving him an excuse to leave quietly, triggers the floozies into action. They force him to recline, ask loudly for a cold knife, and generally make a spectacle which makes the embarrassed David wish that he had cut his throat instead of punching himself. Ann cannot help noticing the furor, and she asks Jeff to take her away.

This scene reveals the essence of Hitchcock's subjective camera. During the first stages, we share David's embarrassment and then we participate in his triumph. Then, suddenly, after the nose incident, we quickly find ourselves on the other side of the fence (although not without some uneasiness) with Mrs. Smith. The shifting subjectivity sparks our laughter and we can identify with both parties, yet since we are not maintaining an objective viewpoint, we are also in a sense laughing at ourselves.

Ann decides to marry Jeff, and his parents (Philip Merivale and Lucile Watson) stop off on their way to Lake Placid to visit the couple at the law office. The happy scene is interrupted by David, however, who asks his former wife if she has washed more underwear for him and then talks about Ann's tendency to get seasick on river cruises. Jeff's parents cannot abide the thought of their son becoming engaged to a woman who has lived with another man. They take their son into the bathroom (one of Hitchcock's favorite locations for private revelations) to try to talk him out of marrying this woman. Jeff convinces them that they do not know the real Ann and arranges to bring her to Lake Placid to spend some time getting acquainted with his parents.

David, of course, shows up at Lake Placid also. Feigning illness, he wins Ann's sympathy temporarily, but she quickly discovers the charade and becomes more determined to marry Jeff. Driving into town with him, however, she weakens in her resolve and convinces her fiancé to return to the lodge with her, where she stages a scene that causes David to become jealous and burst into her room. Jeff's angry parents arrive in the middle of the altercation, and the marriage is off for good. The Smiths reunite and the film ends, leaving the viewer with the impression that the cycle will repeat itself endlessly.

The fact that Hitchcock was not at all intimidated by trying his hand at comedy is evident in the excellent performances that he inspires in his three principal actors. Montgomery, playing David Smith with an insolent smile and knowing eyes, evokes the perfect picture of a man who, although very much in love, becomes careless and overconfident until he discovers that he is losing his wife. Lombard continues a role that she developed into a fine art in her portrayal of a beautiful but not particularly intelligent wife who organizes her marriage around a code of rules and then goes to pieces when she realizes that her marriage is not quite legal. Raymond, making his second film in a midcareer "comeback" that saw him change his hair color from platinum to black, is steady and restrained as the "other man" whose broad shoulders, generosity, and Southern manners do not truly substitute for Ann's husband.

The moving force in this film, however, is Hitchcock's talent, which moves the plot along with stylish fluidity and a naïve comedic artistry in the first reels before stalling, embarrassingly, halfway through. Yet there are a number of amusing sequences and several striking images with which Hitchcock experiments here that provided a transition to his subsequent films. *Mr. and Mrs.*

Smith, with its marital subterfuge, seems something of a rehearsal for the darker interplay of *Suspicion*, in which Lina McLaidlaw (Joan Fontaine) and Johnny Aysgarth (Cary Grant) stretch Ann and David's self-centered little world to a diabolical extreme. In other instances, the subjective images of Ann and Jeff in the high-ride at the carnival recur in *Strangers on a Train* (1951) when Bruno returns to the amusement park and loses his life on the carousel—reminiscent of Ann and Jeff trapped in the ride in *Mr. and Mrs. Smith*.

Finally, in the scene in which Ann dries her hair by the fire in Jeff's apartment, she foreshadows Madeleine in *Vertigo* (1958) warming herself by the fire after jumping into San Francisco Bay. Although the thematic and emotional contexts of these images are entirely different in *Mr. and Mrs. Smith* from what they would be later in the suspense films, they do indicate that Hitchcock not only viewed this film as an opportunity to take a personal approach to an age-old genre of comedy, but that he was also trying out ideas that he would use later to better effect. Thus, *Mr. and Mrs. Smith*, like Hitchcock's other minor works, cannot be written off as a meaningless bit of fluff. Everything had meaning to the "Master of Suspense," and things are not always as they seem at first glance.

Stephen L. Hanson

MR. BLANDINGS BUILDS HIS DREAM HOUSE

Released: 1948
Production: Norman Panama and Melvin Frank for RKO/Radio
Direction: H. C. Potter
Screenplay: Norman Panama and Melvin Frank; based on the novel of the same name by Eric Hodgins
Cinematography: James Wong Howe
Editing: Harry Marker
Running time: 94 minutes

Principal characters:
Jim Blandings	Cary Grant
Muriel Blandings	Myrna Loy
Bill Cole	Melvyn Douglas
Joan Blandings	Sharyn Moffett
Betsy Blandings	Connie Marshall
Gussie	Louise Beavers
Henry Simms	Reginald Denny

In the years immediately following World War II, major demographic changes began to take place in America. Peacetime brought a new prosperity, the postwar baby boom, and a housing shortage which eventually resulted in a mass exodus of young, middle-class families from big cities to the suburbs. In 1948, the trend was ripe for satirization, and H. C. Potter's film adaptation of Eric Hodgins' novel, *Mr. Blandings Builds His Dream House* is a delightful thrust at the rush to get away from it all.

The opening scene is a gem, and it sets the tone for the rest of the film. The narration is a paean to the joys of big city life and offers nothing but praise for the "modern cliff dwellers" who live in the high-rise apartments of New York City. The images on the screen, however, undercut these claims. From rush hour traffic and the teeming sidewalks to the Blandings' crowded bathroom sink, the camera records an existence more suited to a beehive or an anthill than to human beings. The effect is, of course, ironic. The irony is reversed throughout the rest of the film, as Jim Blandings (Cary Grant) doggedly maintains his enthusiasm for life in the country even as his beloved country estate threatens to ruin his life.

In his Manhattan apartment, Jim Blandings strives to maintain a sane and orderly life in an apartment that is far too small for his family. Even the medicine chest is overcrowded, and its contents overflow every time it is opened. In a hilarious scene, both he and his wife Muriel (Myrna Loy) try to use the bathroom mirror at the same time, he to shave and she to apply makeup. Eventually, steam from the shower fogs up the mirror, making it impossible for either one to use it. Thus Potter delineates the Blandings' basic problem even before they sit down to breakfast.

The scene at the breakfast table foreshadows many of the events that will occur later in the film. We meet the rest of the Blandings household, which consists of daughters Betsy (Connie Marshall) and Joan (Sharyn Moffett), as well as Gussie (Louise Beavers), a black live-in housekeeper. Betsy's homework assignment is to write an essay on the decline of the West as reflected in the classified ads. She chooses an ad placed by a man who has been forced by financial reverses to sell his farm. Jim, a $15,000-a-year advertising executive, is alarmed by the anti-advertising bias of his daughter's teacher, and his mood worsens with the arrival of Bill Cole (Melvyn Douglas), an old friend and the family lawyer. Cole informs Muriel that the cost of her proposal to redecorate their apartment in a colonial motif will exceed seven thousand dollars. The entire project is news to Jim, who puts a stop to it immediately.

In this scene, Potter lays the groundwork upon which the rest of the film is built. He touches on the ambiguous role of advertising (which is the Blandings' primary source of income, but which also ultimately induces them to spend their way into debt) in the Blandings' life. In the seemingly offhand mention of a farm, Potter introduces the concept that will eventually turn Jim Blandings into a comic Ahab, monomaniacally pursuing the great white house in the country. Muriel Blandings' penchant for absurdly profligate spending prepares us for an ironic variation on this theme when her thrifty husband joins her in a spending spree. Finally, Bill Cole, who narrated the opening sequence and is the film's voice of common sense, arrives on the scene for the first time.

The film continues in Jim's office. He has been assigned to work full time on a new account, WHAM, a hamlike substance the taste of which Blandings grows to detest. While in his office, however, he sees an ad for a house in rural Connecticut. Suddenly fascinated by the prospect of country living, Jim and Muriel visit the house, which is clearly in need of major repairs, a fact which the Blandings do not seem to notice. They are too busy listening to the Realtor, who tells them that the house dates from the Revolutionary War. Bill Cole advises against the purchase, arguing that the price is too high, but Blandings is enthralled by the rickety old house and will not listen to any criticism. It is like a fine old painting, he says, worth much more than the cost of the paint and canvas. They buy the house.

Everyone they call in for an estimate on the cost of making the house livable tells them to tear it down and start over. The Blandingses are initially horrifed by the thought, but grow intrigued at the prospect of building their dream house from scratch. When architect Henry Simms (Reginald Denny) arrives with the blueprints, they plunge into an orgy of remodeling that makes Muriel's earlier seven-thousand-dollar plans for their apartment look cheap. They become so excited that they give simultaneous and conflicting orders to the architects, which include four bedrooms, each with its own bathroom (the Blandingses have not forgotten the chaos of their early morning mis-adventures) and closet, and result in plans for a house twice as big as the original.

Costs proceed to escalate. Demolishing the original house ahead of schedule costs them six thousand dollars, and a local well-digger drills down 227 feet without finding water, although they get more water than they bargain for when their basement floods. Nevertheless, Bill Cole bails the Blandingses out, and construction proceeds, as Jim, caught up in the proceedings, begins to spend less and less time working on the WHAM account. Suddenly, the Blandingses are evicted from their apartment in the city and are forced to move into their "dream house" before it is finished. A few more inconveniences surface, among them the fact that Jim Blandings will have to rise in the middle of the night to catch the 6:15 A.M. train to the city each day.

As if he did not have enough problems, additional complications enter Jim's life. An old fraternity pin falls out of one of the boxes he is moving into his new home, and it turns out to have belonged to Bill Cole. A surreptitious look into Muriel's old diary reveals that she and Bill were college sweethearts before she began dating Jim. Annoyed that she cared enough about Cole to keep the pin all these years, he angrily confronts her with his discoveries, although, abashed, he soon ends up apologizing when she assures him that there is nothing between her and Bill.

Back in the city, Jim is suddenly ordered to produce the WHAM advertising slogan by the next morning. He stays in his office until dawn, trying unsuccessfully to do so. Finally, he decides to return home, certain that his career is through. Meanwhile, Bill Cole, who had come to visit the Blandingses the day before, is forced to stay overnight in the dream house when a sudden storm causes the river to rise, cutting him off from town. Thus director Potter sets the stage for another comical misunderstanding about the relationship between Muriel and Bill Cole. As Jim arrives home, he is confronted by a contractor who demands payment of an additional $1,247 which Muriel had mistakenly authorized. Before he has time to absorb this shock, he sees Bill Cole strolling downstairs in his robe and pajamas. Jumping to the obvious (to him) conclusion, Blandings begins to rant, blaming all of his problems on his "dream house" and vowing to get rid of it.

He is interrupted by another contractor, but this one wants to return some money. He had been overpaid by $12.36. Blandings is overwhelmed by this small act of honesty and kindness, and his anger subsides, leaving only bewilderment. Bill Cole's presence is soon explained satisfactorily, and everyone sits down to breakfast—an order of WHAM. As Gussie serves it, she proclaims "If you ain't eatin' WHAM, you ain't eatin' ham!" Stunned, Blandings realizes that this is the slogan for which he has been looking, and phones it into his office just in time to save his job. All's well that ends well, and the dream house does not look so bad after all. As Bill Cole remarks, "Maybe there are some things you should buy with your heart and not your head."

Potter elicits topnotch performances from his principal actors. Douglas is fine as Bill Cole, projecting a warmth and calmness that Potter skillfully plays off against the frenetic Blandingses; and Loy is pleasantly scatterbrained as Muriel. Grant, however, as Jim Blandings, carries the film. Grant has a talent for playing amiable eccentrics, and it is a pleasure to watch him in the role of a sane man gone slightly mad in pursuit of his dream.

Potter directs the film with a sure hand, skillfully preparing the viewer for almost every turn of the plot. The one exception to this pattern is the rather sudden introduction of Bill Cole as Jim Blandings' possible rival for Muriel's affections. In a drama, this would have been a serious error, but in this light comedy it is barely noticeable. *Mr. Blandings Builds His Dream House* remains an immensely enjoyable cinematic experience, and one which is not dated despite its reliance on a theme of topical interest to postwar Americans.

James P. Girard

MR. DEEDS GOES TO TOWN

Released: 1936
Production: Frank Capra for Columbia
Direction: Frank Capra (AA)
Screenplay: Robert Riskin; based on the novel *Opera Hat* by Clarence Budington Kelland
Cinematography: Joseph Walker
Editing: Gene Havlick
Running time: 118 minutes

Principal characters:
Longfellow Deeds .... Gary Cooper
Babe Bennett (Mary) .... Jean Arthur
Mac Wade .... George Bancroft
Cornelius Cobb .... Lionel Stander
Amy Faulkner .... Margaret McWade
Jane Faulkner .... Margaret Seddon

Mr. Deeds Goes to Town is a milestone in film history, the epitome of success and innovation in the comedy genre. It won Frank Capra the second of his three Academy Awards for direction, earned Gary Cooper his first nomination for Best Actor, and also launched that special brand of comedy unique to the 1930's, screwball. It was the first film to carry a director's name above the title, initiating a trend which has continued into the 1980's. *Mr. Deeds Goes to Town* was voted the Best Picture of 1936 by the New York Film Critics and the National Board of Review, and was also nominated by the Academy of Motion Picture Arts and Sciences for Best Picture of the Year, losing to M-G-M's *The Great Ziegfeld*. Unlike that film, however, *Mr. Deeds Goes to Town* has continued to be well regarded by film historians and audiences for more than forty years.

Director Capra's comic vision, which had achieved recognition previously in *Lady for a Day* (1933) and *It Happened One Night* (1934), crystallized in *Mr. Deeds Goes to Town*, which became quintessential Capra, containing many of the elements of humor combined with social comment that would become his trademark for the remainder of his career in such films as *Mr. Smith Goes to Washington* (1939) and *It's a Wonderful Life* (1946). In addition to being the first of the type, *Mr. Deeds Goes to Town* is one of the best, being a successful mixture of romance, comedy, and philosophy.

The film's protagonist, Longfellow Deeds (Gary Cooper), hails from Mandrake Falls, Vermont, "Where the scenery enthralls, where no hardship e'er befalls," according to the town motto. Living quietly in his small New England town, Deeds runs the tallow factory, plays the tuba in the town band, and composes poems for greeting cards. A homespun idealist, Deeds is the

romantic "All-American-boy" grown up. The name seems perfectly suited to
the man. He is a poet like his namesake and he is indeed a long-fellow as
portrayed by Cooper. The surname of Deeds is also apropos, for as the story
unfolds, his deeds are what make him famous.

The story is interesting but hardly new, even in 1936. The plot centers on
the age-old situation of boy meets girl, boy loses girl, boy gets girl. The story,
however, is no more than a clothesline upon which Capra hangs his themes
and character studies. The dramatic conflict arises in his characters, their
situations, and their world. Capra pits the city versus the country, the individual versus big business, and the cynic versus the idealist in the conflict
between the innocent Deeds and the hardened city dwellers who prey upon
him. Deeds wins the battle through his generosity, sensitivity, and the solid
moral core that guides his personal and social responsibilities. Director and
cowriter Capra's message is clear and simple: good can and will triumph over
evil.

The conflict begins when Deeds's multimillionaire uncle dies and quite
unexpectedly leaves his nephew a fortune. His uncle's slick New York City
lawyers immediately descend upon peaceful Mandrake Falls with their own
ideas about who should be handling Deeds's finances. They had been skim-
ming money from the millionaire's estate, and they want to make certain that
no country bumpkin will spoil their setup. The heir's priorities are quickly
established, however, when his interest in the millions is diverted by the
special-delivery arrival of a new mouthpiece for his tuba.

Deeds travels to Manhattan where he must settle his uncle's estate. The
money brings him trouble in the form of newspaper reporters and undesired
notoriety. Among the reporters clamoring for his story is Babe Bennett (Jean
Arthur), a wisecracking lady journalist. Babe is tough as nails on the surface,
but is, as we soon discover, a small-town girl underneath. She plays right into
Deeds's weakness when she disguises herself as "Mary," a starving, unemployed stenographer, and faints into his arms. In his mind, she becomes the
"Lady in Distress" of his dreams. Deeds promptly assumes the role of knight-
errant and proceeds to woo his lady fair. The romance blooms as "Mary"
shows Deeds the town. Innocently deeds tells her his hopes and dreams and
Babe surreptitiously relays them to her editor-in-chief Mac Wade (George
Bancroft). Mocking headlines about the "Cinderella Man" appear as the
unknowing Deeds falls in love with his betrayer. Meanwhile, his inheritance
has caused him so much trouble that he decides to put it to better use by
establishing a new community for unemployed farmers.

In order to avoid losing their income from Deeds's inheritance, the lawyers
arrange for relatives to contest the will. They charge Deeds with insanity,
pointing out that anyone would have to be crazy to give away twenty million
dollars. At this point, Babe, finally ashamed of her tricks and by now falling
in love with Deeds, quits the newspaper and is ready to admit her part in the

deception. Even winning the Pulitzer Prize for her "Cinderella Man" series has proven empty. News of her deceit reaches Deeds first. Disillusioned, Deeds falls prey to the scheming lawyers and is tucked away in a sanitarium. Unwilling to defend himself in his sanity trial, he sits silently in the courtroom, embittered toward humanity while a psychiatrist and policeman testify to his insanity.

Mr. Deeds Goes to Town ends in true Capra fashion. The farmers Deeds tried to aid plead with him not to give up the cause, and Babe finally proves that Longfellow's trust was not misplaced. On the stand she publicly confesses her love for him and helps him to win his case with her testimony.

The film's moods are mercurial, ranging from Deeds's café brawl with New York's poetic elite to his romantic Central Park interludes with "Mary," and finally to his philosophical contemplation of Grant's Tomb. Screwball antics abound, mixing physical and verbal comedy. For example, Deeds plays the tuba to think, chases fire engines, and feeds donuts to horses with a seriousness only Cooper could portray. Even Babe practices whimsical magic tricks in the newspaper office. Delightful sequences show Deeds and his uncle's servants trying out the echo in the mansion's foyer and the unforgettable Faulkner sisters testifying that Deeds was "pixilated" in court. These are examples of Capra's flights of fancy that still keep audiences charmed.

Although it is longer than most comedies of the period, *Mr. Deeds Goes to Town* never slows in pace. Capra's genius for rhythm and dialogue keeps the action pulsing. The film expresses Capra's commitment to the power of comedy to express moral ideas. His faith in the common man is seen in the script, which was adapted from the *Saturday Evening Post* serial "Opera Hat." The film is buoyant with a kind of populist optimism that provided welcome relief in the difficult Depression days. Happily, Frank Capra's moralistic message does not inhibit the comedy in *Mr. Deeds Goes to Town*; it only enhances it. As a result, the film still charms modern audiences with its optimism and comic grace.

The actors also add to the charm of the film, both on the star level, with Cooper's disarming innocence pitted against Arthur's street-wise toughness, and on the supporting level, for Capra had a genius for casting supporting roles. The villains were always evil and oily, and the "good guys" always had a certain likable character which lacked hypocrisy. Particularly good in this film is the cigar-smoking, cynical Cornelius Cobb (Lionel Stander), who admires Deeds's homespun naïveté despite his initial skepticism. In Capra's films, the characters who change are always the better for it. Those who are bad remain bad and often lose their fortunes as well, and those who are good never become bad. Even if they temporarily lose sight of "the right track," by the end of the story the "good guys" have triumphed over their adversaries.

Joanne L. Yeck

MR. LUCKY

Released: 1943
Production: David Hempstead for RKO/Radio
Direction: H. C. Potter
Screenplay: Milton Holmes and Adrian Scott; based on the short story "Bundles For Freedom" by Milton Holmes
Cinematography: George Barnes
Editing: Theron Warth
Running time: 100 minutes

Principal characters:
Joe Adams	Cary Grant
Dorothy Bryant	Laraine Day
Hard Swede	Charles Bickford
Captain Steadman	Gladys Cooper
Crunk	Alan Carney
Mr. Bryant	Henry Stephenson
Zepp	Paul Stewart
Mrs. Ostrander	Kay Johnson
Greek Priest	Vladimir Sokoloff

Cary Grant is the epitome of class, wit, and masculine sex appeal. Even into his late fifties, he could believably romance such younger stars as Doris Day, Audrey Hepburn, and Leslie Caron with movie audiences, particularly females, happily depositing their dollars at the box office to see him do so. Grant's rapport with the filmgoer is not based solely on his looks or screen presence; he is also an able performer and an uncommonly talented comedian. *Mr. Lucky*, his first solo starring effort, is far from the best film Grant ever made; in fact, its story line is quite unbelievable and even a bit offensive. The film is uplifted, however, by the participation of its star, and serves as an ideal vehicle for his talents.

Mr. Lucky was released at the height of World War II. Only during that era of national unity under the threat of the Axis onslaught could such a scenario not have been laughed off the screen. Grant stars as Joe Adams, a suave rogue and owner of the gambling ship, *Fortuna*. He is drafted at an inopportune time: he is seeking adequate cash to bankroll the expansion of his operations to Havana. The selfish Adams must therefore dodge the army. He assumes the identity of a deceased crony and hustles his way into a war relief organization which is short of money. After much difficulty, he persuades the group to allow him to operate a gambling concession at a charity ball. The organization thinks he is assisting them in raising $100,000 for medical supplies, while he is actually planning to slip off to the South Atlantic with the winnings.

A couple of plot twists intrude on Adams' plans. His former partner Zepp (Paul Stewart) moves in to grab the take for himself, and Adams learns that his dead friend was an ex-con. One more conviction, and he will be thrown into prison for life. There is, of course, the required happy ending. It is stressed throughout that Joe is a gambler, not a gangster. There is a difference: one is redeemable; the other, according to the Production Code, is beyond contempt. Joe is no criminal, just a misguided, self-centered gambler and draft-dodger. It is not necessary that a term in prison or a seat in the electric chair be his fate; as he is played by Grant, he is lovable and misguided rather than spineless and incorrigible. He is redeemed by a good woman, a virtuous heiress (Laraine Day) who falls in love with him. The film would not be complete if a woman did not succumb to his wit and charm. Likewise, he develops a similar affection for her. In the fairyland of 1940's Hollywood, love conquers all. Her perseverance and support eventually convert Joe into a moral, upright citizen.

Many critics applauded *Mr. Lucky* for its entertainment value and the "originality" of the draft-dodger angle; however, while the film is amusing if not taken seriously, its theme was at the time not unique. Seven years earlier, for example, in M-G-M's *San Francisco*, Clark Gable portrayed a gambler and adventurer, with the slick name of Blackie Norton, who saw the proverbial light via the love of virginal Jeanette MacDonald and the events of the day, the 1906 earthquake. In *Mr. Lucky*, the conversion of the not so sinisterly named Joe Adams (an all-American, everyman appellation even though he is played by a British-accented actor) from depravity to morality is pure corn. It is as realistic as Blackie/Clark giving up gambling, drinking, and skirt chasing for sweet Jeanette and her singing. *Mr. Lucky* is nevertheless still an effective piece of wartime propaganda with a message: even the low-lifes of America must place their own concerns second to the unity of the nation and the defeat of Hitler, Mussolini, and Tojo. The film is also uplifted by the presence of its star, who is essentially the entire show. Almost any other actor in the lead role would have transformed *Mr. Lucky* into a thoroughly implausible trifle.

The author of *Mr. Lucky*, Milton Holmes, was a former professional at the Beverly Hills Tennis Club. He had never written before, but wrote the scenario during a low period in his life. He gathered the courage to show his work to Grant, who agreed to star in the film for RKO. Holmes's dialogue in one sequence is glutted with rhyming slang, a type of gibberish which originated among vagrants in eighteenth century England. For example when Grant requests Day to "hand me the fiddle and flute" and "get your tit-for-tat," he is asking for his best suit and telling her to put on her hat. When Day, who learns the jive talk from a British butler and teaches it to Grant, wants to warn Grant of the presence of the police, she tells him about "a bottle and stopper," meaning "copper." The novice screenwriter did very well for his first film effort. Holmes's modest fee for the *Mr. Lucky* script, which he coauthored with Adrian Scott, was thirty thousand dollars down and a ten-week contract for an additional five thousand dollars.

H. C. Potter's direction is inventive. The film is technically creative in that points are made or characters and relationships established not solely by dialogue but by such cinematic techniques as distorted photography, striking camera angles, and exaggeration of sound on the soundtrack. This was not the only "Mr." film with Grant which Potter directed; five years after the release of *Mr. Lucky*, he worked with the actor again in *Mr. Blandings Builds His Dream House*, a film which was also typical of its postwar era. In the later film, a city couple (Grant and Myrna Loy) attempt to construct a house in the country and luxuriate in the American dream which could then presumably be attained in the wake of the Allied victory.

Mr. Lucky was the seventeenth film in which Grant starred that opened at New York's Radio City Music Hall. The titles of some of the others give evidence of his drawing power and of the quality of his work: *The Philadelphia Story* (1940), *Suspicion* (1941), *The Awful Truth* (1937), *Gunga Din* (1939), *Holiday* (1938), and others. At the time, no other actor had made so many starring appearances on the Music Hall screen. *Mr. Lucky* played to capacity audiences, due mostly to the popularity of its star, and was held over for nearly two months. Despite an excellent supporting cast (Charles Bickford, Alan Carney, Gladys Cooper, and Paul Stewart), Grant's presence dominates the film. The project seemed a worthy enough vehicle for a short-lived television series during the late 1950's, now remembered primarily for its beautiful theme music, in which the now obscure John Vivyan re-created Grant's role.

Rob Edelman

MR. PEABODY AND THE MERMAID

Released: 1948
Production: Nunnally Johnson for Universal
Direction: Irving Pichel
Screenplay: Nunnally Johnson; based on the novel *Peabody's Mermaid* by Guy Jones and Constance Jones
Cinematography: Russell Metty; underwater cinematography, David S. Horsley
Editing: Marge Fowler
Running time: 90 minutes

Principal characters:
Mr. Peabody .... William Powell
The Mermaid .... Ann Blyth
Polly Peabody .... Irene Hervey
Doctor Harvey .... Art Smith

When cinema wanders into the realm of fantasy, the laws of nature can be flouted at the snap of a director's finger: Mary Poppins flies through the air with an umbrella; a statue comes to life and falls in love in *One Touch of Venus* (1948); a man marries a witch and becomes governor of Massachusetts in *I Married a Witch* (1942); and a winged horse bucks its rider through the skies in *Clash of the Titans* (1981). Once the studio has completed its miracles of special effects, the product is generally received by audience and critics as innocent fantasy—escapist fare at worst, or perhaps, at best, a film with a morally uplifting message as in the case of the Academy Award-winning *Mary Poppins* (1964). Yet of all of Hollywood's mythic creations, filmmakers and film critics, in particular, seem to have difficulty in coping with one—the mermaid. Admittedly the mermaid is an awkward creature to have around. She can be a delightfully charming and sexy companion for two or three reels, and then as the protagonist falls in love with her she begins, like most anomalies, to present a problem. She is a fish, after all. Or is she?

A British film *Miranda* fared poorly at the hands of critics in 1949 because it concerned a London doctor (Griffith Jones) who, while fishing off the Cornish coast, was captured and imprisoned by an enterprising mermaid (Glynis Johns). To escape from his damp but emotionally rewarding captivity, the doctor agreed to take her to his home where she was installed as a wheelchair patient with her tail tastefully swaddled in a blanket. There was a purring sultriness about Miranda the mermaid that unnerved the doctor's wife and enslaved a visiting artist and a resident chauffeur. The film's final scene, which showed Miranda in Capri nursing somebody's baby, was scissored out of the American version to avoid offending public sensibilities. The film was a failure.

One other attempt at treating the mermaid myth was made in 1948. *Mr. Peabody and the Mermaid*, an American film, also suffered initially mixed reviews but has grown considerably in critical stature in the thirty-five years since its introduction. It has done so in spite of the fact that most critics still generally regard it a failure as a film of fantasy or whimsy. It is, strangely, as a film of realism that it succeeds remarkably well.

Mr. Peabody and the Mermaid was one of the first and perhaps the best cinematic treatments of the syndrome that has come to be known as "male menopause." Although the emotional side effects of menopause in women had been long recognized by psychiatrists and physicians, the similar psychological upheavals manifesting themselves in men approaching their fiftieth birthday had not been much discussed until comparatively recently. Blake Edwards' recent successful film *10* (1979) provides a textbook example of the syndrome featuring a successful middle-aged man who temporarily jettisons his career as well as a long-standing romantic relationship to pursue a twenty-one-year-old girl who is on her honeymoon. It is a fantasy, a last grasp at romance, but one involving a flesh and blood fantasy figure.

In *Mr. Peabody and the Mermaid*, Dr. Harvey (Art Smith), the film's psychiatrist, explains that the age of fifty is the dangerous age for males, and that a man reaching that age can expect almost anything to happen to him. He, in fact, fell in love with an ice skater when he turned fifty. She was very special. Not only was she beautiful but she was also a remarkable skater, and on a number of occasions she skated through the doctor's office window to keep him company. She gave this practice up, of course, and disappeared after the doctor got safely past the dangerous half-century mark.

The approach of the fiftieth birthday, then, incites in some men the frantic attempt to pursue the romantic illusions of youth, (the perfect "10," for example) one last time before they must turn sedately to the task of growing old. The illusion of romance, not the object of that emotion, is what is important in this last fling. Most men who indulge themselves will later feel foolish concerning the object of their desires but will forever bask in the memory of the emotion of being (or thinking they are) briefly young and vital once more.

Mr. Peabody at fifty is certainly as easy to believe and a lot easier to look at (as played by William Powell) than is the average man passing through a midlife crisis. Mr. Peabody, a Boston aristocrat, takes a Caribbean holiday with his wife Polly (Irene Hervey) to recover from a severe attack of the flu. While fishing, he lands a beautiful mermaid (Ann Blyth) by snagging her in the tail. Although pure fish from the waist down, from the waist up she is pure Hollywood and a fifty-year-old man's dream come true. Instead of throwing her back, Peabody takes the mermaid home and gives her the run of the bathtub, figuring that she will be just what the doctor ordered to relieve his gloom about getting old. Requested by Polly to get rid of that large fish, he moves her to the less confining expanses of the villa's oversized fishpond. Peabody quickly becomes more enamored of the mermaid than seems proper for a married Boston blueblood. She returns his affection, however, and at one point, bites a girl who is flirting with him.

Although Peabody personally loves his new friend just as nature presented her to him, his sense of propriety leads him to go shopping to buy her all of the clothes she will ever need—the upper part of a two-piece swimsuit. In an uproarious scene a flustered Peabody attempts to explain to a confused sales-girl why he only needs half of a bathing suit, and must finally buy it all and throw away the bottom part. The mermaid is now presentable, but, oddly, the only person in the film who ever sees her completely, is Peabody himself. Eventually, his wife, unable to bear up under the strain of her husband's odd behavior and of a situation she is unable to understand, goes back to Boston. Soon the local police, aware of Peabody's increasingly eccentric actions, sus-pect him of killing her, so Peabody forces himself to take the mermaid back to the sea and set her free. Feeling rejected, however, she lures him into the water and nearly drowns him in order to keep him on the bottom with her forever. He is rescued in the nick of time and returns home, where his wife takes him to a psychiatrist who warns him not to tell the story to anyone under fifty. He then attempts to explain Peabody's experience. Men around fifty, he states simply, are liable to start seeing things.

To the audience, Peabody's mermaid is no diaphanous manifestation of the mind. She is, as portrayed by Blyth, a fleshy and finny creature as only Hollywood can create. Some found Peabody's flirtation with a "fish woman" vulgar or a little obscene; yet the film is psychologically sound, and the situation is not any more extreme or necessarily more unrealistic than making love to a perfect "10" to the strains of Ravel's Bolero. Peabody, like T. S. Eliot's J. Alfred Prufrock, has a right to hear the singing of his own particular mermaid.

Nunnally Johnson's script adapted from the novel by Guy and Constance Jones is constructed with high good humor and a steady hand although it may not entirely overcome the fact that mermaids do not lend themselves to happy endings since they cannot settle down and live happily ever after. This fact probably led to the inconclusive drowning sequence at the end of the film. Yet at its best, which is the majority of the film, the script achieves laughter as well as insight into the psychological aspects of aging males.

Powell is perfect as a man who will never see fifty or a mermaid again. He needs all his long experience in playing a flustered man of distinction to confront a mermaid. Blyth needs only to rely upon her costuming to ensure her success in the film; yet she makes her emotions remarkably clear although given no lines at all. In one charming scene she dabs at her tears while under water. No words are possible—or needed. The remainder of the cast gives competent comedic performances, particularly Hervey as the frustrated Polly

Peabody. Irving Pichel's direction of Johnson's script is deft and lighthearted.

Although *Mr. Peabody and the Mermaid* misses the mark as a work of fantasy, it is an unusual film that overcomes its built-in limitations and scores as a piece of psychological realism. As such, it is an interesting entertainment with some insight into the psychology of men. Perhaps, however, it should be seen only by those over fifty.

Stephen L. Hanson

MOBY DICK

Released: 1956
Production: John Huston for Warner Bros.
Direction: John Huston
Screenplay: Ray Bradbury and John Huston; based on the novel of the same
  name by Herman Melville
Cinematography: Oswald Morris
Editing: Russell Lloyd
Running time: 115 minutes

Principal characters:

Captain Ahab	Gregory Peck
Ishmael	Richard Basehart
Starbuck	Leo Genn
Captain Boomer	James Robertson Justice
Stubb	Harry Andrews
Manxman	Bernard Miles
Carpenter	Noel Purcell
Queequeg	Friedrich Ledebur
Father Mapple	Orson Welles
Blacksmith	Ted Howard

Herman Melville's novel *Moby Dick* (1851) is a story of one man's dark
and foreboding obsession with hunting for a great white whale. Filled with
overtones of good and evil, of man struggling with himself and with God,
Moby Dick will always remain a complex, richly contoured tale of man in
combat with his emotions and with his environment. In 1930, Hollywood
attempted a film version of the novel that was, in the end, a poor substitute
for Melville's original story. Starring John Barrymore, the 1930 film changed
the narrative story, converting the passion of Captain Ahab in his search for
the white whale into bad melodrama with little, if any, resemblance to the
original work. *The Sea Beast* (1926) was another film version of *Moby Dick*,
with Barrymore again in the lead role. In 1956, John Huston, who produced
and directed such fine adventure films with subtle psychological touches as
The Maltese Falcon (1941), *The Treasure of the Sierra Madre* (1948), and *Key
Largo* (1948), directed a film of *Moby Dick* that managed to convey a good
deal of the novel's passion and drama. Although Huston did not attempt to
capture all of the complexities of Melville's lengthy discussions of the "nature"
of the sea and the whale as a mysterious creature of God, for example, he
did succeed in converting the novel into a film story of high adventure and
tragedy.

Huston spent nearly two years filming *Moby Dick*. Working with writer
Ray Bradbury on the filmscript, Huston wanted to make the film a study of

Ahab as a man caught up in a madness long nurtured by his solitary years at sea. At the same time, it was necessary for Huston to construct Ahab's world with great care: the whaling vessel *Pequod*, the ship's sailors who are subject to Ahab as lord and master of their lives, and the few characters, especially Ishmael, who are able to understand the source of Ahab's passion. In Huston's *Moby Dick*, everything is subservient to one major narrative purpose: the exploration of the character of Ahab, a man possessed.

The film is a stripped-down version of the novel. It begins with the narration by young Ishmael (Richard Basehart) of his arrival at the Spouter Inn in New Bedford, Massachusetts, the main port of the New England whaling fleets. Naïve, eager, and craving worldly adventure, Ishmael learns about Captain Ahab and his ship. Together with a "strange bedfellow," the harpooner Queequeg (Friedrich Ledebur), whom he meets in a boarding house, Ishmael signs on as a hand on the *Pequod*. Ishmael has heard strange things about Ahab, intimations of the captain's demonic drives, from an old sailor he meets in New Bedford. Still, he is willing to pledge several years of his life to a great adventure. Before he leaves New Bedford, Ishmael finds himself in the seaman's church, presided over by the stern-eyed Puritan divine, Father Mapple—a cameo role played by Orson Welles—who delivers an ominous sermon from the church's prow-shaped pulpit. Father Mapple warns his congregation about the dire consequences that will result if man trifles with God's will. Mapple's bellowing sermon is an ominous beginning for Ishmael's journey with Captain Ahab.

Ishmael soon learns that the real purpose of the *Pequod*'s voyage is the continuation of Ahab's obsessive hunt for the white whale. Ishmael soon becomes aware of the maniacal intentions of Ahab. As his face seems to age with worry, Ahab (Gregory Peck) storms in his cabin, ranting at the injustice to which he has been subjected over the long years: being maimed by the white whale on a previous voyage, and coming close to, but never killing the animal. Through several well-photographed scenes in Ahab's cabin showing the captain's eyes staring at his nautical charts or at the setting sun through the porthole, the intensity of the man's emotions is revealed.

The voyage of the *Pequod* continues. Soon the ship's crew becomes imbued with the vengeful lusts of Ahab. Ishmael turns to the first mate, Starbuck (played by the great English character actor Leo Genn), for advice and counsel. Starbuck tells the young man about Ahab's past, his obsessions, and his need for revenge. For the first time, Ishmael begins to understand the Biblical quality of the whaling vessel's voyage. Every plan and movement of the *Pequod* has been determined by the central purpose of revenge against Moby Dick. Ahab finally sights and overtakes the white whale. Several of the ship's best harpooners, including Queequeg, are sent out with Ahab in long boats to kill the enormous creature. The white whale, as furious in his movements as are the men attempting to kill him, attacks the boats. Ahab flings his great harpoon into the whale's side, ensnaring himself in the weapon's lines. Now firmly lashed to the object of his hatred, Ahab stabs and stabs at his mortal enemy as the whale submerges. With Ahab now hanging lifeless, lashed to its side, Moby Dick attacks the *Pequod*. In a final spasm of hatred and energy, the wounded creature rams the ship. The *Pequod* sinks, and all of her crew except Ishmael are lost.

Almost all of the structural elements brought together by Huston in the filming of *Moby Dick*—the whaling ships, the men who sail them, and the environment that sustains them—are combined with a story line of immense power. There is a keen sense of period awareness, as director, writers, and players convey what it is like to be part of a lost world. Peck, as Ahab, rages at his fate in an accurately designed setting carefully constructed to replicate the trappings of a nearly forgotten time. Huston wanted to capture the flavor of the seagoing world of corruption, idealism, and greed. We see the whalers working on a ship ingeniously crafted to resemble an actual nineteenth century whaling vessel; we listen to the ship's sailors talking in the now-lost cadences of early New England; and we note how these men speak of their lives and of Ahab, the man who governs them. Each man on the *Pequod* has his own reasons for following Ahab, yet each man also shares the captain's passionate desire for vengeance and the kill.

Although Huston does not succeed in capturing all the nuances of Melville's novel, he does effectively focus on the central character of Ahab. Peck makes Ahab a combination of the sinister and the benign, a man set apart by the intensity of his emotions and drives. Ahab's unholy mission becomes a sinister voyage into destruction, and Huston's dramatic rendering of that mission will stand as a well-crafted attempt to envision how man can become as flawed as the imperfect world he despises with such fervor.

Larry S. Rudner

A MODERN HERO

Released: 1934
Production: Warner Bros.
Direction: G. W. Pabst
Screenplay: Gene Markey and Kathryn Scola; based on the novel of the same name by Louis Bromfield
Cinematography: William Rees
Editing: Jim Gibbons
Running time: 70 minutes

Principal characters:

Pierre Rodier	Richard Barthelmess
Mme. Azais	Majorie Rambeau
Joanna Ryan	Jean Muir
Claire Benson	Verree Teasdale
Leah	Florence Eldridge
Hazel Rodier	Dorothy Burgess

In Germany, Georg Wilhelm Pabst was a film director of great importance from the silents in 1923 to the talkies in 1933. He was also the last of the noted German directors to be imported to Hollywood. Warner Bros. brought him over in 1934 and gave him a choice assignment and an equally choice star to direct. The property was Louis Bromfield's novel, *A Modern Hero*, about a heartless young man who rises, step by step, using both men and women to reach the goal to which he aspires. He reaches the top, a man of wealth and property, but is rejected, and his kingdom topples overnight. It is a moral tale, based on the Biblical warning, "For what does it profit a man to gain the whole world, and lose his soul?" The star was Richard Barthelmess, who had acted brilliantly in the silents under directors D. W. Griffith and Henry King; he successfully survived the transition into talkies, and during the first half of the 1930's made some exceedingly popular films at the studio to which he was under contract—Warner Bros/First National.

Yet Pabst's film of *A Modern Hero*, released early in the spring of 1934, puzzled the critics, who found it generally uneven and lifeless, lacking the brilliance that had sparked his German films. Although the popularity of Barthelmess was still stable, his public did not respond to this motion picture, and he made only one more; his contract was not renewed. Pabst was dumbfounded; he had anticipated the kind of success which Ernst Lubitsch, F. W. Murnau, G. A. Dupont, and other émigré directors had known in Hollywood. *A Modern Hero* is interesting, but mostly because it is the only Hollywood film Pabst directed. Nobody seems to know exactly what happened subsequently. Pabst must have had a contract for more than one film, but if he did, the terms were not honored. Very quietly he left for France and then went on to Austria; he was embarrassed, and avoided telling people why he had come back. He was Czech-born and was a very sensitive man; this was the first failure he had been forced to endure, and he could not face it. The assumption in Hollywood, probably correct, was that Warner Bros. had become indifferent to him, finding his one film too downbeat, and had terminated his contract by paying him off, as frequently has happened before and since.

Actually, *A Modern Hero*, as Bromfield wrote it, is a very interesting story very much in the vein of Paul Muni's *The World Changes* (1933) and Edward G. Robinson's *Silver Dollar* (1932). Perhaps it was too much like those two films; or perhaps it was a misguided effort on the part of the studio to turn Barthelmess into an older dramatic player. By 1934, Barthelmess was thirty-nine years old; for the first time he was showing signs of his years and needed a cinematographer with a soft-focus lens.

A Modern Hero is the story of a young circus rider named Pierre (Richard Barthelmess) who will do anything to get up in the world. His mother is Madame Azais (Marjorie Rambeau), a fortune-teller in a sideshow tent who reads the future and knows that her son will gain a fortune but know no happiness. There is a young girl, Joanna (Jean Muir), who in other circumstances might have provided a wonderful love and life for Pierre, but he only betrays her, leaving her pregnant, taking material means from her, and moving on to another woman. This woman, Leah (Florence Eldridge), helps him corner the market on the bicycle trade, and when he has got what he wants from that, he moves on to still another woman and another station of life, manufacturing automobiles. He is completely unscrupulous. All that he wants from the women who help him move up the ladder of success is money and position. He marries one woman Hazel (Dorothy Burgess), in order to get her father's money, and then steps into the upper bracket of wealth in the world of finance and manufacturing. He thinks he has the world in his hands, when he is discarded by Claire Benson (Verree Teasdale), the last woman in his life, who is cannier than he. The riches he had stored up are gone—and so, ultimately, is he.

Pabst was at his best in the earlier sequences in the circus and carnival scenes, for this was the kind of international, glamorous background that appealed to him. Barthelmess is at his best also in these sequences as the handsome young circus rider who has a way with women, and his mother, a gypsy fortune-teller played by Rambeau, gives what is the most colorful performance in the film; her character is the only one really presented dramatically. Muir, a frail blonde who was then the bright hope at Warner Bros., plays Joanna, to whom Pierre at least gives a child, which is more than he gives to any other woman.

On the surface, *A Modern Hero* presented Pabst with the kind of background he had used to advantage in German films. His failure to achieve distinction with the story may have been caused by his unfamiliarity with the English language. He himself spoke English acceptably, but he did not really communicate in the language, a fatal drawback in any director's makeup. He could control the action and the camera, but he had to have a dialogue director to help him guide the players. The cinematography by William Rees is uncommonly good, especially in the circus scenes, because Pabst understood the camera and how to tell a story dramatically with it.

Pabst's first big success had been with a 1925 silent about postwar life in Vienna, *The Joyless Street*, important today because it was Greta Garbo's second big feature and her last in Europe before she was put under contract by Louis B. Mayer and came to Hollywood and M-G-M. In 1928 Pabst directed a realistic romance, a precursor *film noir* called *Pandora's Box*, which brought him great fame and is today the one motion picture by which he may be known, because it has become a cult film, remembered for what he did in it and how he used the talents of an American movie actress, Louise Brooks, who had been misused in Hollywood and abandoned. The next year, 1929, Pabst starred Brooks again in *Diary of a Lost Girl*, which brought him and her additional fame. His talking films in the early 1930's are still outstanding: an antiwar feature, *Westfront 1918* (1930), confirmed his reputation; *The Threepenny Opera* (1931) showed him using melodrama, music, comedy, and all that was bizarre to dramatic effect; *Kameradschaft* (1932) featured a German mining story with much of it filmed in documentary style in a German mining town; *L'Atlantide* (also 1932) was a beautiful film pictorially; and *Don Quixote* (1933) presented the great Russian opera star, Chaliapin.

These and others preceded Pabst's being signed by Warner Bros. and brought to Hollywood. The European films remain unique and prove his versatility in handling all kinds of scenes. The question remains, why did he fail with *A Modern Hero*? It is not a classic story, but neither essentially were *Pandora's Box* and *Diary of a Lost Girl*, and Pabst took those bleak, realistic tales and made them cinema masterpieces. Why were Barthelmess and all the women excepting Rambeau so ineffectual in *A Modern Hero*? Did Pabst see in Rambeau something of the dazzling personality, the glitter that had attracted him in Brooks? Perhaps we shall never know, because Pabst never wanted to discuss *A Modern Hero*. Lotte Eisner has written that Pabst spoke of the obligation of his returning to Europe because of his family's change of situation there, building a string of excuses that seemed perfectly in order, but that in the end only seemed to confirm his lack of success in America as the reason for his departure. In any event, one cannot dismiss *A Modern Hero* as just another movie that did not quite succeed, because its lack of success had such a determining effect on the careers of both Pabst and Barthelmess.

Barthelmess, all too aware of his age and wanting to continue as a film hero, went to England in 1936, ostensibly to film a costume romance, *A Spy of Napoleon*, which he did; but then he went quietly off to a sanitarium and had cosmetic surgery done on his face. Whatever the result, it was not good, for he was idle for two years, presumably in seclusion somewhere. He then returned to acting, but on the stage in the lead of a dramatization of James Cain's *The Postman Always Rings Twice* for the Theatre Guild. This led to his return to films, not as a star, but as a character player. The handsomeness evident in Griffith's *Broken Blossoms* (1919) and *Way Down East* (1920) and the youthful virile sensitivity that Henry King had drawn from him in *Tol'able David* (1921) were gone. So was the attractive modern youthfulness he displayed in *The Patent Leather Kid* (1927) and *The Noose* (1928), both of which brought him an Academy nomination as Best Actor in the first year of the Awards. He played the aviator husband of Rita Hayworth who proves himself in *Only Angels Have Wings* in 1939, and he played several other effective character roles such as The Dealer in the 1942 version of *The Spoilers* with John Wayne, Marlene Dietrich, and Randolph Scott. After that, during World War II, he went into the service, went to sea, and never made another film. *A Modern Hero* had been as much of a turning point for him as it had been for its gifted director, G. W. Pabst.

DeWitt Bodeen

MONSIEUR VERDOUX

Released: 1947
Production: Charles Chaplin for United Artists
Direction: Charles Chaplin
Screenplay: Charles Chaplin; based on an idea suggested by Orson Welles
Cinematography: Roland Totheroh
Editing: Willard Nico
Running time: 123 minutes

> *Principal characters:*
> Henri Verdoux .... Charles Chaplin
> Marie Grosnay .... Isobel Elsom
> Annabella Bonheur .... Martha Raye
> The Girl .... Marilyn Nash

"I like women, but I don't admire them." This statement, spoken by Charles Chaplin in *Monsieur Verdoux*, provides the keynote for the film itself. Henri Verdoux is a contemporary Bluebeard who makes a career out of marrying wealthy women and then murdering them for their fortunes. *Monsieur Verdoux* is Chaplin's most controversial film, as well as one of his personal favorites.

Henri Verdoux is a happily married man, devoted to his crippled wife and their young son. Serious business problems, however, have left him in desperate financial straits, and he has developed a deadly scheme which enables him to support his family. Under various aliases, Verdoux has married a series of women, gained control of their money, and then murdered them. As the film begins, he has just disposed of the body of one of his wives in an incinerator, after which he attempts to seduce Marie Grosnay (Isobel Elsom), a woman who is viewing his house in hopes of buying it. His plan fails, however, and Verdoux proceeds to another town, where he is known as Monsieur Floray. Here, too, he has a wife whom he murders, and whose fortune he takes for himself.

After a visit to his family, Verdoux pays a call on Annabella Bonheur (Martha Raye), yet another illegal wife. His plans for Annabella, however, seem to fail at every turn. She refuses to give him control of her finances, and she unknowingly avoids all of his attempts to kill her. Verdoux learns of a new poison which leaves no trace when the victim's body is examined, and he decides to test its effectiveness on a stranger before using it on Annabella. He meets a destitute young girl (Marilyn Nash) on the streets of Paris and invites her to his apartment for dinner. As Verdoux prepares the meal and mixes the poison with the girl's wine, the two discuss life and love, and he learns that she had been sent to prison for stealing in order to provide for her late invalid husband. Verdoux feels a bond between himself and the girl, and he exchanges her poisoned wine for a fresh glass at the last minute. The girl leaves, thanking him for his kindness, not knowing how close she has come to death.

Verdoux returns to Annabella with a peroxide bottle filled with the poison, but her maid uses the contents of the bottle on her hair and replaces the bottle with another. Verdoux uses this bottle to poison Annabella's wine. She remains unharmed as the bottle contains only peroxide, but her maid loses her hair. Verdoux then takes Annabella out to the middle of a lake in a rowboat, but his attempts to push her overboard result in his falling into the water and being rescued by Annabella.

Verdoux abandons his efforts to murder the seemingly invincible Annabella, and begins, instead, to court Marie Grosnay, whom he has met again. She agrees to marry him, but Annabella arrives at the party beforehand and Verdoux is forced to flee to avoid recognition.

Several years pass, and Verdoux once again encounters the girl he had nearly poisoned. Their positions are now reversed: she is the mistress of a wealthy munitions manufacturer, while Verdoux's wife and son have died and his finances have failed. The girl takes him as her guest to a restaurant, where he is recognized by relatives of one of his murdered wives. Verdoux sees the girl safely out of the restaurant, then gives himself up to the police.

During his trial, Verdoux states that his crimes have been no greater than those of the governments and munitions men who wage wars against one another. He believes that a society involved in large-scale slaughter and corruption leads to the corruption of the individuals who live within it, and that his own crimes are only a pale reflection of the world around him. He goes to his execution telling the priest who visits him that he is at peace with God; his quarrel is with man.

Monsieur Verdoux was the first film in which Chaplin made a complete departure from his famous Tramp character. *The Great Dictator* (1940), with its character of the Jewish barber, had served as a transition away from the Tramp, but it was not until 1947 that Chaplin abandoned his baggy pants and derby for the urbane, immaculately tailored character of Henri Verdoux. Indeed, Verdoux is deliberately as far removed from the Tramp as Chaplin could make him. The Tramp is shy and unlucky with women; Verdoux is irresistibly attractive. The Tramp has a childlike quality of innocence and mischief; Verdoux is a calculating murderer. Finally, and most importantly, the Tramp represents all that is best in man—his courage, love, and perseverance—while Verdoux is a symbol of man's darkest side, of the depths to which he can be brought.

Chaplin's performance as Verdoux is fascinating, and his comic artistry remains at its usual high level. The film suffers, however, from an excess of dialogue, particularly in those scenes involving Verdoux and the girl. Although Chaplin's philosophizing is interesting and unusual, its presence tends to slow the overall pace of the film. Its talkiness aside, however, the film's screenplay is well-constructed and was nominated for an Academy Award.

Along with Chaplin himself, the most memorable presence in *Monsieur Verdoux* is that of Raye. Her performance as Annabella Bonheur is an outrageously funny portrait of good-natured vulgarity. The contrasts between Annabella and Verdoux are brilliantly drawn, and their scenes together are among the film's best. These scenes are made doubly amusing by the fact that Verdoux clearly finds her company unbearable, yet is forced to pretend love for her in order to carry out his plan. Verdoux's cultured, impeccable manner is in a state of constant confrontation with Annabella's noisy lack of refinement, and it is precisely this quality of oblivious coarseness which manages to save her, time and again, from the cunning stealth of his intentions. Verdoux must at last resign himself to the fact that Annabella is impervious to subtlety of any kind, even that involving murder.

The idea for *Monsieur Verdoux* was suggested to Chaplin by Orson Welles, who felt that the story of the French murderer, Charles Landru, would make an interesting film. When Chaplin decided to pursue the project, he paid Welles for the idea, but a controversy grew up over the years between the two men over how much Welles had contributed to the actual script of the film.

The conflict with Welles was only one of the areas of dispute in which the film was involved. Several critics expressed displeasure over Chaplin's comic treatment of murder, commenting that he would do well to return to the Tramp character in his future films. *Monsieur Verdoux* was conceived shortly after Chaplin's much-publicized paternity suit, and much of the film's underlying bitterness is certainly a result of his feelings toward Joan Barry, the young woman in question. In addition, *Monsieur Verdoux*'s release came at the height of Chaplin's difficulties during the McCarthy period, and the film's bizarre tone and antiwar sentiments provided additional fuel for his accusers. As was to happen with *Limelight* (1952) later, *Monsieur Verdoux* became a target for those groups which were angered by Chaplin's refusal to become an American citizen, and a press conference following the film's New York opening was turned into a cross-examination of Chaplin's political beliefs by several members of the audience. *Monsieur Verdoux* did not enjoy the success that Chaplin's previous pictures had had, and it has only been in recent years, with the fading of public feelings against Chaplin, that the film has come to be judged on its own merits. Chaplin's personal fondness for the film was no doubt due, in part, to the many problems it encountered, and there is perhaps a trace of defiance in this statement from his autobiography: ". . . I believe *Monsieur Verdoux* is the cleverest and most brilliant film I have yet made."

Janet E. Lorenz

MONTY PYTHON AND THE HOLY GRAIL

Released: 1974
Production: Mark Forstater for Python Pictures and Michael White for EMI;
  released by Cinema 5
Direction: Terry Gilliam and Terry Jones
Screenplay: John Cleese, Graham Chapman, Terry Gilliam, Eric Idle, Terry
  Jones, and Michael Palin
Cinematography: Terry Bedford
Editing: John Hackney
Music: Neil Innes
Running time: 90 minutes

Principal characters:

King Arthur/and others	Graham Chapman
Sir Lancelot the Brave/ Black Knight/French Knight/Tim the Enchanter/Large Man with Dead Body/and others	John Cleese
Patsy (Arthur's trusty steed)/Soothsayer/and others	Terry Gilliam
Sir Robin the Not-Quite-So-Brave/Roger the Shrubber/Brother Maynard/Cart Driver/and others	Eric Idle
Sir Bedevere/Dennis' mother/Prince Herbert/ and others	Terry Jones
Sir Galahad the Pure/ Dennis/King of Swamp Castle/Soldier With a Keen Interest in Birds/and others	Michael Palin
The Witch	Connie Booth
The Owner of a Duck/and others	Neil Innes

A Very Famous Historian/
The Dead Body Who Says
It Isn't .... John Young
Three-headed Knight .... Terry Jones,
          Graham Chapman, and Michael Palin
The Knights Who Say
"Ni" .... Michael Palin and others

The film's credits may give the viewer the initial impression that *Monty Python and the Holy Grail* is not quite . . . well, normal. It starts off well enough, with the film's title appearing in white letters on a black background; but an instant later a subtitle appears: Mønti Pythøn ik den Hølie Gräilen. This is the first in a series of "Swedish translations" which accompany the credits; "translation" is soon abandoned, however, for the likes of "Wi nøt trei a høliday in Sweden this yër?," and the film's "real" credits are locked in a losing battle with the absurd subtitles. Soon, every other credit seems to have something to do with mooses (or rather, møøses), even though we have been tendered an apology and advised that "those responsible have been sacked." In the wake of the møøse invasion comes another disclaimer: "The directors of the firm hired to continue the credits after the other people had been sacked, wish it to be known that they have just been sacked." Does this herald the return of sanity? Not at all: the "Executive Producer" credit reads "John Goldstone & 'Ralph' The Wonder Llama"; the producer's assistants are "Earl J. Llama, Mike Q. Llama III, Sy Llama, and Merle Z. Llama IX." And so on.

This credits sequence—surely the most bizarre in motion-picture history—is just a typical bit of work for the comedy troupe Monty Python, composed of five Englishmen (John Cleese, Graham Chapman, Eric Idle, Terry Jones, and Michael Palin) and one American (Terry Gilliam). The six first got together in 1968, and scored a big hit on British television with *Monty Python's Flying Circus*, a half-hour show which ran from 1969 to 1974. The program (and their record albums) also gained for them a large following on the other side of the Atlantic. It was first shown in the United States on public television stations beginning in the fall of 1974, and has been shown frequently since then.

The members of Monty Python are masters of the comedy of the absurd and the unexpected. One possible description of their style is "comic anarchy," which invites comparison with the Marx Brothers. On that score, however, it is safe to say that the Pythons make the Marxes look like Republicans. Groucho, Harpo, Chico, and sometimes Zeppo carried out their shenanigans primarily within the restrictions of some of the most narratively uninspired and cinematically pedestrian films in motion-picture history. In marked contrast to the Marx films, the Pythons' television shows and films are among the least inhibited ever made. The group simply runs wild, seizing control of every frame of their films and turning them topsy-turvy. The operative assumption behind their humor is "Be silly, then be sillier, then move on to something else—quickly." Admittedly, this is not everyone's idea of a good time. There are probably many people who consider Monty Python about as funny as death and taxes, but that is all right with them. They are likely to express their sentiments by suddenly cutting away to a room full of, say, nuns and cricket players chanting "Not funny, not funny," and then crush the lot of them beneath a giant cartoon foot. You cannot please *everybody*, especially when it comes to comedy.

At first, the group's *very* British humor (much fun is made of regional accents, among other things) would seem likely to be lost on American audiences. Its underlying basis, however, is simple disrespect for convention—which in various guises has been delighting audiences at least since the days of the Keystone Kops. Nothing, as the saying goes, is sacred, and to the Pythons this includes the medium itself. The basic assumptions which lie at the heart of nearly all films—that is, the orderly progression of incidents towards a unified whole, and the notion of "distance" between performers and audience—are blithely tossed out the window. Anything can happen, and usually does.

There are obvious limitations to this approach. Monty Python's anything-to-be-silly attitude sometimes becomes silly-for-silly's-sake, and the threat of comic overkill is always in the wings. Within the half-hour television format, the formula works superbly; stretched to feature-length, it occasionally wears thin. This was demonstrated by the group's first tentative venture into films, *And Now For Something Completely Different* (1971), a collection of their most popular television skits. It is intermittently hilarious but ultimately tedious and overlong at eighty-eight minutes. *Monty Python and the Holy Grail* (1974), released in the United States in 1975) is a different matter. Its more or less well-observed story line serves nicely as a framework on which to hang numerous short satirical bits, and also provides another set of conventions—the rules of narrative—which, of course, the Pythons take great delight in occasionally subverting (as when a character asks the audience, "Do you think this scene should be cut?").

It is difficult to synopsize *Monty Python and the Holy Grail*, a free-wheeling lampoon of the Arthurian legend of the noble Knights of the Round Table, with a straight face. The film begins as King Arthur, accompanied by his servant Patsy, is seen riding through the English countryside. Well, not "riding," exactly; they do not have any horses, so they just trot along on foot while the servant bangs two half coconuts together in imitation of hoofbeats. This equestrian mockery gets them into an argument with a soldier, which evolves into a discussion of the migratory habits of swallows. In the next scene, a dark and dirty medieval street, a cart driver collects the bodies of plague victims; a large man attempts to dispose of a body despite its protests ("I'm not dead . . . I feel fine!"). Meanwhile, Arthur has a run-in with the peasant Dennis, a member of an anarcho-syndicalist commune, who resents being treated as an inferior by the King; "I didn't vote for you," chimes in Dennis' mother. Moving along, he next finds it necessary to do battle with the Black Knight, who puts up fierce resistance even after Arthur has cut off both his arms and legs ("All right," relents the Knight, "we'll call it a draw"). Entering a village, the King engages the comradeship of Sir Bedevere, whom he assists in attempting to convince a mob of superstitious louts not to burn a young woman they suspect of being a witch. The crowd concludes, however, that because she weighs the same as a duck, she is made of wood, and therefore floats in water, and is a witch. They burn her anyway. During a brief interlude, the turning pages of a book inform us that Arthur has also been joined by Sir Lancelot the Brave, Sir Robin the Not-Quite-So-Brave, Sir Galahad the Pure, and "the aptly named Sir Not-Appearing-In-This Film" (who, of course, does not). They proceed to Camelot, where they discover a music-hall type revue in progress; knights are dancing on tables and singing: "We dine well here in Camelot. We eat ham and jam and Spam a lot." "C.. second thoughts," concludes the King, "Let's not go to Camelot. It is a silly place." There immediately ensues a conversation between Arthur and a rather irritable God (an animated figure peering through animated clouds), who charges the Knights with a sacred task—to seek the Holy Grail. "Good idea, O Lord," says Arthur. "Course it's a good idea!" booms God, insulted.

The film is barely under way. Yet to come is a very famous historian, who delivers a few moments of ponderous historical analysis before being slain by a knight on horseback. He is followed by an incredibly rude French knight, who claims that his master's "already got one" (a Holy Grail, that is), and then bombards Arthur and his men with assorted livestock. Next are the Knights Who Say "Ni," who demand the sacrifice of a shrubbery ("One that looks nice. And not too expensive!"); the battle to the death with a killer rabbit who is finally defeated with the Holy Hand Grenade of Antioch; and much, much more. Things proceed pretty much in this vein until the climactic battle scene is just about to begin. Suddenly the police arrive and arrest Arthur and Bedevere for the murder of the Historian, and the film ends abruptly. Incidentally, they never do find the Holy Grail.

Hopefully, this "synopsis" conveys something of the narrative structure and comic flavor of *Monty Python and the Holy Grail*. Also important, however, is the overall visual design. The film was shot on location in Scotland, and the castles and countryside, along with the excellent costumes and the careful cinematography, contribute to a strikingly authentic period look that effectively counterpoints the absurd goings-on. The direction is credited to Gilliam and Jones, but the film is a collaborative effort in almost every way. All six members of the troupe receive screenplay credit, and they follow the custom of their television show by playing multiple roles, including many of the female characters. Their versatility is amazing and delightful and adds a great deal to the "nothing sacred" spirit. The animated sequences, another staple of the television series, are designed by Gilliam. They are funny because they are so deliberately unsophisticated, with cut-out figures scurrying about the frame, and because they are likely to pop up at any time, usually in the place of expensive special effects. The scenes with God and the ferocious twenty-three-eyed (approximately) Beast of Aaaargh are extremely effective.

Monty Python and the Holy Grail takes satirical aim at everything in sight and hits most of its targets squarely, if sometimes a little sloppily. It is an ambitious undertaking, and although it threatens to bog down occasionally, it is entertaining and inventive throughout. The film's major weakness is inherent in the group's style. Ninety minutes is simply a long time to sustain their nonstop goofiness without any "serious relief." The constant flood of absurdity can become wearing to all but their most ardent fans.

Howard H. Prouty

THE MOON AND SIXPENCE

Released: 1942
Production: David L. Lowe, Jr. for United Artists
Direction: Albert Lewin
Screenplay: Albert Lewin; based on the novel of the same name by W. Somerset Maugham
Cinematography: John F. Seitz
Editing: Richard L. Van Enger
Music: Dmitri Tiomkin
Running time: 89 minutes

Principal characters:
Charles Strickland	George Sanders
Geoffrey Wolfe	Herbert Marshall
Dirk Stroeve	Steve Geray
Blanche Stroeve	Doris Dudley
Dr. Coutras	Albert Basserman
Mrs. Amy Strickland	Molly Lamont
Ata	Elena Verdugo
Tiare Johnson	Florence Bates

The prodigious output of novels, short stories, and plays by W. Somerset Maugham, often regarded as this century's greatest storyteller, has provided the motion-picture medium with many hours of entertainment. The majority of his works that have been adapted to the screen are high-class melodramas in which the female characters—sometimes bordering on the clichéd—are larger-than-life femme fatales. The most famous screen representation of a Maugham heroine is, of course, Bette Davis' brilliant performance as Mildred in *Of Human Bondage* (1934). Other Maugham heroines have been excellently portrayed by Gloria Swanson as Sadie Thompson in *Sadie Thompson* (1928); Jeanne Eagels as Leslie Crosbie in *The Letter* (1929); Joan Crawford as Sadie Thompson in *Rain* (1932); Greta Garbo as Karin in *The Painted Veil* (1934); and Bette Davis as Leslie Crosbie in *The Letter* (1940). Other noteworthy films based on Maugham works include *The Razor's Edge* (1946) and *Quartet* (1949).

While Maugham's female characters have always been fascinating and popular on screen, his 1919 novel, *The Moon and Sixpence*, provides no such heroine, and probably would have been a better novel and film if it had, despite its popular success. The novel basically is a *roman à clef* interpretation of the tormented life of French Impressionist painter Paul Gauguin. Gauguin was born in Paris in 1848 and spent the first thirty-five years of his life in conventional pursuits. He was married, had a family, and was a member of a prosperous brokerage firm, dabbling in painting on the side. He resigned from the brokerage house in 1883 with the firm intention to devote his life to painting. He aligned himself with the Impressionists and participated in their last great exhibition in 1886. He then deserted his family entirely and spent the next five years working in Martinique, Brittany, and Arles (with Van Gogh), and finally, in 1891, he made his famous journey to Tahiti where he developed his revolutionary style. Rejecting his former objective, representational style of painting, he chose to reveal his interpretation of life and beauty via the subjective expression of Impressionism and ultimately discovered entirely new ground in art through the use of vibrant colors and exotic depictions of the primitive life of the South Seas. He died in 1903 on Marquesas Isle.

Maugham told his story in the novel through a third-person narrator (Maugham himself, as in the *The Razor's Edge*), and Gauguin's life bears numerous similarities to Maugham's own. Maugham himself had given up a career as a physician to pursue a life of writing, and his marriage, which produced one daughter, ended in a breach as decisive and final as that of Gauguin. Through the protagonist of *The Moon and Sixpence*, Charles Strickland (George Sanders), and the narrator, Geoffrey Wolfe (Herbert Marshall, who played the character again in *The Razor's Edge*), Maugham endeavored to reveal the reason why a man of genius must mercilessly fight himself, his family, and the conventions and restrictions of society in order to seek that destiny in which he so strongly believes.

With Gauguin's life as his model and inspiration, Maugham set *The Moon and Sixpence* in his native England. In a pleasant English drawing-room, Amy Strickland (Molly Lamont) is entertaining several literary friends. Her mind is not on her guests, but instead on the telephone call she is expecting from her brother-in-law. When the call comes and she leaves the room, her guests delight in commenting on the dullness of her stockbroker husband Charles. On the telephone Mrs. Strickland learns that her husband has deserted her and is in Paris to paint. This artistic mistress is more than Amy can bear, and she exclaims that she hopes he never comes back and that he starves.

In Paris, Charles Strickland is befriended by a fellow-painter, a Dutchman named Dirk Stroeve (Steve Geray), and his wife Blanche (Doris Dudley). It is the cold of winter, and Strickland is lying ill and impoverished in his studio. The Stroeves take him into their studio to recuperate. He begins to paint again, including a nude of Blanche done without her husband's knowledge. Although Strickland harbors an utter disdain for women and the shackles they imply, he enters into an adulterous affair with Blanche. When Strickland announces he is going to the South Seas, Blanche blurts out that she must go with him. Stroeve is shattered by his wife's infidelity with his friend but is too weak-willed to stop her, and walks out on them both. When Strickland cold-bloodedly informs her that she cannot go with him to the South Seas, Blanche, full of remorse and grief at losing both of the men in her life, walks into the bedroom and shoots herself.

Strickland then travels to the South Seas and takes up a life of painting, taking on odd jobs only long enough to earn money to buy painting supplies. He becomes known as "the quiet one," a beachcomber, a drifter. The proprietress of the local hotel, Tiare Johnson (Florence Bates), reproaches him for his desultory life and is finally able to convince him to take a native wife, Ata (Elena Verdugo), who has a small plantation on which he can live a more normal existence and still be free to paint. Strickland does so, and he and Ata have a child. His painting goes well and his life seems idyllic except for a number of brown patches on his face and arms. Dr. Coutras (Albert Basserman), a local resident, visits Strickland and realizes that he is suffering from leprosy. He implores Strickland to go off to the mountains to live alone but Ata will have none of it, saying she will stay with him until he dies. Strickland accepts his fate and makes Ata promise that after his death she must burn their home, on the walls of which is his greatest work: a mural of Adam and Eve in the Garden of Eden.

More than a decade has passed and once again in England, Amy Strickland is hosting a dinner party for a number of art critics who are discussing her late husband. The guests are shown portfolios of Strickland's work, and the celebrity-conscious Mrs. Strickland explains that it was her interest in art and literature which inspired her husband to create his masterpieces. Maugham's irony is both chauvinistic and bitter.

Albert Lewin's presentation of his "brilliant and brooding novel" is faithful to Maugham to a fault, and that is the shortcoming of the film. It is unrelentlessly serious and sombre and, despite good intentions, fails to come alive. This is probably true of almost every film which has ever depicted the life of a creative genius. It absolutely fails in its attempt to illuminate that quirk behind genius which drives the artist in his unscrupulous search for beauty. With the inner fire of the artist remaining an illusion on screen, the film becomes little more than the story of a tormented man with contempt for society, convention, and women. This, too, was a failing of Maugham's novel, which, while holding the creative artist sacred, fails to explain his soul. Many critics felt that in 1942 the novel was already dated and had little relevancy at a time when the world was torn by war.

Sanders is appropriately acerbic and contemptible as Charles Strickland. Sanders recalled in his memoirs that one line of dialogue, which said in effect that the more you beat women the better they are for it, caused him a great deal of anguish with women fans. Despite that fact, he explained, he agreed wholeheartedly with both Maugham and Gauguin on the subject. Marshall as narrator Geoffrey Wolfe appears here for the sixth time in a Maugham film. This was also essentially Marshall's last leading role in his lengthy career, the remainder of which would consist of supporting parts. Previously Marshall had played the lover of Jeanne Eagels in *The Letter*; the husband of Greta

Garbo in *The Painted Veil*; and the husband of Bette Davis in the later version of *The Letter*. Later he played Maugham himself in *The Razor's Edge*.

As cinema, *The Moon and Sixpence* suffers a weakness that seems inherent in the motion-picture medium: the inability to reveal the demon of despair behind genius and the creative process. Attempts have been made to do so, with varying degrees of success, in four noteworthy films about artists made after *The Moon and Sixpence*. *Moulin Rouge* (1952) contains a virtuoso performance by José Ferrer as Henri de Toulouse-Lautrec and remarkably colorful (literally) depictions of Paris life, but the lurid details and sadness which drove this artist to alcoholism and death are fancified for cinematic effect. 1956's *Lust for Life* deals with both Vincent Van Gogh (Kirk Douglas) and Paul Gauguin (Anthony Quinn, who won an Oscar for his supporting role), but the film is based on Irving Stone's romanticized novel and reveals little of the despair and frustration of either artist. *The Agony and the Ecstasy* (1965) stars Charlton Heston as Michelangelo and is quite successful in its analysis of that great genius, but the 1950 Oscar-winning documentary *The Titan* (directed by Richard Lysford and narrated by Fredric March) probably remains the finest cinematic exploration of the life of an artist.

Ronald Bowers

THE MOON IS BLUE

Released: 1953
Production: Otto Preminger
Direction: Otto Preminger
Screenplay: F. Hugh Herbert; based on his play of the same name
Cinematography: Ernest Laszlo
Editing: Otto Ludwig
Running time: 99 minutes

Principal characters:

Donald Gresham	William Holden
David Slater	David Niven
Patty O'Neill	Maggie McNamara
Michael O'Neill	Tom Tully
Cynthia Slater	Dawn Addams
Television performer	Fortunio Bonanova
Taxi Driver	Gregory Ratoff

The film *The Moon Is Blue* is not remembered for the usual reasons. Although the performances are competent, professional, and at times even skillful, they are no more so than the performances given in other more notable films released at the same time. The story or plot is amusing to a degree, but slight and difficult to remember. The artistic effects of *The Moon Is Blue* are adequate but draw no special comment. *The Moon Is Blue* does, however, have historic significance in that it was the first American film made for general distribution to be released without the all-important Code seal issued by the Motion Picture Production Association, that is, the Hayes Office.

The Moon Is Blue concerns the adventures of a twenty-two-year-old girl from Brooklyn, Patty O'Neill (Maggie McNamara), who is picked up on the top of the Empire State Building by young and prosperous architect, Donald Gresham (William Holden). Most of the remainder of the film takes place in Gresham's apartment or the nearby apartments of the Slaters: David (David Niven), a middle-aged playboy, and his daughter Cynthia Slater (Dawn Addams). Cynthia is Donald's estranged fiancée.

Patty informs Donald that while he can hug or embrace her or even attempt seduction if he wants to try, she is not going to give up her virginity until after she is married. The free-talking and very moral Patty is seeking an honorable man in an honorable relationship. However unassailable the heroine's virtue may be, her conversations with the architect are outspoken, and the two of them discuss topics such as virginity, seduction, and pregnancy with much candor. The wide-eyed and cute Patty, wearing Peter Pan collars, asks such forthright questions as "would you try to seduce me?" and "do you have a mistress?" Supplementary action, complications, and contrasts are given to the story by the role of David, who also tries to seduce Patty; the appearance of Michael O'Neill (Tom Tully), Patty's father, who punches Donald in the nose; and the various appearances of Cynthia. Cynthia feels that Donald did her wrong, and part of her grudge is that she feels that he treated her in too gentlemanly a manner on their last date and hence did not show enough interest. *The Moon Is Blue* ends on a highly moral note, as the virtuous Patty, by asking disarming questions and remaining firm, finally gets her man on her own terms, and a marriage is in the offing. A show of real virtue and goodness is able to subdue man's baser instincts.

The violation of several heretofore spoken taboos in *The Moon Is Blue* was calculated; it was hoped that this would cause controversy upon its release in 1953, and indeed it did. The denial of a Code seal, its condemnation by the Catholic Church, and the attendant publicity made the public want to see it even more. If the then-pervading morality led the public to expect a depiction of sin, most viewers were only titillated. *The Moon Is Blue* was a successful commercial film, and its very success permitted later filmmakers to consider more explicit treatments which would be made in the future. Never again would the issuance of a Code seal carry the same weight to American filmmakers, distributors, or the public.

Since the time of the initial release of *The Moon Is Blue*, morals and conventions have changed considerably, both on film and in society. Judged according to current standards, the concepts and reasoning in this film seem quaint, silly, and dated. Today's audience would be more likely to laugh *at* the film (and often they do) rather than laugh in appreciation. Insignificant as it may be in itself, however, *The Moon Is Blue* made a significant contribution in the direction of freedom of expression for the film medium. Prior to this film, certain subjects were treated with broad gestures, by implications, or by mere hints. With the appearance and success of *The Moon Is Blue*, sexual subjects began to be freely discussed and even flippantly mentioned in respectable films. For this reason, even a mediocre film such as *The Moon Is Blue* is always to be remembered in film history.

Mark Merbaum

MOONRISE

Released: 1948
Production: Charles Haas for Republic
Direction: Frank Borzage
Screenplay: Charles Haas; based on the novel of the same name by Theodore Strauss
Cinematography: John L. Russell
Editing: Harry Keller
Running time: 90 minutes

Principal characters:
Danny Hawkins	Dane Clark
Gilly Johnson	Gail Russell
Grandma	Ethel Barrymore
Clem Otis	Allyn Joslyn
Mose	Rex Ingram
Billy Scripture	Henry Morgan
Ken Williams	David Street
Aunt Jessie	Selena Royle
Jimmy Biff	Harry Carey, Jr.
Jerry Sykes	Lloyd Bridges

Theodore Strauss's novel, *Moonrise*, a somber tale of psychic depression and murder in a small Virginia town, was one of the best-sellers of 1947. Garson Kanin had originally planned to film it, with John Garfield in the starring role. Then the film rights were acquired for $125,000 by Marshall Grant Productions, which offered James Stewart $335,000 and approval of casting and director if he would accept the leading role. Thankfully, Stewart turned the offer down, for he was much too old for the part and too relaxed an actor for such a tortured characterization. Eventually, Marshall Grant Productions joined forces with producer Charles K. Feldman and took the project to Republic, where Feldman and his director Frank Borzage were at that time headquartered.

Moonrise was the third and final film Borzage directed for Republic—the other two were *I've Always Loved You* (1946) and *That's My Man* (1947)—and it is considered by many critics to be the director's greatest sound film. It was certainly one of the most important films to come out of Republic in the 1940's, and *Variety* (September 9, 1948) hailed it as "one of the finest produced pictures the valley studio has ever boasted." *Moonrise* was Borzage's last great screen achievement—he directed only two other films after *Moonrise*—and marked the end of a career which had included such triumphs as *Seventh Heaven* (1927), *A Farewell to Arms* (1932), *Man's Castle* (1933), and *The Mortal Storm* (1940). In many respects *Moonrise* is an unusual Borzage film, for it is a complex, psychological drama, lacking the simplistic outlook of his earlier productions, but here, as in most of the director's films, love triumphs over adversity and the young lovers are reunited at the end, even though they must face a far from certain future, with the boy at the least guilty of manslaughter.

The film opens with an execution by hanging, viewed in shadow, with shots of legs walking to the gallows in the pouring rain. As the trap is sprung, there is the sound of a baby's cries on the sound track and a cut to a toy dangling by a string above the baby's cot. Short sequences show the child growing up and being taunted at school by his classmates with cries of "Danny Hawkins' dad was hanged." The next shot is again of a pair of legs—those of Danny Hawkins (Dane Clark)—walking through the swamp for an encounter with Jerry Sykes (Lloyd Bridges, in one of his briefest screen appearances), one of Danny's childhood tormentors. The two men become involved in a bloody fight, and in a fit of drunken rage Danny beats Sykes to death with a piece of rock. He drags the body into the swamp, but in the process loses his pocket knife.

Danny is full of anger, given to irrational outbursts of violence and hatred, a hatred built up inside of him because of what happened to his father. It transpires that Danny's mother had been given the wrong tablets by a doctor and, as a result of the tragic mistake, had died. With the same anger that we see Danny display, the father had gone into town and murdered the doctor. Danny's anger also results in a car crash, soon after he has forced his attentions on Jerry Sykes's girl, Gilly Johnson (Gail Russell), the local schoolmistress. There is also a gentler side to Danny, however, as in his defense of a deaf-mute named Billy Scripture, who is gently and effectively played by Henry Morgan. In a touching scene, later in the film, Billy Scripture finds the footprints he had made as a child in the sidewalk cement, but cannot understand why his feet will no longer fit them.

Danny and the schoolmistress develop a strange fondness for each other, but she is never quite certain of his behavior and is concerned that his erratic actions will damage her standing in the community. They meet in an old abandoned Southern-style mansion, in which the schoolmistress imagines the romanticism of the old South. Across the way from the mansion lives Mose (Rex Ingram), a retired black, who raises dogs for coon hunting. As played by Ingram, the character of Mose is as far removed from Hollywood's stereotyped black as it is possible to be. He is intelligent, a philosopher who ponders why people should wish to retire from the human race. He calls his favorite animal Mr. Dog, because "there isn't enough dignity in the world." Mose is the one totally stable human being in the film, the only person unable to say an unkind or malicious word.

It is Mose and his dogs who find Jerry Sykes's body, while coon hunting with Danny and a group of would-be hunters. At the same time, Billy Scripture finds Danny's knife, but fails to understand its significance or why Danny should make such furious and violent efforts to get it back. Gradually Sheriff Clem Otis, played in a laconic fashion by Allyn Joslyn, suspects Danny of the crime. In one marvelous sequence, the sheriff and his wife survey Danny and his girl as the four ride in a ferris wheel at the county fair. Danny's guilt overcomes him and he leaps from the wheel, giving the sheriff further reason to suspect he is the murderer.

Pursued by the sheriff and—unwillingly—by Mose and his dogs, Danny stumbles through the swamp to the house of his grandmother (Ethel Barrymore) in the hills. She helps him come to terms with his past and face the future and what it may hold for a murderer. Barrymore appears for approximately three minutes in the last reel of the film, despite her sharing top billing with Clark and Russell. Barrymore certainly dominates the scene in which she appears, however, and the playing of a lesser actress in such a crucial role would have severely undermined the film.

Danny walks down the hill to the sheriff's party, to Mose, and to his girl. The two lovers embrace, and Mose welcomes Danny back to the human race. Danny is free of the terrors and the hatreds that have engulfed his young life, and for the first time in the film, there is a scene with an abundance of light.

Moonrise is a dark, somber film, shot entirely on studio sets—even the swamp is an indoor set—and in many ways it is a claustrophobic film, its melancholy gripping not only Danny but also the audience. Its only light moments concern Housley Stevenson as a civil war veteran who keeps asking who Danny is and remarking that he was not a Yankee. Clark is well cast as Danny Hawkins. He is not the screen's usual attractive leading man, and his face has a haunted, somewhat unintelligent quality to it. Similarly, Russell is well cast as the schoolmistress, definitely an actress of the 1940's but not very good-looking.

The film was regarded by many contemporary critics as ninety minutes of monotonous gloom, and its director was attacked for showing too much concern with camera angles and too little interest with entertainment. Certainly the film's box-office potential was limited. Today, however, *Moonrise* has found its proper place in the history of the cinema, and one critic has even gone so far as to describe it as sublimity squared.

Anthony Slide

MORGAN!

Released: 1966
Production: Leon Clore for Quintral/British Lion
Direction: Karel Reisz
Screenplay: David Mercer; based on his BBC television play *Morgan: A Suitable Case for Treatment*
Cinematography: Larry Pizer and Gerry Turpin
Editing: Victor Proctor
Running time: 97 minutes

Principal characters:
Leonie Delt .... Vanessa Redgrave
Morgan Delt .... David Warner
Charles Napier .... Robert Stephens
Mrs. Delt .... Irene Handl
Mr. Henderson .... Newton Blick
Mrs. Henderson .... Nan Munro
Policeman .... Bernard Bresslaw
Wally .... Arthur Mullard
Counsel .... Graham Crowden
Second Counsel .... Peter Cellier
Judge .... John Rae
Best Man .... Angus Mackay

Morgan!, directed by Karel Reisz and based on a BBC television play by David Mercer, begins in London with the private siege of an eccentric young artist who is resisting his upper-class wife's desire to end their marriage in favor of a more stable relationship. It ends on the grounds of a mental hospital, the meaning hanging on what the viewer determines to be victory or defeat, madness or sanity. Reisz, part of the British reaction among filmmakers against conventional cinema techniques, directed *Saturday Night and Sunday Morning* (1960), and then went on to produce *This Sporting Life* (1963), before tackling the ambiguities and vague social dissatisfactions that are at the center of *Morgan!*

The film begins as Morgan Delt (David Warner), ape fancier, irreverent Marxist, and allegedly promising painter, comes back from a holiday in Greece to discover that his wife, Leonie (Vanessa Redgrave), has filed for divorce in his absence and plans to marry Charles Napier (Robert Stephens), a sleek art dealer and former friend of Morgan. An extension of the "angry young man" character of several earlier British films, Morgan feels an anger that focuses itself on defying the conventions of bourgeois marriage, political conformity, and presumably traditional art (although we never see his work) in an attempt to build a society comparable to that of the gentle, herbivorous great apes that he idealizes: a society of warmth and spontaneity.

In an effort to recapture Leonie's love and reestablish his fantasies on firm financial as well as emotional ground, Morgan mounts an escalating campaign of alternating charm and potentially murderous violence that ends with the abduction of his by now irritated wife to a lonely and romantic lake site in Wales.

Depending on whether his situation is seen as the result of narcissistic self-indulgence or the result of unsympathetic forces of class and politics gone haywire, his behavior is more or less explicable and symbolic. His outrage at Leonie's pending marriage expresses itself in shaving hammers and sickles on her poodle and on an angora rug. He plants a skeleton in her bed to discourage her art dealer lover and a bomb under a bed where his former mother-in-law (Nan Munro), is sitting, and even manages to seduce Leonie in a vulnerable moment. Whatever counter impulse she responds to when she chooses the more manageable Napier over Morgan, Leonie is drawn again and again to Morgan's disruptive charm and imagination. It is clear that it will not last, but it is also evident that she feels the pain of knowing this as deeply as he.

Between attacks on Leonie and her lover, Morgan escapes to the home of his mother, a fussy, lovable eccentric (Irene Handl), who, like Leonie herself, helped to buffer him from the need for responsibility. A cockney Marxist who provides much of the warm, sentimental humor in the film, she reminds Morgan at one point that her dead husband ". . . wanted to shoot the royal family and put everyone who had been to public school in a chain gang. He was an idealist, your Dad was." On another occasion she tells him, "We brought you up to respect Marx, Lenin, Harry Pollitt." If Morgan has flaws in his mother's eyes, it is his lapsed political sensibility and his marriage to an upper-class woman in betrayal of the Communism of his parents. If Morgan has a politics, it is not the politics of class but of the personal and the fantastic, the Rousseauian imagination that expends itself in visions of free, tree-swinging primitives like Tarzan and King Kong. Morgan's incongruent violence against Leonie and Napier he explains by asking, "Where has gentleness got me? Violence has a kind of dignity in a loving man."

Even the violence of love and dignity, although mild, has a social cost that Morgan discovers when he disobeys the court injunction by kidnaping Leonie and taking her to Wales. He finds himself in jail and as a consequence trades in his vision of the gorilla as mild-mannered jungle pacifist for an avenging if outnumbered King Kong. He dresses in a gorilla suit and undertakes as a final desperate mission the disruption of Leonie's wedding. It is a curiously sad spectacle for such a theatrical statement, and what is missing is the tension that persists in the early segments of the film, the sense that the tension between Morgan and Leonie has a possibility of resolution. Morgan scales the walls of the London hotel where the reception is taking place, crashes into the room, and when pursued, escapes on a stolen motorcycle and ends up in a charred heap. Morgan in a burning gorilla suit is just one step over the line from the stuffed gorilla in flames early in the film. Now, dazed by the crash, he has a hallucination in which his friends and mentors threaten to destroy him.

The final scene is played out several months later when Leonie, now pregnant, visits Morgan at a mental institution where he is cheerfully tending his symbolic garden of hammer-and-sickle design. When he asks Leonie if the child is his, the answer is an acquiescent smile and a laugh—a kind of Pyrrhic victory considering his incarceration. What is unclear is whether Morgan's commitment to an asylum out of society is meant to stand for an inevitable repression of natural man or whether Morgan, after dependence on Leonie and his mother, has simply opted for another kind of retreat from responsibility. Reisz's subtitle for the film, "A Suitable Case for Treatment," suggests that despite the comic resolution, Morgan's triumph may not be absolute.

Reisz is skilled and effective at getting what he wants out of the camera, using techniques such as speeding up frames or freezing the action to reflect the moods and circumstances of focal character. Clips of the original *Tarzan, The Ape Man* (1932) and *King Kong* (1933) films are edited into the action and effectively demonstrate the intensity with which Morgan leans on his imaginary mentors to shore up his waning success in the real world.

Morgan! launched the careers of Warner, whose work with the Royal Shakespeare Company includes *Henry VI* and *Richard II*, and Redgrave, who was an Academy Award nominee for Best Actress as the flighty, equivocal Leonie. Redgrave did win the Best Actress award at the 1966 Cannes Film Festival for her performance. Although the film is ambiguous and slightly dated today, it has become something of a cult film and is frequently shown in revival houses. It is a worthwhile example of the type of filmmaking which was going on in England in the 1960's, a time which was known as "Hollywood on the Thames."

Joyce Olin

MOROCCO

Released: 1930
Production: Paramount
Direction: Josef von Sternberg
Screenplay: Jules Furthman; based on the play *Amy Jolly* by Benno Vigny
Cinematography: Lee Garmes (AA)
Editing: Sam Winston
Running time: 97 minutes

Principal characters:
Tom Brown .... Gary Cooper
Amy Jolly .... Marlene Dietrich
Kennington (Labissiere) .... Adolphe Menjou
Adjutant Caesar .... Ullrich Haupt

Marlene Dietrich's first American film, *Morocco*, is the second in a collection of films Josef von Sternberg directed starring her. Sternberg had previously made *The Blue Angel* (1930) with her in Berlin, which starred Emil Jannings. Considered by some to be the best of Sternberg's talkies, *The Blue Angel* made history by introducing Dietrich as Lola Lola, who, in the words of one critic, embodied "a new incarnation of sex." Her cool insolence, impassivity, and callous egoism suggested some secret which she provocatively concealed not only in manner but also behind a veiled voice which sang of her interest in "lovemaking and nothing else." Sternberg discovered Dietrich on a Berlin stage and became her mentor, creating the Dietrich mystique and mythology onscreen which carried over offscreen as well. The six pictures he made with her in the ensuing five years, *Morocco*, *Dishonored* (1931), *Shanghai Express* (1932), *Blonde Venus* (1932), *The Scarlet Empress* (1934), and *The Devil Is a Woman* (1935), were progressively drained of action and continuity as the presence of Dietrich and Sternberg's resonate images became all-engrossing for the director until finally even Dietrich's charisma and fame could no longer attract the public. In *Morocco*, however, the melodramatic romance between Dietrich and Gary Cooper provides the needed continuity for Sternberg's abstract considerations of film form.

Sternberg was captivated with images that often were not integral to the story. Emotional relationships and psychological detail were more important to his sensibilities than were story and chronology. There is almost a spiritual quality in his use of light, decor, and minutely observed facial and body gestures. He uses devices such as diffusers and gauzes over the lens to create a heavy, dreamlike atmosphere. His *film noir* lighting would have lent a totally existential ambience if a sharper, more defined and realistic focus had been employed.

Morocco has seldom been equaled as an example of the proper function of dialogue in film, demonstrating Sternberg's pioneering in the use of long silences between speeches in talkies. While the narrative is unfolded primarily through images, sound (only natural sounds were employed to heighten effect), and music, the sparse dialogue perfectly accents and punctuates the story's progress. *Morocco* can be considered a transition film as Sternberg combined a silent film visual technique with sound and a new kind of heroine. The lack of background music in this and others of his early sound films suggests a sharp, immediate quality.

Sternberg's characters are prisoners of their own illusions, and he supports his theme with his visual style, saying, in essence, that we are all prisoners of illusion. His expressionistically exaggerated visual quality, *film noir* lighting, and *mise-en-scène* technique represented the instability of the times, while the subject matter was escapist. His sets, which were always stylized evocations of exotic places rather than realistic or actual locales, his flamboyant costumes, unusual decor, and rich use of detail, as in the cluttered dressing room and apartment of Amy Jolly in *Morocco*, underscore this theme of illusion. A forerunner of *Casablanca*, (1942), *Morocco*'s baroque and expressive exoticism came to the screen complete with the complex light patterns cast by sunlight filtering through overhanging vines and lattices as well as between one of Sternberg's favored pictorial devices, slatted shutters. These shutters and resultant horizontal shadows reappeared in the majority of Sternberg's later films, whether set in Spain, Russia, New Orleans or China. *Film noir* later replaced the shutters with Venetian blinds for a similar effect.

Another central issue, as important to Sternberg's vision as living and dying in illusion, is the gradual loss of strength or power of a once strong human being. A romantic fascination with evil, personified by the *femme fatale*, is integral to the loss. Although still representing hedonism, vice, corruption, and the fatal pursuit of pleasure, Sternberg's fatal woman is not merely a seductress who lures men to destruction; the character takes on new dimensions, becoming more complex. Sternberg enhanced the mystery and added a more direct and honest approach to sex.

Dietrich, the quintessential *femme fatale* of films, sails into *Morocco* on a steamer through a dense fog. The other people on the boat are in light colors and can barely be seen in the mist, but Dietrich wears black which makes her stand out and which also enhances her beautiful bone structure and sensuous lips. Dietrich's natural beauty, accented with exotic make-up (thin, high-arched eyebrows, shadowed cheeks and eyes, long applied lashes, and accented mouth), combine with Sternberg's casual and cool posing of her in draped costumes, feathers, and veils, to epitomize glamorous and sophisticated sex. Dietrich's physical features and presence were perfect for the entertainer-prostitute roles she played in Sternberg's films. Her appeal is not merely sexual, earthy, or voluptuous; rather, it is completely sensual. She is tough yet delicate and combines the aura of a vamp with the mystery of Greta

Garbo. This appeal, and the flexibility of her facial expression, especially the ability to say so much with her eyes together with Sternberg's ability to capture this on the screen, enhanced the prostitute characterization as well as that of the glamorous entertainer. Dietrich's facial expressions could evoke more than one reaction. Sternberg used his polyphonic play of features, which Béla Balázs, the film theorist, defines as ". . . the appearance on the same face of contradictory expressions," to say a great deal. In *Morocco*, the first shot of the actress' expressive face tells the audience that Amy Jolly is world-weary. Sternberg presents her character as having no illusions about life other than maintaining her own illusion, her façade, the *persona* she presents to others. She is searching, as do most of Sternberg's female protagonists, for what she wants but is not quite sure what it is.

In this initial confrontation in *Morocco*, it is not difficult to understand the reactions of the critics and audience to Dietrich. A critic said in 1931, "*Morocco* is notable for the presence of a startlingly beautiful and unusually competent newcomer, the German blonde, Marlene Dietrich, whose . . . acting is an extraordinary exhibition of power, poise, lucidity, and beauty . . . ." He went on to say that Dietrich projected the psychic essences of Greta Garbo and Jeanne Eagles. More recently, Andrew Sarris has said that Sternberg's characters generally make their entrances at moments in their lives when there is no tomorrow and then struggle to discover the truth about themselves and the people they love. For Amy Jolly, there definitely appears to be no tomorrow. She comes to Morocco, the last stop on a path to nowhere, to sing in a café. It is here that Tom Brown (Gary Cooper), a French Foreign Legionnaire, falls in love with her. She is delivering a song in her unique pathos-tinged style. One of the numbers with which she mesmerizes Brown has become infamous as a result of suggested homosexuality. The Dietrich *persona* flirted between male and female, which became part of the mystery. She wore men's clothes on and off the screen, making slacks the fashion rage for women. In this particular sequence in *Morocco*, she appears in a tuxedo and sings her love song to a pretty woman whom she kisses upon the mouth.

Amy Jolly returns Tom's love, but when Tom has to leave to join his regiment, she accepts the marriage proposal of the wealthy Kennington Labissiere (Adolphe Menjou). On the night of their engagement celebration, she hears the legionnaires returning from their expedition and runs from the elegant dinner to find Tom in an Arabian café. Knowing of her engagement, he pretends that he no longer cares for her. After he leaves, she discovers that he has carved her name into the wooden table where he was sitting. The following day, the legionnaires leave once again. Amy gives up a future of security and wealth to follow her love through the desert in a famous scene in which she trails along after a group of prostitutes and native women who make up the "rear guard," following their men despite any hardship and leaving winding footprints across the desert.

Dietrich's delicacy and ability to soften her very expressive face added to the believability of love winning out. Dietrich possessed a dual screen personality. One was the romantic, as in *Morocco*, the other the romantic antithesis, as in *The Blue Angel, The Scarlet Empress,* and *The Devil Is a Woman.* In *Dishonored* there is a conflict between the two personalities with love eventually winning out. In that film she has the power to destroy her lover in the end, for she has won; but instead, she chooses to sacrifice herself to the firing squad. Love is always equated with self-debasement and/or destruction in these Sternberg-Dietrich vehicles.

There were four Academy Award nominations for *Morocco*: Dietrich for Best Actress; Hans Dreier for Art Direction; Lee Garmes for Cinematography; and Sternberg for Directing, but none of them won.

Tanita C. Kelly

THE MORTAL STORM

Released: 1940
Production: Frank Borzage for Metro-Goldwyn-Mayer
Direction: Frank Borzage
Screenplay: Claudine West, Andersen Ellis, and George Froeschel; based on
the novel of the same name by Phyllis Bottome
Cinematography: William Daniels
Editing: Elmo Vernon
Running time: 100 minutes

Principal characters:

Freya Roth	Margaret Sullavan
Martin Brietner	James Stewart
Fritz Marberg	Robert Young
Professor Victor Roth	Frank Morgan
Otto von Rohn	Robert Stack
Mrs. Victor Roth	Irene Rich
Erich von Rohn	William Orr
Mrs. Brietner	Maria Ouspenskaya
Holl	Dan Dailey
Franz	Ward Bond

In June of 1940 before the United States became a combatant in World War II, both Britain and Germany were waging fierce, unofficial propaganda campaigns in America attempting to sway public opinion in favor of their respective causes. Books and films were an integral part of these campaigns. In 1938, Phyllis Bottome wrote the best-selling *The Mortal Storm*, an anti-Nazi book with an emotional plea for men of conscience to fight the menace of Fascism. M-G-M made a movie of the book, placing the story in the Germany of 1933, safely tucked into the category of "history," albeit recent history.

Frank Borzage directed Margaret Sullavan and James Stewart in what at first seems a curious bit of casting. The audience is asked to believe that Stewart, playing Martin Brietner, and Sullavan, playing Freya Roth, are German students caught in the tide of violence that accompanied Hitler's rise to power. Germany was, in this case, a studio backlot designed to look like a European university town. Further, Frank Morgan is cast as Freya's father, Professor Victor Roth, a dignified, "non-Aryan" teacher (non-Aryan was M-G-M's very clumsy way of saying Jew). Morgan had been seen previously in *The Shop Around the Corner*, released in January of 1940, in which he played the cranky but lovable storekeeper, Alfred Kralik, whose gift shop in Budapest employed Sullavan and Stewart as clerks.

Taking this trio from a delightful romantic farce and casting them in a tragedy later the same year would seem to be of dubious value, but *The Mortal Storm* succeeds in spite of its obvious flaws. Backlot scenery and romantic melodrama are overcome by the uniformly excellent performances of both principals and supporting players and by the intelligent restraint exercised in direction.

The story begins as Victor Roth, an eminent professor of physics, celebrates his sixtieth birthday surrounded by his students, faculty, and family. Most of the university gathers as he is presented a commemorative statue by students Fritz Marberg (Robert Young) and Martin Brietner, both of whom are in love with the professor's daughter, Freya. Roth addresses the gathering, reminding his students that the search for scientific truth should not be overshadowed by any other principle. As family and friends gather for a birthday dinner in the professor's home, Fritz announces his engagement to Freya over her objection that she is not ready to say yes. Fritz, amiable but pompous, sweeps aside her reservations, and Freya laughingly consents to the engagement. The family is delighted, and Martin is a good sport—he is Fritz's friend as well as a rival for Freya's affections.

As the celebration continues, the maid interrupts to announce that Adolf Hitler has just been appointed Chancellor of Germany. Fritz and Roth's Aryan stepsons, Otto (Robert Stack) and Erich von Rohn (William Orr), are delighted. They rush to the radio to hear the news, while the professor and his wife (Irene Rich) remain at the table with Freya and Martin exchanging worried looks. When Mrs. Roth asks her jubilant sons what will happen to non-Aryans like their stepfather, they shrug off her fears: "But mother, men like father are an honor to Germany," Otto reassures her.

The professor declares he will wait and see what the "new Germany" brings. Fritz adopts the Nazi outlook, assuming women have no head for politics, and ignores Freya, turning instead to Martin, demanding that he now make up his mind and join the party. Martin, son of an old and honorable farm family, replies, "Peasants have no politics. We keep cows." Fritz persists, however, claiming that those who are not with them are against them, and the confrontation is broken off only when Freya reminds them that this is a family celebration.

All of the attitudes represented here are carefully drawn with a minimum of preaching. The von Rohn boys are exuberant followers, Fritz Marberg a stuffy bore, Martin Brietner a reserved man of the land who keeps his own counsel. In Professor Roth the audience sees a character who partly answers the puzzle presented by so many Jews in Germany. Why did he adopt a wait-and-see attitude when the National Socialists had made their intentions quite clear? Professor Roth considers himself a completely assimilated Jew. He is a respected scholar with prestige and position, honored by all around him. The film thus presents a credible portrait of an intelligent man who decides to remain in Germany because he feels secure in his position.

This security is quickly eroded. In scenes that contrast starkly with those that opened the story, Professor Roth again faces a crowded lecture hall. This time, however, all the students are in uniform, and when he attempts to demonstrate that there is no difference in the composition of Aryan and non-Aryan blood, his class is boycotted. A Nazi bully named Holl (Dan Dailey) calls for the boycott, and Fritz Marberg is among those who walk out. He is a fine student and fully aware that scientifically the Nazi position has no basis, but party loyalty impels him to follow Holl's lead. Young is really the standout here in a fine cast. He does an excellent job of portraying the German whose nationalism faces him with hard choices. The audience wonders what he will not do in the name of duty. His class deserted, Professor Roth carries on experiments in an empty lab, shunned by his students and colleagues. He bears lonely witness to a barbarous and terrifying scene in which students burn the books of Freud, Einstein, and other scholars banned by the National Socialists. The Germany he thought he knew is dying.

When an old tutor is assaulted by Nazi thugs, Martin and Freya rush to his aid, causing a final rupture in Martin's friendship with Fritz and the von Rohns and estranging Fritz and Freya. We see Martin and Freya drawing closer to each other. Professor Roth is then arrested and sent to a concentration camp. Freya, frantic to locate her father, appeals to Fritz Marberg. He gives her the information in the name of their old love. Fritz is becoming a cog in the efficient Nazi machine, but he has not yet completely divested himself of human compassion. Young is never the one-dimensional bad guy, and his struggle with himself is one of the most interesting aspects of the film. When Mrs. Roth visits her husband, she finds him aged and ill, and he tells her to leave the country. The professor has become a tragic victim, but Morgan gives him a dignity that prevents his scenes with Rich from becoming maudlin. The concentration camp scenes, like the book burning, are particularly effective because they are not at all sensationalized. The facts as they were known in 1940 were quite enough to horrify anyone. By avoiding theatrical horrors in favor of factual evidence the director makes a more damning statement.

The professor's family refuses to leave until they hear of his death. They then flee to Austria, but Freya is carrying her father's manuscript and is detained at the border and returned to Germany. She waits in the family house until she receives a message from Martin, who has been unable to reenter the country since he helped an old friend escape to Austria. Freya meets Martin at his home in the mountains, and his mother (Maria Ouspenskaya) sends them off on a perilous flight. They must ski to the safety of Austria through dangerous mountain passes. Franz (Ward Bond) and Holl beat the escape plans out of a young servant girl, and a patrol headed by Fritz Marberg intercepts the couple. Fritz gives the order to fire and Freya is hit. She dies in Martin's arms after crossing the Austrian border. Fritz reports on her death to Otto and Erich, crying, "I had to do it, I had to, it was my duty."

Saddled with a tear-jerking death scene, Sullavan and Stewart perform capably. No one would take them for Germans, but as star-crossed lovers they are hard to beat. This was their fourth feature film together and the third in which they did not live happily ever after. These two act so sincerely in their roles that their personal tragedy sustains the story in spite of the stilted speeches that are forced upon them. The featured players are of special note here. Dailey and Bond are properly menacing as party bullies, and they contrast nicely with Young's pensive Nazi. Stack is very convincing also as Otto von Rohn, a young man who finally realizes his responsibility for the death of his sister and stepfather.

The utter conviction displayed by the entire cast is matched by the intelligence of their direction. Victor Saville is the uncredited producer of the film and is recognized as having handled much of the direction. Being both English and Jewish he had a personal stake in making *The Mortal Storm* something more than mere propaganda. He succeeded in fashioning a film tragedy that delivers a valid and effective message.

Cheryl Karnes

MOTHER WORE TIGHTS

Released: 1947
Production: Lamar Trotti for Twentieth Century-Fox
Direction: Walter Lang
Screenplay: Lamar Trotti; based on the novel of the same name by Miriam Young
Cinematography: Harry Jackson
Editing: J. Watson Webb, Jr.
Running time: 107 minutes

Principal characters:
Myrtle McKinley Burt	Betty Grable
Frank Burt	Dan Dailey
Iris Burt	Mona Freeman
Miriam "Mikie" Burt	Connie Marshall
Bob Clarkman	Robert Arthur
Senor Wences	Himself

From the 1930's into the 1950's the Twentieth Century-Fox studio always had at least one blonde female star who was featured in a series of light-hearted musical films. Alice Faye, Betty Grable, and June Haver were the main "Foxy Blondes," but it was Grable who was the most successful of the three. Indeed, in the early 1940's she was the highest-paid star in Hollywood as well as being the favorite pin-up of American soldiers during World War II. Grable's most popular—and probably best—film was *Mother Wore Tights*.

Like many other Twentieth Century-Fox musicals, *Mother Wore Tights* makes little effort to integrate its musical numbers into the plot, and in fact, the plot is almost as insignificant as possible. The purpose of this film is to give Grable and her costars, Dan Dailey and Mona Freeman, an opportunity to perform some entertaining musical numbers, and it serves that purpose quite well.

We first see an old couple on a front porch, and then a woman's voice offscreen tells us that they are her mother and father and were not always so old and sedate. The story of why Mother wore tights, she tells us, began in Oakland, California, in 1900, and from then on we see the entire story in flashback. Myrtle McKinley (Betty Grable) is graduated from high school in Oakland, but instead of going to business school, she gets a job in the chorus of a vaudeville show in San Francisco. She is soon teamed on stage with Frank Burt (Dan Dailey), and of course, throughout the film we see them perform their musical numbers. At first neither wants to fall in love with anyone because that would get in the way of a career, but soon they begin a short, stormy courtship and are married. They continue traveling the vaudeville circuit until Myrtle becomes pregnant. She wants to quit show business for good, but Frank thinks she is too important to their act. Myrtle's desire prevails, and for several years Frank tours with another partner while Myrtle stays in Chicago with her grandmother (Sara Allgood) and cares for their children, Iris and Miriam. Miriam is called Mikie and is the narrator. (Except when they are small children, Iris and Miriam are played by Mona Freeman and Connie Marshall, respectively.) One day a telegram comes from Frank asking Myrtle to rejoin the act because his partner has quit and he cannot replace her. Urged on by her grandmother, Myrtle rejoins Frank and soon is back in show business to stay.

There are then three fairly minor crises that keep the story going long enough to get in several more musical numbers. First is a Christmas when the parents' engagements keep them away from their daughters for the holiday, but the girls arrive unexpectedly, and all the members of the vaudeville group perform for them at a special party. Notable among these is a specialty act by a Senor Wences (playing himself) in which he does a number combining music and ventriloquism, using his hand as the head of the dummy. Later, the whole family goes to a resort hotel in the Berkshires for a summer vacation, but find the clientele so sedate that the place reminds Frank, he says, "of a well-stuffed morgue." They perform a number in the hotel lobby in an attempt to enliven the group, but are unsuccessful and decide to leave. Three of the "old fogey" guests, however, ask them to stay and "limber up" the place. They do, and a good time is had by all, especially Iris, who begins a romance with Bob Clarkman (Robert Arthur).

This romance produces the third and most serious crisis in the film. Iris becomes ashamed of her parents for being song-and-dance performers while Bob's parents and friends are "so nice and dignified" and go to the opera rather than vaudeville. When all her schoolmates are invited to see her parents perform, Iris is terribly upset, but after the show, in which Frank and Myrtle perform "There's Nothing Like a Song" and "Kokomo, Indiana," Iris is ashamed not of her parents but of her own attitude. When, as the highest honor student in the school of music, Iris sings at the school's graduation, she chooses "You Do" because it is a song her parents introduced in vaudeville.

Mikie, who has continued to narrate the story from time to time, then tells us that Iris married Bob and became a singing star also, and we return to the old couple on the porch, Frank and Myrtle enjoying their retirement.

The most notable feature of the plot, especially compared to those of the countless films and plays about show business, is the lack of any serious problems. In some musical films the protagonists have more trouble putting on one show than Frank and Myrtle have in a lifetime, but for a film like *Mother Wore Tights* the story is used merely to provide a setting for the musical numbers, and no attempt is made to have those numbers serve as part of the plot or characterization. Indeed, *Mother Wore Tights* might better be described as a film about musical performers rather than as a musical *per se*.

The definition does not matter, however, because *Mother Wore Tights* succeeds on its own simple, unpretentious terms by giving us the dancing of Grable and Dailey and the singing of Grable, Dailey, and Freeman.

Although none of the songs from the film has become a classic, as performed in the film two of them—"Kokomo, Indiana" and "This Is My Favorite City"—are especially notable. The latter is sung several times, and each time the favorite city is a different one, depending upon where Frank and Myrtle are performing.

Mother Wore Tights effectively showcases the appealing screen *persona* and talents of Grable and certainly is, as critic John Russell Taylor has written, one of the "admirable examples of formula film-making that worked." In fact, it was one of the top films at the box office in 1947.

Marilynn Wilson

MOVIE CRAZY

Released: 1932
Production: Harold Lloyd for Paramount
Direction: Clyde Bruckman
Screenplay: Vincent Lawrence; based on an original story by Agnes Christine Johnston, John Grey, and Felix Adler, with continuity by Clyde Bruckman, Frank Terry, and Lex Neal
Cinematography: Walter Lundin
Editing: Bernard W. Burton
Running time: 84 minutes

Principal characters:
Harold Hall	Harold Lloyd
Mary Sears	Constance Cummings
Vance	Kenneth Thomson
The Director	Sydney Jarvis
Bill	Eddie Fetherstone
Wesley Kitterman	Robert McWade
Mrs. Kitterman	Louise Closser Hale
Miller	Harold Goodwin
Mr. Hall	DeWitt Jennings
Mrs. Hall	Lucy Beaumont

In a highly favorable review of the 1949 reissue of *Movie Crazy*, the critic of *Time* (July 18, 1949) wrote that Harold Lloyd's films "are warmhearted parodies of old-fashioned American manners and morals." It was an apt description of the films of one of America's greatest comedians, a man whom many agree is on a par with Charlie Chaplin and Buster Keaton. Harold Lloyd (1893-1971) was a graduate of the slapstick era of American comedy, but his films rely little on the violent comedy of slapstick in order to succeed; rather, they give audiences a comic image of themselves, a sometimes naïve, sometimes bumbling American hero who always wins—often against almost insurmountable odds—the football game, the job, the money, the fight, the girl, and even, as in *Movie Crazy*, a movie contract.

The character of Lloyd as the bespectacled, shy hero developed in a series of short films beginning in 1915 with Lloyd as Lonesome Luke and reached its zenith in the 1920's with features such as *Safety Last* (1923), *Girl Shy* (1924), *The Freshman* (1925), *For Heaven's Sake* (1926), *The Kid Brother* (1927), and *Speedy* (1928). Unlike his contemporary comedians (including Chaplin), Lloyd made a remarkably easy transition to talkies, starring in seven successful sound features, beginning with *Welcome Danger* in 1929 and ending with *The Sin of Harold Diddlebock* in 1947.

Movie Crazy was Lloyd's third talkie, directed by veteran Lloyd associate

Clyde Bruckman, who had been responsible for the comedian's two previous sound films and had also written extensively for Keaton in the 1920's. As with all of the comedian's films, however, much of the credit for the direction must go to Lloyd himself, for he was the *auteur* of his films to a far greater extent than most of those directors who, in recent years, have come to be known by that title. For his leading lady, Lloyd chose Constance Cummings, a major dramatic actress in films and later on the stage, who seems a far cry from Mildred Davis, Bebe Daniels, and Jobyna Ralston, who appeared opposite Lloyd during the silent era. At times, Cummings is a colder, less sympathetic heroine than one might wish for such a charmer as Lloyd. She later went on to play hardened, although comical, characters in two well-known British films, *Blithe Spirit* (1945) and *The Battle of the Sexes* (1959).

Like most Americans of the early 1930's, Lloyd's character, Harold Hall, is fascinated with the movies, and the film concerns his efforts to become a part of the industry. *Movie Crazy* is very much a film of comic errors and illusions. It begins with a comic illusion when we, the audience, think we are seeing Harold riding in a chauffeur-driven limousine, when, in reality, he is riding his bicycle alongside the car. The first error occurs when Harold sends off his photograph to a Hollywood film studio and his father substitutes the photograph of another, more attractive, young man. Needless to recount, the studio is taken by the wrong photograph and offers Harold a screen test. The movie-crazy hero, who lives and breathes films, imagining his mother's coffee grinder to be a camera grinding away at a scene, heads for Hollywood.

Just as Colleen Moore had done in *Ella Cinders* some years previous, Harold steps right off the train into the middle of the shooting of a location scene, completely wrecks the shot, and also manages to fall in love with the leading lady, a supposedly Spanish beauty. Our hero then heads for the studio, where he wreaks similar havoc, causing great distress to the studio manager whose straw hat Harold is forever destroying throughout the film. He also falls in love (again) with a girl named Mary (Constance Cummings), whom he fails to recognize as the Spanish leading lady out of makeup. She is taken by his simple charm and by his not having made a pass at her in the first five minutes, christens him "Trouble," and even takes him back to her home.

Complications develop in true Lloyd fashion as Harold overhears a conversation about an excellent screen test which he believes to have been his own and again meets the Spanish beauty, with whom he flirts, unaware that she is Mary, who, in turn, is angered by Harold's fickle behavior. On the back of a party invitation, Mary writes Harold a note telling him she wishes to have nothing more to do with him, but Harold sees only the front of the invitation and heads for the party.

In one of the funniest sequences in the film, Harold arrives at the party and, in the men's room, accidentally dons the jacket of a magician. As he dances with the wife of the studio head, women's underwear appears on a string from his sleeve and the flower in his lapel squirts water in the lady's face. A white rabbit appears, followed by a flock of white mice which cause character actor Grady Sutton, giving one of his inevitable effeminate men performances, to leap on a table, pulling up his trousers in fear.

Back at the studio, Harold is knocked out by an actor who is also in love with Mary. He regains consciousness to find himself in the middle of an action scene set in the hold of a ship, with the other actor and Mary playing a scene together. Believing he is rescuing Mary, Harold engages in a lengthy, sometimes amusing, fight with the other actor which eventually our hero wins after half the set has been flooded with water. It is a curious scene not so much because it is an unusually drawn-out comedy fight but because the scene is played entirely silent without any background music, just as it would be played if it were really a scene being filmed. Lloyd should perhaps be praised for his naturalistic approach to the scene, but also one cannot help but wish for the aid of an orchestra to accentuate the comedy dramatics.

In the end, the studio head's wife sees the scene and is impressed by Harold's comedic talent—she does not realize that he was not trying to be funny. Harold gets both the studio contract and the girl and everything is the way it should be in Lloyd's world of comedic charm.

Movie Crazy was well received by both the critics and the public, and it assured Lloyd of continued financial independence to produce more of his own films without studio interference. *Photoplay* (September, 1932) called the film Lloyd's best talkie, continuing "Lloyd's new one marks a great advance in the use of comedy dialogue. It never slows down the action nor interferes with the gags. It is, as you may gather, a peach of a picture." Reporting on the initial screening at the Rialto Theatre the previous night, Mordaunt Hall in *The New York Times* (September 15, 1932) wrote, "It is virtually a series of slapstick adventures set to sound and as Mr. Lloyd has the good sense to take these experiences with a serious demeanor, they reaped their reward of side-splitting laughter."

In a world satiated with the broad comedy of Keaton and the light, often-disappointing antics of Chaplin, Lloyd comes as a welcome relief. Films such as *Movie Crazy* display the actor's genius not only for comedy but also for telling a comic story without having to stop the plot for the jokes. The comedy and situations vary from the simple to the wild, but the element of fun is always natural and never forced.

Anthony Slide

THE MUMMY

Released: 1932
Production: Carl Laemmle for Universal
Direction: Karl Freund
Screenplay: John L. Balderston
Cinematography: Charles Stumar
Editing: no listing
Running time: 72 minutes

Principal characters:
Imhotep/Ardath Bey .... Boris Karloff
Helen Grosvenor .... Zita Johann
Frank Whemple .... David Manners
Sir Joseph Whemple .... Arthur Byron
Doctor Muller .... Edward Van Sloan
Ralph Norton .... Bramwell Fletcher

The Mummy, along with *Frankenstein* and *Dracula*, is one of the best-known horror films turned out by Universal in the early 1930's. Many of these films were directed by Europeans brought to America by the head of Universal, Carl Laemmle, and showed the influence of German sources. Among these directors were Karl Freund, who had established his reputation as a cinematographer on such German classics as *The Last Laugh* (1924), *Metropolis* (1927), and *Variety* (1925). In America, Freund's credits as a cinematographer include *Camille* (1936), *Murders in the Rue Morgue* (1932), and Tod Browning's *Dracula* (1931). He also directed eight films in the United States, the first of which, *The Mummy* (1932), is by far his most famous.

The Mummy's major themes concern the fear of death and the loss of identity in modern society. Like Dracula, the Mummy's immortality is a lonely curse which causes him to seek out victims from among the living. Similarly, his great strength is the result of mystical forces which modern science is unable to combat. This fear of the unknown and modern technology's inability to cope with it inevitably underscores the concern of these films with the fragility of life. At the same time, the hopelessness of the villain's situation often imbues him with a paradoxical amount of pathos. This in turn is pitted against the immortal one's attempts to take the life of his principal victim (usually a young woman).

Stylistically, the early horror films' main stock-in-trade invariably depends upon the chilling use of darkness and shadow. In this respect *The Mummy* is particularly effective because of Freund's uncanny ability to control the film's mood through his mastery of lighting. Drawing upon many of the techniques used by German Expressionists such as Fritz Lang, *The Mummy* is also noteworthy for its imaginative use of makeup and sets. Combined with the film's suspenseful employment of parallel editing and its dynamic camera movements, these stylistic components make *The Mummy* a continually engaging visual experience.

In terms of its basic story construction, however, *The Mummy* suffers somewhat from an overly convoluted plot. The film begins just after a delegation from the British Museum has discovered the mummy Imhotep, who had been buried alive in ancient Egypt. As is typical of the genre, this act of discovery is immediately followed by an interdiction. Respectful of the death-curse inscribed on the casket, Dr. Muller (Edward Van Sloan) warns his young associate, Ralph Norton (Bramwell Fletcher), not to open it before leaving the crypt to discuss matters further with Professor Whemple (David Manners). Believing that the casket contains the scroll of Thoth and the spell with which Isis raised Osiris from the dead in ancient mythology, Muller advises the Professor to bury it.

Meanwhile, Norton's curiosity has gotten the best of him, and his fate is set. Shot in a very Germanic style, the ensuing sequence utilizes highly atmospheric lighting and the moving camera to create an overwhelming sense of fear and suspense. As the young man begins to transcribe the scroll, the Mummy's eyes start to open. It is at this point that Freund tilts down to the scroll to reveal the Mummy's hand as it slowly enters the frame. Then, without actually showing the Mummy, Freund moves his camera back and forth between Norton and various objects in the room, using the young man's hysterical laughter to convey the utter terror of the situation. Partly because of the seemingly interminable length of Norton's hysteria, the Mummy's resurrection must surely be ranked among the most frightening scenes in any horror film.

This sequence is followed by a flash-forward in which Frank Whemple and a colleague discuss the fact that Whemple's father has not returned to the archaeological site since the day that Norton went mad. Discouraged because their own fieldwork has been unrewarding, the two men are somewhat skeptical when a strange Egyptian who calls himself Ardath Bey (Boris Karloff) offers to lead them to the tomb of Anckesen Amon. Ardath makes good on his promise however, after explaining that he needs their aid because Egyptians are not allowed to exhume their own dead. Shortly thereafter, Bey's true motives are partially revealed in a sequence which makes use of a host of expressionist devices.

Cutting between the Cairo Museum and a fancy dress ball, Freund makes it clear that Ardath Bey is exerting some kind of telepathic power over a young woman whom he associates with Anckesen Amon. Again, both the moving camera and the strong use of light and shadow contribute to the eerie mood as Helen Grosvenor (Zita Johann) begins to respond to Bey's incantations. Leaving the ball in a trance, Helen arrives at the Cairo Museum where she is observed by Frank and his father. After she faints on the doorstep, Frank and Professor Whemple help her back to their apartment. It is here that they learn that Helen is chanting Imhotep, the name of the missing mummy, who is in fact none other than the mysterious Ardath Bey.

Back at the museum, Bey's villainy is confirmed as he murders a guard at the same time that Frank begins to fall in love with Helen. Hearing that Bey was seen in the museum, Dr. Muller realizes what is happening and informs the Professor that Helen is already under Ardath's power. Then, when Bey arrives at the apartment, Muller advises the Professor to hide the scroll which has been in his possession since the first expedition. After tactfully separating Ardath and Helen, Muller proceeds to confront Bey with his suspicions, which results in the latter's unsuccessful attempt to gain control of the Professor and his scroll.

Moments later, however, Bey kills the Professor telepathically and has his Nubian servant bring him the scroll. Bey would probably succeed in killing Helen as well, were it not for the efforts of the persistent Dr. Muller. Playing much the same role that he did in *Dracula* as Professor Van Helsing, Van Sloan's Dr. Muller is the real hero of *The Mummy* because he alone possesses the kind of knowledge needed to ward off the evil fiend. Employing an amulet of Isis instead of a cross (which was used in *Dracula*), he manages to save Frank's life after convincing the young man that it is necessary to "fight magic with magic."

While this transpires, Bey has lured Helen to the Cairo Museum. It is here, amidst the elaborate trappings of ancient Egypt, that Bey contrives to implicate Helen further in his scheme. This is accomplished through the use of a rather long flashback which recounts the infamous story of Imhotep and Anckesen Amon. Arising from the steaming waters of Ardath Bey's pool, this highly stylized vision tells how Imhotep (Boris Karloff) stole the scroll of Thoth in an effort to raise Anckesen Amon (Zita Johann) from the dead. Caught before he could complete his act of sacrilege, the vision ends with Imhotep's condemnation and secret burial.

This striking blend of fantasy and reality sets the stage for Bey's climactic attempt to destroy Helen in order to resurrect her as his beloved Anckesen Amon. When he takes her to the Chamber of Entombment, however, her instincts rebel, and she begins to pray for help in front of a statue of Isis. Then, just after Frank and Dr. Muller arrive, Helen's prayers are answered as the statue sends forth a flash of light which burns the scroll and causes Bey to deteriorate and crumble. Now Frank calls her back from the past, and the film ends with a tilt-down from the burning scroll to the crumpled remains of the Mummy.

Despite its stylized dialogue and the unbelievability of many of its individual scenes, *The Mummy*'s ultimate success is a tribute to Freund's skillful direction and Karloff's remarkable two-part characterization. In this context, Freund's repeated use of the close-up to convey Karloff's sinister ambitions is only one of a number of startling visual devices which more than compensate for some of the film's less effective moments. In a similar vein, the triteness of the love relationship which is established between Frank and Helen is overshadowed by the intensity of the surrounding events. Moreover, it is characteristic of this genre that the young hero is no more than an instrument in the hands of the wise older man, whose knowledge and persistence are the main qualities needed to defeat the forces of evil.

Alan Karp

THE MUPPET MOVIE

Released: 1979
Production: Jim Henson for ITC Entertainment
Direction: James Frawley
Screenplay: Jerry Juhl and Jack Burns
Cinematography: Isidore Mankofsky
Editing: Chris Greenburg
Music: Paul Williams and Kenny Ascher
Special effects: Robbie Knott
Running time: 98 minutes

Principal characters:
Kermit the Frog .... (voice of Jim Henson)
Miss Piggy .... (voice of Frank Oz)
Fozzie Bear .... (voice of Frank Oz)
Rowlf the Dog .... (voice of Jim Henson)
Gonzo .... (voice of Jim Henson)
Dr. Teeth .... (voice of Jim Henson)
Animal .... (voice of Frank Oz)
Talent agent .... Dom Deluise
Doc Hopper .... Charles Durning
Lew Lord .... Orson Welles

Making the transition from television to movies is not always easy; for example, Farrah Fawcett of *Charlie's Angels* in *Somebody Killed Her Husband* (1979) and *Sunburn* (1980) met with little success, and Henry Winkler of *Happy Days* in *Heroes* (1977) and *The One and Only* (1978) was equally unsuccessful. Kermit the Frog, Miss Piggy, Fozzie Bear, and all of their felt and fur puppet friends from *The Muppets*, however, manage quite successfully to move from the small screen to the large one in *The Muppet Movie*, their first full-length motion picture.

Drawing on the characters featured in the successful syndicated television show which is seen in more than one hundred countries, the eight-million-dollar musical comedy-fantasy-adventure features what many consider to be the world's most popular television personalities—the hand, string, and sometimes radio-controlled Muppets. "Muppet" is a word coined by Muppet creator Jim Henson to synthesize "marionette" and "puppet." Like the half-hour television show, which makes use of Kermit the Frog as emcee, the feature film also contains musical numbers and guest celebrities, but whereas the television program is in a revue format, the motion picture has a narrative plot.

The Muppet Movie is a flashback story showing the way the Muppets got together and made it into show business. The rags-to-riches film-within-a-film begins with the Muppets filing into a Hollywood studio screening room to view a film that will tell their history. We watch along with the excited, rowdy group as Kermit the Frog sits in his downhome Georgia swamp and lazily plays his guitar while he sings "The Rainbow Connection." Soon, a vacationing Hollywood talent scout (Dom Deluise) rows by. "I've lost my direction," the scout laments. "Have you tried Hare Krishna?" Kermit replies. The scout then shows Kermit a *Daily Variety* advertisement soliciting "All frogs wishing to become rich and famous." At the suggestion of the agent, Kermit begins a cross-country trek to California, picking up assorted Muppet pals along the way.

In El Sleezo's sleazy saloon, Kermit encounters Fozzie, a not-so-successful song-and-dance bear. Later they are joined by Gonzo the plumber, Camille the Chicken, Dr. Teech and the Electric Mayhem Band, and Miss Piggy, Kermit's sweetheart. Following a hilarious slow-motion love-at-first-sight scene that takes place in a meadow, the seductive but ambitious Miss Piggy temporarily abandons Kermit for show business. Rowlf the Dog commiserates, saying "It's not often you see a guy that green have the blues that bad."

Meanwhile, the coast-to-coast journey becomes a coast-to-coast chase as Doc Hopper (Charles Durning), the villainous human owner of French-fried frogs' legs fast-food franchises, pursues the frog in order to make him "spokesman" for the chain. When Kermit refuses, stating "All I can think of is millions of frogs on tiny crutches," Hopper kidnaps him and hires a mad scientist who unsuccessfully attempts to change Kermit's mind electronically. Miss Piggy, however, beats up this new villain and precipitates a showdown between Doc Hopper and Kermit in a ghost town. Finally a Muppet named Animal saves the day, and the group arrives in Hollywood and soon convinces producer Lew Lord (Orson Welles) to make a film about their recent adventures. It is not coincidental that *The Muppet Movie* was financed by British impressario Lord Lew Grade.

Reminiscent at varying times of old Judy Garland-Mickey Rooney musicals, the Bob Hope-Bing Crosby "road" pictures, the adventures of *Alice in Wonderland* (1933), and the fantasy in *The Wizard of Oz* (1939), *The Muppet Movie* also alludes to the Western, *High Noon* (1952). The showdown between Doc Hopper and Kermit, in fact, was shot at the Columbia ranch where the original Gary Cooper film was made. Appealing to adults and children alike, one does not need prior knowledge of the Muppets to enjoy *The Muppet Movie*, which is immensely entertaining. The exuberant production is well written, with many witty puns, one-liners, and sight gags, by Jerry Juhl and Jack Burns; gorgeously photographed on real outdoor locations in beautiful color by Isidore Mankofsky; and cleverly directed by James Frawley, who also directed such offbeat comedies as *The Big Bus* (1976).

The joyful comedy also makes use of songs written by Kenny Ascher and Paul Williams, who had earlier collaborated on the score for Barbra Streisand's

A Star Is Born (1977). Although some of their tunes are more memorable than others, a few in particular stand out—Kermit's hopeful ballad, "The Rainbow Connection," which won an Oscar nomination; the upbeat "Movin' Right Along" and "Can You Picture That?"; the love song "Never Before, Never Again"; and the finale, "The Magic Store."

The many stars who appear in the film with varying degrees of effectiveness include Durning as Doc Hopper, the greedy rival to Colonel Sanders; Deluise as the vacationing agent; and Bob Hope as an ice cream vendor. Other guests include, among others, Richard Pryor, Elliot Gould, James Coburn, Telly Savalas, Paul Williams, Madeleine Kahn, Carol Kane, Mel Brooks, Cloris Leachman, Steve Martin, and Orson Welles. The late Edgar Bergen and Charlie McCarthy, to whom the film is dedicated, play the judges of a beauty contest.

The film's outstanding aspect, of course, is the Muppets themselves. Not merely two-dimensional, cute figures, they represent a simplified but very human version of the real world. As inventive as Walt Disney's characters, each of the extraordinarily lifelike creatures has a personality, appearance, and vocal quality all its own. Kermit, for example, is a distinct individual who happens to be a frog. He has great expressive range—bashful, self-doubting, lovesick, and morally strong. It is Henson himself, of course, who operates Kermit and provides the frog's voice. We accept the Muppets as real beings and accept their relationships with one another and with the humans with little difficulty. The Muppet world is one of innocence, in which even the most worldly and villainous characters maintain an aura of ingenuousness.

Muppet originator Henson, who directed the 1965 Oscar-nominated short subject *Time Piece*, began experimenting with puppets in the 1950's. His creatures appeared on local Washington television, *The Tonight Show* with Steve Allen, and later on the *Ed Sullivan Show*. Finally his puppets were seen on educational television's *Sesame Street*. Normally Henson likes to keep his Sesame Street characters separate from the Muppets, but in *The Muppet Movie*, we see Big Bird on his way to New York hoping to "break into public television."

Unlike Kukla of Kukla, Fran, and Ollie, who was relegated to a box, or Charlie McCarthy, who was confined to Bergen's lap, the Muppets are seen in the film not only in close-up but also in medium shot and in full body shots. In the Muppet television show, however, the creatures always rest on levels under which the hidden performers manipulate them; in *The Muppet Movie*, we not only see the floor but also see the Muppets, with the help of special effects, walk, run, dance a soft-shoe, play musical instruments, ride a bicycle, and drive a car. In the sequences in which the Muppets *are* hand operated from below, the film's sets were built five feet off the ground to accommodate the people who make the Muppets move. Additionally, because it was difficult for the operators to see what their Muppets were doing, instant video playback systems were constantly used during production. In the film's grand finale, Henson used 137 members of the Puppeteers of America organization to manipulate the 260 Muppets who flock around the gigantic, colorful rainbow. The scene also makes use of a Muppet which resembles the film's director, James Frawley.

One of the most elaborate puppet features ever made, *The Muppet Movie* is full of spunk, verve, and visual excitement. Although there are a few moments that lag, one is inclined to agree with the film's advertising slogan, "it's more entertaining than humanly possible." This advertisement foretold an ironic footnote to the production. Because there had been some half-serious discussion of nominating Miss Piggy for an Oscar for Best Actress, the Academy of Motion Picture Arts and Sciences altered the wording of the official rules for the acting awards to stipulate that the actors must be "human."

The Muppet Movie was very successful and led to another film, *The Great Muppet Caper* (1981), which was not quite as popular, but still did very well at the box office.

Leslie Taubman

MURDER SHE SAID

Released: 1962
Production: George N. Brown; released by Metro-Goldwyn-Mayer
Direction: George Pollock
Screenplay: David Pursall and Jack Seddon; based on the novel *4:50 from Paddington* by Agatha Christie
Cinematography: Geoffrey Faithfull
Editing: Ernest Walter
Running time: 87 minutes

Principal characters:

Miss Jane Marple	Margaret Rutherford
Dr. Quimper	Arthur Kennedy
Emma	Muriel Pavlow
Mr. Ackenthorpe	James Robertson Justice
Police Inspector Craddock	Charles Tingwell
Alexander	Ronnie Raymond
Brian Eastley	Ronald Howard
Cedric	Thorley Walters
Harold	Conrad Phillips
Albert	Gerald Cross
Stringer	Stringer Davis

The detective story has been an enduring staple of popular literature from the late nineteenth century until the present day. It is not, therefore, surprising that filmmakers have frequently turned to this form of fiction as a source for films. Series based upon engagingly eccentric detectives (usually an amateur rather than a professional) have been especially popular with filmmakers and filmgoers just as they have been with detective-fiction readers.

In the late 1950's M-G-M arranged with one of England's most popular writers of detective fiction, Agatha Christie, to make a series of films featuring one of her more delightful detective creations, Miss Marple. The filmmakers decided that Margaret Rutherford, a great character actress most famous for her role as the eccentric medium in *Blithe Spirit* (1946), would be perfect for the part of a woman who looks like a "dotty old maid" but nevertheless solves crimes that baffle the police. Rutherford, however, did not at all want to play in a crime story. The director, George Pollock, finally changed her mind by convincing her that Miss Marple was a good woman who helped people rather than someone with a morbid interest in crime or criminals. In 1961 she began the filming of the first of what was to become a series of four Miss Marple films, and now legions of detective and film fans regard Rutherford as the ideal embodiment of the Christie character.

As is so often true of a series, the first film is the best. In this case part of the superiority of *Murder She Said* can be attributed to the fact that it follows Christie most closely. Other films in the series were based on novels by Christie that did not have Miss Marple in them, and one film in the series, *Murder Ahoy* (1964), was constructed entirely by its screenwriters using nothing from the works of Christie except the character of Miss Marple.

Murder She Said begins innocently enough with Miss Jane Marple (Margaret Rutherford) relaxing in her train compartment with a crime novel. As another train passes hers, she and the occupants of the passing cars regard each other with a mixture of idle curiosity and embarrassment. In one car, however, all of the shades are lowered, but before Miss Marple looks away, one of the shades rises and she sees a man strangling a woman; then the car passes on. Miss Marple tries to convince the conductor on her train that she has seen a murder committed on the other train, but when he sees that she has been reading a crime novel, he patronizingly suggests that she imagined something. She finally convinces the authorities to check the other train, but they find nothing amiss, and later Police Inspector Craddock (Charles Tingwell) comes to her house to talk to her about what she thinks she saw. He too does not take this elderly spinster seriously and says that perhaps the couple she saw were merely honeymooners.

Incensed that she is regarded as just a "dotty old maid," Miss Marple realizes that she will have to solve the mystery herself. She enlists the help of the local librarian, Mr. Stringer (Stringer Davis—in real life Rutherford's husband). Since they have both read hundreds of detective novels, Miss Marple argues, they should understand the criminal mind and be able to solve the case. So the timid, fussy librarian and the strong-willed "dotty old maid" set out to check her hypothesis that the body was thrown off the train before it reached the station.

They find enough evidence to convince Miss Marple that the Ackenthorpe estate is involved. Therefore, to follow the scent further she arranges to take a job as a servant in the household. She soon finds that the family consists of Emma (Muriel Pavlow), a nice young woman, her nephew Alexander (Ronnie Raymond), an impertinent but candid boy, and Emma's father (James Robertson Justice) an irascible old semi-invalid. When the father tries to reprimand Miss Marple by stating that he cannot stand impertinence, she merely replies that they should get along well because "Neither can I."

A cut from young Alexander telling her they expect dinner at eight to a clock showing eleven and Miss Marple exhausted among the dirty dishes tells us that her duties in the household threaten to keep her from her investigation, but she overcomes her fatigue, and before long she has discovered a woman's body in a mummy case in a group of Egyptian artifacts kept on the estate. She surreptitiously has the police notified and soon has the satisfaction of seeing Inspector Craddock at the scene, now unable to dismiss her claim that a crime has been committed.

Alexander has already told Miss Marple that the family is a "pack of vultures" waiting for the inheritance from old Mr. Ackenthorpe. When the police bring the whole family together to check their alibis for the time of the murder, they prove to be not much more attractive than Alexander has said. Besides Emma, there are her three brothers (Thorley Walters, Conrad Phillips, and Gerald Cross) and her brother-in-law (Ronald Howard). The family doctor (Arthur Kennedy), who is in nearly constant attendance on the elder Ackenthorpe, suggests that the corpse is that of a French woman who had married another brother just before he was killed in the War and that she was on her way to establish her claim to part of the inheritance. Before the case is solved two more brothers die, and we discover that the doctor is secretly in love with Emma.

The climax comes with a trap devised by Miss Marple and the police in which she lets it be known that she has the evidence to incriminate the murderer and then waits in her room (with the police hiding nearby) for him to appear. It is, as she deduced, the doctor, and she gets him to explain his plot to kill off all the rest of the family so that he and Emma would have the inheritance to themselves. The woman he strangled on the train was his wife, and the story about the French woman was his own invention. As he begins to strangle Miss Marple, the police rush in and capture him. It is not until a policeman tells her how brave she was that Miss Marple reacts; she faints. Before she leaves, old Mr. Ackenthorpe asks her to marry him, but she refuses and drives off with Mr. Stringer.

The plot is fairly typical of Christie, with numerous characters arousing our suspicions until finally it is the least likely character who is the culprit. The story follows most of the essential points of Christie's original 1957 novel, *4:50 from Paddington* (*What Mrs. McGillicuddy Saw* in Great Britain) with a few major alterations which resulted in a more cohesive, less complicated film. In the novel Miss Marple is a relatively minor character. In the film, however, she takes on the activities of three of the characters from the novel, herself, Mrs. McGillicuddy, who saw the murder take place, and Lucy Eyesbarrow, who was employed as a housekeeper in the Crackenthorpe estate (called the Ackenthorpe estate in the film) and found the body. The character of the librarian was missing in the novel, and several minor characters are missing in the film from the original story. These things aside, however, the film does follow Christie's pattern and tone quite well.

Holding our interest as much as the puzzle, however, is the splendid performance of Rutherford as the elderly amateur sleuth who can hold her own with anyone and proves to be more daring and more perceptive than the police. It is not surprising that Christie dedicated one of her novels (*The Mirror Crack'd, 1962*) to the actress.

Christie's novels have recently provided film audiences with another group of movies based on her stories. *Murder on the Orient Express* (1974) and

Death on the Nile (1978) were successful English-made, star-studded mysteries featuring another Christie detective, Hercule Poirot. Miss Marple appears again in 1980's *The Mirror Crack'd* featuring Angela Lansbury as the stalwart spinster. Onstage, two Christie stories, *Murder in the Vicarage* (1930) and *A Murder Is Announced* (1950), played successful runs on London's West End in the late 1970's and featured Muriel Pavlow, who played Emma in this film, as Miss Marple.

Clifford Henry

THE MUSIC MAN

Released: 1962
Production: Morton Da Costa for Warner Bros.
Direction: Morton Da Costa
Screenplay: Marion Hargrove; based on the Broadway musical of the same name by Meredith Willson and Franklin Lacey
Cinematography: Robert Burks
Editing: William Zieglar
Choreography: Onna White
Music: Ray Heindorf (AA)
Running time: 151 minutes

Principal characters:
Harold Hill .... Robert Preston
Marian Paroo .... Shirley Jones
Marcellus Washburn .... Buddy Hackett
Eulalie Shinn .... Hermione Gingold
Mayor Shinn .... Paul Ford
Mrs. Paroo .... Pert Kelton
Winthrop Paroo .... Ron Howard

For years Hollywood has seemingly reveled in disembowling Broadway musicals while transferring them to the screen. Many times a spirited, moving, exciting show has become a plodding, boring, deadly movie. Yet a handful of shows have actually been brought to the screen not only with their zest intact, but also actually enhanced by the potential of the cinema medium. One of the happiest transitions of all among such fortunate musicals as *The Sound of Music* (1965) and *My Fair Lady* (1964) was 1962's *The Music Man*, Meredith Willson's irresistibly cornpone ode to Iowa.

The Music Man was something of a Cinderella story on Broadway. Stars ranging from Danny Kaye to Phil Harris had turned down the chance to star in it. Ray Bolger finally expressed interest, but ultimately refused when Willson would not allow him to perform a medley of his famous songs in Act II. When the play finally premiered at Broadway's Majestic Theatre on December 19, 1957, Robert Preston, who had so often breathed his last in the final reel of a Western, played Harold Hill, the fast-talking con artist who sells a hick town a boy's band and sets himself up as its leader, without knowing one note from another. The show was a smash hit. The show, which ran for three and a half years in New York, won Preston a Tony Award and began a whole new career for him.

Rarely has a movie property caused so many behind-the-scenes imbroglios as did *The Music Man*. Frank Sinatra desperately wanted to buy the rights and star in the film, and so did Bing Crosby. Willson nixed their offers and finally sold the rights to Warner Bros. who, oddly enough, tried to interest Cary Grant in starring as Harold Hill. Meanwhile, Preston left the Broadway company after twenty-five months and signed a star contract with Warner Bros. Finally, after assorted pleas and tirades from Willson and producer/director Morton Da Costa, who had also directed the Broadway version, Warner Bros. reluctantly presented Preston with the part. Shirley Jones, of *Oklahoma!* (1955) and *Carousel* (1956), was the happy choice for Marian Paroo, the prim librarian; Paul Ford was cast as the malapropic Mayor Shinn with Hermione Gingold as his pretentious spouse. Pert Kelton as Marian's mother and The Buffalo Bills as the barbershop singing councilmen rejoined Preston from the New York show, as did Onna White, the choreographer.

The Music Man opens on a train, where swindler Harold Hill is heading for "wherever the people are as green as the money." He decides that River City, Iowa, fits the bill, and there finds an old partner in crime, Marcellus Washburn (Buddy Hackett), now reformed. After Marcellus tells Harold of the local kids patronizing a pool hall, Harold rips into the famous "Ya' Got Trouble!" number with all the fervor of a revival evangelist, plunging the people into a near hysterical concern for their town boys' purity. Only Marian Paroo (Shirley Jones), the spinster librarian and town piano teacher, fails to fall for Harold's spiel. Pining for a beau ("Goodnight My Someone") and too bright for the yokels of River City, she nevertheless resists Harold's flirtations and determines to expose him as the fraudulent crook that he is.

It is at the Fourth of July celebration that Harold sells his idea of a boy's band, via the classic "76 Trombones." He crows of his revolutionary "Think" system—think the tune and it just comes out, no former musical training necessary—and soon the whole town is at the mercy of his charm. The town council (The Buffalo Bills) becomes a barbershop quartet; the Mayor's wife, Eulalie Shinn (Hermione Gingold), starts a modern dance group for frumps with Harold's blessing; and finally Marian, who sees the great change Harold's promises have made in her shy, lisping little brother Winthrop (Ron Howard), becomes Harold's ally—and his shy romance.

Harold's luck seemingly runs out when a vengeful anvil salesman named Charlie Cowell (Harry Hickox), once tarred and feathered simply for being a salesman after arriving in a town recently fleeced by Harold, comes to River City to expose him. The River City people soon become an angry mob, and Marian, who is nevertheless grateful to Harold for the warmth and love he has awakened in her, ("Till There Was You"), tries to help him escape. He cannot run, however; "For the first time in my life," he tells her, "I've got my foot caught in the door." He is caught and the citizens are gathering tar and feathers when suddenly the band marches in with their instruments. "Think, men—*think!*" pleads Harold as they prepare to play. The noise they make is ghastly, but the proud parents think it is magnificent, plunging them into euphoria and leading into a grand finale of "76 Trombones," led by a triumphant Harold with a glowing Marian on his arm.

Released in the summer of 1962, *The Music Man* was, as all expected, a proverbial "smash." Bosley Crowther of *The New York Times* comforted those who missed the show on Broadway by attesting "It's all here . . . preserved and appropriately made rounder and richer through the magnitude of film," and *Variety* praised it as "Superior entertainment. . . . A building, punching, handsomely dressed and ultimately endearing super musical." It grossed eight million dollars, becoming one of the top money-making films of 1962, entered the Oscar race for Best Picture of the Year (losing to *Lawrence of Arabia*) and won a single Oscar for "Best Scoring of Music, Adaptation or Treatment" for Ray Heindorf. It also placed second in the *Film Daily* "Ten Best" list (between top choice *The Manchurian Candidate* and third pick *The Miracle Worker*). Some of 1962's most laudatory reviews went to Preston, whose performance was rated " . . . as close to a tour de force as is likely to be seen during the calendar year of 1962," according to *Variety*. Strangely, he was neglected by the Academy in the "Best Actor" race.

Perhaps the great charm of *The Music Man* is that it is not at all muted for the screen. Director Da Costa presents it as a *show*, complete with such unabashed theatricality as Harold and Marian being spotlighted in a lover's duet. The self-conscious concern that a song or laugh line is too "big" for the eye of the camera is completely dashed to the winds, and as such, the audience has soon happily surrendered to the exuberance and zest of the musical. Onna White stages the big dance numbers such as "76 Trombones," "Shipoopi," and the precise, toe-tapping "Marian, the Librarian" with all the kicks and energy that detonated on stage. Willson's entire score is employed in the film (although Marian's stage ballad "My White Knight" was revamped into "Being in Love," which contained sections of the original song), and the talented cast has no bashfulness about belting out the lyrics, be it Howard lisping "Gary, Indiana," priceless Gingold leading her innocuous compatriots in a chorus of "Pick-a-Little, Talk-a-Little," or Kelton raising her raucous Irish brogue in the clever "Piano Lesson" exercise. As ever, Jones is a charming musical heroine, and her Marian is a lovely vision in bonnet and ruffles. Her voice is, of course, a constant delight, and her acting is sincere and winning.

Most of all, however, *The Music Man* has Preston, delivering Harold Hill with all the energy, charm, and mesmerism he had perfected in the course of 883 stage performances. Be he twinkling his eyes, tipping his straw boater and waving his hands fervently in "Ya' Got Trouble," or tenderly confessing his love for Marian, Preston *is* Harold Hill. While he shrewdly emphasizes Harold's rascality with bravado and humor, there is always the aura of genuine good feeling in his performance, making his climactic reformation a joy for the audience. Like Yul Brynner's King of *The King and I* (1956) and Rex Harrison's Higgins of *My Fair Lady*, Preston's Harold Hill has itself become solidly established as a screen masterpiece. The fact that these aforementioned actors have all originated their roles on stage, while scores of "name" attractions for movie versions of Broadway musicals are largely (and mercifully) forgotten, should contain a lesson for Hollywood producers.

Today, *The Music Man* is a popular television attraction, and rarely does a Fourth of July pass without at least one local station running it as a special treat for its viewers. Written by Willson as a Valentine to his home state of Iowa, *The Music Man* has transcended its specific setting and become a jubilant piece of Americana.

Gregory William Mank

MY BRILLIANT CAREER

Released: 1980
Production: Margaret Fink for Analysis Film Releasing Company
Direction: Gillian Armstrong
Screenplay: Eleanor Witcombe; based on the novel of the same name by Miles Franklin
Cinematography: Don McAlpine
Editing: Nick Beauman
Running time: 101 minutes

Principal characters:
Sybylla Melvyn	Judy Davis
Harry Beecham	Sam Neill
Aunt Helen	Wendy Hughes
Frank Hawdon	Robert Grubb
Aunt Gussie	Patricia Kennedy
Grandma Bossier	Aileen Brittain
Father	Alan Hopgood
Mother	Julia Blake
Mr. McSwatt	Max Cullen
Mrs. McSwatt	Carole Skinner

My Brilliant Career began as an obscure novel published in 1901 by Miles Franklin, a minor Australian novelist, folklorist, feminist, and literary critic. As a novel, *My Brilliant Career* had a checkered history. Written when Franklin was twenty, the book was generally assumed to be autobiographical, and created a small scandal for that reason. This interpretation so infuriated Franklin that she forbade its republication until ten years after her death. It was, therefore, out of print for more than half a century. She wrote a sequel, *My Career Goes Bung*, in 1903, but declined to have it published until 1946. Thus it was little wonder that her story remained obscure until it was seized upon by a quartet of talented Australian women in 1979 and turned into an internationally successful film.

The film version of *My Brilliant Career* (produced by Margaret Fink, written by Eleanor Witcombe, directed by Gillian Armstrong, and starring Judy Davis in the principal role of Sybylla Melvyn) was one of the group of critically acclaimed films to come out of Australia in the late 1970's. Like her colleagues Peter Weir (*Picnic at Hanging Rock*, 1975, *The Last Wave*, 1979), Fred Schepisi (*The Chant of Jimmie Blacksmith*, 1980), and Philip Noyce (*Newsfront*, 1979), Armstrong has delved into Australia's past for her story. *My Brilliant Career* is no mere period piece from a distant country, however; its subjects— nascent feminism and the drive to fulfill one's own potential no matter how attractive the alternative—transcend the boundaries of chronology and geography. *My Brilliant Career* is a film for all times and places.

The film opens with a shot of Sybylla Melvin, a sixteen-year-old-girl, reading aloud from a manuscript on which she has been working. It seems to be a diary or the beginning of a story she has written, or perhaps it is a bit of both. Sybylla is a young woman of great, if inchoate, ambition. As she muses on the soundtrack about the brilliant career that surely lies ahead for her (in literature, art, or music; she is not sure which), director Armstrong shows us a rather less auspicious scene on the screen.

It is 1897, in Australia. Sybylla lives on a small farm in a remote corner of that continent, and her family is engaged in a losing struggle to make ends meet. To be young, female, rural, and poor in a backward nineteenth century colony is to be handicapped indeed. By the time Sybylla's reveries are interrupted—her family arrives home in the middle of a blinding dust storm—the audience can only assume that the film's title is intended to be ironic.

The title is ironic, of course, but it is also more than a little defiant. Sybylla knows that circumstances are against her first because she is poor, leaving her with little time or energy for creativity (in whatever form it might take), and also because she is a woman, which, in her society, means that any career other than that of wife and mother will be considered frivolous at best and sacrilegious at worst. Still, she pursues her muse, and at no small personal cost.

The film is divided into four sections. The first section takes place on the farm owned by Sybylla's parents (Alan Hopgood and Julia Blake). Although it takes up only a small part of the film's running time, it establishes the givens of Sybylla's life—she is a headstrong and ambitious young woman, born into a society and a class where such attributes mark her as the black sheep of the family. It also establishes the poverty in her branch of the family. Her parents can no longer afford to support her; instead, they send her to live with her wealthy maternal grandmother. The second section of the film takes place at the estate of her Grandma Bossier (Aileen Brittain) and is much longer than the other sections. In it, we are introduced to several important characters in Sybylla's life; and we come to know and like Sybylla herself much better.

Life in the outback has done nothing to prepare Sybylla for the relative luxury of her grandmother's estate. There, among the ladies of society, she is a complete misfit; everything from her table manners to her looks seems to brand her as inferior. She is especially shaken by a picture of her mother as a young woman. The contrast (as she sees it) between her mother's beauty and her own appearance reduces her to tears. "I'm so ugly. Nobody loves me." The scene is important as well as affecting, since it demonstrates that Sybylla has a vulnerable side to go along with her brashness. Sybylla soon gets over her qualms about her looks, however; and indeed, despite the comments of her family and Sybylla herself, she is far from ugly. She is simply not dainty in the manner of the ideal woman of the era. She has wiry hair that resists straightening, freckles, and a minor skin blemish or two; but her face is much more alive than those of the other women her age; it is animated, with eyes that flash with anger, wit, and affection. It is a face with character.

While Sybylla stops worrying about her looks, however, the problem of love is much more persistent. It is a problem that is complicated by Sybylla's own ambivalence about her future. The rest of the film portrays her struggle to choose between a husband and a career. Sybylla has two suitors. The first is Frank Hawdon (Robert Grubb), a prissy but well-to-do Englishman who has come to "rough it" for a year or so as a guest on Mrs. Bossier's ranch. Grandma Bossier thinks he is a perfect match for Sybylla. Predictably, Sybylla cannot stand him, and the filmmakers use Frank Hawdon as the film's comic relief. Her other suitor is Harry Beecham (Sam Neill), who is the complete opposite. Harry is rich, handsome, and virile—a prize catch in every way— but he is also intelligent and sensitive. He and Sybylla are taken with each other almost immediately, but a number of problems impinge on their courtship. One of the problems, money, is ephemeral. Although Grandma Bossier and others make much of the disparity between Harry's wealth and the relative poverty of Sybylla's parents, Harry himself clearly regards this as an irrelevant consideration. More serious, however, are Sybylla's career ambitions. She has decided that she wants to be a writer, and periodically declaims to her shocked relatives that she has no interest in marriage. Her growing affection for Harry is obvious as is his for her, yet expressing this affection proves difficult. Despite their healthy willingness to ignore certain of their society's conventions, Sybylla and Harry are very much products of the Victorian era in their behavior concerning romance. Thus the pair spend much of the film on the verge of articulating their feelings for each other, both verbally and physically, only to freeze at the last moment.

The scene that most effectively illustrates this dilemma is a running pillow fight between the two. They share the physical intimacy of mock combat with a "weapon" that symbolizes their sexual attraction; yet at the end of the fight, when they might have fallen, exhausted but happy, into each other's arms, they back away from each other. Their frustration, and the audience's, is palpable. When Harry finally proposes to Sybylla at a gala dance, he so mishandles the situation (flirting, or appearing to flirt, with one of Sybylla's rivals all evening) that she turns him down in a cold fury. Sybylla's anger soon subsides, but her reservations about marriage remain.

"Loneliness is a terrible price to pay for independence," counsels Harry's Aunt Gussie (Pat Kennedy), a wonderful old woman who has become Sybylla's ally and confidante. Sybylla appears to agree. She goes to Harry and explains her dilemma. She asks for two years time in which to learn where her "brilliant career" will take her. "Then I'll marry you," she says. Harry consents to the lengthy engagement, and they kiss enthusiastically. Almost as soon as they agree to marry, however, they are separated. Sybylla's parents' financial situation has deteriorated further, and she is forced to leave the Bossier household and take a job as a governess for her parents' creditors in order to save the farm.

This section of the film takes place on the McSwatt farm, a terrible place where Sybylla is forced to tutor a brood of dirty, unmannered children. Her flinty resolve gradually wins over the family, however; and director Armstrong uses these scenes to show us that Sybylla is capable of overcoming adversity by dint of hard work. She makes good at her first job and begins to write a novel. Her tenure with the McSwatts ends when the parents (Max Cullen and Carole Skinner) suspect (erroneously; indeed, ludicrously) that she has romantic designs on their eldest son. Nervously, they send Sybylla home, forgiving the remainder of her father's debt.

On her way back home again, she meets Harry. She has heard rumors of infidelity, but Harry denies them. He still wants her to be his wife and is stunned when she explains that she must reluctantly renege on her promise to marry him. "I'm so near loving you, but I'll destroy you, and I can't do that," she pleads. Harry offers her the opportunity for marriage *and* a career—Sybylla is offered no easy choices—but she remains firm. Despite the opportunity of having a well-intentioned and supportive husband, she has learned enough about herself not to trust herself as a wife in the bush. She would have a baby a year and no career at all, brilliant or otherwise. If she is to be a writer, it must be done alone.

The fourth section of the film is really an epilogue. We see Sybylla Melvyn rising at dawn, taking a large package to the mailbox. It is the manuscript of *My Brilliant Career*, her first novel; and the joy and pride that shine on her face tell us as much as we need to know. By this time, the irony in the film's title has taken on a much subtler meaning. For although Sybylla has become a writer (a screen graphic notes that her novel was published in Edinburgh in 1901), the audience has no way of judging the merits of her work; but in a very real sense, this is irrelevant. Given the odds against her, the fact that she has established a career at all is in itself a hallmark of brilliance.

The critical response to *My Brilliant Career* was almost unanimously positive. Further, the film became the most financially successful of Australia's cinematic exports to that time. The script, the acting, and the direction combine to make a nearly flawless film. Witcombe's script follows Franklin's novel closely. Her refusal, under pressure from financial backers, to alter the ending by having Sybylla agree to marry Harry was both courageous and intelligent. Sybylla's final declaration of independence (tinged, to be sure, with regret) is, in view of her development throughout the film, logical and dramatically consistent. For the rest, the script is feminist without being polemical. Subtlety and restraint are the hallmarks of the plot and dialogue.

The acting in the film is of uniformly high quality, both in the major and supporting roles. Grubb is humorously foppish as Frank Hawdon; Brittain is formidable as Grandma Bossier; Kennedy brings a cantankerous charm to the character of Aunt Gussie; Cullen and Skinner are amusing in their brief roles as the McSwatts, the Ma and Pa Kettles of the outback; and Wendy Hughes is lovely in the role of the wistful Aunt Helen. New Zealander Neill, an actor with the looks of a rugged James Mason, is terrific as Harry Beecham. He projects a tenderness and sensitivity that is nevertheless entirely virile. It is easy to see what attracted Sybylla to him; and her final rejection of his love is as hard on the audience as it is on her.

Indeed, were it not for the uniform excellence of Neill and the rest of the supporting cast, the film might have been thrown out of balance by the brilliant performance of Davis as Sybylla Melvyn. Davis was an obscure actress/singer in Australia when she was selected to star in *My Brilliant Career*, and the choice was extremely fortuitous. A young woman of striking presence, she gets inside her character with a naturalness that is utterly convincing. It is, in fact, Davis' thoroughly convincing performance that permits the film's commitment to feminism to shine through without becoming merely preachy. Davis' Sybylla Melvyn embodies the fierce pride, wit, talent, and ambition of the feminist, but she is no cardboard superwoman. Her vulnerability is a necessary leavening in making the character human and endearing. Davis does all of this so winningly that there is no need for Witcombe and/or Armstrong to underline the political aspects of the story.

The pleasant task of putting all of these elements together fell to Armstrong. *My Brilliant Career* was her first feature film (although she was no rank beginner, having previously directed a series of shorter films), and it was an auspicious debut indeed. The narrative flows seamlessly; each scene—indeed, each shot—has a purpose. *My Brilliant Career* is evidence of Armstrong's enormous talent as a filmmaker.

My Brilliant Career, then, is a film with a title that aptly describes its director and star. If *My Brilliant Career* is any indication, Armstrong and Davis, as well as the new national cinema of Australia, can all look forward to brilliant careers.

Robert Mitchell

MY DARLING CLEMENTINE

Released: 1946
Production: Samuel G. Engel for Twentieth Century-Fox
Direction: John Ford
Screenplay: Samuel G. Engel and Winston Miller; based on an original story by Sam Hillman and the novel *Wyatt Earp, Frontier Marshall* by Stuart N. Lake
Cinematography: Joe MacDonald
Editing: Dorothy Spencer
Running time: 97 minutes

Principal characters:

Wyatt Earp	Henry Fonda
Doc Holliday	Victor Mature
Clementine Carter	Cathy Downs
Old Man Clanton	Walter Brennan
Chihuahua	Linda Darnell
Morgan Earp	Ward Bond
Virgil Earp	Tim Holt
Billy Clanton	John Ireland
James Earp	Don Garner
Ike Clanton	Grant Withers

Filmed within a year of the end of World War II, *My Darling Clementine* is John Ford's most positive expression of a recurring major theme in his Westerns, the necessity of the triumph of civilization over the wilderness. As the years passed, providing time for more sober reflection on the lessons of that war, Ford's view was to deepen and darken so that *The Man Who Shot Liberty Valance* (1962) is a much more morally ambiguous examination of the same theme. In 1946, however, the ends seemed to justify the means, and sacrifice to ensure progress was expected of Americans. Using a historic incident from America's past, Ford offered comfort to his audiences by demonstrating the value to be gained as a result of their losses in the war. Beyond that implicit reassurance, Ford also provided an explicit re-creation of an era in America's past, and a major addition to a favorite American film genre, the Western.

My Darling Clementine begins with the Earp brothers—Wyatt (Henry Fonda), Morgan (Ward Bond), Virgil (Tim Holt), and James (Don Garner)—driving a herd of cattle to California near Tombstone, Arizona. The three older Earps leave the cattle with James and ride into Tombstone for shaves. On the way, they encounter Old Man Clanton (Walter Brennan) and his sons. Clanton is a rough, taciturn man with a hint of evil about him. Wyatt and Clanton each recognize a potential and formidable adversary in the other.

The Earps ride on, discovering that Tombstone is a raw, wild, wide-open town, and very proud of it. Wyatt's shave is interrupted by a drunken Indian shooting up the town. When the marshal resigns rather than face him, Wyatt steps in and subdues Indian Joe. The mayor promptly offers the marshal's job to Wyatt, but he refuses, preferring cattle-herding to town-taming.

When the brothers return to the campsite, however, the herd is gone and James has been murdered. Wyatt rides back to Tombstone, accepts the marshal's job, and deputizes his brothers. In a touching graveside scene, Wyatt promises his dead brother to make the country a place where "kids like you can grow up and live safe."

The new marshal begins to establish his authority in the town and immediately confronts Doc Holliday (Victor Mature). Holliday is a gambler, a gunfighter, and a consumptive ex-surgeon from Boston who now runs Tombstone. Wyatt and Doc are immediately attracted to each other and both recognize that they are equals in competence and authority. As the film progresses, Wyatt will gain increasing strength, while Doc's power will wane. Doc has a Mexican mistress, Chihuahua (Linda Darnell), who dislikes Wyatt on sight. Clementine Carter (Cathy Downs), a nurse and Holliday's former love back in Boston, arrives in Tombstone hoping to rehabilitate Doc and persuade him to marry her. Wyatt is extremely attracted to her, and when Doc firmly refuses Clementine's proposal, he begins a shy pursuit of her himself. In a lyrical and exhilarating scene, Wyatt, freshly barbered and perfumed, escorts Clementine to the dedication of the new church. The scene ends in an awkward yet spirited dance in which Wyatt and Clementine declare their feelings for each other through movement and music.

The film now moves swiftly to the climactic gunfight at the O. K. Corral. In order to hide an indiscretion with Billy Clanton (John Ireland), Chihuahua unknowingly implicates Doc in the murder of James Earp. Wyatt confronts Doc, who denies it, and both men then confront Chihuahua. She confesses her lie and mentions Billy, who overhears the conversation and shoots her. Billy is also shot, but manages to escape to the Clanton ranch. Virgil Earp follows him and is shot by Old Man Clanton. The Clantons ride to Tombstone, toss Virgil's body at Wyatt's feet, and go to the O. K. Corral to wait for the inevitable gunfight. In the meantime, Doc has operated on Chihuahua. Seemingly successful, Doc believes he has recovered his surgical skills and can rejoin society as a productive citizen. Chihuahua dies, however, and Doc joins Wyatt, bitter at the loss of his renewed hope. In the gun battle, the Clantons are killed as well as Doc Holliday. Wyatt and Morgan ride off to California to tell their father what has happened, but not before Wyatt has promised Clementine that he will return to Tombstone, where she plans to stay to be the schoolmarm.

Ford indicates that the progress Wyatt makes from unshaven, independent cowboy to slightly dandified, responsible lawman, and the parallel movement of Tombstone from raw frontier settlement to a settled community with a church, a school, and a Shakespearean troupe in the saloon is not only inevitable but also necessary. There are no backward glances at the freedom lost with the wilderness, and no questioning of the sacrifices made by Doc and the dead Earp brothers. These losses may be mourned, but the progress achieved as a result is worth the price. Ford would move from firm convictions in the 1940's to many grave misgivings in the 1960's, most obviously in *The Man Who Shot Liberty Valance*. The Dodge City sequence in *Cheyenne Autumn* (1964) also indicates his suspicions about the blessings of civilization. In that sequence, Wyatt Earp, as played by James Stewart, is a lazy, decadent marshal in sharp contrast to the righteous certitude of Fonda's Wyatt Earp.

My Darling Clementine is of primary interest because it is the foundation of Ford's continuing examination of one of his major themes. It is also satisfying because Ford expands and develops a major convention of the Western genre, the gunfight. The film is the third retelling of the O. K. Corral battle in the sound era, the previous two efforts being *Frontier Marshal* (1939) and *Tombstone* (1942). In addition to his artistic contribution, Ford also brings historical accuracy to the incident. Ford knew Wyatt Earp in the 1920's, and the aging Marshal had described the gunfight to the young director. Ford is careful to avoid the face-to-face confrontation in the middle of the street, but has the Earps and Holliday approach the corral by back alleys and from behind fences, using whatever cover is available in order to get as close as possible. Earp had admitted he was a poor shot, and proximity was crucial.

The film is interesting further because of the relationship between Earp and Holliday. Wyatt is one of the few Fordian heroes allowed a friendship with a man clearly his equal. Most of the heroes in the Ford universe are more comfortable with men than with women, but they tend to form close ties only with men who are obviously subordinate. The Fordian hero must not be encumbered with strong emotional bonds. With Doc, however, Wyatt forms an attachment that is both emotionally satisfying and, more significant in terms of his growth as a responsible citizen, instructive. Doc teaches the raw cowboy the values of the East, the impulse toward law, order, religion, and education, qualities essential in civilizing the wilderness. Doc then steps aside and allows Wyatt literally to marry those Eastern virtues as embodied in Clementine Carter. By learning from Doc, and then pursuing his feminine aspect, Clementine, Wyatt fulfills his destiny as a town-tamer.

Finally, Fonda's contribution to the film must be acknowledged. From 1939 through 1948, Fonda made six films for Ford. Critics Joseph McBride and Michael Wilmington have pointed out the varying uses Ford makes of Fonda's silences in these films. Because of Fonda's physical attributes and his acting style, Ford is able to indicate subtle characterizations of the men Fonda is portraying without dialogue. As Wyatt Earp, Fonda is believable both as the self-reliant cowboy and as the shy, dandified suitor. He conveys the moral force in Earp that, although necessary, borders on rigidity and self-righteous-ness. It is a tribute to Fonda that it is impossible to imagine the other Ford favorite, John Wayne, in the role of Wyatt Earp. *My Darling Clementine* is distinguished, then, by a superb performance by Fonda, by the positive cel-ebration of the settling of the West, and by the genius of Ford, combining to produce a significant contribution to the genre and to American film history.

Don K Thompson

MY LITTLE CHICKADEE

Released: 1940
Production: Lester Cowan for Universal
Direction: Edward Cline
Screenplay: W. C. Fields and Mae West
Cinematography: Joseph A. Valentine
Editing: Edward Curtiss
Running time: 83 minutes

> *Principal characters:*
> Cuthbert J. Twillie .... W. C. Fields
> Flower Belle Lee .... Mae West
> Masked Bandit/Jeff Badger .... Joseph Calleia
> Mrs. Gideon .... Margaret Hamilton
> Amos Budge .... Donald Meek

In 1939, Universal Studios struck paydirt by combining W. C. Fields, an established star, even if, at that time, a somewhat faded one, with Edgar Bergen and Charlie McCarthy, a popular radio comedy act, in *You Can't Cheat an Honest Man.* The film salvaged Fields's cinematic career and made Universal a great amount of money in the bargain. By that time, Mae West, who had also recently come under contract to Universal, was having career problems of her own. The censorship power of the Hays Office over the studios had robbed her films of the freewheeling ribaldry that had made her famous, and, at the age of forty-seven, she was beginning to become something of a box-office liability. It seemed logical to Universal, therefore, to try the same sort of gambit that had rescued Fields's career. Fields and West were paired as Cuthbert J. Twillie and Flower Belle Lee, respectiviely, and thus *My Little Chickadee* was born.

The film is set in the Old West, and opens with a scene highly reminiscent of John Ford's *Stagecoach* (1939), as Flower Belle (Mae West), the town's scarlet woman, is banished from Little Bend for consorting with the notorious Masked Bandit. She is forbidden to return until she can prove that she is "respectable and married." A hatchet-faced spinster named Mrs. Gideon (Margaret Hamilton) not only leads the mob that hounds the lovely Flower Belle out of town, but she also boards the departing train to warn the good folks of Greasewood City, Flower Belle's destination, about her wicked ways. Also on the train is a down-and-out gambler, Amos Budge (played by Donald Meek, who had a similar role in *Stagecoach*).

The train stops to pick up Cuthbert J. Twillie (W. C. Fields), who has a faithful Indian companion named Ugh and a stovepipe hat with an absurdly wide hatband. The action is under way. Fields soon spots Flower Belle and begins to pump Mrs. Gideon for information about her. When the dour spinster replies that she cannot think of anything good to say, Twillie responds impatiently, "I can see what's good. Tell me the rest."

Flower Belle is cool to Twillie's advances until she inspects his baggage, which contains what seems to be a thick wad of money. Warming to Twillie's fulsome praise ("What symmetrical digits," he remarks about her gloved hand), she persuades Budge to pose as a parson, and a marriage ceremony commences: "Of course you're both acquainted with the rules of matrimony," Budge begins. "I've got a pretty good idea," leers Flower Belle.

When they arrive at Greasewood City, however, Flower Belle insists on her own room at the hotel, much to Twillie's consternation. Ugh arrives and asks "Big Chief gottum new squaw?" "New is right," grumps Twillie. "She hasn't even been unwrapped yet." The efforts of the disgruntled Twillie to obtain his conjugal prerogatives from the alluring but aloof Flower Belle (who has discovered that Twillie is not, in fact, fabulously wealthy) form the basis for the rest of the film's plot.

His romantic plans for the evening ruined, Twillie goes to the bar downstairs, where he spends much of his time bantering back and forth with the drinkers and gamblers. He obtains a stake by betting $100 on the cut of a deck. His opponent draws a king, which he shows to Twillie, who feigns embarrassment—a game between gentlemen should be based on trust, he says, no need to show the card. Twillie then cuts a card, which the camera's quick glimpse shows the audience (but not the other gambler) to be a lowly deuce. "Ace," Twillie calmly announces, hurriedly slapping the deck back together. When his opponents protests, Twillie acts wounded. He shuffles through the deck until he finds an ace, and, showing it to the other gambler, he says in a pained voice "There it is, if you must satisfy your morbid curiosity."

Twillie's tactics eventually land him in hot water with the locals, and he is about to be forcibly ejected from the saloon when Flower Belle makes a dramatic entrance. Jeff Badger (Joseph Calleia), the owner of the saloon and the leader of Greasewood City's disreputable element, is immediately smitten with Flower Belle ("Every man I meet wants to protect me," she remarks sarcastically. "I can't figure out what from"), and orders Twillie freed in an attempt to curry favor with her. Indeed, upon hearing Twillie boast of his prowess with a sixshooter, Badger hits upon a plan to win Flower Belle: he makes Twillie sheriff, a job which, in Greasewood City, has a very high mortality rate. As Flower Belle swaggers out of the room with the new sheriff in tow, Badger grins to his cronies, "She's gonna make a very pretty widow."

Flower Belle, meanwhile, has other things on her mind. She has received a note from the Masked Bandit of Little Bend requesting an assignation. Leaving Twillie alone for the evening—he winds up in bed with a goat—she meets the Zorro-like badman on a windswept hill. They pledge their love for each other (although she is a bit frustrated because she has never seen his face), and the Bandit commences a string of robberies in the Greasewood City area.

Twillie, learning of his wife's passion for the Masked Bandit, dons a cape and mask himself and clambers up a ladder into Flower Belle's bedroom window, where he snatches a kiss. This proves his undoing, since Flower Belle, a connoisseur of kisses, immediately realizes that he is not the real Masked Bandit. "You cheat," she accuses. "If a thing's worth having, it's worth cheating for," protests Twillie, but to no avail. Flower Belle forces him from her chambers.

Climbing back down the ladder from her window, Twillie is spotted. He is arrested as the Masked Bandit, and Flower Belle is also jailed as an accomplice. She escapes, but Twillie is left behind. As an angry mob prepares to string him up, Twillie is asked if he has a last request. "I'd like to see Paris before I die," he replies, adding hurriedly, "Philadelphia will do!"

Flower Belle, uncharacteristically stricken by her conscience, goes to Jeff Badger for help in rescuing Twillie. Badger kisses her, and she suddenly realizes that he and the Masked Bandit are one and the same. Agreeing to help, Badger puts in an appearance as the Bandit just as Twillie is about to be hanged. The townsfolk, realizing their mistake, free their shaken sheriff.

The film ends on an ironic note, with the two stars exchanging trademark quips. Flower Belle plans to stay in Greasewood City, and Twillie is leaving town. On his way out of the saloon, Twillie remarks that he is heading north, and, in a passable Mae West imitation, invites Flower Belle to "Come up and see me sometime." Not to be outdone, she grins and replies "I'll do that, my little chickadee." As she turns and wiggles upstairs, "The End" is superimposed over the appropriate portion of her anatomy.

The two stars collaborated on the script (Fields using his own name for a change, instead of one of his ludicrous pseudonyms), with West providing the film's basic plot and Fields supplying his usual devastating comedy to keep things lively. Both writers/stars were well known to screen audiences, and although they gave their characters other names, no one was fooled. W. C. Fields played W. C. Fields, and Mae West played Mae West.

Fields is in fine form, dropping polysyllables like rare pearls in his patented nasal rasp. His acting is highly energetic; he was evidently full of enthusiasm for the project (or at least his portion of it—the stars were rumored to have feuded, although they certainly work well together on the screen). Although *My Little Chickadee*, like *You Can't Cheat an Honest Man* before it, was destined to be remembered primarily as a Fields vehicle, Mae West gives one of her best performances. Matched at last with a screen personality the equal of her own, she does not have to worry about carrying the film by herself. Instead, she relaxes and gives a quintessentially Westian performance. Rolling her eyes and playing to the camera shamelessly, she squeezes *double entendres* out of virtually every sentence in the parody of lust that West made famous.

Universal's faith in the duo was amply rewarded. *My Little Chickadee* was an even greater success than *You Can't Cheat an Honest Man*, and it deserved to be. Fields's career prospered a bit longer, until ill health brought on by his legendary drinking forced an early retirement and an untimely death in 1946. Although Mae West was to outlive Fields by decades, she never recaptured the magic that marked her early career. *My Little Chickadee* was her last truly great moment on the screen. The epic confrontaton between these two legends of film comedy is reason enough to rank *My Little Chickadee* among the masterpieces of cinema.

Robert Mitchell

MY SISTER EILEEN

Released: 1942
Production: Max Gordon for Columbia
Direction: Alexander Hall
Screenplay: Joseph Fields and Jerome Chodorov; based on their play of the
  same name and adapted from short stories by Ruth McKenney
Cinematography: Joseph Walker
Editing: Viola Lawrence
Running time: 95 minutes

Principal characters:
Ruth Sherwood	Rosalind Russell
Robert Baker	Brian Aherne
Eileen Sherwood	Janet Blair
Appopolous	George Tobias
Chic Clark	Allyn Joslyn
Grandma Sherwood	Elizabeth Patterson
Walter Sherwood	Grant Mitchell
Frank Lippincott	Richard Quine
Effie Shelton	June Havoc
The Wreck	Gordon Jones

Rosalind Russell's durable film career embraced myriad roles and numerous genres. In *Sister Kenny* (1946) and *Mourning Becomes Electra* (1947) she deftly handled drama. In *His Girl Friday* (1940) she showed a flair for wisecracking and screwball comedy. She displayed her musical prowess in *Gypsy* (1962), and in perhaps her most famous individual character, she played the eternal *Auntie Mame* (1958). In retrospect, however, she probably remains best known for her "career woman" roles, of which there were more than twenty. Among them, the role of aspiring writer Ruth Sherwood in *My Sister Eileen* (1942) is a hallmark, for in addition to starring in the incisive and delightful film comedy, Russell triumphed in *Wonderful Town*, a musical version of the story, by Betty Comden and Adolph Green, which appeared on Broadway in 1953 and 1954. She also re-created the role in a live CBS television production of *Wonderful Town* in 1958, and portrayed Ruth in a *Lux Radio Theatre* presentation, thus playing the role in all four media, a unique accomplishment.

My Sister Eileen evolved from a series of short stories by Ruth McKenney, which appeared in *The New Yorker* and had real-life origins. The stories were later the basis for a successful Broadway play, which propelled Columbia to pay a then-staggering $225,000 for the film rights. Further proof of the property's durability is the fact that in 1955, Columbia remade *My Sister Eileen* as a musical (different from Comden and Green's version) starring Betty

Garrett, Jack Lemmon, and Janet Leigh. The short stories were also the basis
for a television series in the 1950's, starring Elaine Stritch as Ruth.

The story's enduring popularity is no doubt due to its clever, biting treatment of a long-familiar film theme—that of wide-eyed and innocent girls
seeking careers who suddenly find themselves in awesome New York City.
The adventures of Ruth Sherwood (Rosalind Russell) and her beautiful sister
Eileen (Janet Blair) begin when they rent a studio apartment in Greenwich
Village. The apartment becomes an important catalyst for the madcap hap-
penings that ensue. It is a subterranean apartment with a single window
looking out on the city, but the city also looks back. "Life passes up and down
in front of you, like a parade," says their landlord, the rotund (and scene-
stealing) Appopolous (George Tobias). He fails to tell the women that curious
dogs and cats and peeping toms are also frequent passers-by.

After moving in, Ruth and Eileen make a number of unsettling discoveries.
At various times of the day, the entire building begins shaking, because
workmen are blasting for a subway, just inches beneath their floor. There are
also strange visitors to contend with—since the previous tenant, medium Effie
Shelton (June Havoc), had an all-male clientele. Some of the neighbors are
also odd. The Wreck (Gordon Jones), for example, is a professional football
player biding his time out-of-season. He spends all his days exercising to stay
in shape, and does it right outside Ruth and Eileen's window. As Ruth will
ultimately note, "For a place with a bad location, and no neon sign, we're
doing a heck of a business."

Ruth has come to New York in hopes of becoming a writer. Eileen, who
already has a promising career as a man-attracting ingenue, is an aspiring
actress. Not surprisingly, each will encounter obstacles and surprises along
their respective ways. Ruth's career-minded pursuits are centered on getting
stories published in *Manhatter* magazine, an obvious take-off on *The New
Yorker*. While she seeks out bylines, Eileen blithely goes along, collecting a
string of admirers. In no time at all, Eileen has enticed a drugstore clerk
(Richard Quine), a newspaperman (Allyn Joslyn), and even a dozen members
of the Portuguese merchant marine.

The encounter with the merchant marines—who do not speak English—is
a highlight of the film. Determined to shake the men after a night on the
town, Ruth and Eileen form a conga dance line in a small club. With the men
enthusiastically dancing behind them, the women lead the line out the door
in hopes of breaking away. Instead, however, the line grows as excited passers-
by join in. By the time the line has reached their subterranean apartment,
a near-riot is brewing. Subsequently the girls are jailed, but in keeping with
Eileen's ability to charm, she fast becomes the toast of the police station.
Upon release from jail, she also receives a distinguished service award from
the Portuguese government.

The light-hearted events, however, cannot diminish the fact that Ruth is finding it difficult to crash the writing market, despite the encouragement of *Manhatter* editor Robert Baker (Brian Aherne), who is also taking a romantic liking to her. The girls have a hard time making enough money even to eat, and are forced to subsist on spaghetti. Events culminate with the publication of Ruth's first story, however, thus prompting a celebration at the girls' apartment—where friends and relatives from Cleveland (who comment on how plump Ruth is getting from eating so much spaghetti) have gathered. In the midst of the affair the workmen from the subway accidentally drill their way up through the floor. "Hey Pete! We musta took a wrong turn!" yells one of the men. It is a gag made funnier by the fact that the workmen are none other than The Three Stooges.

Directed by Alexander Hall, who also directed the stage play, *My Sister Eileen* evokes a charming, upbeat mood, as Ruth and Eileen seek success and gain an ensemble of friends and adventures along the way. Russell's performance dominates the production; in fact, it brought her the first of four Best Actress Oscar nominations. (She was later nominated for *Sister Kenny*, *Mourning Becomes Electra*, and *Auntie Mame*. Like her role in *His Girl Friday*, *My Sister Eileen*'s Ruth pointed Russell toward meatier, more sophisticated career-woman parts; it has been reported that she wanted to play Ruth Sherwood after seeing Shirley Booth do the role on Broadway, feeling that she could handle the part and that it could boost her career.

Pat H. Broeske

THE MYSTERY OF EDWIN DROOD

Released: 1935
Production: Universal
Direction: Stuart Walker
Screenplay: John L. Balderston and Gladys Unger; based on Leopold Atlas
   and Bradley King's adaptation of the novel of the same name by Charles
   Dickens
Cinematography: George Robinson
Editing: Edward Curtiss
Running time: 85 minutes

> *Principal characters:*
> John Jasper .... Claude Rains
> Neville Landless .... Douglass Montgomery
> Rosa Bud .... Heather Angel
> Edwin Drood .... David Manners
> Hiram Grewgious .... Walter Kingsford
> Durdles .... Forrester Harvey
> Princess Puffer .... Zeffie Tilbury
> Helena Landless .... Valerie Hobson

Charles Dickens' forte as a novelist was his ability to create character and atmosphere. Plotting, however, is not generally regarded as one of his strongest points. He resolved to work on this deficiency by writing a mystery story—a genre in which skillful plotting is vital. Thus the first of twelve projected installments of *The Mystery of Edwin Drood* (published serially, a chapter at a time, as was Dickens' custom) appeared in April, 1870. Three months and three chapters later, Dickens died. Three more chapters were found in manuscript and quickly published, but the last half of the novel, and the solution to the mystery, followed Dickens to his grave. Over the ensuing century, there has been no shortage of literary critics and creative writers who have ventured their version of the way Dickens would have resolved his story. Among these speculators were John Balderston and Gladys Unger, who wrote the screenplay for Stuart Walker's *The Mystery of Edwin Drood*, the second film version of Dickens' unfinished mystery (the original cinematic adaptation was Arthur Gilbert's British silent version in 1909). Dickens left Balderston and Unger the following "facts" with which to work. Edwin Drood is missing and presumed dead (by the other characters in the novel, if not by all of its readers). The most likely suspect is choirmaster/opium addict John Jasper, who is jealous of Drood's supposed romance with Rosa Bud, Drood's childhood sweetheart. Even Jasper believes himself to be guilty, although the incident is clouded in his mind by the effects of opium. Jasper attempts to throw suspicion on a young Ceylonese named Neville Landless, another rival for Rosa's affections. Meanwhile, a mysterious stranger, wearing an obvious disguise and calling himself Dick Datchery, appears on the scene and begins to investigate Drood's disappearance. Here Dickens' contributions to the tale end.

The filmmakers stick closely to the Dickens fragment, omitting only the development of a number of secondary characters—Sapsea, Crisparkle, Grewgious, and Helena Landless play minor roles in the film; Bazzard, Mr. Honeythunder, and Lieutenant Tartar are left out entirely—their inclusion would have made for a much longer, less focused film. Everything save the relationships between Drood, Jasper, and Landless is pared away.

The film *The Mystery of Edwin Drood* opens, like the novel, in an opium dream of John Jasper (Claude Rains). Bizarre images of the bell tower of the Cloisterham Cathedral and Rosa Bud (Heather Angel) swirl in his head; he awakens in torment and stalks out without paying, thus making an enemy of Princess Puffer (Zeffie Tilbury), the proprietress of the opium den. Princess Puffer's enmity will prove to be Jasper's undoing in the filmmaker's solution to the Drood mystery.

The next scene establishes the arrival of the Landless twins, Neville (Douglass Montgomery) and Helena (Valerie Hobson), in Cloisterham. They have recently arrived from Ceylon in pursuit of an education, but they hate the idea of living in the cold damp of an English December. Neville has an additional handicap: a particularly nasty temper. He is softened only by the sight of the beautiful Rosa Bud.

Walker introduces the rest of the principals in the next scene, a dinner in honor of Rosa's eighteenth birthday. Neville is obviously smitten with Rosa, but we learn that she has been betrothed since birth to Edwin Drood (David Manners). There is more friendship than passion, however, between Rosa and Drood. The third competitor for Rosa's affections is John Jasper himself, the secret opium eater but public paradigm of morality (and also Drood's uncle and guardian). Jasper cannot keep his eyes off Rosa; his piercing gaze follows her everywhere. She eventually faints under the strain of his spooky attention, thus bringing the party to a precipitous close.

Leaving the party in Neville Landless' company, Drood makes a mildly disparaging remark about Rosa. The infatuated Neville takes instant offense, and only John Jasper's timely intervention prevents a heated quarrel. The three men go to Jasper's flat for drinks, where Drood again offends Neville, who, now emboldened by drink, draws a knife on him. Jasper again separates the two, and an abashed Landless heads for home. The incident, however, is not forgotten—Jasper sees to that by telling the story to the town gossip, who spreads an exaggerated version of the tale. Meanwhile, Jasper takes a curious tour of the cathedral's crypt, expressing an unusual interest in the effects of quicklime on the human body. He drugs Durdles (Forrester Harvey), the custodian, and makes a wax impression of the key to the crypt.

It soon becomes apparent that Jasper has devised a scheme to eliminate both of his rivals: he will murder Drood and blame the deed on the hotheaded Neville Landless.

The situation is complicated when Rosa's guardian, Hiram Grewgious (Walter Kingsford), gives Drood Rosa's mother's wedding ring with an admonition to take it only if his love for Rosa is sincere. Drood accepts the ring, but both he and Rosa quickly begin having second thoughts about their impending marriage. They soon decide to break off their engagement but resolve to tell no one until after Christmas so as to avoid spoiling anyone's holiday. Until then, Drood will keep the ring.

Things come to a head on Christmas Eve. Drood disappears, having been last seen in Neville's company late the night before. Jasper accuses Neville, but Landless remains free owing to the lack of any concrete evidence against him. Jasper's plans slowly begin falling apart. He is stunned to learn that Drood and Rosa had broken off their engagement, and he is maddened when Rosa quickly transfers her affections to Neville Landless. He overplays his hand when he approaches Rosa with cryptic hints that she can only save Landless by marrying Jasper himself. Rosa spurns his advances and rushes to Neville with word of Jasper's veiled threats.

It is at this point that Balderston and Unger strike forth on their own to solve Dickens' mystery. The question of the true identity of Dick Datchery (one of the major unresolved questions of the novel) is answered quickly, as Neville Landless dons the wig and whiskers of that peculiar character and, with the advice of Hiram Grewgious, proceeds to accumulate evidence against John Jasper. The big break in the case comes when the frustrated Jasper turns once again to opium to ease his tormented mind. The short-changed Princess Puffer questions him closely while he is under the influence of the drug and learns enough from his ramblings to connect him with the disappearance of Edwin Drood. Jasper later kills her, but not before she has revealed her information to Datchery/Landless.

Things now happen swiftly, as Landless and Grewgious add up their clues. They rush to the crypts of the Cloisterham Cathedral, where Durdles tells them of a newly occupied coffin and some missing quicklime. Jasper pursues the men to the cathedral and sets upon Landless, but he is stopped by the arrival of most of the townsfolk. The coffin is opened; the quicklime has done its work, but Rosa's wedding ring is untouched, and its presence confirms two things: the body is that of Edwin Drood, and John Jasper was his killer. Jasper flees to the top of the cathedral, where he leaps to his death with Rosa's name on his lips. The film ends, ironically, almost as it began, with Jasper's opium visions come true, as Rosa Bud is married—to Neville Landless—while the bells in the cathedral tower peal out with joy.

Thus the Walker-Balderston-Unger version of the story offers a thoroughly orthodox conclusion to Dickens' mystery. All of the conspicuous loose ends are tied up, and the two major plot questions—who was Dick Datchery, and is Drood really dead—are answered in ways consistent with the evidence in the Dickens fragment of the story. Naturally, this conclusion was bound to disappoint a host of more ingenious (or perhaps merely more feverish) fans whose countertheories—most involving the contention that Drood was not dead at all and many suggesting that Datchery was Drood in disguise—have fueled a virtual cottage industry. While the filmmakers' solution to the mystery may have been prosaic, however, their approach to the film was definitely not. Indeed, Walker and his cast treat *The Mystery of Edwin Drood*, not so much as a mystery as a Gothic horror story. While the film may be mediocre Dickens, it is terrific cinema. Credit for this transformation belongs primarily to a trio of men who were at their best in horror films: cinematographer George Robinson, actor Claude Rains, and director Stuart Walker.

Rains as John Jasper is a study in torment as he uses his face, and particularly his eyes, to reflect Jasper's malign anguish. Ironically, in *The Invisible Man* (1934), his first screen role, Rains's face never appeared on camera. This film, released a year later, gave him a chance to show what he could do. Rains specialized in playing villains thereafter and garnered four Academy Award nominations throughout his long and distinguished acting career.

Other noteworthy members of the cast include Montgomery in a fine performance as the hotheaded Neville Landless; Kingsford in the small but likable role of Hiram Grewgious; Tilbury as Princess Puffer; and Angel, aptly named to portray the angelic Rosa Bud. Ironically, Manners as Edwin Drood has relatively little to do, since he disappears after only a few scenes. Harvey as Durdles turns in the most "Dickensian" performance as the drunken custodian of Cloisterham Cathedral's crypts.

Robinson does much to contribute to the Gothic atmosphere of the film. The interplay between light and shadow matches the mood of the film perfectly; and Jasper's opium den reveries are photographed in a swirling style that is particularly effective. Robinson worked on a number of Universal's Frankenstein-Dracula-Wolfman films throughout the 1940's and showed a real flair for the genre. Horror was also director Walker's strongest suit. *The Mystery of Edwin Drood* and *The Werewolf of London* (also in 1935) were the best of the handful of films he directed. He used his cast well, and wisely let Rains carry the movie. A year before tackling this project, Walker filmed a fairly good version of Dickens' *Great Expectations*.

The Mystery of Edwin Drood, however, merits our attention not as filmed Dickens, for the Dickensian elements are sparser in this work than usual. It is, rather, a good if little-known example of the Gothic horror film at which Universal excelled in the 1930's and 1940's, and also a good early showcase for the acting talents of Rains.

Robert Mitchell

THE NAKED CITY

Released: 1948
Production: Mark Hellinger for Universal
Direction: Jules Dassin
Screenplay: Albert Maltz and Melvin Wald
Cinematography: William Daniels (AA)
Editing: Paul Weatherwax (AA)
Running time: 96 minutes

> *Principal characters:*
> Lieutenant Dan Muldoon .... Barry Fitzgerald
> Frank Niles .... Howard Duff
> Ruth Morrison .... Dorothy Hart
> Jimmy Halloran .... Don Taylor
> Willie Garzah .... Ted DeCorsica
> Narrator .... Mark Hellinger
> Dr. Stoneman .... House Jameson

In the years immediately following World War II, there arose in Italy a school of filmmaking known as "neorealism." In reaction to the glossy Hollywood-style productions that seemed to have little relevance to the real world, directors such as Roberto Rossellini (*Open City*, 1945), Vittorio De Sica (*Bicycle Thieves*, 1948, *Umberto D*, 1952), and Luchino Visconti (*L'Ossessione*, 1942) made films that were grimly realistic and almost documentary in style, and which dealt with life at the bottom of society. In the United States, in 1948, producer Mark Hellinger combined this neorealistic style with a voice-over narration common to newsreels and other documentaries to produce *The Naked City*. Directed by Jules Dassin, *The Naked City* follows a squad of homicide detectives through the seamier parts of New York City as they solve a murder case, and, in the process, gives the viewer an unvarnished look at life in "the naked city."

The film opens with scenes of the New York skyline shot from a helicopter above the city. As we watch, Hellinger's voice warns us that *The Naked City* is a different sort of movie. It has been shot on location, and many of the people appearing in it are real, everyday citizens. "This is the city as it is," Hellinger emphasizes. Hellinger continues his commentary throughout the film. Indeed, his narrator becomes as much a character in the film as the actors on the screen. Omniscient and more than a little cynical, the narrator functions as the voice of the naked city itself.

The action begins at 1:00 A.M. one summer morning. As Hellinger tells us that most of the solid citizens are asleep by now, we see vignettes of the night people—workers, partyers, and criminals. We watch two men drown a young woman in her bathtub. At 5:00 A.M., the city stirs. The murderers have a falling out, and one of them kills the other. The original murder victim—Joan Dexter, a former model—is discovered by her housekeeper, and the police are summoned. Lieutenant Dan Muldoon (Barry Fitzgerald) is the 1940's version of Everycop, an Irishman with a thick brogue, a warm heart, and a mind like a steel trap. He is assisted by young Jimmy Halloran (Don Taylor), also Irish, but less stereotypically so.

We watch as Muldoon, Halloran, and their assistants sift through the meager clues: a bottle of prescription drugs, a pair of men's pajamas that the housekeeper identifies as belonging to one Philip Henderson, and a black sapphire ring. The housekeeper also names Frank Niles (Howard Duff) as another of Miss Dexter's close companions. The narrator warns us not to expect any startling breakthroughs. In a city with eight million potential suspects, the police proceed methodically, by trial and error.

As the junior member of the team, Halloran pounds the pavement, as the narrator taunts him about the distance between the clues he is trying to run down. Halloran interviews Miss Dexter's doctor, named Stoneman (House Jameson), who attests to the wild life she led (she "needed a good spanking," he avers), and also Ruth Morrison (Dorothy Hart), one of Dexter's friends at the modeling agency, who informs Halloran that Miss Dexter was fired for flirting with a client.

Meanwhile, Dan Muldoon is attempting, without much luck, to identify the mysterious Philip Henderson. In the interim, he interviews Frank Niles and proceeds to catch him in a series of obvious lies. Niles denies knowing Ruth Morrison, for example, only to have Miss Morrison walk into the room and announce that they are engaged to be married. "Congratulations," Muldoon remarks drily. It soon becomes clear that Niles was involved in some illegal scheme with Joan Dexter; and, although he has an alibi for the night of her murder, Muldoon puts him under twenty-four-hour surveillance.

Interspersed with the criminal investigation are scenes of everyday life in the naked city. Some of these—particularly the scenes involving Jimmy Halloran and his family—are pleasantly domestic; most, however, show the darker side of urban life. In a bit of black comedy, a woman, obviously crazy, confesses to the murder of Joan Dexter; and Miss Dexter's parents, alternately grief-stricken, embarrassed, and furious at their dead daughter, come to identify her body. The scenes involving Mr. and Mrs. Dexter are particularly powerful, and Hellinger and Dassin spare us none of their naked emotion.

As Muldoon and Halloran come under increased pressure to solve the case—the newspapers are quick to sensationalize the "Bathtub Girl" murder—they deduce that Frank Niles (who, under the watchful eyes of the police, has been pawning stolen jewelry all over town) was involved with Miss Dexter in a burglary ring, and that the black sapphire ring in Miss Dexter's room had been stolen from none other than Ruth Morrison.

Muldoon, Halloran, and Ruth Morrison go to Niles's apartment for a confrontation and arrive just in time to prevent him from being murdered. In a particularly well shot and edited scene, Halloran pursues Niles's assailant down the fire escape and through the streets. Much of the scene takes place in shadows, as the filmmakers deliberately obscure the action—just as the solution to the murder remains obscure to Muldoon and Halloran. Frank Niles declines to assist the police in any way, and is promptly thrown into jail. Things begin to clear up a bit when the killer's dead partner is dredged up out of the river. Running through a list of the dead man's known accomplices, Halloran hits upon the name of Willie Garzah (Ted DeCorsica), whose *modus operandi* seems to tie in with the tangled Dexter-Niles case.

As Halloran is tracking down Garzah in lower Manhattan, Frank Niles, succumbing to the threat of twenty years in prison, begins to talk. He identifies the mysterious "Philip Henderson" as Miss Dexter's Dr. Stoneman. When confronted, Stoneman is almost relieved. He admits to being a part of the burglary ring—he tipped off the thieves when one of his wealthy patients was going to be out of town—and names Willie Garzah as the missing accomplice and likely killer of Joan Dexter.

All of the action now converges on the hunt for Garzah. Halloran locates him first, but Garzah disarms the policeman and knocks him cold. "It's a great big beautiful city, copper. Try and find me," snarls the killer as he heads for the streets. The chase continues. Garzah is pursued by Halloran from one direction and by Muldoon and his men from another. As the narrator taunts the killer ("Don't lose your head!"), Garzah climbs onto one of the girders on an elevated train platform. Shots are exchanged, and the filmmakers grant Garzah one last view of the city (ironically similar to the shot that opens the film) before he falls to his death. The story ends as it began, with a summary by the omniscient narrator. "There are eight million stories in the naked city. This . . . has been one of them."

The Naked City succeeds on two levels. The first of these levels is its plot. It is a simple, straightforward detective story which Dassin sees through to its logical conclusion. Writers Albert Maltz and Melvin Wald give him a script with believable characters in believable situations, and the cast brings the script to life with effortless aplomb. Particularly noteworthy are the performances of Duff as Frank Niles, who watches helplessly as his ad-libbed alibies unravel before his very eyes, and DeCorsica as Willie Garzah, the thuggish killer. Only Fitzgerald, who emphasizes the Irish leprechaun side of Lieutenant Muldoon a bit too much, appears to be acting.

It is this realism that forms the basis of the film's second level of success. *The Naked City*, as producer/narrator Hellinger promised, is an unvarnished look at New York City. Hellinger and Dassin, aided by the brilliant cinematography of William Daniels (who won an Academy Award for his efforts), have produced a film of uncompromising realism. *The Naked City* arguably stands as the finest example of American neorealism. Its style was followed by a highly successful television series of the same name during the early 1960's.

Robert Mitchell

THE NAKED SPUR

Released: 1952
Production: William H. Wright for Metro-Goldwyn-Mayer
Direction: Anthony Mann
Screenplay: Sam Rolfe and Harold Jack Bloom
Cinematography: William C. Mellor
Editing: George White
Sound: Douglas Shearer
Music: Bronislau Kaper
Running time: 91 minutes

Principal characters:
Howard Kemp .... James Stewart
Lina Patch .... Janet Leigh
Ben Vandergroat .... Robert Ryan
Roy Anderson .... Ralph Meeker
Jesse Tate .... Millard Mitchell

In *The Naked Spur*, a bounty hunter, along with two other men who cross his path, attempts to deliver an accused killer to the authorities in civilization. A woman traveling with the outlaw becomes a catalyst in the drama, and the hero, who has been nursing a mysterious psychological wound, finally gives up his obsession following a violent and spectacular physical conflict. The plot is that simple, but the film has such a resonance and stark beauty that it renders incidental the humble origins. It is a film which commands attention on three levels. First, the elaboration of the narrative demonstrates persistent invention at the same time that a classic purity is retained. Further, the five characters, created from archetypes within the Western genre, achieve a remarkable degree of individuality as well as compose a fascinating ensemble. Finally, the landscape itself functions significantly in the drama and vividly underscores the film's elemental nature. In the context of an evolved criticism of cinema, none of this is surprising; a lean, unadorned screenplay often provides the strongest material for a film. The cast could not be improved upon. Most crucially, director Anthony Mann is retrospectively regarded as an artist with an uncommon gift for uniting landscape and character and for portraying action with psychological incisiveness.

The very first image imposes upon us the emotional and physical forceful-ness of the film. A serene outdoor setting in the Colorado Rockies, apparently empty of life, is disfigured as an unsettling swish pan reveals in close-up the gleaming spur of the title. The rider, Howard Kemp (James Stewart), turns his horse and moves toward the background of the frame, merging with the landscape. The solitary figure soon discovers another man in a clearing, the old prospector Jesse Tate (Millard Mitchell). Friendly and easygoing, Tate is wary of Kemp, whose tenseness and reserve suggest unprovoked hostility, but he accepts Kemp's assertion that he is a lawman and accepts his offer to help find a wanted man for twenty dollars. The two men travel on, soon encountering Roy Anderson (Ralph Meeker), a young cavalry lieutenant who, it develops, has been dishonorably discharged. The fugitive, Ben Vandergroat (Robert Ryan), is above the men at the edge of a rocky precipice and is throwing rocks down to create a continuing small avalanche. As Jesse covers them, Howard and Roy attempt to scale the steeper face behind Ben. Howard fails and is burned by the rope, but Roy makes it easily and sneaks up behind Ben. He is surprised by Lina Patch (Janet Leigh), Ben's companion, who bites his gun arm. He punches her in the face and jumps Ben.

The two men fight until Howard and Jesse arrive to assist in Ben's capture. Ben reveals to the other men that there is a reward on him but that Howard is not a lawman. Roy and Jesse cut themselves in for equal shares, and Ben immediately begins scheming to find ways to set the three men against one another, knowing that Howard's share of the reward, by itself, will not be enough to buy back the ranch that he has lost. It is at this moment that intense close-ups of Lina and Ben present a foreshadowing of incipient conflict within the group. With his hands bound, Ben holds Lina like a prisoner as the sound of her injured horse being shot is heard offscreen. Numbed by the emotional shock of the loss of her animal, Lina can do nothing but meekly assent to Ben's pathological whisperings.

As the group travels on, we learn more about them. Roy is a man of no moral character. His earlier troubles with the army had been the result of his apparent seduction of an Indian princess so it comes as no surprise when he begins to lust after Lina immediately. Jesse, it develops, has always hoped to make a big gold strike and failed to do so. Lina is the daughter of a dead friend of Ben, and theirs is not a love relationship. Ben and Howard knew each other in Kansas, and there was no personal antagonism between them. All of the characters talk freely about themselves, with the exception of the grim and taciturn Howard, who remains mysterious and aloof. Some insight is provided into his character, however, by Ben, who seems to know him better than he knows himself. In a conversation between the two, Ben pointedly philosophizes: "Choosin' a way to die, what's the difference? Choosin' a way to live—that's the hard part."

In theory, Howard has been designated as the hero of the film by the presence of Stewart in the role, but before half the film has elapsed, sympathetic identification with him has been strained considerably. The villain, Ben, who has done Howard no personal harm, is a much more likable and ingratiating figure. The moral bankruptcy of Roy makes him appear to be the antagonist until the climax reveals the chilling evil of Ben's true nature. Howard, who is repressing his better instincts, sees Roy as an unsettling mirror who reflects the erosion of his own decency. Even in this relationship, however, there is something perversely appealing about the easygoing Roy as opposed to the morosely obsessive Howard. "Loosen up. Spring is here," Roy tells Howard as the group begins its journey. It sounds like a fair request.

In the first scene in which Howard and Lina speak alone, his weak attempts at self-justification at her expense do not make him more endearing. Only the subtle touch of unexpected softness in his voice as he speaks about ranching contradicts this impression, but he quickly reverts to his accustomed harshness. The turning point for his character occurs only after he has been wounded in the leg, the physical wound visually reinforcing the impression that he is emotionally crippled. The outbreak of violence which resulted in the wound is not unexpectedly precipitated by Roy. The Indian princess he claimed to have seduced was apparently unwilling, and he is now being pursued by her tribe. The group sends him on his way, but he subsequently risks their lives by ambushing the Indians further up the trail. In the ensuing fight, a shocking moment occurs. After killing an Indian, Howard, his eyes blazing psychopathically, hits him again and again for no reason. In one of several notably dramatic images used to close major sequences, Howard is the last of the group to ride away from the scene. He turns for a moment, looking back into the frame as he surveys the corpses of the Indians, then bows his head and rides quietly out of the frame.

In the night that follows, the unsettled and unsettling hero finally reveals himself. Screaming hysterically, Howard awakens from sleep, abruptly emerging from below the frame to disrupt again a tranquil image. The other four characters stand over him while Lina tries to comfort him as he trembles with fever and speaks deliriously to a girl he calls Mary. This exposure of vulnerability is enhanced by the appearance of an unexpected musical theme, the tender "Beautiful Dreamer." Finally, Ben explains what Howard's ravings are about, taking great pleasure in telling the story. Howard had left his ranch in his fiancée's name when he went off to fight in the Civil War. She had sold the ranch and used the money to run away with another man.

This remarkable revelation finally provides perspective for Howard's bitterness and solitude. Raging against himself and unwilling to be hurt once more, he lashes out brutally at others with little or no provocation. Our intuitive concern for him, also shared by Lina, is, thus, finally justified. After a few more days of hard riding, the group takes refuge in a cave during a storm. Ben persuades Lina to distract Howard so that he can make his escape, convincing her only through his assurance that if she does not help him, he will try to kill Howard. In a tender scene, Howard finally does "loosen up." Stirred by Lina's warmth and gentleness, he allows himself to respond to her. With moving impulsiveness, he takes her in his arms and kisses her passionately. At this moment, Ben tries to make good his escape, but Howard sees him and subdues him. This time, it is the circumstances which prompt him to resume a violent stance. In the cramped space of the cave, the camera isolates him from the other four members of the group as he stands quivering with a gun in his hand, ready to kill Ben. Unexpectedly, he relents and even prevents Roy from shooting Ben. Again, at the conclusion of this sequence, he is alone in the frame, a tense silhouette staring out from the mouth of the cave into the night sky, trying to force himself to believe that a woman has once more betrayed him.

Howard refuses to go along with Roy in risking Ben's life the next day by placing his neck in a hangman's noose to assume that he will reach the other side of a rushing river. Howard and Roy fight it out. The effort exhausts them both, and Ben takes the opportunity to use Jesse as a means of escape, that night, by convincing the other man that he knows where there is a gold mine that he will give to him. The next morning, Ben overpowers Jesse and, over Lina's horrified protests, kills him in cold blood. He then takes refuge on a high rock overlooking the river and waits to ambush Howard and Roy. He scorns Lina's efforts to dissuade him, but when the two men arrive, she saves them by shouting a warning. Ben responds by hitting her with his rifle. As Ben and Roy fire at each other, Howard, now in greater control of himself, climbs the sheer face of the cliff and throws his spur into Ben's face. Shot by Roy, Ben falls into the river below, his corpse drifting into the shallows away from the torrent. Roy crosses the river by means of a rope and then ties another rope, thrown by Howard, around Ben's body. As he starts back across the river, a huge tree stump hits him and his dead body is washed away in the rushing waters. Pulling Ben's body to safety, Howard coldly insists that he will carry through with his initial plan. With his back to the camera in a forceful forward tracking shot, he drags Ben's body to his horse, then turns with tears in his eyes, as Lina tells him that she will go with him anyway. Emotionally spent, he holds her and sobs. He unties Ben's body to bury him along with Jesse and tells Lina that they will go to California. The camera pans up into the sky as the "Beautiful Dreamer" music is heard, and a final dissolve reveals the couple riding away across a clear landscape.

With the exception of the sequence in the cave, most of *The Naked Spur* was shot in vivid Technicolor on location in Rocky Mountain National Park. The exteriors are awesome. The rushing rivers, jagged rocks, and majestic trees of an unspoiled land provide perfect counterpoint to the emotional delirium of the unsettled protagonist and the raw physicality of the action. Stunt men and doubles are rarely in evidence. The camera reveals quite clearly that the five players actually did most of the fighting, climbing, riding, and crossing of raging rivers. This is not the least of their accomplishments, and it enhances the credibility of their characterizations. Similarly, the cinematography and sound recording, accomplished in rugged settings where the control readily available on a sound stage is not possible, are outstanding achievements.

None of the five roles is secondary, and Stewart, Ryan, Leigh, Mitchell, and Meeker all contribute memorably. Ryan, so adept at bringing nuance and charisma to psychologically unbalanced characters, whether good or evil, often dominates while a sullen Stewart keeps to himself, reacting to the others when called upon to do so. Colorful villains are common in the films of director Mann, providing counterpoint to the moral ambivalence of the heroes. The laughing Ryan, flaunting his keen intelligence and perceptions about life, is often mesmerizing. Roy, as dashing and confident as he is hollow and corrupt, is equally compelling as portrayed by the swaggering Meeker. The guileless but endearing Jesse is wonderfully incarnated by Mitchell, one of this splendid actor's last roles. Leigh, portraying the only character who possesses unambiguous moral goodness, broke out of ingenue roles with this film to become one of the most versatile and interestng actresses of the period. Her beauty is not concealed by the men's clothes she wears throughout, and she has enough presence to hold her own in highly dramatic scenes with actors as skilled as Stewart and Ryan.

As for Stewart, it is commonly observed that his Westerns for Mann represent a deliberate departure from the gentle and idealistic *persona* that had originally made him a star. The harrowing fury one finds in characters like Howard Kemp is not, however, entirely remote from the Capraesque Stewart of earlier years, as exemplified by his performance in Frank Capra's *It's a Wonderful Life* (1947). The gentleness and vulnerability once exposed are more moving because of the tough and callous façade. The climactic moment of the film, occurring when the façade finally breaks down completely, is a devastating catharsis, and Stewart's intensity and immersion in the role seem to be so complete that it is difficult to discern any trace of his professional technique or to perceive the moment as other than the emotional release of a real man.

Chronologically, *The Naked Spur* is the fifth of ten exceptional Westerns made by Mann in the 1950's and his third with Stewart. At this midpoint, it crystallizes the formal and dramatic qualities of his work which had been developed previously and would be elaborated upon in the films still to come. Mann's individual talent, thriving in a genre he plainly adored, is attested by a *mise-en-scène* which becomes more rewarding the more closely it is analyzed. This *mise-en-scène*, which is the result not only of a conscious style but also of absolute belief in the material, attains, in this work, a rare purity which is at once physical and moral. Honed to essentials such as a small group of characters, a single journey, and a neurotic obsessiveness struggling against an impassive landscape, the screenplay by Sam Rolfe and Harold Jack Bloom is an ideal one for Mann. With no incidentals to distract him, he is able to give all of his attention to compositions and camera angles which will most expressively integrate the raw emotions of the characters with the unadorned beauty of settings far from civilization. The film is effective in a manner exemplified by the musical score provided by Bronislau Kaper, dramatically stark and unsentimental with the exception of the three key sequences in which the "Beautiful Dreamer" theme appears. The prevailing tone of the film is as cold and cutting as a spur, and the moments of romantic yearning seem like fragments of a tormenting dream. Perhaps this explains why the hero's ultimate self-renewal carries such uncommon moral and emotional force.

Blake Lucas

NATIONAL VELVET

Released: 1944
Production: Pandro S. Berman for Metro-Goldwyn-Mayer
Direction: Clarence Brown
Screenplay: Theodore Reeves and Helen Deutsch; based on the novel of the same name by Enid Bagnold
Cinematography: Leonard Smith
Editing: Robert J. Kern (AA)
Running time: 123 minutes

Principal characters:
Mi Taylor	Mickey Rooney
Velvet Brown	Elizabeth Taylor
Mr. Brown	Donald Crisp
Mrs. Brown	Anne Revere (AA)
Edwina Brown	Angela Lansbury
Donald Brown	Jackie "Butch" Jenkins
Malvolia Brown	Juanita Quigley
Farmer Ede	Reginald Owen

As popular today as it was upon its release, *National Velvet* has all the earmarks of a truly enduring film classic. Adapted from the English children's novel by Enid Bagnold, *National Velvet* was made at a time when M-G-M was interested in turning out "family fare" and was making many films starring its stable of pre-adolescent and adolescent contract players. The series started with the famed *The Wizard of Oz* (1939), starring Judy Garland. Within the next five years, M-G-M was to employ the talents of Mickey Rooney, Roddy McDowall, Margaret O'Brien, Jackie "Butch" Jenkins and the beautiful Elizabeth Taylor in such films as *My Friend Flicka* (1943), *The Human Comedy* (1943), *The White Cliffs of Dover* (1944), and *Lassie Come Home* (1943). All of these films combined sweetness and light with winning performances from truly talented actors and actresses.

What sets *National Velvet* apart from the rest of M-G-M's family films (aside from Elizabeth Taylor's fine performance in her first starring role) is the beauty of the production and the uniformly excellent performances of the adults in the film. Anne Revere and Donald Crisp play the parents of Velvet Brown (Elizabeth Taylor), and between them they create such a strong aura of warmth and good family feeling that the picture is lifted above the level of children's fare and becomes a human interest story, appealing to everyone. Mickey Rooney proved in *National Velvet* that he was capable of more than the Andy Hardy films, and Elizabeth Taylor was radiant as a twelve-year-old girl completely captivated by horses. The combination of natural beauty, total innocence, and innate intelligence that Taylor brought to her characterization of Velvet Brown made the role hers forever. In the 1978 sequel *International Velvet*, in which Velvet Brown (played by Nanette Newman) is twenty years older, memories of Elizabeth Taylor's freshness and high spirits keep coming back, even with the addition of Tatum O'Neal as Velvet's horse-loving niece.

Because *National Velvet* was made in Hollywood at the M-G-M studio, the English coastal village of Sewels is somewhat mock Tudor, with signs to Brighton pointing to the Pacific Ocean. It matters little to one's enjoyment of the film where it was shot, however, for it has the charm of a modern fairy tale. M-G-M in the 1940's tended to slight accuracy in details of period or place, and what usually emerged was what studio designers thought places *should* look like.

The story is set in prewar England, in the quiet Sussex seacoast village of Sewels. Into the town wanders Mi Taylor (Mickey Rooney). About eighteen years old, he was once a jockey but is now a dispirited itinerant with no family or friends. He meets twelve-year-old Velvet Brown in the village and finds that her mother is the person he is seeking. His recently deceased father had an address book which Mi found among his belongings; in it was listed a Mrs. Brown of Sewels. Mi is immediately taken by Velvet, an appealing girl whose childish dreams center around owning and riding horses. Velvet invites Mi to her home for dinner, and on the way, they admire a beautiful horse belonging to a local farmer. As they watch, the horse easily jumps its high fence and only Velvet, who has a way with horses, is able to prevent it from running away. When they arrive at the Browns' house, Mrs. Brown warmly welcomes Mi after learning that he is the son of the man who had trained her to swim the English Channel years before. Mi had always suspected that his father had been more than a trainer to Mrs. Brown, who gave up her promising career as a swimmer to become the wife of the local butcher. Now content and a mother of four, she leaves her swimming trophies in the attic, but Mi's presence brings back a rush of memories to her, and she persuades her husband to give the boy a job in his shop. Velvet, her sisters, Edwina (Angela Lansbury) and Malvolia (Juanita Quigley), and her little brother Donald (Jackie "Butch" Jenkins), are delighted to have Mi with them, and soon he is like a member of the family.

When Farmer Ede (Reginald Owen), the owner of The Pi (the horse Velvet rescued), decides to raffle his horse because of its wild behavior, Mi buys a ticket for Velvet, and she wins. Velvet and Mi now have a common interest as they proceed to train The Pi. Velvet confides her wild ambition to Mi. She wants to enter The Pi in the Grand National Steeplechase, and nothing he says can dissuade her. Velvet tells her mother of her dream, and Mrs. Brown surprises her by providing the £10 for the entry fee, using the one hundred gold sovereigns that she won for swimming in the channel. In a touching scene, Mrs. Brown encourages Velvet to follow her dream and realize her ambition, betraying just a tinge of regret that she stopped her own career just when she was on her way to fulfillment.

Velvet and Mi spend months training The Pi, with Velvet always riding. Mi refuses to ride and will not tell Velvet his terrible secret: that he was once blamed for the death of a fellow jockey after causing a spill in a race. He hires an excellent jockey to ride The Pi in the Grand National, but the day before the race, the rider admits to Velvet that he does not think the horse has a chance. Angry, Velvet refuses to let the jockey ride, and Mi, now desperate and worried, decides that he will conquer his fear and ride The Pi himself. Velvet has the same idea, however; she has her heart set on riding in the Grand National and persuades Mi to help her disguise herself as a boy. Reluctantly, Mi agrees and cuts her hair and helps her fix a riding outfit. On the day of the race, Velvet fools the officials and rides brilliantly, winning the Grand National.

The most important jumping race in England has been won by an unknown rider, but her triumph is short-lived as she slips from her saddle in a faint right after the race. In the field hospital, her subterfuge is discovered, and The Pi is disqualified. Velvet and Mi still know that their horse is a winner, however, and Velvet has had her moment of glory. They return home to Sewels in honor, and Mi leaves the village. Velvet's faith in him has regenerated Mi and given him the strength to face the world.

Critics were lavish in their praise of *National Velvet*. Made during the war-troubled years of the 1940's, the film contained just the right amount of sentimentality, pathos, and Hollywood hokum to endear itself to all. Especially outstanding in smaller roles were Jackie "Butch" Jenkins, as Velvet's younger brother, and a teenage Angela Lansbury, fresh from England, as Edwina, the older sister of Velvet, who is forever falling in love. Anne Revere won an Academy Award as the strong and loving Mrs. Brown, and Donald Crisp repeated his role as the crusty but lovable father figure that he had played in *Lassie Come Home*. Although the film was only the beginning of stardom for Elizabeth Taylor, she is still often remembered primarily as the girl who was "in love with horses" in *National Velvet*.

Joan Cohen

NIGHT AND DAY

Released: 1946
Production: Arthur Schwartz for Warner Bros.
Direction: Michael Curtiz
Screenplay: Charles Hoffman, Leo Townsend, and William Bowers; based
    on Jack Moffitt's account of the career of Cole Porter
Cinematography: Peverell Marley and William V. Skall
Editing: David Weisbart
Dance direction: LeRoy Prinze
Music: Cole Porter
Running time: 128 minutes

Principal characters:

Cole Porter	Cary Grant
Linda Porter	Alexis Smith
Monty Woolley	Himself
Carole Hill	Ginny Simms
Omar Cole	Henry Stephenson
Mary Martin	Herself

Night and Day is the Warner Bros. version of the life of Cole Porter. The
fact that it is largely fiction is not surprising. One reason is that Hollywood
biographical films are usually careless about factual details, and the genre of
musical biography, which reached its peak in the 1940's, was especially given
to "creative" treatment of reality. Another reason is that for legal reasons
the film studios were usually careful to be sure that any living people portrayed
would not be offended. In addition, the studio had given Porter considerable
control over the production in order to receive his permission to make the
film. (It also paid him a reported $300,000.) Indeed, the credits of *Night and
Day* claim only that it is "based on the career of Cole Porter."

The many differences, both large and small, between the actual life of
Porter and the way it is portrayed in the film are, therefore, largely immaterial
since neither Porter nor Warner Bros. desired historical authenticity. Porter,
for example, asked that Cary Grant play him in the film. This request, which
may have been somewhat facetious, was obviously based on Grant's qualities
as a handsome, romantic film star rather than on any resemblance he bore
to Porter. The studio executives were, of course, virtually certain that a film
featuring Grant and the songs of Cole Porter would be a box-office hit regardless of whether the script was an accurate account of the events of Porter's
life.

Originally the studio hoped to have several name entertainers—such as
Fred Astaire, Danny Kaye, and Sophie Tucker—appear in the film to perform
songs written by Porter, but that plan proved to be too expensive. Instead,

Mary Martin appears as herself to sing "My Heart Belongs to Daddy," the Porter song most associated with her, and most of the other numbers are sung by a character portrayed by Ginny Simms who is called Carole Hall and is a composite of several of the singers, such as Ethel Merman, who introduced Porter's songs. Also, Monty Woolley plays a fictionalized version of himself in the film; instead of being a fellow undergraduate with Porter as he was in real life, he is at the beginning of the film a law professor at the same time Porter is a student.

Indeed, after a title that establishes the year as 1914, the film begins with Professor Woolley being censured by the administration at Yale for not being dignified enough and for neglecting his classes. Woolley agrees with their emphasis upon dignity, but in the very next scene he is in shirtsleeves boisterously leading a student pep rally with a megaphone. Cole Porter is also expected to lead his own song "Bulldog," but first he must be summoned from the Follies Theater, where he is playing the piano.

When Christmas vacation comes, Porter goes back to his Indiana home, taking Woolley with him, ostensibly to help him catch up on the law studies that he has been neglecting. At the opulent family mansion, however, Porter tells his grandfather, Omar Cole (Henry Stephenson), that he is not going back to Yale because he cannot be a lawyer. "Every contract I read turns into a lyric," he says. Porter also meets Linda (Alexis Smith), who is visiting one of Porter's cousins. One image sums up this turning point in Porter's life. His disappointed grandfather sits in the foreground while Porter, Linda, and the other family and guests gather around the piano and sing in the background; in the center of the room is an abandoned set of law books that the grandfather had given Porter for Christmas.

Then Porter and Woolley begin raising money for Porter's first show, *See America First*, which Woolley will direct. They are successful in raising the money and putting on the show, but the show fails because on the same day it opens, the Lusitania is sunk and the attention of the public turns away from musical comedies. In the wake of the show's failure, Porter also decides that he cannot remain on the sidelines and goes to fight in France. We see him sitting with other soldiers in a partially destroyed building writing "Begin the Beguine." Bombs begin to fall, and when the smoke clears, Porter lies wounded.

The next section of the film is devoted to Porter's rehabilitation, which is largely engineered by Linda, who has become a nurse and gone to Europe after Porter left the United States. Porter is depressed and says he does not think that his music is important anymore, but Linda gives him a pep talk and buys him a piano. Soon he is sitting at the piano staring at a clock on the wall, and the words of "Night and Day" begin coming to him—"like the tick tick tock of the stately clock." Then he hears rain outside, and more words come to him, "the drip drip drop of the raindrops," and when Linda enters the room "You, You, You." The music, however, is still giving him trouble, and he continues to play the piano as he talks to Linda. Suddenly he interrupts her. "Wait a minute; I think I've got it," he says, and begins playing the finished melody of the song.

Hollywood has always had trouble portraying artistic or intellectual creation, and this scene is a perfect example of the foolishness that usually resulted when a musician or writer was depicted on the screen. In fact, a segment of M-G-M's *That's Entertainment, Part II* (1976) is devoted to a humorous look at how songs were inspired and composed in that studio's films. *Night and Day* was actually composed more than a dozen years later for Astaire to sing in a Broadway show.

In the film Porter then rejects Linda's attempts to help him financially just as he rejected his family's money and goes back to the United States. He tries to sell his song but is told he lacks "the common touch" and finally is reduced to playing in a music store to promote the sale of sheet music. During a lunch break he and Carole Hill (Ginny Simms), the singer with whom he works, perform one of Porter's own compositions, "What Is This Thing Called Love?," and a crowd gathers.

Porter and Woolley again start raising money for a new show, and soon Porter is a success. Eventually he is invited to England, where he discovers that his success has preceded him and also discovers Linda sitting on a park bench. She is running a children's home in London, and for a moment Porter thinks that all the children he sees around her are hers. When that misunderstanding is cleared up, they are married. Porter's success continues, but Linda becomes increasingly upset by the fact that Porter has, as she tells him, "put me in a small corner of your life." Nearly all of his time and energy goes into planning, writing, and rehearsing his shows.

Linda leaves Porter, and he continues working until he is called back to Indiana by the illness of his grandfather. He arrives in time to have a talk with him before he dies; his grandfather tells him that he is proud of his success as a songwriter. After the funeral, Porter goes horseback riding every day. One day a storm comes up and his horse is frightened; it rears and falls, and Porter's legs are crushed. He must undergo a series of twenty-seven operations, between which he continues to compose and supervise new productions. In the last sequence in the film, he and Woolley go back to Yale, where the glee club honors him by singing "Night and Day." During the song he spots Linda in the audience. The two then go outside and embrace in the moonlight as the last bars of the song are sung and the film ends.

Grant gives a creditable performance within the limitations of the script. He spent some time with Porter to study his mannerisms, but the fact that very little is done to change Grant's appearance in the early scenes when Porter was supposed to be in his early twenties (Grant was over forty) detracts from the portrayal. Smith does well in the role of Linda, and Woolley takes obvious delight in portraying himself as witty, talented, compassionate, and beloved by all but the old fogies.

The songs of Cole Porter are, of course, as important to *Night and Day* as the plot. They are presented in a number of different ways, from informal rehearsals to full-scale production numbers. In fact, Martin's performance begins as her first reading of the song and after a few bars switches to a fully rehearsed and produced number. Simms sings six of the songs in her role as the fictional Carole Hill, and her performances convey the qualities that have made classics of so many of Cole Porter songs. The dance numbers, created and directed by LeRoy Prinz, however, lack the imagination the songs deserve, although they are entertaining.

Night and Day is, in essence, a fairly standard example of the Hollywood musical biography made better than average by such outstanding songs as "Night and Day," "Begin the Beguine," and "You're the Top." It was also one of the most popular films of 1946.

Marilynn Wilson

NIGHT MUST FALL

Released: 1937
Production: Hunt Stromberg for Metro-Goldwyn-Mayer
Direction: Richard Thorpe
Screenplay: John Van Druten; based on the stage play of the same name by
   Emlyn Williams
Cinematography: Ray June
Editing: Robert J. Kern
Running time: 115 minutes

Principal characters:
Danny	Robert Montgomery
Olivia Grayne	Rosalind Russell
Mrs. Bramson	Dame May Whitty
Justin	Alan Marshal
Mrs. Terence	Kathleen Harrison
Dora	Merle Tottenham

Anybody watching a retrospective of M-G-M talking features of the 1930's and 1940's could come to the conclusion that Robert Montgomery was the best male actor that studio had under contract. He had more than the strong antihero image of Clark Gable and more than the lovable tough guy image of Spencer Tracy. Most of the parts assigned him were seemingly similar, yet he managed to individualize and humanize them. Given the right circumstances, he showed that he could play anything: amoral playboy, nice guy, comedian, lover, weakling, or villain. Whatever he did never just faded into the wallpaper. His fifteenth picture, *Shipmates* (1931), was his first starring vehicle; his name was above the picture's title, but otherwise the set-up was the same: he was a lovable sailor in love with the admiral's daughter.

It was not until his fortieth film, released in 1937, that Montgomery showed the world what a marvelous actor he really was. The picture was *Night Must Fall*, adapted by John Van Druten from the play of the same name by Emlyn Williams. The play, starring its author, had been an exciting hit on both the London and New York stages. Montgomery saw it on Broadway and began his campaign to get M-G-M to buy it as a starring vehicle for him. Those in authority at his studio were appalled at the suggestion. They could not deny that the play was engrossing, but it was repulsive, and the hero was a charming young man who was mad, a murderer who liked to beguile old ladies who had befriended him, then strangle them, behead them, and carry their heads around in a hatbox. By 1937 the studio had had its share of trouble with Montgomery, who regularly went to the mat with studio head Louis B. Mayer. There were those in the front office who were all for chastising him this time, but as Montgomery's pleas continued, those in authority reversed themselves.

They reasoned that it might be wiser to buy the property, let Montgomery play the lead, and when it bombed at the box office and Montgomery's prestige dropped, assign him the role of a nice society bounder playing opposite Joan Crawford, Norma Shearer, or one of the other M-G-M ladies. To Montgomery's delight, the studio bought the property and turned it over to Hunt Stromberg to produce, Van Druten to write, and Richard Thorpe to direct. It would not be an overly expensive production; the action would be limited to the interior and immediate exterior of an English country cottage, and Ray June's cinematography would make it all look like a very superior film.

On the outskirts of an English village in Essex is the cottage where Mrs. Bramson (Dame May Whitty), a rich, old, ever-complaining English widow, lives. With her resides as companion and housekeeper her niece Olivia Grayne (Rosalind Russell), who must wearily kowtow to all the foolish demands Mrs. Bramson makes, for Mrs. Bramson, who is confined to a wheelchair, is selfish and demanding, not only of Olivia but also of the cook and housemaid, who are entirely at her mercy.

The village is a typical sleepy little place where nothing of much importance seems to occur. As the picture opens, however, something very unusual is happening. It is a foggy early morning, but in the bordering forest a grave is being dug, in which a corpse is deposited by someone softly whistling the Irish melody "Danny Boy." In the Bramson kitchen there is considerable excitement because the local paper has news about the suspicious disappearance of a rich woman who had been living in the resort hotel. Authorities suspect foul play and are searching the area thoroughly for both the missing body and the killer.

Meanwhile, Dora, the maid (Merle Tottenham), is tearful, because she has been keeping company with Danny (Robert Montgomery), a bellboy at the hotel, and she has let him seduce her. Mrs. Bramson, suspecting the worst, has had Danny fired from his job and summoned him to her presence. Dora would like Mrs. Bramson to force Danny to marry her, but when the boy arrives on the scene, he charms the old lady. Olivia, Mrs. Bramson's niece, is on to Danny at once, suspecting that he is little better than a hustling opportunist, but she is also fascinated by him, for although his way of getting what he wants is all too obvious to Olivia, who is beyond succumbing to flattery, she is secretly amused by the boldness of his conceit and his instinctive knowledge of how to endear himself to a lonely old lady.

Mrs. Bramson is at once taken in by Danny; she blames Dora for leading him on. In her opinion any one can see that Danny is at heart a nice, decent young fellow, a friendly soul and a willing worker. He has agreed to move into the cottage, earning his keep by gardening and wheeling Mrs. Bramson out for daily promenades. Olivia suspects that Danny may be even worse than she had first suspected. She has caught him in several bold lies, and his innocence is disguised by a kind of ruthless cunning. Also, she suspects him because he is able to look anybody straight in the eye and lie without flickering an eyelid. Danny, to her way of thinking, has something to hide and is dangerous. It is her opinion that people who are truly innocent are the ones who cannot outstare an accuser, while the guilty can stare one straight in the eye while they smilingly affirm their innocence.

The police arrive in the neighborhood, searching the underbrush for the missing body. They discover the newly dug grave and unearth the body, a headless corpse. Although the head is missing, the dead woman is identified as the widow who was recently a resident at the nearby resort hotel. The only clue to the woman's murderer is that she has been seen in the company of an unknown young man who is fond of whistling the tune "Danny Boy." Olivia has the evening off with a beau, Justin (Alan Marshal), and as she prepares for the evening, she is aware that Danny has moved into the small servant's quarters and is arranging his few possessions. He is also absent-mindedly whistling to himself the tune "Danny Boy." Olivia turns icy with suspicion, yet she is morbidly fascinated by Danny. She is intelligent and worldly, yet the fact that Danny may be a psychotic capable of murderous evil intrigues her. She is a spinster at war with her own emotions, yet she cannot deny that the machinations of a beautiful young man like Danny arouse her sexually.

Mrs. Bramson and Danny are left alone and spend the early part of the evening in dinner and socializing. Mrs. Bramson is more than ever delighted with Danny as her own special find, but he knows that his time in the Bramson cottage is nearing an end. He has discovered that in his absence Olivia has searched his meager belongings and learned the secret of the black hatbox he carries around with him. Even as Mrs. Bramson plans a gay-hearted future for herself and her newest protégé, Danny twists a cord in his hands, and coming up quietly behind her, throttles her. He hears someone coming and scarcely has time to hide the wheelchair with his dead victim huddled in it.

It is Olivia returning. She is not surprised to find Mrs. Bramson missing and duels with Danny verbally, exposing him for what he is. He admits his guilt and intimates that she too will be a victim. It is too late for him to save himself, however, for the police, having heard his confession, move in on him and take him into custody. He breaks down with a final scene of bravado and self-pitying tears, while the audience, like Olivia, can only choke back their natural liking and sympathy for him in the realization that he is, for all his charm, a dedicated killer, and they must let night fall kindly upon him.

Night Must Fall opened at the Sid Graumann's Chinese Theater in Hollywood and received superlative notices. Louis B. Mayer and some studio executives had been horrified by the picture, and circulars were passed out to those in the Chinese Theater courtyard who had already paid their money to see the film, advising them that the studio was ashamed of the picture and was disowning it. *Night Must Fall*, however, was liked by the public as well as the critics, and M-G-M sheepishly withdrew the circulars disavowing the film as theirs.

When Academy Award time came around, Montgomery received a nomination as Best Actor for his work as Danny in *Night Must Fall*, and Dame Whitty, who had also played her role in the theater, likewise received a nomination for Best Supporting Actress as Mrs. Bramson. The cast was small, but every performer handled himself superbly, including Russell in particular as the spinsterish Olivia forced to betray a young man to whom she is drawn against her better judgment.

Mayer had advised everybody at M-G-M to vote for Spencer Tracy, who was also a candidate that year for his performance in *Captains Courageous*, and it was Tracy who captured the Oscar. Had there been an upset, if Montgomery had won for *Night Must Fall*, Mayer would have been enraged, as his dislike of Montgomery was almost manic. To punish Montgomery for his success, Mayer saw to it that he was loaned out to Marion Davies at Warner Bros. when she requested him for her final picture, *Ever Since Eve* (1937).

Mayer went on to cast Montgomery in several indifferent comedies (*Live, Love and Learn*, 1937, and *The First 100 Years*, 1938). That same year, when Mayer was not looking, Montgomery got another hit both critically and publicly with *Yellow Jack*, and in 1940 he gave a beautiful performance in a very different comedy melodrama, *The Earl of Chicago*, after which he managed several loan-outs, one of which was *Here Comes Mr. Jordan* (Columbia), which brought him a second Academy nomination as Best Actor.

Night Must Fall remains a cinema masterpiece. It was redone in 1964 in England by Albert Finney, but without any of the mood or bright believability that made it one of 1937's shining achievements. As performed by Montgomery and the rest of the cast, *Night Must Fall* holds up as wonderfully suspenseful *film noir*.

DeWitt Bodeen

THE NIGHT OF THE IGUANA

Released: 1964
Production: Ray Stark for Metro-Goldwyn-Mayer/Seven Arts
Direction: John Huston
Screenplay: John Huston and Anthony Veiller; based on the play of the same
    name by Tennessee Williams
Cinematography: Gabriel Figueroa
Editing: Ralph Kemplen
Sound effects: Basil Fenton-Smith
Costume design: Dorothy Jeakins
Music: Benjamin Frankel
Running time: 118 minutes

> *Principal characters:*
> The Reverend
> T. Lawrence Shannon .... Richard Burton
> Maxine Faulk .... Ava Gardner
> Hannah Jelkes .... Deborah Kerr
> Charlotte Goodall .... Sue Lyon
> Judith Fellowes .... Grayson Hall
> Nonno .... Cyril Delevanti
> Hank Prosner .... James Ward

A frequent criticism leveled at films which are adapted from other media
is that the quality of the original work fails to come through on the screen.
John Huston's *The Night of the Iguana* is therefore something of a rarity since
it is a work of quality comparable to, and in many ways better than, Tennessee
Williams' original play of that name which won the New York Drama Critics'
Award for the 1961-1962 season. Huston and Anthony Veiller, who cowrote
the screenplay, made a number of changes in adapting the play for the screen.
This is especially apparent in the ending of the film and in the characterizations. In the film, for example, Maxine Faulk, as played by Ava Gardner, is
a sympathetic, even vulnerable character as opposed to the stage character,
who is disagreeable and has a cruel, biting sense of humor.

The screenwriters also expanded the role of Charlotte Goodall, the teenaged girl whom the Reverend Mr. Shannon seduces while acting as tour guide
for a busload of women vacationing in Mexico. She is a minor character in
the play, but on the screen the role was expanded for Sue Lyon, fresh from
playing the title role in the sexually oriented *Lolita* (1962). Charlotte becomes
an extremely important character. Her seductive movements and her knowledge of how to employ a combination of feigned naïveté and petulance to get
what she wants are visually well depicted, especially when the camera focuses
on her undulating posterior. Her sensuality is used to amplify certain aspects

of the character of the Reverend Mr. Shannon. Shannon's weakness for women is understandable, but by enlarging the Charlotte Goodall role, Shannon's character is affected as well. He is no longer the callous, priggish seducer that he was in the play; he is a man with frailties who is tempted and succumbs to that temptation.

The screenwriters also eliminated certain characters who appeared on stage. The play is set in 1940, and a family of Nazis is vacationing at the Coste Verde Hotel when Shannon arrives. Throughout the play, one of the characters, Herr Fahrenkopf, listens to the Battle of Britain on his shortwave radio, and aside from being stereotypically Aryan in physical appearance and mentality, there are also other obvious symbols used which emphasize the theme of man's inhumanity on a grand scale. Huston does not need to include the family in his film, however, since he reveals the effects of human cruelty through the interaction among the three main characters, Maxine Faulk, Shannon, and Hannah Jelkes.

The story takes place in a small Mexican hotel off the beaten path of the famous tourist spots. Maxine Faulk (Ava Gardner) is a recent widow who owns the hotel. As the action begins, Lawrence Shannon (Richard Burton), a defrocked minister who has become a second-rate tour guide, brings a bus full of female American tourists to the hotel. Hannah Jelkes (Deborah Kerr) and her grandfather Nonno (Cyril Delevanti) also come to the hotel about the same time. Hannah is a very gentle spinster from New England, and Maxine, who is her exact opposite, does not like having Hannah stay at the hotel because she fears that a relationship might develop between Hannah and Lawrence, whom Maxine hopes to marry.

The characterization of Lawrence takes on two separate dimensions. On one hand, he is attracted to the gentle spirituality of Hannah, while on the other, he is sexually attracted to Charlotte Goodall (Sue Lyon), one of the tourists who aggressively pursues him. Charlotte is so deeply infatuated that at one point she actually walks on broken glass in emulation of the mystical Lawrence who becomes so involved in his almost trancelike ravings that he does not realize that he is walking on broken glass. When Lawrence succumbs to the physical temptations of Charlotte, Maxine angrily fires him. When he temporarily goes out of his mind, Maxine has the natives tie him up in a hammock, a parallel to the iguana which the natives have tied up under the hotel porch until they have time to kill and devour it. Hannah talks to Lawrence in his almost deranged state and eventually convinces him to free himself and save the iguana, in order to be "kinder than God." Lawrence, now lucid again, wants Hannah to stay with him, but she gently refuses, so he goes back to Maxine.

Both the play and the film version of *The Night of the Iguana*, when taken in the context of the time in which they were produced, are remarkably open in their treatment of such controversial subjects as lesbianism, fetishism, and statutory rape. Since censorship was still an issue in the early 1960's, however, the references to the lesbian intentions of Judith Fellowes (Grayson Hall) toward Charlotte are veiled in the play. Huston expanded a one-line reference to "dykes" from the play into an entire scene in the film—that of Maxine's diatribe directed at Judith, who is seemingly unaware of her own lesbian tendencies. The fact that Shannon stops Maxine from destroying Judith by making her face the truth after Judith has tried to destroy Shannon emotionally is perhaps a capitulation to the censor by Huston. Rather than presenting Judith as a woman who is comfortable with her lesbianism, Huston depicts her as a pitiable, misguided character.

All of the characters in *The Night of the Iguana* are stereotypes, but that is not a fault of the film. The casting of Burton, Gardner, and Kerr in the principal roles was ingenious because each of them during the course of their respective careers has come to personify certain images. Shannon is the virile but sensitive male stereotype, destroying himself through his indulgence in liquor and women, and Burton, in films made prior to *The Night of the Iguana*, such as *Look Back in Anger* (1959), and even offscreen, has fostered this image. Maxine is the earthy, ribald, sensuous woman, the hooker-with-a-heart-of-gold stereotype, an image which Gardner personified in prior screen roles such as *Show Boat* (1951) and *Mocambo* (1953). Hannah Jelkes typifies another type of the female image: the madonna, the lady, the New England spinster who is repelled by sensuousness but who harbors an innate sense of etiquette and kindness. With her blonde, cool features and reserved demeanor and a long history of portraying ladylike roles, as in *The King and I* (1956), *Tea and Sympathy* (1956), and *An Affair to Remember* (1957), Kerr is perfectly cast in the role.

As a screenwriter, Huston had worked on such films as *Jezebel* (1938) and *High Sierra* (1940) before making his directorial debut with *The Maltese Falcon* (1941), which he also wrote. Huston's subsequent directorial career has been characterized by many productions which he has made on location, usually under arduous conditions. He often collaborates in the writing of screenplays, as he did on *The Battle of San Pietro* (1945), a war department documentary, *Treasure of the Sierra Madre* (1947), which received an Academy Award, and *The African Queen* (1952).

The Night of the Iguana was shot on location in Puerto Vallarta, Mexico, and the director of cinematography was the Mexican, Gabriel Figueroa, who skillfully alleviates the staginess of the play through a high degree of camera mobility and a diversity of camera angles employed when shooting in confined spaces. Most of the action in the film takes place in cramped quarters—inside Shannon's hotel room in Cuernavaca, inside the bus, and on the veranda at the Coste Verde—but Figueroa is able to circumvent the usual problems with his skillful cinematography. High-angle shots in which the camera is mounted on a mobile crane are used to introduce scenes in which the characters reveal their innermost thoughts and desires. The climactic scene in which Hannah helps Shannon through his delirium begins with a high-angle crane shot of the actors, slowly tracking in on the action. Extreme low-angle close-ups and fast pans are used to exaggerate and caricature the busload of vacationing women. The camera swiftly tracks back in low-angle close-up from each woman's face, revealing the ridiculousness of their pointed sunglasses and straw hats and creating a parody of the American female tourist.

The music by Benjamin Frankel has a slow rhythm produced by musical instruments indigenous to Mexico. Coupled with the sound effects by Basil Fenton-Smith, which consist of noises integral to the Mexican countryside—parrots squawking, insects, rain, and so forth—the score creates an atmosphere of waiting which contributes to the aura of timelessness surrounding the events.

The Night of the Iguana was generally well received by critics at the time of its release, with the one notable exception being Bosley Crowther, who gave it a scathing review in *The New York Times*. The film also made money, which heightened Huston's reputation in the eyes of the Hollywood motion picture industry. His two most recent films up to that time, *Freud* (1962) and *The List of Adrian Messenger* (1963), had been box-office failures, although in retrospect they are also very good films.

Anne Kail

THE NIGHT THEY RAIDED MINSKY'S

Released: 1968
Production: Bud Yorkin and Norman Lear for United Artists
Direction: William Friedkin
Screenplay: Arnold Schulman, Sidney Michaels, and Norman Lear; based on the novel of the same name by Rowland Barber
Cinematography: Andrew Laszlo
Editing: no listing
Art direction: John Robert Lloyd; set decoration, William Eckart and Jean Eckart
Choreography: Danny Daniels
Running time: 100 minutes

Principal characters:
Raymond Paine .... Jason Robards
Rachel Schpitendavel .... Britt Ekland
Chick Williams .... Norman Wisdom
Trim Houlihan .... Forrest Tucker
Jacob Schpitendavel .... Harry Andrews
Louis Minsky .... Joseph Wiseman
Vance Fowler .... Denholm Elliott
Billy Minsky .... Elliott Gould
Candy Butcher .... Jack Burns
Professor Spats .... Bert Lahr
Narrator .... Rudy Vallee

Billy Minsky is generally regarded as the man who introduced what is now regarded as burlesque to America at a theater built by his father, the National Winter Garden at Houston Street and Second Avenue in New York City. Of course, "pure" burlesque, meaning burlesques of popular entertainments, was introduced by Weber and Fields in the last century, but Billy Minsky, who died in 1932 at the age of forty-one, was responsible for the raunchier aspects of burlesque, pretty girls with little clothing, and in time Minsky's burlesque lived up to its slogan, "What the Folies Bergere is to Paris, Minsky shows are to New York." *The Night They Raided Minsky's* is a colorful re-creation of the beginnings of Minsky's brand of burlesque, with faithful renderings of many of the popular comedy sketches from burlesque's golden era. The film, like burlesque, is brash and cheerful and moves along at a fast pace. It fails as motion-picture art because it rushes too much; characters are introduced and never fully developed, and the ending is anticlimactic and forced. The film is enjoyable, however, as a collection of some of burlesque's classic "bits."

The Tandem Production Company of multitalented Bud Yorkin and Norman Lear acquired the film rights to Rowland Barber's novel, *The Night They Raided Minsky's*, in August of 1965, and originally planned it as a starring vehicle for Tony Curtis. Curtis subsequently quit after a disagreement over the script, and was replaced by Jason Robards, at which time, presumably, the role of Raymond Paine was somewhat curtailed. It was two years before filming got under way in New York, making the feature one of the first major musical comedies to be shot entirely in that city since the early days of sound. Shooting was undertaken in part on New York's lower East Side, and, in addition, art director John Robert Lloyd and production designers William and Jean Eckart did a beautiful job of re-creating the New York entertainment scene in the mid-1920's, particularly the auditorium and backstage areas of the Minsky theater. It says much for the work of the art direction staff that it is almost impossible to say where the set design ends and when one is actually looking at a New York city street.

The story of *The Night They Raided Minsky's* is fairly simplistic, if a little unbelievable. To Minsky's National Winter Garden Theatre comes Rachel Schpitandavel (Britt Ekland), who has run away from her harsh Amish father Jacob (Harry Andrews) to become a dancer. At the theater, the audience is introduced to the two comics, Raymond Paine (Jason Robards) and Chick Williams (Norman Wisdom), who are rivals both on and off stage, to Billy Minsky (Elliott Gould), whose father (Joseph Wiseman) wants to sell the theater, to Vance Fowler (Denholm Elliott), head of the Society for the Suppression of Vice, who wants to close down the theater, and to Trim Houlihan (Forrest Tucker), a racketeer and burlesque fan. Raymond Paine devises a scheme to have Rachel dance her simple and decidedly wholesome Amish-style routine at the theater in a special midnight show. He will tell Fowler that the highspot of the evening's entertainment is to be an indecent dance by Mademoiselle Fifi from Paris. Fowler will charge in with the police to find only Rachel; he will appear a fool and be forced to apologize to Billy Minsky's father, who, in turn, will agree to keep the theater. Despite the appearance of Rachel's father, all appears to be going according to plan. Rachel goes onstage and tries to emulate the burlesque dancers that she has seen, whereupon her outraged father tries to stop her and tears her dress. Rachel begins to go into a striptease routine, seeing the enthusiastic way in which the audience has received the ripping of her dress. Suddenly she notices the disapproving look of Raymond Paine and, by accident, allows the top of her dress to fall down. Thus in 1925 was the striptease born. Of course, everyone is arrested, but it makes no difference, for Rachel has become a heroine to the crowd. The only person who appears to feel any regrets is Spats (Bert Lahr), an old-time burlesque performer who realizes he has seen the end of burlesque as he knew it.

Lahr was himself a former burlesque comedian. One of the problems that the filmmakers encountered was that he died while the film was still in the shooting stages. The character was left in the finished production, but because of the lack of footage, there is little sense to his being there, and it is hard to understand Spats's feelings at the end of the film without access to a synopsis put out by the producers. *The Night They Raided Minsky's* should have been a splendid tribute to the genius of Lahr, but it is not, and, presumably because of his untimely death, not once do we see him onstage.

Although Robards is supposedly playing the top comedian in the burlesque show, there is no question that the comedy star of the show and of the film is the British comedian Norman Wisdom, who is a joy to watch. *The Night They Raided Minsky's* is the only American film of this comedian, known for his British features such as *Trouble in Store* (1953), *Man of the Moment* (1955), and *There Was a Crooked Man* (1960), and for his portrayal of the Ray Bolger role in the British stage production of *Where's Charley?* Dexter Maitland in the minor role of the burlesque singer, Duffy, handles his songs well. Rudy Vallee is strangely wasted on some voice-overs, and, of course, his casting is questionable from a nostalgia point of view because he never played burlesque.

Ekland, an actress not usually noted for any exceptional talent, is outstanding as the Amish girl determined to perform dances from the Bible and telling Minsky, "All I need is an apple and a snake for props." As her father, Andrews is well cast, suitably harsh and unfeeling. When he asks Minsky Senior if he prays to the same God, back comes the reply, "Only a God who could tolerate me could possibly tolerate you."

William Friedkin came to motion pictures from television and directed *The Night They Raided Minsky's* at the age of twenty-eight. While not Friedkin's most important film—it was followed by *The Boys in the Band* (1970), *The French Connection* (1971), and *The Exorcist* (1973)—*The Night They Raided Minsky's* is certainly his most entertaining. Aside from Lahr's death, there were obviously a number of problems in the film's production; Curtis' departure from the project and the lack of a film editor credit indicates troubles in postproduction. Nevertheless, Friedkin has turned in a fine, if flawed, motion picture, which makes admirable use of hand-held cameras and uses contemporary newsreel footage to advantage.

Budgeted at four million dollars, *The Night They Raided Minsky's* did not do very well at the box office, and reviews were mixed. The trade press tended to be the more critical, while much of the popular press liked the film. One major complaint was that the film painted too charming a picture of burlesque and lacked the vulgarity and sleaziness that was American burlesque. As *Newsweek* (December 30, 1968) commented, "The best thing to do about *The Night They Raided Minsky's* is to go, pay your money, sit there until you've had enough and then leave in good spirits and good conscience."

Anthony Slide

A NIGHT TO REMEMBER

Released: 1942
Production: Samuel Bischoff for Columbia
Direction: Richard Wallace
Screenplay: Richard Flournoy and Jack Henley; based on the novel *Frightened Stiff* by Kelly Roos
Cinematography: Joseph Walker
Editing: Charles Nelson
Running time: 90 minutes

Principal characters:
Nancy Troy	Loretta Young
Jeff Troy	Brian Aherne
Anna Carstairs	Jeff Donnell
Scott Carstairs	Will Wright
Inspector Hawkins	Sidney Toler
Mrs. Devoe	Gale Sondergaard
Bolling	Donald MacBride
Polly Franklin	Lee Patrick
Eddie Turner	Don Costello
Mrs. Salter	Blanche Yurka
Lingle	Richard Gaines
Pat Murphy	James Burke

A Night to Remember, which opened in December, 1942, and quickly disappeared in the holiday rush, has unfortunately surfaced only rarely in the ensuing years and then usually only on late-night television—an undeserved fate for a film that ranks as one of the best of its kind and is also something of a trend-setter. Columbia had intended the Samuel Bischoff production featuring Loretta Young and Brian Aherne as a logical successor to a film type established by the popular "Thin Man" series which would provide approximately ninety minutes of escapist entertainment, alternately frightening and amusing the audience. Yet it was constructed on a rather large scale with comparatively high production values for that type of film. Consequently, it can be viewed in retrospect as a transitional piece that formed part of the bridge between the lower budget "mystery with humor films" such as *The Thin Man* (1934) and the later slick modern comedy-mystery films best exemplified by Stanley Donen's *Charade* (1964). Bosley Crowther, one of the few major critics to note *A Night to Remember*'s passing, wrote it off in January, 1943, as "the tag end of all the cinema traffic that passed through haunted houses last year." Now it is largely forgotten by the general public or, in some cases, confused with the more famous *A Night to Remember*, a 1958 British documentary/drama about the sinking of the ocean liner *Titanic*.

The original *A Night to Remember* was a uniquely successful blend of intelligent writing, solid acting, and high production values of the kind that made *Charade* a sizable hit some twenty years later. Like the Donen film, it is an entertaining example of the "comedy-whodunit" class, and it has slowly earned, despite its relative obscurity, a strong reputation with contemporary film scholars studying the pre-*film noir* mysteries. This reputation is based primarily upon its role as a pace setter in the type of deft craftsmanship that would become a hallmark of a comedy-mystery genre a generation later.

A Night to Remember is based on the mystery novel *The Frightened Stiff*, the second book by a pseudonymous author named Kelly Roos. Roos was actually the composite identity of a husband-and-wife team, Audrey and William Roos, who had taken the mystery world by storm in 1940 with an extremely strong first novel, *Made Up to Kill*. Although each had published other novels in their own names, their collaboration produced the kind of story and characters that were perfect for a Hollywood accustomed to the likes of Nick and Nora Charles and Mr. and Mrs. North. The popularity of these husband-and-wife detective teams created a need for new and interesting plots combining humor with mayhem. Consequently, the studios were constantly on the lookout for scripts with unusual twists and fresh characters. Kelly Roos gave them Jeff and Haila Troy.

In the novel, Jeff Troy is a commercial photographer, and Haila, his clever and competent spouse, is a housewife. They are also amateur detectives, however, whose string of successes in solving baffling cases is a constant source of embarrassment to Lieutenant Hawkins of the Homicide Bureau when these grizzly events throw them together. In making the film, Hollywood took a few liberties with the characters. The script by Richard Flournoy and Jack Henley changes Jeff Troy from a photographer to an author of murder mysteries. Haila undergoes a name change to Nancy, which was no doubt easier for the audience to understand and for the other actors to pronounce.

Nancy (Loretta Young) wants to turn her husband, Jeff (Brian Aherne), away from the murder mysteries that have made him a success in order to have him write a romantic novel about Greenwich Village. To get into the spirit of the idea, they rent a basement apartment in a building at No. 39 Gay Street. Although Nancy thinks that there is something strange about the place and its tenants, she goes about trying to make it comfortable and pays little attention to the eccentricities of the other occupants of the building. To celebrate their first night in the building, Jeff takes her to a nearby restaurant, Polly's Stables, owned by Polly Franklin (Lee Patrick). While making a phone call at the café, Nancy overhears a man in the next booth insist, sinisterly, that someone meet him in the basement apartment at No. 39 Gay Street; the mysterious caller then disappears into the bar. Becoming alarmed, Nancy relates her experience to Jeff, who is talking to Polly. Polly identifies the man as Kaufman, a notorious character. Jeff quickly downs a couple of highballs for courage and confronts Kaufman at the bar. Kaufman slugs him, however, knocking him down, and then leaves.

The rest of the night passes uneventfully for the couple, but the next morning, they find Kaufman dead in a little garden behind their rooms. To complicate matters, the victim was knocked unconscious with a horseshoe belonging to Jeff and then drowned in the Troy bathtub. In the light of the fact that he had hit Jeff earlier that evening, the young mystery writer becomes the prime suspect. This theory quickly vanishes, however, when the police interrogate the landlord, Eddie Turner (Don Costello), who reveals that the building had housed a speakeasy during the prohibition era. The police also suspect Turner of doing away with his business partner who disappeared several years before. The most important discovery, however, is that Kaufman was renting the apartment above the Troys. The apartment turns out to be completely devoid of furnishings when it is searched.

After the police leave, Turner secretly rounds up the other four occupants of the building, Mr. and Mrs. Carstairs (William Wright and Jeff Donnell), a man named Lingle (Richard Gaines), and Polly Franklin. Their discussion reveals that all five are mysteriously forced to live in the building. They are also sure that one of their number killed Kaufman and then transferred all of the victim's furniture into his own rooms in order to hide the evidence. Although Nancy is fearful, Jeff, with much seriocomic blundering, sets out to solve the crime. He cultivates his acquaintance with Polly Franklin and learns about a mysterious man named Andrew Bruhl who is assumed to be Kaufman's real identity. Jeff does not fully accept this idea, however, and writes the supposedly dead Bruhl a letter. Seeing it delivered, the amateur detective figures out that Bruhl is still alive and thus cannot be Kaufman.

That night, Jeff calls the other tenants together and reveals his theory that they are all being blackmailed; yet no one knows the identity of the black-mailer, Bruhl, since he has never shown himself. Jeff reveals that Bruhl is still alive. In doing so, he realizes that he has set himself up as the next victim. He vainly tries to send Nancy away before the killer calls, but when the murderer strikes later that night she is in the thick of the fray; in fact, she accidentally knocks Jeff out. The police arrive in the nick of time, however, and, after the shooting stops, the real Bruhl is found dead of a gunshot wound. The mysterious killer turns out to be the tenant Lingle, and Kaufman is revealed to have been another blackmail victim who would not pay up and was therefore killed by Bruhl.

Richard Wallace directed the production strictly for mass entertainment and to offer wartime audiences a happy alternative to the more grimly mooded, war-reflective films of the period; *A Night to Remember* is therefore an adroit blend of dialogue and contrasting situations. Although some of the events that occur are designed to frighten the audience, others, such as Nancy's mistaken attack on her husband, are designed to amuse. One such scene combining both frightening and amusing elements is pivotal to the story. Nancy and the audience are initially apprehensive about the mysterious man in the bar of Polly's Stables and of his sinister phone conversation. Jeff heightens this feeling by downing several drinks to build up his courage before confronting Kaufman in the bar. Humor sneaks in, however, when Jeff turns his head to show off for Nancy's benefit. This gives Kaufman an opportunity to hit him and escape, but, more importantly, it creates a motive to make Jeff a suspect-revenge. This deft blending of humor and suspense holds the audience's attention throughout and unifies the film into a cohesive whole.

If Wallace conclusively demonstrates an aptitude for mad comedy, so also does his cast. Aherne gives a brilliant portrayal of the mystery writer/amateur sleuth who experiences the pitfalls inherent in such a venture. He creates a character that ranks with his best and deftly delivers some razor-sharp lines with an unerring sense of timing that obtains full value from every laugh. Young plunges herself completely and believably into the role of a nervous wife alternately alarmed, intrigued, and repelled at the efforts of her husband to bring his fiction to life and to follow the model of his private detectives. Also notable are Donnell, who turns in an outstanding performance as the terrified victim of a blackmailer, and Patrick, who succeeds in building a colorful character out of the hostess-owner of Polly's Stables. Sidney Toler and Donald MacBride are standouts as police detectives, and Blanche Yurka does well as the mysterious housemaid.

A Night to Remember changes the thrust of the earlier comedy mysteries by placing most of the emphasis on the humorous elements. Although in its superb blending of the diverse elements of mirth and mayhem the film presages later efforts in the genre, notably *To Catch a Thief* (1955) and *Charade* (1964), it also looks ahead to purer comedies such as *The Pink Panther* (1964) and others in the Inspector Clousseau series in which the inept detective catches the crook in spite of himself. *A Night to Remember* can still be classified as a sleeper forty years after its initial release and is still dependent on enthusiastic word-of-mouth advertising for any exposure it receives.

Stephen L. Hanson

NO LOVE FOR JOHNNIE

Released: 1961
Production: Betty E. Box for J. Arthur Rank
Direction: Ralph Thomas
Screenplay: Nicholas Phipps and Mordecai Richler; based on the novel of the same name by Wildred Fienburgh
Cinematography: Ernest Steward
Editing: Alfred Roome
Running time: 110 minutes

Principal characters:
Johnnie Byrne	Peter Finch
Fred Andrews	Stanley Holloway
Pauline	Mary Peach
Roger Renfrew	Donald Pleasence
Mary	Billie Whitelaw
Tim Maxwell	Hugh Burden
Alice	Rosalie Crutchley
Charlie Young	Mervyn Johns
The Prime Minister	Geoffrey Keen
Flagg	Dennis Price

"*No Love for Johnnie* has the rare distinction of making a political figure alive and human, of making the milieu of politics believable." This was the opinion of Hollis Alpert in his review of the film for the *Saturday Review*, and it characterizes what is best about this commanding film that came out of England in 1961. *No Love for Johnnie* was adapted from the novel by Wilfred Fienburgh, which was published posthumously in 1958. The book managed to convey the impression that politics is important and really matters even though some politicians may be petty and self-seeking. The film changes the theme somewhat, as it emphasizes the question of a man's personal life versus his political life, yet it still takes the business of politics seriously and mirrors the attitude of the English toward their parliamentary institutions.

Peter Finch, one of England's most underrated actors, is entirely convincing as a man consumed with political ambitions who rises to membership in that most select of clubs, Parliament, and then loses touch with the ordinary people whose votes got him there. He is a weak man and an opportunist but, in the sturdy hands of Finch, not a completely unsympathetic character. The film depicts politics as a fairly dirty business and portrays the men around Johnnie Byrne as not much better than he. The difference between him and his associates is that the viewer is allowed to look into Byrne's personal life and gain some understanding of how he turned out the way he did. The film removes the assumption that parliamentary politics must always be trivial and boring, and some of the scenes on the back benches are every bit as exciting as those in *The Last Hurrah* (1958) and *The Candidate* (1972), two American films about politics that received acclaim. In a decade when films dealt with the problems of the working class, *No Love for Johnnie* was a natural extension of that philosophy. The film is a brilliant if cynical statement about how government in England works (or sometimes does not work) and about how politics can consume the life of one man.

The film centers around Johnnie Byrne, a bright, forty-year-old member of Parliament who started life on the back streets of Earnley, the grim Northern industrial town that he now represents in the House of Commons. He has a good-looking, undomestic wife named Alice (Rosalie Crutchley) and a burning ambition to reach the top of the political ladder. After the general election in which Johnnie's party is swept into office by a huge majority, he fails to get a post in the new government. He suspects that part of the reason might be his wife's Communist activities and is very embittered and disappointed. He and Alice have not had a good marriage for some years. She maintains her own separate political activities, as does Johnnie. When he returns to his London apartment after the election, he feels even more estranged from his wife, but his upstairs neighbor Mary (Billie Whitelaw) gives indications that she could care for him if he gave her the chance.

As soon as Parliament reassembles, Johnnie is approached by two members of an extreme left-wing splinter group within his own party who hope to undermine the power of their own leaders and want Johnnie to go along with them. He does not commit himself but keeps their overtures in mind. Returning to his apartment, he finds Mary washing up in the kitchen, and she tells him that Alice has left him. Feeling lonely and rejected both personally and professionally, Johnnie spends the night in pubs and strip clubs, ending up in a call-girl's bedroom. A feeling of revulsion comes over him and he returns to his apartment. He pours out his soul to Mary, who listens sympathetically, hoping that Johnnie will at last appreciate her.

They begin to see each other quite often. At a party with Mary, however, Johnnie meets Pauline West (Mary Peach), the young and beautiful daughter of a provincial doctor. Pauline and Johnnie are instantly attracted to each other, and Mary watches their affair develop with a great deal of jealousy. Meanwhile, Johnnie finally does agree to take part in a political maneuver that might discredit the government. The Prime Minister (Geoffrey Keen) hears of the intrigue and tries in vain to dissuade Johnnie from the leading role that he is to play in it. Johnnie is central to the plan since he is to ask a leading question in the House which will probably disrupt the government by causing a great deal of chaos. The day arrives for his momentous activity, but at the very moment that Johnnie should be asking his question, he is in bed with Pauline. His fellow dissident Parliament members react to his lack of responsibility with a great deal of anger and reject him completely.

After a time, Pauline also sees that Johnnie has thoughts only for his own political career to the exclusion of everything else, and she breaks off the affair and goes to her parents' house. Although he follows her and attempts to resume the relationship, she wants nothing to do with him. By now Johnnie feels rebuffed by everyone—his wife, his mistress, his fellow MP's, and his constituents. He returns to London where he is approached by Alice, who asks him if he wants to give their marriage another try. Alice gives him her phone number and tells him to let her know that evening. Johnnie has almost decided to go back to her when he is called by the Prime Minister. Because of his defection from the splinter group (which the Prime Minister thought was intentional), he has decided to offer Johnnie a post in the government as Assistant Postmaster General. The Prime Minister explains that Johnnie did not get a job sooner because everyone knew that his wife had connections with the Communist Party, but now that they have separated, that problem no longer exists. The Postmaster General beckons Johnnie to the front bench, and as he sits down and rests his head contentedly on the back of it, he tears up his wife's telephone number. Johnnie has found happiness at last.

Finch won a British Academy Award for his performance. He had made many films in England before this, but it was not until he starred in *No Love for Johnnie* that he began to gain international recognition and to get better roles in such films as *Girl with Green Eyes* (1963) and *The Pumpkin Eater* (1964). Also appearing in *No Love for Johnnie* were some of the most stalwart British character actors, including Stanley Holloway, Donald Pleasence, Dennis Price, and Mervyn Johns. Whitelaw received good notices as Mary, the girl upstairs, as did Peach and Crutchley, the other women in Johnnie's life.

The film aroused a good deal of comment in the British press, some of it positive, some of it hostile. Because the British take their politics very seriously, many critics thought the film far too contemptuous of the British system of government and disliked the film's portrayal of a member of Parliament. Others thought the film an important model of how a film about politics should be made. All reviews, however, praised Finch's performance no matter how they felt about the film. England, unlike America, has produced very few films about politics and politicians, and although it is now seldom seen, *No Love for Johnnie* remains fascinating as a study of how political urgencies often clash with private needs.

Joan Cohen

NO WAY OUT

Released: 1950
Production: Darryl F. Zanuck for Twentieth Century-Fox
Direction: Joseph L. Mankiewicz
Screenplay: Joseph L. Mankiewicz and Lesser Samuels
Cinematography: Milton Krasner
Editing: Barbara McLean
Running time: 106 minutes

Principal characters:
Ray Biddle .... Richard Widmark
Edie .... Linda Darnell
Dr. Luther Brooks .... Sidney Poitier
Dr. Wharton .... Stephen McNally
Mute brother .... Harry Bellaver

There emerged in the aftermath of World War II a kind of film which, for lack of a better label, was dubbed the "problem picture." The seeds of these films bore fruit when writers and directors, many having seen the war at first hand, recognized that America and her allies had been engaged in more than a battle between superpowers—that the struggle had been against the kind of insane hatred that had spawned the death camps. With victory, the long overdue dream of equality and social justice seemed possible, and some filmmakers felt a responsibility to help bring the dream about.

Under Darryl F. Zanuck, Twentieth Century-Fox had enjoyed a run of luck with topical films such as Elia Kazan's *Gentleman's Agreement* (1947) and *Pinky* (1949). Indeed, to everyone's surprise, *Pinky*, which featured Jeanne Crain as a black, turned out to be the studio's highest-grossing film of the year. Joseph L. Mankiewicz set out to make the toughest picture about race relations ever to reach the screen, *No Way Out*. The finished product projected a claustrophobic atmosphere more often associated with the big-city crime films of the 1950's. The title refers not only to blacks trapped in an urban ghetto, but also to poor whites, who are equally locked into a vicious cycle of unrelieved poverty and are unable to channel their feelings of frustration into social change, instead venting their anger through unthinking racism. Richard Widmark and Linda Darnell were set to star, with a young black actor, Sidney Poitier, making his film debut in the pivotal role of Luther Brooks, a token black doctor in a large metropolitan hospital.

Luther has hardly started on the job when two brothers are brought in by the police. They are the Biddles, cheap hoodlums gunned down in a failed robbery. Luther wants to take a blood sample from the younger brother, who has lapsed into a coma; Ray, the older brother (Richard Widmark), a virulent racist, is horrified. When his brother dies, through no fault of Luther, Biddle is obsessed with revenge and manages, through his brother's widow, Edie (Linda Darnell), and a third brother, a mute, played by Harry Bellaver, to incite the population of the white slum, Beaver Canal, touching off a race riot.

Against the centerpiece of the impending riot two subplots are presented. One involves Luther's family, to whom he is both a hero and a freak. Partially involved with the white world, he does not particularly wish to gain entrance to it, but, rather, wishes to fulfill his dream of becoming a good doctor. His mother is proud; his brother is embittered by his own inability to make a success of life as Luther appears to be doing; and his wife is attempting to adapt to the long hours of loneliness which come with marriage to a doctor.

The twenty-four-year-old Poitier performed here, for the first time, a role he would be called upon to portray often in future films until his own drawing power and the emergence of other Black stars would allow him to grow as an actor. Throughout the 1950's, however, his *persona* was that of the super Black man who could do anything a white man could, and do it better. Poitier was able to work within these restrictions and still turn in excellent performances. There was a seething quality about him which audiences found intriguing. He was a black Marlon Brando whose soft voice registered a warning that he could be pushed only so far.

The other subplot deals with the defense of Poitier by hospital big-wig Dr. Wharton (Stephen McNally) against a board of physicians who, unwilling to rock the boat, wish the young doctor dismissed using the pretext that he may have caused young Biddle's death.

It was the riot itself, however, which raises the film above earlier efforts. The white mob from Beaver Canal, expecting little resistance, marches into an ambush and is suddenly illuminated by a shot from a flare-gun and routed, with military precision, by the blacks, who have learned of the impending raid and decide to stay and fight. It is a full-scale battle, as people grab bottles, rocks, knives, and whatever else is handy for weapons. There are no comforting images for white audiences to carry out of the theater. Mankiewicz seems to have modeled this scene upon actual newsreel footage of the 1943 Detroit riots, and it proved too strong for many people to take.

When Biddle learns of the rout of the Beaver Canal irregulars, he is driven into an even greater frenzy. He must now personally destroy Luther at all cost. Edie, it turns out, has been involved in an affair with her dead husband's brother. Like them, she is an ignorant poor white who sees little chance of escape from the soul-destroying existence of life in Beaver Canal. Yet she is sensitive enough to feel guilty about the affair and conscience-stricken over the death of her husband. Biddle's powers of persuasion finally convince her that her husband has died at the hands of the "nigger doctor" and make her an accomplice in his escape from the guarded hospital ward.

The confrontation between Biddle and Luther inevitably occurs. Biddle, bleeding from the wound which has reopened during his escape, gun in hand and spewing hate, wants Luther to squirm and beg before he kills him. Luther, as cool as possible, plays Edie against Biddle until he manages to wrest the gun from his antagonist's hand. Trapped, bleeding, and with the sound of police sirens closing in, Biddle continues to taunt Luther, attempting to make him shoot. Luther has the last word, however: "Don't worry, white boy, we'll patch you up." Once again, the quality of goodness imposed on Luther strains credulity. By shooting Biddle he would, for one irrational moment, obliterate the obstacles which have thwarted him his whole life. It is to Poitier's credit that he makes us believe in his ultimate decision. It is to Widmark's credit that he tackled such an unsympathetic role. Although he was afraid of becoming typed as a heavy, Biddle, his final screen maniac, is a masterful creation. He is totally without redemption until the last minutes of the film when he manages to make the character pitiable. Biddle is not evil; like so many others before and since, he has simply been taught to hate.

Largely confined to the night world of the hospital with only the centerpiece of the race riot to represent the exterior universe, the film manages to illustrate that it is the dehumanization of poverty which the two central characters are trying to escape, one through crime, the other through what he has learned to be socially acceptable means.

Michael Shepler

NO WAY TO TREAT A LADY

Released: 1968
Production: Sol C. Siegel for Paramount
Direction: Jack Smight
Screenplay: John Gay; based on the novel of the same name by William Goldman
Cinematography: Jack Priestley
Editing: Archie Marshak
Makeup: Bob O'Bradovich
Costume design: Theoni Aldredge and George Newman
Running time: 108 minutes

> *Principal characters:*
> Christopher Gill .... Rod Steiger
> Kate Palmer .... Lee Remick
> Morris Brummel .... George Segal
> Mrs. Brummel .... Eileen Heckart

If all acting, but especially film acting, functions as an exercise in disguise (both emotional and physical), often elevating it to an art form, there is a peculiarly pronounced genre of films in which the disguise is played largely for its own sake. Audiences generally respond to these films, which include *Kind Hearts and Coronets* (1949), *The Seven Faces of Dr. Lao* (1964), *The List of Adrian Messenger* (1963), and *Theatre of Blood* (1972). No matter what their artistic merits or lacks might be, the enjoyment of a guessing game which transcends the particular "reality" of their screen stories makes those films enjoyable. Such a film is the blackly comic *No Way to Treat a Lady*, which spotlights Rod Steiger portraying seven distinctly different characters.

At the film's opening, impersonating a kindly Irish priest, Christopher Gill (Rod Steiger), an elegant man-about-town, gourmet, and affluent owner of a successful Broadway theater, calls on a lonely widow, succeeds in entering her apartment, charms her, and suddenly strangles her for no obvious reason. He was seen, however, by Kate Palmer (Lee Remick), who tells the detective assigned to the case, Morris Brummel (George Segal), that she probably would not be able to recognize the killer. Kate and Brummel begin a relationship which, over the course of the film, grows into a love affair, at which point Brummel takes her home to meet his mother (Eileen Heckart), a strong, fiercely dominating woman. Brummel offhandedly tells a reporter that the murderer must be extremely clever; and when the statement is published, Gill, disguising his voice, telephones Brummel expressing gratitude for his opinion.

Gill strikes again, this time disguised as a German plumber, then phones Brummel to report his deed. The repeated series of calls soon makes Brummel the butt of his co-officers' jokes. After another murder, Brummel again carelessly remarks to the press that the killer who "signs" each of his victims with a grotesque "kiss"—a pair of lips painted on the their foreheads in garish red lipstick—must be a sexual pervert. Reading this, Gill is enraged and calls Brummel to complain, losing his self-control enough to let slip that he is obsessed with his deceased mother, a famous actress from whom he has expertly learned the arts of makeup, voice, and costuming. Brummel is removed from the case by his superiors for his loose comments to the press, but after another murder, Gill demands that Brummel be reinstated.

Back on the case to try to trap the murderer, Brummel releases to the media details of a "false" murder. When Gill predictably calls to protest, he stays on the line too long, and the call is traced, although the police arrive too late to catch him. To "punish" Brummel, Gill decides to kill Kate and gains entrance to her home disguised as a caterer delivering a surprise dinner from Brummel. The detective appears in time to save his lover and traces Gill, through his earlier remarks about his mother, to the theater. The pair finally confront each other in the flesh, and Brummel, evading Gill's attempt to murder him, finally kills him on the empty stage. As he dies, after an agonizing soliloquy worthy of Shakespeare, Gill pleads, "Mr. Brummel, would you forgive me . . . please?"

Black comedy is extremely difficult to pull off successfully, but *No Way to Treat a Lady* is helped by its precise structure as a conventional cat/criminal versus mouse/detective murder tale. The dialogue by veteran screenwriter John Gay (who was nominated for an Academy Award in 1958 for *Separate Tables*) is witty enough to bring off the comedy. Although the film misses much of the screwy logic and clever ironies of the source novel by William Goldman, who would in the 1970's himself become one of Hollywood's most prolific and well-paid screenwriters, it is improved somewhat by the visual effects of Gill's disguises. Director Jack Smight approached the material as a kind of cartoon and was unable to sustain either the juxtaposition of comedy with horror (the violence of the killings is not covered up) or the quick, suspenseful pacing required of a Hitchcockian story, which must closely involve the viewer in the detective's slow unraveling of the plot and unmasking of the culprit, whose identity we know from the start.

The film thus becomes a study of character and characterizations. Individual sequences are extremely well directed by Smight, who fills the film with a rich sense of detail and mordant humor. For example, Gill reads newspaper accounts of his activities like reviews of his productions, which, essentially, they are. Except for Heckart's grossly overdrawn Jewish mother, and although the characters, including the victims, are basically designed as caricatures (especially Steiger's "roles"), the performances are excellent, including minor characterizations such as Michael Dunn's genuinely absurd bit as a dwarf who "confesses" to the murders. Reviewers regarded the film as a pleasant entertainment which would fall apart if thought about to any degree, although Smight and Gay do well in their Freudian paralleling of Gill and Brummel, both destructively saddled with stern, smothering mothers, and their incorporation of the parallel into the story. All of the victims are elderly women, for example, and no doubt the idea to murder his own mother has occurred to Brummel at least once.

The film is based loosely on the real-life Boston Strangler murders, which grisly tale was being filmed quite seriously with Tony Curtis by Twentieth Century-Fox when *No Way to Treat a Lady* was released. The film was shot entirely in New York at the insistence of producer Sol C. Siegel, a long-time veteran of the industry who began producing films at Republic, where he made John Wayne's early motion pictures and introduced Gene Autry to America. This was Siegel's last production. Smight's use of forty-eight location sites in New York, including Sardi's (in which owner Vincent Sardi plays a cameo), the Metropolitan Opera, the *New York Daily News* newsroom, the Belasco Theater (doubling for Gill's theater), and a 110-year-old mansion on Pierrepont Street in Brooklyn Heights which doubles for various "apartment" sets, all excellently photographed by Jack Priestley, add needed verismilitude. On the whole, the film, designed by George Jenkins, who would win an Oscar in 1976 for *All the President's Men*, aided then-New York Mayor John Lindsay's attempt to bring motion picture production back to the city.

Director Smight received his training in television, where he was associated with such strong New York-filmed series as *Naked City* and *East Side, West Side*. He moved on to direct several interestingly diverse films such as *Harper* (1966), *Rabbit, Run* (1970), and *The Traveling Executioner* (1970). His most recent films have tended to be rather lifeless epics such as *Midway* (1976) and various television movies.

The critics applauded Segal's performance. The film was his thirteenth, having previously been successful in *King Rat* (1965), *Ship of Fools* (1965), *Who's Afraid of Virginia Woolf?* (1966, for which he received an Oscar nomination), and *The Quiller Memorandum* (1966). His previous film, *Bye Bye Braverman* (1968), and *No Way to Treat a Lady* served to typecast him for many years as a sort of sadly comical, much put-upon Jewish nebbish.

Of course, the *raison d'être* of the film was Steiger himself, who was a sought-after actor, having just won the Best Actor Oscar for the immensely popular *In the Heat of the Night* (1967). Steiger was at the height of his popularity (he has since succumbed, with the aid of weak directors, to florid overplaying and self-parody), contributing hard-hitting performances in films such as *The Mark* (1962), *The Harder They Fall* (1956), and *The Pawnbroker* (1965). At one point in *No Way to Treat a Lady*, Steiger does a neat imitation of W. C. Fields, which was remarkably prescient: in 1976 he would portray the troubled comedian in a full-length study for Universal, *W. C. Fields and Me*. If occasionally the makeup (supervised by Bob O'Bradovich), wigs, and costumes by Theoni Aldredge and George Newman are a bit transparent, Steiger's differing voices and accents are masterful. In addition to the seven onscreen characters, which range from a flamboyant gay to a prostitute (the latter, with Steiger in full drag, is inexplicably played with the victim turning out to be a female impersonator), he also throws in a number of still different telephone voices. All in all, Steiger looks as if he is having the time of his life with his bravura performance, acting up a storm in an actor's dream role.

David Bartholomew

NORTH BY NORTHWEST

Released: 1959
Production: Alfred Hitchcock for Metro-Goldwyn-Mayer
Direction: Alfred Hitchcock
Screenplay: Ernest Lehman
Cinematography: Robert Burks
Editing: George Tomasini
Running time: 136 minutes

Principal characters:
Roger Thornhill .... Cary Grant
Eve Kendall .... Eva Marie Saint
Phillip Vandamm .... James Mason
Clara Thornhill .... Jessie Royce Landis
The Professor .... Leo G. Carroll
Lester Townsend .... Philip Ober

Alfred Hitchcock is known as the "Master of Suspense," who with films made on both sides of the Atlantic pleased and scared audiences for some fifty years. Two periods of his directorial career are, however, regarded as being particularly remarkable. The first encompassed his last films made in Britain, from *The Man Who Knew Too Much* (1934) through *The Lady Vanishes* (1938). The second came in the middle of his American career, from *Strangers on a Train* (1951) through *Psycho* (1960). It was in this second exceptional period that *North by Northwest* (1959) was made. The film contains many of Hitchcock's favorite themes, devices, and actors mixed with some new combinations and locations to manipulate the audience artfully and shamelessly. It produces the effects of fear, suspense, and surprise so well that many critics regard the film as the peak of his career, and the public made it one of his biggest money-makers.

The film begins with an amusing scene which sets up the action without the audience having the slightest idea where it might lead. (As it turns out, the protagonist does not have any idea what is going to happen either.) Roger Thornhill (Cary Grant), a Manhattan advertising executive, is rushing to a business luncheon, dictating orders furiously to his secretary in a taxicab. After he arrives at the Plaza Hotel for his meeting, he is mistaken for another man and kidnaped by two thugs. At this point two themes bring the audience into familiar and exciting Hitchcock territory: a person is suspected mistakenly of something he did not do, and an ordinary man suddenly is thrust into extraordinary circumstances. As the film continues, we learn more and more of what is indeed a very complicated predicament into which Roger has stumbled and also that Hitchcock and his screenwriter, Ernest Lehman, have some good new twists on some good old tricks. At times we know no more than Roger himself does and at others we are given extra information, which only increases the suspense.

Roger is taken to a Long Island estate and questioned by Phillip Vandamm (James Mason), who is convinced that Roger is an agent named George Kaplan. Roger cannot change Vandamm's mind and finds himself forced to drink a bottle of bourbon and then placed at the wheel of a moving car. His captors expect a fatal accident; instead, Roger survives a harrowing "drive" down a winding, narrow road by the ocean only to be arrested for drunk driving. Attempting to prove his incredible story about the night's events, Roger goes to the United Nations building to talk to the owner of the estate where he was questioned, but the man, Lester Townsend (Philip Ober), who says that he has not been living there recently is killed suddenly by a knife thrown by one of Vandamm's men. It appears to the crowd that Roger has killed the man, so he has now to escape from both the police and Vandamm. At this point we learn that George Kaplan does not exist and is only an imaginary decoy created by the government to keep Vandamm's spy ring from discovering the real agent.

Not having this vital bit of information, Roger takes the train to Chicago in search of Kaplan so he can clear up the confusion. Seemingly by accident, he meets Eve Kendall (Eva Marie Saint), who hides him in her compartment when the police search the train and then keeps him there overnight (although in possible deference to the censors she says he must sleep on the floor). The next morning we find that she is working for Vandamm, but since Roger does not learn this, he follows her instructions to meet Kaplan at a crossroad on a highway miles from any town. As he waits for the fictitious agent, Roger is suddenly attacked from above by shots fired from a crop-dusting airplane flying just above the ground. This famous Hitchcock scene was thought of by the director as he rode through the flat open country near Bakersfield, California, and watched the crop-dusting airplanes at work. It is an ideal situation for terror, combining the seemingly innocuous setting of open farmland in broad daylight with the unexpected menace from which the hero has no place to hide and no way to defend himself.

When the airplane crashes into a truck, Roger escapes and returns to the city. Attempting to follow Eve now that he knows she had set him up for the attack in the open field, Roger arrives at an antique auction and sees Eve and Vandamm together. He is still unable to convince Vandamm that he is not Kaplan, and when he notices that the spy's agents are waiting for him at the exit, he begins heckling the auctioneer so that the police will come and arrest him and save him from Vandamm. The ploy works, but the police— instead of taking him to jail—take him to "The Professor" (Leo G. Carroll), the head of an unspecified government bureau. The Professor explains that Eve is not only Vandamm's mistress but also a government agent and that Roger must follow Vandamm to South Dakota and pretend to be Kaplan in order to save her life. In order to prevent Vandamm from suspecting that she is on the side of the government, Eve "shoots" Roger with a gun containing blanks, and he and the Professor successfully convince Vandamm that he is wounded and confined to the hospital. Roger later has to go to Vandamm's house to help Eve escape, but they are nearly caught and are chased across the faces of the Presidents carved on Mount Rushmore. The chase ends with the killing of Vandamm and Roger's rescue of Eve as she is about to fall down the mountain. The film ends with a clever transition between Roger pulling Eve up as she is about to fall down the mountain side to him pulling her up into a pullman berth on their honeymoon.

The script was written by Lehman based on his own ideas, some research, and—quite importantly—months of discussions with Hitchcock. For the crop-dusting scene, for example, Lehman says that he and Hitchcock acted out the entire sequence in Hitchcock's living room, and then Lehman wrote it into the script exactly as they had worked it out. Lehman's research trip took him over the same route followed by the hero. He visited the United Nations building, had a judge in Long Island put him through the entire process of getting picked up for drunken driving, took the train to Chicago, and visited Mount Rushmore. If parts of the plot seem far-fetched, one must remember what Hitchcock told French director/critic François Truffaut in a book-length interview: he is more interested in emotion and mood than in strict logic and plausibility. Also, one can see how carefully he withholds or dispenses information so that the audience will be caught up in the surprises rather than in evaluating the believability of each action or event.

Important to the overall effect are the actors, of course. Grant portrays the urbane hero and Mason the suave villain to perfection, but Saint has some trouble with the role of the cool blonde who is both villain and heroine. Some of this can be blamed on the part, however, because she is required to switch from being teasing and seductive for an ulterior purpose in the first scenes to being cold and impersonal to being truly in love at the end. These three are ably supported by Carroll (who appeared in more Hitchcock films than any other actor) as the Professor and Jessie Royce Landis as Roger's mother.

Judith A. Williams

NORTHWEST PASSAGE

Released: 1940
Production: Hunt Stromberg for Metro-Goldwyn-Mayer
Direction: King Vidor
Screenplay: Laurence Stallings and Talbot Jennings; based on the novel of the same name by Kenneth Roberts
Cinematography: Sidney Wagner and William V. Skall
Editing: Conrad A. Nervig
Running time: 115 minutes

Principal characters:
Major Robert Rogers	Spencer Tracy
Langdon Towne	Robert Young
Hunk Marriner	Walter Brennan
Crofton	Addison Richards
Elizabeth Browne	Ruth Hussey
Parson Browne	Louis Hector
Wiseman Claggart	Montagu Love

In 1940, director King Vidor, who had been making films since 1913, made his first color feature. *Northwest Passage* (with the subtitle "Book I: Rogers' Rangers") was adapted by Laurence Stallings and Talbot Jennings from Kenneth Roberts' novelization of the exploits of that great eighteenth century American frontiersman, Major Robert Rogers. The film's title, however, is a bit of a misnomer, since the action ends before Rogers and his Rangers can even begin to search for the fabled Northwest Passage between the Atlantic and Pacific Oceans. According to Vidor, producer Hunt Stromberg and his writers could not agree on a script for the second half of the film; thus, Book II was never shot.

Although *Northwest Passage* takes place almost entirely in New York State and eastern Canada, it must be considered as a film Western, albeit a qualified Western; for the essence of the film concerns life on the American frontier, its hardships and its rewards. Most particularly, *Northwest Passage* is about the relationship between the American settlers and the Indians they inexorably displaced.

Northwest Passage begins and ends in Portsmouth, New Hampshire, in 1759. Although Portsmouth is not a major urban center like Boston or New York, it will, in the scenes that serve as the prologue and epilogue to Robert Rogers' Indian campaign, come to symbolize civilization. Portsmouth is the home of two of the film's three principals, the callow Langdon Towne (Robert Young) and his hard-drinking, wise-cracking companion, Hunk Marriner (Walter Brennan); Vidor wastes little time in introducing us to the two men.

Langdon Towne is a bright, creative young man in his mid-twenties who has just been expelled from Harvard University for drawing a satirical cartoon about the dean. Hunk Marriner is a rebel too, although he expresses his contempt for authority in a less artistic manner. As Langdon makes his way through town to reach his parents' house, he finds Hunk locked in the public stocks in the town square—his punishment for loudly insulting the area's colonial authorities. Marriner is fifteen years older than Towne and considerably less educated, but the two are friends nevertheless. They commiserate over their misfortunes and agree to meet later that evening, when Hunk is freed.

Towne's family takes his expulsion and his newly announced intent to pursue a career as an artist with a minimum of fuss, but the father of his girl friend Elizabeth (Ruth Hussey) is less forgiving. Parson Browne (Louis Hector) derides Langdon's ambitions and orders his daughter to cut her ties with young Towne.

Langdon seeks comfort at a nearby tavern, where, after a few drinks too many, he loudly repeats his friend Hunk's seditious remarks against Wiseman Claggart (Montagu Love), His Majesty's representative in New Hampshire. Sure enough, Claggart and his minions overhear Towne's tirade, and the evening ends in a brawl, with Langdon and Hunk evading arrest only by slipping out into the night and escaping into the woods. They resolve to hike to Albany, and Towne will paint Indians, his favorite subject, along the way.

The two men never make it to Albany. Instead, director Vidor introduces them to Major Robert Rogers (Spencer Tracy), the film's third protagonist, who leads them on a campaign against a tribe of marauding Indians that is fraught with adventure and peril. When Langdon and Hunk return to Portsmouth after what becomes almost a rite of passage, they are no longer outcasts.

On their way to Albany, Towne and Marriner stop at a roadside tavern to slake their thirst. Inside, they help a jovial man in a curious green uniform sober up an Indian companion. To show his gratitude, the uniformed man buys them flagon after flagon of a potent hot rum mixture. The last thing Langdon and Hunk notice before they pass out is that the stranger has evinced a keen interest in Towne's artistic ability, particularly as it might apply to mapmaking; and that he also seemed to be trying to entice them into joining the army. The stranger, of course, is Major Robert Rogers, leader of Rogers' Rangers, a quasi-independent American guerrilla force allied with the British Army against the French and the Indians. When Towne and Marriner wake up, they discover that they have been shanghaied. An amused Rogers calms their protests with a promise that their mission will not be very arduous, and that Towne, in return for making maps for the expedition, will be afforded the opportunity to paint all the Indians he wishes. Somewhat dazedly, the two men agree to join up.

Up to this point, *Northwest Passage* has been strong on comedy and weak on action. All this changes abruptly, however, when the Rangers set about their work, which is killing Indians. Suddenly, the frontiersman's hatred of and contempt for the Indian comes to dominate the film. This attitude is expressed often throughout the remainder of the film, sometimes forcefully, and sometimes in a casual, even jocular manner. The filmmakers' best attempt to explain this hatred occurs as Major Rogers explains his mission to the British officers. "Those red hellions have come down and hacked and murdered us," he says grimly, "burned our homes, stolen women, brained babies, scalped stragglers, and roasted officers over slow fires for five years. If you were in our place, what would you do?"

Rogers' solution is to kill as many "fighting Indians" (he is willing to spare the women and children) as he can. The tribe he is after now is headquartered in Canada, and the Rangers head that way. Their trek takes them through some gorgeous scenery—Vidor makes the most of it for his first Technicolor feature—as Rogers' men fight off the elements, Indians (Towne is severely wounded during the climactic battle in which the Rangers destroy their target, an Indian village), and finally hunger. If no individual scene from this part of the film stands out, it is because they are all powerful.

Rogers' personality comes to dominate the film, just as it dominates his men. He is a bold leader, stern yet obviously fond of his men; and his Rangers just as obviously return his affection. His leadership is threatened only when near starvation brings the men to the edge of mutiny—and madness. One of the Rangers, a man named Crofton (Addison Richards), whose brother had earlier been brutally slain by Indians, beheads an Indian during the sack of the village. While the rest of the men subsist on a handful of corn a day, Crofton secretly devours his trophy. He commits suicide when his cannabalism is discovered.

Rogers himself comes close to breaking when, having driven his men and himself to the absolute limit, he arrives at an intended rendezvous with the British Army, only to find that they, and thus the food, have not yet arrived. Calling on his last reserves of will power, he rallies the Rangers one last time. Suddenly, in the midst of his emotional address to the troops, a faint but unmistakable sound intrudes—a fife and drum, signaling the tardy but welcome arrival of the British. Rogers' Rangers are saved.

The film ends back in Portsmouth. Towne, recovered from his wounds, is reunited with Elizabeth Browne, whom he will marry; Hunk Marriner is reunited with his favorite bartender; and Robert Rogers is being given his new orders. He and his Rangers will search for the Northwest Passage. The final shot shows Major Rogers walking off into the horizon, heading for a sequel that, sadly, was never made.

Northwest Passage is a well-acted, tightly paced, and indeed almost thoroughly convincing film, except in one respect. There is no mistaking the fact that the film is virulently and unambiguously anti-Indian. Native Americans are portrayed as an almost subhuman species, worthy only of the white man's contempt—and a bullet or a well-placed bayonet. Even granting that this attitude may very well have typified that of the average eighteenth century American, it is still more than a little shocking to see such a one-sided presentation. Whatever the inherent unfairness of judging a work of art by the ethical standards of a later age, Vidor's *Northwest Passage*, like D. W. Griffith's *Birth of a Nation* (1915), suffers from its blatantly biased point of view. That said, however, the other virtues of *Northwest Passage* cannot be denied.

The acting, as one might expect from a cast headed by Tracy, Brennan, and Young, is first-rate throughout. Young is just right as the good-hearted but slightly dilettantish Langdon Towne (he was later to play a similar role in Fritz Lang's *Western Union*, 1941). Young's untested but plucky Towne nicely complements Brennan's japes and Tracy's charisma. As Hunk Marriner, Brennan is the ideal sidekick, a role that he was to repeat and perfect years later for Howard Hawks opposite Humphrey Bogart in *To Have and Have Not* (1944) and John Wayne in *Red River* (1948) and *Rio Bravo* (1959). Cantankerous and cynical, Hunk provides *Northwest Passage* with its moments of comic relief.

When Tracy is on the screen, however, he dominates the film. Some of this is due to the script—Robert Rogers is by far the dominant character in the last three-quarters of Stallings' and Jennings' screenplay—but credit must also be given to Tracy. He radiates warmth, courage, and leadership. Indeed, even the script's anti-Indian diatribes sounded somehow less offensive coming from Tracy than they might have from some other actor.

Along with his cast, Vidor deserves a great deal of credit for the strengths of *Northwest Passage*. He integrates great acting and terrific scenery into a well-paced, action-packed "Western." Its unfortunate attitude toward Native Americans aside, the film's major flaw is that, through no fault of Vidor's, it remains unfinished. *Northwest Passage* should therefore more truthfully be referred to as a great half-film.

James P. Girard

NOTHING BUT A MAN

Released: 1964
Production: Michael Roemer, Robert Young, and Robert Rubin for Cinema
Direction: Michael Roemer
Screenplay: Michael Roemer and Robert Young
Cinematography: Robert Young
Editing: Luke Bennett
Running time: 92 minutes

Principal characters:
Duff Anderson	Ivan Dixon
Josie	Abbey Lincoln
Will Anderson	Julius W. Harris
Lee	Gloria Foster
Jocko	Yaphet Kotto

Nothing but a Man was produced and directed in the small-town black ghettoes of the deep South by two white men in 1964. This was also the year that saw riots in the black ghettoes of every major city in the United States; the passage of the Civil Rights Act in the halls of Congress; and the deaths of three white civil rights workers from the Northeast at the hands of white Southern racists. *Nothing but a Man* is a cultural product of its time: it was among the first fiction films made for general release which focused upon the "ordinary" experience of the "average" black American. It followed in the wake of (and surpassed, in terms of recognition and acclaim) the somewhat sentimental *One Potato, Two Potato* (1964), which was the story of an interracial marriage, and *The Cool World* (1964), the abrasive quasidocumentary-style exploration of drugs and violence in Harlem. *Nothing but a Man*, however, transcends its time. It is not a typical 1960's film for two reasons: first, because the film retains an emotional validity, conveying what may be hesitatingly called a "universal" truth about the experience of two human beings; and second, because the film's context—the American South which is ruled by economic deprivation and racial tension—still exists to some extent, despite what the media may say about the New South of prosperity and racial harmony.

The film cost $200,000 to make—an extremely low budget, even in 1964; it was shot by an independent production company on location in Maryland, Mississippi, and other small Southern towns. The principals were the then-little-known Ivan Dixon and Abbey Lincoln (the latter had been a New York jazz and nightclub singer before starring in this film). The filmmakers, Michael Roemer and Robert Young, both had backgrounds in television documentary production, which serves the film well. Its shooting style is an estimable blend of economy, artistic selection, and documentary exposition. The film is remarkably low-key in its exposition of story and character; the dialogue is spare, restrained, and naturalistic. Indeed, while it is fiction and its action is structured, *Nothing but a Man* seems to exist on that highly compelling plane where actual reality and dramatically composed reality sometimes, but rarely, meet in film.

Dixon is Duff, a railroad gang worker whose work has enabled him to escape the constriction of small-town life. He is not drawn to the idea of marriage, a family, and a steady job, but he is attracted to Josie (Abbey Lincoln), the daughter of a preacher. He resists joining her and her world of would-be middle-class aspirations until a visit to his father and his own abandoned son convinces him otherwise. His father (Julius Harris) is older than his years, broken by a life of unskilled labor, unemployment, and alcohol, and held together only by the concern of his mistress. His son, whom he had consigned to the care of an exhausted young woman in a squalid urban slum, is a mute four-year-old, already showing the symptoms of deprivation, both emotional and economic.

The early days of Duff and Josie's marriage are characterized by a gentle sweetness; there is joy and humor in the exposition of two people who are learning how to live together in mutual concern. The outrage of being black in a small Southern town soon emerges from the background, however, to become the central fact in their lives. Until now, Duff had lived in the relatively insulated world of the traveling work crew and had escaped the unrelenting damage which comes from daily being called "boy" and being expected to look at the ground instead of into another man's eyes. He has a hard time finding a job, is harassed and abused, and, finally, fired for attempting to organize ill-treated black factory workers. He is threatened by his wife's pregnancy and galled by his relations with her father, who is a classic accommodating Uncle Tom-type seeking refuge in fundamentalist religion from the reality of economic and psychological castration. Their marriage becomes the scene of angry and frustrated battles, and Duff elects to do what he has so often done in the past: he moves on. His father's early, alcohol-induced death, however, makes him stop to consider how he is living his own life. He reclaims the son whom he had abandoned and returns with him to Josie. The implications for their future are not idealized: they will struggle together to rear their children and to live with decency and self-respect.

The performances of Dixon and Lincoln in this film are highly empathetic and deceptively skillful. The deceptiveness arises from the fact that their style of acting is so controlled and natural that it conveys more a sense of "being" than of "acting." Both actors were much acclaimed for their portrayals, receiving awards at the First Black Film Festival in Senegal in 1966 and high praise at the film's exhibition at the New York Film Festival in 1964 and 1970.

Because it was shot on location in black and white rather than in a studio in color, and because it conveys such a strong sense of actual events and real people, *Nothing but a Man* has often been likened to a documentary. This analogy, however, obscures the fact that it takes a high degree of artistic control and selection to simulate real life on film. Through director Roemer's images, we are allowed to focus on Duff and Josie, but we are never allowed to forget the ominous and oppressive presence of the white Southern town in which they live; we are never able to shrug off the poverty and squalor in which they are forced to struggle. The dirty streets, the workers' ginmills, and the decrepit apartments are wordless, nondidactic arguments against oppression. The camera is constantly moving, exploring without explaining, but it can stop to let a single arresting image—a winged cockroach or a broken-down gameboard with bottle caps for checkers—fill the frame.

Nothing but a Man remains unsurpassed as a film about human beings who happen to be born black in America. Its achievement rests in the fact that without soft-focus photography, without heroic idealizations, and without phenomenal exploits it creates a moving, powerful, and entertaining portrait of two people whose lives are distinguished by their engagement in a struggle for that dignity which ought to be the birthright of every citizen. It is unfortunate that the careers of Dixon and Lincoln have not, to date, grown to major proportions. Lincoln is still known primarily as a singer, and Dixon, an active character player, is perhaps best known for his role as a P.O.W. in television's long-running *Hogan's Heroes* series.

Connie McFeeley

NOTORIOUS

Released: 1946
Production: Alfred Hitchcock for RKO/Radio
Direction: Alfred Hitchcock
Screenplay: Ben Hecht
Cinematography: Ted Tetzlaff
Editing: Theron Warth
Running time: 103 minutes

> *Principal characters:*
> Devlin .... Gary Grant
> Alicia Huberman .... Ingrid Bergman
> Alexander Sebastian .... Claude Rains
> Paul Prescott .... Louis Calhern
> Madame Sebastian .... Leopoldine Konstantin

The postwar years constituted a period of deep transition for Hollywood. No longer able to get by on escapist and war propaganda films, the major directors and producers of the period turned to more realistic reflections of life. Motion pictures of the *film noir* genre as well as "message" pictures such as *Gentleman's Agreement* (1947) and *Home of the Brave* (1949) now became as important as the spectacular musicals of the early 1940's had been. One of the most enduring of all directors, Alfred Hitchcock, was able to adjust his basic concept of suspense to fit easily into the postwar philosophy of witch-hunting, as well as the *film noir* style of filmmaking. With great depth he was able to blend suspense with a love story and a contemporary theme. *Notorious* is as contemporary to the 1940's as it is classic to audiences today. As a contemporary story, it dealt with the postwar suspicions concerning the remaining Nazis who fled to South America, and it starred two of the screen's most important stars of the day, Ingrid Bergman and Cary Grant. On the classic side, the suspense of the story, the romance, and the timelessness of Bergman's and Grant's performances make it as enjoyable today as it was in 1946.

Hitchcock employed many of the techniques which have become his trademarks in *Notorious*, but with nuances which make it unique. It has intrigue, but the audience is more aware of what is transpiring than in such films as *The Man Who Knew Too Much* (1934 and 1956) or *Suspicion* (1941). There are no intricate twists of plot; everything unfolds in a relatively natural, easily comprehensible sequence. Also, the heroes are not innocents caught up in a mysterious trap as in *The 39 Steps* (1935) or *The Lady Vanishes* (1938); instead, the characters seek out their fate and in a sense cause it to happen.

The story follows Alicia Huberman (Ingrid Bergman) and Devlin (Cary Grant) in their attempt to entrap Nazi exiles now residing in Rio de Janeiro.

Devlin, as a government agent, enlists Huberman's help. Her role is necessary in the United States government's investigation because, as the daughter of a convicted Nazi spy, she was well known to many of the top Nazis, and thus would be, in a sense, above suspicion. When Devlin comes to a party in Alicia's home, he tricks her into helping him. While she has been playing the role of the spoiled, drunken society girl, Devlin knows that she has hated her father for his betrayal of the United States. He has "bugged" her home and in so doing recorded her telling her father of her loyalty and love for the United States. Drunk and angry, Alicia struggles with Devlin and calls him a liar, but she knows that her fate is sealed. If she does not help the government, they might be forced to try her for treason, even though they know she is not a spy.

The main action of the film begins when Alicia and Devlin go to Rio to use Alicia as a plant to lure Alexander Sebastian (Claude Rains), suspected of being one of the upper-echelon Nazis now residing there, into revealing information. Sebastian had once been in love with Alicia, but Alicia never returned his devotion. While Alicia and Devlin are waiting for their assignment to begin, they tour the city, and during the course of their sight-seeing, they realize that they are in love. Alicia constantly baits Devlin, tearing herself down as a "drunk" and a "tramp," finally forcing Devlin to admit that he loves her despite what he considers to be her low character.

At a turning point in the film, while Alicia happily prepares dinner for Devlin after their admission of love, Devlin goes to the office of his superiors and learns that Alicia will have to pretend to be in love with Sebastian in order to learn more about his activities. Devlin, always the outward cynic, symbolically leaves a bottle of wine which he bought for his and Alicia's celebration at the office and returns to her to see if she is willing to do what the government wants. Instead of asking her not to do it, Devlin forces her into agreement by not reaffirming their love. The exterior toughness and cynicism of both Alicia and Devlin makes happiness for them elusive throughout the film, and in itself, seems mysterious. It is hard to believe that such a deep love would be so difficult to express, but Grant and Bergman do an excellent job of making their respective characters believable. Of course, as a plot device, this lack of communication between the two is completely necessary, for without it, there would be no story.

After Alicia accepts her assignment, events move rather quickly as she "accidentally" meets Sebastian again while riding, and they begin a romance. There are a number of short scenes showing them together, interrupted by scenes of Alicia telling Devlin or Paul Prescott (Louis Calhern) and the other officials about information she has gotten. At times Alicia tries to reach Devlin, but he behaves very coolly toward her. Finally, she tells Prescott and Devlin that Sebastian wants to marry her, hoping that Devlin will stop her, but he does not. Alicia and Sebastian are married, and after returning to their estate outside Rio, they give a large party, in part on the suggestion to Alicia from Devlin. At this point the mystery of Sebastian's activities becomes as important as the love story between Alicia and Devlin. As it happens, Alicia has learned that there is something strange about a particular vintage of wine in Sebastian's cellar. Neither she nor Devlin know what is important about the vintage, but they suspect that it may contain something other than wine.

In one of the best scenes in the film, and one which is shown repeatedly in documentaries on Hitchcock, Alicia removes the key to the wine cellar form Sebastian's key chain, then tries to hide it in her hand when he almost finds her in the act. It is a perfect example of the type of suspense which Hitchcock himself found most appealing in films. He has said that more suspense can be produced on film if the audience *knows* what is about to happen than if they do not. As Sebastian kisses Alicia, then proceeds to open one of her hands and kiss it, then goes on to open the other hand (which holds the key), the tension is riveting. In a seemingly endless few seconds, Alicia finally throws her arms around Sebastian in an embrace, thus preventing him from discovering the key. The key, in fact, became something of a good-luck charm for Bergman, Grant, and Hitchcock, who passed it among themselves over the years until Bergman gave it back finally to Hitchcock during the American Film Institute's Life Achievement Award ceremonies honoring him in 1979.

During the party, which Devlin joins, to Sebastian's consternation, as he suspects that Devlin is in love with his wife, Alicia and Devlin manage to slip off to the wine cellar. There they discover that the vintage in question contains dirt, which is later discovered to be rich in uranium, which is necessary for atomic research. This information is helpful, but Alicia must continue in her subterfuge in order to discover the location of the mine and research plant.

Just as Devlin and Alicia leave the wine cellar together, Sebastian comes down to the cellar and sees them kissing (which Devlin did to cover the real reason why they were there). Sebastian is extremely jealous, but when he later discovers a bottle which Devlin and Alicia have broken, he realizes that they are American agents and pretends to Alicia that he is not angry. Although initially Sebastian had wanted to kill Alicia out of jealousy, his mother (Leopoldine Konstantin) convinces him to play along with her, but in the meantime to watch her carefully and submit her to slow poisoning. They do this not only to rid themselves of Alicia, but also to protect themselves from the other Nazis, who would undoubtedly kill Sebastian for his stupidity.

Alicia begins receiving the poison in small doses in her coffee. While outwardly sympathetic and concerned, Sebastian and his mother begin increasing the doses to the point that Alicia is barely able to make her weekly visit to Rio to see Devlin. Devlin suspects that Alicia is ill, but again, he is unable to express his true feelings and accuses her of having a hangover. Later, when Devlin tells Prescott about their meeting, which is to be their last because

Devlin was due to leave for Spain on assignment, he says that he is going to see Alicia "as a friend of the family" at Sebastian's estate.

That same day, Alicia discovers what Sebastian has been doing to her when he and his mother become very upset when a friend almost drinks her coffee by mistake. It is too late for her to leave, however, and she collapses on the stairs. They confine her to her room without the telephone and keep her prisoner, although they say that she will have a doctor. Devlin enters the house, sneaks upstairs, and finds the semiconscious Alicia. She is almost incoherent, but tells Devlin what is wrong. He finally confesses his love for her and very tenderly helps her out of bed. As he half carries her down the long staircase, Sebastian and his mother meet him. In order to save himself from exposure to his Nazi friends who are downstairs, Sebastian pretends to help Devlin and Alicia, saying that she must be rushed immediately to the hospital. With false concern, he helps Alicia into Devlin's car and hopes to go to the hospital with them, but Devlin closes the door quickly and rushes off, leaving Sebastian to explain himself to his already suspicious guests, who are waiting in the doorway.

The ending is never spelled out, although it is implied that Alicia will get to the hospital in time, and Sebastian will be held accountable for his crimes, either by the Americans, or, more likely, his own cohorts. The last scene at the car is one of the best in the cinema, allowing both parallel stories a neat ending point.

Although *Notorious* won no Academy Awards and only one nomination, for Rains as Best Supporting Actor, it did do reasonably well at the box office and received fairly good critical reviews. Like a great number of Hitchcock's films, however, contemporary reaction was far less enthusiastic than what it would be later. The same was true of most of Grant's films. Even some of his recognized best works now, such as *Bringing Up Baby* (1936) or this film, did not garner much enthusiasm at the time of their release. Bergman and Rains, on the other hand, were at points in their respective careers when they almost never got bad reviews (Bergman was still being called "Saint Ingrid" by the press). Their performances stand up well even now, but the performance of Grant and the overall merits of the film are much more appreciated today than they were in 1946.

Patricia King Hanson

NOW, VOYAGER

Released: 1942
Production: Hal B. Wallis for Warner Bros.
Direction: Irving Rapper
Screenplay: Casey Robinson; based on the novel of the same name by Olive Higgins Prouty
Cinematography: Sol Polito
Editing: Warren Low
Makeup: Perc Westmore
Costume design: Orry-Kelly
Music: Max Steiner (AA)
Running time: 118 minutes

Principal characters:
Charlotte Vale .... Bette Davis
Jerry Durrance .... Paul Henreid
Dr. Jaquith .... Claude Rains
Mrs. Henry Windle Vale .... Gladys Cooper
Tina Durrance .... Janis Wilson

Now, Voyager today is regarded, along with such films as *Dark Victory* (1939) and *All About Eve* (1950), as a quintessential Bette Davis picture. Oddly enough, however, Davis was almost not in it. When Warner Bros. purchased the rights to film the Olive Higgins Prouty novel, it was announced that Irene Dunne would be borrowed from another studio for the lead role. When Davis heard this, she immediately went to the producer, Hal B. Wallis, and argued that she should have the part, particularly since her New England background enabled her to understand the Bostonian heroine better than anyone else could. Fortunately, her argument was convincing.

The film is the story of Charlotte Vale (Bette Davis), born late and unwanted into an upper-class Boston family. The tyranny of her mother (Gladys Cooper) over her makes Charlotte into a frumpy, unattractive, neurotic woman until she is rescued by the treatment of a psychiatrist, Dr. Jaquith (Claude Rains). The mother's comment when she sees her daughter shattering emotionally is, "No member of the Vale family has ever had a nervous breakdown."

Dr. Jaquith brings Charlotte out of her shell and sends her on an ocean cruise, telling her to be interested in everything and everyone. Her mental health is further restored by her friendship with one of the other passengers, Jerry Durrance (Paul Henreid). As the friendship changes to love, things become very complicated because Jerry has a wife whom he does not love but cannot hurt. Charlotte and Jerry part in South America thinking they will never see each other again, and Charlotte returns to her mother's house with her newfound sense of independence and self-worth. Her mother, however, expects her to "resume the duties of a daughter," and in several scenes Charlotte has to assert herself despite her mother's imperious demands. When Charlotte finally explodes in anger and says, "I didn't want to be born, and you didn't want me to be born," the shock kills her mother. Charlotte returns to Dr. Jaquith's sanitarium, but instead of having another breakdown she finds restoration in helping a young patient (Janis Wilson) who turns out to be Jerry's daughter, Tina. Jerry and Charlotte then establish a platonic relationship in which Charlotte will rear Tina and Jerry will remain married to his wife. When Jerry asks her if she can be happy with that arrangement, Charlotte replies with the film's famous (but often misquoted) last line, "Don't let's ask for the moon, we have the stars!"

One of the most striking aspects of *Now, Voyager* is the transformation of Charlotte's character from that of a neurotic caterpillar into that of an independent butterfly. It is not only the acting talent of Davis but also the talents of the director, Irving Rapper, the makeup man, Perc Westmore, and the costume designer, Orry-Kelly, that make the change both dramatic and believable. The very first time we see Charlotte we have been made curious about her by the conversation of the others. Then she begins descending the stairs and we see her feet in "sensible shoes," then her lumpy figure in a dowdy dress (Davis wore padding for these scenes), and a few shots later we see her unattractive hairdo, heavy eyebrows, and glasses. After she has been treated by Dr. Jaquith and is on the ocean cruise, once again we see her come down a stairway after the others have been talking about her, but this time her shoes, dress, and hair are stylish and her figure slim. This motif is repeated when she returns to her home and walks down steps to join a party for her relatives and family friends. Even later Jerry's daughter, Tina, who has undergone a similar transformation, enters a scene coming down the very same stairs on which Charlotte first appeared.

Now, Voyager is also famous for Jerry's lighting two cigarettes and handing one to Charlotte, but this is not just a gimmick, it is a motif used several times as a symbol of their love. Indeed, he begins their last conversation in the film with the invitation "Let's have a cigarette on it." In the novel from which the film was made the motif was a complicated exchange of lighted matches and cigarettes, but it proved to be unworkable in rehearsals; so Henreid suggested that he simply light both cigarettes and hand one to Davis. It proved to be an inspired improvisation.

The title of the film is taken from a line by the American poet Walt Whitman ("Now, Voyager, sail thou forth to seek and find") that Dr. Jaquith writes on a piece of paper and gives to Charlotte when she is ready to leave his sanitarium.

Although the film is most known for its story of the two lovers and their sacrifices and accommodations, perhaps its strongest theme is the crippling influence of the too demanding mother. The theme gains its accuracy and emotional force from Casey Robinson's script, on which Davis also worked in order to keep it as close to the original novel as possible, and especially from the emotional yet controlled acting of Davis and Cooper, who played her mother. As testimony to the truth of the theme, Davis reports receiving hundreds of letters from children of possessive mothers as well as many from mothers who admitted they saw their own mistakes on the screen.

It is not surprising that Davis still chooses *Now, Voyager* as one of her favorite pictures and that she has nothing but praise for her costars, Henreid, Rains, and Cooper. Nor is it surprising that the film inspired Max Steiner to create one of his most restrained and evocative motion-picture scores, an Academy Award-winning work somewhat reminiscent of the music of Tchaikovsky.

Judith A. Williams

THE NUN'S STORY

Released: 1959
Production: Fred Zinnemann for Warner Bros.
Direction: Fred Zinnemann
Screenplay: Robert Anderson; based on the novel of the same name by Kathryn Hulme
Cinematography: Franz Planer
Editing: Walter Thompson
Sound: George Groves
Running time: 149 minutes

Principal characters:
Gabrielle Van Der Mal/
Sister Luke .... Audrey Hepburn
Dr. Fortunati .... Peter Finch
Mother Emmanuel .... Dame Edith Evans
Dr. Van Der Mal ....Dean Jagger

The Nun's Story is Fred Zinnemann's moving adaptation of Kathryn Hulme's quasibiographical novel about a strong-willed young woman's struggle to become a perfect nun. The film features an outstanding performance by Audrey Hepburn as Sister Luke, who is forced by her own conscience to choose between a career as a nurse and a vocation as a nun. Zinnemann and his screenwriter, Robert Anderson, stress the dichotomy between career and vocation throughout the entire film. A career is something that one actively chooses and pursues out of interest and/or ability. A vocation, however, is, in the literal sense, a calling; one hears the call and chooses (or refuses) to submit to the will of the caller. In the case of the nun, the caller is God. Although *The Nun's Story* is about religion, it rises far above the level of religious tract, for Zinnemann and Anderson are true to the novel that inspired the film. Hulme resisted the temptation to portray faith triumphant: in the end, Sister Luke leaves her order to become a nurse in the secular world.

The film's protagonist is a young Belgian woman named Gabrielle Van Der Mal (Audrey Hepburn), the daughter of a famous surgeon (Dean Jagger). She wants to make a career of medicine, like her father, but she also feels called to become a nun. Thus, despite the fact that she is engaged to be married, she decides to enter a convent. The film opens with Gabrielle slipping the engagement ring off her finger, serene in her decision to become a nun. Zinnemann will use a nearly identical scene at the end of the film, as Gabrielle—by then Sister Luke—has reached her tortured decision to leave her order.

The first hour of the film, set in 1930, has been called by Bosley Crowther "a documentary picture of how a young woman becomes a nun." The girls are taught to regard the bells that call them to worship as "the voice of God" and to respond instantly to the call. Later in the film, Zinnemann will use these bells to illustrate Sister Luke's frustrations with her life as a nun.

Gabrielle's teacher is Mother Emmanuel (Dame Edith Evans), the mother superior of the convent. Mother Emmanuel is a gentle but stern woman who never stops reminding Gabrielle and the other novitiates that the life they have chosen will not be easy, and that the sacrifices they must make will be bearable only through the love of Christ. Their order is a particularly strict one. They will take vows of poverty, chastity, and obedience, and although some of the other would-be nuns may have difficulty with the first two vows, it soon becomes clear that obedience will be Gabrielle's chief hurdle.

It is not that Gabrielle is rebellious in any normal sense of the word; she is simply a very bright, self-confident young woman, who has difficulty subsuming her personality and ambitions to that of her order. She has her heart set, for example, on going to the Congo as a nurse, and she is ideally suited for such a job, but she endures disappointment after disappointment before her dream is fulfilled, watching nuns medically less qualified than she go off to Africa while she stays in Europe. Her superiors are trying to teach her a lesson in humility. "You entered the convent to be a nun," Mother Emmanuel tells her, "not to be a nurse." In truth, Gabrielle is her own harshest critic. Every prideful thought is followed by pangs of conscience at questioning the wisdom of her superiors. Ultimately, her own standards become more rigid than those of her order. "You must learn to bend a little, or you'll break," counsels a more experienced nun. As Zinnemann shows the audience, however, bending is something Gabrielle never masters.

Gabrielle is eventually accepted fully into her order. Her new name is Sister Luke, and she wears the nun's gold bride-of-Christ wedding band. Finally, her ultimate dream comes true: she is sent to the Congo, where she comes as close to fulfillment as she ever gets. She is assigned to work with Dr. Fortunati (Peter Finch), a brilliant, cynical, and irreligious surgeon. Fortunati is an acerbic man who drives himself and his subordinates hard. For a time, Sister Luke thrives on the work, rising at dawn to operate before the tropical sun turns the hospital into an oven, and working late at night in the laboratory. Fortunati is soon won over by her competence, and the two develop a professional respect for each other. The doctor sees in Sister Luke what she has kept from everyone else: the tension between her professional duties as a nurse and her religious obligations as a nun. The bells—those "voices of God"—become a constant trial. She is forced to seek a special dispensation to receive communion each morning in the operating room, which particularly amuses Dr. Fortunati when she almost faints during an operation because of her fasting. Although a mild case of tuberculosis seems to reinforce her piety, it soon becomes clear that Sister Luke loves her profession more than her vocation. Thus, when circumstances force her to return to Belgium, she is devastated. She cannot adjust to the routine of the convent.

Mother Emmanuel is understanding; there are no openings in the Congo, but she does send Sister Luke to a hospital near the border with Holland. She is needed there—World War II has broken out, and there is much work for a nurse. The war affects Sister Luke emotionally as well, however, and she is unable to maintain the façade of neutrality ordered by her superiors when Belgium surrenders. She aids members of the Belgian underground resistance; and when she learns that her father has been killed by the Nazis, she snaps. Despite her best efforts, she cannot forgive the Germans. All she can think of is revenge.

Sister Luke concludes that she is unworthy of her vocation, and resolves to leave her order, despite the pleas of Mother Emmanuel. The last scene in the film mirrors the first. Sister Luke, alone in a room, removes her habit and the ring that marked her as a nun. She opens the door and steps out alone into the secular world. Zinnemann holds the final shot for several long moments as Gabrielle walks into the distance. The shot emphasizes the loneliness of her decision, but also reinforces the impression of her determination to live her own life. The scene is an effective contrast to Gabrielle's serenity at the beginning of the film, and the whole effect is quite moving.

The Nun's Story is a powerful film, and was recognized as such by both the public and the critics. Although it was ultimately swamped by the *Ben Hur* tidal wave, the film was nominated for eight Academy Awards, including Best Picture, Best Director, and Best Actress. The praise was richly deserved. *The Nun's Story* is on a par with Zinnemann's other characteristic works, such as *High Noon* (1952), *From Here to Eternity* (1953), and *A Man for All Seasons* (1966). Zinnemann is a cool, relatively detached director who tells his stories in a straightforward manner. In *The Nun's Story*, he has the help of a marvelous cast and crew. Anderson garnered an Oscar nomination for his screenplay, as did cinematographer Franz Planer, sound man George Groves, editor Walter Thompson, and Franz Waxman, who provided the musical score. Most of these contributions stand up well. Only Waxman's score seems a bit heavy-handed, unnecessarily underlining already effective scenes.

Four actors in *The Nun's Story* stand out. Evans is very good as Mother Emmanuel. Affection and discipline are two attributes that are a challenge to portray at the same time, and Evans carries it off nicely. Finch is likable as the acerbic and perceptive Dr. Fortunati, and Jagger, in a smaller role as Gabrielle's father, also does good work. The film belongs, however, to Hepburn. Gabrielle/Sister Luke is in practically every scene in the film's two-and-one-half hours, and Hepburn handles the role with aplomb, aptly conveying her character's inner turmoil and inner strength. She richly deserved an Academy Award nomination for her portrayal.

The 1950's was a decade of public piety in the United States, and too often filmmakers pandered to the lowest common denominator of this spirit. *The*

Nun's Story never descends into religiosity. It is an intelligent film, carefully crafted and well acted, with some thought-provoking insights on the nature of faith and commitment. As such, it merits our serious attention.

Robert Mitchell

ODD MAN OUT

Released: 1947
Production: Sir Carol Reed for J. Arthur Rank; released by Universal
Direction: Sir Carol Reed
Screenplay: F. L. Green and R. C. Sherriff; based on the novel of the same name by F. L. Green
Cinematography: Robert Krasker
Editing: Fergus McDonell
Running time: 116 minutes

Principal characters:
Johnny McQueen	James Mason
Kathleen	Kathleen Ryan
Dennis	Robert Beatty
Constable	Denis O'Dea
Father Tom	W. G. Fay
Shell	F. J. McCormick
Lukey	Robert Newton
Grannie	Kitty Kirwin
Tober	Elwyn Brook-Jones
Rosie	Fay Compton
Maudie	Beryl Measor

Odd Man Out begins with a disclaimer. Prefatory remarks are superimposed over a long shot of an unnamed Northern Irish City to inform the viewer that the film's purpose is not to judge the British rule of Northern Ireland or to expose any political conflict existing there but rather to explore ". . . the conflict between people when they become unexpectedly involved." It is rare for a film to begin with a statement of a political intention but necessary in this instance because of its intensely controversial subject: the Irish Republican Army. It is also important to remember that these opening remarks are not an indication that the film is "objective." It attempts to be nonpolitical and to use a violent political crime as a dramatic device upon which to draw the universally applicable moral of charity toward one's fellow man.

The film's action spans the last eight hours in the life of rebel leader Johnny McQueen, played with deft understatement by James Mason. McQueen and his four members of "The Organization" rob a mill's safe in the afternoon for money to sustain their revolutionary activities against the British government. Despite Johnny's nonviolent beliefs, he scuffles with an armed millworker and the man's pistol fires accidentally. Johnnny is severely wounded while the mill worker is killed. Johnny's men grab their chief and attempt to make their getaway with him; but Johnny falls from their car. His men are too confused to act quickly enough to rescue him, so Johnny struggles up from the street to hide among nearby buildings. This is the last independent choice Johnny makes in the film.

Even before the robbery it is hypothesized by his fellow group members that Johnny may be physically unfit for the robbery because he has had to hide indoors for six months after escaping from prison. One of his men, Dennis (Robert Beatty), implies that he is not emotionally fit either. Johnny dismisses these fears; but, on the way to the robbery, he is disoriented by the sudden impact of the busy city environment. Reflecting his point of view, the camera expressionistically crosscuts harsh angles of the city's buildings towering across Johnny's vision while fast, blurred traffic rushes by in several directions. An imaginative sound track intensifies the city's noises, which make it impossible for Johnny to compose himself. Usually these techniques confuse an audience, but in *Odd Man Out* they express Johnny's emotional state to the audience at the time of the robbery. Subjective expressionism such as this is effectively used throughout the film to relate Johnny's experience. His dialogue is minimal.

Following the robbery, Johnny finds refuge in a bomb shelter. He is discovered there by a little girl who wanders inside after her ball. In a masterful dissolve which transforms the stooping child picking up the toy into a tall uniformed man holding the ball, Johnny hallucinates, imagining that he is in prison. He speaks to the "guard" and tells him about a wild dream that he has just had in which he commits robbery and kills a man. Although he appears to be released of this hallucination after a few moments, Johnny never fully regains control of his reason and is tormented throughout the film by visions of unreality which are filmed from his point of view. Spilled beer bubbles, for example, become familiar faces speaking to him, and later, other caricatures of his acquaintances emerge from oil paintings to sit in rows before him while he delivers St. Paul's Epistle to the Corinthians.

This quotation from the Bible is the film's most explicit thematic statement: ". . . And though I have the gift of prophecy and understand all mysteries and all knowledge and though I have all faith so that I could remove mountains and have not charity, I am nothing." Christian theology defines charity as the love of God for man or of man for his fellow men. In this speech, Johnny is not only speaking of the lack of charity he receives during his crisis but also of his own lack of giving charity earlier in the film when he rejects Dennis' offer of leadership out of pride and then ignorantly overlooks the love of Kathleen (Kathleen Ryan), the woman who has been hiding him. The implication that Johnny lacks charity and thus is nothing combines with his personal loss of reality at the film's end. He is finally found by Kathleen who urges him to come to her. Johnny says, "If you are real, stretch out your hand to me." A moment later he begs her, "Go back to life, please." He knows he is nothing and is already dead.

Johnny's loss of rational ability results in his inability to make decisions. Thus he loses all control over his fate. In a film filled with religious symbolism, Johnny has lost his free will, his ability to choose. Fallen from grace, he becomes an object to be pushed mercilessly by fate through the night. Wandering helplessly and never asking for anything until he asks for Kathleen's hand, Johnny does not react to situations and people because as an object he is neutral. The people about him exploit him for their own goals or dismiss him from their lives out of fear. Pursued and yet shunned, Johnny is in limbo.

The plot contrasts several pursuers with an almost equal number of discoverers. The constable (Denis O'Dea) directs an intensive manhunt to preserve law and order. Dennis pursues Johnny out of a sense of duty to rescue the organization's chief, but perhaps more because of a desire for glory. He devises a flamboyant decoy to cover Johnny's escape from the bomb shelter but then stupidly lets them be recognized on a tram. Johnny manages to stumble away, but Dennis is captured. Father Tom (W. G. Fay), the parish priest and Johnny's childhood teacher, wants to salvage Johnny's soul. He bargains with a conman, Shell (F. J. McCormick), to learn where Johnny is hiding by promising a "precious article of faith" as barter for the information. Shell is confused about the "faith" and tries to determine what the precious article's value is next to the money the police would give him for the same information. While Shell vascillates, however, Johnny is found by the artist Lukey (Robert Newton), who wants to paint the truth about death which he believes emanates from the rebel's eyes. At Lukey's studio, Johnny is grimly propped up as a model while Lukey's intern friend Tober (Elwyn Brook-Jones) practices his fledgling medical skill upon Johnny even though he believes that it is useless to patch him up.

The fearful discoverers include Rosie (Fay Compton) and Maudie (Beryl Measor), two Protestants who see Johnny fall in the street. They take him into their home, where Rosie's husband sends him back to the street, explaining "I'm not for you and I'm not against you." A cabbie who finds Johnny in his cab drops the rebel off at a junkyard and asks him not to tell the police he helped him but to inform the organization that it was Gin Jimmy. A Biblical parallel is again drawn by these sequences that those who are not for him are against him. These people condemn Johnny by their abandonment of him, despite their words to the contrary. The only pursuer who succeeds in finding Johnny is Kathleen. All of the film's authority figures—the constable, Dennis, her grandmother (Kitty Kerwin), Father Tom, and Johnny himself—tell her not to attempt to help. Her grandmother uses the example of her own life to dissuade Kathleen. Pointing to a photograph of herself as a young and beautiful bride, she righteously explains how she did not run after her rebel husband but stayed and "had her life . . . where's the sense in runnin' toward trouble when you know you can't mend it." Kathleen looks at herself in a mirror and resolves to find Johnny. She takes a gun and leaves the house.

Obviously, the kind of life her grandmother chose has no meaning for Kathleen.

She arranges for Johnny's escape by pleading with a boat captain to wait until midnight to set sail and later explains to Father Tom that she is willing to take Johnny's life rather than let the police get him. The priest asks her where her faith has gone, and she answers that her faith is her love and that she believes that what she intends to do is good.

The film's conclusion casts doubt about anyone's ability to do good. Kathleen struggles to keep Johnny standing despite seeing their ship sail without them in the distance. In front of them the police are closing in, and their flashlights find the fugitives against a wire fence. Kathleen pulls her gun out. The police move closer as two shots are heard and the police return fire. Johnny and Kathleen are shown lying face forward in the snow, dead, while the clock tower tolls midnight. It is ambiguous whether Kathleen fired at the police to force them to kill Johnny and herself or if she did indeed kill Johnny rather than let the police have him.

Odd Man Out was a critical and financial success when it opened in 1947. It was praised for the excellence of its philosophical theme within the framework of a thrilling and timely story although several reviewers considered moments of the film stylistically overbearing or too unrealistic.

Odd Man Out does evidence a stylistic inconsistency. The style shifts reflect the intentions of the film's director, Sir Carol Reed, to translate gradually the social dilemma of a criminal into a metaphysical question. As a morality play, the film's major style elements of cinematography, editing, music, and sound effects shift from daylit neorealism during the robbery to dark naturalism during Johnny's wanderings through the surrealism of the artist's studio and concludes with a transcendent romanticism in which a lover and a rebel fall dead onto purifying white snow while a bell tower tolls solemnly. Additionally, the expressionism of the hallucination sequences conveys the protagonist's subjective experience.

Elizabeth Ward

OH! WHAT A LOVELY WAR

Released: 1969
Production: Brian Duffy and Richard Attenborough for Accord/Paramount
Direction: Richard Attenborough
Screenplay: Len Deighton (uncredited); based on the Joan Littlewood production of the same name and adapted from the BBC radio feature *The Long, Long Trail* by Charles Chilton
Cinematography: Gerry Turpin
Editing: Kevin Connor
Musical direction: Alfred Ralston
Running time: 144 minutes

Principal characters:
Field Marshal Sir John French	Laurence Olivier
Sir Edward Grey	Ralph Richardson
General Sir Henry Wilson	Michael Redgrave
Count Leopold Von Berchtold	John Gielgud
General Von Moltke	John Clements
Kaiser Wilhelm II	Kenneth More
Emperor Franz Josef	Jack Hawkins
Field Marshal Sir Douglas Haig	John Mills
Music Hall Star	Maggie Smith
Sylvia Pankhurst	Vanessa Redgrave
Archduke Ferdinand	Wensley Pithey
Photographer	Joe Melia

For all its appearance of being a somewhat experimental film, a semi-Brechtian, antiwar musical mingling fantasy with reality in its treatment of World War I as "the ever popular war game: songs, battles and a few jokes," *Oh! What a Lovely War* from the start was conceived of as a commercial venture. Financed by Paramount for $3,500,000, the motion picture was made on a spectacular scale utilizing lavish costumes, Panavision, and Technicolor and with a cast that reads like a *Who's Who* of the British acting profession. In terms of the British market, the commercial optimism turned out to be well founded and the film was a hit, although it did rather less well in the United States. The emphasis on commercial viability, however, backed up by Director Richard Attenborough's avowed intention of making an unconventional project accessible to the broad general public, goes a long way toward accounting for the film's strength and limitations.

Oh! What a Lovely War began as a BBC radio feature by Charles Chilton at Christmas, 1961, in which the breezy jingoism of the recruiting songs of the World War I period was contrasted with the horrific reality of life in the trenches. Taken up by radical British theater director Joan Littlewood, *Oh! What a Lovely War* became one of the milestones of British theater in the

1960's. The show was a bitter indictment, not of war in general, but of the particular social, political, and, above all, class system which were all part of World War I.

The film rights were acquired in June, 1967, by photographer Brian Duffy and thriller writer Len Deighton, whose works included *The Ipcress File*. The latter wrote the screenplay, although as a result of complicated contractual disagreements with Paramount, his name did not appear on the credits, which have no screenplay listing. He keeps to the general idea of the stage show, but transfers the action to the seafront at Brighton, a British south coast resort, where the wonderful Victorian pier becomes the setting for a bizarre series of sideshows, with Field Marshal Sir Douglas Haig (John Mills) selling tickets beneath an amusement arcade sign spelling out "World War I." The time is August, 1914, and the long hot summer is drawing to a close. The crowned heads of Europe gather in a beautiful white ballroom to chat and reminisce. A photographer assembles them for a group portrait, and, as the flash bulb goes off, the Archduke Ferdinand (Wensley Pithey) falls dead: World War I has begun, the photographer creeps away, the crowned heads argue among themselves, and the carpet—a map of Europe—is rolled up. This sequence acts as a kind of prologue to the movie, establishing its style as a deliberately unrealistic portrayal of history acted out by very real people.

From here, linked by aural rather than visual dissolves and the omnipresence of the Smiths, a typical working-class family decimated by World War I, *Oh! What a Lovely War* proceeds to chronicle the war by cutting from the carousels, peep-shows, and helter-skelters of Brighton Pier to the trenches and field hospitals of Flanders, although the latter scenes carefully avoid graphic violence. Indeed, not a single person is actually shown being killed in the film; instead, the dead are handed a red poppy. The songs, thirty-three in all, gradually develop from the jaunty numbers of 1914 ("Are We Downhearted?," "Pack Up Your Troubles in Your Old Kitbag") to the bitter but wry complaints of 1917 and 1918, expressed with cynical humor ("When This Lousy War Is Over," sung to the hymn tune of "The Church's One Foundation," "The Bells of Hell," "Never Mind," "Far from Wipers").

Oh! What a Lovely War is the history of World War I presented in a series of superbly performed, often brilliantly succinct charades. A music-hall singer (Maggie Smith) lures young men up on the stage with a provocative rendering of "I'll Make a Man of You"; onstage, they find themselves recruited into the army, and the singer, on closer inspection (a swift change of makeup and mood, from realistic to grotesque) turns out to be a raddled old whore. A French cavalry officer (Jean-Pierre Cassel) leads his men on a murderous charge into enemy machine-gun fire on a carousel. At Christmas, 1914, an impromptu truce occurs: German and British soldiers meet in no man's land and exchange drinks and greetings before the war resumes. Back in England, two society people (Dirk Bogarde and Susannah York) bemoan the austerity of wartime life while sipping champagne at a fund-raising ball. Britain's leading campaigner for women's suffrage, Sylvia Pankhurst (Vanessa Redgrave), makes a pacifist speech to a hostile crowd. Surveying the battlefield from atop the helter-skelter on Brighton Pier, Haig prays "for victory, Lord, before the Americans arrive" (a line from history rather than the writer's imagination), then slides pompously down to ground level.

Perhaps the final sequence—the one most frequently singled out for critical acclaim—typifies *Oh! What a Lovely War* at its best and most effective. The one remaining Smith soldier goes into battle on the eve of the Armistice, led to the front line by a red tape. Emerging out of the smoke, Joe Melia, the actor who was the photographer in the opening sequence and has reappeared in a variety of guises throughout the film, leads him through a concrete blockhouse and into a room where the peace documents are being signed. The red tape takes him round the room and out onto the Sussex Downs where he joins his dead brothers reclining in the sun, the last soldier to die in World War I. The female members of the Smith family, oblivious to their presence, picnic nearby. The Smith boys dissolve into three white crosses, and the camera begins to crane back, revealing the crosses surrounded by rows of others. As Jerome Kern's "They'll Never Believe Me" fades up on the sound-track, the camera cranes further and further back revealing more and more crosses, thousands and thousands, covering the hillside as the light changes with a cloud drifting across the sun. It is a moment of intense emotion, a skillful and apposite summation to the movie.

Oh! What a Lovely War was Attenborough's first project as a director after a twenty-five year career as a film actor, and it became a labor of love: working without a fee but with the promise of a share of the royalties, he persuaded most of the all-star cast to work for reduced fees with similar promises of fuller payment when the film went into profit. Receiving its premiere in London on April 10, 1969, the film received a rapturous welcome, with a seven-minute standing ovation for Attenborough. John Russell Taylor in *The Times* called the film "an almost complete triumph," and Cecil Wilson in the *Daily Mail* was unequivocal in terming it "a masterpiece." The key to Attenborough's commercial success is that he has taken what was a left-wing stage show and turned it into a more broadly based (and therefore inevitably less radical) work. While Littlewood's play had been socialist theater, Attenborough's film is a humanist condemnation of the "folly of war." The army chiefs are held responsible but treated with indulgence. This change of emphasis, inevitable although it may have been, is the film's one real shortcoming: too often it seems a spectacular, all-star exercise in musical nostalgia, not an antiwar film. Certain American critics remarked on this point. Vincent Canby of *The New York Times* thought that it was "so enlarged, stretched out and over-orchestrated that the ultimate effect is dramatically anesthetizing." For him, any attempt to see the film as a comment on Vietnam was misplaced;

it was an exercise in specific nostalgia. Pauline Kael was, as usual, more barbed. The movie was "show-business Marxism . . . in Panavision, and over-poweringly *clean*."

Oh! What a Lovely War is nevertheless an extraordinary cinematic debut. Attenborough achieves the almost impossible in preserving balance between the pier and the trench scenes—seafront and battlefront. Of the individual sequences only a few fall short: the carousel sequence with the French cavalry seems mannered, and the scene in which a soldier in a trench appears to "invent" one of Rupert Brooke's poems is unfortunate. These weak moments are almost negligible, however, compared to sequences such as Maggie Smith's music-hall recruitment drive, the prebattle church service (in a setting strongly reminiscent of the interventionist ending of *Mrs. Miniver*, 1942) in which the hymn gradually gives way to a single voice singing "When this lousy war is over," and the final sequence, which, apparently, even had the critics in tears at the London press show. *Oh! What a Lovely War* is a film made up of fine individual scenes, performed like sketches by an outstanding cast and relying on a cumulative effect. Ironically, for a film adapted via much transformation from a stage show, it is extremely, although not detrimentally, theatrical.

Nick Roddick

THE OLD MAID

Released: 1939
Production: Hal B. Wallis for Warner Bros.
Direction: Edmund Goulding
Screenplay: Casey Robinson; based on the play of the same name by Zoe Akins and a novella by Edith Wharton
Cinematography: Tony Gaudio
Editing: George Amy
Running time: 95 minutes

Principal characters:
Charlotte Lovell .... Bette Davis
Delia Lovell .... Miriam Hopkins
Clem Spender .... George Brent
Dr. Lanskell .... Donald Crisp
Tina .... Jane Bryan
Dora .... Louise Fazenda
James Ralston .... James Stephenson
Lanning Halsey .... William Lundigan

In the first quarter of the twentieth century, Edith Wharton wrote a quartet of novellas illustrative of life as it was in four particular decades of American history during the nineteenth century. The real tearjerker in the tetralogy was *The Old Maid*. Its story was so visual that to read it was to see it in the mind's eye being enacted as if on a stage. Playwright Zoe Akins responded to this appeal by dramatizing the story as a full-length play, which was presented in New York at the Empire Theater in 1935, directed by Guthrie McClintic and costarring Helen Menken and Judith Anderson. It won the Pulitzer Prize and Best Drama for that year and was purchased shortly thereafter by Paramount for a projected film. Paramount did not have two women under contract who would be suitable for the costarring roles, however, and Hal B. Wallis, whose principal female star at Warner Bros. was Bette Davis, purchased it to be filmed with Davis as one of four features she did in 1939.

The story of *The Old Maid* may have been considered old-fashioned and maudlin, but it was a successful tearjerker. Casey Robinson wrote a very appealing screenplay; and it was the kind of woman's picture Edmund Goulding directed to perfection. The thing that intrigued Bette Davis about her role of Charlotte Lovell, the old maid of the title, was that it allowed her to develop from a romantic young woman to a listless, graying spinster who runs a day school for children of working mothers. Also, Davis had never costarred with another woman and was interested in working with Miriam Hopkins, who had been selected to play the role of Delia Lovell, Charlotte's cousin and rival whose busy life has always been a social and domestic whirl. The paths of Bette Davis and Miriam Hopkins had crossed before at George Cukor's theater in Rochester, New York, where Hopkins had once been a star and Davis the ingenue in a play production. Later, on Broadway, Hopkins had starred in the play *Jezebel*, which flopped; but the film starring Davis won her the Academy Award as Best Actress in 1938, the second time she had won the Oscar.

Hopkins gave a clue as to how rocky the shooting was going to be when she appeared on the set for the first day's shooting wearing a costume which Bette Davis had worn in *Jezebel*. Davis paid no heed to the trick, but from that day on, Hopkins tried one trick after another. Finally, one day, by sheer accident, a spotlight plunged down from a catwalk, missing Davis by inches. She looked at Hopkins, who had paled. "I didn't do that!" Hopkins snapped. Davis said nothing. By that time they were not exchanging words unless they were playing a scene together. The Hopkins-Davis feud is probably the best-publicized duel between two women in Hollywood history. Much of it never really happened, but every day the trade papers had a new anecdote about the perils of Bette and the villainies of Miriam. The film was nevertheless completed on schedule, and, when released in August of 1939, proved to be one of the best-liked of all Davis features. It had real female audience appeal, and its quality production and sterling performances were generally favorably received.

The story begins at the time of the American Civil War in a proud old home in Philadelphia, where Delia Lovell (Miriam Hopkins) is about to be wed to a wealthy socialite, James Ralston (James Stephenson). On the very morning of the wedding, however, Delia learns that Clem Spender (George Brent) is returning after a long stay in Paris. Delia had once been engaged to Clem for two years, and now, after several years as a hard-playing, hard-drinking playboy in Paris, he is returning to claim Delia as his bride. Charlotte Lovell (Bette Davis) is sent to the station to bring Clem up to date. A shy person, Delia's wallflower cousin loathes what she must do, and it is obvious that through all these years she has herself silently loved Clem. He pays no attention to what she tries to tell him and comes to Delia's home only a few moments before the ceremony. Delia has been prepared for such an exigency by the family physician, Dr. Lanskell (Donald Crisp), who has exacted a promise from her that no matter what Clem may say or promise, she will go through with the wedding to Ralston. Clem blithely leaves her with a necklace he had bought in Paris as a wedding present and departs. A moment later, Delia goes downstairs on the arm of Dr. Lanskell to be married. Charlotte, however, one of the bridesmaids, slips out of the house and follows Clem. She spends the day with him and most of the night. He leaves her with a tender kiss, for he has enlisted in the Union Army, and is leaving the next day.

Four years pass. Delia is now the mother of two children. Clem Spender was long ago slain in a battle. Charlotte, with the help of the family maid, Dora (Louise Fazenda), has transformed the spacious stables of her family home into a day school, where more than twenty children are cared for as their mothers work for a living. One of the children, the youngest, is called Tina (Jane Bryan), short for Clementina. She is a foundling, but the audience knows that she is the daughter Charlotte bore the now-dead Clem Spender. As the years pass, and Tina grows up, she and Charlotte go to live with Delia, who has been widowed. Tina looks upon Charlotte as her old maid aunt. Charlotte is frustrated with the girl's patronizing manner and intends to take Tina away, going some place far from Philadelphia, but Delia persuades her to stay on so that Delia may adopt the child and assure her a future of security.

In time, Tina falls in love with Lanning Halsey (William Lundigan), a young man from a good family. The night before the wedding, Charlotte wants to go to the girl's room and talk to her as a mother might before a daughter's marriage; but when she reaches the door, Tina hears her and calls out, "Is that you, mother?" Charlotte loses heart, and it is Delia who goes into Tina's room. Delia softens and tells Tina that Charlotte, the old maid aunt, had once loved and relinquished a chance to marry well because it would have meant giving up the little girl, Tina. She makes Tina promise that the next day when she is leaving on her honeymoon, she will save the very last kiss for her Aunt Charlotte. Many things become clear to Tina, and before she leaves the following day, the last kiss she gives is, as she had promised, to Charlotte, who stands watching her daughter drive away with her new husband. Charlotte quietly, happily caresses the cheek that Tina has just lovingly kissed.

The Old Maid proved to be a very effective mother-daughter love story. The two costars, who had feuded so bitterly during production, were acclaimed such an ideal team that Bette Davis, four years later, was approached about costarring again with Hopkins in a movie adapted from John van Druten's play, *Old Acquaintance* (1943), which also had two marvelous parts for women. On finishing *The Old Maid*, Davis had vowed that she would never again appear in any film with Hopkins. This time, however, the days of movie stardom were over for Hopkins, and she was thinking of returning to the theater, where stage lights are kinder to an actress than is a camera. Davis agreed to perform again with her professional enemy in *Old Acquaintance* because her own part was not "sappy," as she had characterized Charlotte in *The Old Maid*; her character would be intelligent, modern, and well-dressed. There were incidents of rivalry during the shooting of *Old Acquaintance*, but nothing as ruinous as had occurred during the filming of *The Old Maid*. Both women even enjoyed one scene in which Davis' character tries to shake some sense into Hopkins'. Obviously a highlight to the story, it could not be cut or played down in any way; it was something Davis must have yearned to do many times during the earlier production of *The Old*

Maid. It was a comeuppance that Hopkins had earned, and she took it in fair grace. It would be six years before she returned to Hollywood, and then it would be to play a succession of character roles, the best of which were in such William Wyler films as *The Heiress* (1949), *Carrie* (1952), and *The Children's Hour* (1961).

Today, *The Old Maid*, although a period piece in more ways than one, is looked upon as one of the brighter jewels in the selection of features Hal B. Wallis produced for Davis. In Edmund Goulding, Wallis selected a director who had drawn some of Davis' most effective performances from her (*Dark Victory* was made that same year, 1939, and in 1941 Goulding would work with Davis again in *The Great Lie*). The entire production has style, which is enhanced by Orry-Kelly's beautiful costume designs and the score written by Max Steiner. The cast of *The Old Maid* is strong. Brent is romantically ideal as the wayward Clem Spender; Stephenson is effectively stalwart as James Ralston. The sympathetic maidservant Dora is well played by Fazenda in her final screen role, and Bryan plays a charming Tina. When viewed today, *The Old Maid* may at first be regarded as a deliberate attempt to play upon the viewer's emotions, but it soon captivates an audience. The competitive performances of Davis and Hopkins are admirable, and both actresses must be applauded for daring to play so skillfully together.

DeWitt Bodeen

THE OLD MAN AND THE SEA

Released: 1958
Production: Leland Hayward for Warner Bros.
Direction: John Sturges
Screenplay: Peter Viertel; based on the novel of the same name by Ernest Hemingway
Cinematography: James Wong Howe
Editing: Arthur Schmidt
Music: Dmitri Tiomkin (AA)
Running time: 89 minutes

> *Principal characters:*
> The old man .... Spencer Tracy
> The boy .... Felipe Pazos

The world's mythology, especially that of the Near East, is replete with accounts of struggles between heroes and monstrous creatures from the depths of the sea. Examples include the Sumerian myth of Enki's defeat of Kur, the Babylonian story of Marduk's triumph over Tiamat, the Greek account of Zeus's battle with Typhon, and allusions to Leviathan in the Hebrew Bible. Literature has continued this tradition in novels such as Herman Melville's *Moby Dick* (1851) and Ernest Hemingway's *The Old Man and the Sea* (1952). The film version of Hemingway's novel captures some of the allegorical and mythical qualities that have consistently characterized depictions of a solitary hero in conflict with the raw power of nature.

Following the Hemingway novel fairly closely, *The Old Man and the Sea* focuses on the quest of an aging Cuban fisherman (Spencer Tracy) who has gone for eighty-four days without a catch. Having lost his luck, he becomes a figure of mockery for the younger fishermen and can turn only to a young boy (Felipe Pazos) for moral, spiritual, and physical support. Undaunted by repeated failure, however, the old man continues to go out alone in his boat each morning. Finally, he hooks a large marlin, which drags him farther out to sea. The film concentrates on the agonizing struggle between the old man and the gigantic fish and then on the old man's attempt to return home with his catch.

Heroism is a central issue in the film. The old man, in his quest for elusive success in fishing, manifests the qualities of a mythic hero. Particular emphasis is assigned to the solitary nature of his endeavor and to the insurmountable obstacles he must face to accomplish his goal. His isolation is apparent throughout the film, for the old man, unlike the younger, more successful fishermen, goes out by himself each morning in search of fish. Formerly the young boy had accompanied him onto the open sea; in fact, the old man had taught him how to fish. The old man's recurrent failures, however, convinced the boy's father that he could benefit more from apprenticeship to a more prosperous fisherman. Consequently, the boy, who still idolizes his mentor, can associate with the old man only on shore, where he prepares his coffee and reads the baseball results in the newspaper with him.

On the sea, the old man is a lonely, solitary figure, his small boat a minute speck on the vast horizon of the Atlantic Ocean. The cinematography of James Wong Howe, who was nominated for an Academy Award for his efforts, underscores the loneliness of the old man. Howe's seascapes capture nature's magnitude in contrariety to the frail old man and reinforce the viewers' sense of the vast power of nature which opposes this miniscule but dignified representative of humanity. Even the scenes shot in a studio tank, although they lack the effectiveness of the location shots, preserve the idea. Thus the film's visual imagery couples with the characterization of the old man to convey the mythic hero's lonely and arduous quest.

The old man's quest is indeed carried out against difficult odds. For one thing, he has apparently lost the luck essential for the successful fisherman. In mythic terms the gods have abandoned him, and he has almost three months of failure to show in proof of their neglect. Moreover, when he does finally hook a fish, it is a huge marlin, a monstrous creature longer than the old man's vessel. This fish, the contest with which constitutes most of the film, taxes his strength almost beyond endurance. The marlin drags the old man's boat far out into the Gulf Stream. There the blistering sun parches the old man with its prostrating heat, his arthritic hands begin to cramp, and the fish continually jerks the taut line through his bleeding fingers. Finally the old man kills the marlin, but he is still not free from obstacles. The body of the great fish, lashed to the side of his boat, attracts an endless horde of hungry sharks. The old man gallantly defends his prize, but the sharks outnumber him and ultimately strip the marlin of its flesh, leaving only the bare bones of the skeleton. Unvanquished, the old man returns home with at least the symbolic essence of his success, proof of his semitriumph over nature. Like Ulysses or Aeneas, he comes home from wanderings on a hostile sea, not totally victorious in his quest, but with dignity and nobility intact.

The sort of mythic heroism represented by the old man requires a primordial context in which the lines of conflict are sharply demarcated. Thus his quest must occur on the sea, for when he returns to his village, his accomplishments can be appreciated only by someone such as the young boy, who is a disciple of mythic heroism. The film clearly shows that the old man's triumph over nature is foreign to the world view of civilized, social humanity when at the end a group of tourists see the marlin's skeleton on the beach and are unable to identify what it is. Earlier in the film, the context requisite for mythic heroism emerges from the old man's reveries. He dreams of his younger days on the coast of Africa when he defeated an adversary in a marathon bout of arm-wrestling. He also dreams of young, vital lions frolicking on the sands of a beach. In their sportive wrestling, the young lions epitomize the mythic contest situation.

The heroic qualities present in the old man are paralleled in the "great DiMaggio," the old man's idol who sometimes visits Havana and whose legendary feats on the baseball diamond are the most interesting events in the newspapers which the old man reads. Like the old man, Joe DiMaggio must perform alone. As he stands in the batter's box, he is in a one-on-one contest situation with the opposing pitcher; as he roams the outfield awaiting a long fly from an opposing batter, he can rely only on his own skills and judgment. Furthermore, DiMaggio's accomplishments occur against heavy odds. For example, his record streak of games in which he hit safely requires him to face the subterfuges of numerous pitchers eager for the honor of ending the streak. Finally, the baseball stadium, like the sea, is a primordial contest arena. Opposing sides are plainly delineated, and each player devotes himself unquestioningly to winning.

The bulk of *The Old Man and the Sea* concentrates on the pursuit of the marlin and the old man's attempt to bring it back home; therefore, Tracy is the only actor on screen for most of the time. Tracy narrates the old man's thoughts and feelings as he acts out in virtual pantomime his fights first with the marlin and then with the sharks that come to ravage the catch before he can get it to safety. A kind of trialogue is set up in the film among the voice of the narrator, the visual images, and the musical score. Each element reinforces the other two in depicting the old man and his epic battle.

Despite the positive features of the film, particularly its reiteration of the mythic dimensions of the action, there are some problems. The filmmaker who sets out to adapt any well-known literary work to the screen faces a dilemma. On one hand, he cannot stray from the plot and theme of the work without violating viewers' expectations. On the other hand, some parts of the literary work may not translate effectively into film. Those responsible for *The Old Man and the Sea* chose to adhere faithfully to the novel; but it was a difficult task to sustain cinematic interest when only one character appeared throughout most of the film. Also, since that character devoted himself singlemindedly to one set goal, some monotony was bound to result. This film, however, is an excellent attempt at working with a difficult property. Along with James Wong Howe, Tracy received an Academy Award nomination. His efforts, along with those of Howe and of Dmitri Tiomkin, whose musical score won the Academy Award, as well as the film's mythic elements, make *The Old Man and the Sea* an interesting and moving film.

Frances M. Malpezzi
William M. Clements

OLD MOTHER RILEY DETECTIVE

Released: 1943
Production: John Baxter for British National
Direction: Lance Comfort
Screenplay: Austin Melford, Geoffrey Orme, Barbara K. Emary, and Arthur Lucan
Cinematography: no listing
Editing: no listing
Running time: 80 minutes

Principal characters:
Mrs. Riley .... Arthur Lucan
Kitty Riley .... Kitty McShane
Inspector Cole .... Ivan Brandt
Kenworthy .... Owen Reynolds
Inspector Moresby .... George Street
P. C. Jimmy Green .... Johnnie Schofield
Bill .... Hal Gordon
Elsie .... Valentine Dunn
Cook .... Marjorie Rhodes
H. G. Popplethwaite .... H. F. Maltby
Lily .... Peggy Cummins
Alfredo Campoli .... Himself

Old Mother Riley is a peculiarly British phenomenon. She is the grand old lady of the British cinema, in the form of a female impersonator who is so much the character he created that not once watching any of the Old Mother Riley films does one ever stop to consider the incongruity of this character, an Irish washerwoman played by a music-hall comedian named Arthur Lucan in drag. Nor does it seem in any way strange that playing opposite Old Mother Riley as her daughter is one Kitty McShane, in reality Old Mother Riley's wife, an unattractive, dowdy, slightly plump actress with no acting or singing ability, but who insists on doing both, and who always ends the films in the arms of the handsome leading man.

Lucan (1887-1954) first conceived of Old Mother Riley in the early 1900's. The character quickly became a favorite of the British music halls, and was brought to the screen in 1936. Between 1937 and 1952, Lucan starred in fourteen Old Mother Riley films—*Old Mother Riley M. P.* (1939), *Old Mother Riley in Business* (1940), *Old Mother Riley at Home* (1944), *Old Mother Riley Headmistress* (1945), and others, all of which were immensely popular in England, particularly in the North. There was no question of artistic merit, for there was not any, and as *Film Weekly* pointed out, the films had "no story value whatever" and were "incredibly badly made." In fact, it was not until 1950 that an Old Mother Riley film played London's West End, and only Old Mother Riley's last film, *Mother Riley Meets the Vampire* (1952), was released in the United States—as *My Son, the Vampire*—and then only because Old Mother Riley's costar was Bela Lugosi.

The female impersonation of Lucan is far removed from what passes for female impersonation today. Even in England, the only female impersonator who comes close is Mrs. Shufflewick (with her catchphrase "I'm broad-minded to the point of obscenity"), but Mrs. Shufflewick is vulgar and crude, whereas Old Mother Riley never said or did anything that would give parents concern about bringing their children to an Old Mother Riley film.

Old Mother Riley's popularity in England, then and now, should not be underestimated. Today, Old Mother Riley is worshiped by British intellectuals and totally misunderstood by Americans, who fail to see in the characterization Old Mother Riley's true significance, as noted by a critic in 1941, who described her as "the champion of the underdog, a hater of sham, a Valkyrie of the back streets"—in other words, everything that a present-day liberal might wish to be. She was an Irish washerwoman, but her Irish was of Liverpool rather than Ireland. *The Manchester Guardian* thought that she kept alive "something of the real squalor of a harsher, vanished age," and that "the eager bony face and the appalling black bonnet were a descant on our own deformity." Old Mother Riley in films and comic strips—for many years she was featured in a weekly called *Film Fun*—is as much an institution in Britain as is Superman in America. The goals of both are much the same, although Old Mother Riley always won her battles in a less sophisticated, down-to-earth, downright working-class way.

Old Mother Riley Detective is typical of the Old Mother Riley series. It cost approximately twenty-seven thousand pounds to produce and earned a profit of seventy-eight thousand pounds. It was produced at a time when Old Mother Riley was Britain's second-favorite film star, losing out only to George Formby.

The film opens with the theft of information concerning foods to be rationed in war-torn England from the Office of the Food Controller. Old Mother Riley (Arthur Lucan), a cleaner in the building who works for nothing because it is her contribution to the war effort, is enlisted by the police to help track down the guilty party, described as a rat eating away at Britain's food supply. As Old Mother Riley says, "Did you ever hear of a rat getting away from an Irish terrier?" She investigates the black market in food, while at the same time providing propaganda for the audience as to how easy it is for everyone to manage with rationing and the importance that women now play in turning out wartime supplies in the man-depleted factories. Eventually, Old Mother Riley learns that the owner of the building in which the Office of the Food Controller is located, a Mr. Kenworthy (Owen Reynolds), is the leading figure in the black market in food, and, after a chase on a borrowed motorbike, she corners him in a haystack and proceeds to jab him with a pitchfork until the police arrive.

Here Old Mother Riley is at her most garrulous and her most endearing. She is the quintessential Irish cleaning lady, running a boarding house on the side, fighting with the police, and, with arms and legs flying in all directions, capturing the villains. She is a saucy old lady when playing strip poker with the police (they lose) and sentimental and quiet while watching her daughter Kitty (Kitty McShane) fall in love with the inspector (Ivan Brandt) investigating the case. As in many of these low-budget British films produced during World War II, the leading men look like, and probably were, army rejects, slightly effete and sickly looking, with little acting talent.

There was always something surrealistic about an Old Mother Riley comedy. In *Old Mother Riley Headmistress*, porcelain horses on the mantlepiece neigh and a piano dances around while Old Mother Riley plays it. In one shot, the director and crew are seen reacting to the performance of the players. Many times Old Mother Riley will look at the camera, as if asking her director or her audience for directions. In *Old Mother Riley Detective*, just before attacking the villain, the old lady advises mothers in the audience to get their children out of the theater because she is about to use language that will make a sergeant major blush. Villains in her films are always rather seedy, and however bright they may be, the old Irish washerwoman is brighter—she has the schooling of a life on the streets of England's slums behind her. She knows how to use her fists and her feet, and her courage is unfailing.

When Lucan died, the London *Times* (May 18, 1954) ran an obituary which ended with a few words which sum up the constant appeal of Old Mother Riley: she was "a bemused old woman, who seemed to those who laughed at her antics to enjoy an existence of her own."

Anthony Slide

ON APPROVAL

Released: 1944
Production: Sydney Box and Clive Brook for General Film Distributors
Direction: Clive Brook
Screenplay: Clive Brook and Terence Young; based on the play of the same name by Frederick Lonsdale
Cinematography: C. Friese-Greene
Editing: Fergus McDonell
Costume design: Cecil Beaton
Running time: 80 minutes

Principal characters:
George, Duke of Bristol	Clive Brook
Maria Wislak	Beatrice Lillie
Helen Hale	Googie Withers
Richard Halton	Roland Culver
Dr. Graham	O. B. Clarence
Parkes	Lawrence Hanray
Mrs. McCosh	Elliott Mason
Landlord	Hay Petrie
Cook	Marjorie Rhodes
Jeannie	Molly Munks
Voice-over	E. V. H. Emmett

Beatrice Lillie, Britain's long-reigning star of musical comedy and revue, has appeared in only a few films, and, strangely enough, only a silent feature, *Exit Smiling* (1926), truly captures the essence of her personality. One British feature, *On Approval*, however, contains enough of the Lillie acerbic wit to serve as a monument to her talent, and, happily, the film contains a great deal more, making it stand out as one of the great British comedies of all time. Aside from Lillie, the film owes its success to two men: Frederick Lonsdale, who wrote the original play on which it is based in 1927, and Clive Brook, a polished actor of the British stage and British and American screens, who produced, directed, and adapted *On Approval*.

The film opens with scenes of warfare, of guns firing and airplanes droning, while the voice of E. V. H. Emmett (commentator for Gaumont British News) asks, "Oh dear, is this another war picture?" He suggests a return to prewar days, but they prove just as noisy and as nerve-jangling, with scenes of motorcycles and speedboats, jitterbugging and other less appetizing aspects of life. Emmett decides to go back further, back to grandmama's day, "When women were women—and they didn't forget it." We see vignettes of Edwardian and Victorian life, quiet, sedate, and elegant—and perhaps a little boring. We go with a party of theatergoers to see the latest play, which is described as "Very modern and terribly daring," and which is, of course, *On Approval*.

The film introduces us to George, the tenth Duke of Bristol (Clive Brook), who is on his way to attend a party at his own townhouse, in which he can no longer afford to live and which he has rented to the only person who can afford to live there, an American heiress named Helen Hale (Googie Withers). At the party, we meet the heiress, in whose money George has more than a passing interest; we meet George's friend, Richard Halton (Roland Culver), whose income is three hundred pounds a year; and we meet Maria Wislak (Beatrice Lillie), whose income is twenty-five thousand pounds a year, and in whom Richard has more than a passing interest. Maria Wislak—even the name is perfect for a Lillie character—has little time for George, whom she tells "If you had a little more brains you'd be in an asylum." She is interested in Richard, however, and she devises a plan to take him away for a month on approval to her Scottish island home. They will spend the days together and each night Richard will row across the lake in a dinghy to the mainland inn.

After the party, George and Richard retire to the quarters of George's former servants and discuss plans. George devises a scheme to send a telegram to the inn, the Dundrannoch Arms, booking all the rooms in the name of an American family, thus allowing Richard to remain with Maria. At the same time George decides to accompany his friend to Scotland. In the morning, however, on learning from her butler that two of the guests have yet to leave her house, Helen visits the servants quarters and finds the sleeping George and Richard and the proposed telegram. When Maria boards the train to Scotland, accompanied by Richard and her dog, she finds George in the same compartment. When she reaches the Dundrannoch Arms, she finds the hotel full, and she also finds Helen, who has decided to join the group.

At Maria's island home, the servants are shocked to discover that neither couple is married, and their Calvanistic outlook is not helped when the housekeeper spies Maria in what appears to be a compromising position with Richard—he is actually trying to get a speck of dust out of her eye—and when Helen, in response to the servant girl's "Yes, mistress," replies "Mistress! Not yet!" The servants depart *en masse*, to which Maria's only response is "Richard, count the silver." The four set out to fend for themselves, which means Richard rows to the mainland each day to fetch mail and supplies and generally busies himself, Helen takes care of the housework, George does nothing, and Maria sits at the piano and sings, "I'm Just Seventeen and I've Never Been."

As the weeks pass, each begins to see the true colors of the others. When George proposes to Helen, she says, "You should only have asked me for my money and not included me with it." She tells him to marry Maria, who is as selfish as he. Meanwhile, Maria is pleased with Richard, but, having brought him to the island to see if she liked him, she discovers he cannot stand her. Richard and Helen decide to leave the island together, and Helen is strangely attracted to Richard after he was able to tell her that her eyes were green, a question George could not answer. Back on the mainland, both experience strange dreams. Helen sees George, Maria, and herself as statues which move around in slow motion, Maria at the railway station hitting George over the head with a hammer, and George strangling her; Richard dreams of Maria and George together, and each time they are surprised saying, "Ho!" ("Ho!" is a favorite expression of Maria throughout the film, used whenever she has no response to George.)

Helen and Richard return to the island to confront Maria and George, and the upraised voices of the four are gradually drowned out by the wedding march. In the next scene, we see Helen showing the family photograph album to her children, and in response to Emmett's question, she admits that she married Richard. We next see Maria and George as two photographs on pages of an album facing each other. George grabs a rope and, in an impersonation of Tarzan, swings across to Maria. Both embrace and say the inevitable "Ho!"

The appeal of *On Approval* lies not only in the fine playing of the principals, but also in the re-creation of an earlier life style, the costumes (designed by Cecil Beaton), and even the Lancers, during which the on-approval scheme is decided upon. Only one obviously fake shot of the island's landing stage is unnecessarily distracting. Lillie, of course, steals every scene in which she appears, delivering with devastating accuracy her lines, some of which, along with the plot, were too daring for the American Hays Office, which refused to give the film a seal of approval.

On Approval has developed a considerable cult following in recent years, but on its initial release in America it garnered little interest. The only reviewer who found the film delightful was the one from *Time* (March 5, 1945), who wrote, "There has probably never been a richer, funnier anthology of late-Victorian mannerisms." *Hollywood Reporter* (February 22, 1945) commented, "Although Brook is English, he is no Noel Coward, and the farce would probably have fared better if the various tasks had been assigned to several hands, each expert in his own line." *Variety* (March 22, 1944) found the film "patently dull" and "not even funny." The critics were decidedly out of step; *On Approval* has stood the test of time well, maturing with age like the brandy and cigars on which Brook thrives in the film.

Anthony Slide

ON DANGEROUS GROUND

Released: 1951
Production: John Houseman for RKO/Radio
Direction: Nicholas Ray
Screenplay: A. I. Bezzerides; based on A. I. Bezzerides and Nicholas Ray's
  adaptation of the novel *Mad with Much Heart* by Gerald Butler
Cinematography: George E. Diskant
Editing: Roland Gross
Art direction: Albert D'Agostino and Ralph Berger
Set decoration: Darrell Silvera and Harley Miller
Music: Bernard Herrmann
Running time: 82 minutes

Principal characters:
Mary Malden .... Ida Lupino
Jim Wilson .... Robert Ryan
Walter Brent .... Ward Bond
Pop Daly .... Charles Kemper
Pete Santos .... Anthony Ross
Captain Brawley .... Ed Begley
Danny Malden .... Sumner Williams
Myrna .... Cleo Moore
Bernie Tucker .... Richard Irving

As *On Dangerous Ground* begins, Jim Wilson (Robert Ryan), a detective
for the city police force, is on the verge of a spiritual breakdown. He lives
alone in a cheerless apartment and knows no one except his partners, Bill
"Pop" Daly (Charles Kemper) and Pete Santos (Anthony Ross), and the
assortment of hoods, thugs, pimps, tramps, and hustlers he encounters as
part of his job. This dispiriting way of life has made Wilson lonely and alienated, and his bitterness is expressed by violent rages which he directs against
the punks he arrests in the course of duty. Daly and Santos try to help him
but he is unresponsive. At last, after one instance too many of being too free
with his fists, he is sent by an angry Captain Brawley (Ed Begley) to assist
local authorities on a case in the upper part of the state. A disturbed teenager,
Danny Malden (Sumner Williams), has molested and killed a girl. In appre-
hending him, Wilson must contend with the girl's irate father, Walter Brent
(Ward Bond), who wants to kill Danny on sight. The search for the boy leads
Wilson and Brent to a blind woman, Mary (Ida Lupino), who turns out to
be Danny's sister. When Brent tries to force information from her, Wilson
intervenes, showing unexpected reserves of compassion. Mary prevails upon
Wilson to try to bring in Danny unharmed, but the interference of Brent
prompts Danny to flee in panic across the snowy landscape. Losing his grip

as he tries to scale some rocks, Danny falls to his death. Wilson consoles Mary, and it appears that their emotional rapport will bring a new beginning for both of them; but a rupture occurs and Wilson heads back to the city. As he drives home, however, his eyes reflect the completeness of the desolation he now feels, and he returns to Mary, who is waiting.

On Dangerous Ground is one of three key *film noir* which quickly established Nicholas Ray as a major figure of cinema. One of the immediately striking aspects of all three works is that they extend the definition of the *film noir* style by establishing the characteristic mood and then departing from it. *They Live by Night* (1949) is transformed from a simple narrative of doomed criminals into a tender love story very similar in feeling to the folk song which is used as its main musical theme ("I Know Where I'm Going"). *In a Lonely Place* (1950) uses its framework of a murder investigation very effectively to explore a love relationship which ends disturbingly but in a manner contrary to melodramatic conventions. *On Dangerous Ground* contains a structural division which creates as the film's subject a journey, on a literal level from city to country and from night to day, and on another level an inner journey of self-realization for its protagonist.

Although the elements of the plot of *On Dangerous Ground* are somewhat arbitrary and contrived, the protagonist, Jim Wilson, is an unusually convincing and compelling character. In the violent and brooding city overture which introduces him, he is an archetypal *film noir* character—a hard and brutal detective, always on the edge of violence and a source of concern to his companions on the job. We feel an instinctive sympathy for this man, however; his aloneness in the dark night of the cityscape is complete even when he is in the midst of throngs of people. He is remote from Pop and Santos, who ineffectually seek the heart inside him. He is full of self-hatred and believes in nothing, and he knows nothing but to manifest these negative feelings in a destructive power. The initial sequences convey this crisis with admirable dramatic directness. The spareness with which the action is related intensifies the feeling of a nightmarish emotional void without an escape route.

Wilson is immediately contrasted to Santos and Daly in the opening scenes as the three men prepare to go to work. Santos is introduced as he says goodbye to his wife, and the older Daly is presented as a man with a large family. Wilson, on the other hand, is introduced looking at photographs of suspects as he eats dinner alone in his apartment. The scene is very short, but Wilson's demeanor and absorption in his work—and a melancholy musical theme by Bernard Herrmann which is heard once more when Wilson returns to the apartment later the same night—quickly establish his solitude. The three men are investigating the murder of a policeman, and as they go about their night's work, Wilson manifests his obsessive behavior, remaining aloof from the friendly conversation of his two companions. Two incidents unrelated to the main investigation under way are especially intriguing. In the first, Wilson almost becomes violent when a falsely identified robbery suspect becomes angry over being detained, and in the second, a girl in a drugstore who is initially friendly to Wilson makes an innocent remark about "going out with a cop" and Wilson turns around in his chair, his momentarily bitter and hurt expression unobserved by the others.

Wilson and Santos pursue a lead after Daly goes home sick, and Wilson's methods bring the desired results. He intimidates a girl named Myrna (Cleo Moore) into revealing the whereabouts of her boyfriend Bernie Tucker (Richard Irving), and his awareness that he has placed her in jeopardy is expressed by a single shot as he walks down the stairs of her apartment building, his look of defeat undercutting the fact that he has accomplished his purpose. Subsequently, his violent interrogation of Tucker, which occurs after Santos has left the room, seems to be fed by each of the preceding incidents. One of the most neurotic and soul-destroying actions in the entire range of cinema, the interrogation gives the impression that Wilson is actually striking out at himself. His face becomes a terrifying mask and his voice a pitiful whine as he moves toward Bernie with gloved hands. "Why do you make me do it?" he asks desperately. "You know you're going to talk. I always make you punks talk." A dissolve on Wilson as he starts to beat up Tucker is followed by a return to the police station. Wilson almost strikes the taunting Bernie once more but is restrained by his partner. A remarkable low-angle shot, poignantly expressive of Wilson's disorientation, immediately follows as he breaks away from Santos and walks off into the night. His return to his apartment is suffused with melancholy, unalleviated by his brief encounter with a friendly paper boy. A single shot once he enters the apartment becomes a gripping vision of loneliness which has few parallels. Wilson looks for a moment at his sports trophies, the only positive symbols left in his life, and bitterly asks "Who cares?" before obsessively washing his hands as the shot concludes.

When the setting changes and the character of the blind girl enters the story, the protagonist mellows and so does the tone of the work. High-contrast lighting pervades the city sequences and the action is harsh and quick, with even the sequences of Wilson alone being concisely stated. Relatively slower, the country sequences are photgraphed more naturally, with visual effect obtained from the beauty of the snowy landscape or from Mary's fireplace as it casts a strange light in her living room. The intense personal feeling evidenced by Ray for the protagonist's emotional state remains constant, however, with subjective shots of the road as he drives recurring, and with other moments rendered subjectively with a hand-held camera, such as the chase of a suspect in the city sequence, or the subduing of the brutal Brent at the center of the film, the latter a moment deeply charged with emotion primarily because the viewer is forced to feel total identification with Wilson's gesture of feeling for Mary.

In common with *They Live by Night* and *In a Lonely Place*, *On Dangerous Ground* is distinguished by a heroine who is intensely sympathetic rather than the destructive predator leading a man to his doom who figures in so many classic *film noir* works (notably Jane Greer as Kathie Moffett in *Out of the Past*, 1947). Mary is both warm and intelligent. Her harmony with her world is characterized by the "natural" decor of her house, especially Danny's ostentatious wood carving, which is calming and nurturing in contrast to the coldness of Jim's neon night world. In a sense, her relationship with Jim is one of the blind leading the blind. He is more vulnerable than she is, and the dialogue between them makes this explicit. Alike in their loneliness and introspection, they are also alike in their powerlessness to control events. Neither of them is able to save Danny. Ultimately, the emotional sustenance which Mary had tried to give Danny is transferred to Jim, who is significantly linked to Danny by a common expression of emotional disturbance through violence. The link between boy and man is tellingly demonstrated by two identical camera set-ups, the first showing Jim's gloved hand in the foreground and a frightened Bernie in the background, the second showing Danny's hand with a knife in the foreground and Jim in the background. While Danny is a genuine victim of mental illness, however, Jim's violence results from a more sensitive soul than those of other men, a soul which cannot withstand the pressures of a violent environment. For this reason, Jim is able to benefit from a relationship with Mary and begins to be liberated from his condition during his first moments with her.

The merits of *On Dangerous Ground* have aroused considerable retrospective attention. Ray's imaginative and adventurous *mise-en-scène* and the modernity of the conception are articulated with the assistance of gifted collaborators. As a scenarist, Ray chose A. I. Bezzerides, an exceptional writer whose participation was similarly crucial in films which rank among the finest efforts of Jules Dassin (*Thieves' Highway*, 1949) and Robert Aldrich (*Kiss Me Deadly*, 1955). The alternately harsh and tender dialogues which help make *On Dangerous Ground* such an intimate and penetrating character study complement the lucidity and lyricism of Ray's approach. Cinematographer George E. Diskant, who also photographed *They Live by Night*, realizes with equal brilliance the contrasting moods of the city and country sections. Herrmann's score is one of his most beautiful and is unusual for its use of horns for the chase and a haunting *viola d'amore* theme for Mary. This score was one of the composer's own favorites and one of Ray's favorites of those found in his work. Finally, there are the mesmerizing presences of Lupino and Ryan, both of whom now seem more central to the American cinema than other more celebrated stars of the period. Lupino characteristically avoids the sentimentality which we often associate with physically vulnerable characters and projects a full range of adult emotions. Of Ryan, it can be said that his face and carriage alone project better than any screenplay the motif of alienation which pervades Ray's films. The instinctive sympathy which the viewer feels for Wilson in the face of the character's brutal actions in the opening reels owes a great deal to Ryan's ability to convey the profound and apparently inconsolable despair of the inner man.

On Dangerous Ground is not, therefore, a difficult film, the virtues of which must be salvaged from beneath an impoverished artistic surface. Nevertheless, it was completely overlooked when originally released and subsequently regarded as a failure even by Ray himself until recent years. Perhaps the elliptical nature of the concluding scenes and the heart-on-the-sleeve romanticism of the final images account for this curious disregard of such a moving and modern work. A series of dissolves (the anguished face of Wilson driving, the country in daylight, the city streets at night), accompanied by voice-overs of thoughts expressed by other characters earlier, abruptly bring Wilson back to Mary's house. They are reconciled on a staircase, their hands reaching out to touch in close-up. Their faces seem to be lit by a state of grace as they move together to kiss. The film ends with a serene view of the still landscape as the camera moves away from the house. On a narrative level, perhaps this resolution is not altogether convincing; but the spiritual progress implied in Jim's journey, described from the beginning by images charged with emotion, makes it the only possible resolution. *On Dangerous Ground* is a cinematic poem of despair and salvation.

Blake Lucas

ON THE BEACH

Released: 1959
Production: Stanley Kramer for United Artists
Direction: Stanley Kramer
Screenplay: John Paxton and James Lee Barrett; based on the novel of the same name by Nevil Shute
Cinematography: Giussepe Rotunno and Daniel L. Fapp (auto race)
Editing: Frederic Knudtson
Running time: 134 minutes

Principal characters:
Dwight Towers	Gregory Peck
Moira Davidson	Ava Gardner
Julian Osborne	Fred Astaire
Peter Holmes	Anthony Perkins
Mary Holmes	Donna Anderson

Stanley Kramer's *On the Beach* presents an apocalyptic nightmare, offering a perceptive and grimly horrifying vision of the end of the world. A masterful exercise in science fiction set in the near future, *On the Beach* delivers a dark portrait of man's last days after an atomic war. What makes those final days so unsettling is the fact that the film concentrates on everyday people who have no recourse but to continue with their normal lives until the end comes.

As the film opens in 1964, atomic war is taking place in the Northern Hemisphere. When all life there is obliterated, the atomic menace begins drifting down to Australia, haven of the last, doomed life. A United States submarine, the fleet's lone survivor, has come to Melbourne for refuge. Captain Dwight Towers (Gregory Peck) and his men have survived because their sub was submerged when America was hit. Although Towers and his men come to Australia bringing word of a dying world, Towers himself continues to be hopeful that his wife and children, back in Connecticut, might somehow have survived.

Towers' men are equally unsure about the extent of the atomic annihilation. A phantom radio signal emanating from San Diego, ultimately sends the submarine back to the northern waters to investigate in hopes of finding life. The sailor who goes ashore in a decontamination suit to trace the signal discovers that an overturned Coke bottle and a flapping window shade are the source of the transmission. Towers and his men then return to Australia with the bleak revelation.

In Australia the populace prepares for the end. Doctors hand out containers of Government Prescription No. 24768, medication to hasten death. While death is impending, however, life goes on. More people than ever turn out for the opening of trout fishing season, and the best wines are carefully rationed at the yacht clubs. Some people are drawn together awaiting the inevitable, while others are realizing some lifelong goals. For example, Julian Osborne (Fred Astaire), an embittered and conscience-stricken atomic scientist, is a sports car enthusiast who achieves his ambition of winning a grand prix race.

In the midst of a party given by young naval officer Peter Holmes (Anthony Perkins) and his wife Mary (Donna Anderson), she cries out, "There is hope—there has to be," vocalizing what many people feel. It is through Peter and Mary that Towers meets Moira Davidson (Ava Gardner), a cynical, hard-drinking woman who is desperately afraid of being alone at the end. Towers is lonely, but is initially unable to comfort Moira because he is haunted by thoughts of his wife. After the submarine returns from the obliterated Northern Hemisphere, however, he is able to face reality and return Moira's love. Peter and Mary face even greater difficulties because they have a baby, and Peter knows the time will come when the child must be given the medication. Mary has problems coming to grips with this eventual reality, and accuses her husband of being a murderer because of his intentions to administer the pills.

On the Beach does not sermonize; it simply shows the way things could be. While the dialogue, with its fatalistic overtones, sometimes becomes heavy-handed, other sequences evoke an almost poetic beauty. For example, when the cruising submarine investigates the radio transmission and looks for other signs of life along the Pacific Coast, a homesick sailor jumps ship through the escape hatch because he wants to die in San Francisco where his parents died. Watching the city's solemn skyline, the sailor then begins to fish the quiet waters. In another scene, he conducts a final conversation with the submarine's periscope, as he says good-bye to the captain.

With its emphasis on the last pocket of humanity, *On the Beach* refrains from exploring the details of the actual war. It is only revealed that a small, irresponsible nation started it. "Somebody pushed a button," explains Osborne. (In Nevil Shute's novel, on which the film is based, Albania started the war by bombing Naples; Russia and China were the next to start fighting.) Similarly, the film does not dwell visually upon the horrors of radiation sickness; only one case is shown. What amplifies the horror of the situation is the calmness with which people accept the inevitable. When Peter and Mary can no longer go on, they take their pills with their tea after giving the baby the medication. With his grand prix dream realized, Osborne is also ready for death and asphyxiates himself in a garage. Towers, who has grown close to Moira, is duty-bound when the submarine's crew votes to sail the vessel out and sink it rather than await death on the shore. As Towers sails out with his men, Moira is left watching on the beach. Equally stirring are the last minutes, in which papers blow across empty streets and a sign, hanging listlessly, reads, "There is still time . . . Brother."

Fred Astaire, in his first straight dramatic role, is particularly good as the cynical scientist. Gregory Peck is a commanding Dwight Towers, and Ava Gardner, in a departure from the glamorous roles with which she is usually identified, and often photographed in an unflattering way, is effective as the hard-living Moira. Anthony Perkins and Donna Anderson are suitably poignant as the young Holmes couple. Interwoven in the film's background is the music for "Waltzing Matilda," the bittersweet melody which is Australia's national anthem.

Producer-director Stanley Kramer has long been able to take a thought-provoking theme and merge it with the most commercially viable elements of film. His films tend to step away from toes, not on them, as witnessed by such films as *Guess Who's Coming to Dinner* (1967), as well as *Judgment at Nuremberg* (1961). *On the Beach* nevertheless remains one of the most effective, disturbing films about apocalypse, utilizing an almost documentarylike technique.

On the Beach is a downbeat film from beginning to end. At the time of its release it generated headlines with its then highly topical subject matter. The film had an "international premiere, . . . opening simultaneously in seventeen major cities throughout the world, including Moscow.

With its stern examination of doomed life following atomic war, *On the Beach* joined a segment of the science-fiction genre reserved for end-of-the-world lessons. The films that helped to initiate the Cold War fear included the thought-provoking *Five* (1951), about a band of struggling survivors, and the corny *Invasion U.S.A.* (1952), about an attack by the Russians and mass hypnosis, among other concerns. Released in 1959, *On the Beach* helped to round out a decade firmly imprinted with the problems of the atomic age. Released the same year was *The World, the Flesh and the Devil*, another end-of-the-world treatise which also examined racism.

Despite some of these valid studies, *On the Beach*, with its big-name cast and important director, emerges as the most chilling prophetic film of its decade. As is so often the case with science-fiction films, *On the Beach* was completely passed over at Oscar time (the year belonged to *Ben-Hur*). Still, the film ranks as a success, in terms of both box-office and critical response. With its thought-provoking vision of the folly of atomic war, *On the Beach* delivers a painful message. Realistic, revealing moments gave the film its horror ("Dogs go into a corner to die alone, ashamed. But what do we do?" someone asks). Indeed, a number of the decade's critics took offense at the film's stark realism, pointing out that *On the Beach* is virtually devoid of any spiritual counsel. Something, they felt, should have been added as a buffer for the script's bleakness.

Pat H. Broeske

ON TRIAL

Released: 1928
Production: Warner Bros.
Direction: Archie Mayo
Screenplay: Robert Lord and Max Pollock; based on the play of the same name by Elmer Rice
Cinematography: Byron Haskins
Editing: Thomas Pratt
Running time: 91 minutes

Principal characters:

Joan Trask	Pauline Frederick
Robert Strickland	Bert Lytell
May Strickland	Lois Wilson
Gerald Trask	Holmes Herbert
Prosecuting Attorney	Richard Tucker
Defense Attorney	Jason Robards, Sr.
Stanley Glover	Johnny Arthur
Doris Strickland	Vondell Darr
Turnbull	Franklin Pangborn
Clerk	Fred Kelsey
Judge	Edmund Breese
Dr. Morgan	Edward Martindale

In November, 1928, Warner Bros. released its fourth all-talking feature, *On Trial*. There were definite imperfections in the recording device used, which led quickly to the studio's abandoning their way of recording dialogue and sound on discs in favor of recording on a sound track, a method which came into effect in 1929 at all studios, and is still in existence.

The screenplay of *On Trial* was written by Max Pollock and Robert Lord, the latter of whom was to become one of the best screenwriters in Hollywood, and it was adapted from a highly successful play by Elmer Rice. The transition of a play to a film was rapidly becoming a common and successful practice in talking picures. It has become something of a theatrical axiom that no play taking place entirely in the courtroom has ever failed. It was to be equally true of the talking film when the story took place in the courtroom. The very device of the courtroom setting as a frame for all the action based on testimonies, acted out in flashback, was perfect for the screen, and especially for something like *On Trial*, which had a large number of sensational denouements.

The film, like the play, opens with Robert Strickland (Bert Lytell) on trial for the murder of Gerald Trask (Holmes Herbert). Strickland had allegedly caught his wife, May Strickland (Lois Wilson), in a lie, which had led to his discovering that she had been secretly visiting his best friend, Trask. He then went to Trask and shot him to death, according to the charges, although Strickland maintains that he is innocent of murder.

Evidence proves that Mrs. Strickland has not been guilty of any adultery; Trask had compromised her years previous to her marriage, when she was only seventeen, and had been blackmailing her. This information would indicate that if Strickland had known it, the murder he is accused of having committed was not one of impulse but of cold deliberation. Strickland maintains that he knew nothing of his wife's dilemma, and that he in fact had only just paid Trask ten thousand dollars owed him. There is, however, no trace of that money.

Joan Trask (Pauline Frederick), widowed and heavily veiled, takes the stand and gives testimony which moves the jurors, and further points to Strickland as a murderer. May Strickland also takes the stand and confesses that Trask had abused her, but her testimony is topped by her small daughter, Doris (Vondell Darr), who is allowed to give evidence. Her testimony clearly sways the jury, and there quickly follows a surprise confession involving Joan Trask which leads to the identity of the real murderer. Strickland, cleared of any guilt, is rejoined to his wife and young daughter and leaves the courtroom, a free man.

Rice had written the play in his younger days, and it originally opened in New York in August, 1914. Rice himself was a lawyer with a devotion to the theater. He wrote *On Trial* at the suggestion of an article written by Clayton Hamilton in the *Bookman*, which had suggested a play with scenes in inverse order. With a courtroom setting, Rice used the more dramatic idea of going back in order to go forward and used what came to be commonly utilized in screen technique: the flashback. Later it was often used in telling a screen story, but *On Trial* was one of the first times it was used in the theater. It therefore worked beautifully when it had to be adapted for the screen.

On Trial had been filmed as a silent in 1917 by Essanay, and was so successful in its first talkie dramatization in 1928 that it was remade by Warner Bros. in 1939. The play had made a great deal of money for Rice, and its various translations to the screen only added to the fortune he made from this one play alone. It allowed him to withdraw from law practice to work exclusively as a playwright. He worked later as one of the organizers of the Federal Theatre and served as president of the Dramatists' Guild. He went on to write many other successful plays, often with a legal background, which were then turned into equally popular films, such as *Counsellor-at-Law* (1933). That film had been a successful stage vehicle for Paul Muni and then Otto Kruger, and it ranks as what is possibly John Barrymore's best screen performance.

Frederick's career was not harmed by the poor recording which handicapped her performance as Joan Trask; her record as a polished stage actress was too secure. Any fault was not in her delivery of lines, but in the method of recording itself. Subsequent engagements accorded her at Warner Bros. as the star of *Evidence* (1929) and *The Sacred Flame* (also 1929) proved her worth and opened the door for her career as an important actress in talking films, in which she continued with pronounced success until her death in 1937 after an asthmatic attack. With *On Trial* Lois Wilson also established herself as a silent star who made the transition to talkies successfully. She had played often with Edward Everett Horton in plays in Hollywood, and later, when her screen career lapsed, she went on to New York, where she continued both on Broadway and in leading stock companies all over the country. Lytell had not only been a top silent star at Metro, but he was also a matinee idol in the theater. *On Trial* was only the first of his many successful appearances in talking pictures. He and the other men in *On Trial* were not victims of the inferior sound system used for that picture. The idiosyncrasies of early recording on discs were not flattering to the female voice, even when the pitch was low, pleasant, and controlled, as it was with both Frederick and Wilson.

The 1928 print of *On Trial* in its sound version apparently is no longer in existence in its entirety. The silent version made simultaneously with this version for release in foreign countries and houses not wired for sound may have survived, although even this seems doubtful. The 1939 remake, however, survives, but is not now in release. *On Trial* was always a suspenseful play, tricky but theatrically effective, and the same may be said of both talking versions. Although the 1928 version was not perhaps a great film, it is unfortunate for purposes of cinema history that so many of the early talking films (and silents) are no longer extant. Deterioration of the old silver nitrate stock which was used for motion pictures, loss of negatives, and general neglect have led to an unfortunate gap for serious students of the early cinema.

DeWitt Bodeen

ONE-EYED JACKS

Released: 1961
Production: Frank P. Rosenberg for Paramount
Direction: Marlon Brando
Screenplay: Guy Trosper and Calder Willingham; based on the novel *The Authentic Death of Hendry Jones* by Charles Neider
Cinematography: Charles Lang
Editing: Archie Marshak
Running time: 141 minutes

Principal characters:
Rio	Marlon Brando
Dad Longworth	Karl Malden
Louisa	Pina Pellicer
Maria	Katy Jurado
Bob Amory	Ben Johnson
Lon	Slim Pickens
Tetley	Timothy Carey
Harvey Johnson	Sam Gilman

In 1961, Marlon Brando made his directoral debut with a Western entitled *One-Eyed Jacks*. Although the film is a considerable achievement, and although Brando was, and is, perhaps one of the most highly regarded actors of his generation, he did not direct again. Given the conservative timidity of most film financiers, it is not hard to understand why. The filming was difficult and beset with controversy from the start. In the early stages of production, Brando dismissed the original director, an emerging talent named Stanley Kubrick, who later went on to direct *2001: A Space Odyssey* (1968) and who, in the tradition of an Orson Welles or a Laurence Olivier, announced that he would direct and star in it himself. The studio agreed, believing *One-Eyed Jacks* to be a relatively inexpensive action feature. As the production schedule lengthened and the budget rose, however, stories in the press about Brando's behavior became more colorful than the film's plot. The director, it was rumored, had deviated wildly from the script and was improvising new scenes. He was waiting all day for "the right wave" to break on the Monterey coast; he and his actors would get drunk for party scenes and revel until they passed out; and he had offered a thousand-dollar bonus to the extra with the most horrified expression on his face. In short, Brando was playing the profligate director of the old school, to the delight of publicists and the dismay of his producers. At a conservative estimate, at least one million feet of film were shot. The director's final cut ran for more than four hours.

As usual in such cases, the resulting compromise satisfied no one. Brando was uneasy with the ending of his film, which was changed drastically following an on-set poll of cast and crew and re-edited by the studio and the two-hour-and-twenty-minute version released by Paramount was not a great success, either critically or at the box office. In the years that followed, however, *One-Eyed Jacks* has acquired an enthusiastic band of admirers, including the directors of several later Westerns.

A self-consciously "traditional" opening title informs us that we are in Sonora, Mexico. The year is 1880, and a small gang of American outlaws is pillaging a bank. Relentlessly pursued by Federales (the film is uncharacteristically liberal in treating Mexicans as formidable human beings instead of jokes), the gang splits up. Rio, as played by Brando, will hold the police off until nightfall while his partner Dad Longworth (Karl Malden) finds them fresh mounts. Dad changes his mind, however, and makes off with the loot. Rio is apprehended and spends five years in jail. When he escapes, he can think only of avenging himself on the old friend who betrayed him. Here the special circumstances of the plot begin to undermine the traditional premise of the revenge Western. Rio is forced into partnership with Bob Amory (Ben Johnson) and Harvey Johnson (Sam Gilman), a pair of ruffians with a plan. "Fourteen days ride from here" Bob tells him "There's a town. And in that town is the fattest bank you ever saw. And it ain't nothing but a cheese box. And—this is gonna tickle you—the sheriff of that town's Dad Longworth."

When Rio catches up with Dad he cannot kill him. The bank is closed for a fiesta; until it opens he must convince the sheriff that they are "still friends." The texture of the tale grows more involved as each character weaves an elaborate skein of lies to mask his true intentions. Dad swears there were no horses to be had; Rio claims the past five years in Mexico have been one long party; Dad's wife Maria (Katy Jurado) and stepdaughter Louisa (Pina Pellicer) conspire to hide the fact that Rio has seduced the girl. Dad, Rio, Rio's gang, Maria, and Louisa—all are like the one-eyed jacks in a deck of cards, concealing their true natures in order to buy time.

As the deceit becomes more involved, the clean "code of the West" is tacitly abandoned. No longer interested in gunfights, Dad surprises Rio and horsewhips him, then smashes his gun-hand in a sadomasochistic scene of such intensity that it could be the climax of the film. *One-Eyed Jacks* does not end here, however; Rio recuperates in a Chinese settlement on the shore, where, under the tender urgings of Louisa, whom he now loves, he decides that he can forget his vendetta. Unfortunately for him, Bob and Harvey rob the bank on their own, kill several people, and lay the blame on Rio. Riding out, he is arrested, tried, and sentenced to death in rapid order. In a sequence closely modeled on one of the more dramatic incidents of Billy the Kid's career, Rio is tormented by Dad's brutal deputy Lon (Slim Pickens) and freed by Louisa's intervention. Dad returns and runs into the escaping outlaw; forced into the face-off he has tried to avoid, Rio shoots Dad and gets the girl.

Perhaps because of material lost in the studio's cut of *One-Eyed Jacks*, the film lacks balance. Subplots and further elaboration of Dad Longworth's character might be preferable to the many brooding close-ups of Rio, while some of the supporting players are hardly seen at all. The exteriors (Monterey seascapes and dust storms in Death Valley) are consistently outstanding, although Charles Lang's visuals are sometimes marred by clumsy mattes or very obvious stage sets. The muted desert browns of the Sonora sequences are particularly impressive. So, too, are the action sequences; fast and deftly choreographed, they are models of their kind. The entire film is a model, in fact, for the New Westerns of the 1960's and 1970's. With its narcissism and its surface realism of dust, dirt, and racial tension, it resembles the later work of Italian director Sergio Leone or of Sam Peckinpah. Leone has utilized the film's religious symbolism and black humor, while Peckinpah has emulated its melancholy romance.

Perhaps the most unusual feature of the film is the standard of its acting, not usually the premier aspect of a Western. The casting is uniformly appropriate, and Brando directs his company particularly well. Malden's Dad Longworth is a civic hypocrite rather than a mere villain, while Brando survives the transition from rogue to tragic hero. Western stalwarts such as Jurado, Johnson, and Pickens are in fine fettle; few Westerns to date had featured such multifaceted personalities in such moral quandaries. Dialogue consistently undercuts myth, as in the early scene where Rio romances a young woman with an overblown lonesome-cowpoke story ("My home is just any place I put my saddle I guess"), only to rob her moments later. Brando is more impressive as a director than as an actor on this occasion. His die-cast features are too finely honed for the rough bandit he portrays, and his sudden change of heart is unconvincing.

At its lowest ebb, *One-Eyed Jacks* is something of a cross between a soap opera and *Hamlet* without the soliloquies. In its best moments, and there are many of them, it is a classic Western full of self-awareness, visual flair, and a keen sense for the complexity of human dealings, heroic or otherwise.

V. I. Huxner

ONE FOOT IN HEAVEN

Released: 1941
Production: Hal B. Wallis for Warner Bros.
Direction: Irving Rapper
Screenplay: Casey Robinson; based on the novel of the same name by Hartzell
Spence
Cinematography: Charles Rosher
Editing: Warren Low
Running time: 108 minutes

Principal characters:
Reverend William Spence	Fredric March
Hope Morris Spence	Martha Scott
Mrs. Lydia Sandow	Beulah Bondi
Elias Samson	Harry Davenport
Mrs. Preston Thurston	Laura Hope Crews
Hartzell Spence	Frankie Thomas
Eileen Spence	Elizabeth Fraser
Fraser Spence	Casey Johnson
Preston Thurston	Gene Lockhart

The affectionate paean to one's father is a commonplace in literature, and effective cinematic adaptation of these stories are, while not common, not unheard of either, as exemplified by Michael Curtiz's film version of Clarence Day's *Life with Father* (1947). *One Foot in Heaven*, Hartzell Spence's story of his father's trials and triumphs, is just such a film, although at first glance its subject might seem an odd choice for a film biography. William Spence was a small-town Methodist minister in Iowa and Colorado from 1904 through the 1920's, a situation which, on the surface, would appear to offer little of interest for a film drama. Nothing very dramatic happens to Reverend Spence. He gets married, he and his wife rear their three children, and along the way he battles genteel poverty and an occasional contrary parishoner. Yet in the steady hands of director Irving Rapper, this humble country parson becomes a genuine hero. A film that is almost entirely devoid of excitement in the conventional sense becomes a moving and ultimately fascinating cinematic experience.

The film opens in Stratford, Ontario, in 1904, and Rapper introduces his two principal characters. Although he will trace the adventures of William Spence (Fredric March) and his wife Hope (Martha Scott) over the next quarter of a century, these two characters do not change much. William Spence is gentle, devout, and stubborn as a young man, and although he bends a bit in the interpretation of the strict Methodist discipline as he grows older, he is basically the same man when the film ends. Hope Spence is good-humored and loyal to her husband (although possessed of an irrepressible streak of independence) when we meet her as a girl in Ontario, and she remains that way throughout the course of the film. Rapper underlines the consistency of the characters by having Hope repeat her initial vows of love to William at the end of the film: "Whither thou goest, I will go."

The film opens with young William Spence announcing to his future bride that he is giving up his medical studies to enter the ministry. Although initially alarmed at the prospect of life on "the American frontier" in Iowa, Hope agrees to accompany her husband on this and subsequent moves. She will never, however, lose her desire to put down roots in comfortable surroundings, just as her husband will never lose the urge to find new ministerial challenges in more primitive areas. Although he wins all of the arguments, she never fails to argue. It is through such scenes that the filmmakers render the characters human and interesting.

A third character, of sorts, is also introduced early on—the parsonage. Although they will live in many places in their lifetime, one thing remains constant. Whether it is the noise from the nearby firehouse in Iowa or the roof with nineteen separate leaks in Colorado, their living quarters are a continual source of frustration to the Spences and often seem to take on personalities of their own. In due course, the Spences fill up their parsonages with three children, Eileen (Elizabeth Fraser), Hartzell (Frankie Thomas), and Fraser (Casey Johnson). A disagreement, humorous to the audience but not to the Spences, over what to name their youngest child leaves Fraser without a name for weeks after his birth.

The children are normal and healthy, albeit sometimes frustrated by the pressures of growing up in a minister's family. "A pastor's family walks a tightrope," explains their father, "balancing with one foot on earth and one foot already in heaven." The Methodist discipline is strict, and Reverend Spence enforces it in his own family, gently but firmly, to the letter—until one day when he discovers that ten-year-old Hartzell has been to see a movie, an activity expressly forbidden by church custom.

A kind and reasonable man, Reverend Spence vows to accompany his son to the theater and point out the pitfalls of this new medium. In what is perhaps the film's most satisfying and affecting scene, the two of them sit down to watch a William S. Hart Western, *The Silent Partner*. As Rapper cuts back and forth between the screen, the audience, and the two Spences, we see Reverend Spence slowly and unwillingly come not only to enjoy the film but to appreciate it as well. He even uses the film's moral as the basis for his next sermon.

The final third of the film is concerned with Reverend Spence's efforts to build a new church in Denver. The struggle takes years. He inadvertently runs afoul of a rich but snooty widow named Lydia Sandow (Beulah Bondi) by visiting Samson (Harry Davenport), her gardener. "You're putting Samson on my social plane," she fumes. "You're *my* pastor, and you'll visit me." When Spence declines to stop his visitations, she and her bank account leave the church: "From this day on, I'm a Baptist!"

Similar squabbles drive away other wealthy and influential donors, including Mr. and Mrs. Thurston (Gene Lockhart and Laura Hope Crews) who quit the congregation in a rage when Spence temporarily replaces Mrs. Thurston and her cacophonous friends in the choir with a group of children. The Thurstons go too far, however, when they spread a rumor that Spence's son Hartzell has made a local girl pregnant. Hartzell is expelled from school on the basis of this rumor, and now it is William Spence's turn to be furious. He produces evidence that the rumor is false and offers the Thurstons a choice: be sued in court and denounced from the pulpit, or put up the money for a new church. Thus the church is built.

One Foot in Heaven ends with an aging but vigorous Reverend Spence ready to press on to a new congregation, accompanied by his reluctant but loyal wife and family. The final scene has a tearful Spence playing "The Church's One Foundation" on a new carillon, as rapt parishoners are drawn to the church from all over town by the beautiful bells.

Despite the seemingly meager story, *One Foot in Heaven* is anything but static and boring. Rapper and his writer Casey Robinson make it clear that the Spences are no plaster saints, that they have the same needs, hopes, and fears as any other human being. The remarkable thing is that Rapper and Robinson are able to do this so effortlessly. Nothing about the film is labored; restraint is the hallmark of the direction, the writing, and the acting.

One Foot in Heaven is a film about character—principally that of William Spence—but also of others in the film, and Rapper relies heavily on closeups of his actors' faces to reveal this character. Thus it was particularly important for the cast to avoid any semblance of overacting or self-parody that would have broken the film's spell. Indeed, understatement is the keynote of all of the important performances. Virtually every member of the cast turns in an excellent performance. In the minor roles, Bondi and Crews are deliciously petty and spiteful as Mrs. Sandow and Mrs. Thurston, respectively; Davenport is affecting as the lonely but pious gardener Elias Samson; and Thomas brings an understated, Andy Hardyish charm to the character of the teenaged Hartzell Spence.

Just as the two most important characters in the film are William and Hope Spence, however, so are the two most important acting jobs those of March and Scott. Scott manages the difficult task of appearing convincingly dutiful and spunky at the same time. Her expressive face shows the character's struggles with the conflicting emotions. March turns in one of the most effective performances of his distinguished career as Reverend Spence. He radiates warmth, serenity, and devotion; but he (and his director and writer) have enough sense to give his character a few flaws to keep the part from cloying.

Spence's stubborness provides the film with many of its best comic moments.

In this, his second film (after *Shining Victory*, 1941), Rapper put a story and a cast together with a skill he seldom matched thereafter. Although the early part of the film is, of necessity, episodic, every transition is smooth, and no scene overstays its welcome. The dramatic heart of the film—Spence's battle to build a new church in the face of opposition from a fractious group of eminent parishoners—is handled equally well. Rapper's direction is restrained without being stiff, and he treats his material with respect but not reverence. The result was *One Foot in Heaven*, a gentle masterpiece.

Robert Mitchell

ONE IS A LONELY NUMBER

Released: 1972
Production: Stan Margulies for Metro-Goldwyn-Mayer
Direction: Mel Stuart
Screenplay: David Seltzer; based on the short story, "The Good Humor Man" by Rebecca Morris
Cinematography: Michael Hugo
Editing: David Saxon
Running time: 97 minutes

Principal characters:
Aimee Brower	Trish Van Devere
Howard Carpenter	Monte Markham
Gert Meredith	Janet Leigh
Joseph Provo	Melvyn Douglas
Madge Frazier	Jane Elliott

The theme of women's liberation is inherent in *One Is a Lonely Number*, a 1972 film which is told from a woman's point of view. She has been abandoned by her husband and, through her eyes, the audience becomes party to the confusion of a crumbled marriage as well as her shaky attempts to pick up the pieces of her life and carry on. The film possesses frequent soap opera touches, including teary moments following several bittersweet revelations. If the film has a somewhat clichéd daytime television delivery, however, it is also peppered with moments of humor and wry observation. This is particularly evident early in the film when the heroine, Aimee (Trish Van Devere), becomes involved with members of the Divorcées League of Marin County, and near the end, when she dives dramatically into a swimming pool to prove her courage.

In spite of the fact that *One Is a Lonely Number* makes valid points about women caught up in the throes of divorce, the film is not without problems. Particularly irritating is the fact that the film is totally one-sided, since the audience never learns the husband's side of the story. We are told only that four years of marriage has ended quite suddenly, and, for Aimee, completely unexpectedly. All she did, she says, was to toss her English professor husband's copy of Milton out the window during an argument. It is an act that he will not forgive, and one which she thinks caused the breakup. A confused, clinging woman, Aimee is bewildered by her husband's demands for a divorce. She hopes for a reconciliation until she learns that her husband, who teaches at Berkeley, has been keeping a mistress of nineteen on the side. It is the first of several stern plot twists to emerge.

Through her sympathetic best friend Madge (Jane Elliott), Aimee meets Gert Meredith (Janet Leigh), a bitchy, five-times-divorced man-hater who has ready advice for her: "Get a job, get a lawyer, and get laid." Aimee's misadventures as a divorcée are just beginning. Now she has a flashy lawyer in tow, who wants her to contest the divorce in order to snare a bigger settlement. The young mistress, he says, will give their case plenty of ammunition. Aimee also has job-hunting problems, including the seedy employment agent, who makes obvious passes. With no training for a specific career, Aimee is left to swallow her pride and take a low-paying job as a lifeguard at a neighborhood pool. Soon she is reluctantly dragging dogs from the water and supervising squealing youngsters. The swimming-pool sequences are loud and bursting with commotion, and as such they parallel Aimee's new, suddenly erratic life. The water is horribly messy, and at one point an ice cream cone even floats by. The pool's awesome high dive seems to sum up all of her fears. Despite the urgings of the pool's friendly staff members, Aimee will not go near the board.

She has still other adjustments to make. Suddenly, nighttime noises are frightening; but if the night holds an uneasy loneliness, then daytime also has it problems of simple basic survival. Aimee is exposed to some of society's inequities, including a hardware store clerk who refuses to extend credit to divorced women.

There are also new friends for Aimee, including the elderly storekeeper, Joseph Provo (Melvyn Douglas). She initially listens to his nostalgic tales, and advice, with only polite attention, but later she warms to his friendship. She also tucks away his words of advice concerning taking chances, in order to enjoy life. Provo himself had a long, happy marriage, until his wife's death. Aimee continues to steer clear of new and uncertain experiences, however, and the high dive at the pool remains unchallenged by her. Then, quite accidentally, she meets handsome Howard Carpenter (Monte Markham), at a cocktail party. He is warm, amusing, and interested in her, and Aimee, who is just not ready to be completely on her own, readily begins an affair with him. Her life now has some semblance of stability, but it is thrown off balance when she and Joseph Provo discuss the death of a young woman. Aimee never knew the woman, but her position is something which she can understand. Alone in life, the woman also lies alone at the morgue. It is a possibility with which Aimee cannot cope. Turning to Howard for solace, she wonders, "Am I the kind of girl you'd marry?" Her face is hopeful, serene, and not ready for Howard's stilted response, "You're the kind of girl I am married to." It is a bitter lesson for Aimee, who feels tricked and manipulated, but a kind of victory awaits her. For when the day of the divorce trial arrives, Aimee stuns her supporters (including Gert, who has come along hoping to witness revenge) by turning and walking away. She no longer wants to contest anything and is now intent on learning to live with her freedom. With a celebration in mind, she heads for Joseph Provo's. When she learns of his sudden death she is stunned, and yet the death serves to reaffirm Provo's belief in the preciousness of life. In the film's final moments, she pushes her fears of the high dive aside, plunging into the pool.

One Is a Lonely Number marked the first major starring role for Van Devere, as Aimee. She had previously appeared in *Where's Papa* (1970) and *The Last Run* (1971), and has since gone on to costar primarily opposite her husband, George C. Scott. Yet as *One Is a Lonely Number* indicates, she can on her own lend credibility to a sympathetic role. Television actor Markham portrays Howard, a likable seducer-turned-cad, thanks to the soapy script. The memory-filled Joseph Provo is portrayed with poignancy by Douglas, and Leigh gives color (and a delicious bitchiness) to the foul-mouthed, man-hating Gert.

At the time of its release, *One Is a Lonely Number* was all but ignored by box office and critics alike. The film's release was badly timed—*Alice Doesn't Live Here Anymore* appeared in 1975 and *An Unmarried Woman* in 1978. Also, while the more contemporary films of this type are showcases for directorial style as well as vehicles for their respective actresses, *One Is a Lonely Number* is marked by a turgid style and less fanfare in the performances. Still, it must be argued that, where thematic content is concerned, *One Is a Lonely Number* is a sound, honest film. By contrast, the heroine of *An Unmarried Woman* is able to breeze from a broken marriage into an affair with never a worry of monetary or legal problems. If the coming years should see a dissection of the many facets of the women's movement, it is possible that *One Is a Lonely Number* will ultimately emerge with new respectability.

Director Mel Stuart cannot be called a major film force since his works are mostly entertainment pieces glossed over lightly with wry social commentary, such as the breezy but carefully insightful *If It's Tuesday, This Must Be Belgium* (1969) and the bittersweet *I Love My Wife* (1970). Stuart's screen pieces are mostly small-budget productions, devoid of name stars. *One Is a Lonely Number* falls easily into this category, but, like Stuart's other films, it manages to deliver a viable, topical message, albeit surrounded by soap opera clichés.

Pat H. Broeske

ONE MORE RIVER

Released: 1934
Production: Carl Laemmle, Jr., for Universal
Direction: James Whale
Screenplay: R. C. Sherriff; based on the novel of the same name by John Galsworthy
Cinematography: John J. Mescall
Editing: no listing
Running time: 90 minutes

Principal characters:
Claire Corven	Diana Wynyard
Dinny	Jane Wyatt
Tony Croom	Frank Lawton
David Dornford	Reginald Denny
Brough	Lionel Atwill
Aunt Em	Mrs. Patrick Campbell
Sir Laurence Mont	Henry Stephenson
General Charwell	C. Aubrey Smith
Sir Gerald Corven	Colin Clive
Lady Charwell	Kathleen Howard
Blore	Robert Greig
Forsythe	Alan Mowbray
The Judge	Gilbert Emery
Chayne	E. E. Clive
Mrs. Purdy	Tempe Pigott

James Whale is best remembered today as the director of classic horror features such as *Frankenstein* (1931) and *The Invisible Man* (1933), but his skills as a stylish and sophisticated director are far better demonstrated by his little-known productions such as *Waterloo Bridge* (1931) and *One More River*. His British stage background never served him better than in those two features. *One More River*, which is, perhaps, as *Photoplay* (October, 1934) commented, "a trifle ponderous for American appreciation," is based on the last, posthumously published, novel of Nobel Prize-winning author John Galsworthy. For the screenplay Universal selected R. C. Sherriff, with whom Whale had worked on *The Invisible Man*. Sherriff took only the bare bones of the Galsworthy novel, ignoring side episodes such as Dinny's unhappy romantic experiences and concentrating on the breakup of Claire's marriage to Sir Gerald Corven. The film is chiefly concerned with Britain's archaic and decidedly sexist divorce laws, a subject which Americans might find rather quaint and ridiculous; but what is even more quaint and ridiculous is that the American production code required a considerable toning down of the subject matter, and some scenes had to be reshot because of censorship problems.

One More River opens with the arrival of Claire Corven (Diana Wynyard) and Tony Croom (Frank Lawton) in England from Ceylon. Claire is running away from her husband who has treated her cruelly, both mentally and physically (beating her with a riding whip). Tony is returning from a tea plantation which went bankrupt. They are very upper-middle-class, and in her case upper-class, English, and as if to remind one of how terribly proper and English they are, "Land of Hope and Glory" is playing on the sound track as the ship docks. The two met for the first time on the ship and an affection has developed between them, although Claire is quick to point out that they should not particularly plan to meet again in England. Diana Wynyard and Frank Lawton are perfectly cast as the young couple; Wynyard is charmingly proper and sincere and has a perfect diction rare in the cinema, and Lawton is boyishly attractive. Meeting Claire at the dock is her sister Dinny, played by Jane Wyatt, a young stage actress making her screen debut, who, in a couple of years, would hit the highspot of her career with the female lead in *Lost Horizon* (1937).

The two girls drive to London, while Dinny fills Claire in as to what has been happening in England while she was away. The country is in a state of crisis, and its only hope is the election of the National Party to political power. The National Party appears to be another name for the Conservative Party, and once the elections have taken place and the National Party swept to power, no further mention is made in the film of England's moment of crisis.

Claire's family's contribution to the National Party is David Dornford (Reginald Denny), and Claire busies herself helping to see him elected. She also meets Tony again; he has been unable to keep away from her and arranges a chance meeting in a country lane. They kiss once, sedately but with affection. In a perfect re-creation of an English village and an English ancestral home, director and screenwriter introduce us to quaint village characters such as Purdy, who has not voted since Mr. Gladstone retired, and his wheelchair-ridden wife (Tempe Pigott); and to Claire's family, including her father (C. Aubrey Smith), her mother (Kathleen Howard, best known for her brilliant portrayal of W. C. Fields's nagging wife in *It's a Gift*), her uncle (Henry Stephenson), and, above all, her Aunt Em (an unmistakably English name), played to perfection by the great British stage actress, Mrs. Patrick Campbell. Mrs. Pat delivers one-liners with all the ease of a stand-up vaudeville comic. Of a sudden twinge of pain, she comments, "I don't know whether it's flatulence or the hand of God." As Mordaunt Hall in *The New York Times* (August 10, 1934) commented, "All the supporting performers rise to what is demanded of them."

Dornford takes on Claire as his secretary, and she takes an apartment in London, above an antique shop. Meanwhile, Claire's husband, Sir Gerald

(Colin Clive), has returned to England and wishes her to come back to Ceylon with him. His position does not permit him to give her grounds for divorce. Clive, with his curling lip and insolent sneer, is excellent as the husband with a sadistic streak. He visits Claire's father for a man-to-man discussion concerning Claire's return to him, but neglects to tell of the incident in which he beat her with a riding crop. One evening Claire fails to show up for dinner at her uncle's house. Corven had come around to her apartment, and although there is only the vaguest hint of this in the film, the viewer is left with the suggestion that he raped her.

Meanwhile, Claire and Tony have been seeing much more of each other, and, unknown to them, Corven, who has returned to Ceylon, has hired two private detectives to watch their movements. These detectives, George and Bert, are played with a fine sense of the comic in their behavior by E. E. Clive and Snub Pollard. On the way back from a trip to Oxford, the lights on the car Tony and Claire are using fail. Rather than risk driving at night without lights, the couple decide to spend the night together in the car, parked in the woods. Claire, somewhat unconvincingly, it seems, tells Tony she has always wanted to find out what it is like to sleep in a car. Nothing happens between the two. Tony smokes his pipe and falls asleep on Claire's shoulder, but it is enough for Corven to file for divorce, naming Tony as corespondent and asking two thousand pounds in damages from him.

The second half of the film is taken up with the trial and offers further superb characterizations from Gilbert Emery as the Judge, Lionel Atwill as the prosecuting attorney, and Alan Mowbray as the attorney for the defense. Despite acquitting herself well on the witness stand, the fact that she spent a night in London with her husband proves damning evidence against Claire, indicating that his supposed sadism (which Claire will not discuss in court, gentlewoman that she is) did not repel her and that their marriage had not ended in Ceylon. The divorce is granted, with Claire being condemned as the guilty, adulterous party. The courtroom sequence is well handled from a directorial point of view, carefully edited and conceived, but one wonders what American audiences made of it all, since it was a courtroom drama so far removed from anything played in an American court. *Variety* (August 14, 1934) found it "arresting if slow-progressing unfolding."

That night, Tony goes to Claire's apartment and is shocked and repelled to find her apparently unconcerned at all that has taken place and only glad that it is over, drinking to his health and apologizing for serving cold cuts. He cannot comprehend how, during the agony of awaiting the jury's verdict, she found time to worry about cold cuts for dinner. He leaves, but returns in the morning to apologize. She tells him that she is pleased he is back, for she does not care to eat breakfast alone. It is a curiously enigmatic and unsatisfactory ending to a film of tremendous literacy and style.

One More River may not be one of the greatest American films of the

1930's, but it is certainly one of which all associated with it should feel proud. It provides a faithful rendering of English society, English customs, and the English environment—a fine tribute to its director and to a studio, Universal, not always recognized for quality production.

Anthony Slide

ONE POTATO, TWO POTATO

Released: 1964
Production: Sam Weston for Cinema V
Direction: Larry Peerce
Screenplay: Raphael Hayes and Orville H. Hampton; based on an original
story by Orville H. Hampton
Cinematography: Andrew Laszlo
Editing: Robert Fritch
Running time: 92 minutes

Principal characters:
Julie Cullen Richards .... Barbara Barrie
Frank Richards .... Bernie Hamilton
Joe Cullen .... Richard Mulligan
Judge Powell .... Harry Bellaver
Ellen Mary .... Marti Mericka
William Richards .... Robert Earl Jones
Martha Richards .... Vinette Carroll

By the early 1960's, the integrationist idealism inherent in the Sidney Poitier films of the previous decade was no longer viable to black film audiences. As blacks began to demand their constitutional rights, newspapers were jammed with incidents of violence: four black girls were killed when a Birmingham, Alabama, church was bombed in 1963; civil rights leader Medgar Evers was murdered that same year; three civil rights workers, after their arrest and release, were found dead under a dam in Mississippi a year later. Race riots erupted in Detroit, Newark, and Los Angeles. Although the intermingling of the races was still the major theme in films which dealt with blacks, such as *Guess Who's Coming to Dinner* (1967), a new type of racial film hinted at the premise that brotherly love was a folly. In such films as *A Raisin in the Sun* (1961), *Nothing But a Man* (1964), and, ultimately, *Sweet Sweetback's Baadasssss Song* (1971), blacks and whites were depicted as being irreparably different. In *One Potato, Two Potato*, a black man and a white woman do fall in love and marry, but their otherwise happy relationship is disrupted by a society which still views a union between the races as no less than perverse.

The interracial marriage theme of *One Potato, Two Potato* had never before been explored in a major motion picture. *Pinky* (1949) is the most notable earlier film which depicted a romance between the races, but an actual marriage had never before been portrayed. Barbara Barrie stars in the film as Julie Cullen, a white woman with a six-year-old daughter who has been deserted by her husband Joe (Richard Mulligan). She meets Frank Richards (Bernie Hamilton), a black man and a coworker at a local machine factory in the small Midwestern town in which they live. The couple falls in love and marries, and the relationship thrives despite the expected social pressures. Richard's parents (Robert Earl Jones and Vinette Carroll), who at first are vehemently against the marriage, grow to love their new daughter-in-law and her child. Julie's former husband learns of the relationship, however, takes his ex-wife to court to win custody of his daughter, and wins. The perplexed child drives off with her father. Her mother and stepfather have been victimized by their love and by the opposite tones of their skin.

One Potato, Two Potato, filmed on location in Painsville, Ohio, is a gloomy film, closer in style to a documentary than to a fictional drama. Its subject matter, however, is presented in a frank, dramatic manner with taste and integrity. Despite the differences in their race, Frank and Julie are husband and wife as well as friends and lovers. In the film, white Julie is in no way superior to her black husband and must even earn acceptance by his parents. Several scenes are exemplary in their warmth and simplicity. The couple playfully courts in the town square, at first playing a child's game (thus, the film's title), and finally embracing in newfound love. The daughter (portrayed by Marti Mericka, a Cleveland schoolgirl who had never before acted) is uncomprehending of the prejudice that has forced her to depart with her father as the pair drives off in the finale; similarly, her mother is helpless to keep the child.

It is apparent from the outset that, unlike the characters in thousands of love stories depicted on screen, this couple will not live happily ever after because they are flouting the norm. Even though Frank Richards is a stable, loving husband and stepfather and Joe Cullen is a wanderer and dreamer, the latter will gain custody of the child solely because he is white. The film's point of view is perhaps a bit too obvious, and the plot device which sets off the conflict—Joe Cullen's sudden, unexpected return and newfound interest in parenthood—is highly unlikely. Despite these objections, however, Raphael Hayes and Orville H. Hampton's script is intelligent in its presentation of the principal characters, while director Larry Peerce effectively unravels the narrative. One critic was moved enough to call Peerce the most promising new director since Stanley Kubrick. While his direction of *Goodbye Columbus* (1969) and *The Incident* (1967) is workmanlike, *One Potato, Two Potato* is easily his best film to date.

Barrie, whose reputation rests mainly on her stellar performances on the stage, is superb as Julie. She renders a perceptive, intelligent portrait of a woman who lives by her instincts and must thus defend her love of husband and daughter against overwhelming odds. She deservedly was awarded the Best Actress citation at the 1964 Cannes Film Festival. Hamilton's Frank is effectively low-keyed, an average, everyday citizen who happens to fall in love with a white woman. He has appeared in films from *The Jackie Robinson Story* in 1950 to *Let No Man Write My Epitaph* a decade later and *Bucktown* in 1975. Unfortunately, *One Potato, Two Potato* was his only opportunity to enact a three-dimensional lead role.

One Potato, Two Potato was produced independently, as were most of the other black "art" films of the era. It is a courageous film for its time. Peerce and producer Sam Weston, both industry newcomers, raised the $250,000 to produce the film. There were forty-three financial backers in all, and investments ranged from $250 to $30,000. Peerce's father, Metropolitan Opera tenor Jan Peerce, contributed $10,000. After shooting *One Potato, Two Potato* in thirty-four days, the filmmakers were turned down by all of the American distributors. The American committee that selects films for the Cannes Film Festival also would not accept it, picking instead *The World of Henry Orient*, a comedy starring Peter Sellers. A French selection committee finally agreed to show the film, and it earned a standing ovation and the Best Actress honor for Barrie. Not since *Marty*, released nine years earlier, had a low-budget American film come to Cannes with such impact.

Donald Rugoff's Cinema V company picked up the film for distribution. The reviews were generally positive, if not spectacular. *The New York Times* named it among the top ten films of the year, and it earned $85,085 in eight New York area theaters during the first five days of its run. Despite the contrived plot device of Joe Cullen's unexpected return, Weston and Peerce produced a film which examines a sensitive topic without sensationalism or sentimentality. *One Potato, Two Potato* "told it like it was" for blacks and was appreciated more by black audiences than were such heralded major studio efforts as *To Kill a Mockingbird* (1962) and the Sidney Poitier films.

Rob Edelman

ONE WAY PASSAGE

Released: 1932
Production: Warner Bros.
Direction: Tay Garnett
Screenplay: Wilson Mizner and Joseph Jackson; based on an original story by Robert Lord
Cinematography: Robert Kurrie
Editing: Ralph Dawson
Running time: 69 minutes

Principal characters:

Dan Hardesty	William Powell
Joan Ames	Kay Francis
Skippy	Frank McHugh
Countess Barilhaus (Barrel House Betty)	Aline MacMahon
Steve Burke	Warren Hymer
Ship's Doctor	Frederick Burton

One of the most successful of all romantic teams on film was that of William Powell and Kay Francis. They played together in four Paramount films (*Behind the Make-Up, Street of Chance,* and *For the Defense,* all in 1930, and *Ladies' Man* in 1931). Then, when the star ranks at Paramount were raided, both stars went over to Warner Bros., but Warners could not resist costarring them in two more films during 1932—*Jewel Robbery* and *One Way Passage.* The last film they made together, *One Way Passage,* is their most memorable; it did so well at the box office that the studio remade it in 1940 as *'Til We Meet Again,* hoping that Merle Oberon teamed with George Brent might generate some of the magic that Powell and Francis had projected. *'Til We Meet Again* was a good film, but it cannot compare with *One Way Passage.*

One Way Passage is a simple but unforgettable love story, a romantic film that offers both comedy and drama, with a happy-go-lucky touch of the supernatural at the finale. It starts in Hong Kong and ends in Agua Caliente in Mexico, with most of the action taking place onboard a passenger liner in the Pacific sailing between China and San Francisco, with a stopover in Honolulu. For all these scenes, the company never left the Warner Bros. lot in Burbank, using stock footage for scenes of the ship's departures and arrivals at various ports of call. Most of the action takes place onboard ship, a standing set on the lot, and the few shots of the principals in Hong Kong and Honolulu were shot on sound stages. There are really no exteriors; production costs were minimal.

The film opens with Dan Hardesty (William Powell), a man wanted for murder, being taken into custody in Hong Kong by a detective named Steve

Burke (Warren Hymer), whose duty it is to bring him back to San Quentin, where his crime will be expiated. Just before the voyage, Dan encounters an attractive, fashionably dressed, rich American girl named Joan Ames (Kay Francis), also bound for San Francisco. She does not know that he is to die at San Quentin, and he does not know that she is an invalid who has a terminal heart ailment, and will soon die.

Steve has handcuffed Dan to him, admitting, however, that he cannot swim. Dan watches for his chance, then pushes down a guard rail, plunging the two men into the sea. Dan rescues Steve, who is so impressed that he does not insist that Dan be manacled to him during the rest of the voyage, although he continues to watch every move his prisoner makes. Meanwhile, Dan presses his romance with Joan. They go through a daily rite in the bar, where they touch cocktail glasses before drinking their Paradise cocktails. By the time the ship nears Honolulu, they are very much in love.

Steve, at the same time, is interested in a traveler named Betty, also known as the "Countess" (Aline MacMahon), who is a clever thief in her own right and who has her fingerprints registered with the police. Skippy (Frank McHugh) is a pal of the "Countess," a happy drunk, and an accomplished pickpocket. Coming into the harbor at Honolulu, Steve tells Dan that he intends to go ashore with the "Countess," so he is locking him in the ship's brig for the duration of their time in Honolulu. Skippy then contrives to pick Steve's pocket, secure the key, and open the brig to let Dan out. Joan has been looking forward to going ashore with Dan, and when she encounters him on deck, she thinks he has come to fetch her. Dan is actually planning to escape while the ship is anchored in Honolulu and has already made arrangements with a freighter captain who is pulling up anchor shortly after the ship docks. He now uses Joan as a front and goes ashore with her. He is just about to desert her when she suffers a heart attack, and he carries her back to the ship instead of boarding the freighter, as he had planned to do. The ship's doctor (Frederick Burton) tells Dan that a shock might kill Joan, and thus he learns that the girl he loves is doomed to die, just as he is, shortly after they reach San Francisco.

When the passengers disembark at San Francisco, Dan is handcuffed once again to Steve, but he manages to cover the handcuffs with his overcoat. He bids Joan a tender *au revoir*, promising to meet her on New Year's Eve at Agua Caliente. She, however, has overheard a steward talking and knows the truth, that Dan will die at San Quentin. Gallantly, both of them pretend that they do not know the truth, and thus part. Skippy and the "Countess" know the truth about Dan and try to free him, but Steve is too smart for them. Steve has personal plans for the "Countess," for he intends to retire from the force shortly and run a chicken farm in Petaluma, California. He knows about her record, but that evidence has "conveniently" disappeared. She is touched, and bows happily to her fate.

The final scene is actually a postscript to the story. In some sense the addition of the final material seems overly sentimental and even "corny," but the film is so well done that the supernatural implication to the epilogue only adds to its romantic charm. The last scene occurs on New Year's Eve at Agua Caliente, which, as usual, is festive. As the New Year is ushered in by the happy crowd, including Steve and the "Countess," there are two cocktail glasses seen on the bar. They are touched and raised by invisible hands, the toast is drunk, and the stems of the glasses are broken for luck. Dan and Joan have kept their rendezvous as they had promised each other they would, and this time it is forever.

DeWitt Bodeen

THE ONION FIELD

Released: 1979
Production: Walter Coblenz for Avco Embassy
Direction: Harold Becker
Screenplay: Joseph Wambaugh; based on his book of the same name
Cinematography: Charles Rosher
Editing: John W. Wheeler
Running time: 126 minutes

Principal characters:
Karl Hettinger .... John Savage
Ian Campbell .... Ted Danson
Gregory Powell .... James Woods
Jimmy Smith .... Franklyn Seales
Pierce Brooks .... Ronny Cox

When Karl Hettinger (John Savage), a major character in *The Onion Field*, resigns from the Los Angeles Police Department under compulsion because he has been accused of shoplifting, someone asks him, "Are you guilty?" That question touches on one of the issues raised by this thematically rich film. Those themes include not only the ambiguous nature of guilt, but also the sometimes meaningless mechanisms of the American legal system. The film also explores how the ramifications of a crime extend beyond its immediate victim to everyone tangentially connected with it. Besides dealing with these several themes, *The Onion Field* also looks at the complex psychologies of its major characters. Although the film's subject matter is violent crime, it resists the temptation to sensationalize and focuses less on the crime itself than on its effects.

The Onion Field is based on screenwriter and best-selling novelist Joseph Wambaugh's nonfiction book about the longest criminal case in California history. On the night of March 9, 1963, patrolmen Karl Hettinger and Ian Campbell (Ted Danson) stop a suspicious vehicle on a Hollywood street. Its occupants, Gregory Powell (James Woods) and Jimmy Smith (Franklyn Seales), parolees en route to a liquor store holdup, kidnap the two officers. After they are driven to a vegetable farm near Bakersfield, Campbell is shot and killed while Hettinger escapes through the field of onions. Both kidnapers are soon apprehended. Their trials and appeals, however, consume years and years. The first half of the film prepares for the crime, juxtaposing the two sets of partners. The second half treats the crime's effects, depicting the characters caught up in a miasma of guilt and misconstrued justice as redolent as the onion field itself.

The film's position on who is responsible for Campbell's death is clearly ambiguous. On the most superficial level, that ambiguity emerges in the problem of which kidnaper actually killed the policeman. Both Powell and Smith agree that Powell fired the first shot, but accuse each other of having pumped four more bullets into the fallen man. Physical evidence assembled by investigator Pierce Brooks (Ronny Cox) from ballistics and fingerprints contributes nothing to solving this problem. The question of guilt and responsibility, however, extends further. In the course of their trial, much is made of how the maniacal Powell's family background has contributed to his character and of how Smith's situation as a child of the slums turned him to crime. Moreover, since both men are parolees, the film suggests that the judicial system which freed them must bear some blame for Campbell's death.

The most sustained examination of guilt in the film, however, is the treatment of Karl Hettinger. Because he surrendered his gun, even though at his partner's request, Hettinger is viewed by some as having violated proper procedure. His own doubts about his responsibility join with the accusations of some police officials to cause him unconsciously to seek punishment. He begins to shoplift and is finally forced to resign to avoid criminal charges for theft. His sense of guilt, reinforced by the times he must recall the onion field incident on the witness stand at each new trial of the kidnapers, turns him into a derelict who stands on the verge of suicide. He also relives the experience in nightmares. The film ironically shows the deep impact of Campbell's killing on Hettinger while its actual perpetrators suffer no apparent emotional trauma.

The second half of *The Onion Field* focuses especially on the American legal system as Powell and Smith exploit every avenue of trial and appeal. Their first trial results in capital convictions for both, but their executions remain in abeyance as they continue to use the legal process. Powell, in fact, becomes a knowledgeable jailhouse lawyer who at the end of the film is offering legal advice to fellow inmates at the penitentiary. The film is not as critical of the legal system's allowing for appeal as of the effects which the lengthy appeal process exacts on everyone involved. Most apparent is the effect on Hettinger, who has to retell the events of the killing at each new trial. The appeals also involve several families, those of Hettinger, of the victim Campbell, and of the kidnapers. Even the attorneys are affected by the process, and one leaves the profession in frustration over the case. Not only is the appeal process long, but also it is seemingly meaningless as each new trial decision leads only to a new appeal.

Although the most obvious victim of the onion field killing is Ian Campbell, its actual ramifications are shown by the film to spread much more widely. As a modern American "crime and punishment," *The Onion Field* shows how a senseless, spur-of-the-moment killing is rooted in the psychologies of its perpetrators and affects them, their surviving victim, and others who are associated with the act. For example, the psychological disintegration of Hettinger from policeman to thief demonstrates almost a reversal of roles. Whereas he was once an authority figure, he becomes dominated by Powell and Smith when he allows their crime to drive him close to self-destruction.

While *The Onion Field* merits attention for its effective handling of several themes, its production history is also interesting. Author Wambaugh, dissatisfied with film treatments of his other books, such as *The Blue Knight* (1973) and *The New Centurians* (1972) bought back the film rights to *The Onion Field*. This film is the result of Wambaugh's desire for artistic and cinematic integrity. That integrity emerges in a very human treatment of a subject that Hollywood has too often been tempted to depict in terms of stereotyped sensationalism. Wambaugh's characters are real people, and his film is effective on intellectual, emotional, sociological, and artistic levels. Critical response to *The Onion Field*, largely positive, emphasized this integrity manifest in the film.

Frances M. Malpezzi
William M. Clements

OPERATION PETTICOAT

Released: 1959
Production: Robert Arthur for Universal
Direction: Blake Edwards
Screenplay: Stanley Shapiro and Maurice Richlin; suggested by a story of the same name by Paul King and Joseph Stone
Cinematography: Russell Harlan and Clifford Stine
Editing: Ted Kent and Frank Gross
Running time: 124 minutes

Principal characters:
Commander Matt Sherman .... Cary Grant
Lieutenant Nick Holden .... Tony Curtis
Nurse Dolores Crandall .... Joan O'Brien
Nurse Barbara Duran .... Dina Merrill
Tostin .... Arthur O'Connell
Hunkle .... Gavin MacLeod

War may be hell, but it is still occasionally good for a laugh; and World War II, as grim a war as any in recorded history, has produced a large share of comedies. The service comedies of the 1940's tended to follow the misadventures of some hapless draftee (Bud Abbott and Lou Costello's *Buck Privates*, from 1941, is a classic of the genre) in the clutches of Uncle Sam, all the while reassuring the audience on the home front that things were going to turn out all right. The best of the 1950's World War II comedies tended to rely less on slapstick and more on higher production values and sophisticated wit. *Operation Petticoat*, made by Blake Edwards in 1959, is one of the best of these sophisticated service comedies.

Although most of the film takes place during World War II, *Operation Petticoat* is framed by beginning and ending sequences that take place in "real time"—that is, the late 1950's. Edwards uses the second half of the frame—the closing sequence—to bring his story to a neatly ironic conclusion. As the film opens, however, all we know is that Admiral Matt Sherman (Cary Grant), head of the American submarine command in the Pacific, is boarding the *U.S.S. Sea Tiger* one last time. The *Sea Tiger* is about to be scrapped, and the Admiral wants a few moments alone in the sub that was his first command. As he leafs through the *Sea Tiger's* logbook, his reminiscences spark the film's narrative.

Sherman's thoughts take us back to the Philippine Islands during late December, 1941, at the beginning of World War II. An attack by a Japanese raiding party has inflicted major damage on the *Sea Tiger*, to put it mildly. "You've been sunk," is one of the more optimistic diagnoses that then Commander Matt Sherman receives. He is determined, however, to make the sub seaworthy once again. Indeed, the rest of the film chronicles Sherman's efforts to make his way to Australia, where complete repairs can be effected.

At this point, Edwards introduces us to a few key crew members. These include the gruff chief mechanic Tostin (Arthur O'Connell) and Seaman Hunkle (Gavin MacLeod), a woebegone sailor whose life was dramatically altered for the worse when, in a drunken moment, he permitted a particularly pornographic portrait to be tattooed on his chest. The most important member of the *Sea Tiger*'s crew, however, is Sherman's new junior officer, Lieutenant Nick Holden (Tony Curtis).

Nick Holden was leading an idyllic life as an admiral's aide in charge of parades and recreation when the war broke out, thrusting the reluctant lieutenant into the thick of the action under Sherman's command. Holden and Sherman are complete, and thus comical, opposites. While Commander Sherman is a conscientious Navy man eager to serve his country, Holden only wants to survive the war unscathed; he is a born hustler who enlisted only to give himself enough social prestige to catch a wealthy wife.

The two men take an instant dislike to each other; it is thus ironic that they need each other to make it through the war successfully. Holden needs Sherman's nautical acumen to get him safely to Australia, and Sherman needs Holden's skill as a promoter to come up—by hook or by crook—with the spare parts needed to get the *Sea Tiger* moving again. "Never have so few stolen so much from so many," mutters Sherman in amazement at Holden's escapades.

A second Japanese attack makes it imperative that the *Sea Tiger* head south immediately, and so she departs chugging shakily off. Even the local island witch doctor, hired by Holden to bless the voyage, is dubious about the sub's chances. The *Sea Tiger* holds together, however, and Commander Sherman, temporarily free from the need for Holden's chicanery, resolves to make his junior officer toe the mark. En route to Australia, the two talk frankly, and Edwards uses this as an opportunity to let the audience in on Nick Holden's background. It seems that he joined the Navy because he felt that a uniform would give him social prestige and impress the girls he was chasing. Evidently he was right; Holden is engaged to a wealthy heiress. As Holden rattles on about his future bride's fortune, Sherman remarks drily "When the preacher says 'Do you *take* this woman,' he won't be kidding, will he?"

The *Sea Tiger* stops to refuel and pick up supplies on an island that has just been savaged by a Japanese attack, and an additional complication is added to Matt Sherman's life: five beautiful nurses who are marooned on the island. Reluctantly, Sherman agrees to take them as far as the next island.

Although Sherman is disgruntled by the presence of women on the ship, the crew—especially Nick Holden—is delighted, and so, obviously, is director Edwards. He and his writers Stanley Shapiro and Maurice Richlin immediately shift the thrust of the film's comedy from the witty verbal sparring between

Sherman and Holden to a broader, more physical comedy involving the difficulties of passing a buxom nurse in a narrow corridor and similar "problems" encountered by Sherman and his crew.

When the *Sea Tiger* lands at Cebu, Sherman is desperate to rid the sub of the nurses, but the military authorities will not hear of it. The war is heating up on Cebu, and Sherman is not only forced to keep the nurses on the sub, but he is also forced to take on several refugee families and their livestock. At this point, Sherman feels like the captain of Noah's Ark, but things get worse. To add insult to injury, there is an insufficient supply of badly needed white lead primer paint on Cebu. To give the *Sea Tiger* a much needed touchup, the crew is forced to mix the white paint with the only other color available—red. The result is a shocking pink submarine. Its embarrassed skipper and his coed crew wearily head for Australia.

By New Year's Day, however, Sherman has apparently made his peace with the nurses and crew. Indeed, he has grown fond of his chief tormentor, the busty but accident-prone Nurse Crandall (Joan O'Brien); and other crew members have similarly paired off although Nick Holden infuriates Barbara Duran (Dina Merrill), the object of his affections, by mentioning his engagement. The Japanese, however, spoil the festivities by strafing the sub. The *Sea Tiger* hurriedly submerges, but not before its radio communications are destroyed.

With its radio out of order, the *Sea Tiger* finds itself the target of attacks from both the Japanese and the Americans (who have no record of a pink submarine on their rolls). Indeed, an American destroyer nearly sinks the *Sea Tiger*, until, in a moment of inspiration, Holden saves the day by jettisoning some of the nurses' underwear, which floats to the surface and is picked up by the American destroyer's crew. Nurse Crandall's bra is the clincher. "The Japanese have nothing like this," says the awed American captain. "Cease fire."

The long flashback ends as the pink submarine docks in Australia to the hoots and jeers of the assembled multitude. The film then reverts to real time, and the now Admiral Sherman greets the *Sea Tiger*'s current commanding officer and his wife: one Captain Nick Holden and the former Miss Barbara Duran. Admiral Sherman informs Captain Holden that a new atomic sub, to be commanded by Holden, will be christened the *Sea Tiger*, and inquires as to the whereabouts of Mrs. Sherman, who was to accompany the Holdens to the dock. On cue, the Admiral's car careens into view. As it smashes into everything within range, the audience knows who will emerge from the carnage. Mrs. Sherman is none other than the inept Nurse Crandall. The old *Sea Tiger* is then sunk, but its comic legacy will live on.

The roles of Nick Holden and Matt Sherman were made to order for Curtis and Grant. Curtis plays the quick-witted, quicker-tongued Holden to perfection. His character initiates most of the film's best comic sequences, and Curtis supplies the necessary verve and vitality to launch them effectively. Grant, on the other hand, as Matt Sherman, wins just as many laughs as Curtis, but he gets them in a different way. As the beleaguered skipper of the *Sea Tiger*, his part is more reactive than active; and no actor is better than Grant at milking laughs with a pained or startled look. Curtis overplays, Grant under-plays, and the result is a perfect mix, and tremendously effective comedy.

Among the supporting cast, O'Connell and MacLeod stand out as the most comical of the pink sub's zany crew. As for the nurses, O'Brien as Nurse Crandall and Merrill as Barbara Duran perform their not terribly demanding tasks as attractive diversions admirably.

The scenes involving the nurses provoked most of the criticism that greeted *Operation Petticoat* when it was first released. Many critics thought the bosom jokes and the double entendres (for example, Nurse Crandall says to an angry Matt Sherman: "When a person's irritable, he's not getting enough of something," innocently handing him a vitamin pill) were downright salacious. By contemporary standards, of course, the sexual humor in this film is astonishingly mild. A more telling criticism of the film might be that Edwards and his writers occasionally let their enthusiasm for the slightly naughty joke run away with them. At 124 minutes, the film is a bit long, and some of the more repetitive bits involving the nurses could have been excised in the name of brevity, if not necessarily decency.

Nevertheless, Edwards was the ideal director for *Operation Pettitoat*. The film is a near perfect example of the service-comedy genre: it emphasizes wit over slapstick (occasionally mixing the two forms), maintains consistently high production values, and utilizes a topnotch cast. Edwards has demonstrated his ability to handle this formula as well as or better than any other contemporary director, as witness 1979's *10*, as well as his triumphs with Peter Sellers in the incredible *Pink Panther* films of the 1960's and 1970's. Like the *Pink Panther* series, *Operation Petticoat* is an eminently enjoyable, thoroughly unpretentious delight.

Robert Mitchell

ORDINARY PEOPLE

Released: 1980
Production: Ronald L. Schwary for Paramount (AA)
Direction: Robert Redford (AA)
Screenplay: Alvin Sargent (AA); based on the novel of the same name by Judith Guest
Cinematography: John Bailey
Editing: Jeff Kanew
Music: Marvin Hamlisch
Running time: 124 minutes

Principal characters:
Calvin	Donald Sutherland
Beth	Mary Tyler Moore
Berger	Judd Hirsch
Conrad	Timothy Hutton (AA)
Swim Coach	M. Emmet Walsh
Jeannine	Elizabeth McGovern
Karen	Dinah Manoff

Relationships and the tenuous state of the family unit are explored in the intense, Oscar-winning drama *Ordinary People*. Delivered in serious, straightforward style, the film is faithfully adapted from the well-received first novel of Judith Guest, and marks the directorial debut of film star Robert Redford. Through his independent company, Wildwood Enterprises, Redford has proven himself adept at choosing projects that are topical, artistically invigorating, and commercially viable—among them *Downhill Racer* (1969), *The Candidate* (1972), and *All the President's Men* (1976). Undeniably, the fact that Redford also starred in these films helped to insure their success. In making his directorial debut, however, Redford chose to stay behind the cameras. Moreover, he selected a property dominated by a melodramatic tone and introspective characterizations—elements that were not in step with then-current screen trends. Additionally, he assembled a unique cast (including television's sweetheart Mary Tyler Moore) that did not have proven box-office success. These elements ultimately proved to be the film's greatest strengths.

Released in September, 1980, *Ordinary People* followed a summertime glut of mostly light comedy films; in fact, the summer's biggest success was *Airplane!*, a hilarious parody of so-called "disaster" films directed and produced by industry newcomers and starring a hitherto unknown actor (Robert Hays) from a television series. *Friday the 13th*, a "slasher" film which glorified gore, was also wildly successful. Of the year's major releases, *The Empire Strikes*

Back, a sequel to 1977's *Star Wars,* attained unprecedented success at the box office and also unleashed another trend toward science-fiction themes. At this same time, major stars such as John Travolta and Clint Eastwood kept their talents confined to light entertainment; Travolta starred in *Urban Cowboy,* while Eastwood played the title role in the affectionate *Bronco Billy.* It was against this light-hearted panorama that *Ordinary People* appeared. The reaction from audiences and critics alike was immediate. With its pensive look at a family's alienation, *Ordinary People* touched a nerve close to many hearts and homes.

Essentially a four-character drama, *Ordinary People* focuses on the troubled Jarrett family of affluent Lake Forest, a Chicago suburb. The central character of the story is Conrad (Timothy Hutton), the teenage son. In the aftermath of a boating accident which takes the life of his older brother Buck, Conrad cannot overcome his feelings of guilt. He attempts suicide and is hospitalized for four months. Upon returning home he struggles for personal redemption, undergoes psychiatric therapy, and tries vainly to communicate with his parents. His father, Calvin (Donald Sutherland), a successful tax attorney, tries to respond, but Beth (Mary Tyler Moore), his mother, is unable to do so. As Conrad eventually discovers, she lacks the capacity to love him because all of her love was reserved for Buck. She is the nucleus of the family's problems. From the film's opening credits, which are presented in somber, simplistic white lettering against a black background and are unaccompanied by music, one senses the unfolding of a serious human drama.

Conrad is first glimpsed as he sings in his high school choir, and scenes depicting his conspicuously troubled state of mind follow. He cannot sleep at night; he is inattentive in class and distant with classmates, even choosing to eat lunch by himself. He is equally ill at ease with this parents. Alluding to Conrad's problems are bits and pieces of dialogue. His father wonders if he has considered seeing a recommended doctor, and through his friends it is learned that Conrad is repeating a school year. ("They didn't pass you on *anything*?" asks his friend). When Conrad at last nervously confronts the rumpled Dr. Berger (Judd Hirsch), he explains, "I'd like to be more in control, I guess." His decision to meet with Berger takes his parents by surprise, and Cal cannot hide either his pleasure or his curiosity about what the two discussed. Beth's only reaction, however, concerns the location of Berger's office and whether it is in a good part of town.

By this point the tension between Beth and Conrad is apparent, although the clues have been subtle. The signs of trouble grow bolder, however; during one disjointed conversation, when Beth explains her reason for coming home early with the remark "I didn't play golf today," Conrad's response is, "How was your golf game?" At another point, when Beth finds Conrad in the backyard during a chilly afternoon, she ventures out and wonders what he is doing. The ensuing conversation reveals their inability to connect, as Conrad reminisces about a pigeon that used to land regularly on Beth's car ("That was the closest we ever came to getting a pet"), which launches Beth into a tirade about a neighbor's barking dog. The two carry on their conversations simultaneously, each oblivious to the other's message.

The most painful encounter between Beth and Conrad occurs during a family gathering with Beth's parents. The Jarretts pose for a family photograph, and afterward Cal takes the camera and asks Beth and Conrad to pose together. Although Conrad shows some reticence, he moves shyly toward Beth, but the moment proves too much for his mother, who ignores the boy standing beside her and pleads with Cal for the camera so that she can take a picture instead. Conrad disrupts the session with a flurry of expletives as he storms away from Beth. Immediately afterward a flustered Beth goes into the kitchen, where she accidentally drops a fine china plate. "I think this can be saved," she says as she holds the broken pieces together. It is an ironic moment which mirrors her refusal to acknowledge her shattered relationship with Conrad.

The sadness behind her sleek, suburban housewife's façade is depicted in numerous scenes. Through sessions with Berger it is learned that Beth never once came to the hospital to visit Conrad; her only reaction was to throw out the towels and rugs bloodied when Conrad attempted to slit his wrists and to have the stained grout replaced in the bathroom. "She fired the maid because she couldn't dust the living room right," Conrad tells Berger, as he finds himself discovering his mother's need for orderliness at all costs. Indeed, although Cal is anxious to deal with the family's problems, Beth refuses to take them seriously. In one scene she says wistfully, "Christmas in London would be like something out of Dickens"; but Cal feels that they should all spend Christmas at home, together. Later, when Cal suggests that the entire family meet with Berger, Beth recoils. "Let's just hold on to what we've got," she says.

Still other characters come into conflict with Conrad's fragile mental state. His swim coach (M. Emmet Walsh) quizzes him about his hospitalization, asking him if he received shock treatment, and is demanding during training sessions. This is especially significant because Conrad's brother was a championship swimmer. Conrad finally decides to quit the team, to the consternation of his friends and teammates. Karen (Dinah Manoff), a girl Conrad met at the hospital, also causes him to question his precarious sanity. While hospitalized, the two had a completely honest relationship—"Nobody hid anything there," Conrad explains to Berger—but when Conrad calls her up and the two meet for a Coke, he discovers a new, seemingly in-control Karen. She is involved in school activities, says she no longer thinks about the problems which resulted in her suicide attempt, and says she decided against seeing a therapist after leaving the hospital. "Conrad, let's have a great Christmas. Let's have a great year," she says enthusiastically. Startled by her newfound confidence, Conrad begins to question his own jittery condition. When he tries to get in touch with her later, however, and learns that she has committed suicide, the depth of her illness becomes obvious. Terrified, Conrad calls Berger in the middle of the night and pleads for a session.

Karen's death causes Conrad to relive, in flashback, the boating accident which took Buck's life. When he reaches Berger's office he is shaking and fearful, but with the doctor's help, in the film's most intense sequence, he is able at last to explain his guilt: he lived, and Buck did not; he was the strong one, and as a result he is angry at Buck and his memory. "If you can't feel pain, then you're not going to feel anything else either," Berger says soothingly to an emotionally drained Conrad. At the close of the session the two embrace in friendship.

While Conrad is embarking on a new period of self-discovery, Cal and Beth are sensing that they are inherently different. During a brief vacation in Texas, they have a bitter verbal battle on the golf course. As they return home on the plane they are silent, although Cal, who has become disturbed by Beth's coldness, remembers a simpler time years ago (illustrated in a flashback) when they danced together romantically.

Upon their return home, they discover a revitalized Conrad who embraces his mother sincerely, saying, "I'm glad you're back." Cal is shocked when Beth fails to return any emotion. Later that night, Beth awakens and finds Cal at the dining-room table, crying. "You can't handle mess. You need everything neat and easy," accuses Cal, who adds, "I don't know who you are. I don't know what we were playing at." After he questions his love for her, Beth goes to their room and begins packing. Conrad is awakened by the slam of a door and rises in time to see his mother getting into a taxi. While still in his pajamas, Conrad descends the stairs and finds his father seated outside, deep in thought. During the chilly early morning hours, father and son come to a new understanding, and Conrad is told not to blame himself for Beth's decision to leave. As the film comes to a close, Conrad and Cal embrace.

Ordinary People is meticulously presented, with a slow and deliberate pace emphasizing characters rather than cinematic style. As a result of this delivery and the story line about family tensions, *Ordinary People* tends to evoke the look and feel of a soap opera, but that does not detract from its impact. Instead, it serves to deepen characterizations and to underline the film's pivotal drama. Although much of the story is sad, other moments are also brightly hopeful.

There is a strong sense of realism in the film which is especially effective when showing Conrad's relationship with his friends. One longtime friend, who also misses Buck, argues, "I don't know why you want to be in this alone." A date with a pretty classmate also proves introspective for Conrad. After at last working up the courage to ask out Jeannine (Elizabeth

McGovern), the two enjoy a night of bowling followed by serious conversation about Conrad's suicide attempt. "It was like falling into a hole and it kept getting bigger and bigger," he tells her earnestly. Embarrassed by the moment of revelation, Jeannine breaks the serious mood when she spies a group of Conrad's friends and joins them in a chorus of "You deserve a break today." Her frivolity, she later explains, was her defense for a situation she found difficult, and she apologizes, hoping that they will date again. As it turns out, Conrad holds no grudges; in fact, it is Jeannine he goes to see following the emotional session with Berger.

Critically hailed and labeled a "performer's film," *Ordinary People* is dominated by powerful acting, including Hutton's portrayal of troubled Conrad. The son of the late actor Jim Hutton, who was best known for his comedy films and his starring role in the television series *Ellery Queen*, young Hutton made his feature film debut with *Ordinary People*. His much-publicized performance brought him an Academy Award for Best Supporting Actor.

As Beth, Moore was also nominated for an Oscar for Best Actress. Next to Lucille Ball, Moore is probably television's most recognizable performer, having spent several successful years as the perky, vibrant Mary Richards of *The Mary Tyler Moore Show*. As Beth, Moore is definitely cast against type, but in tackling the role, she not only destroys a vivid television image, but also manages to infuse Beth with admirable and sympathetic qualities when it would have been easy simply to have portrayed the character as a monster. *Ordinary People* represents a change of career directions for Moore, as also evidenced by her work in the Broadway play *Whose Life Is It, Anyway?*, for which she received a Tony Award for her portrayal of a quadriplegic woman.

Although most critics commended Sutherland for his sensitive portrayal as Cal, he was the only one of the film's principals not to receive an Oscar nomination. Paradoxically, *Ordinary People* represents some of his finest work, as Sutherland convincingly and often painfully elicits Cal's growing realizations about Beth. His agony is especially moving when he confronts Beth about her demands for orderliness at Buck's funeral, when she makes him change his shirt and shoes for the service. As Dr. Berger, Hirsch manages to be hard-edged as well as sensitive. Berger is the film's undisputed voice of reason, but more importantly, he insightfully guides Conrad toward truth and a new future. A frequent performer on Broadway, Hirsch is probably best known for his work in the television series *Taxi* and *Delvecchio*. He also starred in the critically acclaimed miniseries, *The Law*. For his work in *Ordinary People*, Hirsch received a Best Supporting Actor Oscar nomination, but lost to costar Hutton.

Ordinary People was honored with the 1980 Academy Award for Best Picture. Alvin Sargent was also honored with an Oscar for his screenplay, as was Redford for his directorial debut. After accepting the gold statuette, Redford talked with the press and speculated that the film's success might be indicative that "perhaps there is a change coming—one that has to do with the human emotion."

Pat H. Broeske

OTHELLO

Released: 1965
Production: Anthony Havelock-Allan and John Brabourne for British Home
  Entertainments; released by Warner Bros.
Direction: Stuart Burge; based on the National Theatre production directed
  by John Dexter
Screenplay: Based on the play of the same name by William Shakespeare
Cinematography: Geoffrey Unsworth
Editing: William Kellner
Running time: 166 minutes

> *Principal characters:*
> Othello .... Laurence Olivier
> Desdemona .... Maggie Smith
> Iago .... Frank Finlay
> Cassio .... Derek Jacobi
> Emelia .... Joyce Redman
> Roderigo .... Robert Lang
> Brabantio .... Anthony Nicholls

Stuart Burge's *Othello* is a valuable filmed record of a performance by the
National Theatre directed by John Dexter in 1964. More significantly, it records a great performance by Laurence Olivier in the title role. Yet, like many
filmed plays, it does not provide much cinematic perspective. The camera is
fixed and confined to the stage set; there is a repetition of composition, no
exterior shots or special effects, and almost no experimentation with camera
angle. Most shots are close-ups, medium close-ups, or long shots. The effect
is that of the theater, in which action occurs within the confines of the pros-
cenium arch.

Indeed, the film demonstrates the difference between the theatrical and
cinematic modes. Those elements which made Olivier's stage performance
so memorable have the opposite effect on film: the camera magnifies the
actor's makeup, facial expressions, and speech and reveals the functional sets
to be poorly colored and lit. While Olivier's Moor, who writhes, slithers, and
gestures across the stage, may be effective in the theater, he is seen too closely
on film. Thus critics charge that Olivier looks too much like a nineteenth-
century American black-face minstrel to be plausible as a Moor.

The film was shot with three widescreen Panavision cameras, and nothing
was cut from the stage version. There are some effective slow dolly shots in
such scenes as the one in which Othello and Desdemona (Maggie Smith) are
reunited upon his return from the Cyprus wars and Lodovico's curtain speech
at the end of the film, but camera movement and montage are generally static
and uncreative. Constance Brown is almost alone among the critics in her

praise for the filming. She says that the modest and objective camera never seems imprisoned, and the cutting establishes a brisk rhythm.

The film opens outside of Brabantio's house at night as Iago (Frank Finlay) promises to help Roderigo (Robert Lang) woo Desdemona. While the cynical Iago lurks in the shadows, Brabantio (Anthony Nicholls) awakens and comes to the balcony. Then, outside his own lodging, Othello toys with a rose and avoids Iago's warning about Brabantio, who enters with armed men to take Othello to the council. At the council chamber Othello is charged with witchcraft; Desdemona tells of his wooing and confirms her love for Othello.

A simple dissolve introduces this council scene in which Othello confronts Brabantio and soothes the Venetian Senate with sweet rhetoric. Rather than appearing in the crimson of his fellow senators, Brabantio wears a black cloak which contrasts with Othello's white tunic and with the crucifix he wears around his neck. Othello is the most active person in the chamber, however, and clearly in command. He also dominates the cinematic composition. The camera catches, in close and medium shots, Othello's well-disciplined, histrionic stage gestures. He rolls his eyes, twists his neck, and squeezes his hands.

Olivier's acting style is well defined in this opening sequence. He is always somewhat larger than life, flamboyant in dress and costume, but always lyrical in speech. This is the language which won Desdemona, soothed the council, and fills the theater. By contrast, Finlay's Iago is more restrained. His speech is more conversational, often clipped, and his costume blends with the nondescript background. He is the only actor whose performance is more for the camera than the stage, and it is Iago who is seen most intensely in close-up. It is powerful acting that sustains this long film performance.

After the council meeting, Iago tells Roderigo to "put money in thy purse" and follow Desdemona to Cyprus. At the harbor in Cyprus, Cassio's warm greeting to Desdemona is observed by Iago, and Othello announces the Turks are drowned. Iago then urges Roderigo to provoke Cassio (Derek Jacobi) to fight and reveals his plan to ruin Cassio. That night an angry Othello stops the drunken Cassio from fighting with Roderigo and Montano, and Cassio leaves with Desdemona. Iago urges Cassio to ask Othello's forgiveness through Desdemona.

The turning point of the play is the scene in which Othello becomes ensnared in Iago's web. Outside his lodging, the Moor sees Cassio leaving Desdemona as Iago comments "I like not that." Iago feeds Othello's suspicion and jealousy until the tortured man rips off his cross and vows revenge. From this point on, the play is in Othello's control. When Desdemona attempts to intercede for Cassio, Othello's self-assurance begins to weaken. He refuses to believe Emelia's defense of his wife. As he exits, Othello casts coins at Emelia (Joyce Redman) as if to pay for the services of a brothel.

Following a scene in which Iago attempts to get Roderigo to murder Cassio,

Emelia helps Desdemona prepare for bed as she sings a willow song and has a premonition of death. Outside, in the Cyprus night, Roderigo wounds Cassio and is stabbed by Iago. In Desdemona's bedroom Othello wakes his wife and tells her to pray. He denies her pleas of innocence and then smothers and strangles her. Emelia enters and accuses Iago, who stabs her. Once Othello learns the truth, he embraces his dead wife and commits suicide. When Othello realizes his mistake and wails over Desdemona's body, there is nothing fake in his lament. Olivier's stupendous performance contains a magnetism and physical presence that only a great stage actor can command. Smith's spirited but mature Desdemona and Finlay's portrayal of Iago's gratuitous malignancy complement Olivier's proud and arrogant Othello. The film, however, remains merely a classic example of great moments in the theater and a testimony to the skill of one of our great actors.

Andrew M. McLean

OUR MAN IN HAVANA

Released: 1960
Production: Sir Carol Reed for Columbia
Direction: Sir Carol Reed
Screenplay: Graham Greene; based on his novel of the same name
Cinematography: Oswald Morris
Editing: Bert Bates
Running time: 111 minutes

Principal characters:
Jim Wormold .... Alec Guinness
Doctor Hasselbacher .... Burl Ives
Beatrice .... Maureen O'Hara
Segura .... Ernie Kovacs
Hawthorne .... Noel Coward
"C" .... Ralph Richardson
Milly ....Jo Morrow
Cifuentes .... Gregoire Aslan
Carter .... Paul Rogers
Lopez ....Jose Prieto

Our Man in Havana is a blend of slick, satirical political humor with moralistic tragedy. Graham Greene, who adapted the screenplay from his own novel, and director Sir Carol Reed unfortunately have not found a visual or an emotional strategy which enables them to escape entirely from this dichotomy; nor have they provided a structure which allows the audience not to care for their individuals and thus feel less keenly when misfortune strikes them. For this reason, the film, while entertaining on a certain level, fails to be completely successful.

The plot illustrates the point that all the fuss about espionage and international intrigue is really over nothing more important than self-perpetuating bureaucracies and official boondoggles. It concerns Jim Wormold (Alec Guinness), who lives in Havana and allows himself to be recruited as a secret agent by Hawthorne (Noel Coward) because he needs money to support the extravagance of his daughter, Milly (Jo Morrow). Wormold pretends to hire subagents and fakes military installations by incorporating the designs of the vacuum cleaners he sells in fanciful renderings. He soon becomes the best agent in the Caribbean and acquires a staff consisting of Beatrice (Maureen O'Hara) and a radio man. Wormold is alternately menaced and flattered by Segura (Ernie Kovacs), the head of the secret police, who suspects him and lusts after Milly. His friend, Dr. Hasselbacher (Burl Ives), commits suicide under mysterious circumstances, and Wormold realizes that a rival vacuum salesman, Carter (Paul Rogers), intends to murder him, but Wormold beats him to it. Segura has Wormold deported to London, where the secret service discovers it has been duped and tries to cover up. They give him a medal and a job training staff and lecturing. As he departs hand in hand with Beatrice, they spot a sidewalk vendor selling toys made in Japan that look very much like Wormold's vacuum cleaner fantasies. Industry has caught up with science.

Our Man in Havana would be a very good political satire if it did not change tone when Dr. Hasselbacher commits suicide. Obscurely implicated in Wormwold's adventures, Dr. Hasselbacher seems to be nothing more than a physician with a shady past, rather like one of Greene's sad lapsed Catholics. He mumbles wistfully abnout perfecting a strain of blue cheese; then Wormold and Beatrice find him dressed up in his Prussian officer's uniform. Next he is dead at his and Wormold's favorite bar. Greene never tells the audience why.

Another problem is the character played by Kovacs. He is the head of the dreaded secret police, and for all his breezy playing, his air of having stepped out of a musical comedy about a banana republic, he is, after all, guilty of torture and murder. Additionally, there is the murder planned by Carter but executed by Wormold, who takes Carter bar-hopping with an air of friendly menace. Wormold starts the festivities off by shooting Carter's pipe as though he is joking, but ends by killing him. "Everything's legal in Havana," Wormold says, referring to the casual immorality, the steamy, sexy ambience around them, and the hustlers in doorways as though this explains his behavior. This is another curious aspect of *Our Man in Havana*. With all the tropical sensuality for atmosphere, Reed is curiously reluctant to use it. Guinness is a rather prim figure, decorously refusing the prostitutes his assistant offers to procure for him and never going farther than holding Beatrice's hand. Perhaps Greene and Reed were well advised to play down this aspect in favor of the comedic slant. Guinness was never a notably romantic actor; he has somewhat weak, wistful eyes and a prim smile—not the usual equipment of a matinee idol. The one element Reed is not at all hesitant to emphasize visually is the streets of Havana. If it is night, they are invariably wet (to reflect the lights) with a rain that has always just passed, and he has an unsettling penchant for shooting them at odd angles. It is as though he cannot forget how successful this device was in *The Third Man* (1949), although he used it less felicitously in *Outcast of the Islands* (1952) and employs it here to stress the mystery/spy facets of this story.

The one totally successful component of the film is Coward's performance. From the moment he enters, utterly correct in his black British suit, casually ignoring the sensual bustle around him, he is a welcome and loony sight. "Don't let me down. You're an Englishman, aren't you?" he asks Wormold when the latter refuses to accompany him to the men's room. Once there, they engage in a silly drill, flushing toilets and nattering about code books and secret ink. Coward reappears from time to time, bringing a refreshing craziness to events that threaten all too often to lose their comic tone and veer off into tragedy. "Bit bumpy over the Azores," he remarks seriously when asked if he has had a good flight to London. At another point, he effortlessly discusses murder and the merits of a planter's punch in the same breath, his poker face betraying not the slightest hint that this is all quite whimsical and improbable.

The rest of the cast is not as fortunate. Guinness sometimes looks uncomfortable in a role that changes from paternal indulgence to lighthearted chicanery to all-too-serious murder and double-dealing. Kovacs renders the "Red Vulture" with a few sly, facile strokes, providing Segura with a broad accent and an even broader style, playing the role with a sort of leering obviousness that is a comment on his own performance. O'Hara has a fairly hapless time of it as Beatrice. She has to be competent and supportive, but she is not given much with which to work, as the character is operating in the dark most of the time. Ives is genial and dignified in a role that is largely a cipher, but at times his German accent slips alarmingly.

Our Man in Havana starts off as a pleasant, low-key diversion, overlong and rambling, but not much more serious than the dippy individuals who inhabit it. Halfway through it swerves toward tragedy and never regains the light sureness it had before it began to take itself seriously. The film cannot make up its mind if it wants to be a sarcastic dig at political *poseurs* or a cautionary fable on the inadvisability of amateurs getting involved in governmental machinations. Greene describes his lighter works as "entertainments," but *Our Man in Havana* is more often scary than entertaining; it is too easy to believe that this is the way some of our historical nightmares get started.

Judith M. Kass

OUR TOWN

Released: 1940
Production: Sol Lesser for Sol Lesser; released by United Artists
Direction: Sam Wood
Screenplay: Thornton Wilder, Frank Craven, and Harry Chandlee; based on
   the play of the same name by Thornton Wilder
Cinematography: Bert Glennon
Editing: Sherman Todd
Running time: 90 minutes

Principal characters:
Mr. Morgan, the narrator	Frank Craven
George Gibbs	William Holden
Emily Webb	Martha Scott
Mrs. Gibbs	Fay Bainter
Mrs. Webb	Beulah Bondi
Dr. Gibbs	Thomas Mitchell
Rebecca	Ruth Toby
Wally	Douglas Gardiner
Professor	Arthur Allen

Although stage drama and film may seem to be remarkably alike, there are enough differences between the two forms to make adapting a stage play for the screen an unusually difficult task. The primary difference between the two is that film is basically visual while stage drama is basically verbal. Although a single sparsely appointed set may be sufficient for a play, film demands more variety and realism in its settings.

Thornton Wilder's *Our Town* presented the adapters (Frank Craven and Harry Chandlee working with Wilder himself) with especially difficult problems. The original play uses very little scenery—just a few tables, chairs, and ladders. For example, an entire house is represented by a table and a few chairs for the kitchen and a ladder for the upstairs bedroom. In addition, the work was very popular and had won a Pulitzer Prize when it opened in 1938. Producer Sol Lesser, who closely supervised the entire making of the film and corresponded frequently with Wilder about it, was therefore determined to be faithful to the play while ensuring that it was effective in the quite different medium of film.

In addition to the technical problems of adaptation, it was important that the film successfully convey the theme of the play as well as its essential flavor. The play, Wilder has written, "is an attempt to find a value above all price for the smallest events in our daily life." It does so in a deliberately simple and folksy manner, employing the stage manager as one of the characters.

His function is chiefly that of a narrator, directly addressing the audience, introducing the other characters and setting up and ending many of the scenes. The adapters did a masterful job of putting the play on the screen. They wisely abandoned the play's lack of scenery and put everything into standard realistic settings. They also made the stage manager into the local druggist but left his speeches and function largely unchanged. In addition, they left the rest of the play basically untouched except for the ending and some minor excisions and rearrangements.

The film opens with Mr. Morgan (Frank Craven), the narrator, simply speaking directly to the audience. "The name of our town is Grover's Corners, New Hampshire," he says and then goes on to describe it in some detail and tell us that the action we are to see begins on June 7, 1901. We then see Dr. Gibbs (Thomas Mitchell) returning from delivering twins in the Polish section of town. We also see his wife (Fay Bainter) preparing breakfast for the family while Mrs. Webb (Beulah Bondi) does the same for her family in the neighboring house. The narrator continues to give us occasional information, such as telling us that Mrs. Gibbs will die in a few years. We meet the Gibbs children, George (William Holden), who is sixteen, and Rebecca (Ruth Toby), who is considerably younger. The Webbs have two children also: Emily (Martha Scott), who is in the same class at school as George Gibbs, and Wally (Douglas Gardiner), who is considerably younger than Emily.

As the narrator will tell us at the beginning of the next section of the film, this first section is meant to present daily life, but in addition to seeing many of the "minor" details of life in Grover's Corners and hearing the past history of the area from a pedantic professor from the State University (Arthur Allen), we learn a good deal about the main characters. George is chiefly interested in baseball, finds schoolwork difficult, and neglects the tasks he is supposed to do for his mother. Emily, on the other hand, is both bright and pretty and not afraid to admit it. She agrees to give George some help with his homework. Dr. Gibbs is perfectly content with his lot in life, but his wife, although basically happy, longs to visit Paris "where they don't talk in English and don't even want to."

Mr. Morgan announces that the second section is on love and marriage. It takes place on July 7, 1904, the wedding day of George and Emily, although it also skips back to the previous year to show the origin of their romance: one day Emily tells George that he has become conceited since he became captain of the baseball team, and by the time the conversation has been concluded in the soda shop the two realize they were meant for each other. The rest of the section is concerned with the myriad details and emotions of a wedding.

Then the action advances to the summer of 1913 and focuses upon the cemetery of Grover's Corners, where we see the gravestones of several of the characters from the earlier parts of the film. We next hear the voices of the dead and see the funeral of Emily who has died in childbirth. During the service in the rain Emily talks to the others who have died, but not until the service is over and the living have left do we see the departed ones as Emily continues to talk with them. She decides that she wants to relive one day of her life. The others try to persuade her not to return to the living, but she decides to do so anyway. We then see the events of her sixteenth birthday with the 1913 Emily all in white and occasionally transparent watching her younger self and the members of her family. She is appalled at how fast it all goes by and how little the living "realize life while they live it." She begins saying over and over "I want to live" as her image changes to the "real" Emily and we see that her baby has been born and that she has survived. Her death and the following events were only a dream or a hallucination. The narrator then appears to close the film and wish us good night.

In the original play, of course, Emily does die, and there is no awakening from the "dream." At first, the film also ended with Emily dead, but a preview audience felt that conclusion too harsh, and the happier version was prepared. When Wilder saw the new version, he agreed with the change because characters in a film are so much more real than the "halfway abstractions" that they are in a stage play. It would, therefore, be "disproportionately cruel" to have Emily die, he said, and the idea of the play "will have been imparted anyway."

Not only the theme of the play but also many of its original techniques are imparted in the film version even though the use of nonrealistic scenery was necessarily abandoned. The use of such devices as an onscreen narrator, characters speaking directly to the camera, and questions from the "audience" all make the film version of *Our Town* a distinctive experience.

Wilder's remarks about the difference between the characters in the stage version and the film version of his play also suggest the difficulty of the task of the actors and actresses. In the stage version the acting needs to convey chiefly the abstract level that is frequently pointed out by the narrator—for example that the story of George and Emily represents Love and Marriage. In the screen version, the actors must not only reflect the abstract level but also must make their characters real and believable as simple, homespun individuals. The task is so difficult that it is no surprise that only one actor in the film, Mitchell as Dr. Gibbs, is completely successful in fulfilling all the demands of his role. Indeed, Mitchell was one of Hollywood's most accomplished character actors although he received only one Academy Award, that for his supporting role in *Stagecoach* (1939). The rest of the cast is generally effective, especially Craven repeating his Broadway performance as the narrator, but as Emily, Scott (also from the Broadway cast), who was twenty-five at the time of filming, seems too old in the early scenes, and Holden is not yet the accomplished actor he was to become.

All in all, the film of *Our Town* in both its strengths and its weaknesses demonstrates the excellence of Wilder's classic play. Conveying simplicity is not a simple task.

Marilynn Wilson

OUTCAST OF THE ISLANDS

Released: 1952
Production: Sir Carol Reed for Lopert Films; released by United Artists
Direction: Sir Carol Reed
Screenplay: William Fairchild; based on the novel of the same name by Joseph Conrad
Cinematography: John Wilcox
Editing: Bert Bates

Principal characters:
Captain Lingard	Ralph Richardson
Peter Willems	Trevor Howard
Almayer	Robert Morley
Mrs. Almayer	Wendy Hiller
Babalatchi	George Coulouris
Vinck	Wilfrid Hyde-White
Hudig	Frederick Valk
Aissa	Kerima
Nina	Annabel Morley

The film version of *Outcast of the Islands* strays far afield from the plot details of Joseph Conrad's original novel, but it manages to keep its spirit intact. It is that spirit of ambition, passion, and decay which pervades, and at times overwhelms Sir Carol Reed's film, that is Conrad's most potent contribution to the story.

Peter Willems (Trevor Howard), dismissed because of his dishonesty by Hudig (Frederick Valk) for whom he had clerked, is taken by Lingard (Ralph Richardson) from Singapore to Simbar, a lonely Malaysian settlement where Lingard is the chief trader. Lingard installs Willems in the home of his agent Almayer (Robert Morley), who has married Lingard's adopted daughter (Wendy Hiller). There Willems rapidly goes to seed. Besides Willems' moral decline there is the additional issue of a rebellion planned by Babalatchi (George Coulouris), the village's head man. He wants to break Lingard's lock on the local trade and establish a native as a rival to Lingard, but he needs to get his goods downriver—a passage with which only Lingard is familiar. Knowing Willems has learned the route, Babalatchi tries to persuade him to throw in with his group. At the same time, Willems has become infatuated with Aissa (Kerima), the chief's daughter, a native temptress, whom Babalatchi makes run away to force Willems to come to terms with them. He does, running cargo for the natives, and defects with Aissa to live apart from the civilized world.

Although Conrad refuses to judge his protagonists, director Reed is not so reticent or compassionate. He lets the characters cast judgment upon themselves by revealing their flaws and idiosyncrasies as soon as the audience encounters them. There is a pointed vignette at the opening involving Pastor Vinck (Wilfrid Hyde-White). The padre, obsequious and unchristian, sneaks around carrying tales, moralizing hypocritically at Willems' disgrace. Lingard is more forgiving; he found Willems as a boy and now takes him in tow again, finding a place for him at Simbar, but unprovidentially neglecting to provide him with useful employment. With time on his hands, Willems all too rapidly falls apart, a transition accomplished symbolically by noting the changes in his clothing. In Singapore, Willems is well turned out in a tie and clean white suit; in Simbar, he lounges around in loose, ragged clothes with his shirt open down the front. This is the Howard of 1952 when he was still playing romantic, virile leading men as in *The Passionate Friends* (1948), *Odette* (1950), and *The Clouded Yellow* (1951), so his character's fall is convincing. He is not some besotted old reprobate; he is a young man with his future before him. Willems' decay is not seen as a tragedy, however; between the pounding native drums, the oppressive heat, and the general air of sensual lassitude, it is inevitable. For example, when Aissa, sloe-eyed and desirable, slinks around in a sarong, Willems' fate is sealed. This sequence is seen partly through the eyes of an orphaned native boy who hero-worships Willems and follows him around, so the split between innocence and sin, while not underlined, is nevertheless evident. Aissa is, perhaps, less a woman than a force of nature, an Eve in search of a serpent. She never speaks, but her glances and her air of palpable sexuality are more eloquent than any words. When Willems is left alone with her at the end of the film, condemned to live with the person that he has come to hate as well as to worship, his predicament is doubly poignant. Their only link is their lust. They do not speak each other's language, and Willems has come to fear Aissa for her cold ferocity as much as he yearns for her animal heat.

The type of character study embodied in this film is a forte of British filmmakers, whether seen in the deftly limned comic antics of Alec Guinness, the middle-class angst of Michael Redgrave in *The Browning Version* (1951), David Lean directing a Noel Coward script like *Brief Encounter* (1946), or, later, John Schlesinger's failed romantics, *Billy Liar* (1963) and *Darling* (1965). Reed was fortunate in having a number of excellent actors for this cast. He casts Richardson as Lingard, a flinty, stubborn old salt who expresses his dismay at Willems' actions but walks a tightrope in trying not to judge the man. He tells him, "You're not a human being to be destroyed or forgiven. You are my shame." Condemnation is unavoidable, however, for with this statement, Lingard banishes Willems forever to the jungle backwater. The casting of Richardson was a miscalculation, however; he was fifty when he made the movie and he looks younger. His old-age makeup sits inappropriately on his face, emphasizing the fact that there is a younger man under those white whiskers.

Morley's performance as Almayer is a *tour de force* consisting of blubbery toadying and browbeating in alternate scenes. Morley has always been good at this sort of servile bluster, and here he has a perfect companion, his real life daughter, Annabel, to play his pudgy, nasty screen offspring, Nina.

Hiller plays the one wholly sympathetic character. Mrs. Almayer's behavior is generous and otherworldly in contrast to the selfish, infantile squabbling in which the men indulge. She makes a civilized home for her husband in the midst of a jungle and tries to make Willems feel welcome. She has observed Willems stalking Aissa and perceptively asks him, "Are you afraid of what she is or what you might become?" She, too, is unwilling to judge Willems, but she lets him know that she understands and cares. Hiller's performance is reticent. Slight smiles illuminate Mrs. Almayer's features, and a wistful pathos steals over her face as she watches the passion of which she knows nothing.

Howard's Willems is masterful. Whether ardent or besotted, he never strains one's credulity. His rough voice aches with need as he says, "I know only the despair of her presence and the agony of her departure." He makes Willems neither pitiable nor larger than life, neither a creature consumed by a grand passion nor an amoral, mean-spirited human being—just a man caught up in political and sexual situations he cannot control or really understand. He is arrogant, confused, and cavalier by turns, a real person displaying authentic emotions, not an actor playing a part. His coarse good looks, contemptuous demeanor, and compliant affability are those of a man made delirious by passion and zeal, a man whose moral principles were none too well grounded to begin with and which shatter under the pressure of intrigue, lust, and the terrible alienation he experiences when cut off from the civilization that previously sustained him.

Reed's direction is commendable, although he occasionally overstates his case while making a point about the squalid backwater to which Willems finds himself consigned. Once the audience has seen elephants and crocodiles gamboling in the river, fleets of natives paddling swiftly through the water, and sexy native dancers, and has heard the rhthymic, pounding drums, they do not need to go through it again. Reed has made his film literally and figuratively overheated, reiterating those factors which drive Willems to the point of madness without adding anything new to one's comprehension of them. It is almost as though Reed were afraid to take a position regarding Howard's emotional and moral bankruptcy and decided instead to fill the screen with spectacle. He is very well served by his locations—Ceylon, Borneo, and Malaya are truly exotic and fill the screen with that atmosphere of fetid excess so necessary to Willems' deterioration. Because Reed never comes to grips with the issue of Willems' culpability, however, the narrative lacks drive, a center on which to focus all the supercharged sensations. He remains coolly outside, the uninvolved narrator dispassionately relating the fervent scheming of his characters.

Judith M. Kass

THE OUTLAW JOSEY WALES

Released: 1976
Production: Robert Daley for Warner Bros.
Direction: Clint Eastwood
Screenplay: Phil Kaufman and Sonia Chernus; based on the novel *Gone to Texas* by Forrest Carter
Cinematography: Bruce Surtees
Editing: Ferris Webster
Music: Jerry Fielding
Running time: 135 minutes

Principal characters:
Josey Wales	Clint Eastwood
Lone Watie	Chief Dan George
Laura Lee	Sondra Locke
Terrill	William McKinney
Fletcher	John Vernon
Jamie	Sam Bottoms
Little Moonlight	Geraldine Keams
Grannie	Paula Treman

Sprawling and yet delivered in episodic fashion, *The Outlaw Josey Wales* presents a main character and story line taken from the classic Western mold. Stunning cinematography and painstaking attention to gritty realism, along with a heroic main character, allow this film to stand out as one of its decade's most satisfying Westerns. Directed by and starring Clint Eastwood, *The Outlaw Josey Wales* adroitly mixes heavy doses of bloody violence with occasional gentle beauty, creating a film which is as poetic as it is brutal.

Although Eastwood has long been a potent box-office force, his acting abilities for the most part have been under-valued by the major critics. His various screen portrayals have been dismissed critically for a number of reasons. He has been accused of delivering cardboard characterizations. The "macho" quality of the Eastwood screen *persona* also has come under fire. His directorial efforts—a series of films mostly falling within the Western and action-adventure genres—have been similarly ignored. Yet at the box office, Eastwood's films are sensations. Acting ability aside, Eastwood has a strong screen presence. Furthermore, his films can always be counted on to contain a strong code of morality. In an Eastwood film, there are good guys and bad guys, right and wrong, and no shades of gray.

The Outlaw Josey Wales is such a film. A sturdy and often thought-provoking film within its genre, it offers especially vivid characterizations, as well as a story line that serves as a parable, of sorts, about an honest man in a dishonest society. Josey Wales (Clint Eastwood) is the traditional Western hero, a good man who becomes embittered and vengeful following the deaths of his wife and child. Once a peaceful farmer, Wales's character evolves first into a callous gunman, and later into a man seeking renewed meaning in his life.

Wales's evolution comes slowly during the course of the two-and-a-quarter-hour film, with careful emphasis placed on characterizations and setting. The film is richly detailed and presents Wales's Western odyssey in scenes that maintain a realistic flavor. The film opens during the final days of the Civil War. Wales's farm, on territory along the Kansas-Missouri border, is burned by Northern guerrillas, called Redlegs, and Wales's wife and child are slaughtered. Wales himself receives an ugly saber gash across one side of his face. Although he escapes with his life, the gash remains. In a purely visual sense, these opening moments set the mood for the rest of the film. They are swift and violent, marked by full-screen images of horses ridden furiously into senseless battle by guerrillas who remain mostly faceless villains. The camera focuses on closeups of legs, boots in stirrups, and panting horses.

Josey Wales cannot combat the guerrillas alone, so he joins a ragtag band of Southern guerrillas who become a sort of substitute family for Wales. They, too, are slaughtered by the Redlegs, however, when they are tricked into surrender by the Union soldiers. Terrill (William McKinney), their leader, is the same man who led the bloody attack on the Wales farm. After conferring with Terrill, the leader of the Southern band, Fletcher (John Vernon), talks his men into surrender, thus unwittingly sending them to their deaths. Although Terrill's betrayal haunts him, he is also a realist, and when Wales escapes, he and Terrill form an uneasy alliance and begin to hunt Wales down, both realizing that neither of them will be safe as long as Wales is alive. To expedite their mission, they put a bounty on Wales's head.

Wales journeys West, planning eventually to take refuge in Mexico. Wanting only to be his own man and to remain safe, he nevertheless finds himself caught up in a series of adventures with a group of eccentric characters who share a common bond with Wales: they have all known despair and a sense of loss. They range from a philosophical (and, for the audience, humorous) old Indian to a too-proud group of Jayhawkers heading West. Through Wales's encounter with these people, the gentle side of his nature is revealed. He first finds himself caring for Jamie (Sam Bottoms), a young Southern guerrilla who is wounded during the ambush. Jamie, who escapes with Wales, dies on the trail, after first saving Wales from a pair of murderous bounty hunters.

Lone Watie (Chief Dan George) is an old Indian whose woman and child died on the Trail of Tears. His incessant philosophical chatter and offbeat quality grate on Wales, but he can do little to shake the homeless old man. Little Moonlight (Geraldine Keams), the slave-squaw of a cruel storekeeper, wants to stay with Wales and Lone Watie after Wales comes to her rescue, gunning down the merchant. Wales even garners a four-legged traveling companion, a mangy dog. After rescuing members of a Kansas wagon train from a bloodthirsty gang of comancheros, Wales winds up helping to escort an elderly woman (Paula Treman) and her granddaughter, Laura Lee (Sondra Locke), to an Arizona farm, once owned by the woman's son.

As a director, Eastwood successfully keeps the audience firmly on Wales's side throughout his many adventures. There is a great deal of violence in this film, but it always has a purpose in the story line. When Wales's own guerrilla band is ambushed and slaughtered, Wales retaliates by taking charge of a gattling gun, mowing down the opposition. The comancheros are gunned down by Wales as they attempt to rape a terrified Laura Lee. The violence subsides for a period when the Wales party reaches the Arizona farm. The dry, rugged terrain, located near a ghost town populated by aging cowboys and a saloon floozie, appears as a paradise to the homeless stragglers. Their enthusiasm proves catching, as Wales finds himself caught up in the group's efforts to build a new home. Lone Watie and Little Moonlight, now a couple, are eager to pitch in; the grandmother is quick to grab a broom and begin cleaning; even the last residents of the ghost town join in, anxious to see renewed life in the area. Meanwhile, the wide-eyed, virginal Laura Lee has caught Wales's interest. He finds his cynicism beginning to erode briefly, until more violence breaks out.

This time, Wales finds himself playing the role of mediator. A Comanche chieftain and his tribe have attacked the small farm, and Wales must arrange a peace pact, so that everyone—Indians and settlers—can survive. Meeting with the stern chief, he admits "I come here to die with you, or live with you. Dyin' ain't hard for people like you and me. It's the livin' that's hard." After coming to terms with the Indians, the settlers enjoy a brief respite from violence.

When Terrill and Fletcher track Wales down, however, it appears that bloodshed is once again imminent. Wales guns down Terrill, but is able to come to a kind of alliance with Fletcher. "The war's over," says Fletcher, who plans to file a death report on Wales, despite the fact that he knows that Wales is alive. It is Fletcher's way of achieving his own sense of peace.

The Outlaw Josey Wales marks Eastwood's fifth directorial effort, and his most serious-minded one. It is a sturdy Western offering colorful characters against an epic panorama. Eastwood is particularly effective in a role which seems tailor-made for his talents, that of a good man caught up in an odyssey against evil. As a Western, this film is devoid of any tell-tale 1970's slang, and there are no modern-day anachronisms within the story line. *The Outlaw Josey Wales* never falters in its depiction of the heroic Old West. Skillful direction has resulted in a film which delivers the classic Western confrontations in a straight-laced, rather than campy, manner.

Where Eastwood's films are concerned, critical snobbery may be due, in part, to his modest beginnings. Following a costarring role in the television series, *Rawhide*, Eastwood went to Italy and appeared in a trio of "spaghetti" Westerns. As the enigmatic Man With No Name, he literally blasted his way to fame in *A Fistful of Dollars* (1964), *For a Few Dollars More* (1965), and *The Good, the Bad and the Ugly* (1966). After snaring the attention of American filmmakers, Eastwood delivered additional Western characterizations. He also ventured into the action-adventure genre with the role of Harry Callahan, a hard-edged San Francisco cop and a man with a firm moral code, in *Dirty Harry* (1971). *Dirty Harry* was directed by Don Siegel, and the Eastwood-Siegel collaboration has since proved to be a long and successful one, including films such as *Two Mules for Sister Sarah* (1970), *The Beguiled* (1971), and *Escape from Alcatraz* (1979). While Eastwood garnered recognition for his work with Siegel, however, he also branched out on his own. His films include the contemporary thriller *Play Misty for Me* (1971) and a clever Western with supernatural overtones entitled *High Plains Drifter* (1973).

It is *The Outlaw Josey Wales*, however, which best benefits from the Eastwood style. Eastwood is at ease in the Western genre; simply put, he plays a good convincing cowboy. As a director, he also has a special flair for vividly capturing the West as it once might have been. From a distance, *The Outlaw Josey Wales* can be viewed as a classic tale about good versus evil. Up close, the film takes on heavier, more philosophic notes, as Wales becomes a kind of Everyman, temporarily out of touch with a life that has dealt him injustice.

Supporting players lend this film additional strength. Chief Dan George, who is able to merge sly humor with moving tragedy—as he did in *Little Big Man* (1970), for which he was nominated for an Oscar—stars as Lone Watie. Vernon, the veteran character actor often cast as a "bad guy," is the betrayer, Fletcher. Locke, the wispy blonde actress often associated with Eastwood films (such as *The Gauntlet*, 1978, and *Every Which Way But Loose*, 1979), is effective as the dreamy Laura Lee. A fine score by Jerry Fielding, another name often linked with Eastwood's works, gives the film a rousing musical heritage.

As is usually the case with Westerns, *The Outlaw Josey Wales* failed to capture Academy Award interest (with the exception of Fielding's score, which took a nomination). It was successful at the box office, however, and for a change, some of the critics viewed Eastwood's work with interest.

Pat H. Broeske

THE OWL AND THE PUSSYCAT

Released: 1970
Production: Ray Stark for Rastar; released by Columbia
Direction: Herbert Ross
Screenplay: Buck Henry; based on the play of the same name by Bill Manhoff
Cinematography: Harry Stradling and Andrew Laszlo
Editing: Margaret Booth
Running time: 97 minutes

Principal characters:
Doris	Barbra Streisand
Felix	George Segal
Barney	Robert Klein
Dress Shop Proprietor	Allen Garfield
Eleanor	Roz Kelly
Rapzinsky	Jacques Sandulsecu
Mr. Weyderhaus	Jack Manning

The Owl and the Pussycat stars Barbra Streisand, who won an Academy Award for *Funny Girl* (1968), as Doris, the "pussy cat" of the title, and George Segal as the owl, Felix. The romantic comedy reunited several of the notable artists who helped to make *Funny Girl* such a success: producer Ray Stark, director Herbert Ross, and cinematographer Harry Stradling, in addition to Streisand. The screenplay was written by Buck Henry, best known for his screenplay for *The Graduate* (1967) and *Heaven Can Wait* (1978), in which he was also a featured actor.

Based on Bill Manhoff's successful Broadway play of the same name starring Alan Alda and Diana Sands, the film is the zany story of a somewhat improbable romance between a prissy, down-trodden book-store clerk named Felix (born Fred) Sherman and a part-time hooker (who is also a model and would-be-actress) named Doris Wadsworth/Wellington/Waverly/Washington/Winters (born Wilgus). As the film opens, Doris is trying to catch a bus in the rain. Soggy, fake-fur minicoat askew, and white vinyl boots planted defiantly, she snaps her juicy fruit gum and curses at the departing bus in the finest New York tradition.

With a resigned shrug, Doris slouches into a passing car that offers refuge from the rain (and also the prospect of making a few dollars). Her destination is a grubby, brownstone tenement where, with lights blazing, television blaring, and curtains gaping, Doris does what is necessary to make ends meet. At the same time, across the courtyard, Felix Sherman peers intently through his horn-rimmed glasses while crouching over his typewriter trying to complete his elusive potential best-seller. Distracted by the blaring television, Felix gets a pair of powerful field glasses and clinically observes the source of his distraction and subsequent aggravation. Because he is frustrated and because his patience and understanding have been pushed to the breaking point by a publisher's rejection slip received only a few hours earlier, he reports the clandestine liaison to the landlord.

After having been asked very brusquely to leave, Doris goes to Felix's apartment in a rage. Her thunderous knock is greeted by the threatening snarls of a trained doberman on full alert. "Wolf," it turns out, is simply a tape recording, but, coupled with the assortment of locks, chains, and dead-bolts on the inside of the apartment door, the audience's laughter is tinged with uneasiness over the realism that lies beneath the surface of this amusing scene. Bristling with rage, Doris explodes in anger, and when she learns that the "fink" has been training binoculars on her bedroom window, she is even more enraged.

Segal plays the poor, inept intellectual with such authenticity that we find it almost impossible to remember him in his roles as rugged leading men. An actor of much depth and versatility, he earned an Academy Award nomination for his supporting role in *Who's Afraid of Virginia Woolf?* (1966), and has earned critical acclaim for his comic roles in *No Way to Treat a Lady* (1968) and *The Southern Star* (1969).

The scene within Felix's apartment is fast-paced and, at times, hilarious. Having cowed Felix into allowing her to spend the night, Doris slips into a see-through nightgown with large pink hands appliqued across her well-endowed bosom. Complete with pom-poms and a simulated diamond heart situated in a strategic location, her outfit, obviously meant to be provocative, arouses only amusement. Having successfully torn apart Felix's apartment, his life-style, and every facet of his personality, Doris proceeds to attack his physique, a subject that amuses her so much that she develops a bad case of hiccups. Drinking water does not help, and even holding her breath does not stop them, so, in desperation, Felix dons a dusty skeleton costume left over from a halloween party and attempts to scare her out of her hiccups. He looks so patently ridiculous, and his appearance is so incongruous with the image of a serious-minded intellectual, that the entire apartment scene becomes a hilarious spoof. It is Segal at his best, playing the poor fool with a talented comic's fine sense of timing.

The problem of the persistent hiccups is finally solved, but their real problems are just beginning, for the landlord, besieged by complaints from Felix's neighbors, evicts them from the apartment building. The heavy winds and the late hour notwithstanding, they eventually go to the apartment of one of Felix's coworkers, Barney (Robert Klein), who incredulously lets them in and graciously offers them the use of his living room for the night. Unable to sleep without her television to pacify her, Doris asks Felix to read his book; but he barely gets beyond the opening line, "The sun spit morning into Julian's face . . .," when he is stopped by her look of incredulity. A heated argument follows after which Barney and his girl friend leave the apartment in disgust. The night finally ends with the mismatched Doris and Felix making love. In the harsh reality of morning, however, they go their separate ways, because neither is ready to risk exposing the vulnerability that would either cement or destroy their relationship, Felix returns both to the Doubleday Book Store at which he works, and to his rich and virginal fiancée. Doris moves in with her friend Eleanor (Roz Kelly), surviving on the few dollars she picks up in the evenings as a go-go dancer in a sleazy corner bar.

Felix and Doris meet again at Doris' instigation and make love in his fiancée's home. Because the owners are away, Doris and Felix freely make love and smoke marijuana in a bathtub until the family's unexpected return. The climax of the film occurs later in Central Park. Harsh words of criticism are followed closely by tentative confessions of love that strip away the last vestiges of pretense. Doris admits that her true name is Wilgus. She is a small-town girl, toughened on the outside by the big city but still frightened on the inside. Fred throws his fabricated name "Felix" into a pond along with his typewriter, for both are symbols of the idealistic dreams that blinded his perception of reality and consequently of himself.

There is no question that *The Owl and the Pussycat* is an entertaining film, and the cinematography begun by Stradling and completed by Andrew Laszlo captures New York City in all its vibrance and filth. The film has its flaws, however; Streisand's performance is much too stereotyped to be entirely believable; it borders on coarseness with her voice and attitude taking on a hard edge and a belligerency that belie her supposed "heart of gold." The vulnerability lurking beneath her hard exterior is too obscured, and when it surfaces in the final scenes, we tend to doubt its validity. Vulgarity is one of the basic devices employed by Ross and Henry in an effort to give an air of authenticity to Streisand's role and also to create a marked contrast to Felix's intellectual dissertations. Rather than incorporate vulgarity as a normal part of Doris' conversation, however, Ross attempts to derive as much humor from it as possible, and as a result it comes across as obscenity for obscenity's sake.

Segal gives the character of Felix Sherman a sad/funny pathos with which the audience can identify. One may despise him for his weaknesses, but one also feels sorry for his failures and eventually admires him for having the courage to face himself and accept who he really is. Considered separately, both Streisand and Segal give noteworthy performances, but as a couple they do not work well together. She simply overwhelms him with her volatile, explosive personality and scathing satire. Segal's is a subtler humor. He plays a poor fool who smolders occasionally but lacks the combustability to burst into flames. Their attraction is somewhat implausible because their chemistry does not come through on the screen. Oddly enough, the story seemed to work better on the stage where the white Alda and the black Sands made a more believable pair of opposites who have a mutual attraction.

D. Gail Huskins

THE PALEFACE

Released: 1948
Production: Robert L. Welch for Paramount
Direction: Norman Z. McLeod
Screenplay: Edmund Hartmann and Frank Tashlin, with additional dialogue by Jack Rose
Cinematography: Ray Rennahan
Editing: Ellsworth Hoagland
Song: Jay Livingston and Ray Evans, "Buttons and Bows" (AA)
Running time: 91 minutes

> *Principal characters:*
> "Painless" Peter Potter .... Bob Hope
> Calamity Jane .... Jane Russell
> Governor Johnson .... Charles Trowbridge
> Big Joe .... Jeff York
> Patient .... Nestor Paiva

Although Bob Hope's early career included vaudeville and Broadway musical comedy, it was principally in radio that he established the great popularity in the 1930's that led to his screen career. He appeared in his first feature film in 1938, and within three years he was ranked fourth in the annual Top Ten Box Office Stars poll of film exhibitors. Hope achieved this popularity in film in the famous series of Road films with Bing Crosby and Dorothy Lamour, as well as in many other films that were popular at the box office in the 1940's, such as *My Favorite Blonde* (1942) and *Let's Face It* (1943). Widely regarded as Hope's best film, however, is the 1948 Western comedy *The Paleface*. The film costars Jane Russell, who had made her film debut in *The Outlaw* in 1941; but because of problems with censorship, that film had not been widely seen. It had, however, produced a tremendous amount of publicity for Russell as a sex symbol, and thus the combination of Hope and Russell on a marquee virtually guaranteed that *The Paleface* would be a financial success.

Scriptwriters Edmund Hartmann and Frank Tashlin devised a clever vehicle to use the talents and reputations of both Hope and Russell. Hope's usual screen character was wise-cracking, inept, and cowardly. He was by no means a romantic hero, so the idea of having him win the heart of Russell through his personality or through brave deeds would not work. Instead, the plot has Russell marry Hope for an ulterior motive, and it is she who performs the heroic deeds, although Hope gets the credit.

The film is a comic Western, but it is not really a spoof or parody of the genre. Most of the conventions of the film Western are adhered to rather than inverted, and only Hope plays his role in a comic manner. The premise of the film is that Calamity Jane (Jane Russell), a tough woman who is an expert with a gun, is released from jail (in a staged jailbreak) and offered a pardon by the Governor of the state (Charles Trowbridge) if she will find out the identity of the "white renegades" who are smuggling guns to the Indians. She is to abandon her buckskin clothing, dress as a lady, and travel with a wagon train as the wife of a lawyer who is also helping the government.

Jane accepts the Governor's offer, but she soon finds that the lawyer has been killed. A group of outlaws also try to kill her while she is taking a bath, but she shoots all three of them. Meanwhile, in the same building, we have met "Painless" Peter Potter (Bob Hope), a bungling dentist who has to consult a book frequently during his work. When a particularly rough patient (Nestor Paiva) becomes understandably enraged because Potter pulled the wrong tooth, Potter wisely decides to leave town. Jane sees his departing wagon as a way for her to join the wagon train as planned; so she joins him without waiting for an invitation. Then she persuades him to marry her so that she will have a husband with whom to travel. Because she does not explain her mission or her reason for the marriage, numerous scenes of misunderstanding and frustration are set up. The wedding, incidentally, is portrayed in one long close-up that shows only the hands of Potter, Jane, and the minister, and most of the action consists of Potter fumbling with the ring.

In the rest of the plot, Potter accidentally becomes a hero when it appears that he has shot eleven Indians and saved the wagon train. Actually, the shooting was done by Jane, but not even Potter realizes this. He receives the adulation of crowds and believes he is the man they think he is. He puts on an outlandish cowboy outfit, marches into the saloon, and soon orders the meanest man in town, Big Joe (Jeff York), to leave by sundown. When sundown comes, he goes into the streets for the inevitable shootout. Joe and Potter, however, wander around a long time before they see each other. When they do, Jane shoots Joe from her hiding place, and once again Potter gets credit for a heroic deed. All the while, however, Jane has made him keep his distance even though they are husband and wife; she even leaves him briefly, and two or three times she hits him in the back of the head with the butt of a gun while she kisses him. In a variation on this gag, Potter goes around a partition with his eyes closed to kiss Jane, but she is not there; instead there is an Indian, who hits him with his tomahawk.

Finally, after Potter almost captures an outlaw gang by himself and he and Jane are both captured by the Indians, Jane tells him the truth about his "heroic" deeds, but she also tells him that he is the "kindest and bravest man" she has ever known; she even proves that she loves him by kissing him without hitting him. Just as the Indians are going to execute both of them, Potter gets away and considers saving himself by leaving Jane with the Indians, but an offscreen voice convinces him to go back to save her. The voice functions much like the Humphrey Bogart figure Woody Allen used many years later in *Play It Again, Sam* (1972).

In a wild, action-packed finale, Potter rescues Jane and they escape from the Indians and the renegades. The last scene shows Potter and Jane leaving on a real honeymoon. Throughout the film another running gag has been the fact that nearly every time Potter tries to leave some place in his wagon, the horses drag him away by the reins and leave the wagon behind. This time Jane takes the reins, and the horses drag her off through the streets of the town. Potter turns to the camera and says, "What do you want, a happy ending?"

Besides the humorous Western plot, Hope's ability to deliver quips, and Russell's physical charms, *The Paleface* offers an Academy Award-winning song that became a big hit and is now a standard, "Buttons and Bows." In the film, however, the song is given no special treatment; it is sung in an almost offhand manner by Hope. As he sings it in the front of his covered wagon, he fails to watch where he is going, and Russell falls asleep; this causes the wagon to go in the wrong direction and leads them into Indian country, where they are attacked. The song became enormously popular between the time the film was written and its release, causing some people to wonder why it was not given a bigger place in the film.

The Paleface is also interesting to today's audience because it shows the obvious influence Hope has had on Allen. Allen has often cited Hope as one of the comedians he most admires and by whom he has been influenced, and *The Paleface* is ample evidence for that statement. Not only does it have the voice advising the hero cited above, but also the Hope film *persona* is much like the Allen one—the good-hearted but inept man whose main weapon is the wisecrack. Indeed, most of Hope's speeches in this film would fit perfectly into one of Allen's early films. *The Paleface*, therefore, was both a hit with audiences of the 1940's (number twelve at the box office in 1948) and an influence upon today's films.

Marilynn Wilson

THE PALM BEACH STORY

Released: 1942
Production: Paul Jones for Paramount
Direction: Preston Sturges
Screenplay: Preston Sturges
Cinematography: Victor Milner
Editing: Stuart Gilmore
Running time: 88 minutes

Principal characters:
Gerry Jeffers	Claudette Colbert
Tom Jeffers	Joel McCrea
"Princess"	Mary Astor
John D. Hackensacker III	Rudy Vallee
"Wienie King"	Robert Dudley
Toto	Sig Arno

Almost all of Preston Sturges' films can be categorized as comedies of error. Deception, confusion, and mistaken identities abound in his work. *The Palm Beach Story* is no exception to this rule. As the titles appear and the allegro movement from the "William Tell Overture" (intertwined with strains from the "Wedding March") commences, a couple rushes about madly, preparing for their wedding. As each title card is superimposed, the erratic action freezes briefly and then begins again. Although this sequence of events rolls by at a fairly rapid pace, we still manage to notice a few strange and seemingly unexplained occurrences. While the woman, Gerry (Claudette Colbert), is dressing for the wedding, Sturges cuts to a closet where another Colbert is tied up. Concurrently the man, Tom (Joel McCrea), seems to be running *away* from "something" as much as *to* the wedding. For the moment all this remains mysterious, however; and after the sequence ends and the couple is before the altar, the camera tracks back past a title which reads "And They Lived Happily Ever After." As a discordant and crashing note is struck in the "Wedding March," the camera continues to move back until it reveals the final title: "Or Did They?"

Five years pass, and the audience is reintroduced to the happy couple and their now financially plagued marriage. Although both Gerry and Tom Jeffers love each other deeply, Gerry's materialism leads her to desert her inventor-husband in order to find a wealthier prey. After receiving the necessary traveling cash from the half-deaf, love-smitten "Wienie King" (Robert Dudley), she departs for Palm Beach, Florida, the haven of the rich.

Arriving at the train station, she devises a plan to obtain a ticket, having spent most of the money the "Wienie King" gave her on clothes and back rent. A club of millionaires dedicated to hunting (The Ale and Quail Club) are boarding the train at the same time, and deftly exploiting her charms, she manages to wheedle a ticket out of the frugal millionaires (they all contribute to make up her fare after considerable discussion). Frugality is not their only composite quality, however; they also have a monumental disregard for the lives and property of others. While in their private club car, one of the more inebriated members delivers a challenge to another and a shooting spree ensues. Hunting dogs bark, shotguns blast, and furniture and windows are splintered, until at last the three conductors are forced to disconnect the car. As the train deserts them the millionaires fire a few more shots into the air, registering their indignation.

While still on the train Gerry encounters—by climbing on his face to reach her berth—another variant of the species "idle rich." This one is, however, the most highly developed specimen—a billionaire. John D. Hackensacker III (Rudy Vallee), is a rather Victorian gentleman, very much an anachronism. He spends most of his time adjusting his pince-nez and recording each of his expenses, no matter how small, in a notebook. Furthermore, Hackensacker exemplifies a deep distaste for his wealth, or, rather, the peripheral drawbacks of being a billionaire. He says ever so sadly, "When money reaches certain proportions you can't ignore it any more than you can . . ." Gerry: "A horse in a bedroom." Hackensacker: "I wasn't thinking exactly of that, but it'll serve."

Meanwhile Tom has returned to his apartment after an unsuccessful pursuit of Gerry. Again the "Wienie King" appears out of nowhere and like a fairy godfather gives him the money to go and search for his estranged wife. Tom takes a plane to Palm Beach and arrives in time to greet Hackensacker and Gerry and to meet Sturges' final specimen of the idle class. She is an oft-married female, Hackensacker's sister—the "Princess" (Mary Astor), who is not above using her fortune to buy men, especially when they possess physical attributes such as Tom's. Her reply to a later inquiry as to whether she thinks of anything but sex is, "Is there anything else?" The nonchalance with which she flaunts her "kept man," Toto (Sig Arno)—a Max Sennett-like creation who seems to take most of the pratfalls in this film and for whom Sturges invents a nonsensical foreign language—is only surpassed by her "no-holds-barred" attitude in tracking down her newest prey—in this case, Tom.

Although unhappy with the whole situation, Tom is forced by Gerry to pose as her brother. In this way her plans can progress without a hitch. If all goes well, Gerry will have Hackensacker as a husband, and her "brother" will have enough money to finance his revolutionary new airport. For the rest of the film the plot spins dizzily around the complications arising from this masquerade: Hackensacker asking Tom's permission to marry Gerry; the "Princess" proposing to Tom, and so forth. By the final reel, however, the upright Tom has won out, finally seducing his own wife while the unwitting Hackensacker serenades her from below. For once, monetary considerations have been subordinated to love. The next morning they break the news to Hackensacker and his sister. The billionaire is shocked and disappointed, but not enough to keep from asking, "I don't suppose you have a sister?"

In a twist of plot worthy of William Shakespeare or William Congreve, Sturges changes the scene to the same wedding chapel of the titles. There, before the altar, the camera reveals Tom and Gerry, Hackensacker and Gerry's twin sister, and the "Princess" and Tom's twin brother—all united in wedlock. Now, for the first time, we understand the presence of the two Colberts and the seemingly haunted McCrea in the title sequence. Both of the couple's twins obviously had designs on the prospective bride and groom. With this delightful surprise ending, Sturges brings his farce to a properly happy resolution, but not without a tinge of world-weary cynicism. As the camera tracks back, the titles from the opening sequence are repeated: "And They Lived Happily Ever After" and then "Or Did They?"

James Ursini

THE PANIC IN NEEDLE PARK

Released: 1971
Production: Dominick Dunne for Twentieth Century-Fox
Direction: Jerry Schatzberg
Screenplay: Joan Didion and John Gregory Dunne; based on the novel of the same name by James Mills
Cinematography: Adam Holender
Editing: Evan Lottman
Running time: 110 minutes

Principal characters:
Bobby	Al Pacino
Helen	Kitty Winn
Detective Hotchner	Alan Vint
Hank	Richard Bright
Sammy	Warren Finnerty
Marcie	Marcia Jean Kurtz
Marco	Raul Julia
Santo	Vic Ramano

"The intersection at Broadway and 72nd Street on New York's West Side is officially known as Sherman Square. To heroin addicts it is Needle Park." This opening caption tells a great deal about *The Panic in Needle Park*—it is one of the fashionable crop of "New York films" of the late 1960's and early 1970's, shot entirely on location, interiors as well as exteriors, on the Upper West Side; and it is a film about drug addiction. Such basic information was seemingly enough to put most people off, not only because it promised to be a depressing film, but also because it came in the wake of a series of "drug" movies such as *Chappaqua* (1967), *The Trip* (1967), and *More* (1969). This may account for the limited commercial success enjoyed by *The Panic in Needle Park*, despite it's being an official American entry at the Cannes Film Festival and even despite its lead actress, Kitty Winn, bringing back the Best Actress award.

There is, however, one element which is not covered by the opening caption, and an element that everyone connected with the film—producer, writer, director, and stars—have constantly emphasized ever since: it is also a love story. In this respect, *The Panic in Needle Park* is in the best tradition of the story of adolescent lovers trapped in a criminal or semicriminal milieu in which their love becomes impossible or at the very least threatened with doom, like that of Farley Granger and Cathy O'Donnell in *They Live by Night* (1949), or James Dean and Natalie Wood in *Rebel Without a Cause* (1955). At no time, however, does Joan Didion and John Gregory Dunne's screenplay or Jerry Schatzberg's direction adopt a moralizing attitude toward its junkies, as earlier films tended to do. Heroin is a part of their lives, so much a part that it virtually destroys them, and to show that process makes explicit moralizing unnecessary.

The Panic in Needle Park has the appearance of a documentary in the muted tones of Adam Holender's extraordinary location cinematography, both in the streets around Needle Park, on the intersection itself (less a Park than a traffic island), and in the grubby, depressing rooms and hallways of New York's Upper West Side. Coupled with this setting is the plot structure of a melodrama: a girl recovering from an abortion falls in love with a junkie, picks up his habit, and, in order to avoid jail herself, "sells" him to a detective from the Narcotics Bureau. Amazingly, the film is neither documentary nor melodrama, not so much because one cancels out the other as because neither is allowed to get in the way of a straightforward, restrained, and brilliantly economical bit of storytelling.

The cast, all of whom are professional actors, spent a month and a half living on the Upper West Side preparing the picture, and Kitty Winn in particular spent much of her time with Maryann, an ex-addict whose background was very similar to that of Helen in the movie. This kind of preparation is worth stressing because it is a key to the film's style and achievement: it is a compellingly realistic picture of a certain way of life, neither glamorized nor given the appearance of a nightmare, but shown in its everyday concerns: scoring, shooting up, and coming down.

The film became somewhat notorious at the time of its release for the two close-up injection sequences which document the process from the tightening of the strap through to the blood flowing back up the dropper's neck. At the same time, it is equally important to stress that *The Panic in Needle Park* is a *story*, not a documentary, focusing on particular destinies rather than on a general problem. It is about Bobby and Helen, who are drug addicts, rather than being about drug addiction as seen in Bobby and Helen. The distinction is crucial.

Nevertheless, the film's documentary appearance is overwhelming, and the story resembles a case history. Helen (Kitty Winn), a young Midwestern girl from a good family, has just had an abortion done as a favor to her artist boyfriend Marco (Raul Julia), and turns up at his loft obviously in pain. He seems unconcerned. This is not true of Bobby (Al Pacino), a young dealer who has come to sell Marco some marijuana; he sees her shivering on a mattress and gives her his scarf. Later, Helen is admitted to the hospital hemorrhaging. Bobby visits her, supposedly to get his scarf back, but when Helen comes out of the hospital, he is waiting for her. He introduces her to his friends in Needle Park, where there is a "panic" (a shortage): "It's election year. So there's no stuff," it is explained. She meets Bobby's brother Hank (Richard Brite), a burglar ("It's my business. It's what I do well") and learns that Bobby is an addict, despite his own claims that he is "only chipping":

"I chip," declares Hank. "He uses." This statement is true. Helen moves in with Bobby and soon realizes that he has a two-hundred-dollar-a-week habit. He asks Helen to go to Harlem to score for him as a test of how much she will do for him. She agrees, but the score goes wrong, and the pusher is picked up in middeal, and Helen has her first meeting with Hotchner (Alan Vint), a narcotics agent known as Hotch, who lets her go but pressures the pusher into setting up a bigtime dealer. "You must remember," he warns Helen, "a junkie always rats. Always."

Watching Bobby one night after he has taken drugs, Helen takes her first needle. She and Bobby decide to marry, but Bobby is arrested during a robbery set up by Hank. While he is in jail, Helen turns to prostitution to "feed her arm"—a fact which Hotch makes sure he tells Bobby when he gets out. At first upset, Bobby learns to live with it. He is working for a dealer, Santo (Vic Ramano), and doing quite well. They take the ferry to Staten Island and buy a puppy, hoping it will represent a fresh start. "Maybe we ought to move. Get an extra room for the dog," he says. On the ferry back, however, they go into the men's room to take heroin, and the puppy, tired of whining outside the door, wanders off to explore and falls over the side; thus the fresh start ends. Helen is later picked up for robbing a client, and Hotch uses this to put pressure on her. Either she "rats" or she ends up in the Women's House of Detention. "It's like a zoo," he warns her. He really wants Santo, but Helen does not know enough, so he says, "Then give me Bobby." He explains that Bobby knows the score; he will give him Santo and "cop a plea" of nonfelonious possession. Bobby sees Helen as he is arrested and spits at her, "I was going to marry you." When Bobby comes out of jail Helen is waiting outside. He walks past her, but then stops, turns and says "Well?" She goes toward him, and they walk away, not talking, not touching, but together.

The ending of the film is typical, hovering between optimism and bleakness, between sentimental happy ending and pathetic rejection, simply recording a pattern of behavior without indicating the motives or the thought processes. It is for moments like this that *The Panic in Needle Park* is memorable, moments which portray a fragile relationship and the world which surrounds it. Bobby and Helen are no angels. She casually robs her clients, and in one unpleasantly comic scene he catches a prep schoolboy client in bed with his "old lady," takes his wallet, and throws him out half-dressed into the hallway with a taunting epithet. Everybody uses everybody, and the Narcotics Bureau most of all. It would be pretentious to call the film a tragedy, but it operates almost exactly on those terms. Bobby and Helen are crushed between the twin millstones of "a vast destructive industry—and a doubly destructive counter-industry, narcotics law enforcement," according to Jacob Brackman in *Esquire*.

It is possible to question the film's self-imposed limits. It shows, but does not explain; the characters suffer, but they do not learn. Junkies do not learn, however, and explanations do not help. *The Panic in Needle Park* is probably no truer than any film about junkies, for the simple reason that the only place that "the truth about junkies" exists is in tabloid sociology. It is a film about two young people who are in love with each other, take drugs, and almost destroy each other in the course of the story; and they will almost certainly do so again, probably fatally. *The Panic in Needle Park* is, perhaps, a difficult film in a number of ways; it is difficult to watch (especially if one does not like needles), difficult to like, and, most of all, difficult to dismiss. The only sense in which it is inaccessible is that, having acquired a reputation as yet another semidocumentary about drug abuse, it unfortunately is hard to get to see it in a theater.

Nick Roddick

PANIC IN THE STREETS

Released: 1950
Production: Sol C. Siegel for Twentieth Century-Fox
Direction: Elia Kazan
Screenplay: Richard Murphy; based on Daniel Fuchs's adaptation of the novels
  Quarantine and *Some Like 'em Cold* by Edna Anhalt and Edward Anhalt
Cinematography: Joe MacDonald
Editing: Harmon Jones
Art direction: Lyle Wheeler and Maurice Ransford
Music: Alfred Newman
Running time: 96 minutes

> *Principal characters:*
> Clinton Reed .... Richard Widmark
> Police Captain Tom Warren .... Paul Douglas
> Nancy Reed .... Barbara Bel Geddes
> Blackie .... Jack Palance
> Raymond Fitch .... Zero Mostel
> Neff .... Dan Riss
> John Mefaris .... Alexis Minotis
> Poldi .... Guy Thomajan
> Tommy Reed .... Tommy Rettig
> Kochak .... Lewis Charles
> Mrs. Fitch .... Mary Liswood

"[The plague] was a device, a way of getting into the various sides of the society and the city," director Elia Kazan told an interviewer, talking about *Panic in the Streets*. "We were able to use the terrific color and richness of New Orleans." Kazan's New Orleans venture begins when Blackie (Jack Palance), abetted by Fitch (Zero Mostel) and Poldi (Guy Thomajan), murders Kochak (Lewis Charles), a recently arrived illegal alien, in a card game dispute. The morgue attendant who performs an autopsy on the body suspects the worst, and the United States Public Health Service doctor, Clinton Reed (Richard Widmark), confirms the diagnosis that the victim had been dying of pneumonic plague before the murder. Police Captain Tom Warren (Paul Douglas) disagrees that there is any danger of an epidemic, but, assigned to track down Kochak's killer, he cooperates reluctantly with Reed. The mayor goes along with Reed's insistence that there must be no publicity, otherwise the murderer might leave town along with other panicky citizens, thereby spreading the disease. Clues—rustproof paint and shrimp tracings found on the dead man's clothes—lead Reed to a tramp steamer. When the captain denies knowledge of a stowaway, Reed appeals to the crew, who tell him the man had been aboard. He was Armenian, so Reed and Warren start combing Middle Eastern restaurants. Armed with the victim's photograph, they find the right restaurant, but the owner, John Mefaris (Alexis Minotis), does not understand exactly what they are after and sends them away. His wife, contaminated herself, dies of the plague, whereupon Mefaris admits that he recognizes the man in the picture as having been in his place with Poldi. Blackie suspects Kochak brought contraband into the country, which would explain the police activity, and that Poldi now has the goods. He and Fitch locate Poldi, now ill himself, and coax him to tell where the goods are. Following their first decent lead, Reed and the police arrive. With the officers hot on their trail, Blackie and Fitch flee to a waterfront coffee warehouse where an elaborate chase over bags and down chutes ends at water level among the pilings. Blackie wounds Fitch, who wants to surrender, and attempts to escape up a line leading to a fruit boat. He is stopped by the metal guards which prevent rats from leaving ships and falls into the water. With Blackie and Fitch in custody, it will be easier to trace the course of the contamination, and Reed returns home. As Warren drops Reed off, the radio announces that all the contacts have been found.

Panic in the Streets is a chase melodrama, a *policier* whose suspense is not undermined in the least by the audience's knowledge of the murderer's identity. Kazan is clearly at home with location shooting, as he had been with *Boomerang!* (1947) and would be with *On the Waterfront* (1954) and *Wild River* (1960). His New Orleans seethes with details observed in low-life dives, "greasy spoons," and aboard ships. The opening sequence, culminating in Kochak's death, is revealed in high contrast shots of faces swimming out of the dark, racing figures, and shadows on walls. Kazan is equally at home in the morgue where the attendant, preparing to slice up Kochak, matter of factly discusses a spaghetti lunch with a fellow worker.

The film has a pervasive feeling of claustrophobia—even when showing action in a long shot, as in a scene between Blackie and Fitch, with Fitch's wife (Mary Liswood) moving around in the background. Kazan compresses their figures into the foreground, where the urgency of their confrontation enhances the impression of confinement. Kazan crams Widmark into a cheap and dirty diner for an intense, secretive conversation, behind a car in his garage where he removes his contaminated uniform to keep the infection from his family, and in a ship's cabin for a confrontation with an informant. As Kazan said of the last scene, ". . . there was literally only one place to put the camera," so it is shot entirely from a single angle.

Kazan had decided to "make a picture with as many long shots as possible," so there are few close-ups in *Panic in the Streets*. Much of the action takes place in medium shots, then the camera moves in to a close-up. Kazan uses this technique most effectively when Blackie and Fitch are grilling the feverish Poldi trying to find out what the police are after. Blackie stalks around in the background while Fitch nurses Poldi in the foreground. As Blackie moves forward, the camera stays on him, and when he reaches the other two, they are squeezed into a tight angle. Accomplished without cutting, this technique heightens the tension and emphasizes the lunacy of the characters—Blackie with his insistence that Poldi is holding out on him, and Fitch with his obsequious reassurances.

Kazan is well served throughout by his cast: Palance is at his most cadaverous and skull-like; his soft-spoken delivery has the effect of accentuating the aura of menace he gives off. Mostel is a perfect foil, blubbery and stupid, trying with sweaty desperation to outwit the police and stay on Palance's good side. Widmark, in one of the first roles in which he did not play a gangster or a psychopath, is excellent, quiet, understated, exploding only when crossed by anxious, obstructive bureaucrats.

There is a subplot involving Widmark's family life which is not interwoven with the narrative except to make points about his being overworked and underpaid. Barbara Bel Geddes plays his wife Nancy, supportive, sweet, telling him she is expecting the second child he wants so much while they are unable to embrace because he might be contagious. Douglas' familiar gruff, stubborn *persona* is well integrated with the character of Captain Warren, the not-very-bright cop who proves he has more gumption and integrity than Widmark had given him credit for while resisting the efforts of a persistent reporter to get the lowdown on the plague story.

Richard Murphy, who wrote the script, and Kazan appreciate and understand the human foibles which make these people interesting. They are real and complex; getting along with one another is a matter of compromise and comprehension, of the necessity of seeing the other person's point of view for the good of all. Palance's monomaniacal demands and crazed flight are used as counterpoint to the restrained performances of the others.

Judith M. Kass

PAPER MOON

Released: 1973
Production: Peter Bogdanovich for Paramount
Direction: Peter Bogdanovich
Screenplay: Alvin Sargent; based on the novel *Addie Pray* by Joe David
  Brown
Cinematography: Laszlo Kovacs
Editing: Verna Fields
Costume design: Pat Kelly and Sandra Stewart
Running time: 102 minutes

> *Principal characters:*
> Moses Pray .... Ryan O'Neal
> Addie Loggins .... Tatum O'Neal (AA)
> Trixie Delight .... Madeline Kahn
> Deputy Sheriff Hardin/Jess Hardin ...John Hillerman
> Imogene .... P. J. Johnson

The 1930's have long fascinated American filmmakers, but perhaps nowhere has that decade been more lovingly portrayed than in Peter Bogdanovich's *Paper Moon.* The time is 1936, and a young con man, Moses Pray (Ryan O'Neal), is passing through a small Kansas town. He stops to pay last respects to an old girl friend, now deceased, only to find that within minutes of his arrival he has been pressured into taking the dead woman's orphaned nine-year-old daughter, Addie Loggins (Tatum O'Neal), to her aunt in St. Joseph, Missouri. An expert at taking advantage of any situation, Moses soon cons two hundred dollars out of the brother of the man responsible for the death of Addie's mother in a car wreck. Addie, ever-watchful, overhears the arrangement (unbeknown to Moses) and soon creates a scene in a lunch counter by demanding her money. Addie is also beginning to believe that Moses is her father. ("We got the same jaw.") This only adds to Moses' irritability as he quickly realizes that little Addie is no fool and that the only way to keep her quiet is to promise her he will pay her back.

As Moses and Addie take to the road we find out along with Addie the manner in which Moses makes his living. He sells bibles, personally mono-gramed, to widows whose husbands supposedly ordered them just prior to their deaths. Addie quickly proves herself very adept at joining in this con game as well as improvising a routine enabling her to swindle twenty-dollar bills from confused clerks making change in general stores. Moses soon realizes that Addie is an invaluable additon to his game, and the two become partners.

Addie clings to her few possesions as if her life were at stake. She clings to her radio, her cigar box, and her few clothes, and most of all she clings silently to Moses. Her whole world now revolves around the beloved trinkets, memories of her mother, that are in the cigar box, the continuing radio battle between Fibber McGee and his closet, and a determination to please Moses.

Moses and Addie have managed to acquire quite a bit of money from their con games, but this is quickly depleted when Moses becomes infatuated with a carnival dancer named Trixie Delight (Madeline Kahn). For the first time Addie knows jealousy. Determined to destroy this relationship, Addie treats Trixie with sullenness and hostility, and it is not until Trixie confesses to Addie that she is never able to hold a man's interest for long, that the latter becomes more friendly. Moses, however, continues to squander their diminishing funds. Addie, unable to go along with all of this, enlists the aid of Trixie's black maid Imogene (P. J. Johnson). They conspire to have Moses find Trixie in bed with an amorous desk clerk who believes that Trixie will "put out" for twenty-five dollars. The plan succeeds.

Back on the road again, Moses and Addie successfully carry out a scheme to sell a bootlegger (John Hillerman) crates of his own whiskey for six hundred and twenty-five dollars. Moses and Addie are then arrested by Sheriff Hardin (also played by John Hillerman), the bootlegger's brother, and taken to jail. Sheriff Hardin threatens Moses with a long prison sentence unless he turns over the money. Once more taking the initiative, Addie, who has hidden the money in her cloche, instigates a clever escape, during which Moses eludes the Sheriff in a frantic car chase. Feeling for the first time the pressure of the law, Moses trades in his old car for a dilapidated pickup truck. Moses and an unhappy Addie cross the state line into Missouri. Moses, however, has one more "big" job to do, for which he needs Addie's assistance. Then, as he sets out to meet the bigtime operator who will put their plan into operation, he is seized by Sheriff Hardin. Even though Moses cannot be arrested in Missouri, there is no law that says he cannot be beaten up, so Sheriff Hardin takes all the money and leaves Moses a mess.

It is now time to take Addie to her aunt, and all of her pleas to stay with Moses are to no avail. Addie is warmly welcomed into her relatives' home. It is a lovely home, full of everything a small girl could want, a home that appears as if it does not feel the extreme hardship of the Depression. It is clear that this is not what Addie wants after all, however—at least not yet. While her aunt leaves for a moment to get her a drink of lemonade there is no doubt in the viewer's mind that Addie will not stay. Back on the highway Moses is having trouble with the truck. As he sits there he finds the picture that Addie had taken of herself at the carnival, seated on a paper moon. Suddenly Addie can be seen, a small figure carrying all her possessions running down the road toward Moses. Moses tells her he does not want her riding with him anymore, to which Addie firmly retorts, "You still owe me two hundred dollars!" Without another word Addie climbs into the truck (still clinging to the belief that this rather undemonstrative young man is her father), and Moses and Addie drive off.

By the end of the film we feel that these two cast-off people were meant to be together, at least for awhile. The worst thing that can happen to Addie is that she stays with Moses, but she loves him. Whether he loves her or not is conjectural. Moses probably feels some emptiness when Addie is not there, particularly since he has not had much of a relationship with anybody else, but Moses is not communicative. He does not know how to express his emotions or feelings. He probably has them, but he finds it difficult to be honest with other people and with himself. He is only good when he is conning people. Both Moses and Addie are motivated by greed, Moses to make money, Addie to have Moses, but they are sympathetic characters and totally in accord with their time. Director Bogdanovich fills *Paper Moon* with authentic people and handles them lovingly and carefully. Bogdanovich is notorious for making films steeped in the past, and with *Paper Moon* he demonstrates his love and care for the 1930's. The film's ambience is not used only for nostalgia, however; the Depression background enhances the poignance of this unsentimental love story.

Paper Moon is a brilliantly conceived film, from its unpretentious Art Deco titles, to its fine black-and-white cinematography of the Kansas flatlands by Laszlo Kovacs, to its authentic re-creation of a disturbing period in America's history. The film makes the viewer feel as if he is being placed in a time capsule. The acting is superb on all counts. Although the film was nominated for several Academy Awards, only Tatum O'Neal (who in real life is Ryan O'Neal's daughter), as Addie came away with an Oscar, for Best Supporting Actress. *Paper Moon* is an excellent example of all the right ingredients being brought together at the right time. Bogdanovich has captured a mood with care, tenderness, and respectful admiration of the screen's past.

Bonnie Baty

THE PARTY

Released: 1968
Production: Blake Edwards for United Artists
Direction: Blake Edwards
Screenplay: Blake Edwards, Tom Waldman, and Frank Waldman; based on an original story by Blake Edwards
Cinematography: Lucien Ballard
Editing: Ralph E. Winters
Music: Henry Mancini
Running time: 98 minutes

Principal characters:
Hrundi V. Bakshi .... Peter Sellers
Michele Monet .... Claudine Longet
Rosalind Dunphy .... Marge Champion
Waiter .... Steve Franken
Alice Clutterbuck .... Fay McKenzie
Fred Clutterbuck .... J. Edward McKinley
Princess Helena .... Sharron Kimberly
Wyoming Bill Kelso .... Denny Miller
C. S. Divot .... Gavin MacLeod

It is widely recognized that Peter Sellers was a comic genius in addition to being a very fine actor. The vital energy with which he approached each comic role is evident when viewing the various characterizations that he created throughout his career. His innate acting ability was developed and sharpened in a profound way through his early experience on the vaudeville stage with his parents, who were touring performers. This experience provided him with a strong introduction to a comedic world dominated by slapstick and sight gags. As a result, Sellers never thought it necessary to create a sustaining, easily recognizable comic role in the mold of comedians such as Bob Hope or Jack Benny, who essentially play themselves regardless of whatever film they are in. Sellers considered himself a comic actor who rose to the challenge of creating a new character with each role. Significantly, in an interview with *Time*, he stated that *Being There*, a 1979 film which represents his greatest departure from his usual roles, was his best film, and that Chance the gardener was his favorite character of all the ones he had played. Sellers had a deep sense of restraint and economy in handling his comic characters. For example, his Dr. Strangelove, Chance, and Inspector Clouseau are effective characters because their surface seriousness masks an underlying element of chaos or lunacy. These characters are believable only because of the restraint Sellers imposes upon them. In these roles, he has the crucial ability to maintain a necessary balance between both elements; therein lies his success. A lesser actor, without Sellers' economic and thoughtful approach, would easily dilute and therefore cheapen the portrayals.

Sellers was the master of twenty British dialects and, additionally, had a keen ear which enabled him to detect and interpret subtle nuances and inflections of foreign accents of all kinds in spoken English. This ability, in combination with his formidable talent for mimicry, helped Sellers create a substantial list of outstanding and memorable characters. One of these, Hrundi V. Bakshi in *The Party*, superbly combines and demonstrates Sellers' linguistic and slapstick expertise.

In *The Party*, Bakshi (Peter Sellers) is a stage actor who has had some professional theater experience in his native New Delhi. A Hollywood movie studio has imported him to play the leading role in its film *Son of Gunga Din* in order to provide authenticity. During the filming, however, the accident-prone Bakshi manages to blow up the studio's most valuable set. The studio head, Fred Clutterbuck (J. Edward McKinley), becomes outraged and, writing Bakshi's name on a memo, swears that the Indian actor's Hollywood career is over. The memo finds its way into Clutterbuck's secretary's hands, where it is misinterpreted as the name of another guest to be invited to a swank party that Clutterbuck will be giving. An invitation is sent to Bakshi, who promptly accepts. The major portion of the film takes place at Clutterbuck's posh, modernistic home during the party.

Upon arriving at the Clutterbuck home, the bumbling Bakshi immediately loses his shoe in the indoor pond. This is the first clue that the evening will be composed of one Bakshi blunder after another. During the party, Bakshi manages to walk through Clutterbuck's flower bed, and, somehow, his muddy shoe ends up in the hors d'oeurves. He next accidentally pushes a waiter through a plate glass window and then activates the lawn sprinklers and later slides off the roof into the swimming pool. The whole party deteriorates to a state of pandemonium with Bakshi as the unwitting catalyst. Clutterbuck's daughter, Molly, arrives later in the evening with some friends and a young elephant that they have painted with bright, psychedelic colors. Bakshi becomes upset at this and admonishes the youngsters, pointing out that the elephant is a highly honored creature in his native India. Molly and her friends quickly realize the callousness of their act and decide to wash the elephant in the indoor pool. Several of the tipsy dinner guests join Molly's friends and, before long, the house and garden are inundated with soapsuds. At this point, Clutterbuck recognizes Bakshi as the actor he fired and attempts to strangle him; but Bakshi escapes with an attractive starlet, Michele Monet (Claudine Longet), who had befriended him during the party. As they leave, the police and fire departments arrive, along with an ASPCA truck and an ambulance.

The waiter, Levinson, played by Steve Franken, is an alcoholic who drinks all of Bakshi's drinks throughout the party and gets increasingly drunk. He moves in and out of the action, and it is apparent that director Blake Edwards has created him to provide unity for what could have become a disjointed or episodic plot structure. Henry Mancini's music, *Nothing to Lose*, is another unifying element in the film. This effective song is heard at the beginning, played by musicians. Halfway through the film, it is sung by the starlet who befriends Bakshi, and at the end it is heard again, played instrumentally .

The supporting characters attending the party lend a uniquely "Hollywood" flavor. Among the best are a model (known as "Wiggy"), an effeminate hairdresser, a tipsy sexpot, a star of cowboy movies, a European princess, and a professional clubwoman. This motley group of characters was deliberately designed by director, Blake Edwards, to supply the Hollywood party with "authenticity" on several levels.

The viewer is made to understand that these people are all veterans of the Hollywood party circuit and that this will be another standard affair in the tradition of swank studio parties. One trait that all the guests have in common, however, except for Monet, is the way that they treat Bakshi. They completely ignore him or, at best, patronize him. These are all very shallow people who harbor a false sense of their own importance. In fact, most of them are yesmen for Mr. Clutterbuck. Poor Bakshi moves from one guest to another in a vain attempt to join in a conversation and to get acquainted. Michele Monet, who is also an outsider, identifies with Bakshi and is drawn to him. She, too, has problems. She is expected to provide sexual favors in return for a screen test granted her by C. S. Divot (Gavin MacLeod), a producer who brought her to the party. Both she and Bakshi seem to be innocent victims of this arrogant and absurdly callous group.

Much of the absurdity of *The Party* beyond the antics of Sellers is effected by the subtle and innovative camerawork. There are few close-ups; Edwards instead favors the wide angle picture. The viewer is thus able to observe all sorts of interesting comical activity taking place in the background while following the main action in the foreground. Some of the more amusing events in *The Party* are purposely located away from the center of the screen, and this effect is precisely what makes them humorous. It also adds to the feeling of spreading chaos in the Clutterbuck house.

Rarer yet are the reaction shots that are a traditional technique in comedy films. It appears that Edwards, in a daring departure from tradition, decided to pass over filming the responses of the participants of the various comic scenes. This technique implies that if a scene is truly humorous, the audience does not need a cue from the actors to indicate that it is so. Few directors are willing to go so far out on a limb to prove a point, but Edwards has shown that this approach will succeed if the material is amusing to begin with.

While Edwards' innovative direction of *The Party* is interesting in its own right, it is Peter Sellers' quiet and subtle approach to the role of Hrundi Bakshi that makes the film an unqualified success. As Bakshi, the stranger, moves amongst the guests, feigning conversation and blundering into embarrassing situations, the viewer too becomes an outsider, becomes more and more involved in his keen discomfort, and increasingly sees him as a sympathetic figure. Yet Bakshi is not merely a simple-minded, mistake-prone character who ruins everything he touches. Sellers portrays Bakshi as a sensitive and warm-hearted man who desires to be respected as much as he respects others. The viewer learns this during the aforementioned elephant scene, among others. He enlightens the young people with the notion that elephants have feelings too. An elephant should be granted as much dignity as a human would expect to be granted. Unfortunately, at the party, neither Bakshi nor Monet are treated with anything faintly resembling dignity. Given the sort of shallow characters with which fate has surrounded the pair, it is not surprising how remorseless the viewer is when witnessing the destruction of the expensive set and the Clutterbuck home. Indeed, Sellers, through his sympathetic portrayal, has taken these normally disastrous situations, turned them around, and made them exquisitely justified.

Thomas A. Hanson

PARTY GIRL

Released: 1958
Production: Joe Pasternak for Metro-Goldwyn-Mayer
Direction: Nicholas Ray
Screenplay: George Wells; based on an original story by Leo Katcher
Cinematography: Robert Bronner
Editing: John McSweeney, Jr.
Running time: 99 minutes

> *Principal characters:*
> Thomas Farrell .... Robert Taylor
> Vicki Gaye .... Cyd Charisse
> Rico Angelo .... Lee J. Cobb
> Louis Canetto .... John Ireland
> Jeffrey Stewart .... Kent Smith
> Genevieve .... Claire Kelly
> Cooky .... Corey Allen

Nicholas Ray is no John Ford, Alfred Hitchcock, or Orson Welles; he has directed no *The Searchers* (1956), *Psycho* (1960), or *Citizen Kane* (1941). At his best, however, Ray's films are visually exciting, and when considered collectively, they depict a moral ambiguity unusual for the 1950's, the period in which he was most active. It is no surprise, then, that he is a favorite of *auteur* critics and film buffs. According to Ray, every relationship has its own morality, and good and evil cannot be clearly defined. Although *Party Girl* (1958) does not thematically examine specific social or moral dilemmas, it is still classic Ray in its characterizations.

The plot of *Party Girl* is, on the surface, as original as *Oh, God! Book II*, or *Any Which Way You Can*, two predictable 1980 films. The setting is Chicago in the early 1930's. Thomas Farrell (Robert Taylor) is a suave, fast-talking lawyer with a bad leg, the "mouthpiece" for a gang headed by brutal crime boss Rico Angelo (Lee J. Cobb), who had befriended him as a boy. He meets nightclub dancer Vicki Gaye (Cyd Charisse)—nicknamed "Angel" by Rico and, of course, really a "woman of loose morals"—at a party given by the mobster. Vicki asks Farrell to take her home; when they arrive, they discover that her pregnant roommate has committed suicide. When Farrell consoles Vicki, they realize that they are attracted to each other. They see in each other a solution to loneliness.

Farrell uses his disability to play on the sympathies of jurors and earns acquittal on a murder charge for Louis Canetto (John Ireland), an Angelo hoodlum. He meets Vicki again, and a romance begins, even though he has a wife, Genevieve (Claire Kelly), from whom he has long been separated. The lawyer travels to Europe for an operation on his leg, which proves successful. He has fallen in love with Vicki and decides to quit the mob and begin a legitimate practice.

Rico orders him to defend Cooky (Corey Allen), a psychopathic hoodlum, against an indictment, but Farrell rebels. He tells Rico that the only difference between Cooky and the boss is that the former is more unpredictable. Cooky jumps bail, and prosecutor Jeffrey Stewart (Kent Smith) arrests Farrell after a gangland battle. While in jail, his wife decides to divorce him. Despite his fear that Rico will kill him or, worse, get to him by harming Vicki, he exposes the mobster. Rico kidnaps Vicki and threatens to disfigure her to get revenge against the lawyer. Just before the police arrive at his hideout to take him in, Rico is confronted by Farrell. Vicki is brought in with her face wrapped in bandages, but as they are slowly removed, it is revealed that she has not yet been harmed. Rico, however, is now prepared to kill them both. Farrell stalls, using the same techniques he employs to elicit support from jurors. Police sirens are suddenly heard, and bullets spray the room. Rico is killed when acid intended for Vicki is splashed in his own face, and he falls to his death through a window. Vicki and Farrell leave the scene and, finally, Chicago.

Party Girl is, next to *Johnny Guitar* (1954), Ray's most personally realized film. He does not deal with social or moral issues here, as he does in 1951's *On Dangerous Ground* (police brutality), 1956's *Rebel Without a Cause* (juvenile delinquency), 1956's *Bigger Than Life* (drug abuse), or 1958's *Wind Across the Everglades* (ecology). It is closest in story line to *They Live by Night* (1949) in its focus on two outcast lovers in conflict with society. Farrell and Vicki are victims, lacking control of their lives. In *They Live by Night*, however, Ray examines the oppressive conditions which force his characters to "the other side of the law"; in the film, the story of two young, vulnerable lovers on the run, his protagonists are helpless products of a hostile environment. Farrell and Vicki, however, are in a glamorous city, in an atmosphere almost devoid of reality. *Party Girl* is set in an ambience of unreality. No attempt is made to explain Farrell and Vicki, or to understand them; they simply exist.

The settings and presentation of violence are colorfully stylized. An exotically garbed Charisse performs two complete song-and-dance numbers. In one, she is dressed in a skimpy leopardskin outfit. Drums appear in shadow, with grays, beiges, and browns dominating the scene. In the last reel, Rico's hideout is filled with a combination of brightly colored party decorations and broken glass (*Party Girl* was shot by Robert Bronner in CinemaScope and Metrocolor, unusual for a film with such a "low budget" theme). Rico rests himself in a wooden throne, his coat regally draped over his shoulders. When the police arrive, sirens blast on the sound track as searchlights beam into the room. Bullets fly, and more glass is broken. The atmosphere is classic *film noir*.

Superficially, *Party Girl* is just another standard gangster film cliché populated by greedy hoodlums, self-righteous lawmen, and confused heroes caught in between. Contemporary critics viewed the film as such, giving it fair to negative reviews. *Party Girl* is a complex film, however; good and evil are not clearly separated but are in fact intertwined. The hero and heroine who find solace in each other's love are, according to the dictates of society, morally tainted—Farrell is, of course, a lawyer for the mob, and Vicki "picks up a little money on the side" at parties—but Ray does not punish them for their transgressions. They have suffered enough and are allowed to survive the violent finale. While Rico is unmistakably the heavy, he is not completely evil; he is depicted as sentimental and lovable until the last reel. Prosecutor Stewart is no clean-living government official satisfied with doing his duty. He is ambitious for political office; he has simply chosen a different route to power from that of his adversary Rico.

Thomas Farrell is easily the best role of the final decade of Taylor's career. Never a great actor, some of his best films are memorable more for his costars: Greta Garbo (*Camille*, 1936); Margaret Sullavan (*Three Comrades*, 1938); Vivien Leigh (*Waterloo Bridge*, 1940); and Van Heflin (*Johnny Eager*, 1941). In *Party Girl*, however, he is appropriately grim and virile. Charisse, Fred Astaire's last major screen dance partner, is best remembered as Astaire's costar in *The Band Wagon* (1953) and for her wonderful "Broadway Rhythm" number with Gene Kelly in *Singin' in the Rain* (1952). She is well cast and low key as Vicki. As Rico, Cobb generally reprises his Oscar-nominated Johnny Friendly role from *On the Waterfront* (1954), but as always, he is more than adequate.

Party Girl, regarded as a competent but badly dated and uninspired gangster melodrama when released, was not on the *Variety* list of high rental films for 1958, but it has gained a reputation over the years as one of the *film noir* classics of the 1950's.

Rob Edelman

PAT AND MIKE

Released: 1952
Production: Lawrence Weingarten for Metro-Goldwyn-Mayer
Direction: George Cukor
Screenplay: Ruth Gordon and Garson Kanin
Cinematography: William Daniels
Editing: George Boemler
Running time: 95 minutes

Principal characters:

Mike Conovan	Spencer Tracy
Pat Pemberton	Katharine Hepburn
David Hucko	Aldo Ray
Collier Weld	William Ching
Barney Grau	Sammy White
Spec Cauley	George Matthews
Mr. Beminger	Loring Smith
Mrs. Beminger	Phyllis Povah
Charles Barry	Jim Backus

In 1942, *Woman of the Year* launched one of the most popular starring combinations in screen history, with the possible exception of that of Fred Astaire and Ginger Rogers. Its stars, Katharine Hepburn and Spencer Tracy, complemented each other so well that during the run of their M-G-M contracts only the films that they made together were overwhelming successes for the actors. (This, incidentally, was also true of Astaire and Rogers during their tenure at RKO.) The Tracy-Hepburn pairing comprised nine films over a twenty-five year period, ending with 1967's *Guess Who's Coming to Dinner?* Not all of these films were done at M-G-M, however, and Hepburn ended her M-G-M career with a film that broke the mold established by her previous films with Tracy.

Although *Pat and Mike*, like many other Tracy and Hepburn films, is a love story about two apparently mismatched people who turn out to be fully compatible despite the odds, the relationship is so discreetly unfolded that the two stars hardly ever touch. The style of the film is very reminiscent of a Damon Runyon sports novel with its background emphasis on colorful characterizations and petty hoodlums. Screenwriter Garson Kanin, after watching a 1952 tennis match between Hepburn and a professional tennis player, had a hunch that the actress' fans might enjoy seeing her in a film in which she had an opportunity to engage in various sports, so he suggested the idea to his wife and frequent collaborator, Ruth Gordon, and *Pat and Mike* was born.

The romantic comedy concerns Pat Pemberton (Katharine Hepburn), a physical education instructor at a California college. She excels in every sport that she tries, but whenever she attempts to show her stuffy fiancé Collier Weld (William Ching) what she can do, she becomes intimidated by his presence and fails miserably. Collier, an administrator with the college, constantly puts Pat down by pointing out her failures. Actually, he does not want her to excel at anything and would prefer her to acquiesce to his every wish.

One day when Pat is practicing on the golf course, her natural abilities attract the attention of fast-talking, seedy agent Mike Conovan (Spencer Tracy). He likes Pat, but he asks her deliberately to lose a golf tournament in which she is entered in order that he might cash in on a large bet that he will make. She refuses, although she loses the match anyway. Mike is still impressed with her and asks her to look him up in New York if she wants an agent. In a classic Tracy-Hepburn scene, Mike admiringly looks at Pat as she walks away from him and comments that there is not much meat on her, "but it's all churse" (the word, of course, is *choice*, but Mike's Brooklynese talking makes it come out *churse*). After another confrontation with Collier, who was really to blame for Pat's missing a shot and losing the tournament, Pat decides to take Mike up on his offer. Not only does she want to prove to herself that she can compete with the best, but she also wants to show Collier that she is not really the cute, helpless child that he thinks she is (or wants her to be). Pat thinks that Mike's promotion will finally rid her of the inferiority complex which is plaguing her life.

After they agree to work together, Pat and Mike have lunch at Lindy's in New York, where Mike gruffly outlines her rigorous training schedule. After giving a lengthy list of "do's and don'ts," Mike proceeds to order Pat's lunch, to which she sarcastically replies, "Don't forget to throw me over your shoulder and burp me after lunch." "I will if I have to," Mike replies. This sets the pace for their relationship. Mike is the taskmaster and Pat is his star athlete, for no matter how hard Mike drives her, Pat knows that he has confidence in her ability to master any sport.

Pat gradually becomes famous nationwide, performing exhibitions in numerous sports. In addition to the more traditional ones such as golf, tennis, and swimming, she also excels in some sports not usually mastered by women, including boxing, hockey, and even judo. Pat seems invincible, and Mike is happily collecting his percentage for managing her, until a tennis tournament in San Francisco temporarily interrupts her progress. Pat has been the headline stealer of the tournament until one afternoon when Collier comes to watch her play. Suddenly all of her confidence disappears again. As she tries to continue playing, she suddenly imagines the net getting higher and higher, while her racket is getting smaller and smaller. Unable to stand the pressure, Pat faints in the middle of the match.

All through the film, Pat and Mike's relationship has remained platonic. They seem an unlikely pair, but gradually the gruff Mike has fallen in love with Pat. She begins to realize it when, one night during a golf tournament, she wakes up to find Mike by her bed. At first she is upset, but when Mike confesses that he comes into her room every night in order to cover her up if she kicks the blankets off, she is touched. The thing that finally brings them together is Pat's brave judo defense of Mike when some of his former racketeer friends who are secret partners in Pat's contract try to rough him up. They want her to throw the golf tournament (which is the same tournament that she had accidentally lost the previous year), but Mike will not submit to their demands. When Pat has to reenact the scene of her capture of the thugs for a puzzled police captain, the gangsters are embarrassed, but Mike is merely proud. So, at the end, Pat drops Collier and decides to stay with Mike. They shake hands, in true sportsmanlike fashion, and agree to get married.

As in their other eight films together, Tracy and Hepburn's screen relationship is a joy to watch. She is always the cultured, well-educated woman, a perfect complement for the more mundane, rough-hewn Tracy. While Tracy's role sometimes changed, Hepburn's image always seemed to remain the same. The chemistry between them on the screen, which was perhaps enhanced in their fans' minds by their offscreen relationship, is undeniable. This is something that seems to be captured best by their good friends, Kanin and Gordon, who also wrote *Adam's Rib* (1949), which some consider to be their best film. The addition of George Cukor, also from *Adam's Rib* and Hepburn's favorite director, brings all of the proper elements into balance in *Pat and Mike*.

Although Hepburn is known for portraying strong, independent women on film, *Pat and Mike* is, more than any other film, a comedy of equality between the sexes. Mike is rough and superficially antagonistic, but he does not put Pat down because she is a woman. He recognizes her attractiveness and femininity, but he also approves of her excellence in sports. His belief in the equality of the sexes is perhaps best expressed when he tells Pat, "I like a he to be a he and a she to be a she, five-o, five-o."

As a sports film, *Pat and Mike* is unique because it presents a wide variety of famous women athletes; aside from a few television movies, it is, in fact, the only film to do so. Hepburn herself has been a remarkable athlete since childhood, beginning as a tournament-level golfer as a young girl and eventually becoming one of the best tennis players in Hollywood. This film is the only one which showcases her own abilities as well as that of such women as Betty Hicks, Helen Dettweiler, and Alice Marble. Babe Didrikson Zaharias, who, like Pat, was successful in a wide variety of sports, is also featured in a sequence on the golf course. These scenes of tournaments actually give the film a documentary look in some places rather than the stagy stock footage that is frequently seen in sports films.

The supporting players, aside from Ching, who is supposed to be very stiff, are all Damon Runyonesque. Aldo Ray as Mike's dumb boxer is very appealing in an early role, as is Jim Backus, and Charles Buchinski, who later changed his name to Charles Bronson. It is Tracy, however, in his most rough-hewn role with Hepburn, who seems the most like a character written by Runyon. He constantly says "dees," and "dose," and has his own peculiar style of English grammar. When he says, "Let me give you a few statistics or two," it seems to make perfect sense, and we can see what the more cultured Pat finally sees in him.

Janet St. Clair

PATHS OF GLORY

Released: 1957
Production: James B. Harris for United Artists
Direction: Stanley Kubrick
Screenplay: Stanley Kubrick, Calder Willingham, and Jim Thompson; based
  on the novel of the same name by Humphrey Cobb
Cinematography: George Krause
Editing: Eva Kroll
Art direction: Ludwig Reiber
Running time: 86 minutes

Principal characters:
Colonel Dax	Kirk Douglas
Corporal Paris	Ralph Meeker
General Broulard	Adolphe Menjou
General Mireau	George Macready
Lieutenant Roget	Wayne Morris
Private Ferol	Timothy Carey
Private Arnaud	Joseph Turkel
Captain Rousseau	John Stein
German Girl	Susanne Christian

War has been called the great social equalizer; it has often been said that all men are equal in a foxhole. *Paths of Glory*, however, reminds us that not everyone serves in the foxhole. There are those who remain isolated from the ravages of war. Generals and politicians may start the wars but soldiers fight them. *Paths of Glory* is a story about these two groups: the men who give the orders and the men who obey them. Within the context of World War I, Stanley Kubrick, the director and co-writer of the film, implies that war is but a continuation of class struggle in which one group is exploited by another.

The first group is represented by Generals Broulard (Adolphe Menjou) and Mireau (George Macready). Broulard has come to a chateau commandeered by the French for use as a command post by Mireau. Through subtle but persuasive urgings, Broulard induces Mireau to order his men into an attack upon an admittedly impregnable position held by the enemy. In turn, Mireau passes the responsibility to his field commander, Colonel Dax (Kirk Douglas). In so doing, Mireau calmly assures Dax that even with losses conservatively estimated at thirty-five percent, he should be able to hold the position with the surviving sixty-five percent. Dax represents the link between the two groups. He is an officer, but one who must personally lead his men. As a result, he must suffer many of their discomforts and risk the same annihilation.

The attack is a fiasco with many of the men slaughtered before they even get beyond their own defenses. Seeing the men retreating, Mireau emotionally orders the French batteries to fire on their own positions. The battery commander refuses, however, prompting Mireau to threaten him with court martial; the officer still refuses, and eventually calm prevails.

Unable to admit that the attack was ill-conceived, the generals decide to punish the regiment for their cowardice. They decide that one man will be chosen from each of the three companies to stand trial for cowardice. As for the men, they are to be chosen by lot. In one instance, however, Corporal Paris (Ralph Meeker) is chosen by Lieutenant Roget (Wayne Morris) because Paris knows Roget is a murderer and a coward. Colonel Dax, a successful criminal lawyer in his civilian days, volunteers to defend the men. He pleads their case well, pointing out the futility of the attack. Nevertheless, the decision of the tribunal is inevitable, and the men are sentenced to death before a firing squad.

In prison, the three men prepare for their execution. Frustrated and angry, each seeks his own consolation. Private Arnaud (Joseph Turkel) strikes out against the guards, resulting in an injury which leaves him unconscious. Private Ferol (Timothy Carey), a tough, hard-nosed social misfit breaks down in tears and must be consoled by the priest sent to comfort the men. Corporal Paris writes to his wife trying to explain what has happened.

As the time for the execution arrives, they are brought from their cells and shot. Soon after, Dax is visited by Captain Rousseau (John Stein), the officer in charge of the battery ordered by Mireau to fire on the retreating French. Dax, in turn, reports the information to Broulard, who advises Dax that Mireau will stand trial. Believing Dax's motives for telling him this information are selfish, Broulard suggests that Dax will most likely be given Mireau's job. Dax denies that gaining the job was his intent and tells Broulard what he can do with the promotion. Returning to his troops, Dax is surprised to find they are in a bar singing and carrying on. Disappointed by their apparent callousness in regard to the deaths of their comrades, Dax is about to enter when he notices that the apparent gaiety has changed to melancholy and tears, and realizes they were merely hiding their true feelings. When a captured German girl (Susanne Christian) is forced to sing, even though she sings in German, the feelings of the song transcend the language barrier.

The differences between the generals and the men are demonstrated time and again. From the very first, the generals are shown living in palaces, drinking wine, partying, dancing, and generally enjoying the comforts of war. The soldiers are dirty, sick, tired, and living in damp trenchs. To the generals, these men are merely pawns to be moved and slaughtered for the generals' personal glory. The war is shown, by the generals' use of binoculars, to be nothing more than a spectator sport for the high command. When Mireau does appear in the trenchs, his incitements are machinelike: "Hello, soldier!

Ready to kill more Germans?" "Hello, soldier! Ready to kill more Germans?" Mireau is shown to be emotionally isolated from the men he leads. Dax, on the other hand, is seen as one of the men. Through the use of an incredible tracking shot across the battlefield, we follow him, as he leads his men towards the enemy position, in much the same way as his men do.

Stanley Kubrick has never tried to hide his distrust of politicians and generals. In *Dr. Strangelove* (1964) he confirmed many of the points he first made in *Paths of Glory*. The callous disregard for casualties in *Paths of Glory* ("Five percent killed going over the top, another five percent as the advance starts . . . let's say another twenty-five percent in actually taking the Ant Hill, we're still left with enough men to keep it") becomes escalated to General Turgidson's call for all-out nuclear war with Russia resulting in "only ten to twenty million people killed, tops, depending on the breaks."

To the generals, war is a game of numbers and statistics. Men become merely instruments with which to conduct wars. We as viewers, however, are not allowed to forget what war is all about. The attack upon the "Ant Hill," as it is called in the film, is shown in shattering detail. Long tracking shots force us to witness at first-hand the slaughter of men as they futiley make their way toward a distant, almost impossible goal. We never see the enemy. As Yossarian says in *Catch-22*, "the enemy is anyone who is trying to kill you." It is all the more unfortunate when they are your countrymen.

Paths of Glory is, of course, an antiwar film. As Lewis Milestone, the director of an equally famous study of men at war, *All Quiet on the Western Front* (1930), has pointed out, "The good man's only response to war is pacifism." Nevertheless, this response is only incidental to the appreciation of the film. Through the marvelous casting of Menjou as Broulard and Douglas as Colonel Dax, the film takes on a cry for human justice which surpasses the limitations of its being a war film.

With this film, Stanley Kubrick became established. He was no longer the newcomer with potential, but had proven himself as a director with style.

James Desmarais

THE PAWNBROKER

Released: 1965
Production: Roger H. Lewis and Philip Langer
Direction: Sidney Lumet
Screenplay: David Friedkin and Morton Fine; based on the novel of the same
name by Edward Lewis Wallant
Cinematography: Boris Kaufman
Editing: Ralph Rosenblum
Music: Quincy Jones
Running time: 115 minutes

Principal characters:
Sol Nazerman	Rod Steiger
Marilyn Birchfield	Geraldine Fitzgerald
Rodriguez	Brock Peters
Jesus Ortiz	Jaime Sanchez
Oritz's Girl	Thelma Oliver
Tessie	Marketa Kimbrell
Tangee	Raymond St. Jacques
Mendel	Baruch Lumet
Bertha	Nancy R. Pollock

"They're all scum," proclaims Sol Nazerman (Rod Steiger), an embittered
concentration camp survivor, about his fellow man. Because he is numbed
by his experiences in Germany during World War II, Sol, who has become
a pawnbroker, rejects all humanity. He has insulated himself to the point that
he can neither hate nor love, and seems to view the memories of his Nazi
persecutors with the same feelings that he has for the swarming inhabitants
of present-day black and Spanish Harlem, where he works, and his mercenary
sister-in-law, Bertha (Nancy R. Pollack), with whom he lives.

Set in New York twenty years after the war, *The Pawnbroker* is the grim
but powerful story of a disinterested man who ultimately regains his faith in
mankind and his sense of responsibility as a human being. We learn, through
snatches of conversations and flashbacks of varying lengths, that Sol's wife,
who was very beautiful, and his children were killed in a concentration camp.
Now Sol stays in a nice suburban home in Long Island with Bertha's family,
who live on his money. Sol has a very uninvolved relationship with Bertha's
family, preferring to turn a deaf ear to the squabbling which goes on between
her two teenaged children. Sol has a relationship, albeit a shallow one, with
Tessie (Marketa Kimbrell), with whom he sleeps and plays cards, but shares
no emotion. Sol supports Tessie, whose husband died in a concentration
camp, and also her father-in-law Mendel (Baruch Lumet), who is very old
and ill.

Although he was a professor before the war, Sol now owns a pawnshop on 116th Street and Park Avenue in New York City. The racial and social tensions in Harlem seem to parallel those of Nazi Germany, and the sad, lonely, and often desperate customers who frequent Sol's pawnshop also have parallels among the Jews who were persecuted in Nazi Germany. When Sol discovers that his silent partner Rodriguez (Brock Peters), a black racketeer and slumlord, is also involved with prostitution, Sol expresses his first hint of emotion and tells Rodriguez that he wants to terminate their association. We see through quick flashes that Sol's dead wife had been forced into prostitution in the concentration camp, and so he refuses Rodriguez's request for his further fronting of illegal activities. Sol's attitude infuriates Rodriguez, and he has his henchman beat up "the professor." In an almost masochistic way, Sol seems to invite the brutality, because part of him would like to have the memories of the past beaten out of him.

Sol rejects friendship of any kind. When a kind, middle-aged spinster welfare worker named Marilyn Birchfield (Geraldine Fitzgerald) tries to become friends with him, he rejects her, even to the point of insults. He is actually impressed by her offers of friendship, but in an emotional moment when she puts out her hand to him, he merely runs away. Sol is equally unfeeling concerning his Puerto Rican assistant, Jesus Ortiz (Jaime Sanchez), a reformed criminal who wants to go straight, hoping to learn the business from Sol. Jesus half admires and half resents Sol, saying that Sol is "like a teacher" to him, but Sol cruelly lashes out at the boy for his unknowing reminder of the past and says "you are nothing to me."

Jesus, who has been bragging about his knowledge of the pawnshop and his importance there to some of his old buddies who are hoodlums and accuse him of being "straight," becomes enmeshed in a plot to rob the shop. Jesus' girl friend (Thelma Oliver) is a prostitute and promises to give Jesus whatever money he wants, if he will only stay out of the robbery, but Sol's scathing rejection angers Jesus enough to go ahead with the scheme. More than wanting to commit a crime or get money, Jesus wants to get back at Sol, who has hurt him. Because Jesus still has some feelings for the pawnbroker, however, he insists on "no shooting" during the robbery.

The robbery brings the film to its violent climax. Despite Jesus' admonition not to use guns, shots ring out, and Jesus runs to the pawnshop. He arrives in time to save Sol, but gets the bullets intended for the pawnbroker himself. As Jesus lies dying on the street in Sol's arms, Sol suddenly realizes that Jesus has sacrificed his own life for him. With a wide-eyed look of horror and a voiceless howl of recognition, Sol begins to understand just what he has become—a hardened shell of a man, totally devoid of feeling. In order to break that shell, which he himself created, and in order to force himself to *feel* again, Sol deliberately and methodically impales his hand on the metal receipt spindle in his shop. As he feels the agonizing pain of penetration by the spindle, Sol slowly comes alive.

Despite its depressing, violent story, *The Pawnbroker* was an artistic and commercial success. The use of creative editing techniques adds immeasurably to the impact of the film. Early in the film, split-second, almost subliminal flashbacks reveal glimpses of the pawnbroker's recurrent memories of Germany. Gradually these flashbacks become longer, until some scenes of several minutes' duration fill in the details of Sol's past life. In the beginning of the film, Sol is seen as a young, happy family man, frolicking in the country with his wife and children. A sense of distant, faded euphoria and dreaminess is created with the slightly overexposed, slow-motion shots depicting fluttering butterflies and his wife's flowing black hair. The idyllic scene is interrupted when a car carrying Nazi officials comes to take the family away. Later, other flashbacks take shape. A ride on the crowded New York subway reminds Sol of the cattle cars in which his family traveled on the way to the concentration camp, and seeing Jesus' girl friend bare her breasts in front of him reminds him of having been forced to look at his wife naked before a Nazi in the concentration camp brothel. Each flashback reveals the horror of Sol's past more vividly. It is the twentieth anniversary of his wife's death, and this fact, coupled with Jesus' death and all of the other events, eventually lead to Sol's violent catharsis.

Director Sidney Lumet shot most of the film on location in New York. The scenes of Harlem and the pawnshop give an almost documentary texture to the film and allow the audience to feel the characters' sense of claustrophobia in the streets and in Sol's stuffy shop. The film has been criticized by some for having too many heavy-handed symbols, particularly religious ones, but this can be overlooked in the final product because everything relates to the feelings of the main character, Sol, who, from the beginning, is shown to have a different perspective on things from that of anyone else. The other major criticism of the film is that there are many unanswered questions concerning how Sol got involved with gangsters in the first place and how he will get away from them in the future.

These criticisms aside, however, the film is a masterpiece of direction and acting. Steiger, who is a proponent of the "method" school of acting and is often accused of overacting, gives a very controlled performance here. His outbursts are indicative of the character's state of mind, and Steiger never lets them go beyond the scope of the film. He earned a nomination for Best Actor of the year from the Motion Picture Academy for his performance, but lost to Lee Marvin for his comic portrayal of a has-been gunfighter in *Cat Ballou*. Despite rave reviews for the film, the only awards of any significance it received were for Steiger's performance; he won the Best Foreign Actor Award from the British Academy and the Best Actor Award at the Berlin Film Festival.

Leslie Taubman

PENNY SERENADE

Released: 1941
Production: George Stevens for Columbia
Direction: George Stevens
Screenplay: Morrie Ryskind; based on the story of the same name by Martha Cheavens
Cinematography: Joseph Walker
Editing: Otto Meyer
Running time: 125 minutes

Principal characters:
Julie Gardiner Adams	Irene Dunne
Roger Adams	Cary Grant
Miss Oliver	Beulah Bondi
Apple Jack	Edgar Buchanan
Dotty	Ann Doran
Trina (age six)	Eve Lee Kuney
Dr. Hartley	Leonard Willey
Judge	Wallis Clark
Billings	Walter Soderling
Trina (age one)	Baby Biffie

In 1937, the team of Irene Dunne and Cary grant appeared in the film *The Awful Truth*. This successful pairing led to their acting together again in *Penny Serenade*, which is considered to be one of director George Stevens' biggest financial successes. At the time the film was released, the advertising heralded it as the consummate love story. While that may have been the film's primary aim, it also proved to be an enormous tearjerker. The story is told via cutbacks, with most episodes beginning with Irene Dunne listening to a phonograph record. Each tune suggests a memory, and while the music plays, the individual segments unfold. The music and the phonograph provide the connective tissue of the film.

In the opening scenes, Roger Adams (Cary Grant) has left home with a whisky bottle in his pocket. His wife, Julie (Irene Dunne), hears the strains of "You Were Meant for Me" playing on the phonograph. Although she, too, is leaving, Julie cannot resist putting the record on once more. As it plays, the viewer is taken back to an earlier time in New York City. The same song is playing in Julie's place of employment—a record shop. Roger Adams, a fun-loving newspaperman, comes into the store and takes a stack of records into the listening booth. Later, Roger and Julie leave together. He walks Julie home, then asks her if he can listen to music on her Victrola.

Time flows along to New Year's Eve. Julie and Roger have been dating.

At a party, Apple Jack (Edgar Buchanan), who works with Roger, asks Julie of her boyfriend's whereabouts. She replies that she does not know, then goes on to admit she likes Roger, but adds that she never thought about getting married to him. Roger arrives and whisks Julie out to the balcony. He urgently needs to talk to her in private. He tells her he has an offer for a good job in Japan, on a two-year contract. In the next breath, he asks her to marry him immediately, and he will send for her in three months after he gets settled. They get married on New Year's Day and then dash off to the railroad station, where they barely have time to kiss good-bye. Roger asks Julie to promise never to remove her wedding ring. She assures him she will not, no matter what happens. The train pulls out, but Julie does not alight until they are 115 miles away from New York City; the Adamses have begun their married life with a forty-five-minute honeymoon.

The next sequence shows the phonograph playing "Poor Butterfly," which takes Julie back in memory to her brief time in Japan. The pair arrives, via rickshaw, at a large rented house, complete with a hired couple and their three little children who live in and work for Roger. Practical Julie asks how they can afford the place, to which spendthrift Roger replies he received an advance on his salary. A short time later, Julie is seen being fitted for a Japanese dress when Roger bursts in to tell her they are leaving Japan. He has received an inheritance, quit the paper, and intends to take Julie on a trip around the world to make up for the honeymoon they missed. His wife, who is now pregnant, is less enthusiastic. She points out that his fortune is not enough to warrant leaving his job, but to please him she agrees.

Roger's dream vacation does not materialize, however, as there is a severe earthquake and the house collapses, badly injuring Julie, who winds up in a hospital in San Francisco after having a miscarriage. As a result of her injury, she can never have a baby. Roger decides to buy a small newspaper of his own in Rosalia, a small town north of San Francisco. The couple is next seen looking at a structure which combines a newspaper office with an apartment upstairs. One of the rooms obviously used to serve as a nursery, since there are pictures of babies and reminders of children everywhere. They decide to buy the place, and Roger begins to publish the Rosalia Weekly Courier. He sends for his friend Apple Jack, who obligingly comes out from Brooklyn to be Roger's printer. Despite the enthusiasm of the two newspapermen, the circulation stays small.

One day Apple Jack suggests to Julie that she and Roger adopt a child, revealing that he himself was adopted. Roger wants to make Julie happy and agrees to the adoption suggestion, pretending that it is what he wished to do all along. In an amusing scene, the Adamses are in their car en route to the adoption agency in San Francisco. Roger cautions his wife not to grab the first child she sees, insisting that he wants a boy two years old with curly hair and blue eyes; in a pinch, however, he might consider looking at a girl. At the agency, they learn that adoption is not as simple as they thought. The case worker, Miss Oliver (Beulah Bondi), tells them they have no children available at the moment, and besides, there is a long waiting list, at least one year. She also informs them that the agency must make an investigation. When she begins to ask questions about their living quarters and income, Roger exaggerates, saying that he makes one hundred dollars a week. The case worker tells them that someone will be around to see them soon. In parting, Julie informs Miss Oliver that it does not matter if the child does not have curly hair.

When Miss Oliver comes to call, nothing seems to go right; the door is stuck, and the window slams shut. When she asks to see the child's room, however, she is favorably impressed. Outside, she finds Roger making a slide and tells the couple there is a five-week-old girl available, and that she will give them first option. Roger is reluctant, but Miss Oliver says she feels this would be just the child for them, and that she is unique. When Julie pleads with her husband to at least look at the baby, he hesitantly acquiesces.

When they go to the nursery, Julie instantly falls in love with the infant (Baby Biffie), and when the baby grabs hold of Roger's finger, his doubts dissolve, and the couple agrees to the adoption. Miss Oliver says they can have the little girl on a year's probation and that they can take her home immediately. Neither Roger nor Julie knows anything about caring for a baby, and there follow some amusing scenes showing the Adamses attempting to adjust to instant parenthood on their first night together. The next morning, when Roger hears the printing press, he rushes downstairs in his pajamas to tell the printers to stop the noise. When Apple Jack learns about the arrival of the baby, who has been named Trina, he goes upstairs to see her and finds Julie struggling to give the infant a bath. Apple Jack is more experienced at caring for babies, and not only does he bathe the baby, but he also teaches Julie how to fold a diaper and put it on the child.

The audience next hears "My Blue Heaven" emanating from the phonograph. A year has passed and with it the probation period. Miss Oliver visits again and approves the adoption, but says that now the final decision will be up to the judge. She asks the same questions she did when they first applied. When she gets to the part about income, however, Roger confesses he has none. He has had to close the paper down, but says it is only a temporary setback and that he intends to resume publication shortly. Now they must prove to the judge that they can afford to take care of Trina.

Roger drives to the city with the baby in order to face the judge, but Julie remains behind, afraid to face the possibility of losing Trina. The judge (Wallis Clark) checks over the adoption application and decides that Trina must be returned to the orphanage, despite Miss Oliver's favorable report; the lack of income is the key factor in the decision. In an impassioned speech, which is probably the most emotional of Cary Grant's long acting career, Roger pleads his case. He tells how good he and Julie have been to Trina and how they have passed many inspections by Miss Oliver. He explains how he fell in love with the little girl and begs for more time so he can prove he is capable of supporting the child. He says it is for Trina's sake as well as theirs, and he professes that he will do anything to keep the youngster.

When Roger returns home, Julie is anxious. At first, the camera focuses on Roger's legs, then pans up to show him holding little Trina. He tells his wife that the baby is now theirs forever and that nothing can take her from them.

The story next advances six years to a Christmas play. This time the song is "Silent Night," and several children are gathered around a nativity scene. Trina (Eva Lee Kuney) is shown offstage in her sneakers, walking up a ramp, transporting a cardboard cloud across the stage. She hangs up a star, and in a very mature voice, sings as an echo. Before the play ends, however, she slips and falls. On the way home in the car, she tells her parents she ruined everything and will not be able to be an angel next year. When they assure her all will be fine, Trina remarks that she does not know what they would do without Christmas, to which her parents say they do not know what they would do without her. Their statement proves to be ironic. At Christmas the following year, Julie writes a letter to Miss Oliver which discloses that Trina has died suddenly and that the couple has become estranged; she says that Roger does not speak to her any more.

At the Adams' home, Julie tells Roger she wishes he would not go out. Before he leaves, someone knocks at the door. A woman asks if she can use the telephone, as it is raining hard and she wants to call a taxi. The woman has a little boy with her who is scheduled to appear in the Christmas play. Her car has a dead battery and she does not want to arrive at the school late. Julie and Roger offer to drive the mother and son to their destination. When they arrive, the boy dashes out, wearing sneakers. In the background, "Silent Night" is heard. The couple drives away. Roger gets out of the car and tells his wife he is not coming home. He never wants to see anything or anyone who reminds him of his dead child. The next record the audience hears contains the ironic words, "We'll always be together."

In the final part of the movie, the time returns to the present. A recording of "You Were Meant for Me" is playing when Apple Jack comes in with Julie's train tickets. Apple Jack is recalling when he first met Julie. When Roger returns, he tells Julie he does not blame her for leaving him; in fact, she should. He berates himself by saying he never did anything for her. They are still struggling for a living, and he feels defeated. She responds that it is not all Roger's fault. It is just them—they are defeated as a couple. She tells him she needed him, but he has been miles away from her mentally. He replies that he has not been able to think straight. He cannot understand why Trina, who was never sick before, should suddenly fall ill and die. They both express guilt for having scolded her or for occasionally having been impatient with her.

In the midst of their reverie, the telephone rings. It is Miss Oliver, and it seems she has a child available and will again give them the first option. This time the youngster is a two-year-old boy who is the image of the child the Adamses first requested. Julie and Roger decide without hesitation to see the boy, and they immediately go to get the crib out in preparation for their new son. Thus the story ends on a happy note.

Penny Serenade was a popular film among moviegoers at the time it was released. Director Stevens pulls out all the stops. The film begins as a light comedy with plenty of promise, but deteriorates into a soap opera; no chance at irony or sentimentality is missed. On the plus side, however, the acting transcends the subject matter. Cary Grant and Irene Dunne both turn in excellent performances; in fact, Cary Grant received an Academy Award nomination for his role. He himself believes that he did some of his finest acting as Roger Adams and has purchased the rights to the film. Irene Dunne, who had recently adopted a child herself, is also very touching in a role which could easily have become extremely maudlin. Edgar Buchanan is splendid as the ultimate true friend, Apple Jack, and Beulah Bondi lends credible support as the sensitive yet sensible Miss Oliver. To be sure, *Penny Serenade* can still wring tears from the eyes of many viewers.

Fern L. Gagné

THE PETRIFIED FOREST

Released: 1936
Production: Henry Blanke for Warner Bros.
Direction: Archie Mayo
Screenplay: Charles Kenyon and Delmer Daves; based on the play of the
  same name by Robert E. Sherwood
Cinematography: Sol Polito
Editing: Owen Marks
Running time: 83 minutes

Principal characters:
Alan Squier .... Leslie Howard
Gabrielle Maple .... Bette Davis
Duke Mantee .... Humphrey Bogart
Mrs. Chisholm .... Genevieve Tobin
Boze Hertzlinger .... Dick Foran
Jason Maple .... Porter Hall
Gramp Maple .... Charley Grapewin
Mr. Chisholm .... Paul Harvey

Based on a successful Broadway play by Robert E. Sherwood, *The Petrified
Forest* is the story of a wandering writer looking for something worth living
or dying for. His search ends in a small desert café where he and an odd
assortment of other people are held captive by a gangster.

Transferring a play from the stage to the screen is normally a delicate
operation. Stage plays usually depend more upon words and upon the performances of the actors than films do, because a film can use more settings,
real locations, and the resources of the camera and editor to guide the attention of the audience more directly. When a play is made into a film, the usual
practice is to "open it up" by adding new scenes or by changing the settings
of the original scenes so that the film is able to use its own resources to
produce a true film rather than simply a "filmed play," a concept which is
seldom used to good effect. Those who transferred *The Petrified Forest* from
the stage to the screen, however, recognized that one of its greatest strengths
is the power of its words and that part of the motivation that makes the
characters act as they do lies in the fact that they are isolated in the middle
of a very large space—in a tiny café in the desert. There is, therefore, for the
filmmakers as well as for the characters, no place to go. The adapters wisely
recognized this fact and shot nearly all of the scenes in or around the café.

The audience first sees the empty vastness of the desert. Then the camera
comes closer to show Alan Squier (Leslie Howard) walking along a road
attempting to get a ride. Although he does not yet know it, his destination
is a small café and gas station. Operating the place is Jason Maple (Porter

Hall), a superpatriot who is a uniformed member of the Black Horse Vigilantes, a group of middle-aged men playing soldier in order to feel important. His father (Charley Grapewin), called Gramp by everyone, lives in regret that the West is no longer the place of pioneers and desperadoes. He endlessly tells anyone who will listen that Billy the Kid once shot at him and missed. Jason's daughter Gabrielle (Bette Davis), known to everyone as Gabby, is a romantic who dreams of going to France to study painting. At the desert café, however, she waits on tables, keeps the accounts, reads poetry, and copes with the romantic attentions of the football player who runs the gas pumps, Boze Hertzlinger (Dick Foran).

When Alan reaches the café, he orders a meal and Gramp talks to him about Billy the Kid—because he talks to everyone about Billy the Kid. Alan becomes interested in Gabrielle when he sees that she is reading the French poet François Villon, although she cannot pronounce his name. Gabrielle becomes interested in Alan when she finds that he is a writer and has been to France.

Although Gabrielle begins to fall in love with Alan and wishes he would stay until she has the money for them both to go to France, he does not believe that that would work. "I belong," he says, "to a vanishing race—I'm one of the intellectuals"; and to define himself he quotes a phrase from T. S. Eliot: "brains without purpose." When he leaves, she resigns herself to being stuck in the desert and is ready to accept the advances of Boze.

Alan is not, however, gone for very long. He leaves with the Chisholms (Genevieve Tobin and Paul Harvey) and their black chauffeur, a ride that Gabrielle has gotten for him. The car is soon stopped and stolen by Duke Mantee (Humphrey Bogart) and his gang. Throughout the film we have been hearing that this desperate killer is supposed to be in the area on his way to Mexico. When Alan returns to the café to warn Gabrielle and the others, he finds that Mantee and his men are already there, holding everyone at gunpoint while they wait for the rest of the gang. Soon the Chisholms stumble in and are held with the rest.

Gramp is delighted to have a killer around again and insists that Duke Mantee is a desperado, not a gangster, because gangsters are foreigners and Duke is an American. The others are not so delighted, and begin to reveal themselves under the pressure. Mr. Chisholm is, of course, perturbed to find himself in a situation in which his money does him no good. Next, his wife pours out her story. She had given up a chance for a career on the stage because her family did not approve and married Chisholm, a banker, because they did approve.

Now it is Boze's turn. He tells Gabrielle that he really loves her, that he was not just putting on an act. He tries to get one of the gangsters' guns, but Duke shoots him in the hand. While Gabrielle is in the next room tending to him, Alan thinks up a way to help her. He signs his five-thousand-dollar life insurance policy over to her and persuades Duke to kill him just before he leaves the café.

Duke, we discover, is waiting for the rest of his gang before heading for the border because his girl friend is with the others. Even the killer, it seems, has his romantic side. The rest of the gang is captured, however, and the girl friend talks. The police close in on the café and the gangsters use the Chisholms as shields and escape, although not before Alan forces Duke to kill him. Alan dies in Gabrielle's arms. Soon we learn that Duke has been captured. As Alan dies, however, we cannot help remembering the lines from Villon that Gabrielle had read to him hours before: "This is the end for which we/Twain are met."

The Petrified Forest is about people in an existential dilemma. Gramp belongs, or thinks he belongs, to the old West, where men were pioneers and gunfighters were heroes. Mrs. Chisholm has long regretted that she gave up the life she wanted for the wishes of her family. Gabrielle thinks that she belongs in France where things are more artistic than in the desert, and Alan Squier thinks that he no longer belongs anywhere.

The film offers no easy answers. Although he is idolized by Gramp, Duke says that he has spent most of his life in jail and "It looks like I'll spend the rest of my life dead." Although Gabrielle is sure that she will become a good painter if she gets to France where there is "something beautiful to look at, and wine, and dancing in the streets," Alan tells her that after his first novel he spent eight years on the Riviera without writing anything and that artists in France think Arizona would be the perfect place to paint. The characters, however, are romantics at heart. Gabrielle keeps her dream of France, Alan gives up his life to give her the money to get there, and, for love, Duke Mantee gives up his chance for freedom.

The acting honors must go to Howard as Alan Squier. In the role that he also played on the stage, he gives a sensitive portrayal of the frustrated writer and intellectual who cannot accomplish anything, a man perhaps too aware of his limitations. A lesser actor, or one with a different *persona*, would have made the character seem too weak or too pompous to merit our sympathy; but Howard makes us see Alan's appealing side as well.

Davis as Gabrielle distinguishes herself in a role which is quieter and simpler than the ones for which she is best known. At this early stage of her career, however, she is able to convey the romantic qualities of a young woman dreaming of France in a desert café. Notably, it was the role of Duke Mantee that truly launched the screen career of Bogart. Before this role he had appeared in several second-rate films and then had virtually abandoned Hollywood for four years. When he played Duke Mantee on Broadway, however, his performance so impressed Howard that he insisted that Bogart have the role in the film version. The rest of the cast supports Howard, Davis, and Bogart well indeed, especially Grapewin as Gramp, the talkative old codger.

Archie Mayo's direction is competent in the best sense of the word. It is direction which is effective without calling attention to itself. The camera sometimes moves, but only for a good reason; and at times a close shot of two people will show another person between them in the background, although only if that person is relevant to their conversation. Perhaps the main virtue of the directing, however, is its pacing. The film moves along swiftly without ever seeming to hurry. What is important is given its just due and what is not is eliminated.

It must be remembered, however, that the foundation of the excellent acting and directing is the literate script. Credit for the screenplay is given to Charles Kenyon and Delmer Daves, but they only slightly adapted the original play by Sherwood. It is a script in which the characters are revealed as much through their words as through their actions. From the often poetic words of the cerebral Alan Squier to the monosyllabic but still revealing and sometimes poignant speech of Duke Mantee, the artistry of the dialogue is evident. In short, an intelligent, literate script is artistically realized by the sensitive portrayals of actors working under an expert director.

Timothy W. Johnson

PICKUP ON SOUTH STREET

Released: 1953
Production: Jules Schermer for Twentieth Century-Fox
Direction: Samuel Fuller
Screenplay: Samuel Fuller; based on an unpublished story by Dwight Taylor
Cinematography: Joe MacDonald
Editing: Nick De Maggio
Running time: 83 minutes

Principal characters:
Skip McCoy	Richard Widmark
Candy	Jean Peters
Moe	Thelma Ritter
Captain Dan Tiger	Murvyn Vye
Joey	Richard Kiley

Sam Fuller's films occupy a unique position in the commercial film industry. They are determinedly antiintellectual and naïvely pro-American. *Run of the Arrow* (1956) is about "one nation, under God," closing with the title card: "The end of this story will be written by you," while *China Gate* (1958) and *Pickup on South Street* are simplistically anti-Communist. Despite their naïveté, however, they are self-conscious, uncompromising genre films with a directness of emotion that is sometimes breathtaking. This directness is also sometimes embarrassing for more sophisticated modern-day audiences.

Fuller was a writer, director, and often a producer, long before such multifaceted careers became commonplace in Hollywood. He was once a journalist and loves "front page material" in which he can examine not only people caught in events over which they have little control, but also American politics, history, and attitudes. French writer-director Jean-Luc Godard put Fuller in his film *Pierrot Le Fou* (1969), saying that "Film is like a battleground"; Fuller's films (as Godard implies) are particularly full of direct action—his characters, like it or not, are on the front lines. Fuller is admired by Europeans and is one of the most discussed "B"-movie *auteurs* of the American industry. He shoots very fast (*Park Row*, 1952, and *The Naked Kiss*, 1964, were done in a few days each) and controls his pictures from conception to final editing. As a result, his films represent a very tight, coherent body of work.

Pickup on South Street is vintage *film noir*, although with a modern, self-conscious attitude that is unlike classic *film noir*. It is a "B"-picture with an underworld milieu, waterfront locales, and a small-time "dame" and a pickpocket who inadvertently get caught between Communist spies and the FBI. Skip McCoy (Richard Widmark), a "grifter," picks a purse from Candy (Jean Peters) while she is making a delivery for Joey (Richard Kiley), her boyfriend. Unknown to both Candy and Skip, she is carrying film containing secret information and is being watched by the FBI even as Skip interferes with their surveillance by lifting her purse before she can deliver the film to a Communist agent. Moe (Thelma Ritter), a survivor in the waterfront jungle, makes extra money as an informer. She is approached by the police and by Candy, seeking Skip's identity, which she sells to both, even though Skip is her friend. Business is business, and Skip understands her kind of integrity perfectly, wanting to know only how much his name has brought. When she comes to buy back the film, Candy and Skip begin to fall in love, making him even less willing to part with the film cheaply. After many plot twists, in which Moe is killed, Candy beaten, and Skip threatened by both sides, Candy and Skip walk out of the police station. They are free and in love, but there is no indication that they are "reformed" through either their love or the events of the film. It is definitely an upbeat ending, although not unrealistically so.

Pickup on South Street received extremely mixed reviews. *Variety* called it "Unnecessarily violent . . . a sordid, rough shocker staged to emphasize seamy sadism and back alley sex." *Hollywood Reporter* loved it, citing the "gritty, hard hitting, brutal realism." Most other reviews followed along these lines, either praising the film for realism or condemning it for excessive violence. One explanation for this wide divergence of views is the "modern" sensibility at work in the film. Like Godard's work, Fuller's films grow directly from earlier films of the movement. In its visual style and in its narrative, *Pickup on South Street* is self-conscious and requires some prior knowledge on the part of its viewers. Fuller is also like Godard (who virtually defines the modern cinematic attitude) in his relation to story and style: they become stylized, "comic-book," and one-dimensional in order to allow the filmmaker to comment upon—not create within—the movement from which they come. Godard and Fuller work toward very different ends, of course: Godard destroys cinematic language in order to knock it from its ideological foundations and create a new language. Fuller less ambitiously violates "rules" of camera direction and character development in order to shock, to create a film in which tension comes at least in part from the film's failure to meet our expectations. *Pickup on South Street* is outrageous in its presumptive, independent camera, its comic book characters with colorful names such as "Muffin," "Big Thumb," "Tiger," "Whip," "Cannon," "Grifter," "Moe," and "Candy," and its sentimentality about the fringe world of New York.

The two women in the film, Moe the professional "stoolie" and Candy the girl who has "been around," reflect the "modern" aspect of this film as clearly as does the "cut-loose" camera. Like most of the more current films that critics and students began calling *film noir* when they first discovered the movement, such as *Klute* (1971), *Dirty Harry* (1971), *The French Connection* (1971), and *Chinatown* (1974), the women characters are the telling difference. In classic *film noir*, women are powerful, dangerous creatures. They motivate the action and are in control of it, even when it ends (as it usually does) with their own death or destruction. In these modern films, women lack power. They become what women have often been, especially in violent genres, simple archetypal victims (as in *Chinatown* and *Dirty Harry*) or impersonal icons in an uncaring, perhaps mad world (*Taxi Driver*, 1976). Candy is an appealing combination of the classic *film noir* "moll" and the redeeming innocent. The iconography of the gangster film genre presents her to us as a dumb tough girl (used to being slapped around) with a past. She can move in the underworld, is hard and cynical, and has connections in an even more fringe society—that of the Cold War Communists. Candy is untouched by all of it, however, and is essentially more innocent than any character in the film, even the martyred Moe. She can fall in love with Skip in a moment, be outraged when she learns that Joey's work is for the "commies," and embrace Moe as the older woman realizes her love for Skip. Candy "saves" Skip, and they walk off thumbing their noses at the police.

The optimistic romanticism—Moe finds Skip to let him know that "Muffin loves you"—is not developed from the characters, but does not seem "laid on" either, since nothing else in the film is developed in terms of character. The individual characters and their inner states are not nearly as powerful in the modern versions of *film noir* as they are in the classic examples. To be sure, there is a general insecurity, a lack of stability (Skip's house is literally at the end of the world; perched precariously at the end of a pier, generally shrouded in fog), but it seems to come from without to impinge upon the characters, rather than to represent their inner states. Fuller's swooping camera—moving in for close-ups, out for action, always on the move, always in long takes—defines a world in which the instability comes from without rather than from within. The brutal editing and tense action also emphasize a modern viewpoint in which an environment larger than the characters determines their actions and psyches, as opposed to the classic viewpoint in which the characters and their inner states determine the landscape, and the world of the film is simply a reflection of their psyches.

Janey Place

PICNIC

Released: 1955
Production: Fred Kohlmar for Columbia
Direction: Joshua Logan
Screenplay: Daniel Taradash; based on the play of the same name by William
Inge
Cinematography: James Wong Howe
Editing: Charles Nelson and William A. Lyon (AA)
Art direction: William Flannery and Joe Mielziner (AA)
Set decoration: Robert Priestly (AA)
Running time: 115 minutes

Principal characters:
Hal Carter .... William Holden
Madge Owens .... Kim Novak
Rosemary Sidney .... Rosalind Russell
Millie Owens .... Susan Strasberg
Flo Owens .... Betty Field
Alan ....Cliff Robertson
Howard Bevans .... Arthur O'Connell
Elderly Widow .... Verna Felton

Picnic is a powerful drama about the impact of a drifter on the circumscribed lives of five women in a small Midwestern town. Based on the successful play by William Inge and directed by Joshua Logan, the film shows that the man's brief stay in the town forces the major characters—including the drifter himself—to face the loneliness and frustration in their lives. Although each has a different reaction, none will ever be the same again.

The film begins calmly, giving no hint of the turmoil to come. In the early morning Hal Carter (William Holden) arrives in a small Kansas town on a freight train. He is there to look up an old school friend from whom he hopes to get a job, but first he does yard work for an elderly widow (Verna Felton) in return for breakfast. Working in the back yard stripped to the waist Hal gets the rapt attention of the women at the house next door: Flo Owens (Betty Field), her daughters Millie (Susan Strasberg) and Madge (Kim Novak), and Rosemary Sidney (Rosalind Russell), an unmarried schoolteacher who boards with them.

As the film progresses, we find that each of the women has reached a crucial point of anxiety and frustration. Madge is the town beauty dating the son of the town's rich man. She is uncertain about her feelings and is discontented with always being thought of as only beautiful, of only being looked at. Millie is a determined tomboy and determinedly intellectual. Their mother, Flo, is rearing the girls alone, and she is very anxious, especially about Madge; she is worried that Madge will miss her chance to marry Alan (Cliff Robertson), the rich man's son, and will be too old for another chance with someone else, although she is only nineteen. Rosemary, at least twenty-five years older than Madge, pretends to be uninterested in marriage, but she is unable to hide her desperation completely.

Hal himself is no happy-go-lucky adventurer. Being a football star in college was one of the few successes in his life, and that is getting farther and farther behind him as he begins to recognize the futility of his existence. He comes to the town as a man running out of options who hopes for a job from a friend he has not seen for years. The day Hal arrives is Labor Day, the day the town celebrates with a picnic. It is a celebration which includes not only eating but also the selection of the prettiest girl in town as Queen of Neewollah (Halloween spelled backwards) and music and dancing. After Hal has found his friend Alan and been formally introduced to the Owens family and Rosemary, they all go to the picnic.

The story seems to be suspended as the picnic itself is detailed on the CinemaScope screen. We see a barbershop quartet, a pie-eating contest, various games, the Queen's arrival on a river float, children playing, and, of course, eating. James Wong Howe, who photographed the film, liked this section best, and it is easy to see why. Photographed in color, the sequence has a variety of people, action, color, and movement. The cinematography captures the scene without calling too much attention to itself.

The daytime part of the picnic may be an intermission in the developing conflicts, but as night falls temperatures rise. In a small area of the picnic ground lit by Japanese lanterns reflecting on the water, Millie is trying to dance with Hal, but she cannot do the steps. Then Madge comes toward Hal, clapping her hands to the beat of the music; she joins him in a dance that is so sensuous that it makes their mutual attraction obvious to all. Millie is hurt because Hal is supposed to be her date, and she is quite nervous about how to act with a man. She has let down her tomboy defenses and finds her worst fears coming true when she is rejected. Flo is, as always, fearful that Madge will destroy her secure future with Alan.

The sight also inflames Rosemary because the obvious passion expressed in the dance is a sharp contrast to her frustratingly tepid life. She has been drinking and finally breaks in on the couple, demanding that Hal dance with her. When he embarrassedly refuses, she grabs at him, tearing his shirt, and viciously harangues him for being a troublemaker. It is this scene which produces the two most memorable single images of the film: Hal and Madge dancing with the Japanese lanterns in the background, and Hal and Rosemary frozen just after she rips his shirt.

After this incident the tensions and conflicts that have been to some degree submerged come out in the open. Alan denounces Hal and later tries to get him arrested on a trumped-up charge of car theft. Rosemary is remorseful about causing the scene but still just as desperate about her own life. She has been brought to the picnic by Howard Bevans (Arthur O'Connell), a mild-mannered bachelor who has been going with her for some time without proposing marriage. Rosemary abandons her pretense of indifference about marriage and begs Howard to marry her. Even though she completely humbles herself, however, he merely gives her excuses. The next morning when he comes to make further excuses, she assumes he has come to marry her and does not give him a chance to say anything to the contrary. In front of other people she announces that they are to be married, so he has no choice. She achieves her moment of triumph as she rides off with Howard and sticks out her tongue at the school where she will no longer have to teach.

After Rosemary and Alan have attacked him, Hal is terribly angry and upset. When he leaves the picnic in a foul mood, Madge insists on going with him. He intends to catch a freight train out of town, but as Madge soothes and reassures him, he pours out the story of his life. When they part, they part as lovers. The next morning Hal, now hiding from the police because of the charge of car theft, comes to the Owens house to persuade Madge to follow him to Tulsa, where he is going to get a job as a bellhop. Flo urges her not to go, but as Madge tries to make up her mind, Millie tells her to go: "For once in your life do something bright." The film ends with Madge breaking free of her mother's grasp and boarding the bus for Tulsa.

The last few scenes try to persuade us emotionally rather than logically that the ending is a happy one. After all, "boy gets girl" is virtually the definition of a happy ending, and it is very romantic for Madge to leave everything behind for the man she loves. She even gets the blessing of Millie, who has been her antagonist throughout the film. The only character to argue with her is her mother, who has not been portrayed very sympathetically. Once the dramatic ending is over, however, one realizes that Flo is more likely to be right than is Millie. Flo herself made a "romantic" marriage to a man who turned out to be more interested in drink and other women than in supporting his family. (This she strongly implies as she pleads with Madge not to go.) Hal, whom Madge has only known one day, has yet to be successful at anything he has tried.

Logan had also directed *Picnic* on the stage, but with the assistance of Daniel Taradash, the screenwriter, and Howe, the cinematographer, he makes a true film rather than a filmed play. Instead of the play's single set, the film has a variety of settings in the small Kansas town. Indeed, the picnic itself was not shown on the stage, but as depicted in sweeping detail on the CinemaScope screen with the dance between Hal and Madge at the end, it becomes the visual highlight as well as the emotional catalyst of the film.

Before *Picnic*, Logan had worked almost exclusively on the stage. (The only exception was the film *I Met My Love Again* in 1938). Stage directors working in film are often expert at getting good performances from the actors and less expert at using such filmic resources as camera position and editing to take full advantage of the film medium. Logan is no exception. His excellence with the actors, however, overshadows his uncertainty with film. With the possible exception of the somewhat overdone characterization of Russell as Rosemary, Logan seems to have gotten the best possible performance out of each actor within the limits of his or her abilities and the script. His use of the camera and editing, on the other hand, tends to be rather static in the early scenes and unnecessarily frenetic in some later ones. For example, during the picnic, when Hal delivers what is essentially a monologue, the camera constantly switches from one person to another instead of remaining on him. Similarly, Logan's representation of Hal and Madge's lovemaking with a shot of a locomotive rumbling through the night followed by a shot of the harvest moon is clever but not effective because it does not fit the style of the rest of the film.

Crucial to the success of *Picnic*, however, is Holden as Hal. The virtues of the script, direction, and cinematography could not compensate for a weak performance in this role, and Holden is up to the challenge. He presents a three-dimensional portrayal of a man who is often lonely and sometimes confused and uncertain. He successfully conveys that Hal's bravado is only a façade to hide his vulnerability and desperation. Novak is adequate as Madge when she is merely portraying the prettiest girl in town, but she is unable to make us believe she has the depth of character to abandon her family and friends suddenly for a man such as Hal. This is, however, a minor deficiency in the film as a whole. When *Picnic* was released the critics were generally favorable, and the audiences were enthusiastic.

Timothy W. Johnson

PICNIC AT HANGING ROCK

Released: 1979
Production: James McElroy and Hal McElroy for the South Australian Film
  Corporation and the Australian Film Commission
Direction: Peter Weir
Screenplay: Cliff Green; based on the novel of the same name by Joan Lindsay
Cinematography: Russell Boyd
Editing: Max Lemon
Art direction: David Copping
Running time: 110 minutes

Principal characters:

Mrs. Appleyard	Rachel Roberts
Michael Fitzhubert	Dominic Guard
Dianne de Poitiers	Helen Morse
Minnie	Jacki Weaver
Miss MacCraw	Vivean Gray
Dora Lumley	Kirsty Child
Miranda	Anne Lambert
Irma	Karen Robinson
Albert	John Jarratt
Sara	Margaret Nelson

The Australians "arrived" in the United States cinematically in 1978 when
Phillip Noyce's *Newsfront* played at the New York Film Festival. Then came
two films by Peter Weir, *My Brilliant Career* (1980), *The Getting of Wisdom*
(1978), and *The Chant of Jimmy Blacksmith* (1980). All of these films are
intensely regional; they celebrate the lush physical atmosphere of the country,
and they deal with Australian phenomena, with subjects, and personalities
that Americans feel confident are exclusively indigenous to Australia. They
are all assured, accomplished works by a group of filmmakers who have had
to wait too long to make their national voice heard.

The film takes place on St. Valentine's Day, 1900, in the Australian Outback. A class trip to a geological marvel, Hanging Rock, ends in disaster
when three students and a teacher disappear in the course of it. The frightened
party returns to Appleyard College (actually a finishing school) with reports
that all the watches stopped at noon, and to say that Miss MacCraw (Vivean
Gray), one of the chaperones, went after the three missing girls when a fourth,
scared and blubbering, returned to the main group, and never came back
herself. Much later, when the town is still buzzing over the disappearance and
the school has begun to lose some of its pupils because of their parents'
concern, one of the girls, Irma (Karen Robinson), is found through the efforts
of two young men from the region, Michael Fitzhubert (Dominic Guard) and

his servant, Albert (John Jarratt). She recuperates on the Fitzhubert estate, and when she visits the college, the girls cross-examine her. More girls leave the school, including Sara (Margaret Nelson), whose fees have not been paid by her guardian. Mrs. Appleyard (Rachel Roberts) makes a great show of ordering Sara's things packed and saying that the guardian came for her in the night, but her body is found crashed through the greenhouse roof in the morning. Did she jump? Was she pushed? The narrative ends with the statement that Mrs. Appleyard was found dead at the base of Hanging Rock; it is believed she fell while conducting her own search. The disappearances are a mystery to this day.

Director Peter Weir has said in interviews that Joan Lindsay, who wrote the book on which he based his film, is enigmatic about whether her book is fact or fiction. She wrote it as fact, but if it is not, the newspapers, which are depicted as covering the story exhaustively, would reveal the truth. In any event, it is an extremely good story, replete as it is with Jamesian nuances, repressed sexuality, a manacing locale, and an unsolved mystery.

As the day begins, the girls, as lovely as the Valentines they are exchanging, throng the halls, whispering and giggling. Stays are tightened and shimmies dropped over adolescent bodies as the class prepares for the outing. Once ensconced at the Rock, Miss de Poitiers (Helen Morse) declares that the beautiful blonde Miranda (Anne Lambert) is a Botticelli angel while flies and ants collect on a heart-shaped cake. Languor and stifling heat pervade the atmosphere as the four girls go off, their white dresses starched, their hair bouncing in the sunlight. They are watched by the two young men, master and servant, who later find Irma.

Picnic at Hanging Rock is a story of the viewer and the unobservable, the known and the imagined, but most importantly, of the unknown. The unknown is palpable. Everything else is less real. It is also the familiar tale of upstairs/downstairs. First we see the serving girl in bed with the handyman; next Michael Fitzhubert and Albert strike up a desultory conversation while waiting for Fitzhubert's aunt and uncle to finish *their* picnic. The boys spot the girls crossing a stream and later search relentlessly until Fitzhubert finds Irma (Guard's role has unmistakable resonances with his part—as a younger boy—in the 1971 film *The Go-Between*, directed by Joseph Losey, laid in the same era) in the rocks. Albert, we learn, is related to the unfortunate Sara, and the night she dies, he dreams of her for the first time in years. Over all this sublimated chaos stands the brooding figure of Mrs. Appleyard, stern but not hostile, unrelenting but herself fallible.

It is difficult to write about performances in *Picnic at Hanging Rock* because everything is of a piece: the look of the film, the direction, the acting, and the script. Of the performances, however, those of Jarratt and Nelson stand out; they are reserved yet expressive, subdued yet about to burst. Rachel Roberts gives what is by now one of her standard performances, but it is admirable all the same—restrained yet showing Mrs. Appleyard's cracks, the lonely woman whose gradual loss of control over her world drives her to drink and utter indiscreet remarks. The other absorbing performance is that of Guard, as anxious to know why things happen as they do here as he is in *The Go-Between*. In *Picnic at Hanging Rock* his character is denied the natural curiosity of youth, so he has to supply his own answers; and the scene in which he quietly explores with Albert the topics that fascinate him are among the most arresting in the film.

In a film in which surfaces are of as much concern as substance and the unknowable is commonplace, *Picnic at Hanging Rock* reveals itself as something of a Victorian melodrama—that is, it is less profound than it seems upon first examination. It is not Henry James, or Shirley Jackson, or John Collier; it may not even be a real mystery. So it becomes a sort of soap opera, prettier than *General Hospital*, more cryptic than *As the World Turns*, but a movie with a sudsy soul all the same. Here are all these women wringing their hands in various stages of distress, and one or two stout-hearted men to help put things right. Peter Weir's mysteries (*The Last Wave*, 1979, is the other) are less puzzling, less occult that he would like us to believe. They are gorgeous, however—particularly this film; they are lucid, the music is apt, and if Weir does not say anything very deep, it does not matter much. He entertains the viewer.

Judith M. Kass

PINOCCHIO

Released: 1940
Production: Walt Disney
Supervising direction: Ben Sharpsteen and Hamilton Luske
Screenplay: Ted Sears, Otto Englander, Webb Smith, William Cottrell, Joseph Sabo, Erdman Penner, and Aurelius Battaglia; based on the story of the same name by Collodi (Carlos Lorenzini)
Sequence direction: Bill Roberts, Norman Ferguson, Jack Kinney, Wilfred Jackson, and T. Hee
Animation direction: Fred Moore, Franklin Thomas, Milton Kahl, Vladimir Tytla, Ward Kimball, Arthur Babbitt, Eric Larson, and Wolfgang Reitherman
Music: Paul J. Smith, Leigh Harline, and Ned Washington (AA)
Song: Leigh Harline and Ned Washington, "When You Wish Upon a Star" (AA)
Running time: 77 minutes

> *Voices of principal characters:*
> Pinocchio .... Dickie Jones
> Geppeto .... Christian Rub
> Jiminy Cricket .... Cliff Edwards
> The Blue Fairy .... Evelyn Venable
> J. Worthington Foulfellow .... Walter Catlett
> Stromboli and The Coachman .... Charles Judels
> Gideon .... Mel Blanc

Since the beginning of the animated film, the moviegoing public has had a love affair with the world of animation. This affair has continued to grow because film animation is a world made for the children in all of us. Within its boundaries, the animated film is filled with excitement, suspense, and, above all, fantasy. It creates its magic through the medium of the eye and it is experienced in the reality of the heart.

The history of American film animation has had many exciting moments, and most of them can be attributed to one man, Walt Disney. In the late 1920's, Disney, who was not yet thirty, founded a small production company that was destined to become the Disney Studio. From this studio came some of the best feature-length animated films ever made. Among them, *Pinocchio* is perhaps the best of the genre.

The story of *Pinocchio*, like so many of Disney's films, is a simple one. Based on Carlo Collodi's children's story of the same name, *Pinocchio* opens as Jiminy Cricket sings the Academy Award-winning song "When You Wish Upon a Star." Jiminy of course, plays an important role. He is the audience's link to the story, an outsider who becomes more and more involved in the adventures of Pinocchio. At this point in the film, Jiminy sets the stage for the fantasy by asking the audience whether they believe that dreams come true when you wish upon a star. To dispel any disbelief, Jiminy opens a storybook and begins the tale of *Pinocchio*.

The story begins with a flight over a quaint little village to the house of Geppeto, a puppetmaker. It is there that the audience first sees Pinocchio, a pleasant-looking boy puppet. As Geppeto gazes on the Wishing Star, he makes the wish that Pinocchio will become a live boy. Later that night, the Blue Fairy visits the workshop of Geppeto and transforms Pinocchio into a living being, albeit still in puppet form. The Blue Fairy tells Pinocchio that if he can prove himself worthy by being brave, unselfish, and truthful, he will become a real boy. The Blue Fairy also designates Jiminy Cricket to be Pinocchio's conscience. With the main outlines of the plot established, the story begins to unfold as Pinocchio explores the world and attempts to prove himself.

The first test for Pinocchio comes when Geppeto sends him off to school. On his way, Pinocchio meets a sly fox by the name of J. Worthington Foulfellow. In spite of Jiminy's objections, Foulfellow, along with his confederate Gideon, convinces Pinocchio to abandon school and pursue a life on the stage. They introduce the puppet to Stomboli, a wicked puppeteer. Pinocchio has his stage debut with the song "I've Got No Strings," and he is an instant success. Jiminy, feeling that Pinocchio's future is assured, leaves him in Stromboli's care. Stromboli, however, locks Pinocchio in a cage to protect his investment.

When the Blue Fairy appears, she asks Pinocchio how he managed to get into such a predicament. What follows is one of the truly classic scenes in animated fantasy. As Pinocchio tries to lie his way out of the fix he is in, his nose begins to grow. With each lie, his nose becomes a little longer until it finally begins to sprout branches, which offer refuge for a bird with its nest. In spite of his behavior, the Blue Fairy decides to give Pinocchio a second chance, and sets him free.

Together with Jiminy, Pinocchio sets out again to see the world. In no time at all, the two again run into J. Worthington Foulfellow and Gideon. This time the sly fox convinces Pinocchio to join a band of boys headed for Pleasure Island. There Pinocchio, along with the other boys, is encouraged to "live it up" and to make a jackass of himself. He does not know that the purpose of Pleasure Island is to do just that. Just before Pinocchio turns into a jackass, Jiminy comes to the rescue and the two escape from the island.

When Pinocchio and Jiminy return to the workshop, they find Geppeto gone. The Blue Fairy sends Pinocchio a message to let him know that Geppeto went to sea and was swallowed by Monstro, the Whale. The Blue Fairy tells Pinocchio that Geppeto is still alive and living in Monstro's stomach. With little hesitation, Pinocchio and Jiminy start out to save Geppeto's life. With his usual facility, Pinocchio also manages to be swallowed by Monstro. Meeting Geppeto, Pinocchio begins to make plans to escape. Pinocchio lights a fire in Monstro's stomach, causing the whale to sneeze. Pinocchio and Geppeto then escape on a raft, but an angry Monstro begins chasing them across the ocean. Eventually, Monstro catches the pair and destroys the raft. Struggling in the sea, Geppeto begs Pinocchio to save himself, but Pinocchio unselfishly pulls the puppetmaker out of the water. As Geppeto revives, he sees Pinocchio lying on the shore, dead.

Geppeto and Jiminy return to the workshop saddened by the death of Pinocchio. At that moment, the Blue Fairy's voice is heard. She says that Pinocchio indeed has proved himself worthy of being a real boy. As if by magic, Pinocchio awakens, not as a puppet but as a real boy. Seeing what has happened, Jiminy states that this is where he came in and leaves as the chorus begins a reprise of "When You Wish Upon a Star."

Although *Pinocchio* is a delightful fairy tale, the film is also a unique cinematic event. *Pinocchio* was the second attempt by the Disney Studio to create a feature-length animated film. The skills that Disney had developed in the Oscar-winning *Snow White and the Seven Dwarfs* (1937) are here refined and improved, showing great advances in the art of animation. Progress was made in the three areas of artwork, music, and technology. Any one of these in itself would have constituted an improvement on Disney's previous work, but the genius of Disney lay in his ability to merge the art of animation with its technology to create a new film experience.

Anyone who has seen a Disney animated film knows that the artwork is exemplary. In *Pinocchio*, Disney set new standards of excellence in that department. Not satisfied with anything less than perfection, he employed artists who created images that were truly lifelike. In fact, the main complaint of the critics was that *Pinocchio* was *too* lifelike and thus did not resemble previous animated films. To Disney, this was a compliment. His goal in *Pinocchio* was to perfect the art of the animated film, and the Disney staff came closer to that goal than any other group had done. As beautiful as the film's artwork is, the musical score of *Pinocchio* is no less superb. Music has always played an important role in animated films, but in *Pinocchio* its role is changed. Instead of supplying audio cues to the action on the screen, the Academy Award-winning score plays an integral part in the development of the story. As in live-action films, it is used to create moods, to establish characters, and to act as a link between the different parts of the story.

Although the artwork and music in *Pinocchio* were truly superb, the audiences at that time were more in awe of the technology involved. Before the making of *Pinocchio*, the Disney Studio had perfected a new device known as the multiplane animation camera, and *Pinocchio* was the first feature-length animated film to use it exclusively. The unique feature of this camera was its ability to create depth by photographing different layers of artwork. No longer needing to rely on artistic shadowing to create the illusion of depth, the Disney artists took advantage of the multiplane camera to the greatest extent possible.

In addition to the animation camera, Disney made other advancements in the technology of animation. Before *Pinocchio*, action in an animated film occurred within the film frame. Disney felt that this space was confining and extended it by again looking at the live-action film. In *Pinocchio*, he introduced the power zoom shot, the panoramic view, and other techniques. In *Pinocchio*, Disney expanded the world of animation to bring it closer to the reality of live-action motion picture.

The artwork, the music, and the technology of *Pinocchio*, taken separately, are superb. The real genius of the film, however, lies in the fusing of these elements. *Pinocchio* is in every sense a total movie. Its characters are well developed, and the audience is able to relate to them. The music blends well with the visual images and supports the story. The technique of animation creates the illusion of reality. The audience, however, does not consciously focus on these various elements. They appear as an integral unit, and that is a sign of a truly great motion picture.

Dennis K. Smeltzer

THE PIRATE

Released: 1948
Production: Arthur Freed for Metro-Goldwyn-Mayer
Direction: Vincente Minnelli
Screenplay: Albert Hackett and Frances Goodrich; based on the play of the
 same name by S. N. Behrman
Cinematography: Harry Stradling
Editing: Blanche Sewell
Music: Cole Porter
Running time: 101 minutes

> *Principal characters:*
> Manuela .... Judy Garland
> Serafin .... Gene Kelly
> Don Pedro .... Walter Slezak
> Aunt Inez .... Gladys Cooper

The Pirate is one of the wittiest and most interesting musicals of the 1940's.
In addition to the teaming of Judy Garland and Gene Kelly, the film features
the direction of Vincente Minnelli and the music of Cole Porter, and is based
on a play by S. N. Behrman. All of these elements combine to bring to *The
Pirate* a quality of exceptional style and originality.

The story of *The Pirate* is set in a small Caribbean town. As the film opens,
Manuela (Judy Garland) tells her friends of the exploits of Macoco the Pirate.
Manuela longs for adventure and romance, and secretly dreams that Macoco
will appear one day and carry her away from the boredom of her life in the
village. Manuela's Aunt Inez (Gladys Cooper) informs her that she has
arranged for Manuela to marry the town's mayor, Don Pedro (Walter Slezak).
Manuela hopes that marriage to such an important man will bring excitement
to her life, but she discovers, to her dismay, that Don Pedro longs for a quiet,
peaceful life in the village, having seen enough of the world in his youth.

Realizing that her chances for adventure are fading, Manuela persuades
Aunt Inez to take her to the coastal town where her trousseau will be delivered. There she encounters Serafin (Gene Kelly), the star of a band of strolling
players, who has been busy serenading all of the local girls with the song
"Nina." Manuela refuses his attentions, but is stunned by his quick assessment
of her situation. Intrigued by Serafin, she steals out of her room that night
to watch his performance. When Serafin sees her in the audience and hyp-
notizes her as part of his act, Manuela unexpectedly reveals her love for
Macoco and performs a tempestuous song, "Mack the Black," describing him.
Serafin ends her trance with a kiss and Manuela flees from the theater,
humiliated.

Manuela and Aunt Inez return to the village, but they are followed by

Serafin and his troupe. Arriving on her wedding day, Serafin walks a tightrope across the town square to gain admittance to Manuela's bedroom. Don Pedro arrives to throw him out, but when they are alone, Serafin tells the mayor that he was once a victim of one of Macoco's raids and that he recognizes Don Pedro as the infamous pirate. Unaware of Manuela's infatuation with the legend of Macoco, Don Pedro begs Serafin to remain silent. Serafin agrees, and, seeing his opportunity to win Manuela, announces to the villagers that he himself is Macoco. Manuela is overwhelmed and fantasizes a stunning adventure, the "Pirate Ballet," in which she sees Macoco (Serafin) plundering ships and slaying all who oppose him.

Serafin takes over the mayor's house and threatens to sack the town if Manuela is not brought to him. Don Pedro realizes what Serafin is planning, but is unable to speak out for fear of destroying his own reputation in the village. Hoping to foil Serafin's scheme, he leaves town to fetch the militia. Manuela, inwardly thrilled to be the object of "Macoco's" attentions, goes to the mayor's house, but while she is there another member of the acting troupe accidentally reveals Serafin's ruse. Manuela reacts in a fury, throwing everything in the room at Serafin. When he is knocked unconscious, however, she realizes that she loves him, although he is only an actor and not Macoco the Pirate. She sings "You Can Do No Wrong" to him, but they are surprised by Don Pedro and the militia, who arrest Serafin.

Wrongfully implicated by Don Pedro and found quilty of Macoco's crimes, Serafin is sentenced to be hanged. He requests that he be allowed to give one final performance, during which he attempts to hypnotize Don Pedro. When his efforts fail, however, Manuela pretends that she is in a trance and tells the crowd of her love for Macoco and her disgust for Don Pedro. As she sings "Love of My Life" to Serafin, Don Pedro is so overcome with jealousy that he reveals his true identity and is arrested. Manuela joins Serafin's acting troupe, and the film ends with the two of them in costume, giving a rollicking, high-spirited performance of "Be a Clown."

The Pirate is one of the many notable musicals produced at M-G-M by Arthur Freed and his talented filmmaking unit. The film is an outstanding example of the high quality of production values which made the unit famous. The sets and costumes are lavish and rich in detail, and the elaborately staged dance numbers are a swirling feast for the eye.

Although *The Pirate* has now become something of a cult film, it was not well received at the time of its release. This was due primarily to the film's unsentimental, tongue-in-cheek tone, a factor which set it apart from other musicals of the period. The script is witty and fast-paced, and it contains an abundance of sly references to theatrical life and theatrical egos. This type of "inside" humor worked well in *The Pirate*'s original play form when presented to the small world of New York theatergoers, but the wider audiences who saw the film found its tone baffling.

The stars, Garland and Kelly, work well as a team here, as they do in all of their screen appearances together, and it is ironic that their presence in the film added to the audience's confusion. Kelly, who had become known for his brash, good-natured all-American roles, is seen here as a dashing, mustachioed performer. His acrobatic dancing style, however, is ideally suited to such numbers as "Nina" and the "Pirate Ballet," and if the script's sophisticated dialogue was not what his fans had expected, the sight of Kelly walking tightropes and scaling walls did much to reconcile them to his part in the film.

The same was not true for Garland. As Manuela, she reveals her unique flair for comedy in a performance which ranges from slapstick clowning to moments of quiet tenderness. Director Minnelli, who was at that time married to her, clearly hoped to provide her with an opportunity to display her own wry, witty sense of humor, yet her role is so far removed from the uncomplicated, girl-next-door characters of her previous films that audiences of the time resisted her portrayal of Manuela.

Minnelli's skilled hand is felt throughout the film. Minnelli began his career as a theatrical art director, and his use of color is one of the trademarks of his directorial style. In his earlier film, *Meet Me in St. Louis* (1944), also with Garland, he uses color to evoke a mood of warmth and nostalgia. In *The Pirate*, however, his purpose is quite different. The tone of the film is one of fantasy and stylization, and Minnelli's choice of vivid, contrasting colors lends it a feeling that borders on surrealism. The characters and settings are deliberately theatrical, and Minnelli keeps the film's mood on a stylish, self-mocking level.

In this he is aided by Porter's delightful score. Whether the lyrics are those of Serafin's hilarious "Nina" ("Nina . . . I'll be having schizophrenia 'til I make you mine . . ."), or Manuela's touching "You Can Do No Wrong," Porter's songs add precisely the right touch to each scene. Indeed, the combined talents of Minnelli, Porter, Garland, and Kelly result in a film which was sophisticated at a time when musicals were expected only to be lively, and witty when they were required only to amuse. It is not surprising that *The Pirate* has grown in critical acclaim and popularity with the passage of time.

Janet E. Lorenz

PLAY IT AGAIN, SAM

Released: 1972
Production: Arthur P. Jacobs for Paramount
Direction: Herbert Ross
Screenplay: Woody Allen; based on his play of the same name
Cinematography: Owen Roizman
Editing: Marion Rothman
Running time: 84 minutes

Principal characters:
Allan Felix .... Woody Allen
Linda Christie .... Diane Keaton
Dick Christie .... Tony Roberts
Bogart .... Jerry Lacy
Nancy (Allan's ex-wife) .... Susan Anspach

Woody Allen is best known for such films as *Annie Hall* (1977) and *Bananas* (1971) in which narrative is not so important as individual scenes or disconnected gags, but *Play It Again, Sam* concentrates more on telling a story than the typical Allen film. The origin of the film is also atypical. Instead of writing an original screenplay with a collaborator and then directing the script himself as he usually does, Allen first wrote *Play It Again, Sam* as a play (which ran for a year on Broadway), and then, instead of directing the film version himself, he had Herbert Ross do it. These differences make the film more accessible and more controlled than many of his other films but no less imaginative and funny.

The opening of the film is both immediately engrossing and momentarily confusing. Before any credits appear we find ourselves watching the final scene of the 1941 Humphrey Bogart-Ingrid Bergman classic, *Casablanca*. As the scene continues, however, we find that it is being viewed in a theater by Allan Felix (Woody Allen), a writer for a film magazine, who watches it in open-mouthed admiration, sometimes mouthing the well-remembered words as we see the opening credits superimposed over his face.

Allan, we soon see, has strong feelings of his own inadequacy and a deep desire to be like the Bogart he sees on the screen—tough, confident, and attractive to women. Allan's self-esteem is at a low ebb because he has just been divorced. In a flashback he remembers his wife, Nancy (Susan Anspach), telling him why she wants out of the marriage: "I don't find you any fun; I feel you suffocate me; I don't feel any rapport with you, and I don't dig you physically." The fact that Allan wants to see films all the time also irritates Nancy. He is a watcher, she says, and she wants to *do* things.

The film uses a few flashbacks and fantasy scenes, but its chief imaginative device is that Humphrey Bogart (Jerry Lacy) appears to Allan from time to time. Although no one else in the film can see or hear him, Bogart is very real to Allan, who receives frequent advice and encouragement from him. The device is an expressive representation of Allan's preoccupation with the world of films, a preoccupation which makes his own life seem flat and colorless in comparison. Bogart's first advice is, "Dames are simple." He has never known one "that didn't understand a slap in the mouth or a slug from a .45," but this advice is useless to Allan, and he remains depressed.

Determined to help him out of his despondency, his friends Dick (Tony Roberts) and Linda Christie (Diane Keaton) begin trying to get dates for him. This course of action is not at all successful, mainly because Allan does not feel that he is attractive to women, so he goes to absurd lengths to make an impression. Before his first date, we see him dousing himself with cologne (he even drinks some), selecting books to leave half-opened as if he is reading them, and putting in a conspicuous place a track medal which he has bought. He has a brief fantasy about the girl succumbing to his charms ("Until tonight the doctors told me I was frigid"), but by the time she arrives with Dick and Linda, he is so worried about making an impression that he cannot carry on a simple conversation or even walk across the room without knocking over the furniture.

Despite one disastrous experience after another, Dick and Linda continue trying to find the right woman for Allan, and Linda keeps reassuring him between his failures. Dick is a harried businessman, and his continually calling his office to leave a telephone number whenever he arrives at a new place is a running gag in the film. As Dick spends more time on his business and Linda more time on helping Allan, Linda and Allan find themselves growing closer together. With Linda, Allan does not feel he has to put on an act.

He is completely relaxed with Linda until he finally realizes that he is in love with her. This realization occurs on the day Linda is coming to his apartment for dinner while Dick is away on a business trip. His confusion is represented first by a fantasy confrontation in a supermarket between Nancy and Bogart, with Bogart encouraging his romance with Linda and Nancy arguing with both Bogart and Allan. Allan also envisions the possible outcomes of the evening with Linda. In one version, Dick comes to him and announces that he has fallen in love with an Eskimo and would like Allan to take care of Linda. (As he leaves, he gives Allan a phone number—with a Frozen Tundra prefix—where he can be reached.) In another, when he tries to kiss Linda, she starts screaming "rape." When Linda actually arrives, Allan is at first very uncertain and fearful of offending her, but under Bogart's coaching he finally kisses her. In the confusion that follows, they knock over a lamp, and Linda, flustered, decides to leave. Moments later, however, she returns and we see their ecstatic embrace alternating with glimpses of Bogart and Bergman embracing in *Casablanca*. We next see the huge poster for the

Bogart film *Across the Pacific* (1942) which dominates Allan's bedroom; the camera then tilts down to show the two in bed, and we find that it is the next morning.

The physical and mental turmoil which follows involves several fantasies, in one of which Dick commits suicide by walking into the sea just as the faded movie actor Norman Maine did in *A Star Is Born* (1937 and 1954); much telephoning; and the realization by both Allan and Linda that Linda belongs with Dick. The action finally takes all three to the airport where Allan tells Linda to get on the plane in a scene which is nearly identical to the last scene of *Casablanca*. It is the ultimate use of the Bogart legend as well as a credible resolution of the romance. Bogart having pointed out to him that he got "a pretty good dame" to fall for him when he was not being phony, Allan walks away into the foggy evening determined to succeed on his own.

Despite Allen's well-known antipathy for California, *Play It Again, Sam* was shot in San Francisco because of a film strike in New York at the time it was made. Adapting the story to the West Coast setting was skillfully done so that such settings as the beach underscore the unfolding relationship between Linda and Allan, and others, such as an outdoor restaurant over-looking the San Francisco Bay and a cable car, artfully establish the locale without overwhelming the viewer with local color. The background is always background but is not neutral.

Play It Again, Sam abounds in references to other films. The most obvious are those to *Casablanca* (indeed, the title is a common *mis*quotation of a line from that film), but there are many others. Much of the film is reminiscent of *The Seven Year Itch* (1955), in which actor Tom Ewell, whose wife is away for the summer, has many amorous fantasies about his upstairs neighbor, Marilyn Monroe; and Allan's fantasy of curing a woman's frigidity is a reversal of a scene in *Some Like It Hot* (1959) in which Tony Curtis pretends to have the same affliction so that Monroe will try to overcome it. In addition, Linda mentions an Ida Lupino film in which Lupino becomes involved with her husband's best friend and then kills them and herself, and when Allan imagines what Dick will do when he finds out about Allan and Linda, he envisions both a suicide scene like the one James Mason did in *A Star Is Born* (1954) and a scene of revenge done in a style that parodies Italian films.

Keaton is natural, charming, and appealing as Linda, whether she is comparing neuroses and medications with Allan or trying to find a woman for him to go out with. Roberts does a good job of portraying Dick as a basically decent man who temporarily neglects his wife for his business. He must appear sympathetic enough that we see why Linda goes back to him but not so sympathetic that we do not understand why she gets involved with Allan. Woody Allen as Allan gives a good performance, playing much the same character that he plays in several of his other films—the rather incompetent intellectual who is insecure about women. Finally, director Ross expertly balances comedy and romance to make *Play It Again, Sam* both affecting and funny.

Timothy W. Johnson

POINT BLANK

Released: 1967
Production: Judd Bernard and Irwin Winkler for Metro-Goldwyn-Mayer
Direction: John Boorman
Screenplay: Alexander Jacobs, David Newhouse, and Rafe Newhouse; based
   on the novel *The Hunter* by Richard Stark
Cinematography: Philip H. Lathrop
Editing: Henry Berman
Running time: 92 minutes

Principal characters:
Walker	Lee Marvin
Chris	Angie Dickinson
Yost	Keenan Wynn
Mal Reese	John Vernon
Brewster	Carroll O'Connor

Novelist Richard Stark's classic contemporary antihero Parker is given his most vivid screen portrayal as the character Walker, played by Lee Marvin in John Boorman's visually experimental *Point Blank*. After his release from jail, Walker (Lee Marvin), a professional criminal, searches for his wife and for the man who sold him out to the police as the fall guy. His search leads him to his wife, now dead, and to her sister. He convinces Chris (Angie Dickinson), his sister-in-law, to help him avenge his wife's death and take revenge on those responsible for his incarceration. He muscles through a string of punks and petty hoodlums in his search for the boss with violence that is extreme and unusual. He wrecks cars, furniture, and objects of art. He is more concerned with destroying affectations of wealth than with murdering people. After determining who was responsible for the double cross, Walker convinces Chris to proposition the culprit. She is successful, and at the moment of sexual fulfillment Walker, according to plan, interrupts their "bliss" and tosses his ex-partner out a penthouse window. Satisfied, Walker leaves, trying to pick up the pieces of his shattered career as a professional thief.

There is a visual flavor present in *Point Blank* which epitomizes the popular culture of the 1960's in a way that few films have. It is a fascinating blend of elliptical cutting, convoluted time structure, and shocking, violent images. Directed by Boorman, who has placed his unmistakable visual stamp on such films as *Deliverance* (1972), *Zardoz* (1974), and the ambitious *The Exorcist II: The Heretic* (1977), *Point Blank* showcases Boorman's talent for creating tension by contrast. He has the ability to create images in his films which are wild and uncontrollable, yet which have a calculating, intelligent force behind them. Boorman is one of the truly individualistic filmmakers whose work exists on a complex level. His films require a certain amount of audience sophistication in order to generate an aesthetic completeness. *Point Blank* uses the medium of the film to the fullest. Boorman builds his film with a convoluted time structure and in this way freely cuts back and forth in time to use flashbacks as part of the basic narrative technique. This type of film-making is somewhat disturbing for audiences not familiar with the form of film. Regardless of his tendency toward obliqueness, Boorman does make effective use of the medium to create drama. He employs his actors to reinforce the visual effects in much the same way that Alfred Hitchcock did.

The novels of Stark, whose real name is Donald Westlake, are rich in characterization and milieu. The author's ability to suggest the criminal environment is nothing short of brilliant. Various filmmakers have seen the potential for cinematic adaptations of Stark's work. Besides Boorman, Jean Luc-Goddard and Ralph Nelson have tried to interpret various of his novels. Each director approached the character of Parker in a manner characteristic of his style. Goddard's adaptation of Stark's *The Jugger* was an obscure and vague film. Ralph Nelson turned *The Seventh* into a socially relevant crime-melodrama entitled *The Split* (1968), in which "Parker" is transformed into a black man portrayed by Jim Brown. Beyond the basic plot of a well-executed robbery of ticket receipts at a major sporting event, *The Split* ignores most of Stark's original novel, preferring to concentrate on interracial tension and corruption.

In its way, *Point Blank*, adapted from Stark's novel *The Hunter*, is more faithful to its literary roots. The ellipitcal style of Boorman's film approximates the violent world of Parker, and the choice of Marvin to portray the character called Walker is a brilliant stroke of casting genius. Marvin is able to generate a feeling of strength in scenes of both emotional and physical intensity. His action is also enlarged by the use of the wide screen and by Boorman's use of choker close-ups (compositions which tend to isolate particular actors because of the extended rectangular shape of the projected image).

The apparent success of Walker at the end of the film is nontraditional. The use of the antihero had never been exploited to such a degree in crime-melodramas as it was in *Point Blank*. Marvin is able to allow his character to transcend the typical morality of good and evil to such a degree that the element of revenge and eventual murder seems totally justifiable.

Point Blank is characteristic of a new wave of American films which exploded onto the scene in the wake of the multimillion-dollar film epic. It presents intense dramatic conflicts on the wide screen with intimate detail. The existentialism of the characters that populate the film, the use of the urban milieu, the display of violence, and the uncertain morality exhibited by the antihero all point to a radical change in the content of contemporary motion pictures. These attitudes and avenues of development may seem typical at this time, yet during the 1960's when films such as *Point Blank* and the work of Stanley Kubrick and Sam Peckinpah became recognized, the pendulum was certainly poised in the opposite direction.

Carl F. Macek

THE PRESIDENT'S ANALYST

Released: 1967
Production: Stanley Rubin for Paramount
Direction: Theodore J. Flicker
Screenplay: Theodore J. Flicker
Cinematography: William A. Fraker
Editing: Stuart H. Pappe
Running time: 103 minutes

> *Principal characters:*
> Dr. Sidney Schaefer .... James Coburn
> Don Masters .... Godfrey Cambridge
> Kropotkin .... Severn Darden
> Nan Butler .... Joan Delaney
> Snow White .... Jill Banner
> Wynn Quantrill .... William Daniels
> Jeff Quantrill .... Joan Darling
> Bing Quantrill .... Sheldon Collins
> Henry Lux .... Walter Burke

The President's Analyst is a spy spoof made in the wake of the 1960's James Bond craze, and one that actually has something interesting to say. In this fast-moving, visually adept comedy written and directed by Theodore J. Flicker, the key word is satire. Mischievous and clever, the film is a rarity: a coherent black comedy that uses the spy-caper genre as a springboard to examine the betrayal of the so-called American Dream.

The unusual premise is that the President of the United States needs a psychiatrist. Chosen to relieve his anxieties is a New York practitioner, Dr. Sidney Schaefer (James Coburn), a successful Everyman with a basic faith in America. Sidney moves to Washington with his girl friend Nan Butler (Joan Delaney) and is soon being summoned at all hours to secret sessions at the White House. Sharing the President's psychological burden, he becomes convinced that agents of all kinds are after the secrets he carries, following him everywhere he goes. Soon Sidney begins to get unnerved. Just when he feels himself cracking under the mental strain, he discovers that his suspicions are real. Foreign agents *are* after him, and, what is worse, the American "FBR" and "CEA" want him killed as a security leak.

Sidney escapes from Washington with the Quantrills, a family he picks at random from the White House tour, but is appalled by their extremist politics and their fanatical militancy. Their son Bing (Sheldon Collins) turns out to be a junior FBR agent who reports Sidney to his superiors. Out for a walk with his adopted family, Sidney is located and attacked by his pursuers. They prove to be no match for the Quantrills, who gleefully scream "Muggers!"

before stopping the assailants with guns and karate chops. Sidney flees once again, however, this time joining a truckful of hippies.

The only "good spy" pursuing Sidney is the top American agent Don Masters (Godfrey Cambridge), the man who had recruited Sidney for the Washington job and who now feels responsible for him. Don is able to save Sidney from multiple assassination attempts but cannot keep him from falling into the hands of a succession of kidnapers, each with a use for Sidney's secrets. The last is Don's professional friend, the Russian agent Kropotkin (Severn Darden). An old-style romantic at heart, Kropotkin responds to Sidney's offer of psychiatric help, and the two elect to return to the President together.

Sidney is once again abducted, however, this time by the Telephone Company, which seeks to use his influence with the President in a plot to take control of the country. An automated conspiracy, the Telephone Company has sensed a rebellious public attitude toward its inefficient service in the form of vandalism and nonpayment of bills and has decided that the solution is to put a wiretap in the brain of every American at birth. Faced with this common enemy, Kropotkin and Don forget their differences and pool their effort to rescue Sidney and destroy the Telephone Company's headquarters. When freed, Sidney joins the battle and finds himself enjoying the combat. The threesome's victory is not final, however: their subsequent Christmas celebration with Nan is watched from afar by a host of Telephone Company robots, who gaze with synthesized empathy upon the mortals they will surely enslave.

Transcending the pointlessness and triviality of many of the sophisticated spy spoofs so prevalent in 1967, such as Coburn's own *Our Man Flint*, *The President's Analyst* cuts right to the heart of America's preoccupation with espionage, tying it in with, of all things, psychoanalysis. The spies in the film, including the American and Russian heroes, all want analysis, as if a spy by nature needed inner surveillance to balance his external life style. Everyone the psychiatrist meets seems to have some sort of mental problem, including the paranoid computer. Mostly sane, politically neutral, totally confused, and hotly pursued by what seem to be hundreds of espionage agents, Sidney Schaefer moves through a psychotic America ripe for the satiric lampoon of director Flicker. The only target spared is the President himself, who is respectfully not portrayed. The jibes aimed at the thinly disguised FBI and CIA, however, are anything but respectful. The J. Edgar Hoover character, Henry Lux (Walter Burke), is so paranoid that he has staffed his bureau exclusively with agents shorter than himself. The standard spy gadgetry of his various assassins succeeds mostly in helping them kill each other instead of Sidney.

It is when Sidney seeks refuge in the suburban landscape that the satire is in best focus. The "typical American family" turns out to be infected with mindless consumerism and extremist zeal. Wynn Quantrill (William Daniels) is obsessed with extremely loud stereo music, which he calls "total sound." The Quantrill house resembles an armed camp. Wynn has both a "car gun" and a "house gun" and even the "Missus" (Joan Darling) takes karate lessons. Wynn's idea of political liberalism is summarized by his eagerness to send his less enlightened neighbors, "the real fascists," to the gas chamber. America's bleak political future is represented by their son who wiretaps the house phone for the FBR with a Junior Spy kit.

The President's Analyst's science-fiction conclusion was criticized by many contemporary reviewers as cynical, unfunny, and too extreme. The revelation of the ultimate enemy as the HAL-like computer menace of the Telephone Company is actually both ahead of its time and a logical extension of the film's ideas. Technocracy triumphs over chaos; James Bond is enslaved by his own gadgets. Spies will not bug telephones anymore, but will be bugged along with everyone else by mind control. The brilliant final image, with the warm and genuine human celebration being monitored by a dozen animatronic figures, is humorously conceived, but reveals a chilling truth about the direction of modern society. More sinister than the vegetables of *Invasion of the Body Snatchers* (1956 and 1978), these telephone pod-people are mastering the pretense of human emotions.

Like Stanley Kubrick's *Dr. Strangelove* (1964), *The President's Analyst* succeeds as black comedy because of the sincerity of its characterizations. Even in the midst of its comic-book melodramatics, the characters resemble real people with real problems. Much of the credit for this goes to the performers. Darden and Cambridge invest their spy characters with unexpected sentiment behind their tongue-in-cheek banter. As the bigots next door, Daniels and Darling make a remarkably strong impression, especially considering the brevity of the suburbia episode.

Sidney Schaefer is perhaps Coburn's most well-rounded performance. His hawklike features and hesitant manner are as stylized as the film's decor. More importantly, Coburn projects an open-minded quality, a wide-eyed inquisitiveness that wins the interest and identification of the audience. In the last shot of the battle scene, the pacifistic Sidney punches through a cloud of pink smoke, firing his machine gun at the enemies of freedom, laughing like a hero on a Marxist propaganda poster. Sidney's experiences have transformed him from a complacent citizen into a revolutionary soldier. Thanks to Coburn's strong presence, at the fadeout, freedom's chances somehow look good, even with the odds all on the side of the totalitarian computers.

Glenn M. Erickson

PRIDE AND PREJUDICE

Released: 1940
Production: Hunt Stromberg for Metro-Goldwyn-Mayer
Direction: Robert Z. Leonard
Screenplay: Aldous Huxley and Jane Murfin; based on Helen Jerome's dramatization of the novel of the same name by Jane Austen
Cinematography: Karl Freund
Editing: Robert J. Kern
Costume design: Adrian
Running time: 117 minutes

> *Principal characters:*
> Elizabeth Bennet .... Greer Garson
> Mr. Darcy .... Laurence Olivier
> Mrs. Bennet .... Mary Boland
> Mr. Bennet .... Edmund Gwenn
> Lady Catherine de Bourgh .... Edna May Oliver
> Jane Bennet .... Maureen O'Sullivan
> Lydia Bennet .... Ann Rutherford
> Miss Bingley .... Frieda Inescort
> Mr. Bingley .... Bruce Lester
> Kitty Bennet .... Heather Angel
> Mary Bennet .... Marsha Hunt
> Mr. Wickham .... Edward Ashley
> Mr. Collins .... Melville Cooper

Essential to the appreciation of M-G-M's *Pride and Prejudice* is the understanding that the film, like the novel, is a parody of the manners and customs of the society into which English novelist Jane Austen was born. She wrote the novel in 1793 (although it was published twenty years later) as a distorted reflection of aristocratic and near-aristocratic English country life.

In keeping with his personal conviction to "Do it big, do it right, give it class," Louis B. Mayer, head of Metro-Goldwyn-Mayer, dictated that Austen's England be re-created in lavish splendor and her characters depicted in excessive folly. The screenplay was drawn from a faithful dramatization of the novel by Helen Jerome which was presented on the New York stage in 1935. In adapting the play to the screen, however, writers Jane Murfin and Aldous Huxley took liberties with the central character, Elizabeth Bennet. Here, her story is interwoven with those of her family rather than presented as a contrast between her unusual and forceful nature and the constraints of her time and background.

In keeping with the extravagant look of the film, the novel's period was advanced some forty years in order to feature the voluminous and dandified costume styles of the mid-1800's. The restrained, vertical-line style of the classical revival Directoire and Empire costume periods was deemed less suitable, although more historically accurate. Designer Adrian created five hundred hoop-skirted gowns for the film, which actress Marsha Hunt, who portrays Elizabeth's sister, Mary Bennet, recalls as being most difficult to manage in the narrow restroom stalls during the short breaks in filming on the M-G-M sound stages. The gowns, however, were a delight to wear during the daily 4:00 P.M. tea breaks which the company dutifully observed because of the many Britons working on the film.

The drama unfolds in three locales: Longbourn, the country home of the Bennet family; Netherfield Park, the vast estate which is rented for the season by a Mr. Bingley (Bruce Lester), his sister (Frieda Inescort), and their friend, Mr. Darcy (Laurence Olivier); and Meryton, the distant village where the Bennet women encounter their social rivals while shopping.

Mrs. Bennet (Mary Boland), the mother of the five Bennet girls, first glimpses the Bingleys and Mr. Darcy and immediately perceives the matrimonial possibilities in the two men. She has lately exhibited a constant state of nervous agitation regarding her undoweried and still unmarried daughters. She fears that the girls are doomed to spinsterhood, and a penniless one at that, owing to the fact that they will come into no inheritance at their father's death. The Bennet fortune is encumbered; it must pass only to a male heir as decreed by an ancestral benefactor. The current male heir is a distant cousin to the Bennets, the boring and pompous Mr. Collins (Melville Cooper).

Mr. Bennet (Edmund Gwenn), born a gentleman although married to a shopkeeper's daughter, suffers his wife's distress with equanimity. He is not surprised when, returning from shopping with the girls at Meryton, she tells him of sighting Netherfield Park's new residents. When she implores him to arrange a meeting of Mr. Bingley and Mr. Darcy and their daughters, he reassures her that the introductions will take place at the upcoming Assembly Ball.

At the Assembly Ball, the social event of the season, Mr. Bingley favors Jane Bennet (Maureen O'Sullivan) with his attentions but Mr. Darcy remains aloof from the event, which he considers to be "the middle classes at play." Elizabeth Bennet (Greer Garson) overhears his condescending observations, however, and is angered. She is soon able to return his insult to her family and friends by refusing to dance with him when he asks her. He is stunned. She dances instead with a Mr. Wickham (Edward Ashley), to whom Darcy bears a mysterious resentment. Elizabeth is further annoyed by Darcy's "incivility" to Wickham.

In the days following the ball, Jane receives an invitation from Mr. Bingley to have tea at Netherfield Park. Knowing that it will rain, her mother urges her to ride the distance not in a closed carriage but on horseback. As Mrs. Bennet hoped, Jane catches a bad cold en route and is ordered by the doctor for whom Bingley calls to stay in bed at Netherfield for one week. Her sister

Elizabeth is then sent to attend her there by the shrewd mother. During Jane's week of convalescence, Mr. Bingley's affection for her grows. Elizabeth and Mr. Darcy, however, exchange only the barest of courtesies. The eldest Bennet daughter is at once piqued and dismayed at having to avoid Darcy's silent stares throughout the long evenings in Netherfield's drawing room.

Meanwhile, at Longbourn, Mr. Collins charitably offers himself, and his impending fortune, to whomever of the Bennet girls their mother believes to be the most suitable. Upon learning that Elizabeth's week at Netherfield does not hold the promise of a match as Jane's does, Mrs. Bennet suggests Elizabeth as a wife for Mr. Collins. She is horrified at the news. She flees his company when he calls at Longbourn for her and later at a garden fête which the Bingley's hold for the recuperated Miss Jane. At the party, Darcy witnesses one of Elizabeth's flights. Close on her heels is Mr. Collins. Darcy purposely throws him off her trail by misdirecting him. Hiding nearby, Elizabeth overhears, and when Collins disappears, she emerges to thank Darcy for his kindness. As they enjoy the remainder of the party together, their acquaintance becomes friendship. Still troubling Elizabeth, however, is Darcy's shabby treatment of Wickham at the Assembly Ball weeks earlier, but she temporarily dismisses the thought.

Later that afternoon, at the brink of a growing fondness for each other, Darcy and Elizabeth overhear her mother going on at length, "Oh sister! Jane's future is assured now! Dear Mr. Bingley makes no secret of his admiration. That week she was ill at Netherfield completed the conquest. I knew it would. Wasn't it clever of me to send her over in a rainstorm on horseback? Of course, dear Jane will now be able to give my daughters opportunities for meeting all sorts of rich men!" Concealing her embarrassment, Elizabeth immediately excuses herself from Mr. Darcy's company.

It is not long before Jane receives a note from Miss Bingley advising her that they have departed Netherfield for London where it is hoped that her brother will propose to Mr. Darcy's sister. Jane is crushed. Elizabeth is saddened by her sister's inconsolable grief and stifles her own distress at Darcy's leavetaking. She is astonished to meet him again many months later while visiting Mr. Collins and his new wife, Charlotte Lucas, a friend of Elizabeth's. During an evening at the nearby estate of Rosings, the home of the formidable and rich Lady Catherine de Brough (Edna May Oliver), Darcy and Elizabeth renew their acquaintance. Realizing the strength of his love for her, Darcy calls upon her the following day to propose. Moments earlier, however, Elizabeth learned that it was he who intervened between Jane and Mr. Bingley. Elizabeth not only refuses him but also berates him for his misperception of Jane's love for Bingley. She also takes issue with his treatment of Mr. Wickham. This final blow forces him out of the room with a polite good-bye and Elizabeth soon returns home to Longbourn.

At home, Elizabeth learns the news that her sixteen-year-old sister Lydia

(Ann Rutherford) has run away with Mr. Wickham without the benefit of marriage. Darcy soon reappears with the revelation that Wickham had attempted the same despicable act with his fifteen-year-old sister, although they were found out in time. At last Elizabeth understands the real cause of the enmity between the two. Unsuccessful at finding his daughter in London, Mr. Bennet returns home and prepares his family to leave Longbourn until the scandal subsides. Lydia and Mr. Wickham, however, arrive in grand style with the announcement that they are indeed married and that he has come into a sudden, anonymous inheritance. Mrs. Bennet is thus rescued from her impending nervous collapse.

Lady Catherine presents herself in the midst of Lydia's joyous homecoming and proceeds to grill Elizabeth about her designs on Mr. Darcy's fortune. As trustee of his mother's estate, Lady Catherine threatens to cut off his inheritance should her nephew marry Elizabeth. Elizabeth is unfazed at Lady Catherine's intimidations, knowing that Darcy's interest in her is quite extinguished because of her proud and prejudiced behavior toward him. She is astonished, however, to learn from Lady Catherine of Darcy's love for her. "He needs a woman to stand up to him!" says the old dowager. Lady Catherine also reveals that it was Darcy who scoured the back alleys of London in search of Wickham and Lydia, and it was he who set up Wickham with an income and forced him to marry Lydia. Delighted and overwhelmed to learn of her misinterpretations of Mr. Darcy's character, Elizabeth maintains her composure long enough to show Lady Catherine out. Darcy's benefactress is happily persuaded that Elizabeth is not a fortune hunter and gives her blessing concerning the match to Darcy, who waits just outside Longbourn's door.

The final scene presents a jubilant Mrs. Bennet as she surveys three love-struck couples before her: Bingley, whom Darcy managed to reconcile with Jane; Lydia and her new husband; and finally, Darcy and Elizabeth. Nearby are daughters Kitty (Heather Angel) and Mary, who are accompanied by two young suitors at the pianoforte. "Just think!" she effuses to her husband, "Three of them married and the other two just trembling on the brink!"

Modern audiences must view *Pride and Prejudice* as a cloying, lighthearted commentary on a society of long ago, for the story surely does not hold up under scrutiny. The film's enjoyment lies in its spectacle, which unfortunately is in black-and-white, in Boland's characterization of a flustered busybody, in Inescourt's withering stares, in the simpering flirtations of the younger Bennet girls, and in the poised, superbly underplayed character of Elizabeth Bennet. Like the novel's dialogue, the speeches of the players in the film are convoluted and excessively refined to the point that they require close listening. Similarly, the baroque story demands vigilant attention or the jigsaw-puzzle story line will not fit together for the viewer. The film, then, cannot be dismissed an an M-G-M costume extravaganza of little substance. It is a beautifully done period piece which suffers only from its overblown characters. Gwenn's Mr. Bennet provides the much-needed balance to offset the comings and goings of a dithering array of lady birds in plumage. Had he played a greater role, this comedy of manners might have found much-needed dramatic stability.

Audiences did not seem to mind the problems with the film, however, and enjoyed the spectacle. In retrospect, the character actors from the M-G-M stock company, joined by the addition of British players from other studios, make the film most enjoyable.

Nancy S. Kinney

PRIDE OF THE MARINES

Released: 1945
Production: Jerry Wald for Warner Bros.
Direction: Delmer Daves
Screenplay: Albert Maltz; based on Marvin Borowsky's adaptation of the
magazine story of the same name by Roger Butterfield
Cinematography: Peverall Marley
Editing: Owen Marks
Running time: 119 minutes

Principal characters:
Al Schmid	John Garfield
Ruth Hartley	Eleanor Parker
Lee Diamond	Dane Clark
Jim Merchant	John Ridgely
Virginia Pfeiffer	Rosemary DeCamp
Ella Merchant	Ann Doran
Lucy Merchant	Ann Todd
Johnny Rivers	Anthony Caruso

In the March 22, 1943, issue of *Life* magazine, writer Roger Butterfield told the true story of Marine hero Al Schmid, who was credited with machine-gunning some two hundred Japanese soldiers during a fierce night attack on Guadalcanal. Underlining Schmid's courageous act was the fact that he had been blinded by a grenade during the early morning hours. Still, he refused to relinquish his position and fought the enemy by having a wounded buddy tell him where to point his gun.

Pride of the Marines tells Schmid's story, but the film's importance as a hero's biography is surpassed by its attempt to deliver an honest story about handicapped veterans and the personal trials they face upon returning home. At the time of its release (it preceded the more famous *The Best Years of Our Lives* by one year), *Pride of the Marines* was considered by most critics to be Hollywood's most serious attempt at depicting the problems of the war veteran. Delivered in a semidocumentary style which gives believability to the film's real-life origins, *Pride of the Marines* also affected viewers because of an especially powerful war scene, which remains even today a stirring and inspirational screen statement about men in combat.

As the story opens, Al Schmid (John Garfield) is a cocky, fun-loving, twenty-one-year-old Philadelphia machinist who boards with the Merchant family (John Ridgely, Ann Doran, and Ann Todd). Although he sees himself as a determined bachelor, he finds his resistance being broken by Ruth Hartley (Eleanor Parker), with whom he falls in love.

Shortly after the attack on Pearl Harbor (Schmid thinks Pearl Harbor is "somewhere off the Jersey coast" when he and the Merchants hear the news on the radio), Schmid joins the Marines, lightly surmising that "shooting Japs would be more fun than shooting bear." His outlook is less flippant during the courageous night on Guadalcanal, which finds him and several buddies attempting to keep Japanese soldiers from crossing the Tenaru River. Al, Lee Diamond (Dane Clark), and Johnny Rivers (Anthony Caruso) are in a machine-gun nest near the river. Although they valiantly try to hold back the enemy, Johnny is killed, and Lee is wounded in the shoulder and rendered helpless. It remains for Al, who is later blinded by a grenade blast, to face the enemy.

It is a wrenching combat sequence, set off by Al's cry (as the Japanese begin wading across the river), "One big bowling alley! Tear their guts out!" Dramatically effective lighting, which emphasizes Al's sightlessness, later sets the mood, as do the piercing sound effects, which are coupled by taunts in the night from the nearby Japanese ("Marine you die . . . Marine you die tonight"). Dominating the scene is Schmid's undaunted bravery, as he screams out to Lee to point him toward the enemy.

It is an embittered Schmid who is later seen in a United States military hospital in San Diego. Refusing to accept his blindness, Schmid dictates letters to Ruth with the help of kind nurse Virginia Pfeiffer (Rosemary DeCamp), but never reveals his blindness to his sweetheart. Against the advice of the hospital doctors, who feel his condition will be permanent, Schmid also insists on an operation. Sadly, it proves unsuccessful. Angry, and with no sense of hope for his future, Schmid tries to break off his relationship with Ruth. He also refuses any efforts toward rehabilitation, such as learning Braille. When he is ordered back to Philadelphia by his commanding officer in order to receive the Navy Cross ("I traded in my eyes for a Navy Cross"), Schmid feigns indifference with Ruth. "I'm nobody's lap dog. I got too much pride," he maintains, with an equally angered Ruth retorting, "You haven't got the pride to accept being blind like a man." Schmid's buddy, Lee, vents his own frustrations when he reminds Schmid that he does not have a monopoly on handicaps. "There's guys who won't hire me because I celebrate Passover . . ." he says.

Schmid remains obstinate, however, until he attends a Christmas party at the Merchant house. Attempting to make his way about the room without any assistance, he tumbles into a Christmas tree. The embarrassing moment underlines his need for other people—especially Ruth. Once again, they declare their love for each other. They plan to marry, and Schmid—in keeping with the true story—regains partial sight so that he can distinguish shapes and colors.

Simple in story line and inspiring in conviction, *Pride of the Marines* is bolstered by fine, understated performances. Garfield, who had established a reputation for portraying reckless fatalists, was given his most traditionally heroic role as the memorable Schmid, and he did well with it.

Although some scenes occasionally veer into sentimentality—especially during a hospital sequence which finds the men (who embrace various ethnic backgrounds and social strata) airing their gripes about their condition and the country's treatment of them—*Pride of the Marines* stands as a still-effective saga about war and its aftermath. Giving particular credence to Schmid's story is the vivid combat sequence, a memorable depiction of the war which has spawned the tragic need for rehabilitation.

In viewing the film today, it remains a courageous and decidedly patriotic effort. While it might be argued that some of the dialogue about the Japanese is derogatory (during the night on Guadalcanal, for example, their taunting words are heard as "Mreen yoo Dyee . . . Mreen yoo dyee tonight!"), considering the film's wartime release date any ethnic slurs seem intended as an indictment against "the enemy" rather than a nationality. It should also be noted that contemporary offerings about war veterans and their adjustment, such as the Academy Award-winning *Coming Home* (1978), are no more stirring than this film. In fact, because *Coming Home* only deals with the after-effects of war itself, the earlier film may ultimately stand as a more definitive study. It remains for *Coming Home*—which never depicts the horrors that purportedly affected its men—to weather an equally lengthy screen life.

Pride of the Marines is also distinguished by Delmer Daves's direction— which is all the more admirable in light of the fact that Daves had made his directorial debut just two years earlier. His first film, *Destination Tokyo* (1943), also starred Garfield, along with Cary Grant; the story detailed a United States submarine's attempts to invade Japanese waters. In later years, Daves helped to redefine the Western genre (notably with *Broken Arrow* in 1950). The director's filmography, which touches nearly every genre, exemplifies a diverse talent.

While the screenplay for *Pride of the Marines* was nominated for an Academy Award, writer Albert Maltz was later blacklisted. At the time of the film's release, some critics felt that Maltz's script dealt too heavily with "social consciousness." That social consciousness, however, was not depicted by the film's advertising materials—specifically its poster, which shows Garfield, Parker, and Clark with arms linked, walking merrily along.

Pat H. Broeske

PRIDE OF THE YANKEES

Released: 1942
Production: Samuel Goldwyn for RKO/Radio
Direction: Sam Wood
Screenplay: Jo Swerling and Herman J. Mankiewicz; based on an original
story by Paul Gallico, with special assistance by Mrs. Lou Gehrig
Cinematography: Rudolph Maté
Editing: Daniel Mandell (AA)
Running time: 128 minutes

Principal characters:
Lou Gehrig	Gary Cooper
Eleanor Gehrig	Teresa Wright
Sam Blake	Walter Brennan
Babe Ruth	Himself
Hank Hanama	Dan Duryea
Mrs. Gehrig	Elsa Janssen
Myra	Virginia Gilmore

Baseball has been the subject of an occasional film since 1899 when the
first version of *Casey at the Bat* was made. There have been such serious films
made about the sport as *The Bush Leaguer* (1917), *Slide Kelly Slide* (1927),
and *The Big Leaguer* (1953), as well as such comedies as *Elmer the Great*
(1933) and *Alibi Ike* (1935), both with Joe E. Brown, *Fast Company* (1929),
Rhubarb (1951), *It Happens Every Srping* (1949), *Speedy* (1928), with Harold
Lloyd, *College* (1927), with Buster Keaton, and *Ladies' Day* (1943). In
addition, baseball has been the source for a fantasy, *Angels in the Outfield*
(1951), a whodunit, *Death on the Diamond* (1934), and musicals such as *Take
Me Out to the Ball Game* (1949) and *Damn Yankees* (1958).
Nevertheless, it is the biographies of the men who played the sport that
generate the majority of opinion regarding the treatment of the sport on film.
Unfortunately, of the seven feature films made about baseball personalities—
The Stratton Story (1949, with James Stewart), *The Babe Ruth Story* (1948,
with William Bendix), *Pride of the Yankees* (1942, with Gary Cooper as Lou
Gehrig), *The Winning Team* (1952, with Ronald Reagan as Grover Cleveland
Alexander), *The Pride of St. Louis* (1952, with Dan Dailey as Dizzy Dean),
Fear Strikes Out (1957, with Anthony Perkins as Jimmy Piersall), and *The
Jackie Robinson Story* (1950, with Jackie Robinson)—the majority have pro-
vided little insight into either the characters or careers of the men involved.
Furthermore, in some cases (*The Winning Team*, *The Pride of St. Louis*, and
The Babe Ruth Story) the results have been dismal. Cheaply made and miscast,
these films have done much to sustain an image of baseball as intolerably
boring.

Fortunately, there are some films which are at least entertaining, if not insightful, and of these, the best by far is *Pride of the Yankees*. Starring Gary Cooper as the immortal Lou Gehrig and costarring Teresa Wright as his ever-faithful wife Eleanor, the film benefits from Cooper's sincere interpretation of one of baseball's true legends. Perhaps because Gehrig was in fact a quiet, soft-spoken gentleman, Cooper's low-key performance seems especially appropriate. When contrasted with the much more flamboyant Babe Ruth, who makes a cameo appearance as himself in the film, Gehrig appears to be the epitome of what a baseball player should be. Nevertheless, for all of Gehrig's reputed wholesomeness, he provided the country and baseball with years of aggressive but sportsmanslike behavior. To have him immortalized on celluloid by Cooper is both fitting and appropriate.

Given such a model, it is perhaps easier to understand why the film ranks as one of the best sports biographies ever made. Directed with straightforward but compassionate style by Sam Wood, the film follows Gehrig through a childhood in an immigrant slum to his early days at college, where he plays baseball and learns about prejudice and snobbery at the fraternity house where he works. Nevertheless, having convinced a scout for the Yankees of his potential, he is signed and soon playing in Yankee Stadium with Babe Ruth and other legends of the game. Called on to replace an injured player, Gehrig goes on to become known as the "iron man" of baseball by playing in more consecutive games than any other player in history, a record which still stands. Along the way, he amasses records and statistics which amaze even the most ardent of baseball aficionados.

Tragically, however, even the iron man could not last forever. Late in his career, he contracted a very rare nerve disease which now bears his name, and died after a lengthy illness. Nevertheless, in his farewell appearance to the people of New York City, during which he was already weakened by his debilitating disease, he recalled the good times baseball had given him, stating that he considered himself to be the "luckiest man alive."

It is, of course, a tragedy when anyone dies in the prime of life, but it seems even sadder to see someone who has built a career and reputation on his body fall victim to an illness such as his. Film after film has been made in an attempt to capture the drama and sadness of such a tragedy, but few have succeeded as well as *Pride of the Yankees*. Perhaps it is due to the fact that Lou Gehrig was such a symbol of strength that his death was so moving. Surely, the opportunity to say good-bye on both radio and newsreel to the fans who supported and encouraged him over the years helped to immortalize him. All in all, however, Cooper's interpretation will stand as the ultimate tribute to the man.

In the final sequence of the film, in which Gehrig makes his farewell speech, the director intercuts actual footage of the event with closely matched scenes of Cooper delivering the message. The results are moving and dramatic and were instrumental in earning an Oscar for film editor Daniel Mandell. To anyone who has seen the actual newsreel footage, Cooper's performance is doubly satisfying. He captures the strength and courage of a man who knows he is dying and must soon leave the world which bestowed so much honor upon him. For all the apparent tragedy, Gehrig knows he has lived a good life and appreciates its rewards. He does not let his disease deter him from a spirit that always saw the good in life.

Lou Gehrig was an inspiration, and the film is successful because it, too, is inspirational. Like most biographies of that era, the film chooses to emphasize the good and ignore (or at least downplay) the negative. For a man like Gehrig whose life had so many exciting and memorable highlights, the filmmaker's only difficulty was deciding which memories would best represent his incredible career. Unlike other baseball biographies of men such as Babe Ruth, Dizzy Dean, and Jimmy Piersall, who had flamboyant personalities both on and off the field, *Pride of the Yankees* contrasts the quiet man off the field with the exciting, competitive athlete on the field. The results are sometimes schmaltzy, but, considering the man, they are ultimately honest.

In 1977, a television movie entitled *A Love Affair: The Eleanor and Lou Gehrig Story* was made with Edward Herrmann and Blythe Danner in the title roles. Like *Pride of the Yankees*, this film also recognized that much of the real drama in Gehrig's life occurred off the field. This film was based on the book *My Luke and I* by Eleanor Gehrig and Joseph Dorso and told the story of Gehrig's life through his wife's eyes.

It is often very difficult to communicate the inner thinkings and soul of a person in a filmed biography. Many films have tried and failed, but *Pride of the Yankees* must stand as one of the most successful screen biographies and certainly the best film on baseball ever made.

James J. Desmarais

PRINCESS O'ROURKE

Released: 1943
Production: Hal B. Wallis for Warner Bros.
Direction: Norman Krasna
Screenplay: Norman Krasna (AA)
Cinematography: Ernest Haller
Editing: Warren Low
Running time: 94 minutes

> *Principal characters:*
> Princess Maria .... Olivia de Havilland
> Eddie O'Rourke .... Robert Cummings
> Uncle .... Charles Coburn
> Dave .... Jack Carson
> Jean .... Jane Wyman
> Supreme Court Judge .... Harry Davenport
> Miss Haskell .... Gladys Cooper
> Mrs. Washburn .... Minor Watson

Screenwriter Norman Krasna began his career as an eighteen-dollar-a-week department store clerk, progressed to a salary of fifty dollars in the Warner Bros. publicity department, and by 1936, when he was twenty-seven, earned four figures a week as a writer-producer for M-G-M and allegedly owned the longest Rolls-Royce in Hollywood. During the 1930's and 1940's, Krasna concocted some of the era's most delightful comedies. His funniest films focus on the theme of mistaken identity. In *The Devil and Miss Jones* (1941, not to be confused with *The Devil in Miss Jones*, one of the more publicized pornography films of the mid-1970's), the wealthiest man in the world takes a job incognito in a department store he owns to discover why his employees have hung him in effigy. In *It Started with Eve* (also 1941, and remade in 1964 as *I'd Rather Be Rich*), a young man believes his millionaire father is dying and hires a hat-check girl to pose as his fiancée. *Princess O'Rourke* (1943) may not be Krasna's best-remembered film, but it is the first of three films he directed as well as scripted (the others are 1950's *The Big Hangover*, 1956's *The Ambassador's Daughter*, and 1960's *Who Was That Lady?*); and it is also the film for which he received his only Academy Award for writing.

Princess O'Rourke is, like *The Devil and Miss Jones* and *It Started with Eve*, a romantic comedy featuring a "disguised" character: Eddie O'Rourke (Robert Cummings, who also had starred in *It Started with Eve* and *The Devil and Miss Jones*), a young American pilot, falls in love with a young woman (Olivia de Havilland), a princess whom he thinks is a penniless refugee. "Uncle," her guardian (Charles Coburn, star of *The Devil and Miss Jones*), feels that Princess Maria is bored with the quiet life she is leading in New

York and sends her on vacation to California. The princess boards a plane piloted by Eddie and his friend Dave (Jack Carson). She accidently takes an overdose of sleeping pills, and the men cannot wake her when the plane is grounded because of fog. Because she is traveling incognito they cannot establish her identity, so Eddie takes Maria to his apartment and, with the assistance of Jean (Jane Wyman), Dave's wife, puts her to bed. She awakens the following morning, rather dazed and wearing Eddie's pajama top, and finds a note from him asking her for a date that night. She returns to her hotel and, after explaining her absence to her guardian, leaves for the date. She is unaware that she is being followed by a Secret Service agent.

Maria spends a delightful evening with Eddie, Dave, and Jean. She is impressed by their unpretentiousness and lets them believe that she is a refugee, has no money, and is traveling to California to begin employment as a house maid. Eddie has fallen in love with her and asks her to marry him, but the princess declines, as she knows she must wed a man from a royal family.

By now, "Uncle" has prepared a file on Eddie; he learns that the pilot is an honest young man of fine character. Maria is informed that she will be able to marry Eddie; her uncle can tell that she loves the pilot, and the king, her father, will allow the union. Of course, Eddie is flabbergasted when he learns Maria's true identity. He is invited to a White House ceremony, where he is informed by the guardian that, before the wedding, he must renounce his American citizenship. Eddie is angry and cancels the ceremony. When "Uncle" is asleep, however, the princess renounces *her* royal standing with the help of the President and his dog. At midnight, Eddie and Maria are wed in the Chief Executive's study by a sleepy Supreme Court Justice (Harry Davenport).

The finale may be contrived, but Krasna has nevertheless fashioned an amusing, spirited comedy. As befitting a film released at the height of World War II, *Princess O'Rourke* is proudly, unabashedly patriotic. The film's premise is that only in America can an all-American boy—from Brooklyn, no less—who is the opposite of an aristocrat grow up to marry a princess in a ceremony at the White House. The marriage is approved as a gesture toward cooperation between nations. Still, Eddie O'Rourke would gladly, unquestioningly give up the woman he loves if having her means forsaking his country, or in this case, forsaking his United States citizenship.

While de Havilland never became a cult figure (like Joan Crawford) or a living legend (like Greta Garbo or Bette Davis or Katharine Hepburn), she is still one of Hollywood's finest actresses and stars. She is adept at playing both comedy and drama, and is one of the few performers to win two Academy Awards, for *To Each His Own* (1946) and *The Heiress* (1949). She also received nominations for *Gone with the Wind* (1939), *Hold Back the Dawn* (1941), and for what is possibly her greatest performance, as Virginia Cunningham, a young woman in a mental institution, in *The Snake Pit* (1948). *Princess O'Rourke* is far from her greatest film or performance, but she is appropriately charming as Princess Maria.

The boyish, ever-youthful Cummings is dashing and affable as Eddie O'Rourke. Never a great actor, he was a popular screen star who gave able performances in light comedies and was effective in his few dramatic roles (1942's *King's Row* and 1954's *Dial M for Murder*). Coburn is appropriately crusty as the princess' guardian. 1943 was a banner year for this distinguished character actor; in addition to *Princess O'Rourke*, he appeared in *The Constant Nymph* and *Heaven Can Wait* and won a Best Supporting Actor Academy Award for *The More the Merrier*. Carson and Wyman, who were Warner Bros. contract players at the time, offer bright support as Eddie's friends.

Princess O'Rourke received good reviews (Cummings earned some of the best of his career, with one critic even comparing him to James Stewart). While today the film is hopelessly dated, it remains a pleasant, diverting example of period comedy.

Rob Edelman

THE PRIVATE LIFE OF DON JUAN

Released: 1934
Production: Alexander Korda for London Films; released by United Artists
Direction: Alexander Korda
Screenplay: Frederick Lonsdale and Lajos Biro; based on a story of the same name by Henri Bataille
Cinematography: George Perinal
Editing: Russell Lloyd
Interior decoration: Vincent Korda
Running time: 90 minutes

Principal characters:
Don Juan	Douglas Fairbanks
Antonita	Merle Oberon
Dolores	Benita Hume
Leporello	Melville Cooper
Rosita	Binnie Barnes
The Actor Don Juan	Owen Nares
The Girl at the Castle	Patricia Hilliard
Pedro	Clifford Heatherley
Pepita	Gina Malo
Carmen	Joan Gardner
Roderigo	Barry MacKay
An Actress	Heather Thatcher

The film career of Douglas Fairbanks, Sr., was a long and distinguished one. He entered films in 1915, after a lengthy stage career, with *The Lamb*, and was immediately established as a leading film actor. With films such as *Flirting with Fate* (1916), *The Half Breed* (1916), *Wild and Woolly* (1917), and *His Majesty the American* (1919), he consolidated his appeal to film audiences. In 1919, along with Mary Pickford (whom he was to marry a year later), Charles Chaplin, and D. W. Griffith, Fairbanks founded United Artists. The 1920's marked the height of Fairbanks' screen appeal; his films became even more lavish and ambitious and his exploits more daring and exciting. *The Mark of Zorro* (1920), *Robin Hood* (1921), *The Thief of Bagdad* (1923), *Don Q, Son of Zorro* (1925), *The Black Pirate* (1926), and *The Gaucho* (1927) stand as permanent memorials to one of the greatest performers and personalities of the silent screen.

With the end of the silent era, Fairbanks faced problems. His problems were not with sound, because his long years on the stage assured him a good speaking voice, but rather he had problems with his age; he was bordering on fifty when he starred in his first talkie, *The Taming of the Shrew*, in 1929, and it was harder for him to sustain his athletic stunts. Worse still, it was harder for him to accept the reality of his own aging. The idyllic marriage between Fairbanks and Pickford was souring rapidly, perhaps spurred by the King and Queen of Hollywood losing their crowns to newcomers to the screen.

After *The Taming of the Shrew*, Fairbanks starred in four more features. None of them are bad by any means, and at least one, *Reaching for the Moon* (1930), is still extremely entertaining, thanks to its risqué dialogue and the fine comedy performances of Fairbanks and Bebe Daniels. The most interesting of the Fairbanks sound features, however, is his last film, *The Private Life of Don Juan*, not only because it is well made and well acted, but also because of the obvious similarities between the aging Don Juan and the aging Fairbanks.

The Private Life of Don Juan was produced by Alexander Korda, a Hungarian-born entrepreneur who was one of the most colorful figures in British cinema, and who made the British cinema international. *The Private Life of Don Juan* was made immediately after *Catherine the Great* (1934), featuring Douglas Fairbanks, Jr., and a "nature" documentary titled *The Private Life of the Gannets* (1934). (Korda appears to have had a fixation with the private lives of his characters; in 1933 he had produced his first major success, *The Private Life of Henry VIII*.) In starring Douglas Fairbanks, Sr., in the film, Korda furthered his interest in United Artists, the American distributor of his productions. Fairbanks expressed a liking for Korda, possibly helped by the producer's providing him with a lavish English country estate at which Fairbanks could reside in style and also dally with his future wife, the English socialite Lady Sylvia Ashley.

The film opens with the arrival of the middle-aged Don Juan (Douglas Fairbanks) and his wife (Benita Hume) in Seville, where word of the dashing lover's expertise has preceded him. Don Juan's motto is "All girls are different. All wives are alike." An impostor Don Juan, played by the former British stage matinee idol Owen Nares, has taken advantage of the situation and made love to the bored wives of the city. While the actor Don Juan visits the balconies of the beauties of Seville, the real Don Juan is visiting his doctor, who advises a long rest and a healthy diet. Returning from one last fling with the dancer Antonita (played by Merle Oberon, the future Mrs. Korda), Don Juan learns that the impostor has been killed in a duel with an irate husband.

Taking advantage of the situation, Don Juan does not reveal himself, but instead attends his own funeral prior to leaving for a rest in the country, using the pseudonym of Captain Mariano. After six months of rehabilitation, Don Juan tries his hand at love-making once again, but discovers that without the Don Juan name and legend he is nothing more than a middle-aged roué. He cannot even impress a serving maid at the inn, who finds his line of romantic patter stilted and old-fashioned. Don Juan returns to Seville to prove his identity, but nobody will believe him, particularly after his wife denies knowing him. A new, reformed Don Juan, accepting his middle-age and the end of his romantic exploits, returns to his wife and domesticity, perhaps, as one critic at the time wrote, because "he is a little tired of climbing and descending rope ladders."

The script is amusing, but not as sparkling as one might expect, considering the presence of Frederick Lonsdale, one of Britain's most witty playwrights of the day. The sets by Korda's brother, Vincent, are impeccable. *The Private Life of Don Juan* boasts a particularly fine line-up of British film beauties of the 1930's: Benita Hume, Binnie Barnes, Gina Malo, and Merle Oberon, among others. Oberon declares her lasting fidelity to Don Juan's memory by announcing, "No one may touch my lips on a Wednesday." "This assortment of English ingenues," wrote *Variety* (December 18, 1934) "is about the niftiest set of talented lookers in any one film and probably has (and has had) the Hollywood talent scouts doing some hefty scouting." British character actors are equally in evidence, including Melville Cooper, Heather Thatcher, and Athene Seyler.

From a critical point of view, the film fared well in England; but *Variety*'s Abel Green wrote, "Douglas Fairbanks in *The Private Life of Don Juan* seems a mistaken idea," and ended his review with the cryptic and damning comment, "Doubtful for the masses." Andre Sennwald in *The New York Times* (December 10, 1934) was basically favorable, saying, "A visually attractive costume comedy, the film is gently indiscreet in its discussion of the ubiquitous Iberian lover, but its humor is never more violent than that contained in one of its typical polite epigrams: 'Marriage is like a beleaguered city: those who are in it are trying to get out, and those who are out are trying to get in.' "

Korda was unhappy with the production and quickly moved on to his next project, *The Scarlet Pimpernel* (1934), which again relied on Oberon for beauty and love interest. As for Fairbanks, he took a hint—perhaps—from *The Private Life of Don Juan* and settled down to married life, not with Mary Pickford, but with Lady Ashley. Fairbanks never made another film, and died on December 11, 1939.

Anthony Slide

THE PRIVATE LIFE OF SHERLOCK HOLMES

Released: 1970
Production: Billy Wilder for United Artists
Direction: Billy Wilder
Screenplay: Billy Wilder and I. A. L. Diamond
Cinematography: Christopher Challis
Editing: Ernest Walter
Running time: 125 minutes

> *Principal characters:*
> Sherlock Holmes .... Robert Stephens
> Dr. John Watson .... Colin Blakely
> Mycroft Holmes .... Christopher Lee
> Gabrielle Valladon .... Genevieve Page
> Patrova .... Tamara Toumanova

The Sherlock Holmes of Sir Arthur Conan Doyle's immortal stories is all business, keenly intelligent and relentlessly logical. He had his foibles, certainly—his notorious fondness for injecting a seven-percent solution of cocaine to relieve boredom was the most famous—but otherwise Conan Doyle's hero was nearly infallible. Director/screenwriter Billy Wilder, however, had another idea. What if, he wondered, there was another, more human side to the famous detective, a side that his devoted companion and faithful biographer, Dr. Watson, chose to keep hidden from the public lest it tarnish his friend's image? Such speculation on Wilder's part led to his film *The Private Life of Sherlock Holmes*, in which Wilder and his longtime collaborator I. A. L. Diamond show the audience a different side of Sherlock Holmes. Wisely, they do not contradict the Conan Doyle Holmes altogether; instead, they supplement the traditional Holmes, speculating on a side of the detective's personality about which his Victorian creator was, perhaps unavoidably, reticent. *The Private Life of Sherlock Holmes* is about Holmes's sex life, or, rather, his lack of a sex life. The fictional device through which Wilder reveals all this are the secret memoirs of Dr. Watson.

The Private Life of Sherlock Holmes divides neatly into two parts. The first part of the film is a delicious comedy; the latter portion is fairly stock mystery. The two parts are united by a common exploration of Holmes's attitude toward women. "I don't dislike women," Holmes (Robert Stephens) insists to his companion, Dr. John Watson (Colin Blakely), "I merely distrust them." He is in the midst of a good-natured diatribe against the public image of Sherlock Holmes as created in the stories of his adventures that Watson writes for the local press. It is August, 1887, and the great detective is bored. "There are no great crimes anymore," he complains, turning up his nose at a chance to investigate the disappearance of six midgets. His most interesting project is a detailed analysis of the characteristics of ashes from a hundred and forty kinds of tobacco, which process keeps their Baker Street flat blanketed with foul-smelling smoke. Holmes turns to cocaine to relieve the tedium, as Watson clucks disapprovingly. Wilder and Diamond thus paint a picture of humdrum domesticity, all the more comic because it is directly contrary to the dashing detective's image.

Holmes is so bored that he permits Watson to take him to a Russian ballet company's performance of *Swan Lake*. Things liven up a bit when the company's manager invites Holmes and Watson backstage after the performance. While a delighted Watson cavorts with the girls in the cast, Holmes is ushered into the presence of the prima ballerina. It develops that the great Petrova (Tamara Toumanova) has selected Sherlock Holmes (Tolstoy, Nietzsche, and Tchaikovsky having proved unwilling) to be the father of her child. Holmes is both amused and alarmed. Thinking fast, he hits upon a way to avoid the liaison without hurting the Russians' feelings: he claims that he is a homosexual and that Watson is his lover.

In another part of the opera house, the Russian women with whom Watson had been dancing drift away and are gradually replaced by effeminate men, as word about his "relationship" with Holmes spreads backstage. When the befuddled Watson realizes what is transpiring, he is mortified. Rushing back to Baker Street, he is stunned to hear Holmes cheerfully admit to being the source of the rumor. "So there will be a little gossip about you in St. Petersburg," Holmes chuckles, as Watson threatens to move out to avoid a scandal. Gradually, however, Watson's good humor returns. He boasts of his considerable reputation as a ladies' man, and asks Holmes about his own conquests among the fair sex. As the nonplussed Watson stares in amazement, Holmes rebukes him for bringing up the subject.

Thus does Wilder introduce the theme of Holmes's sexual ambiguity. The point is raised humorously, but it is clearly no joke to Holmes. The remainder of the film is devoted to an example of the sort of treachery that put the detective off women in the first place. Shortly after Gabrielle Valladon (Genevieve Page), the female lead, is introduced, Wilder drops the jokes about Holmes's sex life in favor of a mystery. This part of the story is unusual only in that Sherlock Holmes is one step behind everyone else (including the audience) in discovering a solution. Wilder suggests that the very presence of a woman seems to have short-circuited Holmes's famous deductive powers. That, rather than anything overtly sexual, appears to be the source of Holmes's aversion to women.

When Gabrielle Valladon turns up on his doorstep soaking wet in a state of amnesia, Holmes wants nothing to do with her; only Watson's pleas induce him to give her shelter. Gradually, however, her case piques his interest. One of Wilder's final plays on Holmes's possible homosexuality occurs when Gabrielle, still suffering from an impaired memory, mistakes Holmes for her husband. Holmes, hoping to gain information from her, plays along, although just how far he plays is open to conjecture—Wilder ends the scene before we learn whether or not Holmes involves himself carnally with the woman, even for the sake of the case. Watson, however, finds her in Holmes's bed the next morning and jumps to the obvious conclusion. "You cad!" he fumes, as Holmes leers "I found her body very rewarding." As it turns out, he was referring to clues to the woman's identity rather than to anything erotic.

With the establishment of Gabrielle's identity, the film moves into its third stage. Holmes has deduced that Mrs. Valladon is a Belgian who is searching for her husband, a mining engineer working in England who has been missing for several weeks. A visit to his last known address reveals an empty building that seems to function as an arena for the clandestine sale of canaries. Just as Holmes is about to use his famed deductive powers on this apparent mystery, he discovers a letter from his brother Mycroft (Christopher Lee), who imperiously summons the famous sleuth to his club. At the Diogenes Club, Mycroft warns his younger brother to drop the Valladon case—it involves, he says, a matter of national security.

Naturally, Holmes continues his investigation, but Wilder has planted a seed of doubt in the audience's mind. The incident is an important one, for it sets the tone for the rest of the film. From here on, Sherlock Holmes is never quite in control of events. Just as he begins to sort things out, something throws him off balance. His calculations, while often close to the mark, are always slightly askew; and, in the end, it is Mycroft (Sherlock Holmes's smarter brother, according to Gene Wilder's 1977 comedy of that name) who pulls his reknowned brother's irons from the fire.

In the process of his investigations, Holmes grows closer to Gabrielle, and Wilder continues to touch upon the detective's ambiguous sex drive, albeit in more somber tones. Although Holmes and Gabrielle travel as Mr. and Mrs. Ashdown, Holmes never tries to take advantage of the situation. Indeed, he politely declines Gabrielle's offer to share her bed.

Meanwhile, clues abound. Sinister, silent Trappist monks appear and reappear at strategic moments. Holmes, Watson, and Gabrielle travel to Scotland, where, in a cemetery near Loch Ness, they witness a mysterious burial at which the only mourners are midgets. After the midgets leave, Holmes and Watson exhume the coffin, which contains the asphyxiated body of Mr. Valladon and three dead canaries. Then there is the Loch Ness monster, first sighted by an incredulous Watson; the monster overturns the rowboat in which Holmes and his two companions are reconnoitering on the lake. Finally, Gabrielle keeps opening and closing her parasol at odd moments.

Holmes correctly deduces that the monster is actually a submarine. Gabrielle's husband, the canaries, and the six missing midgets (mentioned by Holmes in the film's opening moments) all died during the vehicle's test runs. What he fails to deduce—and Mycroft turns up to explain the situation—is that Gabrielle Valladon is actually Ilsa von Hoffenstahl, a German spy. Gabrielle/Ilsa has tricked the great Sherlock Holmes into leading her and her cohorts (the "Trappists" whom she has been signaling with her umbrella) to the location of the submarine. The German plot is ultimately foiled, but Holmes is shaken and bitter—the more so because of his fondness for the woman he knew as Gabrielle Valladon.

The film's final scene is set back at 221B Baker Street a few years later. Holmes receives a letter from his brother Mycroft, who reveals that Ilsa von Hoffenstahl has died on a mission for the Germans in Japan. She had been living there under the name Gabrielle Ashdown. A grief-stricken look crosses Holmes's face, and he slowly walks toward the medicine chest and the solace of a seven-percent solution of cocaine.

Despite its merits, *The Private Life of Sherlock Holmes* is by no means a perfect film. Page does what she can with the role of Gabrielle Valladon, but the character is curiously lifeless. Gabrielle is supposed to be a master spy, the woman who outsmarted Sherlock Holomes, but Wilder and Diamond offer no onscreen evidence of her cunning. Thus Holmes's failure to see through her machinations makes him seem unduly obtuse.

Much of the credit for the success of *The Private Life of Sherlock Holmes* must go to Stephens and Blakely. Stephens plays Sherlock Holmes as a repressed *heterosexual*; there is no evidence in the film that Holmes is sexually attracted to Watson or to any other man. Stephens' Holmes is a man who is deliberately, willfully asexual. Further, Stephens lets us know that Holmes is aware that this decision cuts him off from much that is good about life. He becomes perceptively more sensitive and more vulnerable once Gabrielle enters his life. He has chosen the absence of pain rather than the possibility of pleasure, and the wounded look on his face tells us that Holmes is constantly at war with himself over this decision.

Blakely wisely plays Dr. Watson as precisely the opposite type. While Stephens' Holmes is cerebral, Blakely's Watson revels in physicality; and this dichotomy is mirrored in the sense of humor that both men bring to the film. Holmes is witty, while Watson galumphs amiably into comic situations. Of equal importance, however, is the chemistry between the two actors, and hence between the characters they portray. If their styles are contrasting, they are nevertheless complementary. We never doubt for a moment that the two men are close friends.

Wilder, of course, was not the first filmmaker to think of adapting Conan Doyle's hero to his own ends. From Basil Rathbone's Nazi-hunting Holmes of the 1940's to *The Adventures of Sherlock Holmes' Smarter Brother* and *The Seven-Per-Cent Solution* in the 1970's, the image of Conan Doyle's invincible detective has been honored more in the breach than the observance. *The Private Life of Sherlock Holmes* belongs at the head of these films. A loving and gently comic look at one of literature's most enduring heroes, *The Private*

Life of Sherlock Holmes is a welcome addition to Holmesiana, and to cinema as well.

Robert Mitchell

THE PRIZE

Released: 1963
Production: Pandro S. Berman for Metro-Goldwyn-Mayer/Roxbury
Direction: Mark Robson
Screenplay: Ernest Lehman; based on the novel of the same name by Irving
　Wallace
Cinematography: William Daniels
Editing: Adrienne Fazan
Running time: 135 minutes

Principal characters:
Andrew Craig	Paul Newman
Dr. Max Stratman	Edward G. Robinson
Inger Lisa Andersen	Elke Sommer
Emily Stratman	Diane Baker
Dr. Denise Marceau	Michelene Presle
Dr. Claude Marceau	Gerald Oury
Dr. John Garrett	Kevin McCarthy
Dr. Carlo Farelli	Sergio Fantoni

An entertaining comedy-melodrama, *The Prize* is a light-hearted mixture of international intrigue, romance, and suspense. The film begins by introducing a number of people who have come to Stockholm to receive Nobel prizes. Max Stratman (Edward G. Robinson), the winner of the prize in physics, is a refugee from the World War II deathcamps and travels with his niece, Emily (Diane Baker), the daughter of his twin brother, who did not manage to escape the Iron Curtain. The American physician, John Garrett (Kevin McCarthy), claims the Italian cowinner of the prize in medicine, Carlo Farelli (Sergio Fantoni), is a cheat. A French couple, Claude (Gerald Oury) and Denise Marceau (Micheline Presle), are cowinners in chemistry but are quarreling because he is "infatuated with another woman's body," as his wife puts it. Andrew Craig (Paul Newman) is an American novelist who is the winner in literature but is an alcoholic who has written nothing but cheap detective fiction under a pseudonym for five years. At a press conference Craig says he is in Stockholm only to collect the money. He says he is more interested in detective fiction than in his art and improvises a plot about the kidnaping of a Nobel prize winner. Inger Lisa Andersen (Elke Sommer) is an attractive Swedish official assigned by the Swedish Foreign Ministry to keep an eye on Craig during his visit.

The main story is set in motion by East German Communist agents who visit Stratman in his hotel room, insisting he defect to his "homeland." When he refuses, the agents reveal their plan to have another man substitute for Stratman for propaganda purposes, and they appeal to Emily for assistance, saying the man they will put in her uncle's place will be her father, whom she believed to be dead. Finally, the physicist is kidnaped and taken to a Russian ship in the harbor. The switch then takes place, and the impostor is ready to use his acceptance speech as a worldwide platform to denounce the United States. Craig, however, who had briefly talked with Stratman, becomes suspicious when the impostor expresses an anti-American attitude, something the real Stratman would never have done.

Since Craig is known to have an interest in detective stories and is known as a hard-drinker, neither the Stockholm police nor, at first, his female caretaker believe his story that the man who claims to be Max Stratman is not the real Stratman. Undaunted, the novelist continues to investigate his hunch. When he discovers a murdered makeup artist, Craig begins to believe his theory is correct, and when he finds himself the object of several murder attempts, he knows he is right. The foreign agents are anxious to silence him in case anyone does begin to believe him.

In one sequence Craig dashes into a building to escape his pursuers only to discover a meeting of nudists taking place inside. In order to remain, he, too, must disrobe, although for some reason he is allowed to wear a towel. The spies are so intent upon catching Craig that they, too, disrobe and go into the meeting. Knowing he will not be able to fend off his pursuers once the speech is finished, Craig begins to heckle the speaker. As his harassment continues, the audience becomes increasingly irritated, until Craig is removed by force—thus escaping the agents. Other harrowing episodes include his having to jump into a river from the top of a ten-story building and having to escape being run down by a car when he is on a bridge.

Finally Craig discovers the real Stratman, almost singlehandedly removes him from the ship on which he had been held, and takes him back to the hotel, where the rescued scientist immediately has a heart attack. The feuding Garrett and Farelli join together to save Stratman's life and, in so doing, patch up their quarrel. We find that the impostor is a professional actor, not Emily's father (who, in fact, had died years earlier in Russia). When he flees the hotel, he is killed by the agents who think he is the real Stratman. Claude and Denise Marceau patch up their quarrel meanwhile, and Craig comes to realize what an honor the Nobel prize is, humbly accepts it, and begins a romance with Inger.

The Prize was a commercial success although most critics seemed unable to accept the film's mixture of comedy and adventure and insisted on taking it more seriously than it took itself. They were unable to recognize that the film is involving even though it does not always earnestly advance its plot and that it is funny even though it keeps us concerned with the fate of its protagonists.

Credit for the tone of the film, which is lightly comic rather than farcical, should be shared evenly by the writer, the director, and the actors. Ernest

Lehman wrote the loose adaptation of the Irving Wallace novel, and certain similarities can be seen to Lehman's script for *North by Northwest* (1959). The scene among the nudists, for example, is nearly a repeat of one in an auction in the earlier film. Director Mark Robson keeps the film moving as the concerns of the other prize winners, including Craig's romantic interest in Inger, intertwine with the kidnap and rescue story, and the comic, romantic, and suspense elements are nicely balanced.

Robinson plays both Max Stratman and the impostor. He is effective in the film's most serious role, which is not surprising since he had played many similar roles before. Sommer, known chiefly for her looks, is able to suggest that Inger truly is an official of the Swedish government as well as a most attractive romantic interest for Craig.

The central character in the film is Newman as Andrew Craig, a part which was a change of pace from his previous roles in such films as *Cat on a Hot Tin Roof* (1958) and *Hud* (1963). Newman was equal to the challenge, proving adept at the engaging mixture of comedy and adventure in *The Prize*, and providing the film with much of its financial success. 1963 was the first year that Newman was on the list of the top ten box-office stars, a list on which he would remain for more than a dozen years. *The Prize* marked a change for Newman which indicated that he could be successful in light roles as well as serious ones. Many of his later successes, such as *Butch Cassidy and the Sundance Kid* (1969) and *The Sting* (1973), also displayed his gift for blending comedy and drama.

Timothy W. Johnson

THE PROFESSIONALS

Released: 1966
Production: Richard Brooks for Columbia
Direction: Richard Brooks
Screenplay: Richard Brooks; based on the novel *A Mule for the Marquesa* by
    Frank O'Rourke
Cinematography: Conrad Hall
Editing: Peter Zinner
Music: Maurice Jarre
Running time: 116 minutes

> *Principal characters:*
> Bill Dolworth .... Burt Lancaster
> Rico .... Lee Marvin
> Hans Ehrengard .... Robert Ryan
> Jesus Raza .... Jack Palance
> Maria Grant .... Claudia Cardinale
> Mr. Grant .... Ralph Bellamy
> Jake Sharp .... Woody Strode

After their highly successful association on the Academy Award-winning *Elmer Gantry* (1960), writer-director Richard Brooks and actor Burt Lancaster came together again to make the action-adventure film *The Professionals*. Mr. Grant (Ralph Bellamy), an American millionaire, hires four soldiers of fortune to rescue his wife Maria (Claudia Cardinale) who, presumably, has been kidnaped and is being held prisoner in Mexico. The group of professionals includes Rico (Lee Marvin), an embittered United States Army veteran; Bill Dolworth (Burt Lancaster), a dynamite expert familiar with Mexico; Hans Ehrengard (Robert Ryan), who is in charge of the horses; and Jake Sharp (Woody Strode), a master at tracking and the use of a bow. This band of rescuers must make their way through some of the most desolate wasteland imaginable in the hope of surprising Jesus Raza (Jack Palance) and his army of 150 trained guerrillas. Their plan is elaborately devised, with Dolworth planting explosives at key points along their escape route in order to provide roadblocks in the path of their pursuers as they make a mad dash to the border with the rescued Mrs. Grant.

The journey to the camp of Jesus Raza is relatively uneventful. It gives the four professionals a chance to discuss their various philosophies as well as to set the stage for the postrescue escape route. Everything goes according to plan, including the nighttime surprise attack on Raza's stronghold. They "rescue" Mrs. Grant only to find that she was not being held as a prisoner but rather was Raza's lover. Her husband had wanted her back and had devised the credible story of her being taken to Mexico as a prisoner. In reality she had left her husband to live in Mexico with her childhood sweet-heart.

At first this situation means little to the band of professional soldiers of fortune. They adhere to their original plan of returning Mrs. Grant and receiving their reward. As they get closer to the border and begin to see the absurdity of a marriage between an elderly millionaire and a young, helpless woman who is in love with another man, the group decides to bend the rules. After battles with bandits and Raza's guerrillas, sandstorms, climbs over nearly impassable mountain peaks, and treks across bleak arid deserts, the remaining professionals count the money as well lost in the cause of love. They release Mrs. Grant at the border while her ruthless husband watches, helpless, as she returns to Mexico and the man she loves.

The film, handsomely produced by Brooks and brilliantly photographed by Conrad Hall, functions on several levels. It is without doubt one of the most stylish pieces of action-oriented filmmaking to appear on American screens for a long time. This style should not be confused with flashy, technical innovation. It comes, rather, from a blending of excellent ensemble acting by Lancaster, Marvin, Ryan, and Strode, a comfortable script which glides with amazing liquidity from one point of view to another, and production values teeming with authenticity.

The attention to detail in *The Professionals* is characteristic of Brooks's work. After starting out as a screenwriter for such "pulpy" films as *Cobra Woman* (1944) and *White Savage* (1943), both starring Maria Montez, Brooks began writing serious films such as *Brute Force* (1947) and even directing such serious films as *Battle Circus* (1952). He has subsequently gone from lavish extravaganzas such as *Lord Jim* (1964) to more intimate dramas such as *Looking for Mr. Goodbar* (1977). Yet for all this diversity of subject matter, the element that remains consistent in much of Brooks's later work is his reliance upon mainstream literary source material.

In *The Professionals*, however, Brooks manages to break out of this pattern. Adapting Frank O'Rourke's pulpish *A Mule for the Marquesa*, he is able to construct a film which epitomizes the dissipation of the nobility of the unci-vilized "Old West." The film shows how a rich, corrupt, self-made demigod like Grant can manipulate the honorable intentions of four ethical adventur-ers. There is a slight conflict of interest in the mercenary approach in which these professionals negotiate for this particular job, but once on the road to Mexico the emphasis shifts to the duties associated with their assignment. In a perverse way Brooks illustrates how the professionals have their basic con-cerns for fair play warped by Grant's personal greed.

The Professionals shares a great deal of ambience with Sam Peckinpah's *The Wild Bunch* (1969). Both of these films deal with small, tight-knit groups of men. Both concentrate on the changing attitudes regarding a nineteenth century chivalry in the face of twentieth century progress. *The Wild Bunch* makes its point with bold, swift strokes. It points to the uselessness and absurdity of violence while granting its necessity. *The Professionals* concentrates on the personalities of its band of soldiers of fortune. Their ultimate realization of the truth allows them to watch their sense of values collapse around them. *The Wild Bunch* depicts a preference to fight and possibly to die rather than surrender to the growing changes of a new environment. The same choice is made in *The Professionals*. The difference comes in dramatic placement. In Peckinpah's film the decision becomes the core of *The Wild Bunch*'s flamboyant depiction of violence. In Brooks's film this decision is a denouement. The two films reach similar conclusions. *The Wild Bunch* provokes a more immediate, physical reaction; *The Professionals* functions on a more intuitive level.

The Professionals enjoys a unique position of being both a highly exciting film and a thought-provoking interpretation of cultural change. Marvin's intensity, Ryan's sincerity, and Lancaster's strength of character contribute to the construction of an outstanding film.

Carl F. Macek

THE PUMPKIN EATER

Released: 1964
Production: Jack Clayton for Romulus Clayton; released by Columbia
Direction: Jack Clayton
Screenplay: Harold Pinter; based on the novel of the same name by Penelope
 Mortimer
Cinematography: Oswald Morris
Editing: James B. Clark
Running time: 110 minutes

> *Principal characters:*
> Jo Armitage .... Anne Bancroft
> Jake Armitage .... Peter Finch
> Bob Conway .... James Mason
> Beth .... Janine Gray
> Philpott .... Maggie Smith

In 1964 a different sort of melodrama was released. *The Pumpkin Eater* was, as the ads promised, "more than just a story of adultery." Jo Armitage (Anne Bancroft) has two "problems." The first is that she goes from husband to husband without really knowing why, and the second is that she is happiest when bearing children. As the number of her children increases, so do her difficulties in communicating with her husbands, and eventually, she feels unable to communicate with anyone at all. Her biggest crisis comes, however, when she feels not only hollow in the quality of her conversations, but also literally hollow because she has a hysterectomy.

The idea that a woman's identity is bound up with her ability to love and bear children was certainly not new to this particular melodrama. Its visual style, however, was markedly different from American melodramas of the 1950's. *The Pumpkin Eater* was, ironically, one of a group of British so-called "kitchen sink" films, films which looked at prosaic realities in less than polished form. The "kitchen sink" films looked at contemporary social problems in a style which reflected a disenchantment with polished Hollywood products. *The Pumpkin Eater*, like other films of its genre, is black-and-white in a time when color was the norm for any major film; black-and-white was chosen because it was felt to have an artistic integrity appropriate to a "serious" film. Along with rather rough cinematography and less than perfect lighting, the lack of color was intended to create a more "real" atmosphere.

The Pumpkin Eater also experimented with narrative structure as an expression of character. Jo sees her story piecemeal, with flashbacks which must be pieced together gradually to make sense. Her memories are not neatly linear, but sparked by random detail or sudden emotion. Through her, the film plays with time. The events of her life are not important so much because one follows the other, but because she remembers them at times of stress in the present. The details are not clear, but the emotions she recalls are. Only the narrative is murky and obscured, as she tries to sort out the causes of those emotions.

The melodrama of *The Pumpkin Eater* takes the form of an interior monologue, spoken by a woman who has lost her faith in conversation. Harold Pinter's screenplay is full of references to the absurdities and opacity of dialogue. It is a theme Pinter plays with in other works. Jack Clayton's direction extends the idea of difficult or opaque communication visually, showing bits and pieces of scenes, like a jumble of building blocks. He uses Jo's face especially as an abstracted, beautiful mask. Both the men and the women she knows are fascinated by her face, but neither they nor she have much insight into what goes on behind it. The viewer comes to see that what is important is not so much why she left a husband or had a child, but that she herself cannot tell us much about it, except that it happened.

We see more of her third husband, Jake Armitage (Peter Finch), than we do of the earlier men. Jake and Jo's estrangement is the film's centerpiece. Their relationship is illustrated by the appearance of children at various ages and by Jake's infidelities. Jo gradually realizes that Jake may be lying to her about his relationship to other women, and because he is having affairs, she cannot trust anything he tells her. As a last try to prove her faith in him, she agrees to an abortion that Jake wants her to have. She already has a small horde of children, some living with them, some away at a boarding school because of Jake's insistence. Everyone tells her that she has had enough children, so Jo has a hysterectomy she does not really want, to keep a man she does want. Then she learns that Jake is still lying to her. There is another woman. The other woman's husband, Bob Conway (James Mason), comes to her with the news of her husband's affair with his wife. The hardest blow for Jo is that this other woman is pregnant.

Jo leaves Jake, almost suicidal not only over the break-up, but also over the loss of her child-bearing capacity. Her identity seems to be lodged in her womb. "My life's an empty place," she repeats to every doctor, relative, ex-husband, or friend she sees. Jo is a pumpkin shell. To her the surgeon's knife has removed not just the womb, but her life. She retreats to the now empty house which she and Jake shared in younger days, when she was bearing children. She comes to a complete dead end, doing nothing but staring out the window. Her eventual rescuers are the people who can prove her fertility. Jake comes walking over the hill, leading her children to the door, and after some hesitation, Jo lets them in. She hardly knows what to say to them, but soon the general clamor of the children makes conversation difficult anyway, and the film ends on this tentative reconciliation.

Clearly the ending does not completely resolve the futility and unhappiness Jo feels about her life. The problems she experiences do not seem to have any ready solution within the world of the film; rather, the world has closed around her. *The Pumpkin Eater* does not allow Jo the out of recognizing the heart of her problems, or of seeing how she fits into her world. Essentially, Jo is a sleepwalking heroine. She is estranged not from her passion, but from any retelling of it. The only love she can capture or prove is the love she literally bears.

The Pumpkin Eater was not a major box-office success, perhaps because of the complexities of the plot and the brooding nature of the film. Like many of Pinter's works, it is not designed for the filmgoer who wants escapist entertainment; as a result, his screenplays and films based on his plays are usually successful critically but only moderately successful at the box office. In retrospect, *The Pumpkin Eater* was perhaps ahead of its time and seems more appropriate for an audience in the late 1970's or early 1980's, when a number of films have delved into the inner consciousness of the leading female character.

Leslie Donaldson

PURSUED

Released: 1947
Production: Milton Sperling (A United States Production) for Warner Bros.
Direction: Raoul Walsh
Screenplay: Niven Busch
Cinematography: James Wong Howe
Editing: Christian Nyby
Music: Max Steiner
Running time: 101 minutes

Principal characters:
Thorley Callum .... Teresa Wright
Jeb Rand .... Robert Mitchum
Mrs. Medora "Ma" Callum .... Judith Anderson
Grant Callum .... Dean Jagger
Jake Dingle .... Alan Hale
Adam Callum .... John Rodney
Prentice McComber .... Harry Carey, Jr.
Jeb (younger) .... Ernest Severn
Adam (younger) .... Charles Bates
Thorley (younger) .... Peggy Miller

Behind the opening credits of *Pursued*, a woman, Thorley Callum (Teresa Wright), rides swiftly across a western landscape. The landscape is that of a remote New Mexico setting, chosen by director Raoul Walsh for its untamed beauty, a place where violent and passionate emotions may find expression. The woman rides to a burnt-out home, which would be long deserted were it not for the fact that Jeb Rand (Robert Mitchum), the hero of *Pursued*, is there, in the company of the unseen furies which have followed him all his life. Speaking softly, he tells Thorley that if he can piece together in his mind the fragments of a dark existence and remember their source, perhaps his obsessions will find rest. The deserted and destroyed dwelling in which he and Thorley are meeting is where it began and where it will end. As Jeb continues to speak, an image of flashing spurs appears on the screen, replacing the image of the couple and introducing a flashback which finds a young boy (Ernest Severn) cowering beneath the floorboards of the home. A woman (Judith Anderson) takes him away from the place, but we are given a close look at his haunted and dazed expression as he passively submits to this maternal act of a stranger. Into the cruel and ungodly desert night, the woman, soon to be identified as Thorley's mother, takes the boy, young Jeb, on a wagon, at such furious pace that it seems as if all the forces of hate must be pursuing them. As if in a dream, Ma Callum and the boy arrive at another home, and Jeb meets the girl, Thorley (Peggy Miller), and boy, Adam (Charles

Bates), who will be his sister and brother.

In this manner *Pursued* begins. It is a film which is at once a dark Western, a tender love story, a vivid adventure, an exegesis of a profound psychological theme, and the modern counterpart of Euripidean tragedy. As Jeb continues to recount his story, we learn of the years which have passed between the events of the first flashback and the present meeting. Jeb tells of how he grew up, never truly being part of the family, being shot at by an unseen stranger when he was ten, finding as an adult that he loved Thorley not as a brother but as an ordinary man, and always remembering those gleaming spurs. Adam (John Rodney), his adopted brother, resents him for intruding on the relationships within the family, but the two men also feel affection for each other, as is poignantly evident when Jeb returns from the Spanish American War and a music box is played, prompting the men to sing "Danny Boy" in a close two-shot which momentarily creates a feeling of serenity absent from the rest of the film until the final frames. The love between Thorley and Jeb, intense, delirious, and mesmerizing, seems forever threatened by some disturbance within the fabric of their lives which seems as though it will burn the sweetness of their affection to ashes. Adam asks Thorley to toss a coin once again, as she had done in order to decide which man went to war, and the loser, Jeb, must quit the ranch and return to being the outsider which he has never really ceased to be.

When this occurs, another ten years have passed, and Jeb, after a brutal fight with Adam, is shot at again the next day. This time he is no longer a boy and shoots back, only to find that he has killed his brother. Becoming a partner with Jake Dingle (Alan Hale) in a gambling house, Jeb must look on as Thorley is courted by the gentle Prentice McComber (Harry Carey, Jr.). After Jeb dares to dance with Thorley, Prentice, like Adam before him, is taunted into violence by Grant Callum (Dean Jagger), the stranger who had shot at Jeb years before, but who is no stranger to Ma. Defending himself, Jeb kills the innocent Prentice, and a remarkable funeral occurs in which the darkness of night seems to pour down into the open air of the day, a darkness broken only by a white light which James Wong Howe directs to the upper face of Thorley, illuminating the vengefulness in her tragic eyes, as Max Steiner scores the Wedding March in a minor key. In the shadow of death, Jeb is permitted to court and marry Thorley, who plans to kill him but loves him too much to pull the trigger. The marriage must remain unconsummated as Grant's hatred reaches its peak and the couple is tracked to the empty house where Jeb finally remembers that the spurs were those of his father, killed by the Callums. Ma Callum had been Jeb's father's lover, and in the violence, her own husband had been killed. Grant's brother had died also. She had always told Jeb to look ahead, but only when she intervenes and kills Grant is her adopted son freed from the past. As a result, a mature romantic union with Thorley is now possible, and a Walshian couple rides away in the final image, not into the sunset, as in most Westerns, but out of the darkness.

Niven Busch, creator of the original screenplay of *Pursued*, is no minor figure in the history of cinema. *Duel in the Sun* (1946) and *The Furies* (1950), two other films made from his stories, show the same love of modern psychology and share the same link to the great dramas of antiquity. All three films are Westerns. It is arguable that no other writer has so thoroughly reflected on cinema, perceived the eternal beauty of its richest genre, and realized that it is here that the most mature and profound themes could find their most meaningful expression in the twentieth century. *Pursued* is one of the first postwar films to observe that the quest for identity is the central crisis faced by man in the modern world. It brilliantly locates this problem of identity within a disturbed family structure and discovers the power of traumatic childhood experience to cripple the individual, leaving him no cause in his existence other than to overcome the loss of that sense of self, so that he might experience life positively. Most movingly, it shows how love between a man and woman suffers when the two people who desire to be a couple are incomplete as individuals.

All of these aspects of *Pursued* are present in Busch's screenplay, which is beautifully written and unfailingly exciting. To his credit, Busch is not pretentious about the seriousness of his ideas. He humbly observes the conventions of the genre, including the classical showdown which results in the death by gunfire of the antagonist. A script is not a film, however, and the lucidity of *Pursued* as a realized work of art is attributable less to Busch than to that old hand of action and adventure films, Raoul Walsh. *The Furies* and *Duel in the Sun* are also works by classical directors, Anthony Mann and King Vidor respectively, and those films, although rich with the qualities expected of Mann and Vidor, are not revelatory in the manner of *Pursued*. Walsh is one artist who has always been given credit for his virile handling of rousing action scenes and for his lusty humor. It is said that he has a flair for adventure stories, and this description conjures up images of men sailing the seas and journeying through the wilderness, images which are certainly not absent from his films. Without wishing away Walsh's virtues as they are customarily understood, however, the audience should cherish with an even greater fervor the director's thoughtfulness and sensitivity.

It is enough to look at the love scenes between Thorley and Jeb, or to watch with empathy as Jeb stands in the middle of a room in the Callum home and questions Ma about his past. In a moment, Walsh is able to turn away from the awesomeness of the rugged exteriors, which are as starkly moving as eternity in his images, and to imbue the most intimate moments with a life-affirming warmth and a yearning for clarity. In Walsh, masculine and feminine traits are balanced in perfect harmony, and it is no surprise that his characters, whether male or female, share this harmony with him. The women Walsh loves in his films are always the strongest and most independent, just as the men identified as his heroes are secure enough not to have to hide their vulnerability. It is appropriate that this director's style, while resolutely classical, is less settled than that of John Ford or Howard Hawks, the directors with whom he most deserves comparison. He moves the camera more than they do, not anxiously or out of uncertainty, but to adjust to that emotional energy which drives his men and women.

It has been noted that the screenplay of *Pursued* demonstrates an awareness of psychology. Walsh has this awareness also, but he does not allow a show of self-pity on the part of Jeb, only a feeling of bewilderment. Walsh's heroes and heroines always resolve their problems in action terms, no matter how severe their psychological wounds. Walsh assures through his pacing and his selection of shots that the film will move forward without being overcome by a listlessness which inevitably threatens the story of an often uncertain hero. The key to the director's interpretation, however, is the actor chosen to play Jeb, and in Mitchum, the director has found the most sympathetic Rand imaginable. Mitchum had to his credit only one challenging role, in *The Story of G.I. Joe* (1945), when Walsh cast him as Jeb, but the restraint and visual expressiveness which have distinguished him in all of his major performances are never more evident than under Walsh's direction. The character always seems capable of dealing with the complexities which challenge him, so that his moments of passivity—in which Mitchum demonstrates an understanding of the camera's power to register the subtlest emotions—never imply a surrender of will.

It is remarkable that Mitchum is brought to maturity as an actor so early in his career as a result of Walsh's perceptiveness; and Walsh elicits similarly outstanding performances from other members of the cast. Anderson gives what is surely her finest performance as Ma Callum. Although Mrs. Danvers in *Rebecca* (1940) is a more famous characterization, the role in *Pursued* is much richer and more challenging, giving Anderson the opportunity to play a woman no less tragic than the protagonist of the Greek tragedy *Medea*. As for Wright, it seems unfair that this extraordinarily attractive and vibrant actress, who is infinitely more appealing as a woman than many more glamorous and celebrated stars, has only twice, in *Pursued* and *Shadow of a Doubt* (1943), been given roles which have called for the full range of her gift for romantic expressiveness. It suffices to add that the great cameraman James Wong Howe and the great film composer Max Steiner are both at the peak of their powers in darkening the film's mood and at the same time enhancing at proper moments the sweet and sensual warmth which is always latent in the interpretation but often necessarily repressed by an atmosphere of violence and revenge.

Pursued was not immediately recognized as a classic of cinema. Although it could not fail to be noticed as an unusual Western, it simply was not a prestige picture, in spite of the integrity and artistry of its direction, writing, cinematography, music, and acting. Slowly, the film is acquiring the reputation it deserves. A work at once traditional and modern, it is one of the most marvelous examples in cinema of a subject stimulating an artist to venture bravely into unfamiliar territory, extending his world.

Blake Lucas